P9-CSV-959

# Acknowledgments

Writing a book requires a great deal of help and support. We realize that it is a cliche to say that it could not have been possible without the following people, but truer words were never spoken.

There are many people who have allowed us to study and learn about community corrections. They all worked with us over the years, and have contributed immeasurably to our knowledge and experience. In particular we would like to thank the following friends and colleagues:

Tim Alley, David Altschuler, Don Andrews, Frank Andrews, Steve Aos, Brandon Applegate, Troy Armstrong, Jean Atkins, Allen Ault, Bob Balboni, John Baron, Cheryl Barrett, Shannon Barton, Julie Baxter, Jeff Beard, Tom Beauclair, Alan Bekelman, Renee Bergeron, Tom Berghausen, Lynn Bielecki, Rick Billak, Claudia Black, Julia Blankenship, Jim Bonta, Paul Book, Sue Bourke, Bob Borst, James Bralley, Ann Brewster, Barb Broderick, Doug Brothers, Kelly Brown, Mike Brown, Bob Brown, Victor Brown, Yvonne Saunders-Brown, Rob Brusconi, Loren Buddress, Nancy Campbell, Ed Camp, Mark Carey, Liz Cass, Norm Chamberlain, Karen Chapple, Steve Chapman, John Chin, Todd Clear, Rob Clevenger, Diane Coates, Alvin Cohen, Marcia Cohen, Anne Frued-Conel, Linda Connelly, Ron Corbett, Jim Corfman, Nancy Cunningham, Marta Daniell, Bob Daquilante, Jim Dare, Patti Davis, Ben de Haan, Steve Devlin, Monda DeWeese, Dennis Dimatteo, Frank Domurad, Mike Dooley, Pam Douglas, Bob Dugan, Joe Ellison, Warren Emmer, Don Evans, Tony Fabelo, Dot Faust, Gretchen Faulstich, Ray Ferns, Joe Fitzpatrick, Nathan Foo, Tonya Gaby, Gene Gallo, Ryan Geis, Paul Gendreau, Bruce Gibson, Steve Gibson, Rosemary Gido, Barry Glick, Robert Gloeckner, Kathleen Gnall, Don Gordon, Mark Gornik Richard Gray, John Gramuglia, Brian Griffiths, Bill Grosshan, Sharon Haines, Ron Hajime, Bill Hamilton, Dena Hanley, Patricia Hardyman, Jennifer Hartman, Steve Haas, Joe Hassett, Sharon Harrigfeld, Tomi Hiers, Ed Heller, Martha Henderson, Domingo Herraiz, Doug Herrmann, Chris Heywood, Rick Hoekstra Buzz Hoffman, Deborah Holmberg, Dorothy Holmes, Steve Holmes, Alex Holsinger Martin Horn, Dana Jones Hubbard, Mindy Hutcherson, Butch Huyandi, Norma Jaeger Linda Janes, Hope Janke, Norma Jaeger, Bob Jester, Maureen Kiehm, Kevin Knight, Authur Jones, Justin Jones, Dan Joyner, Colleen Kadleck, George Kaiser, Sharon Kennedy Bill King, Peter Kinziger Lea Klingler, Melissa Knopp, Rosemary Kooy, Sally Kreamer,

Bill Kroman, Ed Kollin, Don Kuhl, Fred LaFluer, Steve Lamberti, Glen Lammon, Jim Lawrence, Mike Link, Dominic Lisa, Shelley Johnson Listwan, Elaine Little, Mary Livers, Fransaia LoDico, Dan Lombardo, Kirk Long, Denise Lord, Arthur Lurigio, Pam McClain, Scott MacDonald. David McGriff, Alan Mabry, Tom Madeo, Lauren Maio, Joe Marchese, Vicki Markey, Bob Markin, Cheryl Marlow, Carole Martin, Ginger Martin, Betsy Matthews, Tina Mawhorr, Robert Mecum, Harvey Milkman, Linda Modry, Sandy Monfort, Melissa Moon, Marty Magnusson, Tom Muhleman, Linda Murken, Larry Muse, Geraldyne Nagy, Steve Nelson, Maria Nemec, Mike Nickols, Wendy Niehaus, Linda Nixon, Phil Noone, Tom O'Connor, Julie Okamoto, Steve Oldenstadt, Gaylon Oswalt, Beth Oxford, Ted Palmer, Mario Paparozzi, Evalyn Parks, George Parks, Grafton Payne, Geno Natalucci-Persichetti, Dan Peterca, Candi Peters, Sharon Pette, Merel Pickenpaugh, Dianne Poindexter, Bruce Ponder, Vince Polito, Dan Pompa, John Prevost, John Prinzi, Craig Prysock, Nina Ramsey, Brent Reinke, Ed Rhine, Sue Righthand, Bryan Riley, Debbie Rios, Carole Roberts, Denise Robinson, Jim Robinson, Renee Robinson, Claudia Rowlands, Kathy Russell, Loretta Ryland, Reece Satin, John Schneider, Dave Schroot, Richard Seiter, Tim Shannon, Nancy Shomaker Cliff Simonsen Jerry Smith, Linda Smith, Mary Smith, Larry Solomon, Bill Sondervan, Kim Sperber, Mary Spotswood, Barry Stodley, Susan Storm, Tom Strickrath, Kathleen Strouse, Mary Jo Sullivan, Jodi Sundt, Bill Sawyer, Bob Swisher, Mike Tardy, Faye Taxman, Richard Tewksbury, Neil Tilow, Jim Toner, Julie Truschel, Mike Turner, Cecilia Velasquez, Vicki Verdeyen, Ute Vilfroy, Dennis Waite, Myra Wall, Mike Walton, Kathy Waters, Ralph Watson, Beth Weiman, Bonita White, Jim Wichtman, Reggie Wilkinson, Diane Williams, Larry Williams, Gary Yates, George, Yefchek, Gary Zajac, Carole Rapp-Zimmerman, and Linda Zogg.

At LexisNexis we have to thank Kelly Grondin and Carla Hoskinds. The copyediting, proofing, and sundry tasks associated with the production of a book were in the very capable hands of Janice Eccleston. Please accept our sincere appreciation and gratitude. We would be remiss not to mention the assistance and support of our friend Mickey Braswell, and the helpful review of the first edition from Dr. John Whitehead at East Tennessee State University.

A number of current and former graduate students at the University of Cincinnati assisted us (and put up with Ed Latessa) while we were finishing this book: Brian Lovins and Lori Brusman-Lovins, Kate Arnold, Kristin Bechtel, Dave Carter, Kelly Brown, Bill Hansell, Rebecca Schnupp, Amy Stichman, Kate Anderson, Richard Lemke, Jennifer Pealer, Coleen Kadleck, Debbie Shaffer, Tony Flores, and Charlene Taylor. We wish them well with their careers, and hope they adopt the book! Brittany Groot, Tamara Madensen, Jessica Warner and Jessica Halliday gave us some special technical assistance, especially with the figures and charts, and a special word of thanks to Janice Miller, John Schwartz, and Jean Gary for all their help and support.

To our colleagues and friends, without whose support and expertise this book would never have been possible: Harry Allen, Chris Lowenkamp, Larry Travis, Frank Cullen, Jim Frank, Jerry Vito, Bob Langworthy, Robin Engel, Patricia Van Voorhis, John Wright, and Chris Eskridge.

We also have to thank Amy, Jennifer, Michael, and Allison, who reminded us that delinquency prevention begins at home, and to Sara, who will let Paula test early intervention strategies. Finally, to Sally and Frank, who supported, fed, and cared for us. We love you.

Ed Latessa & Paula Smith

# Preface

For those of you that have used the first three editions you will undoubtedly note that Harry Allen is not longer a co-author. Harry continues to enjoy retirement in sunny Palm Springs, but has decided to scale back some of his writing obligations. We wish Harry the very best, and hope we can continue to build on his legacy.

Writing a book on a topic as broad and dynamic as community corrections is a very difficult task. It is extremely hard to know when to stop. The field is changing rapidly and, as a result, information and data are quickly outdated. We believe that we have pulled together some of the most recent and salient information available; however, we accept responsibility for any errors or shortcomings. There are several caveats we would like to make concerning this book.

First, there are a great many charts and tables with data. Memorizing the numbers is not important, they change daily. What is important are the trends over time. We want students to see patterns of what is happening in community corrections.

Second, you will also become aware of our bias. We believe that we incarcerate too many of our citizens, that this is not good social policy, and that they can be supervised in the community without seriously jeopardizing public safety. We believe that much public treasure is wasted and human misery increased while incarcerating low risk offenders. But, as our good friend Frank Cullen often says, "we are liberal, not stupid." We recognize that some offenders—those who are violent and would likely cause serious harm to others—belong in prison. We do not believe however, that all or even a majority of the nearly two million or so incarcerated fit that description.

Finally, there are many who believe that the ills confronting probation and parole are terminal. We do not believe that to be the case. While there is little doubt that the tasks confronting these correctional sanctions are daunting, we believe that the future of community corrections is bright and filled with promise. We hope that the instructors and students that use our book will find the subject of community corrections as interesting and stimulating as we do.

# Table of Contents in Brief

# Table of Contents

# The Criminal Justice System

> It is hard to identify the benefits inmates gain from prison, but the harm done there is readily seen. If you want to increase the crime problem, incite men to greater evil, and intensify criminal inclinations and proclivities, then lock violators up in prison for long periods, reduce their outside contacts, stigmatize them and block their lawful employment when released, all the while setting them at tutelage under the direction of more skilled and predatory criminals. I know of no better way to gain your ends than these.
>
> —Harry E. Allen

Crime is everywhere, in all nations great and small and, in this nation; crime is a violation of criminal statutes passed by elected representatives. The statutes are enforced by a variety of social control agencies specifically designed to fulfill some desired social function. These agencies include law enforcement, prosecution, court, and post-adjudication components that include, among other major units, the probation and parole systems. These varied agencies and actions, along with their philosophical bases and objectives, are usually called the "criminal justice system."

No one imposed this unique blend of agencies on the nation. We invented them ourselves and, if there is something amiss with an agency or mission, it can be changed. One fact about the American criminal justice system is that it is rapidly evolving and changing as a result of the volume of crime, emerging national priorities, available funding, and changing political ideologies. Behaviors thought particularly heinous in one epoch may become regulated, if not accepted, behavior in another. The Great Experiment of Prohibition attempted to protect our national character and youth, increase productivity, lessen collateral problems of idleness and wastrel-like behavior, and improve the moral fiber of those using alcohol, but is no longer a national crusade. As a result, earlier twentieth-century law enforcement efforts lapsed into a phase of tax collection, and controlled-substance, concerned only in large part with keeping alcohol out of the hands of youthful consumers. So it is with the current War on Drugs.

One component of the criminal justice system is corrections, earlier defined as "post-adjudication processing of convicted criminal offenders." This definition, if it were ever adequate, probably best fits the correctional scene of the early twentieth century, when the major sentencing options available to sentencing courts were committing the offender to prison or granting probation. In fact, the study of post-adjudication processing of criminal law offenders was, until about 1969, commonly referred to as "penology."

The field of corrections, like most of the justice system, has undergone rapid change in the past three decades. Programs have been developed to allow prosecutors to suspend prosecution of alleged malefactors provided they became and remained actively involved in seeking personal development and rehabilitation under the "deferred prosecution" program. Pretrial detention of accused law violators is now rare, due to the development of personal recognizance programs

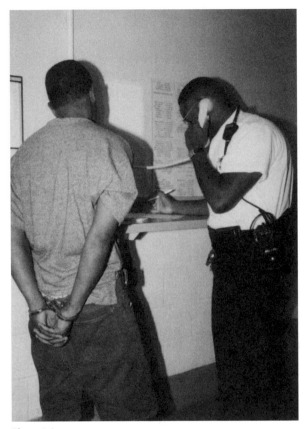

Photo 1.1
Booking in local jail. Photograph by Beth Sanders.

that reduced the importance of the bondsman in the pretrial portion of the system. In addition, the tools of technology have grown greatly in the past two decades, expanding probation supervision into conventional probation, intensive supervised probation, house arrest (with or without electronic monitoring or global position tracking), community service, day attendance centers, and restitution programs. There are even probation variations that combine serving a sentence in jail before probation begins, and several probation programs that require a period of imprisonment prior to return to the community under probation supervision. These latter programs, incidentally, are part of the "intermediate sanctions" that have emerged in the past 25 years: offender control programs that fall somewhere between probation and imprisonment.

What has corrections become? How can we best define it at the present time? For us, corrections is the social control agency that provides societal protection by providing incarceration and community supervision and rehabilitation services to persons accused or convicted of criminal law violating behavior. This definition includes restorative justice and pretrial diversion programs as well as the more traditional probation and parole services. It also embraces intermediate sanctions as well as alternative early-release programs for inmates in prisons across the nation. In sum, corrections is social control of persons whose behavior has brought them to the attention of the justice system. The missions, objectives, procedures, and even principles of corrections have undergone such rapid change recently that we are forced to expand the traditional definition of corrections to include the most recent developments. In another two decades, our current definition may be thought as outdated as the earlier one. We hope to suggest the emerging dimensions as your reading progresses.

## Corrections in the Community

This textbook describes and explains corrections in the community, or "community corrections." This term refers to numerous and diverse types of supervision, treatment, reintegration, control, restoration, and supportive programs for criminal law violators. Community corrections programs, as will be seen later, are designed for offenders at many levels of both the juvenile and criminal justice systems. First, community corrections programs are found in the pre-adjudication level of the justice systems, and include diversion and pretrial release programs, as well as treatment programs provided by private sector agencies, particularly for juveniles (Allen, Latessa, Ponder & Simonsen, 2007; Maloney, Bazemore & Hudson, 2001; Shaffer, Listwan & Latessa, 2001; and Travis & Petersilia, 2001).

As correctional clients move further into the justice system, community corrections programs have been developed and designed to minimize their further processing and penetration into the justice system. These pre-imprisonment programs include restitution, community services, active probation, intensive supervised probation, house arrest, and residential community facilities, such as halfway houses. (All these programs are described in detail in later chapters.) One assumption underlying the effort to minimize offender penetration into the justice system is that incarceration is less effective in reintegrating offenders and is unnecessarily expensive for the good attained. Another assumption is that community corrections is more humane, although there is some contemporary debate over whether corrections ought to be humane rather than harsh. Community corrections is certainly no less effective in reducing recidivism than is prison, and there is strong evidence that community correctional programs, if properly administered can significantly reduce recidivism.[1]

Figure 1.1
**What is the Sequence of Events in the Criminal Justice System?**

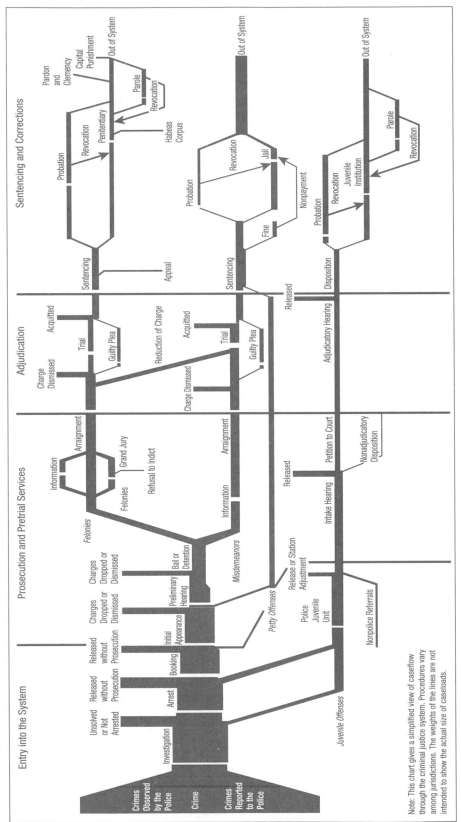

Note: This chart gives a simplified view of caseflow through the criminal justice system. Procedures vary among jurisdictions. The weights of the lines are not intended to show the actual size of caseloads.

Source: Adapted from *The Challenge of Crime in a Free Society*. President's Commission on Law Enforcement and Administration of Justice, 1967.

Community corrections continues after incarceration (and in some cases is combined with incarceration)[2] and among the many programs found at this level are split sentences (jail followed by probation), shock incarceration and shock probation, prison furlough programs, work and educational release, shock parole, and parole programs and services.[3] The various points at which community corrections programs have been developed are suggested in Figure 1.1, which identifies the flow of clients into and through the justice system.

The diagram of Figure 1.1 first appeared in President Lyndon Johnson's Crime Commission report, *The Challenge of Crime in a Free Society* (1969). It outlined the basic sequence of events in the criminal justice process. Police, courts, and corrections were thus viewed as elements that were interrelated and interdependent. The idea was to demonstrate the manner in which successful crime prevention was the goal of the entire system. Community corrections fits squarely into this goal: offenders whose criminal behavior is reduced or eliminated through programs in the community will commit fewer if any crimes in the future.[4]

Two major factors should be pointed out in Figure 1.1. First, the major ways out of the system are probation and parole, shown here as system outputs. The second conclusion is that the number of cases flowing through the system decreases as offenders are processed at the various decision points (prosecutor, court, sentencing, and release from prison). Figure 1.2 depicts the flow of offenders through the system for those arrested for Type 1 felony crimes in 2003.

Figure 1.2
**Outcomes for Arrest for Felony Crime: 2003**

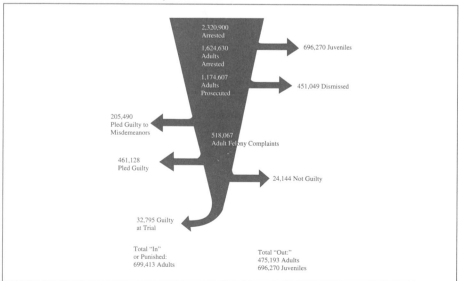

Sources: Federal Bureau of Investigation (2004). *Uniform Crime Report: Crime in the United States: 2003*. Washington, DC: U.S. Department of Justice. Figure adapted from C. Silberman (1978). *Criminal Violence, Criminal Justice*, pp. 257-261. New York, NY: Random House.

Box 1.1

**Probation and Parole**

Probation is a sentence imposed by the court that does not usually involve confinement and imposes conditions to restrain the offender's actions in the community. The court retains authority to modify the conditions of the sentence or to resentence the offender if he or she violates the conditions.

Parole is the release of an offender from confinement prior to expiration of sentence on condition of good behavior and supervision in the community.

The percentage of offenders in each major correctional sanction can be found in Figure 1.3. Non-incarceration sentences were imposed for nearly 60 percent of offenders in 2005. Another 10.9 percent that were sentenced were released from prison onto parole supervision. Together this represents nearly 5 milllion offenders. Even a large part of those offenders sentenced to jail may be released onto probation as part of a split-sentence. It should be obvious that community corrections handles a large proportion of the offenders in the nation. For example, the Bureau of Justice Statistics (2006) reported that one in every 32 adult residents of the nation were under correctional control at the start of 2006. On the basis of 100,000 adult residents in the nation, 1,884 were on probation 347 on parole 738 in prison, and 252 in jail. See Table 1.1.

Figure 1.3
**Correctional Populations in the United States, 2005**

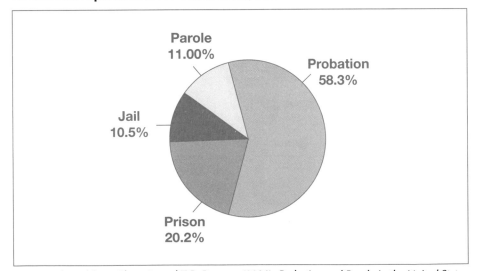

Source: Adapted from Glaze, L. and T.P. Bonczar (2006). *Probation and Parole in the United States, 2005*. U.S. Department of Justice, Office of Justice Programs.

Box 1.2

## Jail

A jail is a confinement facility, usually administered by a local law enforcement agency, intended for adults but sometimes containing juveniles, that holds persons detained pending adjudication and/or persons committed after adjudication for sentences of one year or less. Jails are usually supported by local tax revenues and, as such, are particularly vulnerable to resource reductions.

Additional categories of jail inmates include mentally ill persons for whom there are no other facilities or who are awaiting transfer to mental health authorities, parolees and probationers awaiting hearings, court-detained witnesses and persons charged with contempt of court, federal prisoners awaiting pick up by marshals, and offenders sentenced to state department of corrections for whom there is not yet space but who cannot be released ("holdbacks").

Box 1.3

## Prison

A state or federal confinement facility having custodial authority over criminal-law violating adults sentenced to confinement for usually more than one year.

Table 1.1
**Number of Adults Under Correctional Supervision in 2005 and per 100,000 Residents**

|  | Total | Rate per 100,000 |
|---|---|---|
| Probation | 4,162,536 | 1,884 |
| Parole | 784,408 | 347 |
| Prison | 1,446,269 | 738 |
| Jail | 747,529 | 252 |
| Total correctional population | 7,056,000 | 3,150 |

Source: Glaze, L.E., and T. Bonsczar, (2006). *Probation and Parole in the United States, 2005.* Washington, DC: U.S. Bureau of Justice Statistics.

More than two out of three offenders were living in the community on a given day in 2005. A list of the incarceration rate for each state is shown in Table. 1.2. Louisiana leads the nation with a rate of 797 per 100,000, and Maine has the lowest with 144.

Table 1.2
**Ranking of States by Prison Incarceration Rates, 2005(Inmates per 100,000 Residents)**

| | | | | | | |
|---|---|---|---|---|---|---|
| 1 | Louisiana | 797 | 27 | Wisconsin | 380 |
| 2 | Texas | 691 | 28 | Connecticut | 373 |
| 3 | Mississippi | 660 | 29 | Montana | 373 |
| 4 | Oklahoma | 652 | 30 | Oregon | 365 |
| 5 | Alabama | 539 | 31 | North Carolina | 360 |
| 6 | Georgia | 533 | 32 | Illinois | 351 |
| 7 | Missouri | 529 | 33 | Pennsylvania | 340 |
| 8 | South Carolina | 525 | 34 | Hawaii | 340 |
| 9 | Arizona | 521 | 35 | Kansas | 330 |
| 10 | Florida | 499 | 36 | New York | 326 |
| 11 | Michigan | 489 | 37 | New Mexico | 323 |
| 12 | Arkansas | 479 | 38 | New Jersey | 313 |
| 13 | Nevada | 474 | 39 | Iowa | 294 |
| 14 | Idaho | 472 | 40 | West Virginia | 291 |
| 15 | Delaware | 467 | 41 | Washington | 273 |
| 16 | California | 466 | 42 | Utah | 252 |
| 17 | Virginia | 464 | 43 | Vermont | 247 |
| 18 | Kentucky | 459 | 44 | Nebraska | 245 |
| 19 | Colorado | 457 | 45 | Massachusetts | 239 |
| 20 | South Dakota | 443 | 46 | North Dakota | 208 |
| 21 | Tennessee | 440 | 47 | New Hampshire | 192 |
| 22 | Alaska | 414 | 48 | Rhode Island | 189 |
| 23 | Wyoming | 400 | 49 | Minnesota | 180 |
| 24 | Ohio | 400 | 50 | Maine | 144 |
| 25 | Maryland | 394 | 51 | Federal System | 56 |
| 26 | Indiana | 388 | | | |
| | | | | **U.S. Total:** | **491** |

Source: Beck, A. and P. Harrison (2006). *Prisoners in 2005*. Washington, DC: U.S. Bureau of Justice Statistics, p. 3 (www.ojp.usdoj.gov/bjs/pub/pdf/p00.pdf).

## Probation in America

Nearly 60 percent of the adults under correctional care or custody are on probation, the largest single segment of the community correctional system. As shown in Table 1.3, Texas has the largest number of its citizens on probation, but that Massachusetts had the highest rate: 3,350 per 100,000 adult residents. Seven other states each had a rate of more than 2,500. The lowest state rate was New Hampshire (457 per 100,000).

Table 1.3
**Community Corrections Among the States, End of Year, 2005**

| 10 States with the largest 2004 community corrections population | Number supervised | 10 States with the highest rate of supervision, 2004 | Persons supervised per 100,000 adult U.S. residents* | 10 States with the lowest rates of supervision, 2004 | Persons supervised per 100,000 adult U.S. residents* |
|---|---|---|---|---|---|
| **Probation:** | | | | | |
| Texas | 430,312 | Massachusetts | 3,350 | New Hampshire | 447 |
| California | 388,260 | Rhode Island | 3,091 | West Virginia | 533 |
| Florida | 277,831 | Minnesota | 2,988 | Utah | 578 |
| Ohio | 239,036 | Delaware | 2,828 | Nevada | 709 |
| Michigan | 176,609 | Ohio | 2,745 | Kansas | 723 |
| Pennsylvania | 167,561 | Indiana | 2,583 | Maine | 776 |
| Massachusetts | 165,365 | Texas | 2,580 | Virginia | 788 |
| Illinois | 143,136 | Michigan | 2,350 | North Dakota | 791 |
| New Jersey | 139,091 | Washington | 2,155 | New York | 810 |
| Indiana | 121,014 | New Jersey | 2,117 | South Dakota | 899 |
| **Parole:** | | | | | |
| California | 111,743 | Pennsylvania | 787 | Maine | 3 |
| Texas | 101,916 | Arkansas | 782 | Florida | 34 |
| Pennsylvania | 75,732 | Oregon | 766 | Rhode Island | 41 |
| New York | 53,533 | Louisiana | 712 | North Carolina | 47 |
| Illinois | 34,576 | Texas | 611 | Nebraska | 50 |
| Louisiana | 24,072 | California | 421 | North Dakota | 57 |
| Georgia | 22,851 | Missouri | 414 | Massachusetts | 73 |
| Oregon | 21,499 | South Dakota | 414 | Virginia | 78 |
| Michigan | 19,978 | Wisconsin | 365 | Mississippi | 90 |
| Ohio | 19,512 | New York | 364 | Delaware | 91 |

Note: This table excludes the District of Columbia, a wholly urban jurisdiction, Georgia Probation counts, which included probation case-based counts for private agencies, and Idaho probation counts in which estimates for misdemeanors were based on admissions.

*Rates are computed using the U.S. adult resident population on January 1, 2006.

Source: Glaze, L.E. and T. Bonczar (2006). *Probation and Parole in the United States, 2004.* Washington DC. Bureau of Justice Statistics, p. 3.

In all, it is clear that a great number of convicted persons are now being placed on probation. In most cases, probation agencies monitor the offender's compliance with the conditions of probation release (restitution, community service, payment of fines, house arrest, drug/alcohol rehabilitation, etc.). The crucial roles that probation plays in community corrections and the justice system become even more apparent when institutional and parole population figures are examined.

## The U.S. Prison Population

Because the rate of parole in a given state is affected by the size of the prison population, it is necessary to examine the size of the U.S. prison population before considering parole figures. A census of state and federal institutions is conducted annually and at midyear of each year by the Bureau of Justice Statistics (Harrison & Beck 2006). At the beginning of 2006, the number of people incarcerated in prison was 1,525,924, an all-time high. These figures are even more dramatic when you consider that an estimated 8.1 percent of black males in their late twenties were in prison (Harrison & Beck, 2006:1). Overall, the U.S. prison population rose 34 percent from 1995 to the beginning of 2006, to an all-time high. See Figure 1.4 for the number of persons under correctional supervision in 1995 and 2005.

Figure 1.4
**Correctional Populations in the United States, 1995, 2000, 2005**

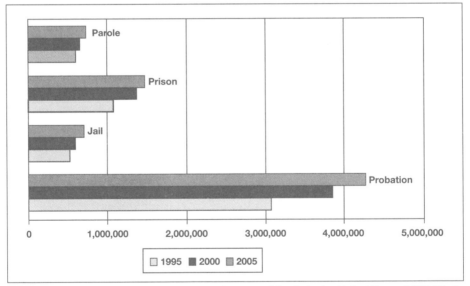

Source: Lauren, E. and T. Bonczar (2006). *Probation and Parole in the United States, 2005.* Washington, DC: U.S. Bureau of Justice Statistics.

These figures are important to the parole rates in part because they represent the source of clients for the parole system. Prisoners enter the parole system by a parole board decision or by fulfilling the condition of mandatory release. Typically, at some time between their minimum and maximum sentences, inmates are released from prison and placed on parole. Mandatory releasees enter parole supervision automatically at the expiration of their maximum terms (minus sentence reductions for time credit accumulated for good time, jail time, and other "gain" procedures). Traditionally, this has been the manner in which a parole system operated under the indeterminate sentencing model presently in force in one-half of the states. The "abandon parole" movement began in 1976, and a number of states have changed their statutes to remove the authority of the parole board to release offenders before the expiration of their sentences. This issue will be discussed in more detail in the chapters that follow.

## Parole in America

Adults on parole at the beginning of 2006 are found in Table 1.1, and totaled 784,408, the highest number ever on parole. Table 1.3 shows that the parole rate ranged from a high of 787 in Pennsylvania to a low of three in Maine). Maine abolished in the late 1970s which explains the low rate.

In sum, the parole statistics reveal the relationship between the size of the prison population and the number of parolees. These figures indicate that both the prison and parole populations dramatically increased from 1995 through 2004. See Figure 1.4. Changes in sentencing options and sentence length have also meant that prisoners were actually serving longer sentences in 2005 than they were in 1995.

## Summary

This brief consideration of statistics from the major components of the correctional system (probation, prisons, and parole) demonstrates their crucial linkage within the criminal justice system. Imagine what would happen if probation and parole were completely abolished and all convicted persons were required to serve their full prison terms. If this had happened in 2004, the prison population could have been nearly seven million! Naturally, the prison system is not equipped to handle such a large number of inmates, nor would it be good social policy to attempt such a foolish venture.

We do not wish to suggest that all offenders could and should be released to community corrections. At least 15 to 25 percent of the prison population are too dangerous or pose too great a threat to community safety to allow their immediate release, even onto "intensive supervised parole" (Allen et al., 2007).

It is the function of probation and its many variants (the so-called "intermediate punishments"), as well as parole, to determine how the population of convicted persons can be managed in a fashion consistent with not only the capacity of the prison population but also the goals of societal protections and offender rehabilitation and reintegration.

In short, the examination of corrections in the community is the theme of this text. We will consider such key issues as: What are the best methods for classifying offenders? For supervising them? What background, education, and training should various community correctional agents possess? How effective are community correctional programs, in terms of public safety? And at what cost? What are the recent innovations in community corrections and intermediate punishments? How effective are these compared to incarceration? The consideration of these (and other) issues will provide readers with the opportunity to form their own opinions and ideas concerning the proper use of community correctional programs, and how to coordinate these in the criminal justice system.

## Review Questions

1. What is corrections in the community?

2. What is meant by the funnel effect, and how does it occur?

3. If probation and parole were completely abolished, what effect would this have on the prison system?

4. Develop an argument for increased use of community corrections.

5. How are offenders generally released from prison?

6. Describe the current distribution of offenders across the main components of the criminal justice system.

## Key Terms

corrections
community corrections
criminal justice system
incarceration

intermediate sanctions
parole
prison
probation

## Electronic Library

Bureau of Justice Statistics www.ojp.usdoj.gov/bjs/

FBI Uniform Crime Reports http://www.fbi.gov/ucr/ucr.htm

National Institute of Corrections www.nicic.org

## Recommended Readings

Allen, H.E., E.J. Latessa, B. Ponder, and C. Simenson (2007). *Correctons in Amercia*. Englewood-Cliffs, NJ: Prentice-Hall.

Latessa, E.J., A. Holsinger (2006). *Correctional Contexts: Contemporary and Classical Readings*. Los Angeles, CA: Roxbury.

## Notes

[1]   An extensive body of research has demonstrated that community correctional programs can have a substantial effect on recidivism provided certain empirically derived principles are met. For a summary of this research see: Latessa, Edward J., and Christopher Lowenkamp (2007). "What Works in Reducing Recidivism." *St. Thomas Law Journal*.

[2]   For example, in Ohio, the state funds "community-based correctional facilities." These facilities are operated by local community corrections boards, are designed to provide treatment, and often utilize local community services. They are, however, secure facilities. For descriptions of the Florida circumstances, see Karl Lucken (1997). "The Dynamics of Penal Reform." Crime, Law and Social Change 26(4):367-384. For a California example, see Harry Wexler et al. (1999). "Three Year Reincarceration Outcomes for Amity In-Prison Therapeutic Community and Aftercare in California." *Prison Journal*, 79/3:321-336.

[3]   Some would argue that many so-called "community" correctional programs are essentially institutional correctional facilities because they are state run. However, we believe that state-operated programs can indeed be considered community correctional programs, provided they include some type of supervision in the community. For a different perspective on this issue see D.E. Duffee (1990). "Community Characteristics: The Presumed Characteristics and Argument for a New Approach." In D.E. Duffee and E.F. McGarrell (eds.) *Community Corrections: A Community Field Approach*. Cincinnati, OH: Anderson Publishing Co. See also Burke, P.B. (1997). *Policy Driven Responses to Probation and Parole Violations*. Washington, DC: U.S. Department of Justice; and Paul Gendreau, Claire Goggin and Paula Smith (2000). "Generating Rational Correctional Policies," *Corrections Management Quarterly*, 4/2:52-60.

4    See Lowenkamp, Christopher T., Edward J. Latessa, and Alex Holsinger (2006). The risk principle in action: What we have learned from 13,676 offenders and 97 correctional programs. *Crime & Delinquency*, 52(1); and D.B. Wilson, C.A. Gallagher and D.L. MacKenzie (2000). "A Meta-Analysis of Corrections-Based Education, Vocation, and Work Programs for Adult Offenders," *Journal of Research in Crime and Delinquency*, 37/4:347-368.

## References

Allen, H.E., E.L. Latessa, B. Ponder, and C.E. Simonsen (2007). *Corrections in America*. Englewood Cliffs, NJ: Prentice-Hall.

Burke, P.B. (1997). *Policy Driven Responses to Probation and Parole Violations*. Washington, DC: U.S. Department of Justice.

Duffee, D.E. (1990). *Community Characteristics: The Presumed Characteristics and Argument for a New Approach*. In D.E. Duffee and E.F. McGarrell (eds.) Community Corrections: A Community Field Approach. Cincinnati, OH: Anderson Publishing Co.

Federal Bureau of Investigation (2004). *Crime in the United States, 2003*. Washington, DC: U.S. Department of Justice.

Gendreau, P., C. Goggin, and P. Smith (2000). "Generating Rational Correctional Policies." *Corrections Management Quarterly*, 4/2:52-60.

Glaze, L.E. and S. Palla (2005). *Probation and Parole in the United States, 2004*. Washington, DC: U.S. Bureau of Justice Statistics.

Harrison, P. and A. Beck (2005). *Prison and Jail Inmates in Midyear 2005*. Washington, DC: Bureau of Justice Statistics.

Latessa, E.J. and C. Lowenkamp (2007). "What Works in Reducing Recidivism." *St. Thomas Law Journal*, 3:521-535.

Lowenkamp, C. T., E. J. Latessa, and A. Holsinger (2006). "The Risk Principle in Action: What We Have Learned From 13,676 Offenders and 97 Correctional Programs." *Crime & Delinquency*, 51(1):1-17.

Lucken, K. (1997). "The Dynamics of Penal Reform." *Crime, Law and Social Change*, 26(4):367-384.

Maloney, D., G. Bazemore, and J. Hudson (2001). "The End of Probation and the Beginning of Community Justice." *Perspectives*, 25(3):22-31.

President's Commission on Law Enforcement and Administration of Justice (1969). *The Challenge of Crime in a Free Society*. Washington, DC: U.S. Government Printing Office.

Shaffer, D.K., S. Listwan, and E. Latessa (2001). *A Description of Ohio's Drug Courts*. Cincinnati, OH: University of Cincinnati Center for Criminal Justice Research.

Silberman, C. (1978). *Criminal Violence, Criminal Justice*. New York, NY: Random House.

Travis, J. and J. Petersilia (2001). "Reentry Reconsidered: A New Look at an Old Question." *Crime & Delinquency*, 47(3):291-313.

Wexler, H., G. Melnick, L. Lowe, and M. Hiller (1999). "Three-Year Reincarceration Outcomes for Amity In-Prison Therapeutic Community and Aftercare in California." *Prison Journal*, 79(3):337-351.

Wilson, D.B., C. Gallagher, and D. MacKenzie (2000). "A Meta-Analysis of Corrections-based Education, Vocation, and Work Programs for Adult Offenders." *Journal of Research in Crime and Delinquency*, 37(4):347-368.

# Sentencing and Community Corrections

## 2

Justice is itself the great standing policy of
civil society; and any eminent departure
from it, under any circumstances, lies under
the suspicion of being no policy at all.
—Edmund Burke

## Contemporary Sentencing Practices

Historically, the American criminal justice system was an adversarial combat between the State and the accused defendant in a criminal trial. The accused denied committing the alleged offense, and the trial jury was charged with determining the fact of innocence or guilt. If found guilty the presiding judge, using all available information and guided by the presentence investigation report previously ordered from the court's investigators, would then impose sentence on the guilty in the interest of justice and to achieve some recognizable correctional objective. Such objectives could include punishment, rehabilitation, reintegration, retribution, reparation, or deterrence.

Perhaps this model typified the justice system a half-decade ago, but it is atypical of sentencing practices in the 2000s. Some 1,510,000 persons were convicted of a felony offense in State courts in 2002, including 197,030 for a violent felony (Durose & Langan, 2005). A large number of convictions were for drug possession and trafficking, about 32 percent of the total number of felony convictions and almost two-and-one-half times the number of convictions for all crimes of violence totaled together (murder, robbery, rape, and aggravated assault). Federal courts convicted 63,217 persons of a felony in 2002. That number represents only six percent of the combined state and federal convictions in that year. See Table 2.1 for the types of sentences imposed by state courts.

Table 2.1
**Types of Felony Sentences Imposed in State Courts, 2002 (in percent)**

| Crime | Non-Incarceration Probation | Incarceration Jail | Sentences Prison |
|---|---|---|---|
| Murder | 5 | 4 | 91 |
| Sexual Assault | 18 | 23 | 59 |
| Robbery | 14 | 15 | 71 |
| Aggravated Assault | 29 | 29 | 42 |
| Burglary | 28 | 26 | 46 |
| Larceny | 33 | 31 | 36 |
| Motor Vehicle Theft | 24 | 39 | 37 |
| Drug Trafficking | 32 | 26 | 45 |
| ALL | 31 | 28 | 41 |

Source: Durose, M., D. Levin, and P. Langan (2004). *Felony Sentences in State Courts, 2002.* Washington, DC: U.S. Bureau of Justice Statistics, p. 2 (www.ojp.usdoj.gov/bjs/pub/pdf/fssc98.pdy).

Determination of guilt, however, seldom employed a jury in 2002 or today. Instead, most of those convicted (95%) pled guilty for considerations, and the judge usually complied with the negotiated plea that had been struck by prosecutor and defense counsel. Only five percent of the total convicted were found guilty through trial, and 60 percent of those were convicted by the judge in a bench trial (Durose & Langan, 2005). A definition of plea bargaining is found in Box 2.1.

Box 2.1

### Plea Bargaining

The exchange of prosecutorial and/or judicial concessions, commonly a lesser charge, the dismissal of other pending charges, a recommendation by the prosecutor for a reduced sentence or a combination thereof, in return for a plea of guilty.

Regardless of the avenue of conviction, 69 percent of those convicted felony offenders were sentenced to incarceration (either prison or jail). The remaining 31 percent were sentenced to probation. Of course, probation is the umbrella under which many other community-based alternatives reside. Before we look at sentencing options it is important to examine overall sentencing approaches.

# The Development of Parole and the Indeterminate Sentence

A basic tenet underlying sentencing in the nineteenth century was a belief in the perfectibility of humans. The American Revolution engendered a great deal of interest and enthusiasm for reform. The emerging nation threw off the dread yoke of British imperialism, including the harsh and widely hated British laws in place throughout the colonies that relied so heavily on the death penalty. In its place, a more rational system of "corrections" arose; the ideal of certain but humane punishment that was believed to most certainly deter offenders from criminal careers. American entered the "Progressive Era" in which "rational men" would be able to pursue their best interests and maximize gain and reward, while avoiding penalties or pain. This famous principle ("hedonistic calculus") was wholeheartedly accepted as a guiding objective in the question being asked by concerned citizens, lawmakers, and public officials: "Who are offenders and what shall we do with them?" Under the British codes, they were seen as inherently evil and thus to be punished, killed, or disabled. Under the Progressive Era, the answer that emerged was quite different: They are people out of touch with God and, given a chance to change by thinking about their crime and relationship with God and fellow humans, they will opt to repent and change. The prison was the answer to the policy question of what to do with offenders, and America embraced prisons with its general zeal for humanitarianism and enthusiasm, building huge "fortress" prisons that emphasized reform and repentance. The American penitentiary ("place to do penance") was a contribution to corrections throughout the world.

Yet in the emerging penitentiary and later reformatory movements, there remained the philosophical quandary: What to do with the reformed offender who continued to be held in prison years after actual reformation. Sentencing codes were determinate or "flat" and inmates were expected to serve their sentences to the day. In this philosophical environment, correctional administrators began to innovate.

In the British outpost of Australia, offenders who had been sentenced to exile by transportation to Australia occasionally continued their violent criminal behavior. Transported felons were failures because they had committed crimes in England; when they continued their miscreant behavior in Australia, they were shipped to Norfolk Island, onto a bleak and inhospitable shore some 1,000 miles to the east. These "double failures" of Australia who were subsequently sentenced to death thanked God, but those sentenced to Norfolk Island sank into the deepest depression and sadness. Such was the place that Captain Alexander Maconochie inherited when he was posted as managing officer in 1842.

Maconochie quickly determined that the violence, treachery, and staff-inmate confrontations had to stop, and seized upon what is now known as the "mark" system (also known now as a form of token economy). Assembling the inmates, he promised that there was hope of freedom if any inmate could amass 100 marks (credits). Each inmate was to be billed for food, clothing, and tools; marks were to be assigned for quantity and quality of work. Through hard work and frugal living, inmates could save marks; when an inmate amassed 100 marks, he was free from correctional control, to marry and live on the island, and conduct himself in proper behavior. Assault and violence immediately declined with this innovative and constructive management approach, but the Royal Marines assigned to prison officer duty thought Maconochie was too lenient and molly-coddled offenders. Maconochie was quickly removed, and Norfolk Island slid rapidly back into the slough of despair it was before Maconochie's innovative management.

Fortunately, Maconochie's ideas spread: imprisonment could be used to prepare an offender for a productive life and eventual return to the community under what could be seen as an "indeterminate sentence." The implications of this demonstration were that sentence length should not be an arbitrary or "flat" sentence but one related to the reform and rehabilitation of the inmate. Sir Walter Crofton in Ireland used Maconochie's concepts when he developed what became known as the "Irish" system.

Crofton reasoned that if penitentiaries were places where offenders reflect on their crimes and would decide to stop their criminal activities ("repent"), then there should be some mechanism or scheme to detect when the reform had occurred, as well as releasing the offender when this had happened. Crofton established a three-stage system, each of which would bring the convict closer to freedom within the community. Phase One consisted of solitary confinement and tedious work, such as picking oakum (separating coconut fibers for the purpose of making rope). After six months, the convict could be assigned to public works on a team, each member of which was responsible for the behavior of every other team member (an early use of "peer pressure"). Anyone who misbehaved would cause all team members to be returned to Phase One. The last phase was assignment to a transitional prison permitting unsupervised day work outside the prison. If the inmate's behavior was good and he could find employment in the community, he was given a "ticket of leave," in effect extending the limits of confinement to include placement in the county on "conditional pardon." While the ex-inmate could not leave the county and was required to produce his "ticket" upon demand by law enforcement agents, he was nonetheless free of correctional control for the duration of his sentence. Of course, if his conduct was bad, the ticket could be revoked and the offender returned to prison (Phase One). In effect, Crofton established conditional liberty in the community, what now would be called parole.

By 1870, prison crowding in the United States had become so massive and the related management problems so complex that a conference was deemed necessary. Prison administrators, wardens, religious leaders, concerned leaders, and innovators met in Cincinnati, Ohio in 1870 in the first meeting of what would become the American Correctional Association. Spurred on by Crofton and empowered by eloquent oratory by Zebulon Reed Brockway, the assembly adopted standards and principles that addressed both new types of buildings to be constructed as well as an early release system. In 1876, Brockway initiated parole in the nation by the ticket of leave system. New York quickly passed enabling legislation and parole became a reality.

Other states responded by changing their sentencing structures as well as by authorizing parole as a mechanism for releasing reformed offenders. The resultant sentencing system was the indeterminate sentence, the dominant sentencing structure in the United States until the mid-1970s.

---

Box 2.2

### Indeterminate Sentencing

Under the indeterminate sentencing system, the sentencing judge pronounces a minimum and maximum period of incarceration, such as from three to five years ("3 to 5") or 5-10, or 1-20, and so on. Correctional personnel were expected to assist the offenders in changing their behavior and preparing for eventual return to the community, and the parole board was to monitor offender behavior and change. The actual decision on parole readiness and release was detailed to a parole board, charged with protecting society and releasing offenders onto community correctional supervision. The actual conditions of parole were set by the parole board, which retained authority to return non-adjusting offenders to the prison for further treatment and punishment. In essence, the sentencing judge shares sentence length determination with the executive branch in which parole boards are located.

---

Box 2.3

### Pretrial Release

The process by which those accused of a crime are released prior to trial. Mechanisms for release include posting bond, or release on recognisance (a promise to return to stand trial).

## Rapid Change in Sentencing

By 1930, most states and federal courts were operating under the indeterminate sentencing structure. The wide range of sentence lengths reflected the dominant rehabilitation goal of the correctional system and the belief that once the offender had been rehabilitated, the parole board would detect the change and then order parole release.[1] Parole boards actually determined the length of the sentence served, using their authority of discretionary release.

Following a very long period of relative inactivity (1930-1974), American sentencing laws and practices began to undergo rapid change, a fundamental restructuring of the sentencing process. The causes have been identified (Allen, Latessa, Ponder, & Simonsen, 2007:67):

1. Prison uprisings (such as at Attica in New York, and others in California, Florida, New Mexico, and Oklahoma) indicated that inmates were particularly discontented with the rhetoric of rehabilitation and the reality of the prison environment.

2. The abuse of discretion caused concerns about individual rights, as prosecutors, judges, and parole boards were immune from review and some practiced arbitrary uses of discretion.

3. Court orders and decisions led to a movement that demanded accountability in official decisionmaking and outcomes.

4. The rehabilitation ideal was challenged, both empirically and ideologically, which undermined the rationale of the indeterminate sentence's "parole after rehabilitation" corollary.

5. Experimental and statistical studies of judicial sentencing found substantial disparity and both racial and class discrimination. Such inconsistencies and disparities fostered the conclusion that sentencing practices were unfair. [Sentencing disparity occurs when offenders committing the same crimes under the same circumstances are given different sentences by the same judge.]

Box 2.4

### Sentencing Disparity

Sentencing disparity is the divergence in the types and lengths of sentences imposed for the same crimes, with no evident reason for the differences. It is also known as unequal treatment of similarly situated offenders.

6. Crime control and corrections became a political football, useful for those seeking election to public office. Such political opportunists led the general public to believe that lenient judges and parole boards were releasing dangerous offenders back into the community, with little concern for public safety.

## New Goals

Although corrections in the 1970s generally reflected the utilitarian goal of rehabilitation, other discussions from the reform movement brought additional correctional goals to the forefront in the 1980s, such as the incapacitation of persons likely to commit future crimes and its variant of selective incapacitation, in which the highest-risk offenders would receive much longer sentences in order to prevent any more criminal activity. The specific deterrence of sentenced offenders—and the general deterrence of those contemplating committing a crime—was legitimized as a social policy goal. One emerging example of this new goal is the "three-strikes" policy states have recently adopted, particularly in California, mandating long-term incarceration (at least 25 years) for those persons convicted of a serious or violent third felony. In addition, retribution as a goal became attractive, inasmuch as it would impose deserved punishment. (Such a "just deserts" strategy looks backward to the offender's personal culpability, focuses on the nature of the act, and considers the harm done.)

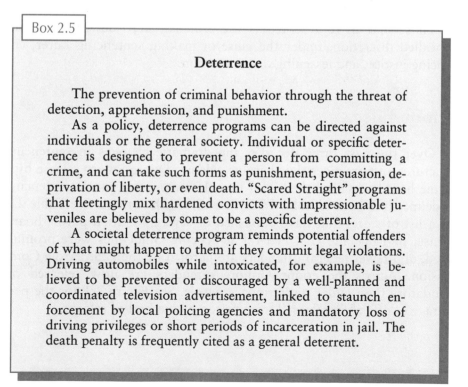

Box 2.5

### Deterrence

The prevention of criminal behavior through the threat of detection, apprehension, and punishment.

As a policy, deterrence programs can be directed against individuals or the general society. Individual or specific deterrence is designed to prevent a person from committing a crime, and can take such forms as punishment, persuasion, deprivation of liberty, or even death. "Scared Straight" programs that fleetingly mix hardened convicts with impressionable juveniles are believed by some to be a specific deterrent.

A societal deterrence program reminds potential offenders of what might happen to them if they commit legal violations. Driving automobiles while intoxicated, for example, is believed to be prevented or discouraged by a well-planned and coordinated television advertisement, linked to staunch enforcement by local policing agencies and mandatory loss of driving privileges or short periods of incarceration in jail. The death penalty is frequently cited as a general deterrent.

## Reform Options

As a result of the reform movement, sentencing practices were changed, in the belief that such practices would limit disparity and discretion, and establish more detailed criteria for sentencing or new sentencing institutions. These contradictory options included:

1. abolishing plea bargaining;

2. establishing plea-bargaining rules and guidelines;

3. setting mandatory minimum sentences;

4. establishing statutory determinate sentencing;

5. setting voluntary or descriptive sentencing guidelines or presumptive or prescriptive sentencing guidelines;

6. creating sentencing councils;

7. requiring judges to provide reasons for their sentences;

8. setting parole guidelines to limit parole board discretion;

9. abolishing parole;

10. adopting or modifying good-time procedures; and

11. routinizing appellate review of sentences (Allen et al, 2007:68-69).

Those options represent only the principal steps designed to limit unbridled discretion, under the guise of making sentencing fairer, enhancing justice, and lessening discrimination.

## Reform Effects

Over the past three decades, the dramatic changes in sentencing structures and practices thus became evident. Discretionary release by a parole board was abolished in at least 18 states, and parole sentencing guidelines had been established in one-half of the others. See Table 2.2 for a list of states that have abolished or severely limited parole board release. In 1987, the U.S. Federal Sentencing Guidelines were promulgated, and fewer federal offenders are paroled by the U.S. Parole Commission. Across the country, more offenders are now released on mandatory than under discretionary parole. See Figure 2.1 for the percentage of offenders released from prison by method of release.

Table 2.2
**States That Abolished or Severely Limit Parole Board Release**

| State | Year |
|-------|------|
| Arkansas | 1994 |
| Arizona | 1994 |
| California | 1976 |
| Delaware | 1990 |
| Florida | 1983 |
| Illinois | 1978 |
| Indiana | 1977 |
| Kansas | 1993 |
| Maine | 1975 |
| Minnesota | 1980 |
| Mississippi | 1995 |
| North Carolina | 1994 |
| Ohio | 1996 |
| Oregon | 1989 |
| South Dakota | 1996 |
| Virginia | 1995 |
| Washington | 1984 |
| Wisconsin | 1999 |

Source: Association of Paroling Authorities International, Parole Board Survey. www.reentry.org

Figure 2.1
**Releases from State Prison by Method of Release (1980-2003)**

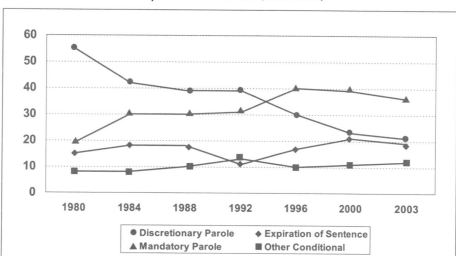

Source: Lauren, E. and S. Pella (2005). *Probation and Parole in the United States, 2004.* U.S. Department of Justice. Office of Justice Programs.

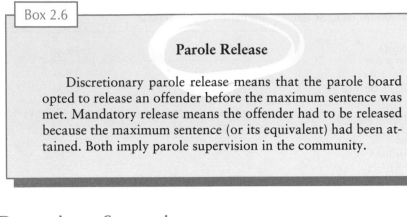

Box 2.6

**Parole Release**

Discretionary parole release means that the parole board opted to release an offender before the maximum sentence was met. Mandatory release means the offender had to be released because the maximum sentence (or its equivalent) had been attained. Both imply parole supervision in the community.

## Determinate Sentencing

Critics have identified several unwarranted and unwanted problems with indeterminate sentencing, as well as parole board decisionmaking. Reformers, neoclassical theorists, politicians, and organized political action groups with punitive agendas coalesced to attack rehabilitation and parole. The primary substitute for the indeterminate sentence is the determinate sentence, a throwback to the tradition of "flat time" in our earlier history. A determinate sentence is a fixed period of incarceration imposed on the offender by the sentencing court. The ideology underlying determinate sentencing is retribution, just deserts, incapacitation, and selective incapacitation.[2]

Travis and Petersilia (2001) found that 18 states have created sentencing commissions whose guidelines have restricted judicial sentencing discretion, that legislation creating mandatory minimum sentences had been enacted in all 50 states, and that 40 states now have sentencing laws requiring inmates to serve at least 50 percent of their sentences in prison. Of those 50 states, 27 (and the District of Columbia) have statutes requiring offenders to serve at least 85 percent of their sentence in prison. See Table 2.3 for a list of Truth-In-Sentencing requirements by state.

## Sentencing Guidelines

Sentencing guidelines for structuring the penalty decisions of judges work by providing decisionmakers with criteria and weights on which the sanction decision should be based (Hoffman & DeGostin, 1975). By explicitly stating the factors that are deemed relevant to the sentence decision, and by providing guidance to the sentencer, these guidelines ensure a greater degree of uniformity in criminal penalties. Explicit sentencing guidelines then work to limit the effect of extralegal factors on the sentencing decision.

Table 2.3
**Truth-in-Sentencing Requirements, by State**

| Meet Federal 85% requirement | | 50% of minimum requirement | 100% of minimum requirement | Other requirements |
|---|---|---|---|---|
| Arizona | Missouri | Indiana | Idaho | Alaska |
| California | New Jersey | Maryland | Nevada | Arkansas |
| Connecticut | New York | Nebraska | New Hampshire | Colorado |
| Delaware | North Carolina | Texas | Kentucky | |
| Dist. of Col. | North Dakota | Massachusetts | | |
| Florida | Ohio | Wisconsin | | |
| Georgia | Oklahoma | | | |
| Illinois | Oregon | | | |
| Iowa | Pennsylvania | | | |
| Kansas | South Carolina | | | |
| Louisiana | Tennessee | | | |
| Maine | Utah | | | |
| Michigan | Virginia | | | |
| Minnesota | Washington | | | |
| Mississippi | | | | |

Source: Ditton, P. and D. Wilson (1999). *Truth in Sentencing in State Prisons.* Washington, DC: U.S. Bureau of Justice Statistics, p. 2 (www.ojp.usdoj.gov/bjs/abstract/tssp.htm).

Such a sentencing structure limits judicial control over sentencing, as the legislature heavily influences the sentence length. Whether there are unforeseen problems in presumptive sentencing remains to be proven, but California's prison population problems may well be due to a corollary of presumptive sentencing: abolition of parole board early release authority that has been used to control prison overcrowding in the past. (California is now the largest single prison system in the world.)

Mandatory prison-term statutes now exist in all states. Those statutes apply for certain crimes of violence and for habitual criminals, and the court's discretion in such cases (regarding, for example, probation, fines, and suspended sentences) has been eliminated by statute. In some states the imposition of a prison term is constrained by sentencing guidelines, such as those shown in Figure 2.2. Guidelines are usually set by a governor's commission, including a cross section of the state population. As noted by a major study (Coleman & Guthrie, 1988:142):

> A sentencing commission in each state monitors the use of the guidelines and departures from the recommended sentences by the judiciary. Written explanations are required from judges who depart from guideline ranges. The Minnesota Sentencing Guidelines Commission states that 'while the sentencing guidelines are advisory to the sentencing judge, departures from the presumptive sentences established in the guidelines

Figure 2.2
**Sentencing Guidelines**

Offender: _____    Docket number: _____

Judge: _____    Date: _____

Offense(s) convicted of: _____

_____

*Crime score:*
   A.   Injury
         0   =   No injury
         1   =   Injury
         2   =   Death                              _____   +
   B.   Weapon
         0   =   No weapon
         1   =   Weapon
         2   =   Weapon present and used            _____   +
   C.   Drugs                                                        ┌─────┐
         0   =   No sale of drugs                                    │     │
         1   =   Sale of drugs                      _____   =    │     │
                                                                     └─────┘
                                                                      Crime
                                                                      score

*Offender score:*
   A.   Current legal status
         0   =   Not on probation/parole, escape
         1   =   On probation/parole, escape        _____   +
   B.   Prior adult misdemeanor convictions
         0   =   No convictions
         1   =   One conviction
         2   =   Two or more convictions            _____   +
   C.   Prior adult felony convictions
         0   =   No convictions
         2   =   One conviction
         4   =   Two or more convictions            _____   +
   D.   Prior adult probation parole revocations
         0   =   None
         1   =   One or more revocations            _____   +
   E.   Prior adult incarcerations (over 60 days)                 ┌─────┐
         0   =   None                                             │     │
         1   =   One incarceration                                │     │
         2   =   Two or more incarcerations         _____   = └─────┘
                                                                   Offender
                                                                   score

Guideline sentence: _____

Actual sentence: _____

Reasons (if actual sentence does not fall within guideline range): _____

_____

Figure 2.2—*continued*

Crime score

| | | | | |
|---|---|---|---|---|
| 4-5 | 4-6 years | 5-7 years | 6-8 years | 8-10 years |
| 3 | 3-5 years | 4-6 years | 6-8 years | 6-8 years |
| 2 | 2-4 years | 3-5 years | 3-5 years | 4-6 years |
| 1 | Probation | Probation | 2-4 years | 3-5 years |
| 0 | Probation | Probation | Probation | 2-4 years |
| | 0-1 | 2-4 | 5-7 | 8-10 |

Offender score

The sentencing judge first determines the crime score, typically concerned with the actual crime, injury, weapon used, and drug sale. Points are assigned as above under "Crime Score." Second, the judge scores the offender's prior behavior, using those items identified under "Offender Score." Determining the guideline sentence entails finding the grid cell that corresponded to the crime and offender score, and then imposing a sentence that falls within the suggested range.

Source: J. Kress et al. (1978). *Developing Sentencing Guidelines: Trainers Handbook.* Washington, DC: National Institute of Criminal Justice.

should be made only when substantial and compelling circumstances exist.' Pennsylvania sentencing guidelines stipulate that court failure to explain sentences deviating from the recommendations 'shall be grounds for vacating the sentence and re-sentencing the defendant.' Furthermore, if the court does not consider the guidelines or inaccurately or inappropriately applies them, an imposed sentence may be vacated upon appeal to a higher court by either the defense or the prosecution.

The range and particular format for sentencing guidelines can include such things as specifically worded statutes and grids with a range of judicial options. Similarly, parole guidelines are sometimes closely prescribed, and sometimes wide discretion is afforded to the parole board. The amount of flexibility in such decisions can directly enhance or detract from the efforts to relieve crowded prison conditions. Because most parole decisions are not based on time but on perceived "risk to the community," tighter and tighter criteria make it difficult to manage prison population size by such decisions.

## Three-Strikes Laws

No discussion of sentencing changes would be complete without exploring "three-strikes" sentencing laws. Although sentence enhancement statutes exist in most states (such as habitual or repeat offender laws), legislation that specifically identified a group of repeat offenders for lengthy incapacitation began to bloom in 1993 when Washington became the first state to enact three strike legislation. Currently 26 states and the federal government have enacted so-called three-strikes laws, all designed to remove offenders convicted of repeated serious offenses from society for a long period of time, if not for life. In California, for example, the minimum sentence under the three-strikes legislation is 25 years, with no "good time" credit. Time served will be no less than 25 years. As one might expect, some unusual cases have arisen in California. For example, one defendant was given a 25 years to life sentence for shoplifting golf clubs (with previous convictions for burglary and robbery with a knife). In one particular notorious case Kevin Weber was sentenced to 26 years to life for stealing four chocolate chip cookies after two previous convictions (Ellingwood, 1995). California also has a two-strikes law that doubles the presumptive sentence. In 2000 California voters did support an amendment to scale back punishment that provides drug treatment instead of life imprisonment for most convicted of possessing drugs, however, in 2004 voters rejected an amendment that would have required the third felony to be either "violent" or "serious" in order for a 25 years to life sentence. See Table 2.4 for a list of states that have enacted some sore of Three Strikes sentencing laws.

While the Supreme Court has upheld the constitutionality of using prior convictions as aggravating factors in determining a sentence, there are many critic os three strike legislation, there is little evidence that three-strikes laws are contributing significantly to reductions in crime rates, and there is no reason to believe that this sentencing effort will be appreciably different from other attempts to limit discretion.[3]

This review of the changes in sentencing practices and their consequences in the last decade clearly shows the shifts that have taken place. Although discretion in determining sentence length has been somewhat removed from the sentencing judge and parole board, it was reduced by legislatures through their enactment of new sentencing structures. In turn, in many jurisdictions, the prosecutor's discretion was increased.[4] The prison populations has continued to climb as more and more offenders are committed and serve longer and longer sentences (Wooldredge, 1996). See Figure 2.3 for the predicted prison population of inmates age 50 or older in California.

Let's now look at some of the other sentencing options that exist.

Table 2.4
**States That Have Some Sort of a Three-Strikes Sentencing Law**

| State | Year Adapted |
|-------|-------------|
| Arkansas | 1995 |
| California | 1994 |
| Colorado | 1994 |
| Connecticut | 1994 |
| Florida | 1995 |
| Georgia | 1994 |
| Indiana | 1994 |
| Kansas | 1994 |
| Louisiana | 1994 |
| Maryland | 1994 |
| Montana | 1995 |
| Nevada | 1995 |
| New Jersey | 1995 |
| New Mexico | 1994 |
| North Carolina | 1994 |
| North Dakota | 1995 |
| Pennsylvania | 1995 |
| South Carolina | 1995 |
| Tennessee | 1994 |
| Utah | 1995 |
| Vermont | 1995 |
| Virginia | 1994 |
| Washington | 1993 |
| Wisconsin | 1994 |

Figure 2.3
**Predicted Prison Population Age 50 and Over Under California's Three-Strikes Law (in percent)**

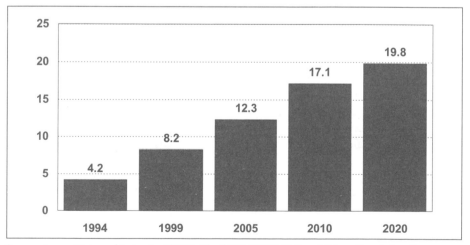

Source: Jones, M.A. and J. Austin (1995). *The 1995 NCCD National Prison Population Forecast*, p. 11. San Francisco, CA: National Council on Crime and Delinquency.

## Sentencing Options

In the plea bargaining process, defense counsel may negotiate sentence outcome to avoid incarceration of the accused. Thus the decision to incarcerate may, in part, depend on the outcome of negotiated justice. The two major incarceration outcomes are imprisonment in a penal facility or in a jail. The major alternative to incarceration is probation and such other intermediate punishments as weekend confinement, house arrest, electronic monitoring, fines, restitution and work centers, intensive supervised probation, and so on. These are discussed below.

If the decision is to place the offender on probation or other intermediate punishment, usually as a condition of probation, the offender is typically supervised by an officer of the local probation department. Conditional freedom under probation requires the probationer to meet certain conditions of behavior, as is noted in Chapter 3. If the probationer is in danger of substantively violating these conditions, or determined to be in need of additional service or more intensive supervision, the supervising officer may request that the judge increase the conditions of supervision to include additional restrictions or program participation. The intent of this practice, often called tourniquet sentencing, is to lessen the risk of failure and recidivism, and assist the probationer to decide to conform to court expectations. The implicit alternative to nonconforming behavior is incarceration, frequently in the local jail, for a period of time to be imposed by the judge. To understand tourniquet sentencing, it is necessary to examine the jail and its roles as a hub of community corrections.

---

Box 2.7

**Tourniquet Sentencing**

Tightening or increasing the conditions of probation to encourage the client to conform to legal and supervisory expectations. A probation officer requests the court to order additional restrictions or to mandate participation in identified programs. The correctional objective is reintegration or avoidance of criminal activity. One example of tourniquet sentencing is the probationer convicted of indecent exposure who continues to consume alcohol. The court may order participation in substance abuse treatment, as well as house arrest with electronic monitoring, or that the probationer take Antebus, a medication that generally sickens the person who imbibes alcohol.

Source: The term "tourniquet sentencing" is attributed to Judge Albert Kramer, District Judge, Quincy, MA. A. Klein (1980). *Earn It: The Story So Far*. Brandeis University, Waltham, MA.

# The Jail

The local detention facility, usually administered by a county law enforcement agency, is generally known as the "jail." There are nearly 3,400 jails across the nation, housing more than 800,000 persons in the beginning of 2006 (Harrison & Beck, 2006). Jails incarcerate a wide variety of persons. Jails receive individuals pending arraignment and hold them awaiting trial, conviction, and sentencing. They also re-admit probation, parole, and bail-bond violators, and absconders, as well as temporarily detain juveniles pending transfer to juvenile authorities. Further, they hold mentally ill persons pending their movement to appropriate health facilities, as well as individuals for the military, protective custody and contempt, and for the court as witnesses.[5] In addition, jails release convicted inmates to the community upon completion of sentence, and transfer inmates to state, federal, and other local authorities. They temporarily incarcerate convicted felons sentenced to prisons but for whom there are no bed spaces (Beck, 1995:1), and relinquish custody of temporary detainees to juvenile and medical authorities (Beck & Karberg, 2001:6). Finally, they sometimes operate community-based programs as work release programs and other alternatives to incarceration, and hold inmates sentenced to short terms (generally under one year). See Table 2.5. It is small wonder that there were more than 25 million entries to and exits from local jails in 2005.

Table 2.5
**Persons Under Jail Supervision: 2005**

| Confinement Status and Type of Program | Number |
|---|---|
| Total Held in Jail | 819.434 |
| Supervised outside of a jail facility [a] | 71,905 |
| Weekender Program | 14,110 |
| Electronic monitoring | 11,403 |
| Home detention, no electronic monitoring[b] | 1,497 |
| Day reporting | 4,747 |
| Community service | 15,536 |
| Other pretrial supervision | 15,458 |
| Other work programs[c] | 5,796 |
| Treatment programs[d] | 1,973 |
| Other | 1,385 |

[a] Excludes persons supervised by a probation or parole agency.
[b] Work release programs, work gangs, other work alternative programs.
[c] Includes persons in work release programs, work gangs, and other work alternative programs
[d] Drug, alcohol, mental health, and other medical treatment.

Source: Harrison, Paige, M, and A. Beck (2005). *Prison and Jail Inmates at Midyear 2005*. Washington, DC: Bureau of Justice Statistics: 7 (www.ojp.usdoj.gov/bjs/pub/pdf/pjim00.pdf).

By permission of Johnny Hart and Creators Syndicate, Inc.

## Other Sentencing Options

Sentencing judges make decisions to incarcerate offenders in jails or prisons, or to place them on probation with its numerous ancillary programs ("in" or "out" decisions). If the decision is to retain the offender in the community under probation or its supplemental programs, the judge increasingly has a large number of supervision and control strategies from which to pick, known as intermediate sanctions (Gowdy, 1993; Allen, Latessa, Ponder & Simonsen, 2007). Obviously, selected programs are not capriciously imposed but are designed to achieve a correctional objective, such as community protection, reintegration, treatment and rehabilitation, and so on. Court officers, usually probation officers, oversee the implementation of and offender compliance with court conditions. If the offender appears to be failing at technical conditions (such as no alcohol, or attending treatment programs), the judge may tighten the requirements by imposing mandatory daily attendance. In extreme cases, a request for medical intervention (e.g., methadone maintenance for heroin addicts) may be issued. If these conditions are not met, or are insufficient for the particular client, the court may further increase the conditions of control by imposing weekend confinement in jail or house arrest. If these are insufficient, the judge may order a short term of jail incarceration to be followed by additional control programs, such as house arrest with electronic monitoring. In extreme cases, the court may order an interlock device installed in the offender's vehicle, as well as intensive supervision. Tightening the conditions and restraints is commonly called "tourniquet sentencing." We turn now to a brief description of major ancillary control ("probation-plus") programs.

## Intermediate Controls

Intermediate punishments are explored in greater detail in Chapter 8. For our purposes, the major intermediate control programs are listed with brief descriptions. The reader will notice that each increases the level of "penal harm" and crime control. For many offenders, such preventive control is necessary for them to begin to deal with their rehabilitation needs.[9] The discussion moves from least to most punishment approaches. See Figure 2.4 for a sample of sanctions ranging from most to least restrictive.

Figure 2.4
**Sample of Sanctions**

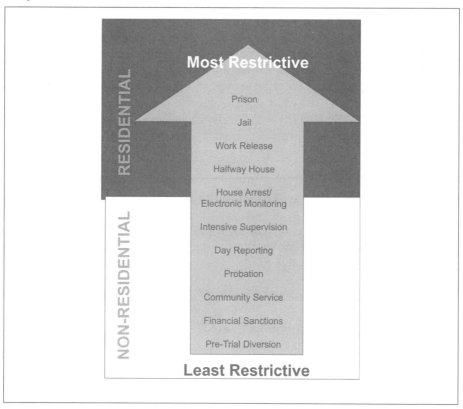

## *Fines*

The penalties courts impose on offenders require specific sums of money be paid, cash payments of a dollar amount. Judges may impose fines based on a fixed schedule published and used throughout the court, or on an individual basis.

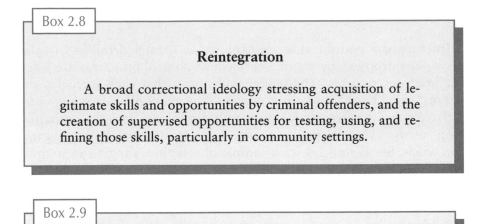

**Box 2.8**

### Reintegration

A broad correctional ideology stressing acquisition of legitimate skills and opportunities by criminal offenders, and the creation of supervised opportunities for testing, using, and refining those skills, particularly in community settings.

**Box 2.9**

### Incapacitation

A crime prevention strategy based on specific deterrence that would disable the potential offender from committing another crime by isolating the instant offender. The most common forms of incapacitation is imprisonment.

**Box 2.10**

### Rehabilitation

Change in behavior of the offender produced by treatment and services. Offender chooses to refrain from new crimes rather than being unable to.

## *Community Service*

Community service or work orders represent court-ordered nonpaid work for a specified number of hours that offenders must perform, usually for some charitable organization or public service such as volunteer hospital orderly, doing interstate and street cleaning, performing maintenance or repair of public housing, or providing service to indigent groups (Anderson, 1998; Caputo, 1999). Professionals such as dentists or doctors can be ordered to provide free services for the indigent, welfare recipients, or probationers, whereas sports stars may be required to speak to youth groups or at schools.

## *Restitution*

This court-ordered condition of probation requires the offender to repair the financial, emotional, or physical damage done (a reparative sentence) by making financial payment of money to the victim or, alternatively, to a fund to provide services to victims. Restitution programs may also be ordered in the absence of a sentence to probation (Seiter, 2000). Restitution is usually a cash payment by the offender to the victim of an amount considered to offset the loss incurred by the victim (medical expenses, insurance deductibles, time lost from work due to victim's injuries, etc.). Payments may be made in installments in most jurisdictions and sometimes services directly or indirectly benefiting the victim may be substituted for cash payments.

---

Box 2.11

### Retribution

Philosophically, this term generally means "getting even" with the perpetrator. Social revenge suggests that individuals cannot exact punishment, but that the state will do so in their name.

Retribution assumes that offenders wilfully chose to commit the evil acts, are responsible for their own behavior, and should receive the punishment they so richly deserve. The just deserts movement in sentencing reflects the retribution philosophy. For many, it provides a justifiable rationale for the death penalty.

---

## *Probation*

Probation is the conditional freedom granted by a judicial officer to an alleged offender, or adjudicated adult or juvenile, as long as the person meets certain conditions of behavior. Unsupervised probation resembles sursis, or "no action by the court as long as there are no further incidents" but, generally, probation includes the requirement to report to a designated person or agency over a period of time.

---

Box 2.12

### Selective Incapacitation

This doctrine of isolating the offender, or causing "social disablement," proposes "adopting a policy of incarcerating those whose criminal behavior is so damaging or probable that nothing short of isolation will prevent recidivism." This "nothing-else-works" approach would require correctly identifying those offenders who should receive long-term imprisonment and diverting others into community corrections. Thus we would be able to make maximum use of prison cells, a scarce resource, to protect society from the depredations of such dangerous and repetitive offenders. The "third strike and you're out" is a continuation of this theme.

Current correctional technology does not permit our correctly identifying those who require incapacitation. Rather, the evidence is that we would probably incarcerate numerous noneligibles (a "false positive" problem) and release to lesser control many of those eligible (a "false negative" problem). Whatever benefits might accrue to this sentencing doctrine have thus far eluded corrections.

---

Box 2.13

### Parole Board

Any correctional person, authority, or board that has the authority to release on parole those adults (or juveniles) committed to confinement facilities, to set conditions for behavior, to revoke from parole, and to discharge from parole. Parole boards also recommend executive clemency through pardon or sentence commutation (shortening), as well as set policies for supervision of parolees.

---

## Day Reporting Centers

Certain persons on pretrial release, probation or parole may be required to appear at a day reporting center on a frequent and regular basis in order to participate in services or activities provided by the center or other community agencies. Failure to report or participate is a violation that could cause revocation of pretrial release, conditional release, or community supervision.

Reports on the national scene indicate that offenders in these programs must not only physically report to their centers but also provide a schedule of planned activities, and participate in designated activities (McDevitt, Domino & Baum, 1997).

## Intensive Supervised Probation

These are court-ordered programs of community supervision by probation officers working with very small caseloads to provide intensive supervision. Such programs are usually linked to impromptu (and scheduled) drug and alcohol testing, curfews, restitution, volunteer sponsors, probation fees, and other punitive intrusions (Anderson, 1998; Maxwell & Gray, 2000).

---

Box 2.14

### Jail

A confinement facility, usually administered by a local law enforcement agency, intended for adults, that holds persons detained pending adjudication and/or persons committed after adjudication for sentences usually of one year or less.

---

## House Arrest

House or home arrest is a more intensive program that requires the offender to remain secluded in his or her own home except for work, grocery shopping, community service, or other minor exceptions. Drug and alcohol use or possession in the residence is a violation of house arrest and can result in increased intervention.[6] Frequently, house arrest may be intensified by requiring the offender to wear an electronic device that signals a computer that the offender is at home, or by requiring electronic breath analyzer testing to determine any alcohol use. House arrest can be used as an alternative to parolees with nonviolent technical violations (Stanz & Tewksbury, 2000).

## Electronic Monitoring

This program requires an offender to wear a bracelet or anklet that will emit an electronic signal, confirming via telephone contact that the offender is located at a specific, required location. Strict curfews are required and restrictions on visitors may be imposed. Some monitoring systems have the capability of emitting signals that can be picked up by cellular listing posts within a community, to signal to a computer monitor that the offender is moving within the community (not at home). Frequently, the electronic monitoring system is buttressed by scheduled probation officer visits, drug testing, and other surveillance options. Electronic monitoring is used with both pretrial releasees and for convicted offenders on community release. In either case, clients pay for at least part (if not all) of the cost of leasing the monitoring equipment.

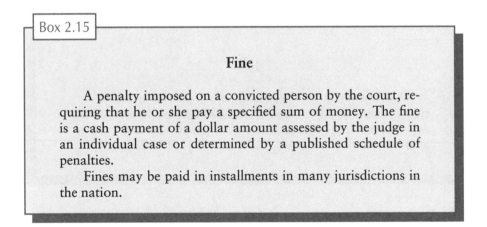

Box 2.15

**Fine**

A penalty imposed on a convicted person by the court, requiring that he or she pay a specified sum of money. The fine is a cash payment of a dollar amount assessed by the judge in an individual case or determined by a published schedule of penalties.

Fines may be paid in installments in many jurisdictions in the nation.

## Global Position Systems

Modern technology has advanced to the point where some offenders can be tracked using global position systems, also known as GPS. These devices are gaining use for sex offenders and domestic violence offenders, and allow a probation officer to track the whereabouts of the offender to make sure that they are not in an area prohibited by the court.

## Community Residential Centers

Formerly known as halfway houses, community residential centers are nonconfining residential facilities for adjudicated adults or juveniles, or those subject to criminal or juvenile proceedings. They are intended as an alternative to jail incarceration for persons in danger of failing on probation or who need a period of readjustment. Increasingly, correctional and victim services (such as services and treatment for battered women, drunk drivers, drug abusers, mentally ill sex offenders, etc.) are offered in these 24-hour facilities.

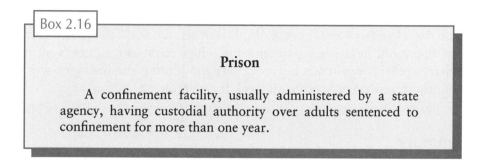

Box 2.16

**Prison**

A confinement facility, usually administered by a state agency, having custodial authority over adults sentenced to confinement for more than one year.

Box 2.17

**Intermediate Sanctions**

Intermediate sanctions, ranging in severity from day fines to shock incarceration ("boot camps"), are interventions that fill the sentencing gap between jails and prisons, at one extreme, and probation at the other. Lengthy incarceration periods may be inappropriate for some offenders; for others, probation may be too inconsequential and may not provide the degree of public supervision necessary to ensure public safety. By expanding sentencing options, intermediate sanctions enable the criminal (and juvenile) justice system to tailor punishment more closely to the nature of the crime and the criminal, to maximize offender compliance with court objectives, and hold offenders strictly accountable for their actions.

## Split Sentences

Frequently, sentencing judges impose a short term of incarceration in the local jail, to be followed by a term of probation. For example, the split sentence (jail plus probation) is the most frequently imposed sentence for felony convictions in California (Lundgren, 2001).

A variation on "jail plus" is weekend confinement. To lessen the negative impacts of short-term incarceration and allow offenders to retain current employment, as well as keep their dependents off welfare rolls, some jurisdictions permit sentences to be served during non-working weekends. Such weekend confinement allows offenders to check into the jail facility on Friday after work and to leave Sunday morning, sometimes early enough to attend religious services. A "weekender" serving his or her sentence over a number of months would generally be credited with three days of confinement per weekend. Some jurisdictions have so many "weekenders" that specific buildings are set aside for their short-term detention. In larger jurisdictions in which sufficient numbers of offenders work on weekends but not every day during the ordinary work week, those buildings operate all week but at reduced staffing levels.

## Summary

The primary mission of the correctional system is protection of the public. Programs must be designed with that objective in mind, or they will be doomed to early failure and public rejection. What seems to be needed is a system that offers as many alternatives to incarceration as are possible for the individuals who appear to have some hope of benefiting from them and who will present little, if any, danger to the community. The residual population may be required to remain in more secure institutions until new treatments can be found for them. The prison, in a modified form, has a valuable place in a correctional system for the estimated 15 to 20 percent of the convicted offenders who require this level of control. For most convicted offenders, however, the use of either partial or total alternatives to imprisonment is a more reasonable and less costly response than is incarceration.

Prisons should be the "last choice" of sentencing judges faced with the difficult decision of how to manage offenders before them, and how best to attain the correctional objective being sought. Judges are increasingly turning to "tourniquet sentencing" as a promising strategy for determining those sanctions.

Whatever good prisons do is difficult to measure, but the damage done is easily detected. If our objective is the protection of society from criminal recidivism, long-term strategies must be developed. If we are determined to control offenders and lower the costs of over-incarceration, it will become necessary to develop a system of community corrections that includes extensive program alternatives and increasing levels of control over the offender in the arms of the law. The process of developing the desired system is discussed in Chapter 12; many of its parts exist in most local communities now. Developing an effective community corrections program will require formulating social policy that requires handling local problems in the community, setting priorities for control of crime, and making resources available to develop and maintain the proposed system. Probation is one of the major elements in such a system.

## Review Questions

1. Compare past sentencing practices to more contemporary ones?

2. What is the difference between a determinate and an indeterminate sentence?

3. What alternatives to incarceration can help alleviated jail crowding?

4. What are sentencing guidelines?

5. How is the jail the center of community corrections?

6. What are the main purposes of imprisonment?

7. What are the alternatives to "bricks and mortar" as a solution to prison overcrowding?

8. How do prisons eventually contribute to the workloads of community corrections?

9. Does your state use determinate or indeterminate sentencing?

10. What is a split sentence?

11. What are some of the causes given for rapid changes in the U.S. sentences laws?

## Key Terms

community service
day reporting centers
determinate sentence
deterrent
electronic monitoring
fine
fixed sentence
incapacitation
indeterminate sentence
intensive supervised probation
intermediate sanctions
jail
mandatory release
overcrowding

parole
parole boards
plea bargaining
prison
restitution
retribution
selective incapacitation
sentencing disparity
split sentence
time credits
tourniquet sentencing
War on Drugs
work-release

## Electronic Library

Bureau of Justice Statistics www.ojp.usdoj.gov/bjs/

Drug Use, Testing and Treatment in Jails (www.ojp.usdoj.gov/bjs/pub/pdf/duttj.pdf).

Electronic Monitoring (www.nlectc.org/txtfiles/ElecMonasc.html).

National Institute of Corrections www.nicic.org

Prisoner Reentry (www.ncjrs.org/pdffiles1/nij/181413.pdf).

## Recommended Readings

Allen, H., E. Latessa, B. Ponder, and C. Simonsen (2007). *Corrections in America*. Upper Saddle River, NJ: Prentice Hall.

Clear, T. (1994). *Harm in American Penology: Offenders, Victims, and Their Communities*. Albany, NY: State University of New York Press.

Irwin, J. and J. Austin (1997). *It's About Time: America's Imprisonment Binge*. Belmont, CA: Wadsworth.

Petersila, J. (2003) *When Prisoners Come Home*. NY: Oxford Press.

Rothman, D. (1980). *Conscience and Convenience: The Asylum and Its Alternatives in Progressive America*. Boston, MA: Little, Brown.

Travis, J. (2000). *But They All Come Back: Rethinking Prisoner Reentry*. Washington, DC: National Institute of Corrections (www.ncjrs.org/pdffiles1/nij/181413.pdf).

## Notes

[1]    Some historians argue that the noble ideals of rehabilitation never really were implemented, and that the "convenience" of punishment won out over the "conscience" of rehabilitation. See D. Rothman (1980). *Conscience and Convenience: The Asylum and Its Alternatives in Progressive America*. Boston, MA: Little, Brown. See also J. Irwin, V. Schiraldi and J. Ziedenberg (2000) "America's One Million Non-violent Prisoners." *Social Justice*, 27(2):135-147.

[2]    DeClan Roche (1999). "Mandatory Sentencing: Trends and Issues." Australian Institute of Criminology, 138(1):1-6.

[3]    King, R. and M. Mauer (2002). *State Sentencing and Corrections Policy in an Era of Fiscal Restraint*. Washington, DC: The Sentencing Project (www.sentencingproject. org/policy/pub9091.pdf).

[4]    J. Austin, J. Clark, and P. Hardyman (1999). "The Impact of 'Three Strikes and You're Out." Punishment and Society, 1(2):131-162; G. Burt, S. Wong, and S. vander Van (2000). "Three Strikes and You're Out." *Federal Probation*, 64(2),3-6; and K. Meehan, supra note 2.

[5]    The "material" witness detained in jails to ensure presence at trial is a seldom-studied actor in the justice system; hence, little is known about this category of jail inmate.

[6]    Technical violators among those on intermediate sanctions can be a large component of the offenders. See F. Taxman (1995). "Intermediate Sanctions: Dealing with Technical Violators." *Corrections Today*, 57(1):46-57. See also Marciniak, L. (2000). "The Addition of Day Reporting to Intensive Supervised Probation." *Federal Probation*, 64(2):34-39.

## References

Allen, H., E. Latessa, B. Ponder, and C. Simonsen (2007). *Corrections in America*. Englewood Cliffs, NJ: Prentice-Hall.

Anderson, D.C. (1998). *Sensible Justice: Alternatives to Prison*. New York, NY: New Press.

Beck, A. (1995). *Profile of Jail Inmates: 1989*. Washington, DC: U.S. Department of Justice.

Beck, A. (2000). *State and Federal Prisoners Returning to the Community: Findings from the Bureau of Justice Statistics*. www.ojp.usdoj.gov/bjs/pub/pdf/sfprc.pdf (July 20, 2001).

Beck, A. and P. Harrison (2001). Prisoners in 2000. Washington, DC: U.S. Bureau of Justice Statistics, p. 3 (www.ojp.usdoj.gov/bjs/pub/pdf/poo.pdf).

Beck, A. and J. Karberg (2001). *Prison and Jail Inmates at Midyear 2000*. Washington, DC: Bureau of Justice Statistics.

Harrison, P., and A. Beck (2006). *Prisoners in 2005*. Washington, DC: Bureau of Justice Statistics (www.ojp.usdoj.gov/bjs/pub/pdf/p00.pdf).

Caputo, G. (1999). "Why Not Community Service?" *Criminal Justice Policy, Review* 10(4):503-519.

Coleman, S. and K. Guthrie (1988). *Sentencing Effectiveness in Preventing Crime*. St. Paul, MN: Criminal Justice Statistical Analysis Center.

Durose, M. and P. Langan (2001). *State Court Sentencing of Convicted Felons, 1998*. Washington, DC: Bureau of Justice Statistics (www.ojp.usdoj.gov/bjs/pub/pdf/scscf98.pdf).

Ellingwood, K. "Three-Time Loser Gets Life in Cookie Theft." *Los Angeles Times*, 28 October 1995, 1.

Gowdy, V. (1993). *Intermediate Sanctions*. Washington, DC: U.S. Department of Justice.

Hoffman, P. and L. DeGostin (1975). "An Argument for Self-Imposed Explicit Judicial Sentencing Standards." *Journal of Criminal Justice*, 3:195-206.

Lundgren, D. (2001). *Crime and Delinquency in California, 2000: Advance Release*. Sacramento, CA: Department of Justice.

Maxwell, S. and K. Gray (2000). "Deterrence." *Sociological Inquiry*, 70(2):117-136.

Seiter, R. (Ed.) (2000). "Restorative Justice." *Corrections Management Quarterly*, 4(3):1-85.

Stanz, R. and R. Tewksbury (2000). "Predictors of Success and Recidivism in a Home Incarceration Program." *Prison Journal*, 80(3):326-344.

Travis, J. and J. Petersilia (2001). "Re-entry Reconsidered: A New Look at an Old Question." *Crime & Delinquency*, 47(3):291-313.

# Probation

> I can forgive, but I cannot forget, is only another way of saying, I will not forgive. Forgiveness ought to be like a canceled note—torn in two, and burned up, so that it never can be shown against one.
>
> —Henry Ward Beecher

As the above quote implies, probation is a way of giving an offender another chance. As such, probation represents one of the unique developments within the criminal justice system. The development of this method of minimizing offender penetration into the correctional system was a crucial aspect of the rise of the rehabilitation model in this country. Any study of probation must begin with an analysis of its predecessors. This chapter will begin with an historical review that will help explain how probation, both for adults and juveniles, developed into its current forms and practices. The second portion of this chapter will focus on the granting of probation, and how it exists today.

Probation is a conditional sentence that avoids incarceration of the offender—it is an alternative disposition available to the court. While probation is an outcome of the offender's conviction in a criminal court, it neither confines him or her in an institution nor allows the offender's release from court authority. Supervision by a probation officer is almost always a condition of release.

---

**Box 3.1**

### Definition of Probation: Adults

A sentence not involving confinement that imposes conditions and retains authority in the sentencing court to modify the conditions of sentence or to resentence the offender if the offender violates the conditions. Such a sentence should not involve or require suspension of the imposition or execution of any other sentence.

---

As indicated by the National Advisory Commission on Criminal Justice Standards and Goals (1973a:115-17), probation can also refer to other functions, activities, and services. It is a status, given to the convicted offender, that falls somewhere between that of free citizen and incarcerated felon (or misdemeanant). As a subsystem of criminal justice, it refers to the agency or organization that administers the probation process. As a process, it refers to those activities that include the preparation of reports for the court, the supervision of probationers, and providing of services for those probationers. These activities are undertaken by the probation officer as a part of his or her regular duty. Finally, as Reed (1997) notes—probation can serve to lower prison populations.

The rationale for the use of probation has been clearly stated by Dressler (1962:26):

> . . . the assumption that certain offenders are reasonably safe risks in society by the time they appear in court; it would not facilitate their adjustment to remove them to institutions, and the move might well have the opposite effect. Meantime, the community would have to provide for their dependents. And the effect of such incarceration upon the prisoner's family would be incalculable. If, then, the community would not be jeopardized by a defendant's presence, and if he gave evidence of ability to change to a law-abiding life, it served both society and the individual to give him the chance, conditionally, under supervision and guidance.

Probation is thus clearly tied to the correctional goals of rehabilitation and reintegration, providing potential benefits to the offender as well as the community.

## Founders of Probation

John Augustus of Boston is commonly recognized as the originator of probation, but there were other contributors to its development both before and after his unique contribution.

Dressler (1962:12-13) cites the 1841 activities of Matthew Davenport Hill of Birmingham, England. In Warwickshire, Hill observed that, in the case of youthful offenders, magistrates often imposed token sentences of one day with the special condition that the defendant remain under the supervision of a guardian. This experiment represented a mitigation of the punishment; no other conditions were imposed and there was no provision for revocation. When Hill became a magistrate, he modified this procedure; he suspended the sentence and placed the offender under the supervision of a guardian, under the assumption that "there would be better hope of amendment under such guardians than in the [jail] of the county." Hill's program has some of the same elements as Augustus's method: selected cases, suspended sentences, and if the defendant got into trouble again no sanctions were levied. Hill was not unwilling to take action against repeaters, however: "That the punishment should be such as to show that it was from no weakness, from no mistaken indulgence, from no want to resolution on the part of the court to perform its duty" that the previous sentence had been suspended. Hill also demonstrated his concern for the safety of the community by requesting that the superintendent of police investigate the conduct of persons placed under a guardian's supervision.

In this country, one of the earliest proponents of leniency was Judge Peter Oxenbridge Thatcher of Boston. By 1836, Massachusetts passed legislation promoting the practice of releasing petty offenders upon their recognizance with sureties at any stage of the proceedings.[1]

It is a court volunteer, John Augustus, who is most often given credit for the establishment of probation in the United States. Augustus first appeared in police court in Boston when he stood bail for a man charged with drunkenness, and then helped the offender find a job. The court ordered the defendant to return in three weeks, at which time he demonstrated great improvement. Instead of incarcerating this individual, the judge imposed a one-cent fine and ordered the defendant to pay costs.

From this modest beginning, Augustus proceeded to bail out numerous offenders, supervising them and offering guidance until they were sentenced. Over an 18-year period (from 1841 until his death in 1859), Augustus "bailed on probation" 1,152 men and 794 women (Barnes & Teeters, 1959:554). He was motivated by his belief that "the object of the law is to reform criminals and to prevent crime and not to punish maliciously or from a spirit of revenge" (Dressler, 1962:17). Augustus obviously selected his candidates carefully, offering assistance "mainly to those who were indicted for their first offense, and whose hearts were not wholly depraved, but gave promise of better things." He also considered the "previous character of the person, his age and influences by which he would in the future be likely to be surrounded and, although these points were not rigidly adhered to, still they were the circumstances which usually determined my action" (United Nations, 1976a:90). In addition, Augustus provided his charges with aid in obtaining employment, an education, or a place to live, and also made an impartial report to the court. The task was not without its frustrations, as Augustus noted (Barnes & Teeters, 1959:554):

> While it saves the country and state hundreds and I might say thousands of dollars, it drains my pockets instead of enriching me. To attempt to make money by bailing poor people would prove an impossibility. The first two years of my labor I received nothing from anyone except what I earned by my daily labor.

His records on the first 1,100 individuals whom he bailed out revealed that only one forfeited bond (Dressler, 1962:18). It is also important to note that virtually every basic practice associated with probation was initiated by Augustus, including the idea of a presentence investigation, supervision conditions, case work, reports to the court, and revocation of probation supervision (Probation in the United States, 1997). When Augustus died in 1859, he was destitute—an unfitting end for a humanitarian visionary.

## Philosophical Bases of Probation

Probation emerged in the United States during the nineteenth century, a period of considerable social turmoil and conflict. It was a development widely influenced by certain thoughts, arguments, and debates in Europe. In a larger sense, probation is an extension of the Western European philosophical arguments about the functions of criminal law and how offenders should be handled and punished. The punishment philosophy generally advocated by the kings, emperors, and other rulers of Europe focused on the crime, and attempted to treat all crimes equally. They viewed the purposes of criminal law as to punish, to deter others, and to seek revenge and vengeance for violations of the "king's peace." Widespread use of the death penalty, torture, banishment, public humiliations, and mass executions resulted from "disturbing the king's peace."

In the eighteenth century, French philosophers created a controversy by focusing on liberty, equality, and justice. Famous French philosophers and lawyers attempted to redefine the purpose of criminal law in an effort to find some way to make the criminal justice system of their time more attuned to the humanitarian ethos of the Age of Enlightenment. A major figure of the time was Cesare Beccaria, a mildly disturbed Italian genius who only left his country once—when invited to visit Paris to debate the French philosophers.

When Beccaria published his classic work, *An Essay on Crimes and Punishments* (1764), he established the "Classical School" of criminology, which attempted to reorient the law toward more humanistic goals. This would include not torturing the accused in order to extract confessions, no secret indictments and trials, the right to defense at a trial, improvement of the conditions of imprisonment, and so on. His work focused on the offense and not on the offender. He believed that punishment should fit the crime. His work was widely read throughout Europe, and even attracted the attention of Catherine the Great, the Russian empress, who invited Beccaria to revise Russian criminal law. Unfortunately, he never took her up on her offer.

The philosophical ferment of the period quickly spread to England and, from there, to the colonies. When the United States emerged from the Revolutionary War, the remaining vestiges of the harsher English penal codes were resoundingly abandoned. What emerged was a constitutional system that incorporated the major components of the humanitarian philosophy, along with a populace imbued with the belief in the inherent goodness of humankind and the ability of all persons to rise to their optimal level of perfectibility.

The difference between the earlier approach to handling offenders (harsh punishments openly administered, and corporal and capital punishments) and the emerging reformation emphasis of the last decade of the eighteenth century, were primarily in (1) the way offenders were viewed and (2) the focus and intent of the criminal law. Prior to the Revolutionary War offenders were seen as inherently evil, deserving punishment so that they might "Get right with God." After the Civil War, Americans had generally recognized that humankind was not basically evil. The focus shifted to dealing with individual offenders, rather than focusing on the crime that had been committed. The Civil War further added to the movement toward democracy, the rise of the reformation movement, and to the further individualization of treatment and punishment. Eventually the question arose: Do all offenders need to be imprisoned in order for them to repent and stop their criminal behavior? It was in this philosophical environment that Massachusetts began to answer the question, and the concern was juvenile probation.

## The Growth of Probation

Buoyed by Augustus's example, Massachusetts quickly moved into the forefront of probation development. An experiment in providing services for children (resembling probation) was inaugurated in 1869, under the auspices of the Massachusetts State Board of Health, Lunacy, and Charity (Johnson, 1928:7). A statute enacted in that year provided that, when complaints were made in court against a juvenile under 17 years of age, a written notice must be furnished to the state. The state agent was then given an opportunity to investigate, attend the trial, and to safeguard the interest of the child.

Despite the early work of Augustus and others with adult offenders, probation was more readily supported for juveniles. It was not until 1901 that New York passed the first statute authorizing probation for adult offenders, more than 20 years after Massachusetts passed a law for juvenile probation (Lindner & Savarese, 1984c). Although the development of probation for adults lagged that of juveniles, by 1923, most states had a law authorizing probation for adults, and by 1956 all states had adopted adult and juvenile probation laws. Historical data on select states can be found in Table 3.1. Surprisingly, it was the Federal Government that resisted probation.

Table 3.1
**States with Juvenile and Adult Probation Laws: 1923**

| | Years Enacted | |
| States | Juvenile | Adult |
|---|---|---|
| Alabama | 1907 | 1915 |
| Arizona | 1907 | 1913 |
| Arkansas | 1911 | 1923 |
| California | 1903 | 1903 |
| Colorado | 1899 | 1909 |
| Connecticut | 1903 | 1903 |
| Delaware | 1911 | 1911 |
| Georgia | 1904 | 1907 |
| Idaho | 1905 | 1915 |
| Illinois | 1899 | 1911 |
| Indiana | 1903 | 1907 |
| Kansas | 1901 | 1909 |
| Maine | 1905 | 1905 |
| Maryland | 1902 | 1904 |
| Massachusetts | 1878 | 1878 |
| Michigan | 1903 | 1903 |
| Minnesota | 1899 | 1909 |
| Missouri | 1901 | 1897 |
| Montana | 1907 | 1913 |
| Nebraska | 1905 | 1909 |
| New Jersey | 1903 | 1900 |
| New York | 1903 | 1901 |
| North Carolina | 1915 | 1919 |
| North Dakota | 1911 | 1911 |
| Ohio | 1902 | 1908 |
| Oklahoma | 1909 | 1915 |
| Oregon | 1909 | 1915 |
| Pennsylvania | 1903 | 1909 |
| Rhode Island | 1899 | 1899 |
| Tennessee | 1905 | 1915 |
| Utah | 1903 | 1923 |
| Vermont | 1900 | 1900 |
| Virginia | 1910 | 1910 |
| Washington | 1905 | 1915 |
| Wisconsin | 1901 | 1909 |

Source: Adapted from F.R. Johnson (1928). *Probation for Juveniles and Adults,* pp. 12-13. New York, NY: Century Co.

## Probation at the Federal Level

Although probation quickly became almost universal in the juvenile justice system, no early specific provision for probation was made for federal offenders, either juvenile or adult. As a substitute, the federal courts suspended sentence in instances where imprisonment imposed special hardships. However, this practice was quickly called into question by several sources.

The major question was a legal one: Did federal judges have the constitutional authority to suspend a sentence indefinitely, or did this practice represent an encroachment upon the executive prerogative of pardon and reprieve and was it, as such, an infringement upon doctrine of separation of powers? This issue was resolved by the U.S. Supreme Court in the *Killits* decision (Ex parte U.S. 242 U.S. 27-53, 1916). In a case from the northern district of Ohio, John M. Killits suspended the five-year sentence of a man who was convicted of embezzling $4,700 from a Toledo Bank. The defendant was a first-time offender with an otherwise good background and reputation, who made full restitution for this offense. The bank officers did not wish to prosecute. The government contended that such action was beyond the powers of the court. A unanimous opinion, delivered by Chief Justice Edward D. White, held that the federal courts had no inherent power to suspend sentence indefinitely and that there was no reason "to continue a practice which is inconsistent with the Constitution, because its exercise in the very nature of things amounts to a refusal by the judicial power to perform a duty resting upon it and as a consequence thereof, to an interference with both the legislative and executive authority as fixed by the Constitution." However, instead of abolishing this probationary practice, the *Killits* decision actually sponsored its further development. Interested parties interpreted the reversal of the "doctrine of inherent power to suspend sentences indefinitely" to mean that enabling legislation should be passed that specifically granted this power to the judiciary.

At the federal level, the National Probation Association (then headed by Charles Lionel Chute) carried on a determined educational campaign and lobbied for federal legislation. These efforts did not go unopposed, however. For example, prohibitionists feared that the growth of probation would take the sting out of the provisions of the Volstead Act.[2] As Evjen (1975:5) has demonstrated, letters from judges to Chute clearly denounced the practice of probation.

> What we need in this court is not a movement such as you advocate, to create new officials with resulting expense, but a movement to make enforcement of our criminal laws more certain and swift . . . In this county, due to the efforts of people like yourselves, the murderer has a cell bedecked with flowers and is surrounded with a lot of silly people. The crimi-

nal should understand when he violates the law that he is going to a penal institution and is going to stay there. Just such efforts as your organization is making are largely responsible for the crime wave that is passing over the country today and threatening to engulf our institutions.

Objections also arose from the Justice Department. For example, Attorney General Harry M. Daugherty wrote that he hoped "that no such mushy policy will be indulged in as Congress turning courts into maudlin reform associations . . . the place to do reforming is inside the walls and not with lawbreakers running loose in society." A memorandum from the Justice Department further revealed this sentiment against probation: "It is all a part of a wave of maudlin rot of misplaced sympathy for criminals that is going over the country. It would be a crime, however, if a probation system is established in the federal courts."

Approximately 34 bills to establish a federal probation system were introduced in Congress between 1909 and 1925. Despite such opposition, a bill passed on its sixth introduction to the House. The bill was sent to President Coolidge who, as a former governor of Massachusetts, was familiar with the functioning of probation. He signed the bill into law on March 4, 1925. This action was followed by an appropriation to defray the salaries and expenses of a limited number of probation officers, to be chosen by civil service (Meeker, 1975; Lindner & Savarese, 1984a; Burdress, 1997). Table 3.2 highlights some of the significant events in the development of probation.

## Probation Today

Because probation is a privilege and not a right, it is essentially an "act of grace" extended by the sentencing judge who presided over the trial (although a few states permit the jury that determined guilt to award or recommend probation). Of all the principal groups of offenders under correctional control in America—probationers, jail inmates, prison inmates, and parolees—the largest group is probationers. Figure 3.1 shows how the number of adults on probation has grown over the past 20 years, from just under 2 million in 1985 to over 4 million in 2005. The United States Bureau of Justice Statistics (2006) found that nearly 60 percent of all convicted offenders were on probation, 11 percent were on parole, 20 percent were in prison, and about 10 percent were in jail. Numerically, at the beginning of 2006, there were over 4 million probationers supervised by at least 20,000 probation officers. Although the average caseload size varies tremendously from jurisdiction to jurisdiction, it is estimated that the average caseload is about 180 offenders per officer. It is estimated that about 50 percent of offenders on probation are for felonies, with the other half for misdemeanors.

Table 3.2
**Significant Events in the Development of Probation**

| Date | Events |
|---|---|
| Middle Ages | *Parens patriae* established to protect the welfare of the child in England. |
| 1841 | John Augustus becomes the "Father of Probation." |
| 1869 | Massachusetts develops the visiting probation agent system. |
| 1875 | Society of the Prevention of Cruelty to Children established in New York, paving the way for the juvenile court. |
| 1899 | The first juvenile court in America was established in Cook County (Chicago) Illinois. |
| 1901 | New York passes the first statute authorizing probation for adults. |
| 1925 | Congress authorizes probation at the federal level. |
| 1927 | All states but Wyoming have juvenile probation laws. |
| 1943 | Federal Probation System formalizes the Presentence Investigation Report. |
| 1954 | Last state enacts juvenile probation law. |
| 1956 | Mississippi becomes the last state to pass authorizing legislation to establish adult probation. |
| 1965 | Ohio is first state to create "shock probation," which combines prison with probation. |
| 1967 | *In re Gault* decided by the U.S. Supreme Court. |
| 1969 | Jerome Miller is appointed Youth Commissioner in the State of Massachusetts and begins to decarcerate state institutions. |
| 1971 | Minnesota passes the first Community Corrections Act. |
| 1973 | National Advisory Commission on Criminal Justice Standards and Goals endorses more extensive use of probation. |
| 1974 | Congress passes the Juvenile Justice and Delinquency Prevention Act establishing the Federal Office of Juvenile Justice and Delinquency Prevention.<br><br>Restorative justice and victim/offender mediation programs begin in Ontario, Canada. |
| 1975 | The State of Wisconsin receives funding from the Law Enforcement Assistance Administration to develop a case classification system. Four years later the Risk/Needs Assessment instruments are designed and implemented. |
| 1980 | American Bar Association issues restrictive guidelines to limit use of preadjudication detention. |
| 1982 | "War on Drugs" begins. |
| 1983 | Electronic monitoring of offenders begins. Georgia establishes the new generation of Intensive Supervised Probation program. |
| 1984 | Congress passes Sentence Reform Act to achieve longer sentences, "just deserts" and equity in sentencing. |
| 1989 | President Bush displays clear plastic bag of crack on prime time television. |
| 1994 | American Bar Association issues proposals to counteract the impact of domestic violence on children. |
| 1998 | National Institute of Corrections begins national correctional training on implementing community restorative justice programs. |
| 2000 | American Probation and Parole Association issues monograph: *Transforming Probation through Leadership: The Broken Windows Model*. |
| 2001 | Evaluation of sex-offender notification on probation in Wisconsin finds high cost to corrections in terms of personnel, time and budgetary resources. |
| 2003 | Evaluation of strategies to enforce drug court treatment by aggressive probation officer involvement results in significant drop in drug use in Maryland. |

Source: Compiled by authors.

Figure 3.1
**Adults on Probation: 1985-2005 (in millions)**

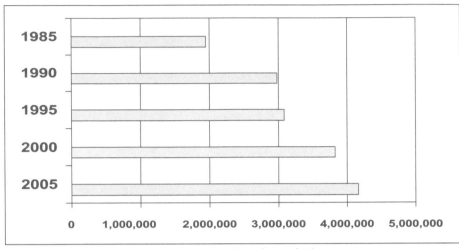

Source: Bureau of Justice Statistics (2006). (www.ojp.usdoj.gov/bjs/

Table 3.3 illustrates the most serious offense for offenders on probation in 2005. So, what is probation, why it is so frequently used, and what is the process by which so large a proportion of offenders are placed on probation?

Table 3.3
**Adults on Probation in 2005: Most Serious Offense**

| Offense | Percent |
|---|---|
| Sexual Assault | 3 |
| Domestic Violence | 6 |
| Other Assault | 10 |
| Burglary | 5 |
| Larceny | 12 |
| Fraud | 6 |
| Drug Law Violations | 28 |
| DUI | 15 |
| Minor Traffic Offenses | 5 |

Source: Glaze, L.E. and T. Bonsczar, (2006). *Probation and Parole in the United States, 2005.* Washington, DC: U.S. Bureau of Justice Statistics.

## Objectives and Advantages of Probation

As stated earlier, both state and federal jurisdictions enacted statutes that permit the granting of probation, as well as define certain categories of offenses for which probation may not be granted. These acts could include all crimes of violence, crimes requiring a life sentence, armed robbery, rape or other sex offenses, use of a firearm in a crime, or multiple-convicted offenders.

Yet, despite the existence of legislatively defined exclusion, granting probation is a highly individualized process that usually focuses on the criminal rather than the crime. The following are the general objectives of probation:

1. Reintegrate amenable offenders.

2. Protect the community from further antisocial behavior.

3. Further the goals of justice.

4. Provide probation conditions (and services) necessary to change offenders and to achieve the above objectives.

While probation granting is individualized, judges and corrections personnel generally recognize the advantages of probation:

1. Use of community resources to reintegrate offenders who are thus forced to face and hopefully resolve their individual problems while under community supervision.

2. Fiscal savings over imprisonment.

3. Avoidance of prisonization, which tends to exacerbate the underlying causes of criminal behavior.

4. Keeping offenders' families off local and state welfare rolls.

5. A relatively successful process of correcting offenders' behavior (60 to 90% success rates have been reported).[3]

6. A sentencing option that can permit "selective incapacitation."

Probation, the most frequent disposition for offenders and widely recognized for its advantages (Dawson, 1990:1), has also received strong endorsement from numerous groups and commissions, including the prestigious National Advisory Commission on Criminal Justice Standards and Goals (1973a), the General Accounting Office (1982), and the American Bar Association (1970). The National Advisory Commission recommended that probation be used more extensively, and the ABA endorsed probation as the presumed sentence of choice for almost all non-violent felons. Others have argued (Finn, 1984) universal use of probation would reduce prison populations. It is important to remember that prison space is a limited and, some would say, scarce resource. The economics of corrections are such that probation is essential if the system is going to effectively manage its finite resources (Clear, Clear & Burrell, 1989). Figure 3.2 illustrates the cost per offender for probation supervision. Even when we consider specialized supervision (e.g., intensive, electronic), the daily supervision still averages less than $4 per day. When is probation an appropriate sentence and how is it granted?

Figure 3.2
**Average Daily Cost per Probationer by Supervision Type**

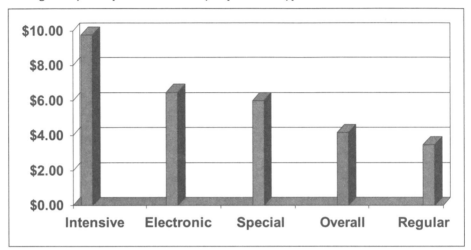

Source: Camp, C. and G. Camp (2003). *The Corrections Yearbook 2002*. Middletown, CT: Criminal Justice Institute, p. 206.

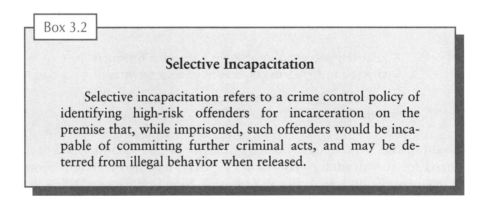

Box 3.2

### Selective Incapacitation

Selective incapacitation refers to a crime control policy of identifying high-risk offenders for incarceration on the premise that, while imprisoned, such offenders would be incapable of committing further criminal acts, and may be deterred from illegal behavior when released.

## Granting Probation

Sentencing is a complicated process, and sentencing judges frequently find that the disposition of the case (sentence) has already been determined—by the prosecutor, not the judge! This is because, prior to the determination of guilt, the prosecuting attorney and defense counsel have engaged in plea bargaining. During this interaction, any (or even all) of the following trial elements may have been negotiated:

1. The defendant's pleading guilty to a lesser crime but one that was present in the illegal behavior, for which the penalty is considerably more lenient.

2. The frequency of the crime ("number of counts") to which the defendant will plead guilty.

3. The number of charges that will be dropped.

4. Whether the prosecutor will recommend that the defendant receive probation or be sentenced to incarceration in jail or prison.

5. The recommended length of time (months or years) of incarceration.

6. If sentence will be consecutive or concurrent.

It appears that the judiciary tend to accept and acquiesce to the negotiation outcomes (Glaser, 1985; Dixon, 1995). However, in many cases, judges still decide the sentence, one alternative of which may be probation.

---

Box 3.3

### Sentencing: Concurrent or Consecutive?

If the offender is to be sentenced for more than one crime and receives a *concurrent* sentence, the offender would start serving time for all his crimes, beginning on the day of arrival in prison. If a *consecutive* sentence is imposed, the offender generally must serve the minimum sentence for the first crime before beginning to serve time for the second offense. Offenders obviously prefer the concurrent over the consecutive sentence option, because they would be eligible for release from prison much earlier!

---

The process of granting probation begins after the offender either pleads guilty (frequently for favorable personal considerations) or is adjudicated guilty following a trial. For those offenders whose crime falls within the list of probation-eligible offenses, or in those states where mandated by law, a presentence investigation will be ordered. One of the major functions of a presentence investigation report is to assist the court in determining the most appropriate sentence.

Based on observations of the defendant at trial—including demeanor, body language, evidence of remorse, and behavior—as well as the recommendation in presentence reports and the prosecutor's recommendation for sentence, judges attempt to determine the appropriate sentence for a particular individual. Judges are aware that individualized justice demands that the sentence fit not only the crime but also the criminal.[4]

As one might expect, probation tends to be granted more prevalently for nonviolent offenders. Table 3.3 shows that in general offenders convicted of nonviolent crimes (e.g., drug law violations) were more likely to received probation than those convicted of violent offenses (e.g., sexual assault).

A number of factors can influence the sentencing decision, such as the nature of the offense, the demeanor of the offender, the harm done the victim, judicial and community attitudes, and many other considerations. Many of these factors are brought forth in a document called the presentence investigation report, or PSI.

Perhaps the most important criteria is the recommendation of the probation officer who composes the PSI. The role of the presentence report recommendation is a major factor, for the extent of concurrence between the probation officer's recommendations and the judge's sentencing decision is quite strong. Liebermann, Schaffer, and Martin (1971) found that, when probation were recommended, judges followed that recommendation in 83 percent of the cases; Carter (1966) found an even stronger agreement: 96 percent of the cases. Liebermann et al. (1971) also found that, when the recommendation was for imprisonment, the judge agreed in 87 percent of the cases. Macallair (1994) found that defense-based disposition reports for juveniles that recommended probation alternatives consistently lowered commitments to state correctional facilities. So what is the PSI?

## The Presentence Investigation Report

One of the primary responsibilities of probation agencies is investigation. This includes gathering information about probation and technical violations, facts about arrest, and, most importantly, completing the presentence investigation report for use in sentencing hearings.

DOONESBURY                                                by Garry Trudeau

DOONESBURY © 1973 G.B. Trudeau. Reprinted with permission of UNIVERSAL PRESS SYNDICATE. All rights reserved.

The concept of the presentence investigation report (PSI) developed with probation.[5] Judges originally used probation officers to gather background and personal information on offenders to "individualize" punishment.[6] In 1943, the Federal Probation System formalized the presentence investigation report as a required function of the federal probation process. The PSI can have a great deal of significance in the sentencing process, because 80 to 90 percent of defendants plead guilty and the judge's only contact with the offender is during sentencing ("The Presentence Report," 1970). The judge's knowledge of the defendant is usually limited to the information contained in the presentence report. As Walsh concludes (1985:363), "judges lean heavily on the professional advice of probation."

In a study of the acceptance of the PSI recommendation, Latessa (1993) examined 285 cases in Cuyahoga County, Ohio (which includes the city of Cleveland). He found that judges accepted the recommendation of the probation department in 85 percent of the cases when probation was recommended, and in 66 percent when prison was the recommendation.

As mandatory minimum sentences have become more popular some jurisdictions report that fewer PSIs are being prepared. However, for others the PSI remains an important function for probation. For example, in terms of the agency workload, almost one-half (45%) of the agencies that conduct presentence investigations reported that more than 25 percent of their workloads were devoted to these reports.

At the Federal level, Federal Sentencing Guidelines have increased the importance of the presentence investigation and the role and responsibility of the probation officer. (Dierna, 1989; Jaffe, 1989; McDonald & Carlson, 1993; Steffensmeier & Demuth, 2000).

## Functions and Objectives

The primary purpose of the PSI is to provide the sentencing court with succinct and precise information upon which to base rational sentencing decisions. Judges usually have a number of options available to them: they may suspend sentence, impose a fine, require restitution, incarcerate, impose community supervision, and so on. The PSI is designed to aid the judge in making the appropriate decision, taking into consideration the needs of the offender as well as the safety of the community.

Over the years, many additional important uses have been found for the presentence report. Basically, these functions include:[7]

1. Aiding the court in determining sentence.

2. Assisting correctional authorities in classification and treatment in release planning.

3. Giving the parole board useful information pertinent to consideration of parole.

4. Aiding the probation officer in rehabilitation efforts during probation.

5. Serving as a source of information for research.

In those jurisdictions in which probation and parole services are in the same agency, the PSI can be used for parole supervision purposes.

A presentence investigation report includes more than the simple facts about the offender, as is seen below. If it is to fulfill its purpose, it must include all objective historical and factual information that is significant to the decision-making process, an assessment of the character and needs of the defendant and the community, and a sound recommendation with supporting rationale that follows logically from the evaluation (Bush, 1990). A reliable and accurate report is essential, and the officer completing the report should make every effort to ensure that the information contained in the PSI is reliable and valid. Information that has not been validated should be indicated.

## Content

The presentence investigation report is not immune from a lack of consistency across jurisdictions, but there seem to be some common elements that illustrate the uses and content of the PSI. A survey of 147 probation agencies across the nation (Carter, 1976) revealed that the cover sheets contained 17 pieces of identical information in more than 50 percent of the agencies surveyed. The information that appears most often across the various jurisdictions is included in Table 3.4.

Table 3.4
**Common Elements Contained in Presentence Reports**

| | | | |
|---|---|---|---|
| 1. | Name of Defendant | 10. | Plea |
| 2. | Name of Jurisdiction | 11. | Date of Report |
| 3. | Offense | 12. | Sex |
| 4. | Lawyer | 13. | Custody or Detention |
| 5. | Docket Number | 14. | Verdict |
| 6. | Date of Birth | 15. | Date of Disposition |
| 7. | Address | 16. | Marital Status |
| 8. | Name of Sentencing Judge | 17. | Other Identifying Numbers |
| 9. | Age | | |

Source: R.N. Carter (1976). "Prescriptive Package on Pre-Sentence Investigations." Unpublished draft. Washington, DC: Law Enforcement Assistance Administration.

While the content requirements for a presentence investigation vary from jurisdiction to jurisdiction, there appear to be some common areas that are included and these generally consist of the following:

1. Offense
    Official Version
    Defendant's Version
    Codefendant Information
    Statement of Witnesses, Complainants, and Victims

2. Prior Record
    Juvenile Adjudications
    Adult Record

3. Personal and Family Data
    Defendant
    Parents and Siblings
    Marital Status
    Employment
    Education
    Health (physical, mental, and emotional)
    Military Service
    Financial Condition
    Assets
    Liabilities

4. Evaluation
    Alternative Plans
    Sentencing Data

5. Recommendations

Basically, these areas reflect the recommendation of Carter (1976:9), who states that "in spite of the tradition of 'larger' rather than 'shorter,' there is little evidence that more is better." At a minimum, the PSI should include the five basic areas outlined above. This permits flexibility by allowing for expansion of a subject area and increased detail of circumstances as warranted. On the other hand, a subsection may be summarized in a single narrative statement.

Carter believes it is not necessary to know everything about an offender. Indeed, there is some evidence that in human decisionmaking, the capacity of individuals to use information effectively is limited to five or six items of information. Quite apart from the questions of the reliability, validity, or even relevance of the information, are the time and workload burdens of collecting and sorting masses of data for decisionmaking. The end result may be information overload and impairment of efficiency. Figure 3.3 is a sample outline of a presentence report from the Montgomery County Adult Probation Department (Dayton, Ohio). The PSI contains information related to the present character and behavior of the offender.

A sample outline of a presentence investigation report from the Montgomery County Adult Probation Department (Dayton, Ohio) is shown in Figure 3.3. A thorough PSI is not complete without a plan of supervision for those individuals selected for probation. If this type of information is developed while preparing the PSI, supervision can begin on day one, not several weeks into the probation period. During the development of the PSI, special attention is also given to seeking innovative alternatives to traditional sentencing dispositions (jail, fines, prison, or probation). Recently, there has been increased attention given to the victim (Umbreit, 1994; Roy, 1994). Many probation departments' now include as part of their PSI report a section pertaining the victim. An example of a victim statement from the Montgomery County is presented in Figure 3.4. This section includes an assessment of the harm done to the victim, and may include their comments concerning the offense and offender.

## Evaluation and Recommendation

Two of the most important sections of the presentence investigation report are the evaluation and the recommendation. Although the research evidence is mixed, there appears to be a high correlation between the probation officer's recommendation and the judge's decision (Hagan, 1975; Walsh, 1985). There is also some evidence that the sections most widely read by the judge are the PSI evaluation and recommendation.

The evaluation should contain the probation officer's professional assessment of the objective material contained in the body of the report. Having gathered all the facts, the probation officer must now consider the protection of the community and the need of the defendant.

Figure 3.3
**The Montgomery County Common Pleas Court Adult Probation Department Presentence Report**

---

Prosecutor:                                                Defense Attorney:

—————————————————————— I. Case Information ——————————————————

A.  Case No.:                               C.  Jail Status:
        Referred:                                   Amount of Bond:
        Disposition:                                Days in Custody:

B.  Name                                    D.  Urinalysis Ordered Yes___ No___
        Alias(es):                                  Urine(s) Collected:
        Address:                                    Result(s) Positive:
                                                    Result(s) Negative:
        Phone:                                      Probation Officer:

    Date of Birth:                          E.  Codefendant Status:

    Social Security No.:                    F.  Restitution:

—————————————————————— II. Charge Information ——————————————————

A.  Current Adjudicated Charge(es)/
        O.R.C./Penalty:
                                            D.  Other Pending Cases/Detainers:

                                            E.  Prior Felonies:
B.  Indicated Charge:
                                            F.  Repeat Offender Status:

C.  Original Jurisdiction:                  G.  Eligibility for Conditional Probation:

—————————————————————— III. Client Information ——————————————————

A.  Physical
        Sex_____ Race_____ Height_____
        Weight_____ Eyes_____ Hair_____
        Present Health _____

B.  Social
        Marital Status _____
        No. of Dependents _____
        Custody of Children if Sentenced _____
        _____
        Employment Status _____
        Last Grade Completed _____
        Social Service Involvement _____
        Past _____
        _____
        Present _____
        _____
        Limitations:
                        Rec. Bailiff_____ Date/Time_____

Figure 3.4—*continued*

Part I. The Offense

Part II. Criminal Record Section

A.    Juvenile

B.    Adult

Part III. Employment/Other Pertinent Data

Part IV. Recommendation

Reasons:

1.

2.

3.

4.

Respectfully Submitted,

_____

Team Supervisor_____

Source: The Montgomery County Adult Probation Department.

Figure 3.4
**Victim Impact Statement**

Judge:

Case No.:

Name of Defendant:

Disposition Date:

A.   Economic Loss

B.   Physical Injury

C.   Change in Personal Welfare or Familial Relationships

D.   Psychological Impact

E.   Comments

Source: The Montgomery County Adult Probation Department.

First, the probation officer should consider the offense. Was it situational in nature, or indicative of persistent behavior? Was violence used? Was a weapon involved? Was it a property offense or a personal offense? Was there a motive?

Second, the community must be considered. For example, does the defendant pose a direct threat to the safety and welfare of others? Would a disposition other than prison deprecate the seriousness of the crime? Is probation a sufficient deterrent? What community resources are available?

Finally, the probation officer has to consider the defendant and his or her special problems and needs, if any. What developmental factors were significant in contributing to the defendant's current behavior? Was there a history of antisocial behavior? Does the defendant acknowledge responsibility or remorse? Is the defendant motivated to change? What strengths and weaknesses does the defendant possess? Is the defendant employable or supporting any immediate family? The probation officer should also provide a statement of sentencing alternatives available to the court. This does not constitute a recommendation, but rather informs the court which services are available should the defendant be granted probation.

A sound recommendation is the responsibility of the probation officer. Some of the alternatives may include:

| | |
|---|---|
| anger management programs | restitution |
| cognitive behavioral groups | fine |
| probation | mandatory drug treatment |
| work release | house arrest/electronic monitoring |
| incarceration | community service |
| split sentence | psychiatric treatment |
| shock probation | day fines |
| halfway house | victim mediation |
| family counseling | shock incarceration |
| day reporting | no recommendation |

If commitment were recommended, the probation officer would indicate any problems that may need special attention on the part of the institutional staff. In addition, if the defendant were considered a security risk, the investigator would include escape potential, as well as any threats made to or received from the community or other defendants.

Regardless of the recommendation, the probation officer has the responsibility to provide supporting rationale that will assist the court in achieving its sentencing goals.

## Factors Related to Sentencing Decisions

As mentioned previously, the PSI involves a great deal of a probation department's time and resources. The presentence report is the primary comprehensive source of information about the defendant that is available to the sentencing judge. Although most judges agree that the PSI is a valuable aid in formulating sentencing decisions, there appear to be some differences of opinion about the value of the recommendations section of the report.[8]

Several studies have attempted to identify those factors that appear to be of primary importance to sentencing judges. Carter's 1976 survey found that the two most significant factors were the defendant's prior criminal record and the current offense. An earlier study by Carter and Wilkins (1967) found that the most important factors for judges in making a decision to grant probation included the defendant's educational level, average monthly salary, occupational level, residence, stability, participation in church activities, and military record. But, again, when factors were ranked according to their importance in the sentencing decision, the current offense and the defendant's prior record, number of arrests, and number of commitments were ranked most important. Welch and Spohn (1986) also concluded that prior record clearly predicts the decision to incarcerate, however, their research suggests that a wide range of indicators have been used to determine "prior record," but that the safest choice to use is prior incarceration.

In another study, Rosecrance (1988:251) suggests that the PSI report serves to maintain the myth that criminal courts dispense individualized justice. His conclusions are, "that present offense and prior criminal record are the factors that determine the probation officer's final sentencing recommendation." Rosecrance (1985) also believes that probation recommendations are designed to endorse pre-arraigned judicial agreements, and that probation officers structure their recommendations in the "ball park" in order to gain judicial acceptance. Rogers (1990) argues, however, that the presentence investigation individualizes juvenile justice.

In another study, Latessa (1993) examined both the factors that influenced the probation officers recommendation, as well as the actual judicial decision. He found that offenders were more likely to be recommended for prison if: they were repeat offenders, committed more serious offenses, there was a victim involved, and they had a prior juvenile record. The factors that influenced the actual sentencing decision included: the recommendation, drug history, mental health history, seriousness of offense, and having been incarcerated previously in a state prison. Latessa concluded that in this jurisdiction sentencing factors are based mainly on offense and prior record factors, and other relevant information, such as the presence of a victim. It is important to note that demographic factors, such as race, sex, and age did not play a factor in either the recommendations or the decisions of the judges.

## Conditions of Probation

When probation is granted, the court may impose certain reasonable conditions on the offender, which the probation officer is expected to monitor in the supervision process. These must not be capricious, and may be both general (required of all probationers) and specific (required of an individual probationers). General conditions include obeying laws, submitting to searchers, reporting regularly to the supervising officer, notifying the officer of any change in job or residence, and not being in possession of a firearm, associating with known criminals, refraining from excessive use of alcohol, or not leaving the court's jurisdiction for long periods of time without prior authorization. A partial list of services provided by probation jurisdictions can be found in Figure 3.5.

Figure 3.5
**Percentage of Probation Agencies Offering Specific Services**

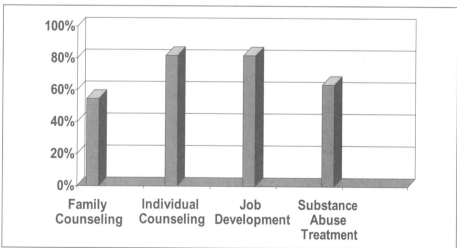

Source: Camp, C. and G. Camp (2003). *The Corrections Yearbook: Adult Corrections, 2002*, p. 215.

Specific conditions are generally tailored to the needs of the offender or philosophy of the court. For reintegration or other such purposes, the court may impose conditions of medical or psychiatric treatment; residence in a halfway house or residential center; intensive probation supervision, electronic surveillance, house arrest, community service, active involvement in Alcoholics Anonymous; participation in a drug abuse program; restitution or victim compensation; no use of psychotropic drugs (such as cocaine or marijuana); observing a reasonable curfew; no hitchhiking; staying out of bars and poolrooms (particularly if the probationer is a prostitute); group counseling; vocational training; or other court-ordered requirements. Such required conditions are specifically designed to assist the probationer in the successful completion of probation. An example of the standard conditions of probation from the Federal Courts is presented in Figure 3.6.

Figure 3.6

PROB 7A
(Rev. 10/89)          **Conditions of Probation and Supervised Release**

**UNITED STATES DISTRICT COURT**

**FOR THE**

_____

Name _____     Docket No. _____

Address _____

    Under the terms of your sentence, you have been placed on probation/supervised release (strike one) by the Honorable _____, United States District Judge for the District of _____. Your term of supervision is for a period of _____, commencing _____.

    While on probation/supervised release (strike one) you shall not commit another Federal, state, or local crime and shall not illegally possess a controlled substance. Revocation of probation and supervised release is mandatory for possession of a controlled substance.

## CHECK IF APPROPRIATE:

☐ As a condition of supervision, you are instructed to pay a fine in the amount of _____ ; it shall be paid in the following manner _____ .

☐ As a condition of supervision, you are instructed to pay restitution in the amount of _____ to _____ ; it shall be paid in the following manner _____ .

☐ The defendant shall not possess a firearm or destructive device. Probation must be revoked for possession of a firearm.

☐ The defendant shall report in person to the probation office in the district to which the defendant is released within 72 hours of release from the custody of the Bureau of Prisons.

☐ The defendant shall report in person to the probation office in the district of release within 72 hours of release from the custody of the Bureau of Prisons.

Figure 3.6—*continued*

**It is the order of the Court that you shall comply with the following standard conditions:**

(1)    You shall not leave the judicial district without permission of the Court or probation officer;

(2)    You shall report to the probation officer as directed by the Court or probation officer, and shall submit a truthful and complete written report within the first five days of each month;

(3)    You shall answer truthfully all inquiries by the probation officer and follow the instructions of the probation officer;

(4)    You shall support your dependents and meet other family responsibilities;

(5)    You shall work regularly at a lawful occupation unless excused by the probation officer for schooling, training, or other acceptable reasons;

(6)    You shall notify the probation officer within 72 hours of any change in residence or employment;

(7)    You shall refrain from excessive use of alcohol and shall not purchase, possess, use, distribute, or administer any narcotic or other controlled substance, or any paraphernalia related to such substances, except as prescribed by a physician;

(8)    You shall not frequent places where controlled substances are illegally sold, used, distributed, or administered;

(9)    You shall not associate with any persons engaged in criminal activity, and shall not associate with any person convicted of a felony unless granted permission to do so by the probation officer;

(10)    You shall permit a probation officer to visit you at any time at home or elsewhere, and shall permit confiscation of any contraband observed in plain view by the probation officer;

(11)    You shall notify the probation officer within 72 hours of being arrested or questioned by a law enforcement officer;

(12)    You shall not enter into any agreement to act as an informer or a special agent of a law enforcement agency without the permission of the Court;

(13)    As directed by the probation officer, you shall notify third parties of risks that may be occasioned by your criminal record or personal history or characteristics, and shall permit the probation officer to make such notifications and to confirm your compliance with such notification requirement.

**The special conditions ordered by the Court are as follows:**

Upon a finding of violation of probation or supervised release, I understand that the Court may (1) revoke supervision or (2) extend the term of supervision and/or modify the conditions of supervision.

Figure 3.6—*continued*

> These conditions have been read to me. I fully understand the conditions, and have been provided a copy of them.
>
> (Signed) _____    _____
>                          Defendant                              Date
>
>
> _____    _____
>         U.S. Probation Officer/Designated Witness        Date

## *Probation Fees*

As part of the conditions of probation, many jurisdictions have included probation fees as part of the probation experience. These fees are levied for a variety of services including the preparation of presentence reports, electronic monitoring, ignition interlock devices, work-release programs, drug counseling and testing, and regular probation supervision (Ring, 1988; Lansing, 1999). The fees range anywhere from $10 to $120 per month, with the average estimated to be about $32 per month. The imposition of supervision fees has increased dramatically over the years, with only 10 states reported user fees in 1980, at least 25 states by 1986, and by 2000, 43 states had authorized the imposition of some form of supervision fee (Baird, Holien & Bakke, 1986; Lansing, 1999; Camp & Camp, 2003). In addition, some states, such as Ohio, now require probation officers to assist in collecting child support payments from parents under probation supervision.

The critics of probation fees argue that it is unfair to assess a fee to those most unable to pay. Others argue that probationer fee's will result in a shift from treatment and surveillance to fee collection, and that it will turn probation officers into bill collectors.

Others however, believe that probation fees can be a reasonable part of the probation experience (Wheeler, Macan, Hissong & Slusher, 1989; Wheeler, Rudolph & Hissong, 1989). Harlow and Nelson (1982:65) point out that successful fee programs serve a dual purpose, "both an important revenue source and an effective means of communicating to the offender the need to pay one's own way."[9]

It appears that probation fees are rapidly becoming a fixture in probation. Not only is it a means of raising revenue and offsetting the costs of supervision, treatment and surveillance, but it can also be used to as a form of punishment (or to promote responsible behavior depending on your viewpoint).

## Restitution and Community Service

Two more recent but related trends in the conditions the court may impose are restitution and community work orders. Restitution requires the offender to make payment (perhaps monetary) to a victim to offset the damages done in the commission of the crime. If the offenders cannot afford to repay at least a part of the loss suffered by the victim, it is possible to restore the victim's losses through personal services. Probation with restitution thus has the potential for being a reparative sentence and Galaway (1983) argues that it should be the penalty of choice for property offenders. Restitution can lessen the loss of the victim, maximize reconciliation of the offender and community, and marshal community support for the offender, perhaps through enlisting a community sponsor to monitor and encourage the offender's compliance. A good example of this can be seen in California, where in 1982 voters passed a Victim's Bill of Rights. Part of this initiative was a Crime Victim Restitution Program that enables the court to order offenders to repay victims and the community through restitution or community service (see van Dijk-Kaam & Wemmers, 1999).

Community work orders as conditions of probation appear to be increasingly used in conjunction with probation, particularly if there are no direct victim losses or the nature of the crime demands more than supervised release. Examples of community work orders would include requiring a dentist convicted of driving while intoxicated to provide free dental services to a number of indigents, or ordering a physician to provide numerous hours of free medical treatment to jail inmates, perhaps on Saturday mornings. Juveniles may frequently be ordered to work for community improvements through litter removal, cutting grass, painting the homes of the elderly or public buildings, or driving shut-ins to market or to visit friends and relatives. Both restitution and community work orders can serve multiple goals: offender punishment, community reintegration, and reconciliation. The four reasons most commonly cited for using community service are:

1. It is a punishment that can fit many crimes.

2. The costs of imprisonment are high and are getting higher.

3. Our jails and prisons are already full.

4. Community service requires an offender to pay with time and energy.

Another increasingly popular probation program is day reporting, a slightly structured nonresidential program often using supervision, volunteers, sanctions, and services coordinated from a central location. Providing offenders with access to treatment services, day attendance centers can help reduce jail and prison over crowding, hold offenders accountable for their behavior, and help them address such risk factors as unemployment, addiction, and lack of education (see Williams & Turnage, 2001).

## Alternative Probation Procedures

In addition to the most frequent procedures described above, there are six other variations of granting probation that need to be discussed before we consider the legal process of revoking probation of those who cannot or will not abide by court-imposed conditions of liberty in the community:

1. prosecutorial probation,

2. court probation without adjudication,

3. shock probation,

4. intermittent incarceration,

5. split sentences, and

6. modification of sentence.

While probation most frequently is imposed by a trial judge after a guilty plea or trial, it may also replace the trial completely, in which case it is called "probation without adjudication." In practice, the process embraces two separate programs, one operated by the prosecutor (a form of deferred prosecution) and the other by the judge in those limited number of jurisdictions in which state legislation permits a bifurcated process (determining guilt, followed by adjudication as a felon). Both result in probation but are vastly different.

## Deferred Prosecution Probation

Part of the broad power accorded a prosecutor in the United States is the ability to offer the accused deferred prosecution. In those programs in which the prosecutor grants deferred prosecution, the accused will generally be asked to sign a contract accepting moral (but usually not legal) responsibility for the crime and agreeing to make victim restitution, to undergo specific treatment programs (substance abuse, methadone maintenance, anger management, etc.), to report periodically to a designated official (usually a probation officer), and to refrain from other criminal acts during the contract period. If these conditions are satisfied, the prosecutor dismisses (nolle pros) the charge. If the accused does not actively participate and cooperate in the program the prosecutor can, at any time during the contract period, carry the case forward to trial. Deferred prosecution can, although it is infrequent, lead to a unique probation organization within the office of the prosecutor.

## Probation by Withholding Adjudication

This process refers to a judge's optional authority that is available in those states (such as Florida) where statutes permit a bifurcated process: first determine guilt and then declare the defendant a convicted felon. By refraining from the declaration of a guilty felon, the judge can suspend the legal process and place the defendant on probation for a specific time period, sometimes without supervision being required (a "summary" or nonreporting probation). Thus the judge gives the offender a chance to demonstrate his or her ability and willingness to adjust and reform. The offenders know that they can still be returned to court for adjudication of guilt and sentencing, and frequently imprisonment.

The advantages of this option fit squarely in the general philosophy of probation, and may be of particular use in intimate-partner assaults (Canales-Portalatin, 2000). Not only is treatment in the community emphasized, but the collateral benefits are considerable (Allen, Friday, Roebuck & Sagarin, 1981:361-362):

> (The judge) places him or her on probation without requiring him to register with local law enforcement agencies as a previously convicted felon; without serving notice on prospective employers of a previous conviction; without preventing the of-

fender from holding public office, voting, or serving on a jury; without impeding the offender from obtaining a license that requires "reputable character;" without making it more difficult than others to obtain firearms; in short, without public or even private degradation.

## Shock Probation

In 1965, Ohio became the first of at least 14 states that enacted an early release procedure generally known as "shock probation." Shock probation combined the leniency of probation with a short period of incarceration in a penal institution. The assumptions and features underlying this innovative program were described by the then-director of the Ohio Adult Parole Authority (Allen & Simonsen, 2001:226). It was:

1. A way for the courts to impress offenders with the seriousness of their actions without a long prison sentence.

2. A way for the courts to release offenders found by the institution to be more amenable to community-based treatment than was realized by the courts at time of sentence.

3. A way for the courts to arrive at a just compromise between punishment and leniency in appropriate cases.

4. A way for the courts to provide community-based treatment for rehabilitable offenders while still observing their responsibilities for imposing deterrent sentences where public policy demands it.

5. [A way to afford] the briefly incarcerated offender a protection against absorption into the "hard rock" inmate culture.

Critics have argued that shock probation combines philosophically incompatible objectives: punishment and leniency. Other criticisms (Reid, 1976) are that the defendant is further stigmatized by the incarceration component of shock probation, and the existence of a shock probation sentence may encourage the judiciary to rely less on probation than previously. But the most damaging criticism is by Vito and Allen (1981:74):

> . . . the fact of incarceration is having some unknown and unmeasurable effect upon [the more unfavorable] performance of shock probationers. . . . It could be that the negative effects of incarceration are affecting the performance of shock probationers.

Vito has drawn some conclusions about shock probation based on his long-term work in this area (1984:26-27):

1.  The level of reincarceration rates indicate that the program has some potential.

2.  If shock probation is utilized, it should be used with a select group of offenders who cannot be considered as good candidates for regular probation.

3.  The period of incarceration must be short in order to achieve the maximum deterrent effect while reducing the fiscal cost of incarceration.

4.  In this time of severe prison overcrowding, the use of shock probation can only be justified as a diversionary measure to give offenders who would otherwise not be placed on probation a chance to succeed.

Although shock probation has been in use for more than 40 years, it is not a widely used disposition, and the overall effects and effectiveness remain unknown.

## Combining Probation and Incarceration

There are a number of alternatives to placing an offender on probation, other than shock probation, that include a period of incarceration (Parisi, 1980). The U.S. Department of Justice (Bureau of Justice Statistics, 1997a) notes:

> Although the courts continue to use (probation) as a less severe and less expensive alternative to incarceration, most courts are also given discretion to link probation to a term of incarceration—an option selected with increasing frequency.

Combinations of probation and incarceration include:

> Split sentences: where the court specifies a period of incarceration to be followed by a period of probation (Parisi, 1981).

> Modification of sentence: where the original sentencing court may reconsider an offender's prison sentence within a limited time and change it to probation.

> Intermittent incarceration: where an offender on probation may spend weekends or nights in jail (Bureau of Justice Statistics, 1997a).

It is not known how frequently sentencing judges use these options, but the entry status for those offenders entering probation in 2005 can be found in Table 3.5.

Table 3.5
**Adults Entering Probation in 2005: Status Entry**

| Status: | Percent |
| --- | --- |
| Direct imposition | 57% |
| Sentence Suspended | 22 |
| Split Sentence | 10 |
| Imposition Suspended | 9 |
| Other | 2 |
| Total: | 100% |

Source: Glaze, L.E. and T. Bonsczar, (2006). *Probation and Parole in the United States, 2005.* Washington, DC: U.S. Bureau of Justice Statistics.

## Probation Revocation

The judge usually imposes the conditions that must be observed by the offender while on probation and has absolute discretion and authority to impose, modify, or reject these conditions. Some examples of conditions a judge might impose are routine urine testing to detect drug use and abuse; participation in a substance abuse program if the probationer has a drug or alcohol problem; driving limits, restitution to victims of the probationer (but probation may not be revoked if the offender cannot make payments because of unemployment: *Bearden v. Georgia*, 1983);[10] and not leaving the court's jurisdiction without prior approval. Many cases have challenged the conditions that courts might impose, but case law has determined any condition may be imposed if it is constitutional, reasonable, clear, and related to some definable correctional goal, such as rehabilitation or public safety. These are difficult to challenge and leave the court with broad power and tremendous discretion in imposing conditions. Such discretion has contributed to the volume of civil rights suits (del Carmen, 1985).

Once placed on probation, offenders are supervised and assisted by probation officers who are increasingly using existing community agencies and services to provide individualized treatment based on the offender's needs. Assuming the offender meets the court-imposed conditions, makes satisfactory progress in resolving underlying problems, and does not engage in further illegal activities, probation agencies may request the court to close the case. This would terminate supervision of the offender and probation. Probation may also be terminated by the completion of the period of maximum sentence, or by the offender having received "maximum benefit from treatment." Figure 3.7 shows the various ways that adult offenders terminated probation in 2005. Fortunately, most offenders successfully completed their term of probation (59%).

Figure 3.7
**Adults Leaving Probation in 2005**

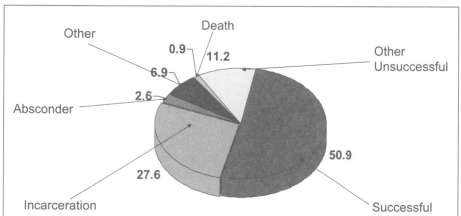

Source: Adopted from Glaze, L.E., and T. Bonczar (2006). *Probation and Parole in the United States, 2005.* U.S. Department of Justice Programs.

In supervising a probationer, officers should enforce the conditions and rules of probation pragmatically, considering the client's particular and individual needs, legality of decisions they must make while supervising clients (Watkins, 1989), the clarity of anticipation by probationer of assistance from the supervising officer (and expectations of the probationer), and the potential effects of enforcing rules on a client's future behavior and adjustment (Koontz, 1980). Many clients have alcohol and drug problems, and must be tested for substance abuse. In 2000, 24 percent of probation clients were on probation for a drug law violation, and 18 percent for driving while intoxicated.

Probationers vary in their ability to comply with imposed conditions, some of which may be unrealistic, particularly those that require extensive victim restitution or employment during an economic period of high unemployment (Smith, Davis & Hillenbrand, 1989). Some probationers are also indifferent or even hostile, unwilling, or psychologically unable to cooperate with their probation supervisor or the court. Others commit technical violations of court orders that are not per se new crimes but are seen as harbingers of future illegal activity. In these circumstances, probation officers must deal with technical probation violations.

Probation officers, charged with managing such cases, may determine that technical violators need a stern warning or that court-imposed conditions should be tightened (or relaxed, depending on

individual circumstances). These determinations may lead to an offender's reappearance before the court for a warning or redefinition of
conditions. Judges and probation officers, ideally, collaborate in such
cases to protect the community or increase the probability of successful
reintegration. Offenders are frequently returned to probation, and supervision and treatment continue.

If the warning and new conditions are not sufficient, or the offender
repetitively violates conditions of probation, or is arrested for an alleged
new crime, a probation revocation hearing may be necessary. If the probationer is not already in jail for the alleged new crime, a warrant may
be issued for his or her arrest. Reasons for probation revocation in 2001
can be seen in Figure 3.8.

Figure 3.8
**Reason for Failure on Probation During 2001**

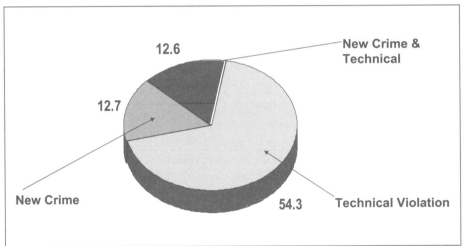

Source: Camp, C. and G. Camp (2003). *The Corrections Yearbook: Adult Corrections 2002.* Middletown, CT: Criminal Justice Institute, Inc., p. 200.

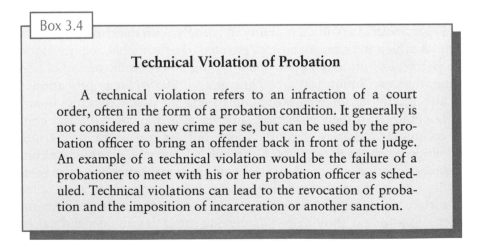

Box 3.4

### Technical Violation of Probation

A technical violation refers to an infraction of a court
order, often in the form of a probation condition. It generally is
not considered a new crime per se, but can be used by the probation officer to bring an offender back in front of the judge.
An example of a technical violation would be the failure of a
probationer to meet with his or her probation officer as scheduled. Technical violations can lead to the revocation of probation and the imposition of incarceration or another sanction.

It is also clear that technical violations can be a major source of failures on probation, and that the rates can vary considerably from jurisdiction to jurisdiction. Figure 3.9 illustrates this point with data from a recent recidivism study conducted in Ohio. As part of this study recidivism rates were compared for probation agencies across the state, by the size of the county. Probation departments in the medium and small counties were more likely to use technical violations for probation revocation and incarceration than the larger counties.

Figure 3.9
**Reason for Subsequent Incarceration by Probationers by County Size**

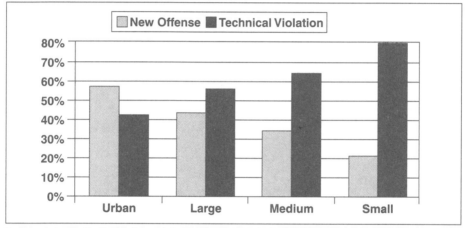

Source: Latessa, E., F. Travis, and A. Holsinger (1997). *Evaluation of Ohio's Community Correctional Act Programs by County Size.* Cincinnati, OH: Division of Criminal Justice, University of Cincinnati.

A probation revocation hearing is a serious process, posing potential "grievous loss of liberty" for the offender. Both probation officers and judges vary considerably as to what would constitute grounds for revoking probation and resentencing to imprisonment. Punitive probation officers may contend that technical violations are sufficient for revoking probation; judges may believe that the commission of a new crime would be the only reason for revocation.

## Revocation and Legal Issues

Probation is a privilege, not a right (del Carmen, 1985). This was decided in *United States v. Birnbaum* (1970).[11] Once granted, however, the probationer has an interest in remaining on probation, commonly referred to as an entitlement. The due process rights of probationers at a revocation hearing were generally ignored until 1967, when the United States Supreme Court issued an opinion regarding state probationers' rights to counsel at such a hearing (*Mempa v. Rhay*). This case provided right to counsel if probation were revoked under a deferred sentencing statute, but this decision did not specify that a court hearing was required. That issue was resolved in *Gagnon v. Scarpelli* (1972), a landmark case in due process procedures in probation. The U.S. Supreme Court ruled that probation cannot be withdrawn (revoked) unless certain basic elements of due process are observed. If a court is considering removing the offender from probation (through a "revocation" hearing), the following rights and procedures must ensue: The probationer must: (1) be informed in writing of the charge against him or her, (2) have the written notice in advance of the revocation hearing, and (3) attend the hearing and be able to present evidence on his or her own behalf. The probationer also has a right (4) to challenge those testifying against him or her, (5) to confront witnesses and cross-examine them, and (6) to have legal counsel present if the charges are complicated or the case is so complex that an ordinary person would not be able to comprehend the legal issues.[12]

---

Box 3.5

### Modifications of Conditions of Sentence

Probation officers supervise clients assigned by sentencing courts and, during the period of community release, may find that certain probationers refuse to abide by the court-imposed rules, or that their clients' personal circumstances change so markedly that additional court direction may be needed.

If the client has difficulty accepting the legitimacy of community control, probation officers may recommend additional surveillance or treatment options. These range from imposing house arrest to electronic monitoring, or daily surveillance by the officer. Clients may also be required to reside in a residential setting, such as a halfway house, or appear daily at a day reporting program, until their behavior or circumstances change.

Increasing the requirements for conformity to court-ordered liberty is frequently referred to as "tourniquet sentencing." Conditions may be relaxed as behavior improves.

---

The probation officer is responsible for seeing that the conditions imposed by the court are met and, if not, calling the violations to the attention of the court. As such, the probation officer functions both as a helper and as a supervisor of the probationer. Legal liability is greater for the probation officer than the court; although an agent of the court, the probation officer does not enjoy the absolute immunity from liability that the court enjoys.

Some areas of potential liability for the probation officer include acts taken or protective steps omitted. For example, a probation officer may be liable for failing to disclose a probationer's background to a third party if this results in subsequent serious injury or death. Case decisions have generally held that the probation officer should disclose the past behavior of the probationer if able to reasonably foresee a potential danger to a specific third party. This would include an employer hiring a probationer as an accountant in a bank when the instant crime was embezzlement, or hiring a child molester to work in a grade school position. Insurance for certain liabilities can be obtained from the American Correctional Association. [13]

As a counselor to probationers, probation officers are often faced with the problem of encouraging their clients to share their problems and needs. Frequently, during the monthly contact, a probationer will reveal involvement in criminal activities. Under these noncustodial circumstances, probation offers are required to warn the probationer against self-incrimination through the *Miranda* warnings[14] or the evidence cannot be used in a court of law. Any discussion with a probationer under detention circumstances must be preceded by the *Miranda* warnings. Litigation is so extensive within the probation area that the probation officer must frequently take an active role as a law enforcement officer rather than a helper, a sad development from the original role John Augustus initiated and correctional personnel usually pursue.

## Summary

This chapter began by tracing the historical, philosophical, and legal developments in the field of probation over the last two centuries. While John Augustus is given credit as the "father" of probation, we have seen that many others played an important part in developing and shaping probation. Probation continues to serve the bulk of adult offenders. This chapter also described the court options and procedures for placing offenders on probation, as well as some issues in supervising offenders. It should be obvious that probation requires a judge to weigh the "individualization" of treatment as well as the "justice" or "just deserts" associated with the crime that was committed. In addition, this chapter has examined the presentence investigation report. Because the PSI is one of the primary responsibilities of probation agencies, its importance is highlighted by the fact that the vast majority of defendants plead guilty, and that their only contact with the judge is during sentencing.

Finally, the imposition of conditions, and the probation officer's monitoring of offender's behavior is an important part of the probation process. Accordingly, revoking probation is not an action that is taken lightly, since it often results in the incarceration of the offender. Granting probation and supervising probation clients are complicated procedures requiring considerable skill and dedication, issues that are also raised in granting parole.

## Review Questions

1. How did philosophical precursors of probation contribute to its development?

2. Why was probation established much earlier for juvenile offenders than for adult offenders?

3. Define probation.

4. Should probation be the disposition of choice for most nonviolent offenders?

5. What are the general objectives of probation?

6. Describe the advantages of probation.

7. How is justice individualized?

8. What functions does the presentence investigation serve?

9. What is the potential value of a victim impact statement?

10. Identify and define five supervision conditions that might be included in the PSI recommendation.

11. List five conditions of probation that are generally required of all probationers.

12. What are three grounds for revoking probation and sentencing to incarceration?

13. List five possible sentencing recommendations that can be made.

14. Explain why probation revocation rates might be higher in rural versus urban areas.

## Key Terms

Cesare Beccaria
concurrent sentencing
conditions of probation
consecutive sentencing
individualized justice
John Augustus
*Killits* decision
presentence investigation report

probation
probationer fees
restitution
revocation
victim impact statements
sentencing hearing
shock probation
split sentence

## Electronic Library

American Correctional Association Probation and Parole Directory, 2004-2006 http://www.aca.org/publications/

Juvenile offender probationers and victims (www.ncjrs.org.html/ojjdp/nationalreport99.toc.html).

National Probation and Parole Association (www.appa-net.org).

Probation and parole populations http://www.ojp.usdoj.gov/bjs/

Sentencing in State courts (www.ojp.usdoj.gov/bjs/fssc98.pdf).

Substance abuse and treatment of adults on probation (www.ojp.usdoj.gov/bjs/pdf.satap95.pdf).

## Recommended Readings

del Carmen, R. (1985). "Legal Issues and Liabilities in Community Corrections." In L.F. Travis (ed.) *Probation, Parole and Community Corrections*, pp. 47-70. Prospect Heights, IL: Waveland. This chapter does an excellent job of summarizing the legal issues surrounding probation, including release, conditions, and supervision.

Dressler, D. (1962). *Practice and Theory of Probation and Parole*. New York, NY: Columbia University Press. A cogent and well-documented analysis of the historical development of probation.

Evjen, V. (1975). "The Federal Probation System: The Struggle to Achieve It and Its First 25 Years." *Federal Probation*, 39(2):3-15. A very thorough description of the rise of the Federal probation system.

Gowdy, V. (1993). *Intermediate Sanctions*. Washington, DC: U.S. Department of Justice. An excellent overview of the range of and issues surrounding intermediate punishments.

Johnson, H. and N. Wolfe (2003). *History of Criminal Justice*, Third Edition. Cincinnati, OH: Anderson Publishing Co. This book provides a history of criminal justice, and probation and examines the philosophy of individualized justice.

Lindner, C. and M. Savarese (1984). "The Evolution of Probation: Early Salaries, Qualifications and Hiring Practices;" "The Evolution of Probation: The Historical Contributions of the Volunteer;" "The Evolution of Probation: University Settlement and the Beginning of Statutory Probation in New York City;" "The Evolution of Probation: University Settlement and Its Pioneering Role in Probation Work." *Federal Probation*, 48(1-4). This four-part series examines the early rise of probation in the United States.

Rothman, D. (1980). *Conscience and Convenience: The Asylum and Its Alternatives in Progressive America*. Boston, MA: Little, Brown. Chapter 3 provides a critical assessment of the early use of probation and the development of the presentence investigation.

## *Notes*

[1]    Sureties refers to cash, property, or bond posted by an offender, to be forfeited if he or she fails to conform to such conditions as to appear in court for trial, or to avoid further criminal behavior over a specified time period. It can also refer to a pledge by another responsible person to assure that the accused will appear or behave properly.[2] The Volstead Act authorized the enforcement of anti-alcohol legislation—the "Great Experiment" of the Thirteenth Amendment to the U.S. Constitution.

[3]    While some dispute the effectiveness of probation (Petersilia, 1985), other researchers (McGaha et al., 1987; G. Vito, 1986) have found probation generally to be effective. This issue is discussed in greater detail in Chapter 11.

[4]    There is some evidence that sentencing is in part influenced by judges' personal goals, such as potential for promotion to a higher court. M. Cohen (1992). "The Motives of Judges: Empirical Evidence from Antitrust Sentencing." International Review of Law and Economics, 12:13-30. Macallair, D. (1994). "Disposition Case Advocacy in San Francisco's Juvenile Justice System: A New Approach to Deinstitutionalization." *Crime & Delinquency*, 40:84-95.

[5]    For a thorough discussion of the early development of the presentence investigation report see "The Presentence Report: An Empirical Study of Its Use in the Federal Criminal Process" (1970). *Georgetown Law Journal*, 58:12-27.

[6]    See E. Sieh (1993). "From Augustus to the Progressives: A Study of Probation's Formative Years." *Federal Probation*, 57(3):67-72.

[7]    These functions are adapted from the Administrative Office of the U.S. Courts (1978). *The Presentence Investigation Report*. Washington, DC: U.S. Government Printing Office. See also T. Marvell (1995). "Sentencing Guidelines and Prison Population Growth." *The Journal of Criminal Law and Criminology*, 85:696-707.

[8] For example, in Cincinnati, Ohio, a single probation department serves both the Municipal Court and the Court of Common Pleas, yet each court requires a different presentence investigation report. The Court of Common Pleas does not permit probation officer recommendations to be included in the report, but the Municipal Court requires one.

[9] For a description of the Texas Program, see P. Finn and D. Parent (1992). *Making the Offender Foot the Bill: A Texas Program.* Washington, DC: U.S. Department of Justice.

[10] 461 U.S. 660 (1983).

[11] 421 F.2d 993, *cert. denied*, 397 U.S. 1044 (1970).

[12] 411 U.S. 778, 93 S. Ct. 1756 (1972).

[13] The current mailing address for the American Correctional Association is 4380 Forbes Boulevard, Lanham, MD 20706-4322 (www.corrections.com/aca).

[14] *Miranda* warnings: 1. That the suspect has the right to remain silent; 2. That any statement he does make may be used as evidence against him; 3. That he has a right to the presence of an attorney; 4. That if he cannot afford an attorney, one will be appointed for him prior to any questioning if he so desires. See *Black's Law Dictionary* (1994), 5th ed., St. Paul, MN: West.

## References

Allen, H., P. Friday, J. Roebuck, and E. Sagarin (1981). *Crime and Punishment.* New York, NY: The Free Press.

Allen, H. and C. Simonsen (2001). *Corrections in America.* Upper Saddle River, NJ: Prentice Hall.

Allen, H. and C. Simonsen (1989). *Corrections in America.* New York, NY: Macmillan.

American Bar Association (1970). *Project Standards for Criminal Justice: Standards Relating to Probation.* New York, NY: Institute of Judicial Administration.

American Correctional Association (2001). *Probation and Parole Directory 2000-2003.* Lanham, MD: ACA.

Baird, C., D. Holien, and J. Bakke (1986). *Fees for Probation Services.* Washington, DC: National Institute of Corrections.

Barnes, H. and N. Teeters (1959). *New Horizons in Criminology.* Englewood Cliffs, NJ: Prentice-Hall.

*Bearden v. Georgia*, 461 U.S. 660 (1983).

Beccaria, C. (1764). *Essay On Crimes and Punishments.* Translated by H. Paulucci (1963). Indianapolis, IN: Bobbs-Merrill.

Burdress, L. (ed.) (1997). "The Federal Probation and Pretrial Services System." *Federal Probation*, 61(1):5-111.

Bureau of Justice Statistics (1997a). *Correctional Populations in the United States.* Washington, DC: U.S. Department of Justice.

Bureau of Justice Statistics (2001). National Correction Population Reaches New High, Grows by 126,400 During 2000 to Total 6.5 Million Adults (www.ojp.usdoj.gov/bjs/pdy.ppus00.pdf).

Bush, E. L. (1990). "Not Ordinarily Relevant? Considering the Defendant's Children at Sentencing." *Federal Probation*, 54 (1):15-22.

Camp, C. and G. Camp (1997). *The Corrections Yearbook*. South Salem, NY: The Criminal Justice Institute.

Camp, C. and G. Camp (2003). *The Corrections Yearbook Adult Corrections 2002*. Middletown, CT: The Criminal Justice Institute.

Canales-Portalatin, D. (2000). "Intimate Partner Assailants." *Journal of Interpersonal Violence*, 15(8):843-854.

Carter, R. (1976). "Prescriptive Package on Pre-Sentence Investigations." Unpublished draft. Washington, DC: Law Enforcement Assistance Administration.

Carter, R. (1966). "It Is Respectfully Recommended . . ." *Federal Probation*, 30(2):38-40.

Carter, R. and L. Wilkins (1967). "Some Factors in Sentencing Policy." *Journal of Criminal Law, Criminology and Police Science*, 58(4):503-514.

Citizens Committee for Children (1982). *Lost Opportunities: A Study of the Promise and Practices of the [New York City] Department of Probation's Family Court*. New York, NY: Citizens Committee for Children.

Clear, T.R., V.B. Clear, and W.D. Burrell (1989). *Offender Assessment and Evaluation: The Presentence Investigation Report*. Cincinnati: Anderson Publishing.

Cornelius, W. (1997). *Swift and Sure: Bringing Certainty and Finality to Criminal Punishments*. Irvington-on-Hudson: Bridge Street Books.

Dawson, J. (1990). *Felons Sentenced to Probation in State Courts*. Washington, DC: U.S. Department of Justice.

del Carmen, R.V. (1985). "Legal Issues and Liabilities in Community Corrections." In L.F. Travis (ed). *Probation, Parole and Community Corrections*, pp. 47-70. Prospect Heights, IL: Waveland.

del Carmen, R.V. and G. Bonham (2001). "Overview of Legal Liabilities." *Perspectives*, 25(1):28-33.

Dierna, J. (1989). "Guideline Sentencing: Probation Officer Responsibilities and Interagency Issues." *Federal Probation*, 53(3):3-11.

Dixon, J. (1995). "The Organizational Context of Criminal Sentencing." *American Journal of Sociology*, 100:1157-1198.

Dressler, D. (1962). *Practice and Theory of Probation and Parole*. New York, NY: Columbia University Press.

Dubois, P. (1981). "Disclosure of Presentence Reports in the United States District Courts." *Federal Probation*, 45(1):3-9.

DuRose, M., D. Levin, and P. Langan (2001). *Felony Sentences in State Courts, 1998*. Washington, DC: Bureau of Justice Statistics (www.ojp.usdoj.gov/bjs/fssc98.pdf).

Evans, S. and J. Scott (1983). "Social Scientists as Expert Witnesses: Their Use, Misuse and Sometimes Abuse." *Law and Policy Quarterly*, 5:181-214.

Evjen, V. (1975). "The Federal Probation System: The Struggle to Achieve It and Its First 25 Years." *Federal Probation*, 39(2):3-15.

*Ex parte* U.S. 242 27-53 (1916).

Finn, P. (1984). "Prison Crowding: The Response of Probation and Parole." *Crime & Delinquency*, 30:141-153.

Fruchtman, D. and R. Sigler (1999). "Private Pre-sentence Investigation: Procedures and Issues." *Journal of Offender Rehabilitation*, 29(3/4):157-170.

*Gagnon v. Scarpelli*, 411 U.S. 778, 93 S. Ct. (1972).

Galaway, B. (1983). "Probation as a Reparative Sentence." *Federal Probation*, 46(3):9-18.

General Accounting Office (1982). *Federal Parole Practices*. Washington, DC: GAO.

Gitchoff, T. (1980). *Expert Testimony of Sentencing. American Jurisprudence Proof of Facts*, 21:1-9. Rochester, NH: Lawyers Cooperative Publishers, 1980.

Gitchoff, T. and G. Rush (1989). "The Criminological Case Evaluation of Sentencing Recommendation: An Idea Whose Time Has Come." *International Journal of Offender Therapy and Comparative Criminology*, 33(1):77-83.

Glaze, L.E. and T. Bonsczar, (2006). *Probation and Parole in the United States, 2005*. Washington, DC: U.S. Bureau of Justice Statistics.

Glaser, D. (1985). "Who Gets Probation and Parole: Case Study Versus Actuarial Decision-Making." *Crime & Delinquency*, 31:367-378.

Gowdy, V. (1993). *Intermediate Sanctions*. Washington, DC: U.S. Department of Justice.

Granelli, J. (1983, May). "Presentence Reports Go Private." *National Law Journal*, 15:1-23.

Greenwood, P. and S. Turner (1993). "Private Presentence Reports for Serious Juvenile Offenders: Implementation Issues and Impacts." *Justice Quarterly*, 10:229-243.

Hagan, J. (1975). "The Social and Legal Construction of Criminal Justice: A Study of the Presentence Report." *Social Problems*, 22:620-637.

Harlow, N. and K. Nelson (1982). *Management Strategies for Probation in an Era of Limits*. Washington, DC: National Institute of Corrections.

Higgins, J. (1964). "Confidentiality of Presentence Reports." *Albany Law Review*, 28:31-47.

Hoelter, H. (1984). "Private Presentence Reports: Boon or Boondoggle?" *Federal Probation*, 48(3):66-69.

Jaffe, H. (1989). "The Presentence Report, Probation Officer Accountability, and Recruitment Practices: Some Influences of Guideline Sentencing." *Federal Probation*, 53(3):12-14.

Johnson, F. (1928). *Probation for Juveniles and Adults*. New York, NY: Century Co.

Johnson, H. and N. Wolfe (2003). *History of Criminal Justice*, Third Edition. Cincinnati, OH: Anderson Publishing Co.

Kane, R. (1995). "A Sentencing Model for Modernizing Sentencing Practices in Massachusetts' 68 District Courts." *Federal Probation*, 59(3):10-15.

Koontz, J.B. (1980). "Pragmatic Conditions of Probation." *Corrections Today*, 42:14-44.

Kulis, C. (1983). "Profit in the Private Presentence Report." *Federal Probation*, 47(4):11-16.

Lansing, S. (1999). *Parental Responsibility and Juvenile Delinquency*. Albany, NY: New York State Division of Criminal Justice Services.

Latessa, E. (1993). *An Analysis of Pre-Sentencing Investigation Recommendations and Judicial Outcome in Cuyahoga County Adult Probation Department*. Cincinnati, OH: Department of Criminal Justice, University of Cincinnati.

Latessa, E., F. Travis, and A. Holsinger (1997). *Evaluation of Ohio's Community Correctional Act Programs by County Size*. Cincinnati, OH: Division of Criminal Justice, University of Cincinnati.

Liebermann, E., S. Schaffer, and J. Martin (1971). *The Bronx Sentencing Project: An Experiment in the Use of Short-Form Presentence Report for Adult Misdemeanants*. New York, NY: Vera Institute of Justice.

Lindner, C. and M. Savarese (1984). "The Evolution of Probation: Early Salaries, Qualifications and Hiring Practices." *Federal Probation*, 48(1):3-9.

Macallair, D. (1994). "Disposition Case Advocacy in San Francisco's Juvenile Justice System: A New Approach to Deinstitutionalization." *Crime & Delinquency*, 40:84-95.

Macallair, D. (1996). "Violence in America: How We Can Save Our Children." *Stanford Law and Policy Review*, 7(1):31-41.

Marshall, F. and G. Vito (1982). "Not Without the Tools: The Task of Probation in the Eighties." *Federal Probation*, 46(4):37-40.

McDonald, D. and K. Carlson (1993). *Sentencing in the Federal Courts: Does Race Matter?* Washington, DC: U.S. Bureau of Justice Statistics.

Meeker, B. (1975). "The Federal Probation System: The Second 25 Years." *Federal Probation*, 39(2):16-25.

*Mempa v. Rhay*, 389 U.S. 128 (1967).

National Advisory Commission on Criminal Justice Standards and Goals (1973). *Corrections*. Washington, DC: U.S. Government Printing Office.

Parisi, N. (1981). "A Taste of the Bars." *Journal of Criminal Law and Criminology*, 72:1109-1123.

Parisi, N. (1980). "Combining Incarceration and Probation." *Federal Probation*, 46(2):3-10.

Parker, L. (1997). "A Contemporary View of Alternatives to Incarceration in Denmark." *Federal Probation*, 61(2):67-73.

The Presentence Report: An Empirical Study of Its Use in the Federal Criminal Process (1970). *Georgetown Law Journal*, 58:12-27.

The Presentence Investigation Report (1978). Federal Rules of Criminal Procedure, Rule 32 (Appendix A). Washington, DC: Administrative Office of the United States Courts, Publication No. 105.

Reed, T. (1997). *Apples to Apples: Comparing the Operational Costs of Juvenile and Adult Correctional Programs in Texas*. Austin, TX: Texas Criminal Justice Policy Council.

Reid, S. (1976). *Crime and Criminology*. Hinsdale, IL: Dryden Press.

Ring, C.(1988). *Probation Supervision Fees: Shifting Costs to the Offender*. Boston, MA: Massachusetts Legislative Research Bureau.

Rogers, J. (1990). "The Predispositional Report: Maintaining the Promise of Individualized Justice." *Federal Probation*, 54(1):43-57.

Rodgers, T., T. Gitchoff, and I. Paur (1979). "The Privately Commissioned Pre-Sentence Report: A Multidisciplinary Approach." *Criminal Justice Journal*, 2:271-279.

Rosecrance, J. (1985). "The Probation Officers' Search for Credibility: Ball Park Recommendations." *Crime & Delinquency*, 31:539-554.

Rosecrance, J. (1988). "Maintaining the Myth of Individualized Justice: Probation Presentence Reports." *Justice Quarterly*, 5:235-256.

Roy, S. (1994). "Victim Offender Reconciliation Program for Juveniles in Elkhard County, Indiana: An Exploratory Study." *Justice Professional*, 8(2):23-35.

Shockley, C. (1988). "The Federal Presentence Investigation Report: Sentence Disclosure Under the Freedom of Information Act." *Administrative Law Review*, 40(1):79-119.

Sieh, E. (1993). "From Augustus to the Progressives: A Study of Probation's Formative Years." *Federal Probation*, 57(3):67-72.

Smith, B., R. Davis, and S. Hillenbrand (1989). *Improving Enforcement of Court-Ordered Restitution*. Chicago, IL: American Bar Association.

Sourcebook of Criminal Justice Statistics, 2001. *Adults on Probation, in Jail or Prison, and on Parole*. Albany, NY: State University of New York.

Steffensmeier, D. and S. Demuth (2000). "Ethnicity and Sentencing Outcomes in U.S. Federal Courts," *American Sociological Review*, 65(5):705-729.

Umbreit, M. (1994). *Victim Meets Offender: The Impact of Restorative Justice and Mediation*. Monsey, NY: Criminal Justice Press.

United Nations (1976). "The Legal Origins of Probation." In R.N. Carter and L.T. Wilkins (eds.) *Probation, Parole and Community Services*, pp. 81-88. New York, NY: John Wiley and Sons.

*United States v. Birbaum*, 421 F2d. 997, cert. denied, 397 U.S. 1044 (1970).

van Dijk-Kaam, J. and J. Wemmers (eds.) (1999). *Caring for Crime Victims*. Monsey, NY: Criminal Justice Press.

Vito, G.F. (1978). "Shock Probation in Ohio: A Comparison of Attributes and Outcomes." Unpublished doctoral dissertation, Ohio State University.

Vito, G. (1984). "Development in Shock Probation: A Review of Research Findings and Policy Implications." *Federal Probation*, 48(2):22-27.

Vito, G. and H. Allen (1981). "Shock Probation in Ohio: A Comparison of Outcomes." *International Journal of Offender Therapy and Comparative Criminology*, 25:70-75.

Walsh, A. (1985). "The Role of the Probation Officer in the Sentencing Process." *Criminal Justice and Behavior*, 12:289-303.

Watkins, J.C. (1989). "Probation and Parole Malpractice in a Noninstitutional Setting: A Contemporary Analysis." *Federal Probation*, 53(3):29-34.

Welch, S. and C. Spohn (1986). "Evaluating the Impact of Prior Record on Judges' Sentencing Decisions: A Seven-City Comparison." *Justice Quarterly*, 3:389-407.

Wheeler, G., T. Macan, R. Hissong, and M. Slusher (1989). "The Effects of Probation Service Fees on Case Management Strategy and Sanctions." *Journal of Criminal Justice*, 17:15-24.

Wheeler, G., A. Rudolph, and R. Hissong (1989). "Do Probationers' Characteristics Affect Fee Assessment, Payment and Outcome?" *Perspectives*, 3(3):12-17.

Williams, D. J. and T. Turnage (2001). "Success of a Day Reporting Center Program." *Corrections Compendium*, 26(3):1-2,26.

Zastrow, W.G. (1971). "Disclosure of the Presentence Investigation Report." *Federal Probation*, 35(4):20-23.

# Juveniles and Community Corrections

**4**

> When we are out of sympathy with the young, then I think our work in the world is over.
>
> —George MacDonald

## The Juvenile Crime Problem

The challenge of crime in the United States remains a major social problem that has serious and sometimes deadly consequences but, in the last half-decade, the size of the problem has abated as the nature of crime has changed. For example, the Federal Bureau of Investigation reports that the volume of crime, while unacceptably high, actually decreased over 16 percent from 1995 to 2005, and the crime rate decreased over 19 percent (FBI, 2006). See Figure 4.1. Unfortunately, the murder rates for juveniles under age 18 rose nearly 20 percent between 2004 and 2005. Once arrested, many youth are processed through the juvenile justice system as demonstrated by Figure 4.2 below. This diagram shows a simplified view of caseflow through the juvenile justice system.

The juvenile crime rate is considered a problematic aspect of the crime problem. Youth under age 18 now commit almost one in six of the most serious crimes in the nation and account nearly one-half of the arrests for arson and about one-quarter of the arrests for robbery, burglary, larceny-theft, and motor-vehicle theft (See Figure 4.2). When arrests for juveniles are compared to those for adults over the last twenty years, the percent of crimes committed by juveniles have been declining. (See Table 4.1). Table 4.2 indicates that juvenile arrests for violent crimes decreased over 25 percent (compared to 9% for adults), and over 43 percent for property crimes, compared to 9.5 percent for adults. Major drops can be seen in arrests for every major index crime including murder, forcible rape, robbery, aggravated assault and arson. Almost two out of every 10 juvenile murder arrests involve a victim under age 18 and, of those, 88 percent were under age 14. Unfortunately, homicide victimization is concentrated among minority groups: the victimization rate for black youth is more than four times the rate for white youth (Snyder, 2005:1).

Figure 4.1
**Crime Index in United States, 1995-2005**

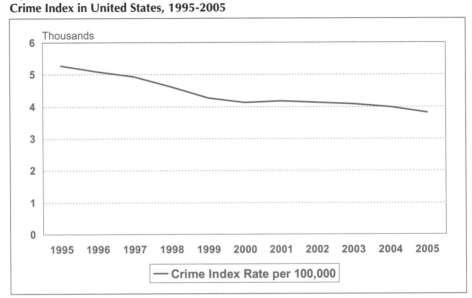

Source: Federal Bureau of Investigation (2006). *Uniform Crime Reports.*

Figure 4.2
**Of Total Arrest in 2005, Percent of Arrests for Juveniles.**

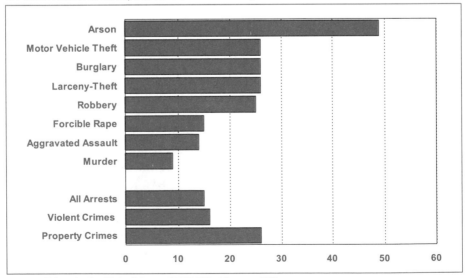

Source: Crime in the United States 2005 (Washington, DC).

Table 4.1
**Percentage of Juvenile (under 18) Arrests Among All Arrests, 1996, 2000, and 2005.**

| OFFENSE: | 1996 | 2000 | 2005 |
|---|---|---|---|
| Total | 31 | 17 | 15 |
| Murder | 15 | 9 | 9 |
| Forcible Rape | 17 | 16 | 15 |
| Robbery | 32 | 25 | 25 |
| Aggravated Assault | 15 | 14 | 14 |
| Burglary | 37 | 33 | 26 |
| Larceny-Theft | 34 | 31 | 26 |
| Motor Vehicle Theft | 42 | 34 | 26 |
| Arson | 53 | 53 | 49 |
| Violent Crimes | 19 | 16 | 16 |
| Property Crimes | 35 | 32 | 26 |

Source: Federal Bureau of Investigation (2006). *Uniform Crime Reports.*

Table 4.2
**Ten Year Arrest Trends 1996-2005 (in percent)**

| OFFENSE: | Juvenile | Adult |
|---|---|---|
| Total | -24.9 | +0.7 |
| Murder | -46.8 | -11.3 |
| Forcible Rape | -25.3 | -18.1 |
| Robbery | -33.7 | -8.3 |
| Aggravated Assault | -19.9 | -9.0 |
| Burglary | -44.4 | -1.5 |
| Larceny-Theft | -42.7 | -13.1 |
| Motor Vehicle Theft | -54.0 | +8.8 |
| Arson | -24.5 | -5.7 |
| Violent Crimes | -25.2 | -9.3 |
| Property Crimes | -43.8 | -9.5 |

Source: Federal Bureau of Investigation (2006). *Uniform Crime Reports.*

Much of the juvenile crime in the 1980s and early 1990s was due to the emergence of crack cocaine, juvenile gangs, and violence as major aspects of gang culture (Allen & Simonsen, 2001:475-476). These crime issues and changes caused the society as a whole to rethink rehabilitation, to advocate "get-tough" approaches, to waiver in their acceptance of juvenile courts, and to bind juveniles over for trial in adult courts. There are more almost 4,000 inmates in American prisons who are under age 18, down from 7,100 in 1986 (Sourcebook of Criminal Justice Statistics 2003). Fortunately, most juvenile offenders who come to the attention of the juvenile court will receive treatment and non-incarcerative dispositions.

As was the case with adult offenders, the development of community corrections has led to probation, currently the most frequently used disposition for juvenile offenders. In the United States, 62 percent of the cases that reach the juvenile court dispositional stage result in probation (Livsey, 2006:1).

Probation for juvenile offenders is defined as a legal status created by a court of juvenile jurisdiction. It usually involves (President's Commission, 1967:130):

1. A judicial finding that the behavior of the child has been such to bring him within the purview of the court;

2. The imposition of conditions upon his continued freedom; and

3. The provision of means for helping him meet those conditions and for determining the degree to which he meets them.

Probation thus implies more than indiscriminately giving the child "another chance." Its central thrust is to give him or her positive assistance in adjustment in the free community.

---

Box 4.1

### Juvenile Probation

Juvenile probation is the oldest and most widely used vehicle through which a range of court-ordered services is rendered. Probation may be used at the "front end" of the juvenile justice system for first-time, low-risk offenders or at the "back end" as an alternative to institutional confinement for more serious offenders. In some cases, probation may be voluntary, in which the youth agrees to comply with a period of informal probation in lieu of formal adjudication. More often, once adjudicated and formally ordered to a term of probation, the juvenile must submit to the probation conditions established by the court.

Source: Office of Juvenile Justice and Delinquency Prevention (1996). *Juvenile Probation: The Workhorse of the Juvenile Justice System*. Washington, DC: U.S. Department of Justice, p. 1 (http://www.ncjrs.org/txtfiles/workhors.txt).

## Historical Background

The historical precursors of juvenile probation are as generally outlined earlier. The legal underpinnings of modern juvenile probation were established in England during the early Middle Ages, under the principle of parens patriae: "The King, being father of His country, must protect the welfare of the children."

As with adult probation, John Augustus is viewed as the "father of juvenile probation," because many of his charges were female juveniles in trouble with the law. His work contributed to the development of the first visiting probation agent systems in Massachusetts (1869) and passage of the first enabling legislation establishing probation for juveniles (1878). In the same era, the Society for the Prevention of Cruelty to Children (1875) was established. Their proposed policies and activism directly contributed to the first juvenile court in America specifically set up to address the care, treatment, and welfare of juvenile offenders: the Cook County (Chicago), Illinois juvenile court in 1899. See Table 3.1 in Chapter 3.

The Cook County juvenile court emerged from the concerns of a group of compassionate, humanitarian, and wealthy women in Chicago who wished each child to receive the care, custody, and treatment as their natural parents ought to have provided (Lindner & Savarese, 1984a). The juvenile court was one project devised to attain these objectives,[1] and utilized individualized treatment based on extensive diagnosis of the child's personality and needs, with the judge serving as a counselor to the patient (juvenile). It was widely argued that the juvenile court would safeguard presumed superconstitutional rights[2] (the child would receive more than his or her just deserts) and avoid the stigma of criminal conviction through informal court proceedings based on benevolent attention, understanding the juvenile, humanitarian intervention, solicitous care, and regenerative and restorative[3] treatment. To attain these objectives, procedural safeguards guaranteed under the U.S. Constitution were abandoned; the focus was on the child, not the deed. Box 4.2 contains three selected Amendments to the U.S. Constitution that pertain to rights guaranteed to adults.

Juvenile court proceedings were informal, conducted in the absence of legal counsel, closed to the public, and individualized to maximize guidance and outcome. To protect and serve the "best interests of the child," records were confidential. Legal challenges were rare.

Juvenile courts were quickly established throughout the various states, federal government, and Puerto Rico. By 1927, all but two states had enacted enabling legislation establishing both juvenile court and probation. The theoretical assumption of juvenile probation was that providing guidance, counseling, resources, and supervision would assist low-risk juveniles to adapt to constructive living, thus avoiding the necessity of institutionalization.

---

Box 4.2

## Selected Amendments to the U.S. Constitution

**Fourth Amendment:** The right of the people to be secure in their persons, houses, papers, and effects, against unreasonable searches and seizures, shall not be violated, and no warrants shall issue, but upon probable cause, supported by oath or affirmation, and particularly describing the place to be searched, and the person or things to be seized.

**Fifth Amendment:** No person shall be held to answer for a capital, or otherwise infamous crime, unless a presentment or indictment of a Grand Jury, except in cases arising in land or naval forces, or the Militia, when in actual service in time of War or public danger; nor shall any person be subject for the same offense twice put in jeopardy of life or limb; nor shall be compelled in any criminal case to be a witness against himself, nor to be deprived of life, liberty or property, without due process of law; nor shall private property be taken for public use, without just compensation.

**Sixth Amendment:** In all criminal prosecutions, the accused shall enjoy the right to a speedy and public trial, by an impartial jury of the state or district wherein the crime shall have been committed, which district shall have been previously ascertained by law, and to be informed of the nature and the cause of the accusation; to be confronted with the witnesses against him, to have compulsory process for obtaining witnesses in his favor, and to have the Assistance of Counsel for his defense.

---

The primary goals of probation became to assist juveniles in dealing with their individual problems and social environments. Resolving underlying causes of the youthful offenders would permit their reintegration into the community. It was argued that probation, rather than incarceration, should be the disposition of choice, because:

1. Probation provides for community safety while permitting the youthful offender to remain in the community for reintegration purposes;

2. Institutionalization leads to prisonization, the process of learning the norms and culture of institutional living (Clemmer, 1940). This decreases the ability of the juvenile to function as a law-abiding citizen when released, and thus leads to further involvement as an adult offender;[4]

3.  The stigma of incarceration is avoided (Schur, 1971);

4.  The negative labeling effects of being treated as a criminal are avoided;

5.  Reintegration is more likely if existing community resources are used and the youth continues to engage in social and familial support systems (family, school, peers, extracurricular activities, employment, friends, etc.); and

6.  Probation is less expensive than incarceration, arguably more humanitarian, and is at least as effective in reducing further delinquent behavior as is institutionalization.[5]

The "child saving movement" underlying the development of the juvenile court is clearly seen here.[6]

## The Legal Rights of Juveniles

It is obvious that the juvenile court, as it developed over the twentieth century, addressed juvenile offenders under civil rather than criminal procedures (civil suits deal with individual wrongs, while criminal prosecutions involve public wrongs). The most important objective of the original creators of the juvenile court was to create a separate court system for delinquent, dependent, and neglected children. Following the doctrine of parens patriae, the juvenile court system suspended or ignored the legal rights constitutionally guaranteed to all citizens: the right to trial and against self-incrimination, and other rights. Constitutional rights were thought unnecessary for juveniles, as the court would focus on and uphold the best interests of a child in a civil setting. Many juvenile judges and child advocates perceived inequity and attempted to provide constitutional safeguards. Beginning in the 1960s, questions about juvenile court proceeding fairness and the constitutionally guaranteed rights of juveniles were brought to the U.S. Supreme Court. Significant changes were made. It is necessary to review those decisions to comprehend their impact on the juvenile justice system and especially contemporary juvenile probation.

### Kent v. United States

In 1966, the U.S. Supreme Court was asked to consider the issue of the transfer ("waiver") of a juvenile to the criminal court system.[7] The issue was the legislative waiver of the juvenile court procedures (Grisso & Schwartz, 2000). The Court stated:

> There is much evidence that some juvenile courts . . . lack the personnel, facilities, and the techniques to perform adequately as representatives of the State in a parens patriae capacity, at least with respect to children charged with law violation. There is evidence, in fact, that here may be grounds for concern that the child receives the worst of both worlds: that he gets neither the protections accorded to adults nor the solicitous care and regenerative treatment postulated for children (*Kent v. United States*, 1966).

This case portended more important issues on which the Court was asked to rule (Merlo, Benekos & Cook, 1997).

## In re Gault

In 1967, the Court decided its first major issue in the area of juvenile court procedures. In Arizona, Gerald Gault, then age 16, allegedly telephoned a neighbor woman and used obscene phrases and words. The use of such language over the telephone violated an Arizona statute. Gerald Gault was subsequently adjudicated a juvenile delinquent after a proceeding in which he was denied basic procedural safeguards otherwise guaranteed to any adult. This landmark decision[8] categorically granted the following to all juveniles charged with delinquent acts that might result in such grievous harm as commitment to a correctional institution:

1. Right to know the nature of the charges against them, to prepare for trial;

2. Right to counsel;

3. Right against self-incrimination; and

4. Right to confront and cross-examine accusers and witnesses.

The *Gault* decision not only returned procedural rights to juveniles, it also ended the presumption that juvenile courts were beyond the purview and scope of due process protections (Sanborn, 1994).[9]

## In re Winship

This 1970 decision further defined the rights of juveniles. Proof used in a court finding of delinquency must show "beyond a reasonable doubt" that the juvenile committed the alleged delinquent act (Sanborn, 1994), the same proof standard used for adults in criminal trials. The

Court specifically found unpersuasive the argument that juvenile proceedings were noncriminal and intended to benefit the child (*In re Winship*, 1970).[10] Currently, juveniles in juvenile court do not have the constitutional right to trial by jury (*McKeiver v. Pennsylvania*, 1971), although some states have extended this right to juveniles.

These three major decisions by the U.S. Supreme Court created the due process model for the juvenile court. The *McKeiver* decision seemed to indicate that the Court was moving away from increased rights for juveniles but, in 1975, the Court ruled (*Breed v. Jones*) that, once tried as a juvenile, that person cannot be tried as an adult on the same charges.[11] In 1979, (*Fare v. Michael C.*), the Court ruled on interrogation, and indicated that a child cannot voluntarily waive his privilege against self-incrimination without first speaking to his parents and without first consulting an attorney.[12] In 1984, the Court distinctly departed from the trend toward increased juvenile rights by reaffirming parens patriae (*Schall v. Martin*, 1984). As Allen and Simonsen (1998:643) note:

As a result of Supreme Court cases, the juvenile court is now basically a court of law. . . .

Thus far, the procedural rights guaranteed to a juvenile in court proceedings are as follows:

1. The right to adequate notice of charges against him or her;

2. The right to counsel and to have counsel provided if the child is indigent;

3. The right of confrontation and cross-examination of witnesses;

4. The right to refuse to do anything that would be self-incriminatory;

5. The right to a judicial hearing, with counsel, prior to transfer of a juvenile to an adult court; and

6. The right to be considered innocent until proven guilty beyond a reasonable doubt.

Juvenile probation, as seen in court proceedings and used in juvenile courts, is currently vacillating between these two models, and major changes are forthcoming (Rogers & Mays, 1987). On one hand, we see liberal reformers who call for increased procedural and legal safeguards for juveniles; on the other hand, we have a conservative movement that focuses on the victim (Torbert, Gable & Hurst, 1996) and seriousness of the crime (Clear & Cole, 1990).[13] As one conservative put it, "You are just as dead if a 15-year-old shoots you as you are if a 25-year-old does."[14]

## Criticisms of the Juvenile Court and Parens Patriae

Criticisms of and disenchantment with the parens patriae juvenile court and its procedures (Moore & Wakeling, 1997) have been voiced by such groups as the American Bar Association, the judiciary, the federal government, practitioners, private nonprofit organizations, researchers, and voluntary organizations, among others. Such efforts, when coupled with decisions by the U.S. Supreme Court, have created major changes in the juvenile justice system and particularly diversion of offenders, status offenders, decriminalization and deinstitutionalization. We will see these changes as we review the contemporary juvenile justice system and juveniles in community corrections.

## The Contemporary Juvenile Justice Scene

### Juvenile Court Processing

Although there are some similarities between the adult and juvenile systems, there are also some fundamental differences. Figure 4.3 shows a simplified version of caseflow through the Juvenile Justice System. Figure 4.4 shows the ages of juveniles upon referral to juvenile court. As has been the pattern for many decades, the highest rate was for 16 year olds, followed closely by 15 and then 17 year olds. Very few were under age 13.[15] Figure 4.5 shows the referral offense for males and female offenders in 2003. Between 1980 and 2003, the juvenile arrest rate for simple assaults increased 102 percent for males and 269 percent for females. In addition, between 1994 and 2003 juvenile arrests for drug

Figure 4.3
**The Juvenile Justice System Flow Chart**

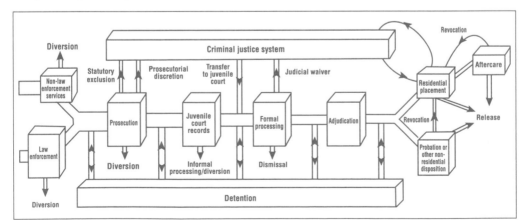

Source: Office of Juvenile Justice and Delinquency Prevention (2001). Caseflow Diagram (http://ojjdp.ncjrs.org/facts/casejpg.html).

abuse violations increased 56 percent for females but only 13 percent for males. About one in four arrests were for female juveniles, continuing a decades long trend. Female involvement in the juvenile justice system continues on a steady course upward.

Figure 4.4
**Age at Referral to Juvenile Court in 2003**

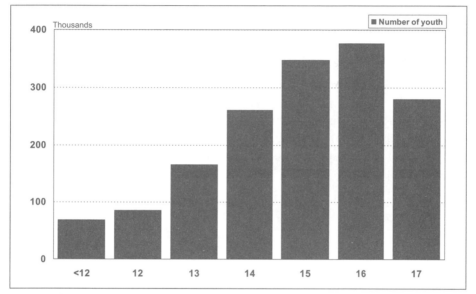

Source: Stahl, A., T. Finnegan, and W. Kang (2006). "Easy Access of Juvenile Court Statistics: 1985-2003." Online. Available: http://ojjdp.ncjrs.gov/ojstatbb/ezajcs/

Figure 4.5
**Referral Offense for Males and Females**

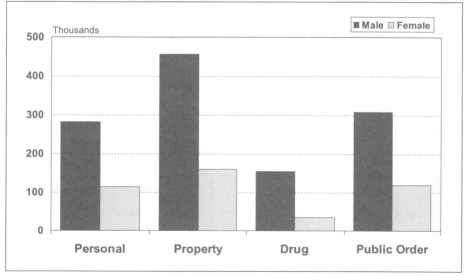

Source: Stahl, A., T. Finnegan, and W. Kang (2006). "Easy Access of Juvenile Court Statistics: 1985-2003." Online. Available: http://ojjdp.ncjrs.gov/ojstatbb/ezajcs/

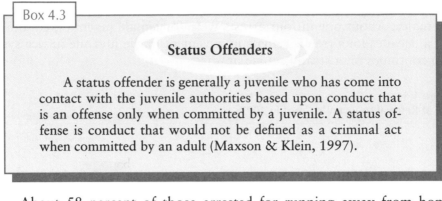

Box 4.3

**Status Offenders**

A status offender is generally a juvenile who has come into contact with the juvenile authorities based upon conduct that is an offense only when committed by a juvenile. A status offense is conduct that would not be defined as a criminal act when committed by an adult (Maxson & Klein, 1997).

About 58 percent of those arrested for running away from home were female,[16] and some four in 10 runaways were under the age of 15. These figures have been declining markedly over the past 10 years for both males and females. See Figure 4.6. Curfew violations and running away from home are viewed as status offenses that can only be committed by juveniles.

Figure 4.6
**Arrests for Runaway: 1996 and 2005**

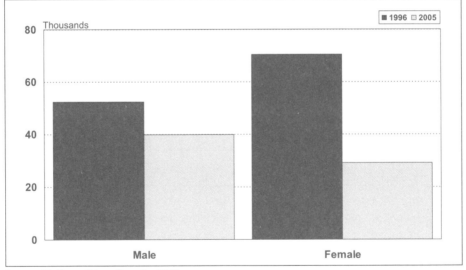
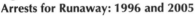

Source: Uniform Crime Reports, 2005.

Juvenile court processing of delinquency cases can be handles in several ways. At intake, referred cases are often screened by an intake officer who might decide to dismiss the case for lack of legal sufficiency or to resolve the matter formally or informally. Informal dispositions could include a voluntary referral to a social agency for services, informal probation, or payment of fines or restitution. Formally handled cases are petitioned to juvenile court and scheduled to an adjudication (or waiver) hearing. Of those youth referred to juvenile court in 2005, about 58 percent were counseled and then released. The remaining 42 percent were referred to juvenile court jurisdiction, and of those about one in 138 were waived to criminal or adult court.

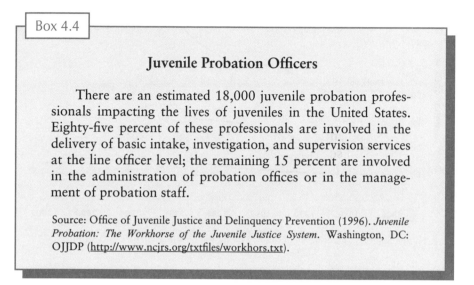

Box 4.4

### Juvenile Probation Officers

There are an estimated 18,000 juvenile probation professionals impacting the lives of juveniles in the United States. Eighty-five percent of these professionals are involved in the delivery of basic intake, investigation, and supervision services at the line officer level; the remaining 15 percent are involved in the administration of probation offices or in the management of probation staff.

Source: Office of Juvenile Justice and Delinquency Prevention (1996). *Juvenile Probation: The Workhorse of the Juvenile Justice System*. Washington, DC: OJJDP (http://www.ncjrs.org/txtfiles/workhors.txt).

At the disposition hearing, the juvenile court judge determines the more appropriate sanction or set of sanctions, generally after reviewing a predisposition ("presentence") report prepared by a probation department. Here the range of options available to the judge is wide and typically includes commitment to an institution, placement in a foster or group home or other residential facility, probation, referral to an outside agency, day treatment or attendance center, mental health program, community correctional center (halfway house), or imposition of a fine, restitution or community service. As can be seen from Figure 4.7, probation is the most often imposed sentence. Probation services (for regular or intensive probation) must cope with heavy caseloads every year.

For some youth, out of home placement can occur. Residential placement could be in a public or private facility and Figure 4.8 provides details on juveniles in facilities intended to hold juvenile offenders. In 2003, there were over 102,000 young persons assigned beds in 1,182 public and 1,773 private residential facilities. Group homes made up 38 percent of all facilities and held 12 percent of juvenile offenders (Sickmund, 2006:5). Sometimes out-of-home placement can be a very traumatic experience for a juvenile, and suicide was the most common cause of death for youth held in custody in 2002. See Figure 4.9. Most of the young offenders resided in public facilities owned and operated exclusively by State or local governmental agencies. Private facilities are those owned and operated by various nongovernmental organizations that provide services to juvenile offenders.

Figure 4.7
**Placement of Juveniles, 1986-2002**

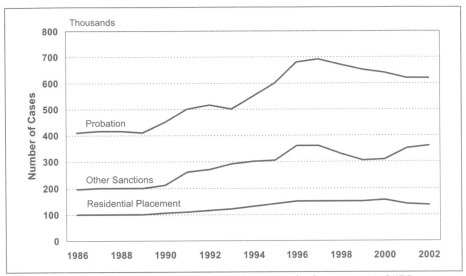

Source: Livsey, S. (2006). Juvenile Delinquency Probation Caseloads, 1985-2002. OJJDP.

Figure 4.8
**Residential Placement for Juvenile Offenders in 2003**

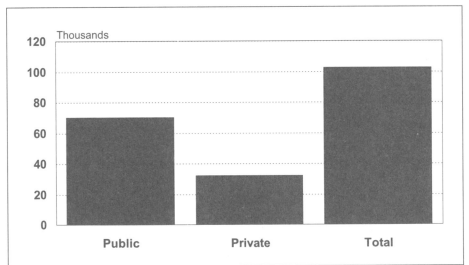

Source: Sickmund, M. (2006). *Juvenile Residential Facility Census, 2002: Selected Findings.* Washington, DC: OJJDP.

Figure 4.9
**Cause of Death for Juveniles in Custody in 2002**

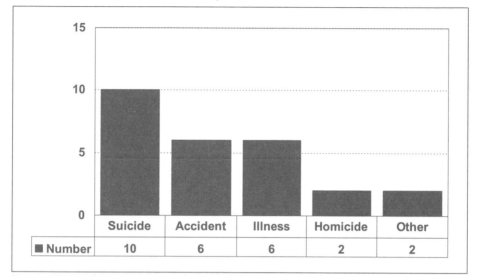

| | Suicide | Accident | Illness | Homicide | Other |
|---|---|---|---|---|---|
| ■ Number | 10 | 6 | 6 | 2 | 2 |

Source: Sickmund, M. (2006). *Juvenile Residential Facility Census, 2002: Selected Findings*. Washington, DC: OJJDP.

## Juveniles Waived to Criminal Court

It will be remembered that all states set an upper age jurisdiction for juvenile courts, and it should be noted that all states have legal mechanisms that, under certain circumstances, permit youth to be tried in criminal court as if they were adults. These mechanisms were primarily developed over the past quarter century (Feld, 2001) and are major changes from previous philosophical bases of juvenile court proceedings.

Such changes were brought about in part by *Kent v. United States*, a case in which the U.S. Supreme Court began to require due process in juvenile waivers and lawmakers tried to construct simple and expedient alternatives to juvenile waiver hearings. Mechanisms included automatic exclusion based on specific age or offense criteria; authorization of prosecutors to direct-file juvenile cases in criminal court; or empowering judges to sentence directly to adult correctional institutions or blend dispositions by imposing both a juvenile institutional commitment to be followed by commitment to adult criminal facilities (Ullman, 2000). These changes were fueled in part by alarm over an increase in juvenile violence, an expanding caseload of juvenile drug offenders, and judicial assessments that many adjudicated delinquents were no longer amenable to treatment (Snyder, Sickmund & Poe, 2000). In addition, offense exclusion provided a politically attractive strategy for "get tough" public officials who proposed to "crack down" on increased youth crime. Figure 4.10 shows juveniles waived to criminal court from

1990 through 2003, the most recent available picture. The offenses for which waivers were sought included offenses against the person and property, drug law violations, and public order. Waivers have decreased since 1994, when they peaked.

Figure 4.10
**Number of Juveniles Waived to Adult Court 1990-2003**

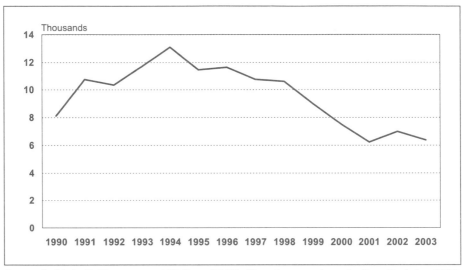

Source: Stahl, A., T. Finnegan, and W. Kang (2006). "Easy Access ot Juvenile Court Statistics: 1985-2003." Online. Available: http://ojjdp.ncjrs.gov/ojstatbb/ezajcs/

Advocates of juvenile waiver mechanisms asserted that juvenile court sanctions and service constitute neither just nor effective responses to predatory and savvy youthful offenders, and that criminal prosecution would ensure more proportionate punishment, more effective deterrence, and greater incapacitation. It was believed that, by focusing on the offense rather than the offender, public safety would be strengthened and recidivism would be reduced. It was also believed that habitually violent juveniles belonging to gangs, abusing substances, and wielding guns should be arrested, charged as adults, and sentenced to prisons. In sum, authority was shifted from the judiciary to the prosecutor, although some states increased the authority of both. The correctional objective was selective incapacitation. It is important to note that the number of both juvenile arrests and cases waived to criminal court have declined since 1994 (Puzzanchera, 2001), reflecting the similar trend of decreasing involvement of juveniles in lives of crime and violence. Of those juveniles waived in 2003 63 percent were white and 37 were black. Only 8 percent were females.

---

Box 4.5

### Selective Incapacitation

This doctrine of isolating the juvenile offender, or "social disablement," proposes a policy of incarcerating those whose criminal behavior is so damaging or probable that nothing short of isolation will prevent recidivism. This "nothing-else-works" approach would require correctly identifying those offenders who would be eligible for long-term incarceration, and diverting others into correctional alternatives. Thus we would be able to make maximum effective use of detention cells, a scarce resource, to protect society from the depredations of such dangerous and repetitive offenders.

Current correctional technology does not permit correctly identifying those who require incapacitation. Rather, the evidence is that we would probably incarcerate numerous non-dangerous juveniles (a "false-positive" problem). Yet there is evidence of effectiveness of some prediction scales to identify low-rate juvenile offenders for selective early release (Hayes & Geerken, 1997). This would be selective "decapacitation"! Whatever benefits might accrue to this sentencing doctrine have thus far eluded corrections.

Yet chronic repeat offenders (those with five or more arrests by age 18), who make up a very small proportion of all offenders, commit a very high proportion of all crimes. More research into correct classification of juvenile and adult offenders is needed.

---

Studies of the effectiveness of waiver programs are ongoing. Risler, Sweatman, and Nackerud (1998) examined the impact of Georgia's waiver legislation and found no significant reduction in the mean arrest rates (no deterrence), and suggested that such laws do not reduce serious violent crime. Redding (1999) argues that, while juveniles are more likely to receive a longer and more serious sentence in criminal court, they may actually serve less time than they would in a juvenile facility. He found that criminal court adjudication generally produces higher recidivism rates for most offenders, and that juveniles incarcerated in adult facilities receive fewer age-appropriate rehabilitative, medical, mental health, and educational services. Bishop (2000) reviewed the effects of juvenile waiver and concluded that expansive transfer policies send many minor and nonthreatening offenders to the adult system, exacerbate racial disparities (McNulty, 1996), and move youth with special and high needs into correctional systems ill-prepared to provide treatment. Bishop also argued that there is creditable evidence that prosecution and punishment in the adult system increase recidivism and expose young people to heightened vulnerability and to potentially damaging experiences and penal outcomes. It will be interesting to observe additional outcome studies on judicial waiver legislation and practices.

Ed Stein. Reprinted courtesy of the Rocky Mountain News.

## Community Corrections

It should be obvious that the juvenile court makes decisions about youthful offenders based on assessments of needs, risks, and rehabilitation. Whether working on an informal basis in the smallest juvenile court or using structured prediction and actuarial instruments that are combined with clinical experience, as in the most sophisticated and largest juvenile settings, the juvenile justice system is winnowing cases, attempting to match sanctions with needs and control. Allen and Simonsen (2001:95) refer to the process as "filtering" offenders into sanction options that address individual needs, community safety and reintegration.

In the juvenile court, disposition decisions are based on individual and social factors, offense severity, and youths' offense history. The dispositional philosophy include a significant rehabilitation emphasis as well as many dispositional options that cover a wider range of community-based and residential services. Dispositional orders can be and often are directed to people other than the offender (family members, in particular), and dispositions may be indeterminate, based on progress toward correctional goals and treatment objectives. In some cases, authority of the juvenile court can extend to majority age (as defined by individual states).

As fascinating as "detention" and "incarceration" might be and are certainly necessary for some offender control, our focus here is on prevention, alternatives to incarceration, probation, and a variety of programs designed to divert juveniles from residential settings and provide treatment and control in the community.

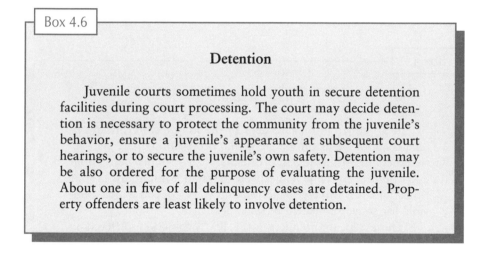

Box 4.6

**Detention**

Juvenile courts sometimes hold youth in secure detention facilities during court processing. The court may decide detention is necessary to protect the community from the juvenile's behavior, ensure a juvenile's appearance at subsequent court hearings, or to secure the juvenile's own safety. Detention may be also ordered for the purpose of evaluating the juvenile. About one in five of all delinquency cases are detained. Property offenders are least likely to involve detention.

## Juvenile Probation

Probation is the oldest and most widely used community-based corrections program. During probation, the juvenile usually remains in the community and can continue such normal activities as attending school or work. In exchange for this freedom, the juvenile must comply with a number of conditions. This compliance could be voluntary as in informal probation in lieu of formal adjudication, but it may also be mandatory. If the disposition results from a formal adjudication and probation, the juvenile must comply with conditions of probation as imposed by the court. Slightly more than one-half of the juvenile probation dispositions are informal (enacted without formal court adjudication or court order).

A juvenile might be required to meet regularly with a probation officer or supervisor, attend counseling, observe a strict curfew schedule, and/or complete a specified period of community service or even restitution. Such orders also imply the authority of the court to revoke probation should the juvenile violate conditions. If there is a revocation hearing, the court may reconsider its original disposition, impose additional conditions, or impose such severe alternatives as placement in a state youth authority.

At juvenile probation intake, juveniles are frequently assigned to caseloads based on their identified "risks" and "needs." High-risk youth who may be in danger of becoming chronic offenders may be assigned to special programs with strict supervision and individually designed treatment programs, including involvement of the youths' families in court-ordered activity (parenting classes, for example). Treatment might also include counselling on alcohol and drug abuse, mental health interventions, employment preparation and job placement, community service projects, and afternoon programs. See Box 4.7. Such programs seek to reduce the number of chronic recidivists through a coordinated program of aggressive early intervention and treatment.

---

**Box 4.7**

### The 8% Solution

In an effort to make a dent in the long-term crime problem, the Orange County (California) probation department researched first-time juvenile offenders and found that about eight percent of the juveniles were arrested a minimum of four times within a three-year period and were collectively responsible for some 55 percent of the repeat cases.

These repeat offenders ("the 8% problem") differed in dramatic ways from those arrested only once, and these differences were evident at the time of first arrest and referral to the juvenile court. [These differences could not have emerged from exposure to the juvenile justice system.] At the time they entered the system, they had become involved in crime at an early age and had a complex set of problems ("risk factors"):

- a multi-problem set of significant family problems (abuse, criminal family members, lack of parental control, neglect, lack of family supervision),

- problems at school, such as failing one course, recent suspension or explusion, or truancy),

- alcohol and drug abuse, and

- such behaviors as gang involvement, running away, and stealing.

It was decided to focus resources on the most problematic group where the need and the potential benefits were greatest.

Those first-time offenders under age 151/2 who exhibited at least three of the four risk factors were determined to be high-risk youth. The objective was to increase structure, supervision and support for families, hold the "8 percenters" accountable for their actions, ensure that youth and their families

Box 4.7, *continued*

understood the importance of school, and promote prosocial values, behavior, and relationships. Teams of probation agents and other youth-serving agencies offered full-service support for the high-risk group, secured funds from the California repeat offender program, and referred high-risk youth to Youth and Family Resource Centers. Services included:

- an on-site school for students in the junior and senior high school levels

- transportation to and from home

- counseling for alcohol and drug abuse

- mental health evaluations and service

- employment preparation and job placement services

- afternoon programs (recreation, life skills, community service projects, and so on)

- intermittent evening classes for the whole family (such as parenting classes)

- Saturday community service activities twice a month.

Preliminary conclusions:

- the number of chronic juvenile recidivists can be reduced through a coordinated program of early intervention and treatment of high-risk youth and families.

- significant risk factors are often overlooked at key points of the juvenile justice system because of a lack of critical information.

Such a concentration of resources and efforts has resulted in participants having committed fewer additional and less serious offenses and serving less time in custody than their counterparts receiving standard probation services. The program had a favorable impact on community safety and on the future of many youth who otherwise would become high-rate persistent offenders.

Sources: Office of Juvenile Justice and Delinquency Prevention (2001). *The 8% Solution* (www.ncjrs.org/pdffiles1/ojjdp/fs200139.pdf), and (www.oc.ca.gov/Probation/e8%25Solution/b8%ProblemStudyFindings.asp).

Investigation and diagnosis of other juveniles, usually at the intake or predisposition report level, may suggest treatment needs for mental health care, drug abusing behavior (of juveniles and their families), or other precipitating factors contributing to the acting out behavior of juveniles before the court. Some are diverted from further court processing and others placed in residential facilities, frequently in the private sector service providers. Probation officers are sometimes required to supervise these juveniles. We first examine diversion programs and then aftercare ("parole") of juveniles exiting residential settings.

---

Box 4.8

**Challenges to Probation**

The field of probation is staffed by dedicated individuals who believe that young persons who break the law can change their behavior in favor of law-abiding activities. Probation departments cannot, however, limit their intake of probationers like private providers or State training schools, which routinely operate over capacity and often have caps on admissions. In that sense, probation is the "catch basin" of the juvenile justice system and is being confronted with increasing and more dangerous caseloads.

Source: Office of Juvenile Justice and Delinquency Prevention (1996). *Juvenile Probation: The Workhorse of the Juvenile Justice System* (Washington, DC: OJJDP) (http://www.ncjrs.org/txtfiles/workhors.txt).

---

## Diversion of Juveniles

The *Gault, Kent,* and *Winship* cases defined those constitutionally guaranteed rights that must be accorded every juvenile, and formed the basis of the due process model noted above. This model requires adherence to minimally guaranteed legal procedures,[17] a voluntary and helping relationship, and the least restrictive environment necessary to treat the juvenile. It also requires a demonstrated need for detention[18] and, absent this, a mandatory noncommitment to an institution (del Carmen, 1984; 1998).

The question of whether incarcerated juveniles have a mandatory right to treatment has been addressed in several federal cases. The most significant of these was *Nelson v. Heyne* (1974), which upheld a categorical right to treatment for confined juveniles under the due process clause of the Fourteenth Amendment. The appellate court stated that the parens patriae principle of the juvenile court could be justified only if committed delinquent youth receive treatment:

> . . . the right to treatment includes the right to minimum acceptable standards of care and treatment for juveniles and the right to individualized care and treatment. Because children differ in their needs for rehabilitation, individual need for treatment will differ. When a state assumes the place of a juvenile's parents, it assumes as well the parental duties, and its treatments of its juveniles should, so far as can be reasonably required, be what proper parental care would provide. Without a program of individual treatment, the result may be that the juveniles will not be treated, but warehoused (*Nelson v. Heyne*).

Despite the implications of Nelson, a nationwide survey of state, local, and privately run juvenile detention facilities found serious problem areas ranging from inadequate living space and crowding, to high numbers of injuries to confined juveniles through "alarmingly widespread" suicidal behavior.[19]

There appears to be no consensus on which youth are best served by residential (versus community) care, although one recent study found that very high risk youth responded best to residential placement, while low and moderate risk youth were best served on probation (Lowenkamp & Latessa, 2005).

The due process model and the Nelson requirements have significantly contributed toward the diversion process of juveniles. Cost is another factor; the American Correctional Association (2001) reports the cost of one juvenile institution as $34,600 and $110,200 for Minnesota and Pennsylvania, respectively. Allen, Latessa, Ponder and Simonsen (2007:336-337) define diversion as:

> The official halting or suspension, at any legally prescribed processing point after a recorded justice system entry, of formal juvenile justice proceedings against an alleged offender, and referral of that person to a treatment or care program administered by a nonjustice agency or to a private agency. Sometimes no referral is given.

Diversion programs function to divert juveniles out of the juvenile justice system, encourage the use of existing correctional facilities and agencies for such offenders, and avoid formal contact with the juvenile court. These programs include remedial education programs,[20] foster homes, group homes, community drug treatment,[21] attendance centers,[22] and local counseling facilities and centers. The effectiveness of such programs is not yet definitively documented but preliminary evaluation reports indicate high efficacy.

---

Box 4.9

### Family Empowerment Intervention

Family empowerment intervention (FEI) expands the focus of change to include not only the juvenile offender but also the family. Team members help families address roles of parents and rule construction and enforcement, as well as unintended parental actions that encourage delinquency. Drug use, relapse prevention and drug avoidance are frequently stressed. An investigation of a family empowerment intervention program in Florida compared juveniles randomly assigned to monthly telephone contacts (with referrals as appropriate) with juvenile offenders and their families receiving three hour-long, home-based meetings per week for 10 weeks from a clinician-trained paraprofessional (FEI youths).

Those receiving FEI services reported fewer drug sales, getting very high or drunk on alcohol less often, and less marijuana use. FEI youth had a lower hair-test positive rates for marijuana use, and had better psychosocial outcomes than the comparison youth. These outcomes provide consistent evidence of the efficacy of family empowerment intervention.

Source: Dembo, R., W. Seeberger, M. Shemwell et al. (2000). "Psychological Functioning Among Juvenile Offenders 12 Months after Family Empowerment Intervention." *Journal of Offender Rehabilitation*, 32(1/2):1-56.

---

## Drug Courts and Diversion

The predisposition report may have also discovered that youth, either status offenders or those who have committed offenses, are experimenting, abusing or chemically dependent on controlled substances, pharmaceuticals prescribed for others but coming under the control of juveniles, or other illicit drugs. In an increasing number of jurisdictions, such youth are afforded access to individually tailored treatment programs under juvenile drug courts. There, a formidable array of specific services may be available and may address not only the juvenile but family, friends, and employers. Studies to date suggest that drug court participants have lower recidivism rates and were less likely than comparison groups to be arrested in any category of offense. Thus drug courts not only reduce recidivism but also enhance public safety (See: Latessa, Shaffer, and Lowenkamp, 2002; and Koetzel-Shaffer, 2006) .

> **Box 4.10**
>
> ### Juvenile Drug Courts
>
> Juvenile drug courts are intensive treatment programs established within and supervised by juvenile courts to provide specialized services for eligible drug-involved youth and their families. Cases are assigned to a juvenile drug court docket based on criteria set by local officials to carry out the goals of the drug court program.
>
> Juvenile drug courts provide (1) intensive and continuous supervision over delinquency and status offense cases that involve substance-abusing juveniles and (2) coordinated and supervised delivery of an array of support services necessary to address the problems that contribute to juvenile involvement in the justice system. Service areas include substance abuse treatment, mental health, primary care, family and education. Since 1995, more than 140 juvenile drug courts have been established in the United States, and more than 125 are currently being planned.
>
> Source: National Drug Court Institute. www.ndci.org/courtfacts.htm

## Deinstitutionalization

The concept of deinstitutionalization, also known as decarceration, is recent; 1969 is considered its inception. In that year, Jerome Miller began deinstitutionalization of incarcerated juvenile offenders in Massachusetts. Asserting that the era of confinement of children in larger correctional facilities was over and that an era of more humane, decent, and community-based care for delinquents had begun, Miller closed the major juvenile institutions. Confined charges were placed in small homes, using other, already existing community-based correctional programs and services (Sherrill, 1976a & 1975b).

Initial program evaluations found the community-based juvenile group did worse in terms of recidivism (74% vs. 66%) than earlier juveniles[23] processed through the correctional units (McCord & Sanchez, 1983). However, closer analysis of the data revealed that, when community-based programs were properly implemented, recidivism rates were equal or slightly lower than the institutional group.

Box 4.11

### Costs and Benefits of Early Childhood Intervention

A series of small-scale programs attempted to assess the costs and benefits of early childhood (prenatal through age 4) intervention, asking if early interventions targeted at disadvantaged children benefit participating children and their families, and might government funds invested early in the lives of children yield compensating decreases in later government expenditures?

Peter Greenwood examined five of the most rigorously designed programs for younger children; programs had a matched control group that was randomly assigned at program onset. In particular, he found:

- IQ differences between program participants and control group members approached or exceeded 10 points at the end of the program.

- The difference in rates of special education and grade retention at age 15 exceeded 20 percent (Abecedarian project).

- Participating children experienced 33 percent fewer emergency room visits through age four than children in the control group (Elmira, NY Prenatal/Early Infancy Project).

- Mothers were on welfare 33 percent less time in the same Elmira Project.

- Earnings at age 27 were 60 percent higher among program participants (Perry Preschool Program).

- Benefits outweighed costs and savings were $25,000 versus $12,000 for each family participating in the Perry program, and $24,000 versus $6,000 for each higher-risk family participating in the Elmira program.

In addition, other advantages to program participants (relative to those in the control group) were decreased criminal activity, improved educational outcomes, and improved health-related indicators such as decreased child abuse, improved maternal reproductive health, and reduced substance abuse.

Carefully targeted early childhood interventions can yield measurable benefits and some of those benefits endure for some time after the program has ended.

Source: Peter Greenwood (1999). *Costs and Benefits of Early Childhood Intervention, Office of Juvenile Justice and Delinquency Prevention* (www. ncjrs.org/pdffiles1/fs9994.pdf).

While no other state has fully followed Massachusetts' lead, several have developed smaller more community-based facilities including Missouri and Utah, which closed a 350-bed training school and placed the 290 youth in community-based programs modeled on Massachusetts' program. Again, researchers concluded there was no evidence that public safety had been compromised. There was strong evidence that Utah saved considerable money when compared to past correctional practices (Krisberg, Austin & Steele, 1987).

In 1995, Ohio began a program entitled RECLAIM Ohio (Reasoned and Equitable Community and Local Alternatives to Incarceration of Minors). This statewide initiative is designed to assist counties in providing community services to adjudicated juvenile offenders. Essentially, local juvenile courts are given an allocation of funds to use for community-based alternatives. In turn, they must pay for all youths who are incarcerated in a state institution from their allocation. Results indicated that they are successfully reducing the commitment rate of juveniles to state facilities. Figure 4.11 shows the number of admissions to state facilities before and after the implementation of RECLAIM. As shown, there has been a significant reduction in commitments to state institutions within the Department of Youth Services. RECLAIM has also strengthened local juvenile courts; private sector service providers increased their participation; and cooperation across prosecutor, court, and court services increased. Failure rates were not unusually high and the percentage of youth participating in RECLAIM who were eventually committed to state institutions has remained low. Project RECLAIM is a constructive example of coordination and use of community corrections to avoid sending youth to secure institutions (Lowenkamp & Latessa, 2005).

Figure 4.11
**DYS Felony Admissions FY 1991-2004**

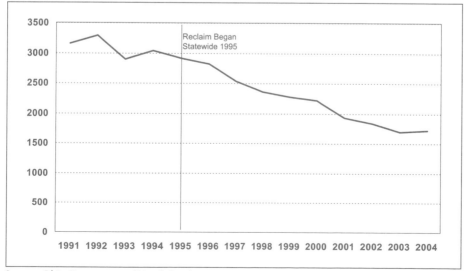

Source: Ohio Department of Youth Services.

Those favoring placement of juveniles in secure institutions cite the public's fear of violent youth crime as a rationale for incarcerating young offenders. They also argue that "getting those thugs" off the streets prevents further offending (selective incapacitation), provides the structure and control necessary for treatment and educational programs (rehabilitation), and prevents other juveniles from committing serious offenses (general deterrence). Deinstitutionalization advocates counter that many incarcerated juveniles were not committed for serious violent offenses, institutionalization is costly, the deterrence evidence is almost nonexistent, the evidence of effective rehabilitation in correctional facilities is weak, and community alternatives are just as effective. Finally, opponents of institutionalization argue that local community alternatives, when coupled with child advocates, can substantially reduce commitments to state juvenile correctional institutions.[24]

---

Box 4.12

### Juvenile Accountability

Holding a juvenile offender "accountable" in the juvenile justice system means that once the juvenile is determined to have committed law-violating behavior, by admission or adjudication, he or she is held responsible for the act through consequences or sanctions, imposed pursuant to law, that are proportional to the offense. Consequences or sanctions that are applied swiftly, surely, and consistently, and are graduated to provide appropriate and effective responses to varying levels of offense seriousness and offender chronicity work best in preventing, controlling, and reducing further law violations.

Source: Office of Juvenile Justice and Delinquency Prevention (2001). *Juvenile Drug Court Programs*. Washington, DC: OJJDP, p. 1 (www.ncjrs.org/pdffiles1/ojjdp/184744.pdf).

---

## Aftercare and Community Corrections

The majority of juveniles committed to state-managed residential facilities and training schools are serious, chronic offenders. They will eventually be released to the community through parole and onto aftercare. Previous research has shown that recidivism rates among juvenile parolees are unacceptably high, ranging from 55 percent to 75 percent (Krisberg, Austin & Steele, 1991). A large percentage of previously incarcerated juvenile offenders continue their criminal involvement into adulthood. A major portion of the problem is that an already overburdened juvenile corrections and aftercare system is increasingly likely to face the kind of youth whom the system had either ignored or failed: serious, chronic offenders. What is needed with this population are effective intervention, intensive supervision and services, a focus on reintegration while incarcerated, and a gradual transition process that utilizes community resources and social networks. This includes aftercare planning, parole officer contact during the institutional phase, and community-based providers working within the residential setting. The latter would include multifamily counseling and life skills services, supervised trips to the community, overnight or weekend home passes, substance abuse services, and money management skills. Virginia, Colorado, and Nevada are implementing such efforts (Office of Juvenile Justice and Delinquency Prevention, 2000).

## The Future of Juvenile Probation and Community Corrections

Several conclusions are suggested by this review of current trends and developments. It is obvious that juvenile justice and juvenile probation are in a period of rapid change, and that juvenile policy is vacillating between the old parens patriae and the newer due process model. Further, the roles and functions of the juvenile probation officer are undergoing change and enlargement. The various state juvenile systems and jurisdictions are moving toward diversion, waiver of juvenile offenders into the criminal justice arena, removal of the status offender from juvenile court jurisdiction, and deinstitutionalization of juveniles. In addition, faced with the legal constraints, requirements for treatment of incarcerated youth, and the high costs of juvenile institutions, probation officers are facing emerging and divergent demands. Finally, to divert and refer juveniles to social services, there must be increased community and private service programs and agencies to provide local community services to juveniles. States can encourage these developments with subsidies and legislation that enable local and county community corrections (Harris, 1996). In other chapters, we explore privatization of juvenile services, technologies applied to juvenile supervision (electronic monitoring, classification devices, specialized service providers, and so on), and newer supervision strategies, such as house arrest, day attendance centers, intensive supervised probation, and specialized caseloads. Reintegrative and restorative approaches are being implemented across the nation, including restitution, victim-offender mediation, compensation, and community work orders. The issues surrounding crowding, changing faces of probation clients, and training needs can be found in later chapters.

---

Box 4.13

### Accountability and Parole

Dean Haumschilt is a Parole Agent in the California Division of Juvenile Justice (DJJ)—formerly the California Youth Authority (CYA)—and concerned with responsibility to the public after a ward's parole. He oversees an institutional treatment group preparing juvenile charges for return to the community and for keeping the public safe. The Impact on Victims program requires wards to make changes in their belief system and behavior so they never hurt anyone else.

The program attempts to neutralize delinquent, victimizing or gang type of attitudes, values and behavior. More than the minimum number of hours in program are required. Wards must incorporate what they learn about their victims, their hurts, fears, nightmares, and wanting some assurance that the ward who victimized them will not victimize them again (or someone else).

Role-playing, modeling, behavior change, and cognitive therapy are part of the program. In the end, the group resource leader assesses the ward and asks:

> Has he or she demonstrated a 180-degree turn in behavior and values: dress, attitude, associations, speech, body language, commitment to change, and empathy? Change is measured by final written examination as well as oral interview and observation.

If the answer is "no," leaders recommend that wards retake the course and continue to get time additions until either they change their values and the way they think and behave, or they run out of DJJ jurisdiction. Wards must become responsible for their behavior.

Source: Dean Haumschilt, "The Responsibility to the Public in Parole." *CYA Today*, 2(2):4 (www.cya.ca.gov/news/cyatoday/vic0401.pdf).

---

Since juvenile probation services, as agents of court supervision for young offenders, depend on the philosophy of the juvenile court, court administrators, and referral agencies, a patchwork of temporizing procedures, responses, and programs is emerging. Some Federal funding of coordinated efforts suggest that it is possible to implement intensive community-based aftercare programs. Yet with a shortfall in resources facing almost every court agency, innovation and strategic planning are required. There is no quick fix for the quandary of juvenile probation and corrections, and we conclude this section by pointing out that new demands will continue to emerge.

# Summary

Our examination of the development of juvenile probation identified those historical events of the nineteenth and twentieth century that contributed first to the development of the juvenile court and then to a reexamination of the legal rights of juveniles. Beginning with the first juvenile court in Chicago (1899), the constitutionally guaranteed rights of juveniles were ignored in favor of a benevolent venue intended to provide each child such care, treatment, and welfare as ought to have been provided by natural parents.

By the 1960s, child advocates and concerned organizations began to ask if the juvenile court were running rough-shod over the rights of its charges while, at the same time, perhaps not delivering on promised benefits. A series of U.S. Supreme Court decisions eventually reasserted such constitutionally guaranteed protections as the right to trial, to remain silent, to present evidence on one's own behalf, to question and challenge the evidence presented against the charge, and most other rights available to adults.

Three major changes emerged. First, many jurisdictions undertook deinstitutionalization, moving their charges from state-controlled institutions into community corrections. Second, the emergence of juvenile drug gangs and increased violence led to demands for more punishment, such as waiver to adult court to stand trial as adults and assumedly be punished more severely. Third, increasingly productive efforts were made to marshal a coordinated network of social and treatment programs that would provide rehabilitative and reintegrative services to youth and their families. Evidence of effectiveness as indicated by a research on program outcomes suggests that such a coordinated program can yield significant reductions in juvenile delinquency, violence, and recidivism. The three major changes continue, and perhaps the best prediction of future directions in juvenile probation would that change will increase in speed and intensity. There is much work yet to be done to prevent delinquency and increase public safety.

## *Review Questions*

1. Why was probation established across the nation much earlier for juveniles than for adult offenders?

2. Why should probation be the disposition of choice with juvenile offenders?

3. Identify and describe three major court cases that have affected juveniles.

4. What is deinstitutionalization, and what state led the way in this movement?

5. Argue the case for binding over serious juvenile offenders as adults; against this practice.

6. How can public safety be enhanced with juvenile aftercare?

7. Identify five major innovations in juvenile community corrections.

8. Can early childhood intervention reduce juvenile offending?

9. Do drug courts reduce recidivism?

10. How has juvenile probation changed in the past decade?

## Key Terms

accountability
decarceration
deinstitutionalization
diversion
drug courts
Fourteenth Amendment

juvenile court
parens patriae
selective incapacitation
status offender
waiver

## Recommended Readings

Krisberg, B. (1997). *The Impact of the Justice System on Serious, Violent, and Chronic Juvenile Offenders.* San Francisco, CA: National Council on Crime and Delinquency.

Schissel, B. (1997). *Blaming Children: Youth Crime, Moral Panic and the Politics of Hate.* Halifax, CN: Fernwood Publishing.

Whitehead, J. and S. Lab (2003). *Juvenile Justice,* Fourth Edition. Cincinnati, OH: Anderson Publishing Co.

## Notes

[1]    Chicago courts continue to innovate to handle juvenile offenders. See U.S. Bureau of Justice Statistics (1994b). *Night Drug Courts: The Cook County Experience.* Washington, DC: U.S. Bureau of Justice Statistics. For a critical view of the Illinois juvenile justice system, see Berger, R. "Illinois Juvenile Justice: An Emerging Dual System." *Crime & Delinquency,* 40(1):54-68. See also Getis, V. (2000). *The Juvenile Court and the Progressives.* Chicago, IL: University of Chicago Press.

[2]    Critics argue that this has not happened. See Feld, B. (1993). "Criminalizing the American Juvenile Court." In Tonry, M. (ed.) *Crime and Justice: A Review of Research,* pp. 197-280. Chicago, IL: University of Chicago Press; and Getis, supra note 1.

[3] Umbreit, M. (1994). *Victim Meets Offender: The Impact of Restorative Justice and Mediation.* Monsey, NY: Criminal Justice Press. See also Bazemore, G. and M. Umbreit (1995). "Rethinking the Sentencing Function in Juvenile Court: Retributive or Restorative Responses to Youth Crime." *Crime & Delinquency*, 41(3):296-316; and Umbreit, M. and B. Vos (2000). "Homicide Survivors Meet the Offenders Prior to Execution." *Homicide Studies*, 4(1):63-87.

[4] The perceived relationship between juvenile delinquency and adult criminality has been seriously challenged by recent research. Arguing that evidence is not sufficient to establish accurate predictions about whether juvenile delinquents would eventually become adult offenders, Lyle Shannon also found that the relationship that does exist can in large part be explained by the effects of processes within the juvenile and criminal justice systems, as well as the continued delinquent behavior of the juvenile. See Shannon, L. (1982). *Assessing the Relationship of Adult Career Criminals to Juvenile Careers.* Washington, DC: U.S. Government Printing Office.

[5] See Solomon, K. and M. Klein (1983). *National Evaluation of the Deinstitutionalization of Status Offender Programs.* Washington, DC: U.S. Department of Justice.

[6] Not all scholars agree that the moving force behind early juvenile court development was benevolent. For example, A.M. Platt believes that the rationale for saving the youth was part of a larger social movement that attempted to strengthen the position of corporate capitalism in the United States. He argues that the juvenile court was a means of preserving the existing class system. See A. Platt (1977). *The Child Savers: The Invention of Delinquency.* Chicago, IL: University of Chicago Press.

[7] Lee, L. (1994). "Factors Determining Waiver to a Juvenile Court." *Journal of Criminal Justice*, 22(4):329-340. See also Jenson, E. and L. Metzger, "A Test of the Deterrent Effect of Legislative Waiver on Violent Juvenile Crime." *Crime & Delinquency*, 40(1):96-104; and Merlo, A., P. Benekos, and W. Cook (1997). "'Getting Tough' on Youth: Legislative Waiver as Crime Control." *Juvenile and Family Court Journal*, 48(3):1-15.

[8] *In re Gault,* 387 U.S. 1 (1967). See also Sanborn, J. (1994). "Remnants of Parens Patriae in the Adjudicatory Hearing." *Crime & Delinquency*, 40(4):594-615; and Manfredi, C. (1998). *The Supreme Court and Juvenile Justice.* Lawrence, KS: University Press of Kansas.

[9] See also Sanborn, J. (1994). "Constitutional Problems of Juvenile Delinquent Trials." *Judicature*, 78(2):81-88; and Feld, B. (1999). *Bad Kids: Race and the Transformation of the Juvenile Court.* New York, NY: Oxford University Press.

[10] Historical data identifying main sources of the growth of juvenile prosecutions in London Court (1790-1820) can be found in King, P. and J. Noel (1994). "The Origins of the Problem of Juvenile Delinquency: The Growth of Juvenile Prosecution in London." In Knafla, L. et al., *Criminal Justice History: An International Volume*, pp. 17-41. Westport, CT: Greenwood Press.

[11] This would be a grievous case of double jeopardy. See also Sanborn, supra note 9.

[12] In *Fare v. Michael C.* (1979), a juvenile murder suspect consented to an interrogation after he was denied the opportunity to consult with his probation officer. The U.S. Supreme Court ruled that there is no constitutional mandate to allow a suspect to speak

with his probation officer. The Court indicated that the trial court judge should take into consideration the totality of the circumstances of the youth's waiver of his or her rights. Factors such as age, maturity, intelligence, and experience should be taken into consideration.

[13]    Berger, R. (1994). "Illinois Juvenile Justice: An Emerging Dual System." *Crime & Delinquency*, 40(1):54-68. Cohn is more pessimistic: Cohn, A. (1994). "The Future of Juvenile Justice Administration: Evolution v. Revolution." *Juvenile and Family Court Journal*, 45(3):51-63.

[14]    See Sheley, J., Z. McGee, and R. Wright (1994). *Weapons-Related Victimization in Selected Inner-City High School Samples*. Washington, DC: Bureau of Justice Statistics. Bastian, L. and B. Taylor (1994). *Young Black Male Victims*. Washington, DC: Bureau of Justice Statistics; and Rapp-Paglicci, L. and J. Wodarski (200). "Antecedent Behaviors of Male Youth Victimization." *Deviant Behavior*, 21(6):519-536.

[15]    Office of Juvenile Justice and Delinquency Prevention (1998). *The Youngest Offenders, 1996*. Washington, DC: OJJDP (http://www.ncjrs.org/pdffiles/fs-9887.pdf).

[16]    Office of Juvenile Justice and Delinquency Prevention (1998). What About Girls? Washington, DC: OJJDP (http://www.ncjrs.org/pdffiles/fs-9884.pdf).

[17]    Sanborn, supra note 9.

[18]    Bazemore, G. (1994). "Understanding the Response to Reform Limiting Discretion: Judges' Views on Restrictions on Detention Intake." *Justice Quarterly*, 11(2):429-452.

[19]    Abt Associates (1994). *Conditions of Confinement: Juvenile Detention and Corrections Facilities*. Washington, DC: Office of Juvenile Justice and Delinquency Prevention.

[20]    An example of this is Project READ, San Jose State University.

[21]    Mauser, E., K. Van Stelle, and Paul Moberg (1994). "The Economic Impacts of Diverting Substance-Abusing Offenders into Treatment." *Crime & Delinquency*, 40(4):568-588; and Sarre, R. (1999). "Destructuring and Criminal Justice Reformers." *Current Issues in Criminal Justice*, 10(3):259-272.

[22]    McDevitt, J., M. Domino, and K. Brown (1997). *Metropolitan Day Reporting Center: An Evaluation*. Boston, MA: Center for Criminal Justice Policy Research, Northeastern University.

[23]    Similar finding emerged when Maryland's Montrose Training School was closed. Gottfredson, D. and W. Barton (1993). "Deinstitutionalization of Juvenile Offenders." *Criminology*, 31(4):591-610.

[24]    Macallair, D. (1994). "Disposition Case Advocacy in San Francisco Juvenile Justice System: A New Approach to Deinstitutionalization." *Crime & Delinquency*, 40(1):84-95. See also Macallair, D. (1993). "Reaffirming Rehabilitation in Juvenile Justice." *Youth and Society*, 25(1):104-125.

# References

Abt Associates (1994). *Conditions of Confinement: Juvenile Detention and Corrections Facilities*. Washington, DC: Office of Juvenile Justice and Delinquency Prevention.

Allen, H., E. Latessa, B. Ponder, and C. Simonsen (2007). *Corrections in America*. Upper Saddle River, NJ: Prentice Hall.

Allen, H. and C. Simonsen (1998). *Corrections in America*. Upper Saddle River, NJ: Prentice Hall.

(2001). *Corrections in America*. Upper Saddle River, NJ: Prentice Hall.

American Correctional Association (1986). *Directory of Juvenile and Adult Correctional Departments, Institutions, Agencies and Paroling Authorities*. College Park, MD: ACA.

(1997). *Directory of Juvenile and Adult Correctional Departments, Institutions, Agencies and Paroling Authorities*. Lanham, MD: ACA.

(2001). *Directory of Juvenile and Adult Correctional Departments, Institutions, Agencies and Paroling Authorities*. Lanham, MD: ACA.

Bazemore, G. (1994). "Understanding the Response to Reform Limiting Discretion: Judges' Views on Restrictions on Detention Intake." *Justice Quarterly*, 11(2):429-452.

Bazemore, G. and M. Umbreit (1995). "Rethinking the Sentencing Function in Juvenile Court: Retributive or Restorative Response to Youth Crime." *Crime & Delinquency*, 41(3):296-316.

Berger, R. (1994). "Illinois Juvenile Justice: An Emerging Dual System." *Crime & Delinquency*, 40(1):54-68.

Bishop, D. (2000). "Juvenile Offenders in the Adult Criminal Justice System." In Tonry, M. (ed.) (2000). *Criminal and Justice: A Review of Research*, Vol. 27. Chicago, IL: University of Chicago Press, pp. 81-167.

*Breed v. Jones*, 421 U.S. 519 (1975).

Clear, T.R. and G.F. Cole (1990). *American Corrections*. Pacific Grove, CA: Brooks/Cole.

Clemmer, D. (1940). *The Prison Community*. New York, NY: Rinehart and Company.

Cohn, A. (1994). "The Future of Juvenile Justice Administration: Evolution v. Revolution." *Juvenile and Family Court Journal*, 45(3):51-63.

Dembo, R., W. Seeberger, M. Shemwell et al. (2000). "Psychological Functioning Among Juvenile Offenders 12 Months After Family Empowerment Intervention." *Journal of Offender Rehabilitation*, 32(1/2):1-56.

del Carmen, R. (1984). "Legal Issues and Liabilities in Community Corrections." Paper presented at the annual meeting of the Academy of Criminal Justice Sciences, Chicago, IL.

del Carmen, R., M. Parker, and F. Reddington (1998). *Briefs of Leading Cases in Juvenile Justice*. Cincinnati, OH: Anderson Publishing Co.

*Fare v. Michael C.*, 442 U.S. 707 (1979).

Feld, B. (1999). *Bad Kids: Race and the Transformation of the Juvenile Court*. New York, NY: Oxford University Press.

Federal Bureau of Investigation (2005). *Crime in the United States, 2005*. Washington, DC: U.S. Department of Justice (www.fbi.gov/ucr/00cius.htm).

Gottfredson, D. and W. Barton (1993). "Deinstitutionalization of Juvenile Offenders." *Criminology*, 31(4):591-610.

Government Accounting Office (1994). *Residential Care: Some High Risk Youth Benefit But More Study Is Needed*. Washington, DC: U.S. Government Accounting Office.

Grisso, T. and R. Schwartz (2000). *Youth on Trial: A Developmental Perspective on Juvenile Justice*. Chicago, IL: University of Chicago Press.

Harris, K. (1996). "Key Differences Among Community Corrections Acts in the United States: An Overview." *Prison Journal*, 76(2):192-238.

*In re Gault*, 387 U.S. 1 (1967).

*In re Winship*, 397 U. S. 358 (1970).

Hayes, H. and M. Geerken (1997). "The Idea of Selective Release." *Justice Quarterly*, 14(2):353-370.

Haumschilt, G. (2001). "The Responsibility to the Public in Parole." *CYA Today*, 2(1):4. Sacramento, CA: California Youth Authority (www.cya.ca.gov/news/cya today/vic0401.pdf).

*Kent v. United States*, 383 U.S. 54 (1966).

King, P. and J. Noel (1994). "The Origins of the Problem of Juvenile Delinquency: The Growth of Juvenile Prosecution in London." In L. Knafla (ed.) *Criminal Justice History: An International Volume*. Westport, CT: Greenwood Press.

Krisberg, B. (1997). "The Impact of the Justice System on Serious, Violent and Chronic Juvenile Offenders." San Francisco, CA: National Council on Crime and Delinquency.

Krisberg, B., J. Austin and P. Steele (1991). *Unlocking Juvenile Corrections*. San Francisco, CA: National Council on Crime and Delinquency.

Krisberg, B., J. Austin, K. Joe, and P. Steele (1987). *The Impact of Court Sanctions*. San Francisco, CA: National Council on Crime and Delinquency.

Latessa, E., M. Moon, and B. Applegate (1995). *Preliminary Evaluation of the Ohio Department of Youth Services RECLAIM Ohio Pilot Project*. Cincinnati, OH: University of Cincinnati.

Latessa, E., D. Shaffer, and C. Lowenkamp (2002). *Outcome Evaluation of Ohio's Drug Court Efforts: Final Report*. Center for Criminal Justice Research, University of Cincinnati.

Lee, L. (1994). "Factors Determining Waiver to a Juvenile Court." *Journal of Criminal Justice*, 22(4):329-340.

Lindner, C. and M. Savarese (1984a). "The Evolution of Probation: Early Salaries, Qualifications and Hiring Practices." *Federal Probation*, 48(1):3-9.

Livsey, S. (2006). *Juvenile Delinquency Probation Caseload, 1985-2002*. Washington, DC: U.S. Office of Juvenile Justice and Delinquency Prevention.

Lowenkamp, C., and E. Latessa (2005). *Evaluation of Ohio's RECLAIM Funded Programs, Community Corrections Facilities, and DYS Facilities*. University of Cincinnati, Center for Criminal Justice Research. http://www.uc.edu/criminaljustice/ResearchReports.html

Macallair, D. (1994). "Disposition Case Advocacy in San Francisco Juvenile Justice System: A New Approach to Deinstitutionalization." *Crime & Delinquency*, 40(1):84-95.

Macallair, D. (1993). "Reaffirming Rehabilitation in Juvenile Justice." *Youth and Society*, 25(1):104-125.

Maxson, C. and M. Klein (1997). *Responding to Troubled Youth*. New York, NY: Oxford University Press.

Mauser, E., K. Van Stelle, and P. Moberg (1994). "The Economic Impacts of Diverting Substance-Abusing Offenders into Treatment." *Crime & Delinquency*, 40(4):568-588.

McCord, J. and J. Sanchez (1983). "The Treatment of Deviant Children: A Twenty-Five Year Follow-Up Study." *Crime & Delinquency*, 29(2):238-253.

*McKeiver v. Pennsylvania*, 403 U.S. 528 (1971).

McNulty, E. (1996). *Arizona Juvenile Transfer Study*. Phoenix, AZ: Administrative Office of the Courts, Arizona Supreme Court.

Merlo, A., P. Benekos, and W. Cook (1997). "'Getting Tough' with Youth: Legislative Waiver as Crime Control." *Juvenile and Family Court Journal*, 48(3):1-15.

Moore, M. and S. Wakeling (1997). "Juvenile Justice: Shoring Up the Foundations." In Tonry, M. (ed.) *Crime and Justice: A Review of Research*, pp. 253-301. Chicago, IL: University of Chicago Press.

*Nelson v. Heyne*, 491 F.2d 352 (7th Cir. 1974).

Office of Juvenile Justice and Delinquency Prevention (1996). *Juvenile Probation: The Workhorse of the Juvenile Justice System*. Washington, DC: OJJDP (www.ncjrs.org/pdffiles/workhors.pdf).

(1999). *Costs and Benefits of Early Childhood Intervention*. Washington, DC: OJJDP (www.ncjrs.org/pdffiles1/fs9994.pdf).

(2000). *Implementation of the Intensive Community-Based Aftercare Program*. Washington, DC: OJJDP (www.ncjrs.org/pdffiles1/ojjdp/181464.pdf).

(2001). *Juvenile Court Statistics, 2005*. Washington, DC: OJJDP (www.ncjrs.org/pdffiles1/ojjdp/180864.pdf).

(2001). *The 8% Solution*. Washington, DC: OJJDP (www.ncjrs.org/pdffiles1/ojjdp/fs200139.pdf).

Orange County Probation Office (2001). *8% Problem Study Findings* (www.oc.ca.gov/Probation/e8%25Solution/b8%ProblemStudyFindings.asp).

Platt, A. (1977). *The Child Savers: The Invention of Delinquency*. Chicago, IL: University of Chicago Press.

President's Commission on Law Enforcement and Administration of Justice (1967). *Juvenile Delinquency and Youth Crime*. Washington, DC: U.S. Government Printing Office.

Rausch, S. and C. Logan (1982). "Diversion from Juvenile Court: Panacea or Pandora's Box?" Paper presented at the annual meeting of the American Society of Criminology, Toronto, Canada.

Redding, R. "Juvenile Offenders in Criminal Court and Adult Prison." *Juvenile and Family Court Journal*, 50(1):1-20.

Risler, E., T. Sweatman, and L. Nackerud (1998). "Evaluating the Georgia Legislative Waiver's Effectiveness in Deterring Juvenile Crime." *Research on Social Work Practice*, 8(6):657-667.

Rogers, J. and G. Mays (1987). *Juvenile Delinquency and Juvenile Justice*. New York, NY: John Wiley.

Sanborn, J. (1994). "Constitutional Problems of Juvenile Delinquency Trials." *Judicature*, 78(2):81-88.

Sanborn, J. (1994). "Remnants of Parens Patriae in the Adjudicatory Hearing." *Crime & Delinquency*, 40(4):599-615.

Sarre, R. (1999). "Destructuring and Criminal Justice Reform." *Current Issues in Criminal Justice*, 10(3):259-272.

Schumaker, M. and G. Kurtz (2000). *The 8% Solution*. Thousand Oaks, CA: Sage.

Schur, E. (1971). *Labeling Deviant Behavior: Its Sociological Implications*. New York, NY: Harper and Row.

*Schall v. Martin*, 467 U.S. 253, 104 S. Ct. 2403, 81 L. Ed. 2d 207 (1984).

Koetzel-Shaffer, Deborah (2006) *Reconsidering Drug Court Effectiveness: A Meta-analytic Review*. Doctoral Dissertation, University of Cincinnati.

Shannon, L. (1982). *Assessing the Relationship of Adult Career Criminals to Juvenile Careers*. Washington, DC: U.S. Government Printing Office.

Sheley, J., Z. McGee, and J. Wright (1995). *Weapons-Related Victimization in Selected Inner-City High School Samples*. Washington, DC: Bureau of Justice Statistics.

Sherrill, M. (1975a, February). "Jerome Miller: Does He Have the Answers . . .?" *Corrections Magazine*, 1(2):24-28.

Sherrill, M. (1975b, February). "Harvard Recidivism Study." *Corrections Magazine*, 1(2):21-23.

Sickmund, M. (2006). *Juvenile Residential Facility Census, 2002: Selected Findings*. Washington, DC: Office of Juvenile Justice and Delinquency Prevention.

Snyder, H. (2005). *Juvenile Arrests 2003*. Washington, DC: U.S. Office of Juvenile Justice and Delinquency Prevention.

Snyder, H., M. Sickmund, and E. Yamagata (1996). *Juvenile Offenders and Victims*. Washington, DC: U.S. Office of Juvenile Justice and Delinquency Prevention.

(2000). *Juvenile Transfers to Criminal Court in the 1990s*. Washington, DC: Office of Juvenile Justice and Delinquency Prevention.

Solomon, K. and M. Klein (1983). *National Evaluation of the Deinstitutionalization of Status Offender Programs*. Washington, DC: Office of Juvenile Justice and Delinquency Prevention, U.S. Department of Justice.

*Sourcebook of Criminal Justice Statistics 2003* (31st edition) Online.

Torbert, P., R. Gable, and H. Hurst (1996). *State Responses to Serious and Violent Juvenile Crime*. Washington, DC: U.S. Office of Juvenile Justice and Delinquency Prevention.

Umbreit, M. (1994). *Victim Meets Offender: The Impact of Restorative Justice and Mediation*. Monsey, NY: Criminal Justice Press.

U.S. Bureau of Justice Assistance (1994a). *Drug Night Courts*. Washington, DC: USBJS.

U.S. Bureau of Justice Statistics (1994b). *Night Drug Courts: The Cook County Experience*. Washington, DC: USBJS.

Whitehead, J. and S. Lab (2003). *Juvenile Justice*, Fourth Edition. Cincinnati, OH: Anderson Publishing Co.

Wu, B. (2000). "Determinants of Public Opinion Toward Juvenile Waiver Decisions." *Juvenile and Family Court Journal*, 50(1):9-20.

# Parole in America

5

The most vivid disagreements over the matter of rights were caused by the ticket-of-leave system. There were only three ways in which the law might release a man from bondage. The first, though the rarest, was an absolute pardon from the governor, which restored him all rights including that of returning to England. The second was a conditional pardon, which gave the transported person citizenship within the colony but no right of return to England. The third was the ticket-of-leave.

—Robert Hughes

A couple was driving through the country one fall day when they came upon a large house with a sign hanging from the porch. The sign said: "Dr. E. Smith, Veterinarian and Taxidermist." This seemed like an odd combination, so the couple drove closer. Under the name, it said: "Either way, you get your dog back."

—Anonymous

## The Development of Parole

The way prisoners are released has changed dramatically over the past few years (Solomon, 2006). Some are released by a parole board (about 22% in 2005), others finish their entire sentences and are released with no supervision (19%) and still others are given mandatory release with supervision (39%). We also know that parole is implemented differently from state to state. So what is parole, and how did we get to this point?

Parole is a correctional option that often evokes strong feelings. There are those who argue that it should be abolished entirely, while others believe that it provides men and women with an opportunity to demonstrate that they can re-enter society and lead law-abiding and productive lives. Regardless of one's position, parole is an important part of the American correctional scene. Furthermore, because it is estimated that nearly 6,500,000 inmates are released to the community each year, many of whom will be under some form of correctional supervision, it is important that we understand the roots of parole and how it is granted.

Although the percentage of prisoners released on discretionary parole is at the lowest rate since the federal government began keeping track, parole remains a commonly used mechanism by which offenders may be released from a correctional institution after completion of a portion of the sentence (see Figure 5.1). Contemporary parole also includes the concepts of supervision by state, release on condition of good behavior while in the community, and return to prison for failing to abide by these conditions or for committing a new crime. As we shall see, earlier parole practices saw the development of these elements.

Figure 5.1
**Adults Exiting from Prison: 2005**

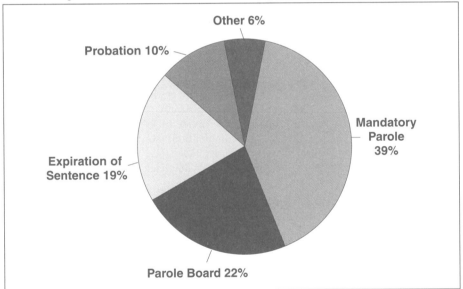

Source: Glaze, L. and T. Bonczar (2006). *Probation and Parole in the United States, 2005. Bureau of Justice Statistics.*

## The Roots of American Parole

Parole from prison, like the prison itself, is primarily an American innovation.[1] It emerged from a philosophical revolution and a resulting tradition of penal reform established in the late eighteenth century in the newly formed United States. As with many other new ideas that emerged in early America, parole had its roots in the practices of English and European penal systems.

Early punishment for offenses were often what Langbein (1976:35-63) called "blood punishments." Capital and corporal punishment were accepted penal practices in Europe and the United States well into the nineteenth century. This was so, in part, because the technology and economy of these principally rural societies were unable to process and control large inmate populations, and also because these societies had strong traditions of corporal punishment that were rooted in the Old Testament.[2]

---

**Box 5.1**

### Retribution

Philosophically, this earlier policy generally meant getting even with the perpetrator. *Social revenge* suggests that individuals cannot exact punishment, but the state will do so in their name.

Retribution assumes that offenders willfully chose to commit their evil acts, are responsible for their own behavior, are likely to commit similar acts again, and should receive the punishment they so richly deserve. Retribution requires the state to make the offender suffer for the sake of suffering.

There has been a rebirth of retribution during the last decade, as seen in minimum mandatory prison sentences, abolition of parole releases in some states, habitual offender statutes, and the "three strikes" laws.

---

In the late seventeenth and early eighteenth centuries, two massive social changes occurred that altered the direction of Western civilization and, consequently, had an impact on criminal law and penalties. The first was the Enlightenment, which gave rise to a conception of the human being as a rational and ultimately perfectible being and, along with this, a belief in basic human equality.[3] Second, urbanization and the earliest movements toward industrialism simultaneously changed the nature of social interactions and created a new social class, the urban working class.

The writing of such thinkers as Locke, Voltaire, Beccaria, and Montesquieu both created and reflected a changing conception of man and the social order. These writers believed that government or society existed because individuals allowed it to exist. In other words, a "social contract" governed society. In order to be secure in their persons and possessions, free and equal individuals banded together and surrendered certain of their freedoms to the government on condition that it protect them from their enemies.

Among those enemies were criminals. The state assumed the responsibility of controlling crime and, by administering justice, punishing offenders. Individuals surrendered their "rights "to seek revenge and to commit crimes or avenge themselves. The social contract was the product of rational, free individuals. And because rational and free people had control of their own fates, they could be held responsible for their actions.

A crime was considered a "breach of contract," an offense against all parties to the social contract and not just the injured party. This state of affairs enabled the establishment of a central body of law (such as the Common Law in England), and centralized control of enforcement. Finally, rational individuals, presumed to have prior knowledge of the law and its penalties, were expected to perceive that it was in their own interest not to violate the law and suffer the penalties. Deterrence was the rationale of the criminal law and its sanctions, which were severe so as to enhance the deterrent effect of the law (Beccaria, 1764). (In fact, more than 200 offenses carried the death penalty in England at one time. During the reign of Henry VIII, some 74,000 major and minor thieves were sent to the gallows. Under the reign of his daughter, Elizabeth I, 300 to 400 at a time were hanged, attracting large crowds where pickpockets flourished—even though pick pocketing was an offense punishable by death (Rennie, 1978:6-7).

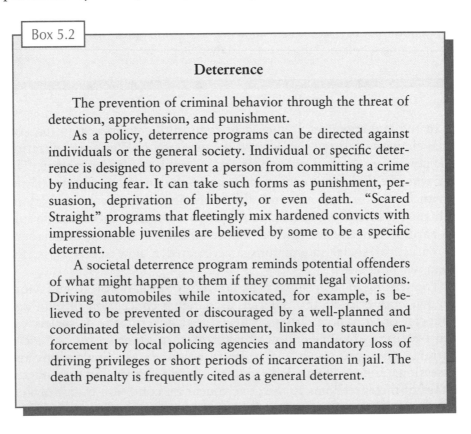

Box 5.2

**Deterrence**

The prevention of criminal behavior through the threat of detection, apprehension, and punishment.

As a policy, deterrence programs can be directed against individuals or the general society. Individual or specific deterrence is designed to prevent a person from committing a crime by inducing fear. It can take such forms as punishment, persuasion, deprivation of liberty, or even death. "Scared Straight" programs that fleetingly mix hardened convicts with impressionable juveniles are believed by some to be a specific deterrent.

A societal deterrence program reminds potential offenders of what might happen to them if they commit legal violations. Driving automobiles while intoxicated, for example, is believed to be prevented or discouraged by a well-planned and coordinated television advertisement, linked to staunch enforcement by local policing agencies and mandatory loss of driving privileges or short periods of incarceration in jail. The death penalty is frequently cited as a general deterrent.

Because the criminal law in colonial America developed from the English Common Law, it was also very harsh. Judges and magistrates in the English system had the option to impose a variety of penalties less severe than death, such as branding, maiming, the stocks, fines, or any combination of these. As a reaction against cruel punishments, the "benefit of clergy" was developed to mitigate punishment for clerics and the wealthy. Initially designed to separate church and state, the "benefit" was eventually extended to all literate British citizens, even to those who could feign literacy (Clear, 1978:6-7; Briggs, Harrison & McInnes, 1996).

The reluctance of juries to convict and judges to impose sentences that were perceived to be disproportionate to the severity of most offenses did much to detract from the deterrent effect of the law. In addition, the inequity evident in sentencing, coupled with the potential and actual practices of abuses of the power to suspend sentences altogether, led to calls for reform in the English eighteenth-century criminal code, particularly for a reduction in the severity of penalties. A gradual shift in the conception of humankind and concomitant re-evaluation of the effectiveness and severity of punishment contributed significantly to the origins of parole as it exists today (Fogel, 1975:30-35).

Other writers, however, felt that poverty and lack of education, or heredity and biological inferiority, were the factors that gave rise to crime. The shifting conception of mankind as being at least partly at the mercy of forces beyond their control reduced the degree to which they could be held responsible for criminal actions, and paved the way for a reduction in the severity of many penalties. These changes in the philosophical conception of crime and punishment brought a new factor into the determination of sentences. Instead of imposing uniformly harsh sanctions for nearly all offenders, judges began to mitigate penalties for those "unfortunates" whom they "deemed to be worthy."

In England, orders of transportation were thought to be a severe punishment. In the eighteenth century, banishment, a common penalty for the aristocracy or nobility for centuries, was imposed on the common offender for the first time. The judge would order the common offender transported to the colonies rather than to the gallows or pillory. The criminal would be allowed to go at liberty in the new land, sometimes for a period of indenture (Pisciotta, 1982), on the condition of not returning to England for a specified time period (such as 10 years), if at all (Hawkins, 1971:Chapter 1). The concept of transportation thus avoids the extreme harshness of existing criminal law while at the same time serving incapacitative purposes of those penalties. The serious felony offender, of course, was still sentenced to death.

While transportation was a partial solution to England's crime problem and, for a time helped to settle and develop the new lands (the colonies, however, had no similar outlet for their offenders, with the exception of casting them into the wilderness, with usually the same results as the death penalty), it was only a temporary one. As a result of the American Revolution, England was forced to transport her convicts elsewhere (Campbell, 1994), and for a time they were sent to Australia; until, eventually, even Australia closed its doors to English convicts.[4]

---

**Box 5.3**

### Incapacitation

A crime prevention strategy based on specific deterrence that would disable the potential offender from committing another crime by isolating the instant offender. Common forms of incapacitation include transportation to other countries or colonies, committing the offender to an asylum or mental hospital, and life-long imprisonment.

A contemporary version of this strategy is "selective incapacitation," a policy that would reserve prison beds for the most hardened, rapacious, and dangerous offenders. It would also require the use of community corrections for less severe offenders.

Two major problems with selective incapacitation are the inability of corrections to devise classification devices that would accurately predict which offenders would repeat (recidivate) or would not commit another crime. The second problem is more intractable: the widespread, but erroneous belief that all offenders are dangerous and cannot be controlled in the community. The latter has been a major impediment to the creation of community corrections.

---

Criminologists commonly accept punishment by transportation as the principal forerunner of parole (Hawkins, 1971). They argue that transportation was an organized, uniform process by which thousands of convicts were punished in a manner short of execution or corporal punishment, as it was a system wherein offenders eventually obtained their freedom. In addition, transportation did not necessarily involve a period of incarceration.

## The Rise of Early Prison Reform

The Treaty of Paris in 1783 acknowledged the creation of the first republic in Western civilization since the fall of the Roman Empire. The United States of America, free from the English monarchy and founded on the teachings of the Enlightenment, became a fertile ground for the development of a new system of criminal justice.

While the influence of English Common Law, with its harsh penalties, was strong in the new republic, even stronger were anti-British sentiment and the desire to abandon the oppressive regime of the English king. American reformers moved away from the archaic, tyrannical sanctions of colonial law and toward a more humane and rational penalty of incarceration.[5] It was argued that fair, simple laws, backed by certain and humane punishment, would eradicate crime.

Chief among the reform groups were the Quakers (Offutt, 1995). The Judiciary Act of 1789 established imprisonment as the penalty for most crimes in Pennsylvania. In a nation that had newly acquired independence, what more fitting penalty could be found than the deprivation of liberty? When Patrick Henry uttered his now-famous line, "Give me liberty or give me death," little did he know that he had identified the perfect penalty for crime. The prison replaced the penalty of death and yet denied liberty to its inmates. Much to the dismay of these first reformers, their efforts were not rewarded by a reduction in crime. Rather, the first penal institutions were dismal failures (Rothman, 1971:62):

> The faith of the 1790s now seemed misplaced; more rational codes had not decreased crime. The roots of deviancy went deeper than the certainty of punishment. Nor were the institutions fulfilling the elementary task of protecting society, since escapes and riots were commonplace occurrences.

The search for the causes of crime continued. The reformers still believed that offenders were rational people who would strive to improve themselves, but the manner in which they could be convinced to obey the law was still unknown. In a time of rapid social change and movement from an agrarian to an industrial society, environmental factors came to be viewed as criminogenic: cities, poverty, and idleness were believed to be the hotbeds of crime.

The proposed solution that emerged was: remove the offender from bad environments and teach benefits of industry and morality. Offenders needed to be shown the error of their ways. Criminal law was required to do more than punish and deter; it should change the prisoner into a productive citizen. Punishment should serve to allow the prisoner to repent, to be trained, and to be reformed into a good citizen. A place to repent was thus needed, and prisons were developed to fulfill that need.

The original basis of the prison was the reformation of the offender, and the ideal of reformation placed high value on discipline and regimentation. In short, in the newly created free society, incarceration itself was punishment and, while incarcerated, the goal was to reform the prisoner. Offenders were expected to obey strict rules of conduct to work hard at assigned tasks (Johnson, 1994). In this milieu, it was believed, the offender would learn the benefit of discipline and industry.

The founders of the penitentiaries were mindful that the prison was a means to an end; their successors were not (Rothman, 1971:245-256). Reformation of inmates came to be identified solely with confinement, and custody eventually grew to be the ultimate goal of incarceration (Rothman, 1971:238). Furthermore, inmates posed significant threats to the security of the penitentiaries. Prison officials resorted to severe corporal punishments in order to maintain control within the prison—a penalty the development of prisons was supposed to replace.

The second generation of prison officials also saw another way of keeping the inmates out of trouble. American industry in the middle 1800s was labor-intensive, and prison populations were ideal sources of cheap labor. Inmate labor was expected to generate the money necessary to run the prisons, and prison administrators were thus receptive to offers to hire entire populations. This situation led to grossly underpaid prison labor, antagonism from unemployed free citizens, and the emergence of the labor contractor as major force in institutional administration.[6] The Report of the Massachusetts General Court Joint Special Committee on Contract Convict Labor (1880:16) illustrates the problem.

> In the State Prison, contracts have been made which have no clause [giving] the State power to annul [them] . . . Such bargains are bad, and, carried out to the fullest extent with large contracts, may naturally be expected to lead to a condition of affairs that has existed in other States given ground to the popular assertion that contractors, and not the State, control the prison.

## Early Practices in Other Nations

The first operational system of conditional release was started by the governor of a prison in Spain in 1835. Up to one-third of a prison sentence could be reduced by good behavior and a demonstrated desire to do better (Carter, McGee & Nelson, 1975:200). A similar system was enacted in Bavaria in the 1830s, and many prison reformers in France in the 1840s advocated the adoption of similar conditional release systems. In fact, the term "parole "comes from the French parole d'honneur, or "word of honor," which characterized the French efforts to establish parole release. Prisoners would be released after showing good behavior and industry in the prison,[7] and on their word of honor that they would obey the law.

Despite the fact that these efforts predate those of Alexander Maconochie, it is he who is usually given credit as being the father of parole. In 1840, Captain Maconochie was put in charge of the English penal colony in New South Wales at Norfolk Island, about 1,000 miles off the coast of Australia. To this colony were sent the criminals who were "twice condemned." They had been shipped from England to Australia, and then from Australia to Norfolk (Allen & Simonsen, 2001:42-43). Conditions were allegedly so bad at Norfolk Island that men reprieved from the death penalty wept and those who were to die thanked God (Barry, 1957:5). The conditions on Norfolk Island were so unbearable that suicide became a means of escape and an act of solidarity. Hughes (1987:468) describes it in vivid terms:

> A group of convicts would choose two men by drawing straws: one to die, the other to kill him. Others would stand by as witnesses. There being no judge to try capital offenses on Norfolk Island, the killer and witnesses would have to be sent to Sidney for trial—an inconvenience for the authorities but a boon to the prisoners, who yearned for the meager relief of getting away from the "ocean of hell," if only to a gallows on the mainland. And in Sidney there was some slight chance of escape. The victim could not choose himself; everyone in the group apparently, had to be equally ready to die, and the benefits of his death had to be shared equally by all survivors.

It was under these conditions that Maconochie devised an elaborate method of granted conditional release. Maconochie's plan was based on five basic principles (Barnes & Teeters, 1959:419):

1.  Release should not be based on the completing of a sentence for a set period of time, but on completion of a determined and specified quantity of labor. In brief, time sentences should be abolished, and task sentences substituted.

2.  The quantity of labor a prisoner must perform should be expressed in a number of "marks" which he must earn, by improvement of conduct, frugality of living, and habits of industry, before he can be released.

3.  While in prison he should earn everything he receives. All sustenance and indulgences should be added to his debt of marks.

4.  When qualified by discipline to do so, he should work in association with a small number of other prisoners, forming a group of six or seven, and the whole group should be answerable for the conduct of labor of each member.

5.  In the final stage, a prisoner, while still obliged to earn his daily tally of marks, should be given a proprietary interest in his own labor and be subject to a less rigorous discipline, to prepare him for release into society.

Under his plan, prisoners were awarded marks and moved through stages of custody until finally granted release. His system involved indeterminate sentencing, with release based upon the number of marks earned by prisoners for good conduct, labor, and study. The five stages, based upon the accumulation of marks, each carried increased responsibility and freedom, leading to a ticket of leave or parole resulting in a conditional pardon and, finally, to full restoration of liberty.

Maconochie has been described as a zealot (Hughes, 1987); however, his reforms made life bearable at Norfolk Island, and can be described as revolutionary in comparison to the horrible conditions that existed there before his arrival. While Maconochie's reforms transposed Norfolk Island from one of despair to one of hope, it was short lived. Petty bureaucrats, and a general mistrust of Maconochie's ideas led to his recall as Commandant in 1843.

Sir Walter Crofton, director of the Irish prison system in the 1850s, built upon foundations laid by Maconochie. He decided that a transitional stage between prison and full release was needed, and developed a classification scheme based upon a system in which the prisoner progressed through three stages of treatment. The first was segregated confinement with work and training provided to the prisoner. This was followed by a transition period from confinement to freedom, during which the prisoner was set to work on public projects with little control being exercised over him. If he performed successfully in this phase, he was released on "license" (Clare & Kramer, 1976:69-70; Maguire, Peroud & Dison, 1996).

Release on license was constrained by certain conditions, violations of which would result in reimprisonment. While on license, prisoners were required to submit monthly reports and were warned against idleness and associating with other criminals. Prisoners on license, then, had to report, could be reimprisoned for violating the conditions of release, and had not been pardoned. These distinctions from earlier systems of release were large steps toward modern parole.

## Early American Practices

Convicts sentenced to prison in America in the early 1800s received definite terms; a sentence of five years meant the offender would serve five years in prison. This strict sentencing structure led to overcrowded prisons and widespread problems in the institutions. It was not uncommon for a governor to grant pardons to large numbers of inmates in order to control the size of prison populations. In some states, this pardoning power was even delegated to prison wardens (Sherrill, 1977:5).

This method of rewarding well-behaved prisoners with reductions in sentence was first formalized in 1817 by the New York State legislature. In that year, the first "good-time" law was passed. This law authorized a 25 percent reduction in length of term for those inmates serving five years or more who were well behaved and demonstrated industry in their prison work. By 1869, 23 states had good-time laws, and prison administrators supported the concept as a method of keeping order and controlling the population size (Sherrill, 1977:6).

---

**Box 5.4**

### Pardon

An act of executive clemency that absolves the offender in part or in full from the legal consequences of the crime and conviction.

Probably the most famous example is President Gerald Ford's pardon of President Richard Nixon for his role in the Watergate crimes.

Executive clemency can include gubernatorial action that results in the release of an inmate from incarceration, as well as pardoning current and former inmates. Camp and Camp (2000) report that pardons and other acts of clemency were awarded to 722 inmates.

Camp, C. and G. Camp (2000). *The 2000 Corrections Yearbook: Adult Corrections*. Middletown, CT; Criminal Justice Institute, Inc., p. 61.

---

The liberal use of the pardoning power was continued in those states that did not have good-time laws, and the mass pardon was not uncommon even in those states that already allowed sentence reductions for good behavior. These developments are important because they represent the first large-scale exercise of sentencing power by the executive branch of government, the branch in which parole boards would eventually be located.

Another philosophical base for American parole was the indenture system established by the New York House of Refuge. Although not called parole, for all intents and purposes a parole system was already operational for juveniles committed to the House of Refuge in New York. The House of Refuge had developed a system of indenture whereby youths were released from custody as indentured servants of private citizens. Unfortunately, this system permitted corruption.[8]

To combat these abuses, the New York House of Refuge developed a system supervising the indentured. A committee was formed that selected youths for indenture, defined the conditions under which they served their indentureships, and established rules both for the superintendent of the House of Refuge and for the persons to whom youths were indentured.

Box 5.5

### Parole Board

Any correctional person, authority, commission, or board that has legal authority to parole those adults (or juveniles) committed to confinement facilities, to set conditions for behavior, to revoke from parole, and to discharge from parole.

Parole boards also can usually recommend shortening a prisoner's sentence (commuting sentences), recommend pardons to a Governor, set parole policies and, in some jurisdictions, recommend reprieve from execution. An example of parole policy would be a "zero-tolerance" policy for parolees whose urine samples indicate recent use of illicit drugs, usually resulting in certain return to confinement.

There was no formal mechanism for releasing the youths from custody, but they were able to work off their contracts and thus obtain their freedom. Their masters could break the contracts and return the youths to the House of Refuge at any time. In essence, a parole system was operating.

In addition to these forms of release from custody before the expiration of the maximum term, the concept of supervising released offenders had also been operationalized. It is important to note, however, that supervision of released prisoners prior to the creation of parole in America only required providing assistance and not crime control duties.[9]

In 1845, the Massachusetts legislature appointed a state agent for discharged convicts and appropriated funds for him to use in assisting ex-prisoners in securing employment, tools, clothes, and transportation. Other states followed this example and appointed agents of their own. As early as 1776, however, charitable organizations, such as the Philadelphia Association for the Alleviation of Prisoners' Miseries, were already providing aid to released convicts (Sellin, 1970:13). By the late 1860s, dissatisfaction with prisons was widespread and a concerted effort to establish a formal parole release and supervision system began. In 1867, prison reformers Enoch Wines and Louis Dwight reported that "There is not a state prison in America in which reformation of the convicts is the one supreme object of discipline, to which everything else is made to bend" (Rothman, 1971:240-243).

In 1870, the first meeting of the American Prison Association was held in Cincinnati, Ohio.[10] Reform was the battle cry of the day, and the meeting took on an almost evangelical fervor (Fogel, 1975:30-31). Both Sir Walter Crofton and American warden F.B. Sanborn advocated the Irish system (Lindsey, 1925:20).

Armed with the success of the meeting, the focus of prison reformers shifted from incarceration as the answer to crime and, instead, concentrated on the return of offenders to society. Prisons remained central, but they were now seen almost as a necessary evil, not as an end in themselves. Prison reformers everywhere began to advocate adoption and expansion of good-time laws, assistance to released prisoners, the adoption of the ticket of leave system, and parole. In 1869, the New York State legislature passed an act creating the Elmira Reformatory and an indeterminate sentence ". . . until reformation, not exceeding five years."

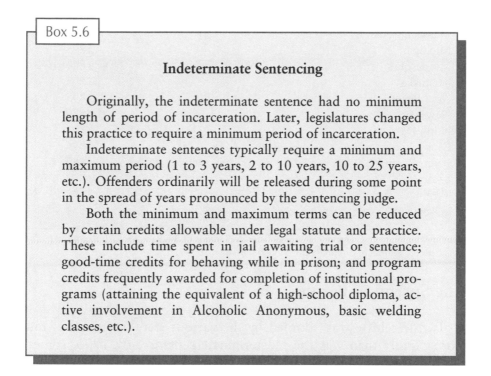

Box 5.6

### Indeterminate Sentencing

Originally, the indeterminate sentence had no minimum length of period of incarceration. Later, legislatures changed this practice to require a minimum period of incarceration.

Indeterminate sentences typically require a minimum and maximum period (1 to 3 years, 2 to 10 years, 10 to 25 years, etc.). Offenders ordinarily will be released during some point in the spread of years pronounced by the sentencing judge.

Both the minimum and maximum terms can be reduced by certain credits allowable under legal statute and practice. These include time spent in jail awaiting trial or sentence; good-time credits for behaving while in prison; and program credits frequently awarded for completion of institutional programs (attaining the equivalent of a high-school diploma, active involvement in Alcoholic Anonymous, basic welding classes, etc.).

This law created the reformatory as a separate institution for young offenders, expressly designed to be an intermediate step between conviction and return to a law-abiding life. The administrators of the reformatory were empowered to release inmates upon demonstration of their reformation. Such release was conditional, and released offenders were to be supervised by a state agent (Lindsey, 1925:21-23).

With the passage of this law, parole in the United States became a reality. It soon spread to other jurisdictions, and by 1944, every jurisdiction in the nation had a parole authority (Hawkins, 1971:64). Table 5.1 illustrates the rapid growth of parole in the United States up to the year 1900. Between 1884 and 1900, parole was adopted in 20 states. The rapid growth of parole, however, was fraught with difficulties and criticism.

Table 5.1
**States with Parole Laws by 1900**

| State | Year Enacted |
| --- | --- |
| Alabama | 1897 |
| California | 1893 |
| Colorado | 1899 |
| Connecticut | 1897 |
| Idaho | 1897 |
| Illinois | 1891 |
| Indiana | 1897 |
| Kansas | 1895 |
| Massachusetts | 1884 |
| Michigan | 1895 |
| Minnesota | 1889 |
| Nebraska | 1893 |
| New Jersey | 1895 |
| New York | 1889 |
| North Dakota | 1891 |
| Ohio | 1896 |
| Pennsylvania | 1887 |
| Utah | 1898 |
| Virginia | 1898 |
| Wisconsin | 1889 |

Source: Adapted from E. Lindsey (1925). "Historical Origins of the Sanction of Imprisonment for Serious Crime." *Journal of Criminal Law and Criminology,* 16:9-126.

## The Spread of Parole

Parole release was adopted by the various state jurisdictions much more rapidly than was the indeterminate sentence. By 1900, some 20 states had adopted parole; by 1944, every jurisdiction had a parole system (See Table 5.2). The expansion of parole has been characterized as being a process of imitation (Lindsey, 1925:21-23), yet a great deal of variation in the structure and use of parole was observed.[11]

The growth and expansion of modern parole was assisted by a number of factors. One of the most important was the tremendous amount of support and publicity that prison reformers gave the concept at the National Congress on Penitentiary and Reformatory Discipline. Its inclusion in the congress's Declaration of Principles, coupled with the publicity of Alexander Maconochie's work in New South Wales, provided the necessary endorsement of correctional experts.

In addition, it was quickly recognized that a discretionary release system solved many of the problems of prison administration. A major factor in favor of parole was that it supported prison discipline. A number of writers pointed out that by placing release in the inmate's own hands, the inmate would be motivated both to reform and to comply with the rules and regulations of the prison.[12] Finally, parole provided a safety valve to reduce prison populations, which were generally overcrowded (Wilcox, 1929:345-354).

Table 5.2
**Significant Developments in Parole**

| Date | Development |
|------|-------------|
| 1776 | Colonies reject English Common Code and begin to draft their own codes. |
| 1840 | Maconochie devises mark system for release of prisoners in Australian penal colony, a forerunner of parole. |
| 1854 | Crofton establishes ticket-of-leave program in Ireland. |
| 1869 | New York State legislature passes enabling legislation and establishes indeterminate sentencing. |
| 1870 | American Prison Association endorses expanded use of parole. |
| 1876 | Parole release adopted at Elmira Reformatory, New York. |
| 1931 | Wickersham Commission criticizes laxity in early parole practice. |
| 1944 | Last state passes enabling legislation for parole. |
| 1976 | Maine abolishes parole. |
| 1979 | Colorado abolishes parole release. |
| 1984 | Federal system abolishes parole as an early release mechanism. |
| 1985 | Colorado reinstates parole release. |
| 1996 | Ohio becomes eleventh state to abolish parole. |
| 2004 | An estimated 600,000 inmates will be released from prison. |

Source: Compiled by authors.

A third contributory factor was that the power to pardon was being liberally exercised in a number of states. The effect of liberal pardoning policies was to initiate parole even though it was not yet authorized by law.

These early parole systems were controlled by state legislators that, in general, rigidly defined which prisoners could be paroled. Most legislation authorizing parole release restricted it to first offenders convicted of less serious crimes. Through the passage of time and a gradual acceptance of the idea of discretionary early release, the privilege was eventually extended to serious offenders.

Early parole systems were primarily operated by persons with a direct interest in the administration of prisons. So the decisions on parole release and those who acted as parole officers were institution-based. Eligibility was strictly limited, at the inception of parole, and only gradually expanded to include more serious offenders. Supervision of released inmates was nominal, and the seeds of corruption and maladministration were present.

## Early Public Sentiments

The decade between 1925 and 1935 was a turbulent time, including both the economic boom (and the Prohibition Era) as well as the Great Depression. Crime—particularly as sensationalized in the mass media—appeared to be rampant. As crime rates increased, the public felt more and more that crime was "public enemy number one."[13] This period also saw the rise of attempt by the federal government to stem interstate crimes, particularly kidnapping, bootlegging, bank robbery, and a host of newly enacted legislation that considerably widened the net of crime the government would seek to prevent and prosecute. Two significant events, reflecting public concern about crime,[14] were the establishment of the maximum security federal prison on Alcatraz, and a crusade headed by J. Edgar Hoover, chief of the Federal Bureau of Investigation, against interstate crime. His pronouncements assumed a political nature, as he strongly advocated neoclassical responses to crime: long-term prison sentences, abolition of parole, increased incarceration of offenders, and use of the death penalty, etc.[15]

Both the releasing and supervision functions of parole were sharply and roundly criticized. The major concern of these criticisms was the failure of parole to protect the public safety. The Report of the Advisory Commission on Penal Institutions, Probation and Parole to the Wickersham Commission in the 1931 summarized the problems with parole, stating:

> Parole is defective in three main respects:
>
> 1. In the chasm existing between parole and preceding institutional treatment.
>
> 2. In the manner in which persons are selected for parole.
>
> 3. In the quality of supervision given to persons on parole.

In short, parole was seen as failing to be effective in attaining the promised and lofty goals. The primary arguments were that convicted criminals were being set loose on society, inadequately supervised, and unreformed. The concept of parole and the general ideology of reform were not yet under attack; it was the means and not the ends that were being criticized.

The decade of the 1930s saw the publication of two documents concerning parole, the 1931 Wickersham Commission Report, noted above, and, in 1939, the Attorney General's Survey of Release Procedures (Hawkins, 1971:47). As with the reports of Wines and Dwight and the International Prison Congress of more than 50 years earlier, the 1931 and 1939 documents pointed to flaws in the operation of American corrections and advocated reforms to improve both prisons and parole services.[16]

Simultaneously, the correctional medical model was on the rise. This criminogenic approach was based on a belief that human beings are basically moral, and that crime is deviation from humankind's basic behavior inclinations. Unlike the earlier views that humans were, at heart, bestial, but restrained their primitive drives because reason informed them that by doing so they would be safe, the idea that humans are basically good led to the inevitable conclusion that there must be something fundamentally wrong with those who were bad. The job of corrections should then be to diagnose the problems, prepare and administer the treatment programs, and make offenders well again. Offenders committed crimes when social, personal, or psychological forces and factors overwhelmed them. Hence, the instillation of new habits, the threat of deterrent sanctions, and the giving of religious instruction dealt only with the symptoms of a deeper disorder. The real causes of crime remained deep within the personality structure of the offender. If the prisons were to be hospitals, the parole board was to release the patient when "well," that is, when able to deal with all phases of everyday life. This development had significant implications for parole.

---

Box 5.7

### Parole

Release of an inmate from confinement to expiration of sentence on condition of good behavior and supervision in the community. This is also referred to as post-incarceration supervision, or in the case of juveniles, aftercare.

---

Between the adoption of parole release in Elmira in 1876 and the enactment of enabling legislation for parole in Mississippi in 1944, the concept of parole faced two critical challenges. The first involved the issue of legality of executive control over sentencing and indeterminate sentences. The second centered on the administration of parole systems. Toward the end of the first quarter of the twentieth century, a new behavioral technology came into its own and grew to be a predominant goal of corrections and sentencing. The rehabilitative ideal gave new legitimacy to parole, endorsing discretion.

## Legal Challenges to Parole

The basic legal challenge raised against parole was that the placing of control over sentence length and criminal penalties in the hands of a parole board was unconstitutional. The specific arguments varied across individual lawsuits, but they were basically of two types. First, the questions of infringement on the principle of the separation of powers clauses of the federal and state constitutions were raised in several states (Lindsey, 1925:40-52).

These suits claimed that parole release was an impairment of judicial sentencing power, an improper delegation of legislative authority to set penalties, and usurpation of the executive branch's power of clemency (Hawkins, 1971:47). For the most part, parole authorities emerged victorious from these court battles, and those constitutional questions of parole were laid to rest.

A further rationale behind challenges to the constitutionality of parole release were based on the Eighth Amendment prohibition against cruel and unusual punishment. Although the issue was weighty, most criminal penalties were limited by legislatively set maximum terms. The most common judicial response to these arguments was that indeterminate sentences could be interpreted as sentences that would not extend the maximum terms as set by the legislature or judge, thereby rendering moot the issue of cruelty by virtue of uncertainty (Hawkins, 1971:49).

---

Box 5.8

### Eighth Amendment

Excessive bail shall not be required, nor excessive fines imposed, nor cruel and unusual punishment inflicted.

---

## Administrative Challenges

We have seen that, in the late nineteenth and early twentieth centuries, parole practices were criticized for failing to protect the public. The basic arguments were that parole authorities were not following procedures that would lead to the release of only deserving inmates, and that the lack of subsequent parole supervision placed the community in danger. Such were the complaints reflected by the Wickersham Commission and the Attorney General's Survey. These were not the only critical voices.[17]

One salient argument, supported by ample evidence, was that parole had become a commonplace method of reducing prison populations. In several states, most inmates were released immediately upon expiration of their minimum terms. Only those inmates whose conduct records within prison showed a failure to conform were held longer. The problem was defined as inadequate or improper release decisionmaking.

Blanket release policies were felt to be inappropriate for several reasons. First, because parole boards failed to consider risk, and parole supervision was inadequate, such wholesale release practices were felt to endanger public safety. Second, because most parole boards were dominated by prison officials, it was believed that too much weight was attached to prison conduct and the needs of the prison administration. Finally, failure to consider reformation efforts of the inmate, or the prison, worked to hamper the success of prisons in reforming criminals.

Proposed solutions were varied and involved beefing-up parole supervision staffs and increasing post-release surveillance of parolees. It was believed that these actions could enhance public protection. Additionally, there were calls for professional parole boards comprised of trained, salaried, full-time decisionmakers who would be removed from the pressures of day-to-day prison administration and its needs, and were skilled in identifying those inmates who were reformed.

These proposals arose at about the same time behavioral sciences expanded into the world of public policy. Psychology and sociology were beginning to develop practical components in addition to their traditional theoretical bases. The new professions of clinical psychologist, social worker, and criminologist were developing. An ability to predict, change, and control undesirable human behavior was promised.[18] Corrections and parole seemed ideal places in which these professions could have their most positive impact. The dawn of the rehabilitative model was at hand, and this model caused radical changes in the practice and organization of the American parole system, as we shall see.

## Granting Parole

As was noted above, parole was originally implemented as a method of releasing reformed inmates at the ideal time. The primary focus of parole was the rehabilitation and eventual reintegration of the offender to society, although it also functioned to incapacitate violent and dangerous offenders whose probability of reoffending was believed to be unacceptably high. Parole also serves as a decompression period that helps the offender make the adjustment between the institution and the outside world. As such, parole is an integral component of reentry process. Figure 5.2 shows how the percentage of prisoners released on parole has declined over the past 65 years. Despite the decline in the percentage released on parole, the actual number of parolee has increased. See Figure 5.3.

Figure 5.2
**Percentage of U.S. Prisoners Released on Parole: 1940-2005**

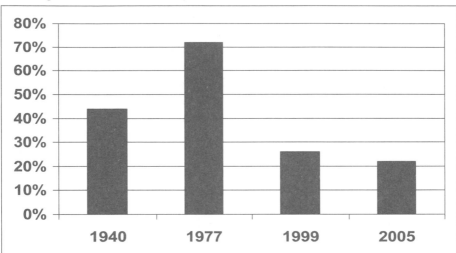

Source: Bottomly, K. (1990). "Parole in Transition: A Comparative Study of Origins, Developments, and Prospects for the 1990s." In M. Tonry and N. Morris (eds.), *Crime and Justice: Review of Research*. Chicago, IL: University of Chicago Press, pp. 319-374; and Glaze, L. and T. Bonczar (2006). *Probation and Parole in the United States, 2005*. Bureau of Justice Statistics.

Figure 5.3
**Parolees in America: 1985-2005**

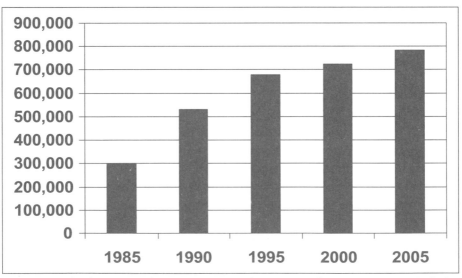

Source: Sourcebook on Criminal Justice Statistics, and GLaze, L. and T. Bonczar (2006). *Probation and Parole in the United States, 2005*. Bureau of Justice Statistics.

# Overview of the Parole Process

The parole process begins in the courtroom when the judge sentences an individual to a prison determinate or indeterminate sentence. The latter includes fixing a term by stating the minimum and maximum length of time the individual is to serve. At the expiration of a certain portion of that sentence, less credit granted for good behavior and performance of duties, an individual becomes eligible for parole. The amount of the sentence that must be served and the amount of credit that can be given for good behavior and performance of duties vary from state to state. In Nebraska, an individual sentenced to a three- to five-year term can become eligible for parole at the end of two years and five months if they have behaved "properly" within the institution.[19] This does not mean that a release will actually occur; it only means that the individual is eligible to be released. There are a number of states that have mandatory parole release statutes that state that at the expiration of a certain portion of the sentence, inmates must be released onto parole, unless the inmate chooses not to be released. A small number of inmates refuse to be released onto parole because they do not want to be subject to a parole officer's supervision and consequently they choose to serve their entire prison sentence ("max out").

Regardless of whether these individuals wish to max out or receive parole, institutional officers compile information concerning their personal characteristics and backgrounds. Treatment progress is continually updated and, at some point in time, the staff begins working with offender's friends, family, and employers to develop a release plan.

The information, along with the presentence and institutional progress reports, is periodically brought to the attention of the releasing authority, usually a parole board. Some states review inmates' progress on a yearly basis, even though they are not eligible for release. In accordance with the eligibility guidelines and an interview with the offender, the parole board decides whether to release the offender on parole. If the decision is to deny release, a future rehearing date is usually set. If a release is to be effected, the parole board then determines when and where the release is to be made. A contract, usually including very specific conditions of parole, is also established. Once a release has been achieved, inmates (now called parolees) come under the supervision of parole officers.

Box 5.9

## Good Time Credits

Statutes in almost every state allow for the reduction of a prison term based on an offender's behavior in prison ("good time"), or for participation and completion of certain educational or treatment programs ("program time"). Reduction in time is awarded; such awards reduce the date to the parole board or minimum sentence, and maximum time to be served.

Good time credits are earned by a formula established within correctional settings, sometimes set into law but usually decided by institutional administrators in collaboration with the parole board. In California, the award is four months for each eight months served (four for 8, or 1:2). If an offender is serving a three-year sentence (36 months) and earns maximum good time, that offender will be in prison no more than 24 months.

Some jurisdictions award time for pretrial detention and post-conviction jail time while awaiting transport to prison. There are thousands of jail inmates who have been sentenced to prison but are being held back pending availability of prison space and transport to prison. These inmates generally earn "jail credits" at a 1:1 ratio, and will bring those credits to the parole board, further reducing the maximum time they will serve as prison inmates.

Finally, to encourage participation in institutional work and rehabilitation programs, credits may be awarded for participation in and completion of specific programs: welding, masonry, car repair, GED, drug treatment, etc. The awards across jurisdictions vary, but usually approximate the "good time credit" ratio.

Thus an inmate sentenced to three years in prison but detained four months on a pretrial basis and held four months in jail after sentencing before being transported to prison would bring eight months of jail time credit and would generally receive an additional four months for good time, the equivalent of serving one year against the term of punishment. If the offender participates in and graduates from a drug treatment program within the first 12 months, that offender will usually serve less than 16 months before being released as having served the maximum sentence ("max out"): 36 months.

---

Box 5.10

### Discretionary and Mandatory Release

Discretionary release is parole of an inmate from prison prior to the expiration of maximum sentence, according to the boundaries set by the legislature and sentence. Discretionary release is associated with the indeterminate sentence and implies that the offender is ready for release and continued treatment within the community.

Mandatory release is the *required* release of the offender by the parole board because the statutes mandate release of any inmate who has served the equivalent of the maximum sentence. Mandatory release implies that the parole board refused to release an inmate prior to attainment of maximum sentence imposed by the court. Mandatory release means the time served behind prison walls, when added to time credits for jail time, good time and earned time, total the sentence imposed by the sentencing court. About four in ten inmates leave prison under mandatory release.

---

## Current Operations

Parole is a complex procedure and has many functions and processes that differ from one jurisdiction to another. Traditionally, parole includes five basic functions:

1. Selecting and placing prisoners on parole;

2. Establishing conditions of supervision (frequently case-specific);

3. Aiding, supervising, assisting, and controlling parolees in the community;

4. Returning parolees to prison if the conditions of parole are not met; and

5. Discharging parolees when supervision is no longer necessary or when sentence is completed.

Parole, unlike probation, is an administrative process located within the executive branch of every state, as well as the federal government. This may soon change, however, for a number of states (Arizona, California, Delaware, Florida, Illinois, Indiana, Kansas, Maine, Minnesota, Mississippi, North Carolina, Ohio, Oregon, Virginia, Washington, Wisconsin and the federal prison system, have virtually eliminated the discretionary release power of these parole boards. Connecticut abolished parole in 1981 but reinstated it nine years later, after prison costs surged.[20] Similarly, Colorado abolished parole release in 1979 and reinstated it in 1985. Thirty other jurisdictions have developed various systemwide parole guidelines that have restricted the discretionary powers of the parole boards.[21] The operation of parole, obviously, is not all uniform.[22]

---

**Box 5.11**

### Parole Board Members

Governors appoint parole board members in 45 jurisdictions, usually with the advice and consent of the state legislature. The most frequent term is four years, and most states stagger the terms of office of members, to achieve continuity of parole boards regardless of changes in the governor's mansion or philosophy. Five-, six-, and seven-year terms are found in Alabama, Arizona, Georgia, and so on. Ohio parole board members serve an indefinite term. In Utah, parole board members are appointed by the Board of Corrections and serve six-year terms.

There are no *statutory* qualifications for parole board membership in 29 jurisdictions, but the other 22 jurisdictions have qualifications that speak to length of time and experience in corrections (or such related field as welfare, religion, or law enforcement). Seven jurisdictions set the minimal educational level as at least a bachelor's degree.

---

State parole systems vary widely in terms of their organizational makeup and administrative process.[23] Most parole boards are independent state agencies that only administer parole. Depending on the state, there are anywhere from three to 19 members on a parole board (Camp and Camp, 2003). Only 22 states have any statutory requirements for specific qualifications for parole board members, and even those are usually stated in such broad terms as "possessing good character" or "judicious temperament." In 1967, the President's Commission on Law Enforcement and Administration of Justice recommended that parole board members be appointed solely on the basis of competence, however, in many states appointment to the parole board appears to be based on political considerations. For example, only two states, Wisconsin and Ohio, appoint parole board members from a civil service list. The governor is directly responsible for parole board appointments in 45 states.

## Parole Selection Process

In most jurisdictions, individual cases are assigned to individual members of the parole board. They review each case and make initial recommendations. These recommendations are usually accepted, although occasionally the board as a whole may seek to obtain more details. While there are some jurisdictions that make the final release decision solely on the basis of written reports, most states conduct some type of a formal hearing. The hearing may be with one member of the parole board, the assembled board as a whole (en banc), or handled by a hearing examiner with no members of the board present. Occasionally, prison staff are also interviewed. Some states send the board members and/or hearing examiners to the institutions to conduct the hearings, while others bring those to be interviewed to the board/examiners.

Parole selection guidelines differ widely from state to state. The U.S. Supreme Court has consistently held parole to be a privilege and, consequently, held that a full complement of due process rights do not need to be afforded at parole-granting hearings (Greenholtz v. Inmates of the Nebraska Penal and Correctional Complex, 99 S. Ct. 2100 (1979). As a result, the states have been given the opportunity to establish whatever inmate privileges they feel are appropriate at parole-granting hearings.

Inmates are permitted the use of counsel in 21 states and are allowed to present witnesses in 19 states. The rationale for the parole decision must be formally articulated in 11 parole jurisdictions. Most states have established regulations as to the amount of time an inmate is required to serve prior to parole eligibility. In 16 states, eligibility is obtained upon completion of the minimum sentence. In 10 states, as well as the federal system, eligibility is achieved upon completion of one-third of the maximum sentence. Other states use the number of prior felony convictions and length of prior sentences to calculate eligibility rules. Even in the states that use the same eligibility guidelines, there is such a wide variation in the length of the minimum and maximum prison terms handed down for the same offense that, in reality, there are literally as many variations in eligibility as there are parole jurisdictions.[24] In addition to time factors, some states restrict the use of parole for those convicted of various serious personal offenses, such as first degree murder, kidnapping, aggravated rape,[25] etc.

If an inmate does not meet parole standards, the sentence is continued, and a date set for the next parole review. If parole is approved, the individual is prepared for release to the parole field service authority. Just how long an inmate must wait to hear the verdict varies greatly. The inmate receives word immediately in many jurisdictions. In others, and in those jurisdictions where no hearings are held, inmates are notified by the prison staff or by mail. Receipt by the inmate of formal written notification varies from immediately in several states to as long as three to four weeks in New Jersey.

---

Box 5.12

### Sexually Violent Predators

California enacted a statute in 1996 that seeks to ensure that sexual predators in prison who are suffering from mental disorders and deemed likely to re-offend are treated in a secure facility through civil commitment, and are not prematurely released into society to victimize others.

The Board of Prison Terms screens cases to determine if inmates meet the criteria specified in the statute and then refers inmates to the California Department of Mental Health for clinical evaluations by two clinicians. If both clinicians concur that the inmate meets the criteria, a county district attorney may file a petition for civil commitment.

If the judge determines that probable cause exists, the prisoner is scheduled for a court trial. A jury hears the case and, based on the "beyond a reasonable doubt" test, may determine that the offender meets the statutory criteria. In such cases, the offender is civilly committed to a Department of Mental Health facility for two years of treatment. Annual examinations are conducted; the offender may petition the court for conditional release (parole). At the end of two years, the prisoner is re-evaluated and the court may enter an order for new trial to seek a new commitment of the offender. Since 1996, more than 300 sex offenders have been found to be sexually violent predators and committed to the Department of Mental Health for treatment.

---

The parole-granting hearing is a very significant event for inmates. Regardless of the outcome, the result will greatly affect their lives. They realize that a single inappropriate word or action could jeopardize their freedom for years to come. Yet despite the significance of the decision, the national average is probably between 12 and 15 minutes per case. This means that parole boards are hearing approximately 15 to 20 cases per day. It is difficult to determine exactly how long a parole board deliberates because they operate in relative secrecy. In many cases, parole hearings are at least partially closed, and decision-making criteria are not really known to outsiders. Indeed, a major criticism of the parole process is a reluctance on the part of most parole boards to clearly articulate standards and guidelines for release.

Box 5.13

### Flopped

Flopped is inmate argot for being denied early release by the parole board for failing to meet parole board standards or expectations. When flopped, the inmate is usually given a "next review date" by the board, and his or her case will be heard again at that time. Frequently the board suggests treatments, programs or goals the offender is expected to complete before the next review (learning to read and write, AA involvement, Life Skills, etc.).

## Factors Influencing Parole Decisions

In theory, parole decisions should be based upon the factors outlined in state statutes. In practice, however, it appears that parole boards are influenced by a wide variety of criteria, not all of which are articulated by law. Furthermore, some states do not have any legal guidelines.

In one of the first studies to examine parole board release decision criteria, Scott (1974) studied 325 males and 34 females facing a parole decision in a Midwest state in 1968. He determined that the seriousness of the crime, a high number of prison disciplinary reports, age (older inmates), a low level of education, a marital status of single, and (surprisingly) a good institutional record were factors that lengthened an inmate's sentence. Prior record and race were determined to have no effect upon the parole decision.

However, in his study of 243 inmates in an eastern facility, Carroll (1976) found that race did play a significant role in this determination. A number of factors that were not related to the parole decision for white prisoners were important for blacks. Blacks who participated in treatment programs or were older were more likely to be released. The supposition is that these blacks were perceived as nonmilitant and therefore less likely to cause problems upon release.

As suggested by Dawson (1966) there appear to be three major release criteria that influence parole boards:

1.  Factors for granting parole based upon the probability of recidivism.

2.  Factors for granting parole other than probability of recidivism.

3.  Factors for denying parole other than probability of recidivism.

## Probability of Recidivism

Perhaps the most basic aspect of the decision-making process is estimating the probability that an individual will violate the law if and when released on parole.[27] This is known as the recidivism factor. Parole boards, as quasipolitical entities, are extremely sensitive to the public criticism that may arise when parolees violate parole, especially if they commit a serious offense. Just how parole boards determine the probability of recidivism is unclear. As early as 1923, Hart (1923) advocated the need to develop methodologically sound prediction tables for potential parolees that were based upon data. Since this observation, many such scales and tables have been developed (Burgess, 1928, Babst, Inciardi & Jarman, 1970; Bromley & Gathercole, 1969; Gottfredson, Babst & Ballard, 1958; Glaser, 1962; Wilkins & MacNaughton-Smith, 1964; Gottfredson & Gottfredson, 1993; Loza & Loza, 2000). For more than 50 years, the value of prediction devices has been recognized as a means of standardizing parole release and more accurately assessing recidivism probability. At least one-half of all parole boards use formal risk assessment (Burke, 1997).[28]

## Factors for Granting Parole Other Than Probability of Recidivism

There are occasions when inmates are granted parole despite the parole board's belief that they possess a relatively high probability of recidivism. In instances when offenders are believed not likely to commit a crime of a serious nature, the parole board may vote to grant parole. This factor is often accompanied by a determination that the inmate will gain little additional benefit from further institutionalization. For example, although an inmate may be an alcoholic with a long record of public intoxication arrests, the parole board may grant a release because it feels that the individual is relatively harmless, and that continued institutionalization will very likely have little further impact upon the alcoholism problem. Compassionate release of inmates dying of cancer and AIDS also fall under this category (Pagliaro & Pagliaro, 1992).[29]

Occasionally, situations arise when inmates have but only a short period of time to serve before the completion of their sentences. When such circumstances arise, parole boards frequently parole these individuals, despite what may be a high perceived probability of recidivism, in order to provide even a brief period of supervisory control and, more importantly, to assist the parolee in the environmental decompression and social reintegration process.

An additional criterion that may swing a parole board, despite an apparent high recidivism probability, is the length of time served. If an inmate has failed to respond to institutional treatment but has served a relatively long sentence, the parole board may grant parole under the conviction that these individuals have paid their dues, and that perhaps they will succeed on parole to avoid being sent back. Occasionally, the maturation process will play an important role. When lengthy sentences are mandated for young persons, the parole board may affect an early release, noting the general process of maturation that will enable these individuals to adopt more acceptable patterns of behavior once released.

## Factors for Denying Parole Other Than Probability of Recidivism

There are circumstances when individuals may not be granted a release despite a relatively low recidivism probability. For example, when inmates have demonstrated occasional outbursts of violent and assaultive behavior, parole boards tend to be somewhat reluctant to grant release. As previously noted, parole boards are extremely sensitive to public criticism, and while the probability of a violent attack may be very small, the seriousness of the incident would likely attract considerable media attention. Consequently, release in such a situation will often be denied. Community attitudes and values often play major roles in overriding the recidivism probability factors. For example, murderers have traditionally been good parole risks in terms of likelihood of parole success. However, whether and how quickly they should be paroled is often a function of community attitudes. If a community attitude is unfavorable, parole is likely to be denied, for the release of such an inmate might expose the parole board to bitter public criticism, and most parole boards prefer to keep an inmate in prison rather than incur the public's anger.

There are also occasions when parole is used as a tool to support and maintain institutional discipline. Individuals may possess very high potential for success on parole, but continually violate institutional rules and regulations. In these situations, parole will frequently be denied. Occasionally, an inmate with a drug abuse problem may be counseled by the parole board to enroll in an existing drug-dependency program, sending a clear message to the inmate population that such rehabilitation programs are appropriate and functional for release. In this way, parole can be viewed as an incentive for good behavior and a sanction against inappropriate conduct. There are even situations when parole may be denied so as to benefit the inmate. Circumstances occasionally arise when inmates are making rapid progress in academic pursuits, or may be receiving and responding to necessary medical and/or psychological treatment. The parole board may temporarily postpone such a case for a few months to give these individuals the opportunity to complete their high school work, for example, or recover from medical treatment they are undergoing.

---

**Box 5.14**

### Parole Board Functions

The most visible function of a parole board is the discretionary release of an inmate from confinement prior to the expiration of sentence, on condition of good behavior in the community. This is commonly known as the parole release decision. But parole boards have extensive authority to undertake a variety of other functions seldom acknowledged in the justice area.

**Setting Policy.** The parole board enunciates and refines broad policy governing specific areas of parole, such as directives to community supervision officers on offenders whose drug tests show illicit drug use. Some policies require the officer to hold a revocation hearing under *Morrissey v. Brewer*; other jurisdictions may only suggest that officers tighten up the conditions of parole ('motivational' jail time, house arrest, or NA). When parole boards establish a "zero-tolerance" policy, a large portion of drug-abusing parolees may be returned to prison.

**Modification of Presumed Release Date.** If an offender is given a presumed release date, it usually is based on conformity to institutional rules. When inmates persistently violate those, a decision may be made to delay release ("extend the time") based on institutional behavior. In effect, the parole board reinforces control of prison inmates and encourages participation in institutional programs.

**Commutation of Sentence.** Inmates serving life sentences or double-life or life-plus-a-day or minimum sentences of several hundred years have few hopes of ever leaving the facility alive. It is possible, however, to petition the executive branch for commutation, a reduction in sentence length. A parole board, whose recommendation for commutation is seriously considered by the Governor, usually hears the initial plea. "Lifers" who receive commutations usually leave the penal institution shortly thereafter.

**Revocation from Parole.** If a supervising officer requests a hearing for revocation of parole under *Morrissey* and the hearing officer finds reasonable cause, the case will be heard by the parole board (or its authorized designee), and the offender's grant of parole maybe revoked. The offender is then returned to prison to serve additional time.

> ┌─ Box 5.14, *continued* ─────────────────────────────┐
>
> **Pardon.** Only the executive branch may grant a pardon, absolving the offender in part or full from the legal consequences of the crime and conviction. Governors usually receive such petitions after they have been considered by the parole board, generally authorized to advise the Governor on these matters.
>
> **Reprieve.** A reprieve is a stay in imposition of sentence, typically associated with death row inmates nearing their execution date. Parole boards, sometimes in conjunction with the Governor's Cabinet, may recommend reprieve to a Governor.
>
> **Incapacitation.** Some offenders have demonstrated a pattern of violent and dangerous criminal behavior that continues unabated in prison. By denying parole and thus forcing such inmates to serve longer prison sentences, parole boards protect the public through disabling future violent crime. This function is seldom recognized.

Finally, there are situations when the parole board may feel that individuals are good risks but ineligible for release because they have not served the minimum terms as fixed by the sentencing judge. Some have expressed a concern over the fact that the courts occasionally err in handing down sanctions more severe than are necessary. Correctional officials, after more careful observation and evaluation than the courts could originally consider, may clearly document greater progress than the court expected. Nevertheless, as previously noted, state parole statutes may mandate a minimum time to be served (calculated as a percentage of the minimum or maximum sentence) that even the parole board cannot ignore. Such inmates may be released, however, under work furlough programs.

## Parole Board Release Decisions

All persons who are eligible for parole are not automatically granted a release. Occasionally, parole boards will not release individuals who could be safely released. This is partially a desire by parole boards to minimize the number of persons who are classified as good risks and released, but whom the board feel are, in reality, bad risks and expected to fail on parole. Failed parole is a problem the boards seek to minimize (Wiggins, 1984).

Our ability to predict future recidivism has improved over the years, however, it is not without its critics (Smykla, 1984; Monahan, 1981;

Gottfredson & Gottfredson, 1994). Furthermore, our ability to predict future violent behavior is limited, and as a result, there is a general tendency to overpredict dangerousness, and this results in more persons being classified as bad risks,[30] fewer persons being granted parole, and an increase in prison populations (Monahan, 1981). Although such tendencies have come under intense criticism, overprediction of dangerousness continues (Morris, 1974; Smykla, 1984). This is probably due to the perception that overprediction is viewed as having smaller short-term costs. In the short-run, it may be cheaper to incarcerate larger numbers of offenders than to permit a few dangerous persons to roam the streets and commit crimes. Such an approach is quite costly in the long-run, however, as more and more persons are housed and cared for within the prison system. Furthermore, there are indications that after the extended prison sentences are served, some former inmates will commit more serious crimes more frequently than they would have prior to their incarceration.

While the courts have ruled that parole cannot be denied on the basis of race, religion, or national origin,[31] they have really not become involved in parole board policies and practices. This is due in large part to the fact that the Supreme Court has defined parole as a privilege rather than a right (Greenholz, 1979). Consequently, there is no constitutional mandate that there even be any formal parole release guidelines, no right to obtain access to institutional files, and no right to counsel at the hearing. Indeed, there is no constitutional requirement that there even be a formal hearing. The state is under no constitutional obligation to articulate the reason for denial of parole and there is no right of appeal, except as given by an individual state.

Most states have adopted laws and/or administrative policies that outline parole procedures. Some allow inmates access to their files and permit the presence of legal counsel. As of 1977, the U.S. Parole Commission[32] and 23 states offered inmates the opportunity to internally appeal parole release hearing decisions (O'Leary & Hanrahan, 1977:42-47). Up to this point, however, the courts have continued to refuse to become involved in any type of review of a negative parole board decision.

## Conditions of Parole

Parole is in essence a contract between the state and the offender. If the offender is able to abide by the terms of the contract, freedom is maintained. If a violation of these conditions occurs, or if a parolee is charged with a new crime, the parole board may revoke parole and return the offender to prison. The offender must abide by the contract, and stay under parole supervision for the period of time outlined by the parole board. While every state has its own policies and procedures, parole usually lasts more than two but less than seven years. Some states in fact permit discharge from parole after a very short time, as long as the offender has diligently adhered to the pre-release contract. While the exact content of the contracts varies from state to state and from individual to individual, the following federal guidelines[33] cover the majority of the conditions that are usually adopted:

- You shall go directly to the district showing on this CERTIFICATE OF PAROLE (unless released to the custody of other authorities). Within three days after your arrival you shall report to your parole advisor if you have one, and to the United States Probation Officer whose name appears on this certificate. If in an emergency you are unable to get in touch with your parole advisor, or your probation officer or his office, you shall communicate with the [United States Parole Commission, 5550 Friendship Blvd., Suite 420, Chevy Chase, MD 20815-7286].

- If you are released to the custody of other authorities, and after your release from physical custody of such authorities, you are unable to report the United States Probation Officer to whom you are assigned within three days, you shall report instead to the nearest United States Probation Officer.

- You shall not leave the limits of this CERTIFICATE OF PAROLE without written permission from the probation officer.

- You shall notify your probation officer immediately of any change in your place of residence.

- You shall make a complete and truthful written report (on a form provided for that purpose) to your probation officer between the first and third day of each month, and on the final day of parole. You shall also report to your probation officer at other times as he directs.

- You shall not violate any law. Nor shall you associate with persons engaged in criminal activity. You shall get in touch immediately with your probation officer or his office if you are arrested or questioned by a law enforcement officer.

- You shall not enter into any agreement to act as an "informer" or special agent for any law-enforcement agency.

- You shall work regularly, unless excused by your probation officer, and support your legal dependents, if any, to the best of your ability. You shall report immediately to your probation officer any change in employment.

Figure 5.4
**Oregon Parole Board Conditions of Parole**

---

<u>GENERAL/SPECIAL PAROLE AND POST-PRISON SUPERVISION CONDITIONS</u>

Parole/Post-Prison Supervision is subject to all listed General Conditions and the designated Special Conditions. Prior to release the Board may modify the conditions at any time. After parole/post-prison supervision has commenced, conditions may be added upon your signed consent or after opportunity to be heard, orally or in writing.

Parole may be revoked for violation of any of these conditions and/or you may be returned when parole is not in your best interest or the best interest of society.

The Board may, at its discretion, sanction violations of Post-Prison Supervision Conditions; sanctions may include returning you to the Department of Corrections custody.

As used in this exhibit, the following words have the following meanings: "Offender" means persons released to parole or post-prison supervision. "Parole Officer" shall also mean the supervisory authority under the post-prison supervision system.

<u>GENERAL CONDITIONS</u>

1.  Pay supervision fees, fines, restitution, or other fees ordered by the Board.

2.  Not use or possess controlled substances except pursuant to a medical prescription.

3.  Submit to testing of breath or urine for controlled substance or alcohol use if the offender has a history of substance abuse or if there is a reasonable suspicion that the offender has illegally used controlled substances.

4.  Participate in a substance abuse evaluation as directed by the supervising officer and follow the recommendations of the evaluator if there are reasonable grounds to believe there is a history of substance abuse.

5.  Remain in the State of Oregon until written permission to leave is granted by the Department of Corrections or a county community corrections agency.

6.  If physically able, find and maintain gainful full-time employment, approved schooling, or a full-time combination of both. [Any waiver of this requirement must be based on a finding by the court stating the reasons for the waiver.]

7.  Change neither employment nor residence without prior permission from the Department of Corrections or a county community corrections agency.

8.  Permit the supervising officer to visit the offender or the offender's residence or work site, and report as required and abide by the direction of the supervising officer.

9.  Consent to the search of person, vehicle, or premises upon the (required) *request* of a representative of the supervising officer if the supervising officer has reasonable grounds to believe that evidence of a violation will be found, and submit to fingerprinting or photographing, or both, when requested by the Department of Corrections or a county community corrections agency for supervision purposes.

Figure 5.4—*continued*

10.  Obey all laws, municipal, county, state, and federal.

11.  Promptly and truthfully answer all reasonable inquiries by the Department of Corrections or a county community corrections agency.

12.  Not possess weapons, firearms, or dangerous animals.

<u>SPECIAL CONDITIONS</u>

1.  Offender shall be evaluated by a mental health evaluator and follow all treatment recommendations.

2.  Offender shall follow a psychiatric or psychotropic medication monitoring program with a physician per the physician's instructions.

3.  Offender shall have no contact with minor females and shall not frequent any place where minors are likely to congregate (e.g., playgrounds, school grounds, arcades) without prior written approval from their supervising officer.

4.  Offender shall have no contact with minor males and shall not frequent any place where minors are likely to congregate (e.g., playgrounds, school grounds, arcades) without prior written approval from their supervising officer.

5.  Offender shall submit to random polygraph tests as part of a sex offender surveillance program. Failure to submit to the tests may result in return to Department of Corrections custody. Specific responses to the tests shall not be the basis for return to Department of Corrections custody.

6.  Offender shall enter and complete or be successfully discharged from a recognized and approved sex offender treatment program which may include polygraph and/or plethysmograph testing and a prohibition on possession of printed, photographed, or recorded materials that the offender may use for the purpose of deviant sexual arousal.

7.  Offender shall pay court-ordered restitution to the clerk of the court of the county of sentencing (ORS 137.106, OAR 255-65-005).

8.  When criteria applies, the Department of Corrections may notify the community of the sex offender's status pursuant to ORS 181.507-509, OAR 291-28-010 to 291-28-030.

9.  Offender shall not use intoxicating beverages.

10.  Other: Special conditions may be imposed that are not listed above when the Board of Parole and Post-Prison Supervision determines that such conditions are necessary.

11.  Offender shall have no contact with those listed below:

The authors are indebted to Lawrence Travis for providing this document.

- You shall not drink alcoholic beverages to excess. You shall not purchase, possess, use, or administer marijuana or narcotics or other habit forming or dangerous drugs, unless prescribed or advised by a physician. You shall not frequent places where such drugs are illegally sold, dispensed, used, or given away.

- You shall not associate with persons who have a criminal record unless you have permission of your probation officer.

- You shall not have firearms (or other dangerous weapons) in your possession without the written permission of your probation officer, following prior approval of the United States Board of Parole.

- You shall, if ordered by the Board pursuant to Section 4203, Title 18, U.S.C., as amended October 1970, reside in and/or participate in a treatment program of a Community Treatment Center operated by the Bureau of Prisons, for a period not to exceed 120 days.

The U.S. Parole Commission's authority and reach is rapidly declining.[34]

## Parole Revocation

In 1972, the U.S. Supreme Court established procedures for parole revocation with the case of *Morrissey v. Brewer*, 408 U.S. 471 (1972). In this case, the Supreme Court said that once parole is granted, it is no longer just a privilege but a right. Consequently, the Court ruled that parolees should be granted certain due process rights in any parole revocation proceeding. While the Court did not grant a full array of due process rights in *Morrissey*, it did advance the mandate of fundamental fairness. The Court required the following minimum due process rights in the event of a parole revocation proceeding.

- Parolee given advanced written notification of the inquiry, its purpose, and alleged violation.

- A disclosure to the parolee of the evidence against him or her.

- The opportunity to be heard in person and present witnesses and documentary evidence.

- The right to confront and cross-examine adverse witnesses.

- A neutral and detached hearing body.

- A written statement by the hearing body as to the evidence relied upon and reasons for revoking parole.

The *Morrissey* case also established a dual state procedure, including a preliminary inquiry at the time of the alleged parole violations as well as a formal revocation hearing. Left unanswered, however, was the right to counsel, and whether or not the Exclusionary Rule should apply to revocation cases. One year later, in the case *Gagnon v. Scarpelli*, 411 U.S. 778 (1971), the Court held that parolees do have a limited right to counsel in revocation proceedings and that the hearing body must determine, on a case-by-case basis, whether counsel should be afforded. While it need not be granted in all cases, ". . . Counsel should be provided where, after being informed of his right, the . . . parolee requests counsel, based on a timely and colorable claim that he had not committed the alleged violation or, if the violation is a matter of public record or uncontested, there are substantial reasons in justification or mitigation that make revocation inappropriate."

The Exclusionary Rule issue remains unanswered. While illegally seized evidence cannot be used in a criminal trial, many states do permit such evidence to be used in parole revocation cases, where the standard is "probable cause." To date, the courts have generally upheld this practice.

## Problems with Parole Board Discretionary Power

Beginning in the 1970s, dramatic shifts began in the field of corrections. Dissatisfied with high recidivism rates, many states opted to amend the traditional indeterminate sentencing model and adopt some of the aspects of a determinate or fixed sentencing model (see Table 5.3). The use of the indeterminate sentence in the United States represented a grand experiment in controlling if not eliminating criminal behavior. Indeterminate sentencing, in which the judge sets limits within legislatively determined minimum and maximum sentences (e.g., one to seven years for burglary), would focus upon the individual criminal and his or her needs, rather than establishing a fixed penalty for certain types of crime. It sought to maximize the possibility of criminal rehabilitation through the use of various educational, vocational, and psychological treatment programs in the institution, and the use of parole board that would release the inmate on parole at the optimum moment when change had occurred.

Through this "medical model of corrections," it was argued that such parole board decisionmaking would offer several benefits:

- It would provide an incentive for rehabilitation by linking it to release from prison.

- This incentive would also apply as a mechanism to control the prison population, ensuring inmate discipline and safety.

Table 5.3
**Sentencing Models by State**

| State | Type of Sentencing | Mandatory Sentencing | Mandatory Offenses |
|---|---|---|---|
| Alabama | Determinate | Yes | Repeat felony |
| Alaska | Determinate, presumptive | Yes | Murder, kidnapping, firearms, repeat felony |
| Arizona | Determinate, presumptive | Yes | Firearms, prior felony convictions |
| Arkansas | Determinate | Yes | Robbery, deadly weapons |
| California | Determinate, presumptive | No | |
| Colorado | Determinate, presumptive | No | |
| Connecticut | Determinate | Yes | Sex assault with firearm, burglary, repeat felony, assault on elderly |
| Delaware | Determinate | Yes | Murder, kidnapping, prison assault, robbery, narcotics, deadly weapons, habitual criminal, obscenity, others |
| Florida | Indeterminate | Yes | Drugs |
| Georgia | Determinate | Yes | Armed robbery, burglary, drugs |
| Hawaii | Indeterminate | No | |
| Idaho | Determinate | Yes | Firearms, repeat extortion, kidnap or rape with bodily injury |
| Illinois | Determinate | Yes | Major offenses, specified felonies and offenses, repeaters, weapons |
| Indiana | Determinate, presumptive | Yes | Repeat felony, violent crime, deadly weapons |
| Iowa | Indeterminate | Yes | Forcible felonies, firearms, habitual offenders, drugs |
| Kansas | Indeterminate | Yes | Sex offense, firearms |
| Kentucky | Indeterminate | No | |
| Louisiana | Indeterminate | Yes | Drugs, violent crime |
| Maine | Determinate | No | |
| Maryland | Determinate, guidelines | Yes | Repeat violent offenders, handgun |
| Massachusetts | Indeterminate | Yes | Firearms, auto theft, drug trafficking |
| Michigan | Indeterminate | Yes | Murder, armed robbery, treason, firearms |
| Minnesota | Guidelines | No | |
| Mississippi | Determinate | Yes | Armed robbery, repeat felony |
| Missouri | Determinate | Yes | Dangerous weapons, repeat felony |
| Montana | Indeterminate | Yes | Firearms |

Table 5.3—*continued*

| State | Type of Sentencing | Mandatory Sentencing | Mandatory Offenses |
|---|---|---|---|
| Nebraska | Indeterminate | No | |
| Nevada | Determinate | Yes | 2nd degree murder, 1st degree kidnapping, sexual assault, firearms, repeat felony |
| New Hampshire | Indeterminate | Yes | Firearms |
| New Jersey | Determinate, presumptive | Yes | Sexual assault, firearms |
| New Mexico | Determinate, presumptive | Yes | Firearms |
| New York | Indeterminate | Yes | Specified violent and nonviolent felonies |
| North Carolina | Determinate, presumptive | Yes | Armed robbery, 1st degree burglary, repeat felony with firearm |
| North Dakota | Determinate | Yes | Firearms |
| Ohio | Determinate | Yes | Rape, drug trafficking, firearms |
| Oklahoma | Determinate | No | Repeat felony |
| Oregon | Indeterminate, guidelines | Yes | Drugs |
| Pennsylvania* | Indeterminate, guidelines | Yes | Selected felonies with firearms, within 7 years of prior convictions, in or near public transportation |
| Rhode Island | Indeterminate | No | |
| South Carolina | Determinate | Yes | Armed robbery, drugs, bomb threat |
| South Dakota | Indeterminate | No | |
| Tennessee | Determinate, indeterminate | Yes | Specified felonies, firearms, repeat felony |
| Texas | Determinate | Yes | Repeat felony, violent offenses |
| Utah | Indeterminate | No | |
| Vermont | Indeterminate | Yes | Drugs, violent crime |
| Virginia | Determinate | No | |
| Washington | Indeterminate | Yes | Firearms, rape, repeat felony |
| West Virginia | Indeterminate | Yes | Firearms in felony |
| Wisconsin | Indeterminate | No | |
| Wyoming | Indeterminate | No | |

*Pennsylvania updated as of December 1982.

Sources: Richard S. Morelli, Craig Edelman, and Roy Willoughby (September, 1981). "A Survey of Mandatory Sentencing in the U.S." Pennsylvania Commission on Crime and Delinquency; Criminal Courts Technical Assistance Project (January, 1982). "Judicial and Executive Discretion in the Sentencing Process: Analysis of Felony State Code Provisions." Washington, DC: American University; Michael Kanvensohn (December, 1979). "A National Survey of Parole-Related Legislation." San Francisco, CA: Uniform Parole Reports.

- Another latent function of parole would be to provide a mechanism to control the size of the prison population.

- Similarly, the parole board would share the responsibility for societal protection with the judiciary through its control over prison release procedures. The board could also serve as a check and balance to judicial discretion by reducing sentencing disparities (such that inmates who committed the same crime would serve approximately the same amount of actual time in prison).

However, a number of factors combined to question the efficacy and fairness of medical model. Penologists, such as Martinson (1974) and MacNamara (1977), reviewing the outcome of research reports on correctional rehabilitation programs, concluded that the medical model failed to cure criminals, reduce recidivism, or protect the public.[35] Others (Morris, 1974) argued that the medical model harmed the inmates because the program participation was tied to, and dependent upon such participation. From the inmates' point of view, the decisions of the board were arbitrary, capricious, prejudicial, unpredictable, and not subject to external review by any other governmental body (Irwin, 1977). In fact, a number of studies (see Goodstein, 1980) have indicated that inmate frustration over failure to obtain release on parole is a factor that contributes to prison violence (Hassine, 2004).

## Parole Board Decision-Making Guidelines

Concerns over some of these issues led a number of jurisdictions, including the Federal Parole System, to adopt parole release guidelines. The U.S. Parole Commission developed its system of parole decision-making guidelines in 1974. The major complaint against parole board decisionmaking has been, and remains, the great amount of discretionary power. The parole decision-making guidelines propose to structure this discretionary power to promote equity and fairness,[36] and also to reduce sentencing disparity. The task was to make the decisions of the parole board less arbitrary and more explicit.

These guidelines usually involve a consideration of the seriousness of the commitment offense and a "risk" score that includes factors predictive of failure or success on parole. Recommended terms of incarceration are predetermined. For example, if the offender is rated as a "good" risk level, and has committed a less serious offense his or her recommended term of incarceration might fall between 6-9 months. Conversely, an offender rated as "high risk" and convicted of a more serious offense might serve a much longer term prior to consideration for parole.

---
Box 5.15
---

### Presumptive Sentencing

One alternative to limiting sentencing disparity is the presumptive sentencing system, a variation of the determinate sentence. In presumptive sentencing, the state legislature sets minimum, average, and maximum terms, allowing the judge to select a term based on the characteristics of the offender and any aggravating or mitigating circumstances proven in court. The sentence imposed will be the time served, less any credits against that sentence that the offender earns (jail time, good time, and program time). California has a presumptive sentencing structure that provides three options to the sentencing judge, as seen here for the crime of burglary.

1. aggravating circumstances: seven years

2. presumptive (average) sentence: five years

3. mitigating circumstances: three years

Ordinarily, the judge would decide if the offender should be placed on probation or imprisoned (the "in-out" decision). Assuming imprisonment to be the answer, the judge would impose the average or presumed term of five years, unless mitigating circumstances were present at the time of the offense (such as the offender being under the influence of a controlled substance at the time of the offense, or had a weak personality and was easily led into committing crime for peer approval, etc.). If mitigating circumstances were proven, the judge would impose the least sentence (three years). On the other hand, if aggravating circumstances were proven in court, the judge must impose the highest sentence (seven years). Examples of aggravating circumstances are gross bodily harm to the victim, prior incarceration in prison, victim extremely vulnerable (blind, frail, paraplegic, over 60 years of age, and so on).

In this fashion, the guidelines system attempts to structure the discretionary power of the parole board while at the same time maintaining equity and fairness (Hoffman, 1983).

Board examiners are also permitted to deviate from the guidelines. The examiners can shorten or lengthen the amount of time specified by the guidelines when, in their judgment, the case at hand appears to merit such consideration. However, when such a step is taken, the examiner is usually required to state the specific factors present that led to such a judgment.

Research indicates that guidelines appear to have some effect in reducing sentencing disparity among inmates. Sentencing disparity is divergence in the types and lengths of sentences imposed for the same crimes, with no evident reason for the differences. The use of parole board decision-making guidelines attempts to deal with the traditional problems of the parole process. They do not represent a panacea, but they are an alternative to either the typical method, outright abolition, or the use of determinate sentencing. There is evidence of more widespread adoption and use of formal risk assessment, as well as toward structural revocation decisionmaking (Runda et al., 1994; Samra, Pfeifer & Ogloff, 2000).

## Get-Tough Sentences

While some criminologists and practitioners have been content to alter various aspects and procedures of the parole process, others have called for its complete abolition. A number of states have, for all intents and purposes, abolished parole. Whatever the change, one should be aware of the argument by Bill Woodward, former Director of Criminal Justice in Colorado (Gainsborough, 1997:3). "The problem with abolishing parole is you lose your ability to keep track of the inmates and the ability to keep them in treatment if they have alcohol and drug problems." As seen in Table 5.4, the attack on parole release has been ongoing for more than 20 years.

Table 5.4
**Significant Events in the Abolition of Parole**

| | |
|---|---|
| 1976 | Maine abolishes parole. |
| 1978 | California abolishes indeterminate sentences and discretionary parole release. |
| 1980 | Minnesota abolishes parole. |
| 1983 | Florida abolishes parole. |
| 1984 | Washington abolishes parole. |
| 1985 | Colorado reestablishes parole. |
| 1986 | Congress abolishes parole at the Federal level. |
| 1990 | Delaware abolishes parole. |
| 1993 | Kansas abolishes parole. |
| 1994 | Arizona and North Carolina abolish parole. |
| 1995 | Virginia abolishes parole. |
| 1996 | Ohio abolishes parole. |
| 1998 | New York passes *Jenna's Law* which eliminaties discretionary release for all violent felony |

Source: Compiled by authors.

Box 5.16

### Sentencing Guidelines

In an attempt to limit if not remove sentencing disparity, many jurisdictions have implemented a set of guidelines to help judges decide what sentence ought to be imposed, given the seriousness of the offense and the characteristics of the offender. Guidelines are based on past experience by a large number of sentencing judges, and represent average sentences imposed by sentencing peers in similar cases. Obviously, inasmuch as the determinations are guidelines, judges are not required to impose the recommended sentence (but at least must state in writing why they are deviating from the recommended range).

One such guideline to determine sentence length is from Minnesota. Across the top of the guideline grid is a score for the characteristics the offender brings to the sentencing hearing: number of prior juvenile adjudications, adult convictions for misdemeanors and felonies, number of time the offender has been previously incarcerated, employment status and educational attainment, and so on. Obviously, the higher the score, the worse the criminal history and longer the recommended sentence length.

The severity of the offense is found on the left side of the grid, ranked from the least severe to highest offense. After the judge calculates the criminal history score, she or he locates the offense category and reads across to see what other judges have done in terms of sentence length. The sentencing judge then imposes a sanction within the suggested range. Obviously, such a guidelines must be revalidated frequently.

One example of shifts in sentencing can be seen in the development of "three-strikes" sentencing statutes across the U.S. While some argue that they have the potential to reduce violent crime committed by repeat offenders by selective incapacitation of up to 25 years, the multiple-billion dollar costs for prison construction, operations, and maintenance are considerable. Further, locking up second and third time offenders for long periods of time will not (1) address the successive waves of juveniles and young offenders who will take the place of those incarcerated for 25 years, nor (2) reduce the risk factors of individuals involved in crime, nor (3) be accurate enough to isolate the truly dangerous from the truly stupid. "Three-strikes" sentencing assumes offenders operate as rational persons in a middle-class background and are driven by free will to commit crimes. Most criminals are neither so simplistic nor pure.

At least 22 states and the federal government have enacted these laws since 1993 (Campaign for An Effective Crime Policy, 1996). California has used these statutes more extensively than other states, and at least 49,000 offenders have been sentenced to at least twice to three times the sentence they would have received, absent these "enhancement" laws. One untoward outcome is that geriatric inmates (those over age 50) will become an increasing proportion of California's prison population, leading one wag to refer to the California prison system as the largest "old-age home" in the nation.

Figure 5.5
**Parole Jurisdictions Using Electronic Monitoring Devices: 1998-2004**

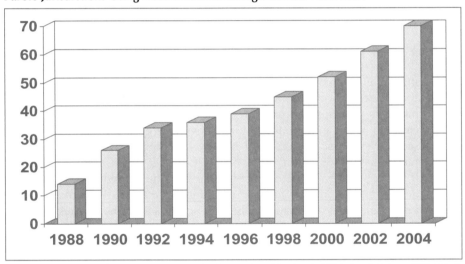

Sources: C. Camp and G. Camp (2003). *The Corrections Yearbook 2002*. South Salem, NY: Criminal Justice Institute Inc.; Data for 2004 are extrapolated.

## Reentry: The New Challenge

The large number of incarcerated offenders in the U.S. has lead to the inevitable result—a large number of offenders who will reenter society each year. In fact reentry has become the new buzz work used by policy makers to describe the process by which offender come back into the community. Some have argued that parole is essential to this process (Travis & Petersilia (2001), while others (Austin, 2001) believe that because a high percentage of offenders pose minimal risk to public safety, parole supervision should be eliminated or shortened to about six months. Given estimates that a significant percentage of offenders who will be returning to the community have a number of important needs (Lowenkamp and Latessa, 2005, Lurigio, 2001), there is little doubt that services and treatment in the community should be an important part of the reentry process. Indeed, several states have already created reentry programs designed to coordinate efforts and services between the institution, parole, and community correctional programs and treatment providers.

## Summary

Although the early beginnings of parole can be traced to Europe and Australia, the process as it is known today is almost exclusively an American invention. Once embraced by early reformers, parole quickly spread and, by 1944, every state jurisdiction had a parole system. In spite of the growth, parole was not without its detractors. Early criticism of parole included a suspicion of the way in which prisoners were selected for release, concern over a lack of community supervision, and extensive abuse by prison authorities. Many of the criticisms leveled at parole continue today.

There is considerable contemporary discussion relative to the value of parole. Indeed, there are those who oppose the indeterminate sentencing mode in general and wish to see parole abolished in particular. Concerns over these issues, and the perceived ineffectiveness of the present parole system, have led jurisdictions to either abolish parole altogether or dramatically adjust the entire parole process. Of all community programs, parole faces perhaps the greatest challenge. There are new indications, however, that pragmatism in the form of simple economics may renew an interest in parole. As our jail and prison populations swell above capacity, criminal justice planners and politicians will be forced to either continue to construct new facilities or develop alternative models. Parole emerges as a relatively inexpensive alternative model and, perhaps more importantly, one that is already in place. There is a need, though, to improve both the parole process and supervision so as to overcome the deficiencies detailed above.

Even if this apparent renewed interest in parole phases out, and parole as we know it is abolished in a stampede toward the determinate sentencing model, the need to assist inmates in their transition from the institution to the free community will remain. The problems facing released inmates are usually temporal or material: obtaining employment, suitable housing, financial aid, alcohol and drug abuse, etc.

As parole moves toward structuring release and revocation decisions to remove unwanted discrepancies, and jurisdictions consider abolition of parole as a release mechanism (whether assisted by guidelines or from clinical experience), two facts remain. First, parole has always served as a "release valve" or mechanism to prevent (or lower) prison overcrowding, a fact sadly ignored by policymakers and politicians. Second, discretionary parole has within it the authority to retain dangerous persons whose behavior would lead reasonable persons, citizens, and experienced correctional practitioners alike, to protect society by not paroling dangerous offenders. If the nation is to avoid the even more extreme of hiking sentences by multiples of current statutory terms, parole authorities should have the ability to protect the public by selective incapacitation of those who have several convictions for crimes against the person (murder, rape, aggravated assault, robbery, etc.). Of course it is important to remember that parole board members are human, and as such they cannot be expected to be infallible. Some inmates invariably are released who should not be, and others are kept far longer than necessary. Outcomes such as these require consideration of ways and means to intended objectives, as well as justice.

## Review Questions

1. Contrast the punishment model with the reform model of corrections.

2. How did Maconochie contribute to the development of parole?

3. How did parole develop in the United States?

4. What were the early criticisms of parole in America?

5. What were three elements of corruption that emerged in American corrections between 1790 and 1930?

6. Contrast the view of criminals offered by Maconochie with that of J. Edgar Hoover.

7. How did the decade from 1925 to 1935 affect attitudes of the American public toward parole?

8. Debate the following resolution: Discretionary parole from prison should be abolished.

9. What functions do parole boards serve?

10. If parole boards could not release offenders into the community, would they be abolished? Why or why not?

11. How do sentencing guidelines work? Parole guidelines?

12. How can parole boards use and implement intermediate sanctions?

13. How can three-strikes laws affect corrections?

# Key Terms

American Prison Association
conditional release
determinate sentence
deterrence
flopped
good-time credits
incapacitation
indeterminate sentence
mandatory release
mark system
pardon
parole
parole board

parole conditions
parole guidelines
parole revocation
penal colony
penitentiary
program credits
reformatory regime
retribution
selective incapacitation
sentencing disparity
sentencing guidelines
transportation

# Electronic Library

Civil liabilities in parole (www.nicic.org/pubs/2001/017068.pdf).

The criminal justice system and racial equality (www.nccd-crc.org/policy/crimjust.htm).

American Probation and Parole history (www.appa-net.org/about%20appa.history.htm).

Directory of community-based programs for women offenders (www.nicic.org/pubs/2000/016671.pdf).

Electronic monitoring (www.appa-net.org/about%20apppa/electron_l.htm).

Handbook for new parole board members (www.nicic.org/pubs/pre/006823.pdf).

Imprisonment and parole policy: American Society of Criminology policy paper (www.asc41.com/policypaper1.html).

Organizational response to change (www.appa-net.org/about%20appa/organiza_1.htm).

Parole policy (www.appa-net.org/about%20appa/parole_1,htm).

Parole supervision fees (www.appa-net.org/about%20appa.supervis.htm).

Responding to women offenders in the community (www.nicic.org/pubs/2000/period.180.pdf).

U.S. Parole Commission history (www.usdoj.gov/uspc/history.htm).

## Recommended Readings

Hassine, V. (2004). *Life Without Parole: Living in Prison Today*, 3rd Edition. Los Angeles, CA: Roxbury.

Hughes, R. (1987). *The Fatal Shore*. New York, NY: Alfred A. Knopf. This is the definitive book on the history of Australia as a penal colony, and the beginning roots of parole as developed by Captain Maconochie.

Rothman, D.J. (1980). *Conscience and Convenience: The Asylum and Its Alternatives in Progressive America*. Boston, MA: Little, Brown. A fastidious discussion of the modern effort to reform the programs that have dominated criminal justice in the twentieth century.

Rothman, D.J. (1971). *The Discovery of the Asylum: Social Order and Disorder in the New Republic*. Boston, MA: Little, Brown. This book presents an excellent history of the use of punishments and corrections in early colonial America.

## Notes

[1]    Various forms of conditional release from incarceration were developed in other countries before an American state adopted a parole system. However, the core elements of a parole system administrative board making release decisions and granting conditional, supervised release with the authority to revoke it, were first created by legislation in New York State (1869).

[2]    For a recent view of the impacts of conservative Christian beliefs on punishment of offenders, see Harold Gramich and Anne McGill (1994). "Religion, Attribution Style, and Punitiveness Toward Offenders." *Criminology*, 32(1):23-46. In the area of impact of evangelical and fundamentalist religion on the death penalty, see Harold Gramich, John Cochran, Robert Burish, and M'Lou Kimpel (1993). "Religion, Punitive Justice, and Support for the Death Penalty." *Justice Quarterly*, 10(2):289-314. For contrasting evidence, see M. Sandys and E. McGarrell (1997). "Beyond the Bible Belt: The Influences (or Lack Thereof) of Religion on Attitudes Toward the Death Penalty." *Journal of Crime and Justice*, 20 (1):179-190; and S. Johnson (2000). "The Bible and the Death Penalty." *Journal of Contemporary Criminal Justice*, 11(1):15-23.

[3]    For an excellent reading of the movement as it relates to the study of crime, see Y. Rennie (1978). *The Search for Criminal Man*. Lexington, MA: Lexington Books, D.C. Heath.

[4]    For an excellent description of transportation to Australia, see Robert Hughes (1987). *The Fatal Shore: The Epic of Australia's Founding*. New York, NY: Knopf. Pre-transportation detention usually was in hulks, dilapidated and unseaworthy naval vessels. See Charles Campbell (1994). *The Intolerable Hulks: British Shipboard Confinement*. Bowie, MD: Heritage Books.

5   For a conflicting interpretation of the political purposes intended for prisons, see A.M. Durham (1990). "Social Control and Imprisonment During the American Revolution: Newgate of Connecticut." *Justice Quarterly*, 7:293-323.

6   For a review of the contemporary issues in the prison privatization movement, see David Shichor (1993). "The Corporate Context of Private Prisons." *Crime, Law and Social Change*, 20(2):113-138. See also Vardalis, J. and F. Decker (2000). "Legislative Opinions Concerning the Private Operations of State Prisons." *Criminal Justice Policy Review*, 11(2):136-148.

7   See Ellen Chayet (1994). "Correctional 'Good Time' As a Means of Early Release." *Criminal Justice Abstracts*, 26(3):521-538.

8   It was not uncommon for juveniles to be indentured without a careful investigation of those who would hold the indenture contracts. Thus, juveniles were sometimes indentured to criminals, and the conditions of their indentureships were virtually uncontrolled.

9   The first legislatively authorized "parole officer" position was established in 1937 in Massachusetts. The officer was charged with assisting released convicts to obtain shelter, tools, and work. The legislation made no mention of any surveillance duties.

10   For a history of the American Correctional Association, see A. Travisono and M. Hawkes (1995). *Building a Voice: The American Correctional Association, 125 Years of History*. Landham, MD: ACA (www.corrections.com/aca/history/html).

11   See E. Lindsey (1925). "Historical Sketch of the Indeterminate Sentence and Parole System." *Journal of Criminal Law and Criminology*, 16:9-126. Lindsey writes, "There has been considerable modification and variation in various phases of the system as it has spread from one state to another. Methods of administration are also widely different." For an update on parole practices, see John Runda, Edward Rhine, and Robert White (1994). *The Practice of Parole*. Lexington, KY: Council of State Government.

12   Perhaps chief among these were E.C. Wines and T.W. Dwight who, in 1867, published a report to the New York Prison Association that was titled, *Prisons and Reformatories of the United States and Canada*. Albany. Other state committees echoed the call for a parole system. See Report of the Massachusetts General Court Joint Special Committee on Contract Convict Labor (1880). Boston. See also Roberts, J., J. Nuffield, and R. Hahn (2000). "Parole and the Public." *Empirical and Applied Criminal Justice Research Journal*, 1(1):1-25 (http://qsilver.queensu.ca/rcjnet/journal/eacjr.html).

13   For a remarkably similar view of contemporary corrections and public fears, see J.W. Murphy and J. Dison (eds.) (1990). *Are Prisons Any Better? Twenty Years of Correctional Reform*. Newbury Park, CA: Sage. See also Chiricos, T., K. Padgett, and M. Gerz (2000). "Fear, TV News and the Reality of Crime." *Criminology*, 38(3):755-785.

14   On media influence on citizen perception and fear of crime, see Melissa Barlow, David Barlow and Theodore Chiricos (1995). "Economic Conditions and Ideologies of Crime in the Media: A Content Analysis of Crime News," *Crime & Delinquency*, 43(1):3-19; Richard Bennett and Jeanne Flavin (1994). "Determinants of the Fear of Crime: The Effects of Cultural Setting." *Justice Quarterly*, 11(3):357-381; and John Wright, Francis Cullen, and Michael Blankenship (1995). "The Social Construction of Corporate Violence: Media Coverage of the Imperial Food Products Fire." *Crime & Delinquency*, 41(1):20-36; and T. Chiricos, S. Escholz, and M. Gertz (1997). "Crime News and Fear of Crime." *Social Problems*, 44(3):343-357.

[15]    But see C. DeLoach (1995). *Hoover's FBI: The Inside Story by Hoover's Trusted Lieutenant.* Washington, DC: Regenery.

[16]    The authors of these reports were joined by others. Reformers wanted full-time, paid parole authorities who had to meet certain qualifications and who were as far removed as possible from political patronage. See W. Colvin (1922). "What Authority Should Grant Paroles? If a Board, How Should It Be Composed?" *Journal of Criminal Law and Criminology,* 12:545-548.

[17]    Field, H.E. (1931). "The Attitudes of Prisoners as a Factor in Rehabilitation." *The Annals,* 157, 162. For sentiments of inmates denied parole, see West-Smith, M., M. Pogebrin and E. Poole (2000). "Denial of Parole: An Inmate Perspective." *Federal Probation,* 64(2):3-10.

[18]    Predicting post-release behavior is difficult. See Stephen Gottfredson and Don M. Gottfredson (1994). "Behavioral Prediction and the Problem of Incapacitation." *Criminology,* 32(3):441-474; and Heilbrun, K., W. Brock, and D. Waite et al. (2000). "Risk Factors for Juvenile Criminal Recidivism." *Criminal Justice and Behavior,* 27(3):275-291.

[19]    The offender's mandatory release date in Nebraska is calculated as follows:

For all odd-numbered maximum terms MR=(MAX-1)/2+11 months

For all even-numbered minimum terms MR=Max/2+5 months

[20]    Editors (1995). "APPA and APAI Go On the Offensive for Parole." *American Probation and Parole Association Perspectives,* 19(3):12.

[21]    Runda, J., E. Rhine, and R. Wetter (1994). *The Practice of Parole Boards.* Lexington, KY: Council of State Governments.

[22]    Such intrastate variations may also be true within states. For example, Sutton recently observed that the decision to place an individual in prison or not, and the length of the sentence per se, may be more a function of the county where the sentence was handed down than the nature of the offense. See Paul L. Sutton (1981). *Criminal Sentencing in Nebraska: The Feasibility of Empirically Based Guidelines.* Williamsburg, VA: National Center for State Courts, 1981. But see M. Turner, F. Cullen, and J. Sundt (1997). "Public Tolerance for Community-Based Sanctions." *Prison Journal,* 77(1):6-26.

[23]    Rhine, E., W. Smith, and R. Jackson (1992). *Paroling Authorities: Recent History and Current Practices.* Laurel, MD: American correctional Association.

[24]    Florida Office of Program Policy Analysis and Government Accountability (1996). Information Brief of Control Release Workload of the Florida Parole Commission. Tallahassee: FOPPAGA.

[25]    English, K., C. Colling, and S. Pullen (1996). *How Are Adult Felony Sex Offenders Managed on Probation and Parole: A National Assessment.* Denver, CO: Colorado Department of Public Safety.

[26]    New York State Division of Parole (1999). *The Ninth Annual Shock Legislative Report: 1997.* Albany, NY: NYSDOP.

27    Oregon Intermediate Sanctions for Female Offenders Policy Group (1995). *Intermediate Sanctions for Females*. Salem, OR: Oregon Department of Corrections.

28    Sutton, supra note 22.

29    P. Pagliaro and A. Pagliaro (1992). "Sentenced to Death: HIV Infections and AIDS in Prison—Current and Future Concerns." *Canadian Journal of Criminology*, 34(2):201-214. See also Hammett, T., L. Harrold, and M. Gross (1994). *1992 Update: HIV/AIDS in Correctional Facilities: Issues and Options*. Washington, DC; U.S. Department of Justice. See T. Hammett, L. Harrold, and J. Epstein (1994). *Tuberculosis in Correctional Facilities*. Washington, DC: U.S. Department of Justice.

30    Monahan, J. and H. Steadman (eds.) (1994). *Violence and Mental Disorder: Developments in Risk Behavior*. Chicago, IL: University of Chicago Press.

31    See *Block v. Potter*, 631 F.2d 233 (3d Cir. 1980); *Candelaria v. Griffin*, 641 F.2d 868 (10th Cir. 1980); *Farris v. U.S. Board of Parole*, 384 F.2d 948 (7th Cir. 1973).

32    Gottfredson, S. and D. Gottfredson (1994). "Behavioral Prediction and the Problem of Incapacitation." *Criminology*, 32:441-474.

33    Hoffman, P. (1994). "Twenty Years of Operational Use of a Risk Prediction Instrument: The United States Parole Commission's Salient Factor Score." *Journal of Criminal Justice*, 22:477-494.

34    Violators of federal statutes sentenced after November 1, 1987 do not fall under the authority of the U.S. Parole Commission but are instead sentenced under the new federal sentencing guidelines, a form of determinate sentencing that emphasizes just deserts. Sentencing guidelines were developed by the U.S. Sentencing Commission and are quite similar to the system used under the Parole Commission.

35    The weight of evidence has shifted against the "nothing works in corrections" argument. Overwhelming evidence shows that programs specifically designed for offenders' needs and delivered in a coherent manner by trained intervention personnel assisted by competent supervisors work and are effective. See Cullen, F and P. Gendreau (2001). "From Nothing Works to What Works: Changing Professional Ideology in the 21st Century." *Prison Journal*, 81(3):313-338.

36    As defined by Gottfredson, Hoffman, Sigler, and Wilkins (1980:7), equity and fairness means that "similar persons are dealt with in similar ways in similar situations. Fairness thus implies the idea of similarity and of comparison."

## References

Allen, H.E. and C.E. Simonsen (1998). *Corrections in America*. Upper Saddle River, NJ: Prentice-Hall.

———— (2001). *Corrections in America*. Upper Saddle River, NJ: Prentice-Hall.

American Correctional Association (2001). Directory. Laurel, MD: ACA.

———— (2001). *Probation and Parole 2001-2003*. Lanham, MD: ACA.

Austin, J. (2001). "Prisoner Reentry: Current Trends, Practices, and Issues." *Crime & Delinquency*, 47:314-334.

Babst, D.V., J.A. Inciardi, and D.R. Jarman (1970). *The Uses of Configural Analysis in Parole Prediction Research*. New York, NY: Narcotics Control Commission.

Barlow, M., D. Barlow, and T. Chiricos (1995). "Economic Conditions and Ideologies of Crime in the Media: A Content Analysis of Crime News." *Crime & Delinquency*, 43:3-19.

Barnes, H.E. and N.D. Teeters (1959). *New Horizons in Criminology*. Englewood Cliffs, NJ: Prentice-Hall.

Barry, J.V. (June 1957). "Captain Alexander Maconochie." *The Victorian Historical Magazine*, 27:1-18.

Beccaria, C. (1764). *On Crimes and Punishments*. Translated by H. Paulucci (1963). Indianapolis, IN: Bobbs-Merrill.

Beck, A. (2000). *Prisoners in 1999*. Bureau of Justice Statistics, Bulletin. Bureau of Justice Statistics. Washington, DC: U.S. Department of Justice.

Beck, A. (2000). "State and Federal Prisoners Returning to the Community." Washington, DC: Bureau of Justice Statistics, p. 3 (www.ojp.usdoj.gov/bjs/sfprc.pdf).

Bennett, R. and J. Flavin (1994). "Determinants of the Fear of Crime: The Effects of Cultural Setting." *Justice Quarterly*, 11:357-381.

Bottomley, K.E. (1990). "Parole in Transition: A Comparative Study of Origins, Developments, and Prospects for the 1990s." In M. Tonry and N. Morris (eds.) *Crime and Justice: A Review of Research, Vol. 12*. Chicago, IL: University of Chicago Press.

Briggs, J., C. Harrison, and A. McInnes (1996). *Crime and Punishment in England: An Introductory History*. New York, NY: St. Martin's Press.

Bromley, E. and C.E. Gathercole (1969). "Boolean Predication Analysis: A New Method of Prediction Index Construction." *British Journal of Criminology*, 17:287-292.

Burgess, E.W. (1928). "Factors Determining Success or Failure on Parole." In B. Harmo, E.W. Burgess, and C.L. Landeson (eds.) *The Workings of the Indeterminate Sentence Law and the Parole System in Illinois*. Springfield, IL: Illinois State Board of Parole.

Burke, P. (1997). *Policy Driven Responses to Probation and Parole Violators*. Washington, DC: U.S. National Institute of Justice.

Camp, C. and G. Camp (2000). *The 2000 Corrections Yearbook: Adult Corrections*. Middletown, CT: Criminal Justice Institute.

Campaign for an Effective Crime Control Policy (1996). *The Impact of "Three Strikes and You're Out" Laws: What Have We Learned?* Washington, DC: CFECP.

Campbell, C. (1994). *The Intolerable Hulks: British Shipboard Confinement*. Bowie, MD: Heritage Books.

Carroll, L. (1976). "Racial Bias in the Decision to Grant Parole." *Law and Society Review*, 11:93-107.

Carter, R.M., R.A. McGee, and K.E. Nelson (1975). *Corrections in America*. Philadelphia, PA: J.B. Lippincott.

Chayet, E. (1994). "Correctional 'Good Time' As a Means of Early Release." *Criminal Justice Abstracts*, 26:521-538.

Chiricos, T., S. Escholz, and M. Gertz (1997). "Crime, News and Fear of Crime." *Social Problems*, 44(3):342-357.

Chiricos, T., K. Padgett, and M. Gerz (2000). "Fear, TV News and the Reality of Crime." *Criminology*, 38(3):755-785.

Clare, P.K. and J.H. Kramer (1976). *Introduction to American Corrections*. Boston, MA: Holbrook Press.

Clear, T.R. (1978). *A Model for Supervising the Offender in the Community*. Washington, DC: National Institute of Corrections.

Cornelius, W. (1997). *Bringing Certainty and Finality to Criminal Punishments*. Irvington-on-Hudson, NY: Bridge Street Books.

Dawson, R.O. (1966). "The Decision to Grant or Deny Parole: A Study of Parole Criteria in Law and Practice." *Washington University Law Quarterly*, (June):248-285.

DeLoach, C. (1995). *Hoover's FBI: The Inside Story by Hoover's Trusted Lieutenant*. Washington, DC: Regenery.

Ditton, P. and D. J. Wilson (1999). *Truth in Sentencing in State Prisons*. Washington DC: U.S. Department of Justice, Bureau of Justice Statistics.

*Farris v. U.S. Board of Parole*, 384 F.2d 948 (7th Cir. 1973).

Fogel, D. (1975). *We Are the Living Proof . . .* Cincinnati, OH: Anderson Publishing Co.

*Gagnon v. Scarpelli*, 411 U.S. 788 (1972).

Gainsborough, J. (1997). "Eliminating Parole is a Dangerous and Expensive Proposition." *Corrections Today*, 59(4):23.

Gendreau, P. (1996). "The Principles of Effective Intervention with Offenders." In A. Harland (ed.) *Choosing Correctional Options That Work: Defining the Demand and Evaluating the Supply*. Thousand Oaks, CA: Sage.

Gendreau, P., C. Coggin, and T. Little (1996). *Predicting Adult Offender Recidivism: What Works!* Ottawa, CN: Solicitor General Canada.

Glaser, D. (1962). "Prediction Tables as Accounting Devices for Judges and Parole Boards." *Crime & Delinquency*, 8:239-258.

Goodstein, L. (1980). "Psychological Effects of the Predictability of Prison Release: Implications for the Sentencing Debate." *Criminology*, 18:363-384.

Gottfredson, D.M., D.V. Babst, and K.B. Ballard (1958). "Comparison of Multiple Regression and Configural Analysis Techniques for Developing Base Expectancy Tables." *Journal of Research in Crime and Delinquency*, 5:72-80.

Gottfredson, S. and D. Gottfredson (1994). "Behavioral Prediction and the Problem of Incapacitation." *Criminology*, 32:441-474.

Gottfredson, S. and D. Gottfredson (1993). "The Long-Term Predictive Utility of the Base Expectancy Score." *Howard Journal of Criminal Justice*, 32:276-290.

Gramich, H. and A. McGill (1994). "Religion, Attribution Style, and Punitiveness Toward Offenders." *Criminology*, 32:23-46.

Gramich H., J. Cochran, J. Burish, and M. Kimpel (1993). "Religion, Punitive Justice, and Support for the Death Penalty." *Justice Quarterly*, 10:289-314.

*Greenholtz v. Inmates of the Nebraska Penal and Correctional Complex,* 442 U.S. 1 (1979).

Hammett, T. and M. Gross (1994). *1992 Update: HIV/AIDS in Correctional Facilities: Issues and Options*. Washington, DC: U.S. Department of Justice.

Hammett, T., L. Harrold, and J. Epstein (1994). *Tuberculosis in Correctional Facilities*. Washington, DC: U.S. Department of Justice.

Hart, H. "Predicting Parole Success." *Journal of Criminal Law and Criminology*,14:405-414.

Hassine, V. (2004). *Life Without Parole: Living in Prison Today*, 3rd. Los Angeles, CA: Roxbury.

Hawkins, K.O. (1971). "Parole Selection: The American Experience." Unpublished doctoral dissertation, University of Cambridge, England.

Heilbrun, K., W. Brock, and D. Waite, et al. (2000). "Risk Factors for Juvenile Criminal Recidivism." *Criminal Justice and Behavior*, 27(3):275-291.

Hoffman, P. (1983). "Screening for Risk." *Journal of Criminal Justice*, 11(6):539-547.

Hoffman, P. (1997). "History of the Federal Parole System. Part I (1910-1972)." *Federal Probation*, 61(3):23-31.

Hoffman, P. and J.L. Beck (1980). "Revalidating the Salient Factor Score: A Research Note." *Journal of Criminal Justice*, 8:185-188.

Hughes, R. (1987). *The Fatal Shore*. New York, NY: Alfred A. Knopf.

Irwin, J. (1977). "Adaptation to Being Corrected: Corrections from the Convict's Perspective." In R.G. Legar and J.R. Stratton (eds.) *The Sociology of Corrections*, pp. 276-300. New York, NY: John Wiley and Sons.

Johnson, E. (1994). "Opposing Outcomes of the Industrial Prison: Japan and the United States Compared." *International Criminal Justice Review*, 4(1):52-71.

Johnson, S. (2000). "The Bible and the Death Penalty." *Journal of Contemporary Criminal Justice*, 11(1):15-23.

Langbein, J.H. (1976). "The Historical Origins of the Sanction of Imprisonment for Serious Crime." *Journal of Legal Studies*, 5:35-63.

Lindsey, E. (1925). "Historical Origins of the Sanction of Imprisonment for Serious Crime." Journal of *Criminal Law and Criminology*, 16:9-126.

Lowenkamp, C., and E. Latessa (2005). "Developing Successful Reentry Programs: Lesson Learned From the 'What Works' Research." *Corrections Today* (April).

Loza, W. and F. Loza (2000). Predictive Validity of the Self-Appraisal Questionnaire (SAQ)." *Journal of Interpersonal Violence*, 15(11):1183-1191.

Lurigio, A.J. (2001). "Effective Services for Parolees With Mental Illnesses." *Crime & Delinquency*, 47:446-461.

MacNamara, D.E.J. (1977). "The Medical Model in Corrections: Requiescat in Pax." *Criminology*, 14:435-438.

McCleary, R. (1978). *Dangerous Men*. Beverly Hills, CA: Sage.

Maguire, M., B. Peroud, and J. Dison (eds.) (1996). *Automatic Conditional Release: The First Two Years*. London, UK: Her Majesty's Stationery House.

Maguire, K. and A. Pastore (1997). *Sourcebook of Criminal Justice Statistics 1997*. Washington, DC: U.S. Department of Justice.

Martinson, R. (1974). "What Works? Questions and Answers About Prison Reform." *Public Interest*, 25(Spring):22-25.

Monahan, J. (1981). *Predicting Violent Behavior: An Assessment of Clinical Techniques*. Beverly Hills, CA: Sage Publications.

Monahan, J. and H. Steadman (eds.) (1994). *Violence and Mental Disorder: Developments in Risk Assessment*. Chicago, IL: University of Chicago Press.

Morelli, R.S., C. Edelman, and R. Willoughby (1981). *A Survey of Mandatory Sentencing in the U.S.* Pennsylvania Commission on Crime and Delinquency.

Morris, N. (1974). *The Future of Imprisonment*. Chicago, IL: University of Chicago Press.

*Morrissey v. Brewer*, 408 U.S. 471 (1972).

New York State Division of Parole (1999). *The Ninth Annual Shock Legislation Report: 1997*. Albany, NY: NYSDOP.

O'Leary, V. and K. Hanrahan (1977). *Parole Systems in the United States: A Detailed Description of Their Structure and Procedure*, Third Edition. Hackensack, NJ: National Council on Crime and Delinquency.

National Commission of Law Observance and Enforcement (1939). George W. Wickersham, Chairman. Report on Penal Institutions, Probation and Parole. Washington, DC: U.S. Government Printing Office.

Offutt, W. (1995). *Of "Good Laws" and "Good Men:" Law and Society in the Delaware Valley, 1680-1710*. Chicago, IL: University of Chicago Press.

Pagliaro, P. and A. Pagliaro (1992). "Sentenced to Death: HIV Infections and AIDS in Prison—Current and Future Concerns." *Canadian Journal of Criminology*, 34(2):201-214.

Petersilia, J. (2001). "Prisoner Reentry." *Prison Journal*, 81(3):360-375.

Pisciotta, A. (1982). "Saving the Children: The Promise and Practice of Parens Patria, 1838-1898." *Crime & Delinquency*, 28(3):410-425.

President's Commission on Law Enforcement and Administration of Justice (1969). *The Challenge of Crime in a Free Society*. Washington, DC: U.S. Government Printing Office.

Rennie, Y. (1978). *The Search for Criminal Man*. Lexington, MA: D.C. Heath.

Report of the Massachusetts General Court Joint Special Committee on Contract Convict Labor (1880). Boston, MA: State of Massachusetts.

Roberts, J., J. Nuffield, and R. Hahn (2000). "Parole and the Public." *Empirical and Applied Criminal Justice Research Journal*, 1(1):1-25 (http://qsilver.queensu.ca/rcjnet/journal/eacjr.html).

Rothman, D.J. (1971). *The Discovery of the Asylum: Social Order and Disorder in the New Republic*. Boston, MA: Little, Brown.

Runda, J., E. Rhine, and R. Wetter (1994). *The Practice of Parole Boards*. Lexington, KY: Council of State Governments.

Samra, G., J. Pfeifer, and J. Ogloff (2000). Recommendations for Conditional Release Suitability." *Canadian Journal of Criminology*, 42(4):421-447.

Sandys, M. and E. McGarrell (1997). "Beyond the Bible Belt: The Influence (or Lack Thereof) of Religion on Attitudes Toward the Death Penalty," *Journal of Crime and Justice*, 20(1):179-190.

Scott, J. (1974). "The Use of Discretion in Determining the Severity of Punishment for Incarcerated Offenders." *Journal of Criminal Law and Criminology*, 65:214-224.

Sellin, T. (Spring-Summer 1970). "The Origin of the Pennsylvania System of Prison Discipline." *The Prison Journal*, 50:13, 15-17.

Sherrill, M.S. (1977, September). "Determinate Sentencing: History, Theory, Debate." *Corrections Magazine*, 3:3-13.

Smykla, J.O. (1984). "Prediction in Probation and Parole: Its Consequences and Implications." Paper presented at the Annual Meeting of the Academy of Criminal Justice Sciences, Chicago, Illinois.

Solomon, A. (2006). "Does Parole Supervision Work? Research Findings and Policy Opportunities." *Perspectives*, 30(2): 26-37.

*Sourcebook of Criminal Justice Statistics* (2001). Albany, NY: University of Albany.

Sutton, P.L. (1981). *Criminal Sentencing in Nebraska: The Feasibility of Empirically Based Guidelines*. Williamsburg, VA: National Center for State Courts.

Travis, J. and J. Petersilia (2001). "Reentry Reconsidered: A New Look at an Old Problem." *Crime & Delinquency*, 47:291-313.

Turner, M.G., J.L. Sundt, B.K. Applegate, and F.T. Cullen (1995). "Three Strikes and You're Out Legislation: A National Assessment." *Federal Probation*, 59(3):16-35.

Vardalis, J. and F. Decker (2000). "Legislative Opinions Concerning the Private Operations of State Prisons." *Criminal Justice Policy Review*, 11(2):136-148.

West-Smith, M., M. Pogebrin, and E. Poole (2000). "Denial of Parole: An Inmate Perspective." *Federal Probation*, 64(2):3-10.

Wiggins, M.E. (1984). "False Positives/False Negatives: A Utility Cost Analysis of Parole Decision Making." Paper presented at the Annual Meeting of the Academy of Criminal Justice Sciences, Chicago, Illinois.

Wilcox, C. (1929). "Parole: Principles and Practice." *Journal of Criminal Law and Criminology*, 20:345-354.

Wilkins, L.E. and P. MacNaughton-Smith (1964). "New Prediction and Classification Methods in Criminology." *The Journal of Research in Crime and Delinquency*, 1:19-32.

Wines, E.C. and T.W. Dwight (1867). *Prisons and Reformatories of the United States and Canada*. Albany, NY: New York Prison Association.

# Roles of Probation and Parole Officers

> . . . **A** parole officer can be seen going off to his/her appointed rounds with Freud in one hand and a .38 Smith and Wesson in the other hand. It is by no means clear that Freud is as helpful as the .38 in most areas where parole officers venture . . . Is Freud backup to the .38? Or is the .38 carried to support Freud?
>
> —David Fogel

As Fogel (McCleary, 1978:10-11) succinctly indicates, the role of the probation or parole officer (PO)[1] has traditionally been viewed as a dichotomy (American Correctional Association, 1995). The supervision role involves both maintaining surveillance (societal protection) over as well as helping or treating the offender (counseling, rehabilitation, reintegration). Supervising officers are often left to their own devices with regard to which role would be most appropriate in supervising their caseloads (Figure 6.1). This dilemma is likely to remain with us even though calls from several quarters of the criminal justice system point toward coming changes in the role of the supervising officer (Taxman & Byrne, 2001; Reinventing Probation Council, 2001). This chapter describes and outlines the boundaries of this role conflict as it has developed over time, the problems associated with it, and the responsibilities of probation and parole agencies.

## Responsibilities of Probation and Parole Agencies

To begin, it is necessary to examine what duties and responsibilities are held in common by probation and parole agencies. O'Leary (1974) has argued that parole resembles probation in several ways. With both, information is gathered and presented to a decision-making authority (either a judge or a parole board). This authority has the power to release (parole) or suspend the sentence (probation) of the offender. In turn, the liberty that the offender enjoys is subject to certain conditions that are imposed by the decision-making authority. If these conditions are not obeyed, the offender may be sentenced, or returned, to prison (Oregon Department of Corrections, 1992).

Figure 6.1
**Average Caseload for Probation and Parole Agencies**

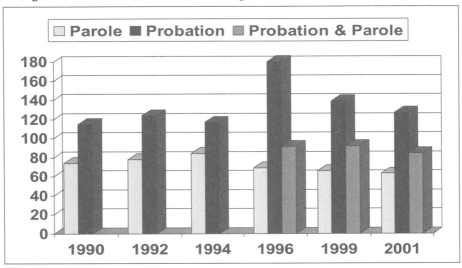
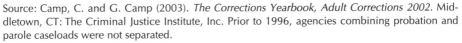

Source: Camp, C. and G. Camp (2003). *The Corrections Yearbook, Adult Corrections 2002.* Middletown, CT: The Criminal Justice Institute, Inc. Prior to 1996, agencies combining probation and parole caseloads were not separated.

On the other hand, parole differs from probation in distinct ways. The offender on parole has served a portion of his or her sentence in a correctional facility. The decision to release the offender from prison is usually an administrative one, made by the parole board. The decision to grant probation lies entirely with the court. As Wallace (1974:950) has written, "Probation is more than a process; it connotes an organization, basically a service agency, designed to assist the court and to perform particular functions in the administration of criminal justice."

Despite these differences, probation and parole agencies share one particular and significant function: They provide supervision of offenders in the community. The basic question remains: What is the purpose of supervision? To Wallace, the function of supervision, drawn from the social work field, is based upon the casework model. Supervision is the basis of a treatment program. The officer uses all the information available about the offender to make diagnosis of that person's needs and to design a treatment plan. One example of a treatment plan for probationers, emphasizing the need for reintegration, was first suggested by the President's Task Force on Corrections (1967:30):

. . . developing the offender's effective participation in the major social institutions of the school, business and church . . . which offer access to a successful career.

Yet, providing treatment is only on aspect of supervision. In addition, the PO is expected to maintain surveillance of those offenders who make up the caseload.

A classic definition of surveillance was provided by the National Conference of Parole (Studt, 1978:65):

> Surveillance is that activity of the parole officer which utilizes watchfulness, checking, and verification of certain behavior of a parolee without contributing to a helping relationship with him.

Although these statements indicate that the treatment and surveillance roles of the probation/parole officer are almost diametrically opposed, several authors have indicated that they coexist as a part of the agency's mission. Some authors—such as Glaser (1969), McCleary (1978), and Studt (1978)—have noted that the PO has two missions: to rehabilitate the offenders who are amenable to treatment, while simultaneously protecting society from those who prove to be dangerous.

In his study of parole officers at work, McCleary (1978:112) discovered that parole officers typically reviewed their caseload to identify the presence of "dangerous men." This term refers to the offender who is irrational or unpredictable. The dangerous man does not respond in a rational manner to the threats or promises made by the PO. It is this responsibility that leads the parole officer to label him or her dangerous and, as such, a prime candidate for surveillance. Despite this evidence, other scholars have suggested that parole officers perceive their role in different ways because of their particular view of the job as well as the appropriate role that they perceive should follow.[2] From this perspective, it is the PO's perception of the purpose of supervision that determines which of the two goals is most appropriate in a given client's case.

Carlson and Parks (1979:155-157) have listed four major responsibilities of a probation or parole agency:

- Surveillance: While the term "surveillance" usually means simply "watching" in a police sense it should be pointed out that a helping purpose is also intended. When surveillance is properly carried out, the client is continually sensitized to the possible results of a course of action that has made him vulnerable in the past. Just as an alcoholic or narcotics addict who is trying to change his life derives support from frequent contact with others who have successfully conquered their problems, so also can many clients derive beneficial results from frequent meetings with the probation officer.

- Investigation: The investigation function includes reporting violative behavior, or actual violation on the part of probationers, and gathering facts about arrests and reporting suspicions to supervisors.

- Concrete Needs Counseling: This type of counseling includes the following areas: employment, education, training, housing, clothing, financial, medical, dental, legal, and transportation.

- Emotional Needs Counseling: The services that a probation officer provides depend on the needs of clientele they serve. These needs can include: marital/family relationships, companions, emotional stability, alcohol and drug usage, mental ability, and sexual behavior.

## Role Typologies

In one of the first studies of types of officers, Ohlin and his associates (1956:211-225) developed the following typology of PO styles:

- The punitive officer, who perceives himself as the guardian of middle-class morality; he attempts to coerce the offender into conforming by means of threats and punishment, and emphasizes control, the protection of the community against the offender, and the systematic suspicion of those under supervision.

- The protective officer, who vacillates literally between protecting the offender and protecting the community. His tools are direct assistance, lecturing, and, alternately, praise and blame. He is perceived as ambivalent in his emotional involvement with the offender and others in the community as he shifts back and forth in taking sides with one against the other.

- The welfare officer, who has as his ultimate goal the improved welfare of the client, achieved by aiding him in his individual adjustment within limits imposed by the client's capacity. Such an officer believes that the only genuine guarantee of community protection lies in the client's personal adjustment, because external conformity will only be temporary and, in the long run, may make a successful adjustment more difficult. Emotional neutrality permeates his relationship. The diagnostic categories and treatment skills which he employs stem from an objective and theoretically based assessment of the clients needs and capacities.

Glaser (1969:293) later extended this typology to include, as a fourth category, the passive officer, who sees his job as a sinecure, requiring only minimum effort. For example, Erickson (1977:37) has satirically offered the following gambit to officers who wish to "fake it" and have an "ideal, trouble-free caseload:"

> "I'm just so busy—never seem to have enough time." A truly professional execution of this ploy does require some preparation. Make sure that your desktop is always inundated with a potpourri of case files, messages, memos, unopened mail, and professional literature . . . Have your secretary hold all your calls for a few days and schedule several appointments for the same time. When, after a lengthy wait, the probationer is finally ushered into your presence, impress him (or her) with the volume of your business . . . Always write while conversing with the subject, and continue to make and receive telephone calls. Interrupt your dialogue with him to attend to other important matters, such as obtaining the daily grocery list from your wife or arranging to have your car waxed. Apologize repeatedly and profusely for these necessary interruptions and appear to be distracted, weary, and slightly insane. Having experienced the full treatment, it is unlikely that the probationer will subsequently try to discuss with you any matters of overwhelming concern. He could even feel sorrier for you than he does for himself. You should henceforth be able to deal with him on an impersonal basis, if indeed he tries to report anymore at all.

The complete typology is presented in tabular form in Figure 6.2. The key distinction in this figure is the manner in which the supervising officer personally views the purpose of the job of supervision. Personal preference and motivations of the PO will often determine the style of supervision that is followed.

A similar typology was developed by Klockars (1972:550-552), based on the working philosophy of the officer. The first style that he presented is that of the "law enforcer." Such officers are primarily motivated by: (1) the court order and obtaining offender compliance with it, (2) the authority and decision-making power of the PO, (3) officer responsibility for public safety, and (4) police work—the PO as police officer of the agency.

The second category is that of the "time server." This individual feels that the job has certain requirements to be fulfilled until retirement—"I don't make the rules; I just work here." The third type is the "therapeutic agent," a supervising officer who accepts the role of administrator of a form of treatment (usually casework oriented) to help the offender.

Figure 6.2
**Typology of PO Supervision Styles**

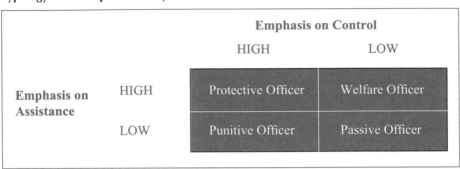

Source: Jordan, F. and J. Sasfy (1974). *National Impact Program Evaluation: A Review of Selected Issues and Research Findings Related to Probation and Parole*, p. 29. Washington, DC: Mitre Corporation.

Finally, the "synthetic officer" attempts to blend treatment and law enforcement components by "combining the paternal, authoritarian, and judgmental with the therapeutic." The synthetic officer attempts to solve what Miles (1965a) terms criminal justice (offender is wrong but responsible for own behavior) with treatment (casework, offender is sick) goals. In sum, Klockars' typology rounds out the original scheme developed by Ohlin et al. (1956) by providing an example through which the PO can integrate the best of each possible role.

Czajkoski (1973) expanded on the law enforcement role of the officer's job by outlining the quasi-judicial role of the probation officer. He develops his thesis on five lines of functional analysis. The first line examines the plea bargaining, Czajkoski cites Blumberg's (1974) argument that the probation officer serves to "cool the mark" in the confidence game of plea bargaining by assuring the defendant of how wise it was to plead guilty. In this fusion, the PO certifies the plea bargaining process—a task that can significantly undermine the helping/counseling role of the PO.

The second line of quasi-judicial functioning by the probation officer occurs at the intake level. For example, at the juvenile level, the officer is often asked which cases are appropriate for judicial processing. Like the prosecutor, this function permits the probation officer to have some control over the intake of the court.

The third quasi-judicial function of the probation officer concerns setting the conditions of probation, a power the judge often gives the probation officer. This often leads to discretionary abuses, since indefinite conditions (often moralistic or vague in terms of offender's behavior) can become a vehicle for maintaining the moral status quo as interpreted by the probation officer. In addition, probation conditions can become substitutions for, or even usurp, certain formal judicial processes. For example, the monetary obligations[3] of the probationer (such as supporting dependents) can be enforced by the probation officer, rather than by a court that is specifically designed to handle such matters (Schneider, Griffith & Schneider, 1982).

The fourth quasi-judicial role is concerned with probation violation procedures. Czajkoski contends that such procedures are highly discretionary, especially in view of the vague and all-encompassing nature of the probation conditions, which are usually not enforced until the officer has reason to believe that the probationer is engaged in criminal activity. Petersilia and Turner (1993) noted that increased surveillance increases the incidence of technical violations (Marciniak, 2000), jail terms, and incarceration rates, as well as program and court costs.

The final quasi-judicial role of the probation officer concerns the ability to administer punishment. Since the officer may restrict the liberty of his or her charge in several ways, this is tantamount to punishment. In this fashion, Czajkoski highlights some of the actions officers take that relate to his or her function as a quasi-judicial official, and illustrates more ways in which the PO uses discretionary power in judicial-like ways.

Tomaino (1975) also attempts to reveal some of the hidden functions of probation officers. Figure 6.3 summarizes the Tomaino typology. Once again, concern for control is contrasted with concern for rehabilitation. To Tomaino, the key probation officer role is the "Have It Make Sense" face. This role attempts to integrate the often-conflicting concerns of societal protection and offender rehabilitation. Accordingly, Tomaino recommends that the officer stress goals, not offender personality traits, to ". . . organize legitimate choices through a collaborative relationship which induces the client to act in accord with prosocial expectations." Perhaps, as Lindner (1975) suggests, the probation officer can create a learning situation for the offender and induce a desire for change.

A different but more recent view of the related role for of the probation officer is also advocated by Taxman (2006:43). Arcaya (1973) argues there are four main goals of a probation officer's contact with an offender:

1. Engagement: To assist the offender in taking ownership of their supervision contract and behavioural plan.

2. Early Change: To assist the offender in addressing dynamic criminogenic factors in a manner meaningful to both the offender and the criminal justice system.

3. Sustained Change: To goal is to transfer external controls from the formal government institution to informal social controls (e.g., parents, peers, community supports, employers).

4. Reinforcers: The goal is to reinforce the change process.

In sum, these authors indicate that the supervising officer has a range of choices concerning the style of supervision to be followed and the ultimate goal of the entire probation/parole process. There is a strong emphasis here upon blending the need for control with the need for counseling. The officer must choose which style to adopt based upon the individual client (severity of the offense, amenability to treatment) and the nature of the situation. Supervising officers clearly have the discretionary power to either enforce the law (i.e., conditions of supervision) or offer help and treatment. No doubt, the world view of the PO also plays a crucial role in this decision.

Figure 6.3
**The Five Faces of Probation Supervision**

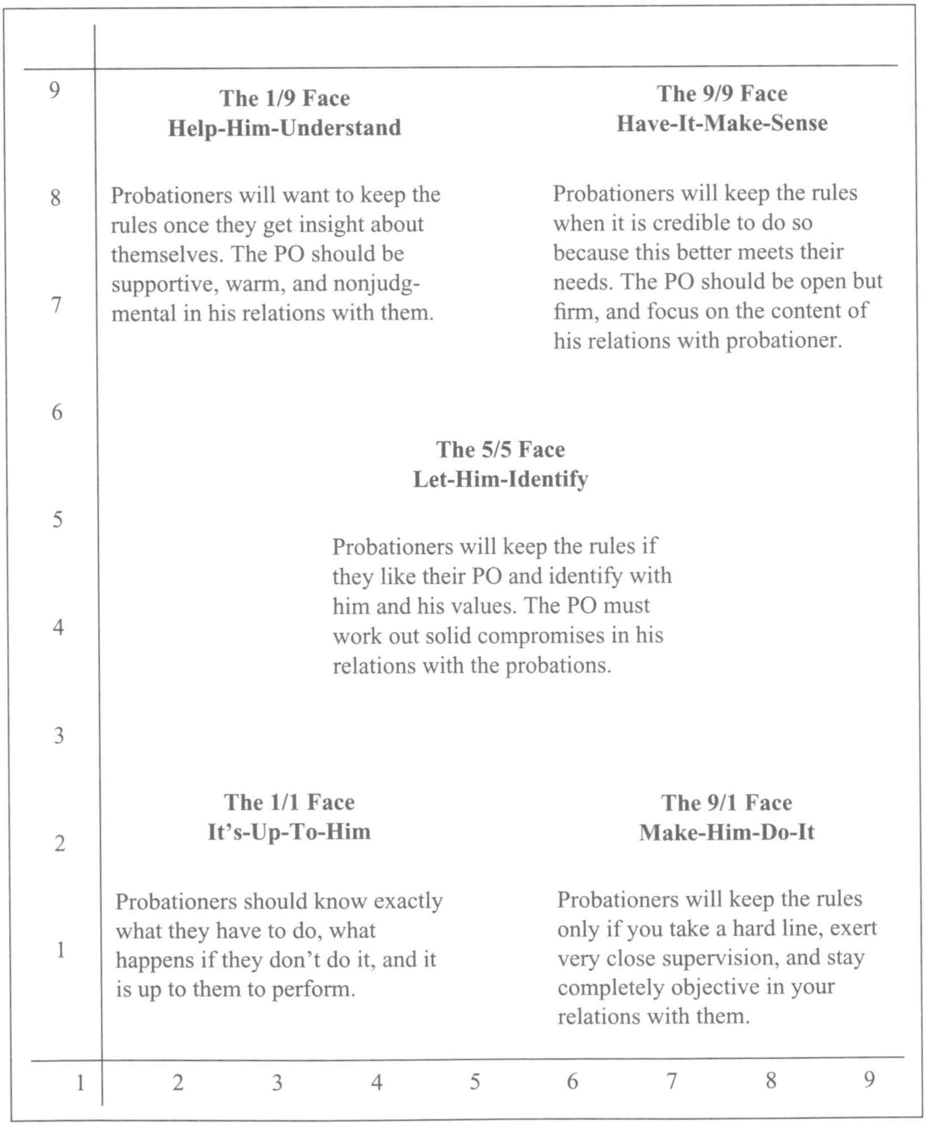

| | |
|---|---|
| 9 | |
| | **The 1/9 Face**  **Help-Him-Understand** |
| 8 | Probationers will want to keep the rules once they get insight about themselves. The PO should be supportive, warm, and nonjudgmental in his relations with them. |
| 7 | |

**The 9/9 Face**
**Have-It-Make-Sense**

Probationers will keep the rules when it is credible to do so because this better meets their needs. The PO should be open but firm, and focus on the content of his relations with probationer.

6

**The 5/5 Face**
**Let-Him-Identify**

5

Probationers will keep the rules if they like their PO and identify with him and his values. The PO must work out solid compromises in his relations with the probations.

4

3

**The 1/1 Face**
**It's-Up-To-Him**

2

Probationers should know exactly what they have to do, what happens if they don't do it, and it is up to them to perform.

**The 9/1 Face**
**Make-Him-Do-It**

Probationers will keep the rules only if you take a hard line, exert very close supervision, and stay completely objective in your relations with them.

1

| 1 | 2 | 3 | 4 | 5 | 6 | 7 | 8 | 9 |

Source: L. Tomaino (1975). "The Five Faces of Probation." *Federal Probation,* 39(4):43.

## Characteristics of Effective Change Agents

What are the characteristics of effective probation and parole officers? Andrews (1979) suggests that effective change agents have several characteristics. First, they are able to develop a quality interpersonal relationship with the probationer or parolee. Warmth, genuineness, and flexibility characterize such relationships. Second, they are able to model behavior in concrete and vivid ways. Third, they are a source of not simply punishment, but of reinforcement for positive behavior. Finally, an effective change agent engages in disapproval with strong, emphatic statements of disagreement about an offender's negative attitudes and behaviors. Unfortunately, as Shichor (1978:37) points out, such characteristics are in sharp contract to current probation and parole practices that are more oriented toward "people processing than people changing."

## The Self-Image of Probation and Parole Officers

How do probation and parole officers see themselves and their work? Over the years there have been several studies focused upon agents to secure their views concerning what the appropriate goals of supervision should be and, within the criminal justice system, where such agents primarily identify with their allegiance.

In an early study, Miles (1965b) surveyed all 116 probation and parole officers on duty in Wisconsin on a single day. In addition, 48 officers were interviewed and accompanied into the field by the researchers. On the basis of these data, Miles discovered that a majority of these officers basically identified with the field of corrections (61.5%). The clear majority of individuals identified themselves as probation officers when dealing with judges (81%), social agencies (69%), and potential client employers (79%). These officers emphasized their identification with correctional work and did not wish to have this primary link absorbed by another area (for example, social work). The survey also uncovered

Box 6.1

### All Things to All People

For larger probation departments, specialization has become more common. There are Presentence Investigation Units, assessment units, fugitive and warrant units, surveillance officers, and specialized caseload units. In rural departments it is still common to have every probation officer perform all of these tasks.

what is considered to be the basic dilemma of probation in terms of its primary goal: offender rehabilitation versus societal protection.

A survey of probation and parole agencies in 2002 revealed several service functions for probation and parole officers,agencies, shown in Figure 6.4 (Camp & Camp, 2003). Making referrals and apprehending absconders were the most frequently cited services.

Figure 6.4

**Percentage of Probation and Parole Agencies Providing Services by Type**

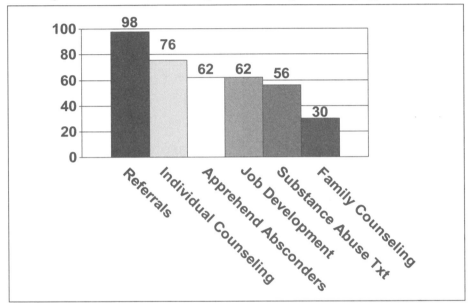

Source: Camp, C. and G. Camp (2003). *The Corrections Yearbook, Adult Corrections 2002*. Middletown, CT: The Criminal Justice Institute, Inc., p. 226

In a study of job tasks, Colley and her associates (1987) surveyed 70 juvenile probation officers in Illinois. Table 6.1 illustrates the tasks performed by at least 40 percent of the sample. While most studies of probation officers have been conducted in urban areas, it is important to note what appear to be differences in the roles and tasks performed between urban and rural probation officers. Rural officers perform a wider range of tasks than urban officers, and are less specialized (Colley, Culbertson & Latessa, 1986). It is also interesting to note that, the majority of probation and parole officers are now females (see Figure 6.5). When viewed in light of their average starting salaries (Figure 6.6), one glimpses the dedication of most PO staff.

Overall, the studies examined reveal that POs are aware of the surveillance/treatment dichotomy that exists with regard to style of supervision. A number of factors (age, education, years of job experience) are related to or influence the PO's style and method of supervision. Yet, in general, there is a distinct lack of consensus over which style of supervision should dominate.

Table 6.1
**Tasks Performed by at least 40 Percent of the Respondents on a Weekly or Daily Basis**

| Skills | Percent |
|---|---|
| COURT | |
| Attends court hearings with client | 58.6% |
| Takes court notes on court proceedings of clients | 47.2% |
| Confers with State's Attorney about cases | 64.2% |
| | |
| SUPERVISION—CASELOAD MANAGEMENT | |
| Meets with minor in office, home, and at school | 57.1% |
| Listens to complaints and problems | 72.9% |
| Asks minors about any general problems and disturbances | 56.5% |
| Inquires about police contacts | 44.3% |
| Consults teachers, therapists, significant others, community services agencies | 44.3% |
| Intervenes in crisis situations | 42.9% |
| Counsels parents | 47.8% |
| Confers with dean of students or school counselors | 47.8% |
| | |
| CASE NOTING | |
| Accounts for the entire history of the case | 65.7% |
| | |
| MONTHLY STATISTICS | |
| Documents all intakes, transfers, terminations, etc. | 44.9% |
| | |
| STAFFINGS | |
| Confers with other staff on informal basis about cases | 60.8% |

Source: L.R. Colley, R.G. Culbertson, and E.J. Latessa (1987). "Juvenile Probation Officers: A Job Analysis." *Juvenile and Family Court Journal*, 38(3):5.

Figure 6.5
**Percentage of Probation and Parole Officers in the United States: Male and Female**

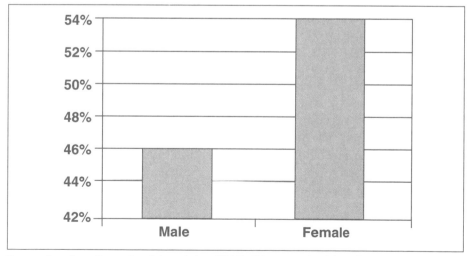

Source: American Correctional Association (2001). *Directory of Adult and Juvenile Correctional Departments, Institutions, Agencies, and Probation Authorities.* Lanham, MD: ACA, p. 56.

Figure 6.6
**Average Probation and Parole Staff Salaries on January 1, 2002**

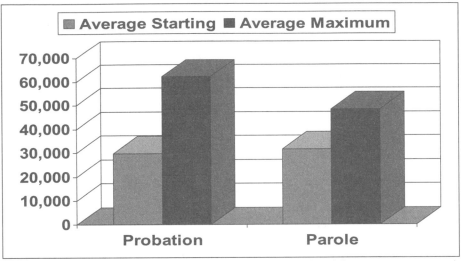

Source: Camp, C. and G. Camp (2003). *The Corrections Yearbook, Adult Corrections 2002*. Middletown, CT: The Criminal Justice Institute, Inc., p. 226

## Social Work or Law Enforcement?

The split between treatment and surveillance has attracted a great deal of attention, but very little in terms of empirical studies. Most authors seem to interpret role conflict as somehow tragic, intractable, and overwhelming. The most common solution has been to advocate that one orientation must be emphasized over all others (Gettinger, 1981). Simply put, is it the role of the probation or parole officer, or that of the helper or the cop?[4]

The roots of role conflict often are attributed to inconsistencies that exist in the three main functions of supervision: to enforce the legal requirements of supervision (the "law enforcement" role), to assist the offender in establishing a successful community adjustment (the "social worker" role), and to carry out the policies of the supervision agency (the "bureaucrat" role). The existence of this role conflict has been seen as a major source of staff burnout (Lindquist & Whitehead, 1986; Whitehead, 1989). Others have recommended abandoning one of the roles, either social work (Barkdull, 1976) or law enforcement (Stanley, 1976). Interestingly, no one seems to believe seriously that the bureaucratic role can ever be eliminated (Rosecrance, 1987; Lipsky, 1980; Takagi, 1967).

One critic of surveillance is Conrad (1979:21), who writes:

> We can hardly justify parole services on the basis of the surveillance model. What the parole officer can do, if it should be done at all, can better be done by the police. The pushing of doorbells, the recording of "contacts," and the requirement of monthly reports all add up to expensive pseudoservices. At

best they constitute a costly but useless frenzy of activity. But more often than not, I suspect, they harass and humiliate the parolee without gaining even the illusion of control.

Clear and Latessa (1993:442) believe that role conflict is common to most professions.

College professors face the age-old conflict of research and teaching; lawyers confront the conflicting demands of client advocacy and case management; even ministers must consider whether they represent the interest of deities to the world or the needs of lost souls (and requisite bodies) in the world.

Certainly, probation or parole officers have no monopoly on role conflict. Many feel that the true "professional" finds a way of integrating various role expectations, balancing them and weighing the appropriateness of various expressions of the roles. There is even some evidence that the roles of "social worker" and "law enforcer" are not incompatible, and that organizational policy can have a direct impact on the attitudes and behavior of probation and parole officers (Clear & Latessa, 1993).

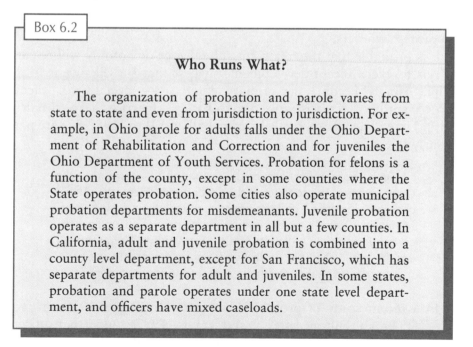

**Box 6.2**

### Who Runs What?

The organization of probation and parole varies from state to state and even from jurisdiction to jurisdiction. For example, in Ohio parole for adults falls under the Ohio Department of Rehabilitation and Correction and for juveniles the Ohio Department of Youth Services. Probation for felons is a function of the county, except in some counties where the State operates probation. Some cities also operate municipal probation departments for misdemeanants. Juvenile probation operates as a separate department in all but a few counties. In California, adult and juvenile probation is combined into a county level department, except for San Francisco, which has separate departments for adult and juveniles. In some states, probation and parole operates under one state level department, and officers have mixed caseloads.

A recent development in PO work is the increased level of assault by clients, leading to demand for arming or increased firepower (or both) of POs.[5] The exact number of critical incidents is unknown, as there is no state of federal bank that tracks the dangers faced by probation, parole, and even pretrial persons. However, a recent survey of probation and parole officers in Minnesota (Arola & Lawrence, 1999) found that 19 percent reported one of more physical assaults during their career, and 74 percent reported being verbally or physically threatened at least once. A similar study in Florida in 1999 found one in 20 probation and parole officers were battered each year.[6] With the emerging emphasis on supervision and surveillance within community corrections, the potential for crisis will increase. Another study of the extent of serious assault on community correctional personnel (Bigger, 1993) found 1,818 incidents since 1980, probably only the tip of the iceberg. Camp and Camp (20003) report more than 16,400 assaults by inmates on prison correctional staff in 2002; about one in four required medical attention. A national study concluded that 14 percent of juvenile justice institutional staff were assaulted in 1999 (Office of Juvenile Justice and Delinquency Prevention, 1999).

Not only is there a need for a central information bank that would track critical incidents, there is a need for in-service training and orientation that would lessen the incipient danger. Brown (1993) suggested that PO safety could be enhanced by physical training as well as being mentally prepared for such crises, including crisis rehearsal, understanding the continuum of force, kinesics (using force), and positive thinking ("self-thought"). Perhaps there is "no farewell to arms" in the offing, and administrators might implement training sessions to reduce liability and protect workers.[7]

It is probable that the treatment-surveillance dichotomy will remain with us forever. Recent developments suggest that surveillance is likely to increasingly become the primary emphasis—especially for clients who constitute a demonstrable risk to society (Harris, Clear & Baird, 1989). Here, conclusions made by Marshall and Vito (1982:37) are particularly relevant.

> . . . It is the manifest duty of the probation officer to keep the court aware of the conduct of the probationer. Here, the official charge to the officer and the directive to the client is most clear: Maintain or abide by the conditions of probation or face the consequences (i.e., violation and incarceration). The argument can be made that the protection of society was always paramount; the helping or treatment role was always secondary.

In a recent study of probation and parole officer attitudes in two states, Stichman, Fulton, Latessa, and Travis (1997) found that officers who had strong support for treatment strategies also placed more importance on control tasks. Conversely, they found that officers with more control attitudes led to placing more importance on treatment tasks. One explanation for this finding is that, as Morris (1978) states, control and treatment in corrections is a false dichotomy. In probation and parole agencies, control of offenders is always important, even if treatment is strongly supported. For example, for an officer to determine whether an offender is attending treatment and changing his or her behavior will require the officer to monitor the offender's behavior and compliance with the conditions of supervision. Stichman, Fulton, Latessa, and Travis (1998) also found that officers' attitudes and orientations may not have a significant effect on their own performance or on the performance of their clients. It may be possible that, similar to Clear and Latessa's (1993) findings that regardless of their own preferences, officers are able to perform the tasks that their organizational policy requires. The effect of officer attitudes and orientations on offender outcome is a very important question, and merits further study.

A final word about PO work, job performance, and satisfaction. Most POs find their work satisfying and their roles challenging, although many would hope for better work conditions, leadership, and quality of work. The federal probation system, which provides both probation and parole services, has begun to explore how to achieve better management through "total quality management" (TQM), widely implemented in corporate settings. TQM has certain management principles (Janes, 1993):

- leadership;

- customer-driven quality;

- continuous improvement of the work process;

- employee empowerment;

- blaming the system (not the people);

- ownership; and

- partnership.

Perhaps the quality of PO work would improve even more if administrators would implement team building through quality circles and self-managed teams.[8]

## Beyond Punishment and Treatment: The Restorative Role

Recently, there have been those who have argued that both retributive punishment (Braithwaite, 1989; Wilkins, 1991; Garland, 1990; Strang & Braithwaite, 2000), and treatment responses (Byrne, 1989; Reiss, 1986) are practically and conceptually incomplete. Bazemore and Umbreit (1995:301) believe that both punitive and treatment interventions place offenders in a passive role—as the objects of treatment or services on the one hand, and punishment and surveillance on the other. They offer as a new paradigm for supervision—a restorative model that shifts the focus of offender accountability from the state to the victim. Table 6.2 illustrates both the current system and a model of restorative justice.

With a restorative model, focus shifts from punishment, or even individual treatment, to accountability and restoring the community. Table 6.3 shows the differences in the messages espoused by the treatment, punishment, and restorative models. Recently, several states, in-

Table 6.2
**Current and Restorative Assumptions**

| Current System | Restorative Justice |
|---|---|
| Crime is an act against the state, a violation of the law, and abstract idea | Crime is an act against another person and the community |
| The criminal justice system controls crime | Crime control lies primarily in the community |
| Offender accountability defined as taking punishment | Accountability defined as assuming responsibility and taking action to repair harm |
| Crime is an individual act with individual responsibility | Crime has both individual and social dimensions of responsibility |
| Punishment is effective<br>  a. threat of punishment deters crime<br>  b. punishment changes behavior | Punishment alone is not effective in changing behavior and is disruptive to community harmony and good relationships |
| Victims are peripheral to the process | Victims are central to the process of resolving a crime |
| The offender is defined by deficits | The offender is defined by capacity to make reparations |
| Focus on establishing blame or guilt, on the past (did he/she do it?) | Focus on problem solving, on liabilities/obligations, on the future (what should be done?) |
| Emphasis on adversarial relationship | Emphasis on dialogue and negotiation |
| Imposition of pain to punish and deter/prevent | Restitution as a means of restoring both parties; goal of reconciliation/restoration |
| Community on sideline, represented abstractly by state | Community as facilitator in restorative process |

Source: G. Bazemore and M. Umbreit (1995). "Rethinking the Sanctioning Function in Juvenile Court: Retributive or Restorative Responses to Youth Crime." *Crime & Delinquency*, 41:303. Adopted from Zehr, 1990. Reprinted by permission of Sage Publications, Inc.

cluding Vermont and Ohio have begun to systematically introduce restorative into the correctional system. A public survey conducted in Vermont (Perry & Gorczyk, 1997) found that the public supports community-based sentences, but that they want accountability from the offender. Specifically, they want the following from offenders:

- Full acceptance of responsibility of the crime;

- Acknowledgement of guilt;

- Full restitution;

- A commitment never to repeat; and

- Some good to come from it.

Table 6.3
**"The 'Messages' of Sanctions"**

|  | Individual Treatment | Retributive Punishment | Restorative Accountability |
|---|---|---|---|
| Offender | You are "sick" or disturbed and your behavior is not your fault. We will provide treatment or services in your best interests. | You are a bad person who willfully chose to commit an offense. We will punish you with swiftness and severity proportionate to the seriousness of the crime. | Your actions have consequences; you have wronged someone or the community through your offense. You are responsible for your crime and capable of restoring the victim or repaying the damages. |
| Victim | Our fundamental concern is the needs of the offender. | The first concern of the system is to make offenders suffer the consequences of their crime. You will benefit because the offender will be punished. | The system believes you are important and will do its best to ensure that the offender repays the debt incurred to you from the crime. |
| Community | We will do our best to rehabilitate offenders through providing appropriate treatment and services. Highly trained professionals will solve the problem. Leave it to us. | We will do our best to punish offenders to teach them that crime will not be tolerated. Threats are the best way to control behavior. | Requiring offenders to repay victims and the public for their crimes receives highest priority in the justice system. We need the help of the community. The community is a key player in holding offenders accountable. |

Source: G. Bazemore and M. Umbreit (1995). "Rethinking the Sanctioning Function in Juvenile Court: Retributive or Restorative Responses to Youth Crime." *Crime & Delinquency*, 41:303. Adopted from Schneider, 1985.

Tables 6.2 through 6.4 compare three justice paradigms: Traditional Justice, Offender Rehabilitation, and Restorative Justice. With the Traditional model the emphasis is on deterrence, punishment, and incapacitation. The Offender Rehabilitation model focuses on reducing recidivism through the successful treatment of the offender. Finally, Restorative Justice attempts to restore the harm that has been done through reparation and improved quality of life for the community. Table 6.4 illustrates some of the differences among the three paradigms. It should be noted that some believe that the restorative justice model can be supplemented by key principles from the rehabilitation model, and combined to create a new model of justice and supervision (Rhine, Neff & Natalucci-Persichetti, 1998). Figures 6.7, 6.8 and 6.9 illustrate the traditional, rehabilitative, and restorative models. Whether this can be effectively accomplished is still open to debate.

A recent meta-analysis of studies of restorative justice programs by Latimer, Dowden, and Muise (2005) revealed several interesting findings:

- Participation in restorative justice programs resulted in significantly higher victim satisfaction ratings815

- Restorative justice programs had a moderate to weak positive impact on offender satisfaction

Table 6.4

**Comparison of Restorative Justice, Offender Rehabilitation, and Criminal Justice Models**

| Criteria | Restorative Justice | Offender Rehabilitation | Criminal Justice System |
|---|---|---|---|
| Primary Focus of Attention | Victims & Community | Higher-Risk Offenders | The Criminal Offense |
| Goals | Safe communities with improved quality of life for all citizens, restoration of victims and community; reparation of harm | Safe communities with improved quality of life for all citizens, rehabilitate offenders and reduce probability of re-offending | Safe communities with improved quality of life for all citizens, deterrence, retribution, and incapacitation |
| Role of Government | Limited | Moderate | Extensive |
| Principle Methods Used | Personal interactions | Cognitive/Behavioral Interventions | Surveillance and isolation of offenders from community |
| Community Members Involved | Victim, offender, community members, community agencies | Primarily offenders, criminal justice agencies, and select community agencies | Offenders and criminal justice agencies, and personnel |
| Flow of Resources | From offenders to victims to community | From offenders, victims and community to treatment programs | From victims and community to criminal justice services |

Source: A.H. Crow (1998). "Restorative Justice and Offender Rehabilitation: A Meeting of the Minds." *Perspectives*, 22:32.

- Offenders in restorative justice programs were more likely to complete restitution agreements

- Restorative justice programs had a very slight effect on recidivism rates (on average, about 6% less than comparison groups).

The authors concluded that while restorative justice programs produced some reductions in recidivism, the rates were considerably less than "appropriate correctional treatment."

Despite the growing call for a shift to a more restorative justice model, there are some critics. Levrant (1998) raises a number of potential concerns related to restorative justice programs. She divides these issues into three categories: staffing, programming, and clientele. Staff issues revolve around the problem of motivation and support of staff for reparative efforts. Vermont, for example, found staff resistance and differing philosophies of punishment were obstacles in program implementation (Dooley, 1996). Programmatic issues stem from the problems associated with changing the underlying manner in which programs operate. Despite efforts to the contrary, most programs remain offender-oriented, and continue to ignore the other criminal justice clientele. Restorative programs may also be easier to implement in communities that are better able to organize, thus possibly eliminating some of the

Figure 6.7
**Traditional Justice**

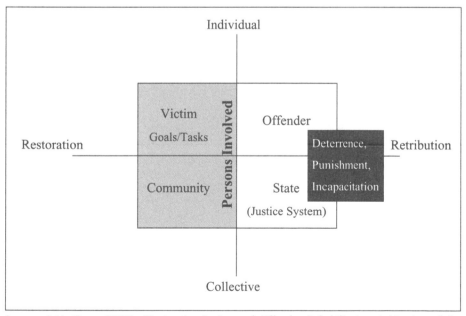

Source: A.H. Crow (1998). "Restorative Justice and Offender Rehabilitation: A Meeting of the Minds." *Perspectives*, 22:30-31.

Figure 6.8
**Offender Rehabilitation**

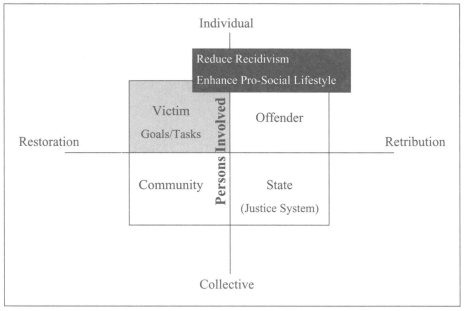

Source: A.H. Crow (1998). "Restorative Justice and Offender Rehabilitation: A Meeting of the Minds." *Perspectives*, 22:30-31.

Figure 6.9
**Restorative Justice**

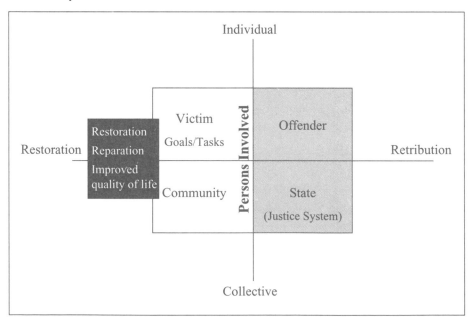

Source: A.H. Crow (1998). "Restorative Justice and Offender Rehabilitation: A Meeting of the Minds." *Perspectives*, 22:30-31.

more disadvantaged communities (where crime most often occurs). Clientele issues include the possibility of net-widening,[9] especially because of the increased willingness for victims and offenders involved in minor crimes to mediate the conflict (Niemeyer & Shichor, 1996; Campbell & Retzlaff, 2000). There is some evidence that many victims and offenders are unwilling to participate in these programs (Umbreit, 1992). A more recent study criticized restorative justice programs for not fulfilling the basic justice tenet that like offenders should be treated equally, that only a small percentage of cases consistently linked harm with repair, that "harm" is often ill-defined (and thus repair is difficult), and that program failure to link harm to repair may contribute to retributive contracts between offender and victim, including the community (Karp, 2001).

---

Box 6.3

### Motivating Offenders

Recently, many probation departments have begun training officers on motivational interviewing. First developed by Miller and Rollnick (1991), and based on Prochaska and DiClemente's (1983) stages of change, motivational interviewing is a technique designed to help prepare offenders to change their lifestyles. Officers are taught skills that can be used to help move an offender from the "not ready" to "ready" stage of change, and then keep them there.

---

## The "Broken Windows" Approach

Recently, there have been some leaders of probation and parole who have called for a dramatic change in the way in which community supervision achieves public safety.[10] This new model is called the "broken windows" approach. Borrowing heavily from community policing, the application of the broken windows model in probation and parole calls for a new partnership with the community. With this approach, the probation officer is asked to collaborate with the community and victim, hold the offender accountable, and improve and expand the leadership of probation. The key strategies outlined with this model include (Arola & Lawrence, 2001):

- Placing public safety first
- Working in the community
- Developing partners in the community

- Rationally allocating scarce resources
- Enforcing conditions and penalizing violations
- Emphasizing performance based initiatives
- Encouraging strong and steady leadership

While the goals of the broken windows approach are lofty, it is not without its critics. Taxman and Bryne (2001) argue that the model is filled with rhetoric, unrealistic, and based on a flawed approach. Furthermore, they contend that it ignores the significant body of research that indicates that the most effective way to achieve public safety is through well-designed and implemented treatment. Table 6.5 illustrates the differences between what Taxman and Bryne call the proactive supervision model and the broken windows model. This debate is just beginning; however, it remains to be seen if the broken windows model can live up to its promises.

Table 6.5:
**Fixing Broken Windows Probation: A Comparison of Two Strategies**

|  | **The Broken Windows Model** | **The Proactive Supervision Model** |
|---|---|---|
| **Definition of the Public Safety Problem** | Probation should be held responsible for the level of public safety in each community, including crime rates, fear of crime, school safety, and quality of life. | Probation should be held responsible for the supervision and control of all offenders under their direct supervision. |
| **The Duties of Probation Officers** | Probation officers should be involved not only in offender surveillance and control, but also in crime prevention efforts and various forms of advocacy and community change. | Probation officers should focus their efforts on the direct supervision of offenders while the responsibility for resource development and coordination should be completed by creating a new "resource specialist" position within probation. |
| **The Location of Probation Officers** | Probation officers should supervise offenders exclusively in the community rather than in the office. Supervision should be *place*-based rather than *offender*-based. | Probation officers should utilize a combination of office and field visits, but the purpose of the contract is always the supervision of the offender, not the place. |
| **The Role of the Probation Officers** | The probation officer should be a "generalist" with the ability to supervise a wide range of offenders (e.g., drug offenders, alcohol offenders, nonviolent offenders, sex offenders, mentally ill offenders), utilizing a classic brokerage model. | Probation officers should be hired and trained with the skills to handle a specialized caseload (e.g., drug offenders, alcohol offenders, nonviolent offenders, sex offenders, mentally ill offenders) including assessment procedures, counseling techniques and a comprehensive knowledge of the treatment network (in-patient and out-patient). |

Table 6.5—*continued*

|  | **The Broken Windows Model** | **The Proactive Supervision Model** |
|---|---|---|
| **The Acquisition and Allocation of Probation Resources** | Probation departments need to develop improved strategies for the rational allocation of *existing* resources, focusing on two primary agency needs: (1) better assessment of offender "risk" to public safety (e.g., sex offenders, gang members, drug dealers); (2) the assignment of field staff to areas with greatest public safety needs. | Probation departments need to "make the case" for increased resources for offender treatment and supervision, by proposing legislation that mandates minimum levels of probation (e.g., *case load size services*) and allows agents to use sanctions as a tool to improve public safety. |
| **Enforcement of Probation Conditions** | Probation officers utilize a range of field surveillance techniques to identify offender noncompliance and quickly respond to violations. A structural heirarchy of sanctions will be used for initial violations with revocation and (return to) prison/jail for repeat "offenders." | Probation departments develop strategies (in conjunction with local judiciary) to reduce the number of conditions established and to enforce the conditions set, using a structured hierarchy of non-incarcerative sanctions. |
| **Location of Absconders** | Probation Departments establish separate probation absconder location and apprehension units to better protect the community. | Probation departments develop a task force to better understand the nature (and impact) of the absconder problem. Utilizing a problem-oriented probation strategy, probation officers will be required directly to focus on addressing the cause(s) of the problem, rather than the consequences. |
| **Partnerships in the Community** | A wide range of probation-community partnerships will be developed, including both crime prevention and community betterment activities. | Probation departments will focus on improving the treatment networks in their community and on those related activities that will enhance the supervision function. |

Source: Taxman, F. and J. Byrne (2001). "Fixing Broken Windows Probation." *Perspectives*, 25(2):26.

# Education and Training of Probation and Parole Officers

During the past 30 years, several national commissions and studies have recommended formal education as a means of significantly improving the delivery of justice in this country (President's Commission, 1967; American Bar Association, 1970; National Advisory Commission, 1973a; National Manpower Survey of the Criminal Justice System, 1978; Sherman, 1978). Graduate-level education and frequent in-service training for probation and parole officers have also been advocated for many years. The emerging philosophy now requires undergraduate degree education as a prerequisite for quality probation and parole service, and continuous in-service training as a means of maintaining and improving both service and skills (President's Commission, 1967; Loughery, 1975; National Advisory Commission, 1973b; Senna, 1976).

Since 1959, the National Probation and Parole Association has recommended that all probation and parole officers should hold at least a bachelor's degree, supplemented by at least one year of graduate study or full-time field experience. This recommendation reflects the assumption that an educated officer is more competent and mature and thus in a better position to efficiently perform the varied functions of probation and parole. However, it was not until the 1967 President's Commission on Law Enforcement and Administration of Justice Task Force Report, which led to the Law Enforcement Education Program, that federal funds were made available for higher education of justice system personnel, including a college education for probation and parole officers. In 1970, the American Bar Association (1970:92) reaffirmed the National Probation and Parole Association's minimum standards, and suggested that probation and parole officers should hold a master's degree. It is also important to note that the American Correctional Association Accreditation Guidelines for Probation and Parole (1981) require entry-level probation and parole officers to possess a minimum of a bachelor's degree. They consider this an important guideline for accreditation.

Photo 6.1
Training session. Photograph by Betsy Fulton.

From the data in Table 6.6, it can be seen that more than 80 percent of the jurisdictions in this country require at least a bachelor's degree for initial employment of probation and parole officers. A 1987 survey of Texas probation officers (Philips, 1987) found that more than 92 percent had a bachelor's degree or higher. Similarly, results from Illinois reported that more than 84 percent of probation officers had a four-year college degree or higher (Colley, Culbertson & Latessa, 1987a).

In addition, many jurisdictions require specific areas of college study, as well as various levels of training and experience. In a survey of all 50 state and the District of Columbia, Reddington and Kreisel (2000) gathered information about trainging requirents for juvenile probation officers. They found that 45 percent (20 states) certify the juvenile probaton officer position, and 82 percent (36 states) mandated training. While there is some consensus as to the level of education needed (bachelor's

Table 6.6
**Entry-Level Requirements for Parole and Probation Officers**

| Jurisdiction | Parole Officers | Probation Officers |
|---|---|---|
| Alabama | BS | BS |
| Alaska | BS | BS |
| Arizona | High school | BS |
| Arkansas | BS | BA |
| California | Some college | Varies, set by counties |
| Colorado | BS | BS + Test |
| Connecticut | BS | BS |
| Delaware | BS | BS |
| Florida | BS | BS + Experience |
| Georgia | BS | BS |
| Hawaii | BS | MS in CJ, or BS + Experience |
| Idaho | Some college | High School |
| Illinois | BS | BS |
| Indiana | AS | BS |
| Iowa | High School | High School |
| Kansas | AS | BS |
| Kentucky | BS | BS |
| Louisiana | BS or Experience | BS or Experience |
| Maine | BS | BS |
| Maryland | BS | BS |
| Massachusetts | High School | BS |
| Michigan | BS | BS |
| Minnesota | High School | High School |
| Mississippi | BS | MS in related field, or BS + Experience |
| Missouri | BS | BS |
| Montana | BS | BS + Experience |
| Nebraska | Not Known | BS |
| Nevada | BS | BS + Experience |
| New Hampshire | BS | BS |
| New Jersey | BS | BS |
| New Mexico | BS | BS |
| New York | BS | BS |
| North Carolina | BS | BS |
| North Dakota | BS + Experience | BS + Experience |
| Ohio | BS | BA |
| Oklahoma | BS | BS |
| Oregon | BS | BS |
| Pennsylvania | BS | BS |
| Rhode Island | High School | BS |
| South Carolina | BS | BS |
| South Dakota | BS + Experience | BS |
| Tennessee | BS | BS |
| Texas | BS | BS |
| Utah | Unknown | BS |
| Vermont | Unknown | BS |
| Virginia | BS | BS |
| Washington | BS | BS |
| West Virginia | AS | AS |
| Wisconsin | BS | BS |
| Wyoming | BS | BS |

Sources: American Correctional Association (2001). *Probation and Parole Directory 2001-2003.*
(Lanham, MD): 10-11, and adapted from "Survey" (1987). *Corrections Compendium*, October 9-13.

degree), the exact content of undergraduate study is still a matter of some debate. Generally speaking, however, aspiring probation and parole personnel would better prepare themselves for agency entry by enrolling in various criminal justice, sociology, counseling, social work, and psychology courses. There is also some evidence that a comprehensive approach to training and development can effectively instill in officers the supervision attitudes that are most conducive to promoting offender change (Stichman, Fulton, Travis & Latessa, 1997).

## Summary

In summary, the conflict between counseling and surveillance is simply part of the job of the PO and a duality that makes their positions in the criminal justice system vital, unique, and necessary. While some see role conflict as a reason for eviscerating some of the less salient tasks, others believe that the profession can find a way of integrating and balancing various role expectations.

The role of probation and parole agencies are varied and range from investigating violations to assisting offenders in obtaining employment. Accordingly, the skills and education required of probation officers are often considerable. The need for college-educated staff has been advocated for many years and is becoming a reality. There has come to be a general acceptance of formal education as a prerequisite of quality probation and parole service, and of in-service development as a means of maintaining and improving that service. This need has been identified and encouraged by several national commissions and organizations, as well as by numerous individual writers and researchers. A decade from now, the entry-level educational requirement may be a master's degree.

Finally, although in many ways probation and parole officers perform the same basic duties that they did when the profession first began, there are many who argue that a change is in order. Restorative justice and the broken windows models represent new paradigms for the field.

### Review Questions

1.  What are the four primary responsibilities of a probation or parole agency?

2.  What are the quasi-judicial roles of probation officers?

3.  How does a probation/parole officer serve a law enforcement role? A social work role?

4. List those tasks that a probation or parole officer can undertake to assist an offender, and those to control an offender.

5. List the seven categories of tasks ranked by probation officers in the von Langingham study.

6. According to Andrews, what are the characteristics of effective agents of change?

7. What are the principles of restorative justice and how does it differ from a more traditional approach?

8. What are some of the criticisms of the restorative model, and what do we know about its effectiveness?

9. What is the "broken windows" model and how does it differ from a proactive supervision approach?

## *Key Terms*

broken windows
conditions of probation
investigation
proactive supervision
protective officer

punitive officer
restorative justice
surveillance
welfare officer

## *Electronic Library*

American Probation and Parole Associaton (http://www.appa-net.org/)

Assault on probation officers (http://www.ojjdp.ncjrs.org/jjbulletin/9808/scope.html).

Battery of probation officers (www.fcc.state.fl.us/fcc/reports/final99/2sr.html).

Broken windows probation (www.manhattan-institute.org/html/broken_windows.htm).

California Probation, Parole, and Correctional Association (www.cppca.org).

A look into the job of a parole agent (http://www.pappc.org/journal/spring-2001/6.htm).

National Association of Probation Executives (http://www.correctionssoftware.com/nape/).

Officer and staff safety (www.doc.state.nc.us/NEWS/1999/9909news/dcc.htm).

Probation safety survey (www.correctionssoftware.com/nape/surveys_page.htm).

Two models of probation: BARJ and broken windows (http://www.pappc.org/journal/spring-2001/7.htm).

## Recommended Readings

Conrad, J. (1979). "Who Needs a Doorbell Pusher?" *The Prison Journal*, 59(1), 17-26. Building upon his experience as a probation officer, a noted scholar gives his opinions on the role of supervision.

Ditton, J. and R. Ford (1994). *The Reality of Probation: A Formal Ethnography of Process and Practice*. Aldershot, UK: Avebury.

McCleary, R. (1978). *Dangerous Men: The Sociology of Parole*. Beverly Hills, CA: Sage Publications. Based on participant observation, this is an in-depth examination of a parole agency and the supervision styles of its officers.

Parent, D., D. Wentworth, and P. Burke (1994). *Responding to Probation and Parole Violators*. Washington, DC: U.S. National Institute of Justice.

Ward, R. and V. Webb (1981). *Quest for Quality*. New York, NY: University Publications. This is the report of the Joint Commission on Criminology and Criminal Justice Education and Standards. It examines the issues surrounding the education of criminal justice professionals.

## Notes

[1]    Throughout this chapter, when the abbreviation PO is utilized, it is meant to designate both probation and parole officers. Their views with regard to their role, as well as the dilemmas that they face, are so intimately related that this abbreviation will not misrepresent the opinions, findings, and conclusions of the various authors.

[2]    Nowhere is the dichotomy of rehabilitation-casework versus surveillance-control more evident than between juvenile and adult probation officers. Juvenile officers support the former by a wide margin, but felony probation officers, particularly males, are more likely to endorse law enforcement strategies. R. Sluder and F. Reddington (1993). "An Empirical Examination of Work Ideologies of Juvenile and Adult Probation Officers." *Journal of Offender Rehabilitation*, 22:115-137. See also Brown, M. and J. Pratt (Eds.) (2000). *Dangerous Offenders: Punishment and Social Order*. London, UK: Routledge.

[3]    Most probationers satisfy financial obligations as ordered by the court. G. Allen and H. Treger (1994). "Fines and Restitution Orders: Probations' Perceptions." *Federal Probation*, 58(2):34-40. For fines levied on corporations, see Clarkson, C. (2000). "Corporate Risk-Taking and Killing." *Risk Management*, 2(1):7-16.

[4]    For a discussion of law enforcement officers as agents of reintegrative surveillance, see S. Guarino-Ghezzi (1994). "Reintegrative Police Surveillance of Juvenile Offenders: Forging an Urban Model." *Crime & Delinquency*, 40:131-153.

[5]    North Carolina Department of Corrections News (1999). Officer and Staff Safety a Top Priority for Department of Corrections (www.doc.state.nc.us/NEWS/1999/9909news/dcc.htm).

[6]    Florida Corrections Commission (2000). Special Risk for Correctional Probation Officers (www.fcc.state.fl.us/fcc/reports/final99/2sr.html).

[7]    Janes, R. (1993). "Total Quality Management: Can It Work in Federal Probation?" *Federal Probation*, 57(4):28-33; F. Chavaria (1994). "Building Synergy in Probation." *Federal Probation*, 58(3):18-22; and National Institute of Corrections (2001). Topics in Community Corrections: Collaboration an Essential Strategy (www.nicic.org/pubs/2001/period200.pdf).

[8]    Bazemore, G. and L. Leip (2000). "Victim Participation in the New Juvenile Court." *Justice System Journal*, 21(2):199-226. See also Cullen, F., B. Fisher, and B. Applegate, "Public Opinion about Punishment and Corrections." In Tonry, M. (Ed.) (2000). *Crime and Justice: A Review of Research*, Vol. 27:1-29.

[9]    Mears, D. (2000). "Assessing the Effectiveness of Juvenile Justice Reforms." *Law and Society*, 22(2):175-202.

[10]    The Reinventing Probation Council that drafted the initial report on broken windows and probation were: Ronald Corbett, Dan Beto, John DiIulio, J. Richard Faulkner, Bernard Fitzgerald, Irwin Gregg, Norman Helber, Gerald Hinzman, Robert Malvestuto, Mario Paparozzi, Rocco Pozzi, and Edward Rhine. See Reinventing Probation Council (2001). Transforming Probation through Leadership: The Broken Windows Model (www.manhattan-institute.org/html/broken_windows.htm).

## *References*

American Bar Association (1970). *Standards Relating to Probation*. New York, NY: American Bar Association.

American Correctional Association (1995). *Field Officer Resources Guide*. Laurel, MD: ACA, 1994.

American Correctional Association (1981). *Standards for Adult Probation and Parole Field Services*. Rockville, MD: Commission on Accreditation for Corrections, ACA.

American Correctional Association (2001). *Probation and Parole Directory, 2001-2003*. Laurel, MD: ACA.

Andrews, D. (1979). *The Dimensions of Correctional Counseling and Supervision Process in Probation and Parole*. Toronto, CN: Ontario Ministry of Correctional Services.

Arola, T. and R. Lawrence (1999). "Assessing Probation Officer Assaults and Responding to Officer Safety Concerns." *Perspectives*, 23(3):32-35.

Arola, T. and R. Lawrence (2000). "Broken Windows Probation." *Perspectives*, 24(1):27-33.

Barkdull, W. (1976). "Probation: Call It Control and Mean It." *Federal Probation*, 40(4):3-8.

Bazemore, G. and M. Umbreit (1995). "Rethinking the Sanctioning Function in Juvenile Court: Retributive or Restorative Responses to Youth Crime." *Crime & Delinquency*, 41:296-316.

Bigger, P. (1993). "Officers in Danger." *APPA Perspectives*, 17(4):14-20.

Blumberg, A. (1974). *Criminal Justice.* New York, NY: New Viewpoints.

Braithwaite, J. (1989). *Crime, Shame and Reintegration.* New York, NY: Cambridge University Press.

Brown, M. and J. Pratt (eds.) (2000). *Dangerous Offenders: Punishment and Social Order.* London, UK: Routledge.

Brown, P. (1993). "Probation Officer Safety and Mental Conditioning." *Federal Probation*, 57(4):17-21.

Byrne, J.M. (1989). "Reintegrating the Concept of Community into Community-Based Corrections." Crime & Delinquency, 35:471-499.

California Probation, Parole and Correctional Association, History (www.cppca.org/history.htm).

Camp, C. and G. Camp (20003). *The Corrections Yearbook: Adult Corrections 2002.* Middletown, CT: The Criminal Justice Institute.

Carlson, E. and E. Parks (1979). *Critical Issues in Adult Probation.* Washington, DC: National Institute of Law Enforcement and Criminal Justice.

Clarkson, C. (2000). "Corporate Risk-Taking and Killing." *Risk Management*, 2(1):7-16.

Clear, T. and E. Latessa (1993). "Probation Officer Roles in Intensive Supervision: Surveillance Versus Treatment." *Justice Quarterly*, 10:441-462.

Chavaria, F. (1994). "Building Synergy in Probation." *Federal Probation*, 58(3):18-22.

Colley, L., R. Culbertson, and E. Latessa (1987). "Juvenile Probation Officers: A Job Analysis." *Juvenile and Family Court Journal*, 38(3):1-12.

Colley, L., R. Culbertson, and E. Latessa (1986). "Probation Officer Job Analysis: Rural-Urban Differences." *Federal Probation*, 50(4):67-71.

Conrad, J. (1979). "Who Needs a Door Bell Pusher?" *The Prison Journal*, 59:17-26.

*Corrections Compendium* (October, 1987). Survey, pp. 9-13.

Crowe, A. (1998) "Restorative Justice and Offender Rehabilitation: A Meeting of the Minds." *Perspectives*, 3:28-40.

Cullen, F., B. Fisher, and B. Applegate, "Public Opinion about Punishment and Corrections." In Tonry, M. (ed.) (2000). *Crime and Justice: A Review*, Vol. 27, pp. 1-79.

Czajkoski, E. (1973). "Exposing the Quasi-Judicial Role of the Probation Officer." *Federal Probation*, 37(2):9-13.

Dooley, M. (1996). "Reparative Probation Boards." In B. Fulton (ed.) *Restoring Hope Through Community Partnerships: The Real Deal in Crime Control*, pp. 185-192. Lexington, KY: American Probation and Parole Association.

Erickson, C. (1977). "Faking It: Principles of Expediency as Applied to Probation." *Federal Probation*, 41(3):36-39.

Florida Corrections Commission (2000). Special Risk for Correctional Probation Officers (http://www.fcc.state.fl.us/fcc/reports/final99/2sr.html).

Fogel, D. (1975). *We Are the Living Proof* . . . Cincinnati, OH: Anderson Publishing Co.

Fulton B., A. Stichman, L. Travis, and E. Latessa (1997). "Moderating Probation and Parole Officer Attitudes To Achieve Desired Outcomes." *The Prison Journal*, 77:295-312.

Garland, D. (1990). *Punishment and Modern Society: A Study in Social Theory.* Chicago, IL: University of Chicago Press.

Gettinger, S. (1981, April). "Separating the Cop from the Counselor." *Corrections Magazine*, 7:34-41.

Glaser, D. (1969). *The Effectiveness of a Prison and Parole System.* Indianapolis, IN: Bobbs-Merrill.

Harris, P., T. Clear, and S. Baird (1989). "Have Community Supervision Officers Changed Their Attitudes Toward Their Work." *Justice Quarterly*, 6:233-246.

Janes, R. (1993). "Total Quality Management: Can It Work in Federal Probation?" *Federal Probation*, 57(4):28-33.

Jordan, F. and J. Sasfy (1974). *National Impact Program Evaluation: A Review of Selected Issues and Research Findings Related to Probation and Parole.* Washington, DC: Mitre Corp.

Karp, D. (2001). "Harm and Repair: Observing Restorative Justice in Vermont." *Justice Quarterly*, 18(4):727-757.

Klockars, C. (1972). "A Theory of Probation Supervision." *Journal of Criminal Law, Criminology and Police Science*, 63:550-557.

Latimer, J., C. Dowden, and D. Muise (2005). "The Effectiveness of Restorative Justice Practices: A Meta Analysis." *Prison Journal*, 85(2):127-144.

Levrant, S. (1998). "Restorative Justice: Emerging Paradigm or Fleeting Panacea." Master's Thesis. Cincinnati, OH: Division of Criminal Justice, University of Cincinnati.

Lindner, C. (1975). "The Juvenile Offender's Right to Bail," *Probation and Parole*, 7(3):64-68.

Lindquist, C. and J. Whitehead (1986). "Correctional Officers as Parole Officers: An Examination of a Community Supervision Sanction." *Criminal Justice and Behavior*, 13:197-222.

Lipsky, M. (1980). *Street Level Bureaucracy.* New York, NY: Russell-Sage.

Loughery, D. (1975). "College Education: A Must for Probation Officers?" *Crime and Corrections*, 3:1-7.

Marciniak, L. (2000). "The Addition of Day Reporting to Intensive Supervision Probation." *Federal Probation*, 64(2):34-39.

Marshall, F. and G.F. Vito (1982). "Not Without the Tools: The Task of Probation in the Eighties." *Federal Probation*, 46(4):37-40.

McCleary, R. (1978). *Dangerous Men: The Sociology of Parole.* Beverly Hills, CA: Sage Publications.

Mears, D. (2000). "Assessing the Effectiveness of Juvenile Justice Reforms." *Law and Society*, 22(2):175-202.

Miles, A. (1965a). "The Reality of the Probation Officer's Dilemma." *Federal Probation*, 29(1):18-22.

Miles, A. (1965b). "Wisconsin Studies the Function of Probation and Parole." *American Journal of Corrections*, 25:21-32.

Miller, W. and S. Rollnick (1991). *Motivational Interviewing: Preparing for Change*. New York: Guilford Press.

Morris, N. (1978). Conceptual Overview and Commentary on the Movement Toward Determinacy. Determinate Sentencing: Reform or Regression? Washington, DC: U.S. Government Printing Office.

National Advisory Commission on Criminal Justice Standard and Goals (1973a). *Criminal Justice System*. Washington, DC: U.S. Government Printing Office.

National Advisory Commission on Criminal Justice Standard and Goals (1973b). *Corrections*. Washington, DC: U.S. Government Printing Office.

National Association of Probation Executives (1999). Probation Safety Survey: Executive Summary (www.correctionssoftware.com/nape/surveys_page.htm).

"National Probation and Parole Association Standards for Selection of Probation and Parole Personnel" (1959). In D. Dressler (ed.) *Practice and Theory of Probation and Parole*, pp. 221. New York, NY: Columbia University.

Niemeyer, M. and D. Shichor (1996). "A Preliminary Study of a Large Victim/Offender Reconciliation Program." *Federal Probation*, 60(3):30-34.

Office of Juvenile Justice and Delinquency Prevention (1998). Youth Gangs: An Overview (www.ojjdp.ncjrs.org/jjbulletin/9808/scope.html).

Ohlin, L., H. Piven, and M. Pappenfort (1956). "Major Dilemmas of the Social Worker in Probation and Parole." *National Probation and Parole Association Journal*, 2:21-25.

O'Leary, V. (1974). "Parole Administration." In D. Glaser (eds.) *Handbook of Criminology*, pp. 909-948. New York, NY: Rand McNally.

Perry, J. and J. Gorczyk (1997). "Restructuring Corrections: Using Market Research in Vermont." *Corrections Management Quarterly*, 1(3):26-35.

Petersilia, J. and S. Turner (1993). "Intensive Probation and Parole." In M. Tonry (ed.) *Crime and Justice: A Review of Research*, 17:281-336.

Philips, P. (1987). *Task Analysis Report on the Job of Adult Probation Officer*. Sam Houston, TX: Criminal Justice Research Center, Sam Houston State University.

President's Commission on Law Enforcement and Administration of Justice (1967). *Task Force Report: Corrections*. Washington, DC: U.S. Government Printing Office.

Prochaska, J., and C. DiClemente (1993). "Stages and Processes of Self-Change in Smoking: Toward an Integrative Model of Change." *Journal of Consulting and Clinical Psychology*. 51 (3):390-395.

Reddington, F. P., and B.W. Kreisel (2000). "Training Juvenile Probation Officers: National Trends and Patterns." *Federal Probation*, 64(2):28-32.

Reinventing Probation Council (2001). Transforming Probation through Leadership: The "Broken Windows" Model (www.manhattan-institute.org/html/broken_windows.htm).

Reiss, A. (1986). "Why Are Communities Important in Understanding Crime?" In A. Reiss and M. Tonry (eds.) *Communities and Crime*, pp. 1-33. Chicago, IL: University of Chicago Press.

Rhine, E., A. Neff, and G. Natalucci-Persichetti (1998). "Restorative Justice, Public Safety and the Supervision of Juvenile Offenders." *Correctional Management Quarterly*, 2(3):16-28.

Rosecrance, J. (1987). "Getting Rid of the Prima Donnas: The Bureaucratization of a Probation Department." *Criminal Justice and Behavior*, 14:138-155.

Schneider, A. (1985). *Guide to Juvenile Restitution*. Washington, DC: U.S. Department of Justice, Office of Juvenile Justice and Delinquency Prevention.

Schneider, P., W. Griffith, and A. Schneider (1982). "Juvenile Restitution as a Sole Sanction or Condition of Probation: An Empirical Analysis." *Journal of Research in Crime & Delinquency*, 19:47-65.

Senna, J. (1976). "The Need for Professional Education in Probation and Parole." *Crime & Delinquency*, 22:67-74.

Sherman, L. (1978). *The Quality of Police Education*. San Francisco, CA: Jossey-Bass.

Shichor, D. (1978) "The People Changing Versus People Processing Organizational Perspective: The Case of Correctional Institutions." *LAE-Journal of the American Criminal Justice Association*, 4(3):37-44.

Simon, J. (1993). *Poor Discipline: Parole and Social Control of the Underclass, 1890-1990*. Chicago, IL: University of Chicago Press.

Smith, A. and L. Berlin (1974). "Self-Determination in Welfare and Corrections: Is There a Limit?" *Federal Probation*, 38(4):3-6.

Stanley, D. (1976). *Prisoners Among Us: The Problem of Parole*. Washington, DC: Brookings Institute.

Stichman, A., B. Fulton, E. Latessa, and F. Travis (1998). "Probation Officer Attitudes and Offender Performance: Is There a Link?" Paper presented at the Academy of Criminal Justice Sciences, Albuquerque, NM.

Stichman, A., B. Fulton, E. Latessa, and F. Travis (1997). "From Preference to Performance: Exploring the Relationship Between Role Definition and Role Performance Among Probation Officers." Paper presented at the Academy of Criminal Justice Sciences, Louisville, KY.

Strang, H. and J. Braithwaite (eds.) (2000). *Restorative Justice: Philosophy to Practice*. Aldershot, UK: Ashgate.

Studt, E. (1978). *Surveillance and Service in Parole*. U.S. Department of Justice: National Institute of Corrections.

Takagi, P. (1967). *Evaluation and Adaptations in a Formal Organization*. Berkeley, CA: University of California.

Taxman, F. (2006). "What Should we Expect From Parole (and Probation) Under a Behavioral Management Approach?" *Perspectives*, 30(2):38-465.

Taxman, F. and J. Bryne (2001). "Fixing Broken Windows: Probation." *Perspectives*, 25(2):23-29.

Tomaino, L. (1975). "The Five Faces of Probation." *Federal Probation*, 39(4):41-46.

Umbreit, M. (1992). "Mediating Victim-Offender Conflict: From Single-Site to Multi-Site Analysis in the U.S." In H. Messmer and H. Otto, *Restorative Justice on Trial: Pitfalls and Potentials of Victim-Offender Mediation—International Research Perspectives*, pp. 431-444, Boston, MA: Kluwer Academic Publishers.

Wallace, J. (1974). "Probation Administration." In D. Glaser (ed.) *Handbook of Criminology*, pp. 949-969. New York, NY: Rand McNally.

Whitehead, J. (1989). *Burnout in Probation and Corrections*. New York, NY: Praeger.

Wilkins, L. (1991). *Punishment, Crime and Market Forces*. Brookfield, VT: Dartmouth Publishing Co.

Zehr, H. (1990). *Changing Lenses: A New Focus for Crime and Justice*. Scottsdale, PA: Herald Press.

## 7

# Strategies for Classifying, Managing, and Providing Services to Offenders

It is hard to change when the only model we have to copy is ourselves.

—Anonymous

## Introduction

In terms of community safety, the most significant responsibility of a probation or parole agency is supervising offenders. Underlying this duty are the dual objectives of protecting the community and helping the offenders. As we have already learned, these objectives are not always compatible.

Depending upon the jurisdiction in which the agency is located, offenders placed on probation and parole may have committed almost any type of criminal offense, and may range from first-time offenders to career criminals. The number of offenders placed on probation or released on parole will also vary considerably over time, depending upon political and fiscal climates in the jurisdiction, existing law in the jurisdiction, size of the prison overpopulation, and the prevailing philosophy toward the use of probation and parole.

The bulk of probation and parole clients are under regular supervision, although about one in eight are under some other management program, such as intensive supervision, electronic monitoring, house arrest, or other special program (Camp & Camp, 2003). Two trends emerging over time are the increased number of clients under correctional control (see Table 7.1), and the increasing use of alternatives to regular supervision. The implications of these supervision strategies are explored below.

In addition, there is likely to be variation among probationers and parolees with respect to the type and extent of conditions imposed upon them by the court or the parole board. Finally, individuals being super-

Table 7.1
**Persons Under Adult Correctional Supervision, 1995-2005**

| Year | Total Estimated Correctional Population | Community Supervision | | Incarceration | |
|------|------|------|------|------|------|
| | | Probation | Parole | Jail | Prison |
| 1995 | 5,342,900 | 3,077,861 | 679,421 | 507,044 | 1,078,542 |
| 2000 | 6,445,100 | 3,826,209 | 723,898 | 621,149 | 1,316,333 |
| 2001 | 6,581,700 | 3,931,731 | 732,333 | 631,240 | 1,330,007 |
| 2002 | 6,758,800 | 4,024,067 | 750,934 | 665,475 | 1,367,547 |
| 2003 | 6,924,500 | 4,120,012 | 769,925 | 691,301 | 1,390,279 |
| 2004 | 6,995,300 | 4,143,466 | 771,852 | 713,990 | 1,421,911 |
| 2005 | 7,056,000 | 4,162,536 | 784,408 | 747,529 | 1,446,269 |

Source: Bureau of Justice Statistics (2006). *Probation and Parole in the United States, 2005.* Washington, D.C.: Bureau of Justice Statistics, p.1 (http://www.ojp.usdoj.gov/bjs/abstract/ppus05.htm).

vised will vary considerably in the types of problems they face (family difficulties, educational or employment needs, mental illness, alcohol or drug abuse). See Table 7.2. As with other major responsibilities of a probation or parole agency, supervision necessitates an organizational structure that will enable the agency to protect the community efficiently and effectively, and to provide the necessary support to aid the offender.

Table 7.2
**Examples of Problems Faced by Offenders Under Supervision**

| Correctional Client Group: | Substance Abuse: | | Mentally Ill | Prior Mental or Physical Abuse Reported |
|------|------|------|------|------|
| | Alcohol | Drug | | |
| Probationers | 40% | 14% | 16% | 16% |
| Jail Inmates* | 41 | 36 | 11 | 16 |
| State Prisoners | 37 | 33 | 10 | 19 |

*Substance abuse for jail inmates was defined as under the influence of drugs or of alcohol at the time of the offense.

Sources: C. Harlow (1999). *Prior Abuse Reported by Inmates and Probationers.* Washington, DC: Bureau of Justice Statistics, p.1; C. Mumola (1999). *Substance Abuse and Treatment, States and Federal Prisoners, 1997.* Washington, DC: U.S. Bureau of Justice Statistics, p. 1; C. Maurschak and A. Beck (2001). *Medical Problems of Inmates, 1997.* Washington, DC: U.S. Bureau of Justice Statistics, p. 3.

Considering the complexity involved in complying with these duties, it is obvious that the agency will be faced with a number of critical management problems and alternatives from which to choose. Many of these that will be discussed separately are, in reality, closely intertwined. They are not "either/or" alternatives. In fact, many strategies can easily be mixed into a variety of combinations.

This chapter addresses the broad area of service delivery and the ways in which probation and parole agencies handle offenders assigned for supervision. The philosophical models of treatment delivery are examined, as well as the planning process of supervision, different levels of caseload size, ways in which offenders are classified and assessed, and new developments in the area of contracting for services and managing community resources.

## Caseload Assignment Models

Offenders are assigned to a probation department by the court, to a parole department by the parole board, and to other community correctional agencies, such as halfway houses, by both.[1] Because the vast majority of offenders supervised in the community are first placed on probation or parole, we will examine the ways in which offenders are individually assigned to probation or parole officers.

How cases are individually assigned to available probation and parole officers varies from jurisdiction to jurisdiction. Carter and Wilkins (1976:391-401) have developed a useful typology of caseload models that includes the major variations in assignment strategies. Underlying their typology is the assumption that the offender population will vary considerably across any characteristic in question (Sigler & Williams, 1994).

The first model is called the conventional model and it ignores the differences and similarities among offenders; cases are randomly assigned to available probation and parole officers. Because of the random distribution of the offender population among caseloads, each officer handles a mixture that is generally a miniature reproduction of the entire offender population including, of course, wide variation in personal characteristics. With the conventional caseload model, then, probation or parole officers must be able to supervise any type of offender who happens to be assigned to their caseload.

Closely related to the conventional model is what is called the numbers game model. This type may also ignore differences and similarities across offenders. The object of this model is to numerically balance all caseloads within the department. This balancing may or may not take the personal characteristics of individual offenders into account because the numbers game model can be approached in two ways. First, the number of cases to be supervised can simply be divided by the number of officers available to the department. For example, if a probation department has 10 probation officers and 800 probationers, every officer will handle a caseload of 80. Alternatively, the department can select an "ideal size" for each caseload and divide the number of offenders by the ideal size, yielding the number of necessary officers. Under this method, if a department has 800 probationers and has selected 50 as its ideal size caseload, then it must provide 16 probation officers. Variations of the numbers game model may also be used with the other models discussed below.

The third assignment model is called the conventional model with geographic considerations. This one differs from the conventional model in one important respect: the caseload is restricted to residents in one type of geographic area (urban, suburban, or rural). Given the travel time necessary to supervise an entirely rural caseload, the size of a rural caseload is generally smaller than suburban or urban caseloads. Such caseloads, however, are not differentiated on the basis of the personal characteristics of the offenders, except to the extent that the characteristics of urban, suburban, and rural offenders may vary. In a large urban area, probation and parole departments may have satellite offices. When this is the case, geographic distinctions may be based on the side of town in which an offender resides.

The other two assignment techniques recognize the presence of important similarities and differences among offenders. The more elementary of these techniques is called the single-factor specialized caseload model. This groups offenders together on the basis of one single characteristic that they all share. Examples include drug and or alcohol abuse, mental retardation, sex, age, type of offense, and high potential for violent behavior ("risk"). Despite the existence of a shared characteristic, offenders on each single-factor specialized caseload may vary widely on other characteristics. For example, a caseload restricted to offenders between the ages of 18 and 21 may still include individuals who differ considerably on such variables as type of offense or potential risk to community.

Finally, the most complex assignment model, the vertical model, classifies offenders on the basis of two or more factors or characteristics. Often this classification is accomplished by using one of the various prediction devices that estimates the chances of a particular offender's succeeding or failing while under supervision. Prediction devices take a wide variety of individual characteristics into account and stress the similarities among individuals. Once all offenders in the agency are screened according to their probability of success, this classificatory scheme can then be used to create caseloads composed of offenders who have roughly the same chances of success or failure. This model is called vertical because it divides the range of offender characteristics into vertical slices in order to create caseloads.

Caseload size can be varied across both the single-factor and the multifactor classifications. For example, the size of caseloads, when based in the vertical model, are usually varied; it can be decreased in those composed of offenders with a high risk of failure, or increased for those composed of low-risk offenders.

Today, many departments employ workload formulas to determine caseload size. This technique takes into account the fact that not all offenders are the same and some will require more attention than others. Here, cases are screened according to a number of factors, such as risk. Table 7.3 shows an example of a monthly work unit ledger from the Montgomery County Adult Probation Department (Dayton, Ohio). In this particular department, a standard workload is 250 work units, based on 107.5 available hours per month. A high-risk case is equal to four work units, while a Pre-Sentence Investigation (PSI) is equal to 14. Each type of case and activity is given a weight, based on a time study that was used as the basis for their formula. This is an excellent example of how work can be equally distributed across a department by taking into account differences between offenders and certain activities.

Table 7.3
**Work Units Monthly Ledger Summary**

| (Team) | | | | | | | | | | | (Month/Year) | | |
|---|---|---|---|---|---|---|---|---|---|---|---|---|---|
| SUPERVISION CLASSIFICATION | | | | INVESTIGATIONS | | | | | | | WORK UNITS | | |
| OFFICER | MAX | MED | MIN | NEW | ITS | UNS | CURT | TLC | INS | INC | PATH | PSI | SHCK | MISC |
| | | | | | | | | | | | | | | |
| | | | | | | | | | | | | | | |
| | | | | | | | | | | | | | | |
| | | | | | | | | | | | | | | |
| | | | | | | | | | | | | | | |
| | | | | | | | | | | | | | | |
| | | | | | | | | | | | | | | |
| | | | | | | | | | | | | | | |
| TOTALS | | | | | | | | | | | | | | |

| | |
|---|---|
| MAX — Maximum Supervision | 4 wk units |
| INS — Intercounty Transfer | 1 wk unit |
| MED — Medium Supervision | 2 wk units |
| PATH — Pay Thru | 1 wk unit |
| MIN — Minimum Supervision | 1 wk unit |
| PSI — Bond or Jail | 14 wk units |
| NEW — Not Yet Classified | 5 wk units |
| SHCK — Shock Report | 2 wk units |
| ITS — Intensive Treatment | 8 wk units |
| UNS — Unsupervised-Court | ½ wk units |
| MISC — Affidavit, Victim | 1 wk unit |
| CURT — Courtesy Supervision | 1 wk unit |
| TLC — Treatment in Lieu of Conviction | 1 wk unit |

(Supervisor)

Adopted from the Montgomery County Adult Probation Department.

Another creative example of how one probation department handles its caseloads can be seen in the Lucas County Adult Probation Department (Toledo, Ohio). Here, all cases are screened according to risk (high, medium, and low). In addition, screening devices are used to identify alcoholics, drug abusers, sex offenders, and offenders with high mental health needs. One probation officer, along with a team of volunteer probation officers, handles all of the low-risk offenders. High-risk offenders that do not require the assistance of a specialist are supervised in a "High-Risk Unit." Those special needs offenders are placed in one of the four specialty units (e.g., alcohol, mental health). The caseloads for the high-risk and specialty units are considerably smaller. Offenders without these needs that fall in the medium-risk category are supervised by regular treatment officers. In addition, this department has an intensive supervision unit that handles offenders of all types, provided they have been diverted from a state penal institution. PSIs are conducted by a separate unit. Using this scheme, Lucas County is able to divert a considerable number of low-risk, minimum supervision cases and focus their attention on offenders who require more specialized treatment or increased surveillance.

Once the general strategy for managing offenders is established, the officers must deliver needed services to their clients. The remainder of this chapter discusses different strategies employed by probation and parole agencies to deliver those services to offenders under supervision. Although we discuss these strategies separately, they are not mutually exclusive, and "pure" types are seldom found in actual supervision practices.

## Casework Supervision versus Brokerage Supervision

The two major orientations or approaches to supervision are casework and brokerage. We will examine each approach, the assumption underlying its use, its advantages and disadvantages, and the major operational concerns. We are discussing "pure" types as though the approaches were mutually exclusive, as if a department would adopt either a caseload or a brokerage approach, but could not combine any feature of the two. In reality, the two approaches are so mixed that it would be unusual if any two departments exhibited precisely the same approach as extreme positions. Most departments adopt positions somewhere along the continuum.

## Casework Supervision

The traditional approach to probation and parole supervision has been the casework approach. Casework is not synonymous with social work; rather it is just one of the three major specialties of social work (the others are community organization and group work). Many definitions of casework and social casework have been offered. Bowers (1950:127) has provided this frequently cited definition:

> Social casework is an area in which knowledge of the science of human relations and skills in relationships are used to mobilize capacities in the individual and resources in the community appropriate for better adjustment between the client and all or any part of his total environment.

Meeker (1948:51-52) has elaborated further:

> The modern emphasis in social casework is upon discovering the positive potential within the individual and helping him exploit his own capabilities, while at the same time revealing external resources in his social and economic environment which will contribute to his ability to assume the mature responsible obligations of a well-adjusted individual.

It is apparent that the basic element in casework is the nature of the relationship between the caseworker and the individual in trouble. It is also obvious from these definitions that casework emphasizes changing the behavior of the offender through the development of a supportive one-to-one relationship. Because of the closeness, this approach views the caseworker as the sole, or at least the primary, agent of treatment for the client.

By following a casework approach, the supervising officer will also follow the basic assumptions of social work. Trecker (1955:8-9) divides these assumptions into four categories: people, behavior problems, the social worker, and the relationship between society and the offender. One of the assumptions about offenders is that ". . . people can and do change in their behavior when they are given the right help at the right time and in the right amount."[2] With respect to behavior problems, it is assumed that, because people's problems are complex and intertwined with the person's total living situation, treatment of those problems must be individualized. The primary treatment agent is assumed to be the social worker, and his or her most important tool is the quality of the relationship created with the client. Finally, it is assumed that the client must be motivated to participate in the treatment process; consequently, a key element of the working relationship between the social worker and the client must be the development of the client's desire to change his or her behavior.

Photo 7.1
Probation officer with an offender. Courtesy of Talbert House, Inc.

A common thread running through these assumptions is the idea that the offender must enter the casework relationship voluntarily, or at least willingly. The relationship involved in correctional supervision, however, does not usually rest on the offender's voluntary participation, but rather on the authority of the probation or parole officer. Under the casework approach, then, it is important to resolve the conflict between the voluntary self-determination of the offender and the authority inherent in the supervising officer's position.

Many authors characterize the authority of the probation or parole officer as an important tool that can be used in the treatment process. Mangrum (1975:219) refers to the use of "coercive casework" and states, "While it is true that effective casework is not something done to or for the client, but with him, it is also true that sometimes it is a matter of some action which gets his attention or holds him still long enough for him to recognize that there is motivation from within . . ." (emphasis added). Studt (1954:24) notes that it is important for the offender to learn that ". . . authority is power to help as well as power to limit . . ." Hardman (1959:249-255) feels that authority, if properly used by the probation officer, can be an extremely powerful tool in the social service. He believes that all individuals, including probationers, entertain both positive and negative feelings toward authority, and that a primary responsibility of the caseworker is to help the client understand and accept those conflicting feelings and to learn new ways of controlling and expressing them.

Casework is so extensively used in probation and parole supervision that it is considered the "norm" as a service provision strategy. It basically follows the medical model of corrections in which the supervising officer, through a one-to-one relationship, diagnoses the offender, formulates a treatment strategy, implements that strategy and, finally, evaluates the offender in light of the treatment.

In reality, however, the supervising officer does not have the time or energy to devote to individual cases. Perhaps the most basic criticisms of the casework approach are that the probation and/or parole officer tries to be all things to all people, and does not adequately mobilize the community and its support systems. In addition, large caseloads, staff shortages, and endless report writing leave supervising officers unable to perform all the tasks called for by casework. Coupled with the trend away from the medical model, probation and parole administrators have initiated both the brokerage approach and community resource management teams.

## Brokerage Supervision

Almost diametrically opposed to the casework approach is the brokerage approach, in which the supervising officer is not concerned primarily with understanding or changing the behavior of the offender, but rather with assessing the concrete needs of the individual and arranging for the probationer or parolee to receive services that directly address those needs. Because the officer is not seen as the primary agent of treatment or change, there is significantly less emphasis placed on the development of a close, one-on-one relationship between the officer and the offender. With the brokerage approach, the supervising officer functions primarily as a manager or broker of resources and social services that are already available from other agencies. It is the task of the probation or parole officer to assess the service needs of the offender, locate the social service agency that addresses those needs as its primary function, refer the offender to the appropriate agency, and follow up referrals to make sure the offender has actually received the services. Under the brokerage approach, it can be said that the officer's relationship with community service agencies is more important than the relationship with an individual client. Both the brokerage and casework approaches share the importance of the offenders' participation in developing their own supervision plans.

The National Advisory Commission on Criminal Justice Standards and Goals (1973:320) recommended that the probation system should "redefine the role of probation officer from caseworker to community resource manager." The Commission report (1973:322-323) characterized this approach in the following way:

> To carry out his responsibilities as a community resource manager, the probation officer must perform several functions. In helping a probationer obtain needed services, the probation officer will have to assess the situation, know available resources, contact the appropriate resource, assist the proba-

tioner to obtain the services, and follow up on the case. When the probationer encounters difficulty in obtaining a service he needs, the probation officer will have to explore the reason for the difficulty and take appropriate steps to see that the service is delivered. The probation officer will have to monitor and evaluate the services to which the probationer is referred.

The Commission also addresses the problems of the individual probation officer's providing services that may be available elsewhere. They encouraged (1973:32) the reliance of probation departments on other social service agencies by suggesting that:

> Probation systems should not attempt to duplicate services already created by law and supposedly available to all persons. The responsibility of the system and its staff should be to enable the probationer to cut through the barriers and receive assistance from social institutions that may be all too ready to exclude him.

With its emphasis on the management of community resources, the brokerage approach requires intimate knowledge of the services in the community and the conditions under which each service is available. It may not be feasible for each officer to accumulate and use this vast amount of information about all the possible community service sources. It has been frequently suggested, therefore, that the brokerage of community services might be more easily handled if individual probation or parole officers were to specialize in gaining knowledge about and familiarity with an agency or set of agencies that provide related services. For example, one officer might become extremely knowledgeable about all community agencies that offer services for individuals with drug-related problems, while another officer might specialize in all agencies that handle unemployed or underemployed individuals. Regardless of whether officers decide to specialize or would prefer to handle all types of community agencies, the essential requirements under the brokerage approach are for the supervising officer to develop a comprehensive knowledge of the resources already available in the community and to use those resources to the fullest extent for the benefit of clients.

Closely related to the brokerage approach is the role of advocate. Several authors have recently stressed the advocacy role for probation officers.[3] Recognizing the fact that some of the services the offenders need will not be available in the community, these authors suggest that, rather than trying to supply those needed services themselves, probation and parole officers should concentrate on working with community agencies to develop the necessary service. This will ensure that these services will be available not only to probation or parole clients, but also to other individuals within the community who might require them.[4]

---

Box 7.1

### Static Versus Dynamic Risk Predictors

Static risk predictors refer to those factors or characteristics of an offender that cannot change. An example would be criminal history. The number of prior arrests, age at first arrest, number of times incarcerated, etc., are good predictors of risk. However, once in place they cannot change. Dynamic risk predictors are those factors or characteristics of an offender that contribute to their risk, but are changeable. For example, peer associations, substance abuse, criminal thinking, lack of employment, etc. These factors also help predict reoffending, and provide the probation or parole officer with areas to target.

---

The essential tasks of the brokerage orientation to probation and parole are the management of available community resources and the use of those services to meet the needs of offenders. There is little emphasis on the quality of the relationship that develops between the officer and the offenders; rather, more emphasis is placed upon the close working relationship between the officer and the staff members of community social service agencies. Counseling and guidance are considered inappropriate activities for the probation and parole officer; no attempt is made to change the behavior of the offender. The primary function of the officer is to assess the concrete needs of each offender and make appropriate referral to existing community services. Should the needed service not be available in the community, it is the responsibility of the officer to encourage the development of that service.

In contrast to the medical model, the brokerage approach is based upon the reintegration model, which emphasizes the needs of correctional clients for specialized services that can best be provided by established community agencies. As a rehabilitation device, brokerage replaces the casework approach. The brokerage task requires the assessment of client needs and the linkage of available community services with those needs.

Obviously, a pure brokerage approach has its drawbacks. Besides the lack of a strong relationship between the probation or parole officer and the offender, community services may not be readily available. This is often the case in more rural communities, and even if these service agencies are available, they may not be willing to accept an offender population. As a rule, there appear to be more offenders in need of specialized treatment than there is program space available. Cutbacks in government funding have also resulted in fewer programs, which raises the question: "How can a probation or parole officer be a broker if the services are not available?"

This discussion of casework and brokerage—the major orientations for probation and parole supervision and service provision—has highlighted the essential tasks of each approach and has emphasized their differences. Another major issue in supervision is one of form.

## Case Management Classification Systems

As mentioned previously, case classification screening devices have become an integral part of probation and parole agencies. While the use of classification and prediction in probation and parole is not a new development (Kratcoski, 1985), they have become more popular (Clear & Gallagher, 1985; Clear, 1988). In the case of parole, case screening is usually done by the parole board.[5] Given the widespread use of some form of guidelines, or prediction devices, the parole officer usually has a very good idea of the type of case he or she is receiving. With probation, much of this information is gathered with the PSI report, or during the first visit between the probation officer and the offender. Perhaps the best way to explain the concept of case management classification is to recognize that each client needs to be supervised. Some offenders pose a greater risk[6] to the community (Champion, 1994) or have more needs, whether they are emotional, physical, or mental. Some offenders accept, indeed even welcome, the added support and help; others do not, and may be resistant or hostile to supervision. It will help the probation officer to have this information before supervision actually begins. Not only can they develop a more tailored (or individualized) supervision plan, but they can also begin to identify the special services or programs that might be of assistance to this offender.

## The Evolution of Classification

For our purposes, risk refers to the probability that an offender will reoffend. Thus, high-risk offenders have a greater probability of reoffending than low-risk offenders. How is offender risk determined? This is obviously a very important question, because it can affect public protection, and the manner in which an offender is supervised (or whether they are even released) in the community.

The prehistory of risk assessment in criminal justice refers to the use of "gut feelings" to make decisions about the risk of an offender. With this process, information is collected about the offender, usually through an interview or file review. The information is then reviewed and a general assessment or global prediction is made: "In my professional opinion. . . ." The problems with this approach are considerable, and have been delineated by Wong (1997) and Kennedy (1998):

- Predictions are subject to personal bias;

- Predictions are subjective and often unsubstantiated;

- Decision rules are not observed;

- It is difficult to distinguish levels of risk; and

- Information is overlooked or overemphasized.

The first generation of formal classification instruments was pioneered by Bruce, Harno, Burgess, and Landesco in 1928. The development of a standardized and objective instrument was brought about by the request of the Illinois Parole Board, which wanted to make more informed decisions about whom to release on parole. Bruce and his colleagues reviewed the records of nearly 6,000 inmates. Table 7.4 illustrates the factors found by Bruce et al. (1928) in their risk prediction instrument. While many of these categories seem out-of-date today, the Burgess scale was one of the first attempts to develop an actuarial instrument to predict offender risk. There are several pros and cons to this approach (Wong, 1997; Kennedy, 1998):

Pros—
- Is objective and accountable;
- Covers important historic risk factors;
- Is easy to use, and reliable; and
- Distinguishes levels of risk of reoffending.

Cons—
- Consists primarily of static predictors (i.e., factors that are immutable);
- Does not identify target behaviors; and
- Is not capable of measuring change in the offender.

The second generation of risk prediction recognized that risk is more than simply static predictors. The best example can be seen in the Wisconsin Case Management Classification System. First developed and used in Wisconsin in 1975, the Client Management Classification System (CMC) is designed to help identify the level of surveillance for each case, as well as determine the needs of the offender and the resources necessary to meet them. With adequate classification, limited resources can be concentrated on the most critical cases—those of high risk (Wright, Clear & Dickson, 1984). Following Wisconsin's development of the CMC, the National Institute of Corrections (NIC, 1983) adopted it as a model system and began advocating and supporting its use throughout the country. It has been proven satisfactory in many jurisdictions, including Austin, Texas (Harris, 1994).

Table 7.4
**Factors in the Bruce, Harno, Burgess, and Landesco Scale**

General Type of Offense (e.g., fraud, robbery, sex, homicide)
Parental & Marital Status (parents living, offender married)
Criminal Type (first timer, occasional, habitual, professional)
Social Type (e.g., farm boy, gangster, hobo, ne'er-do-well, drunkard)
Community Factor (where resided)
Statement of Trial Judge and Prosecutor (recommended or protests leniency)
Previous Record
Work Record (e.g., no work record, casual, regular work)
Punishment Record in Prison
Months Served Prior to Parole
Intelligence Rating
Age when Paroled
Psychiatric Prognosis
Psychiatric Personality Type (egocentric, socially inadequate, emotionally unstable)

Source: A.A. Bruce, A.J. Harno, E.W. Burgess, and J. Landesco (1928). *The Workings of the Indeterminate-Sentence Law and the Parole System in Illinois.* State of Illinois.

The foundation of the system is a risk/needs assessment instrument that is completed on each probationer at regular intervals. Cases are classified into high, medium, or low risk/needs. In turn, these ratings are used to determined the level of supervision required for each case. Tables 7.5 and 7.6 illustrates the Wisconsin risk and needs assessment components of this system.

Once an offender is classified into a risk/needs level, a more detailed assessment of that case can be made with a profiling interview that helps to determine the relationship between the officer and the offender. This element of the system is called the Client Management Classification System, and is comprised of four unique treatment modalities:

- **Selective Intervention.** This group is designed for offenders who enjoy relatively stable and prosocial lifestyles (e.g., employed, established in community, and minimal criminal records). Such offenders have typically experienced an isolated and stressful event or neurotic problem. With effective intervention, there is a higher chance of avoiding future difficulty. The goals of treatment for these individuals include the development of appropriate responses to temporary crises and problems, and the re-establishment of pro-life patterns.

- **Environmental Structure.** The dominant characteristics of offenders in this group consist of deficiencies in social, vocational, and intellectual skills. Most of their problems stem from their inability to succeed in their employment or to be comfortable in most social settings, an overall lack of social skills and intellectual cultivation/ability. The goals for these persons include: (a) developing basic employment and social skills; (b) selecting alternatives to association with criminally oriented peers; and (c) improving social skills and impulse controls.

- **Casework/Control.** These offenders manifest instabilities in their lives as evidenced by failures in employment and domestic problems. A lack of goal-directedness is present, typically associated with alcohol and drug problems. Offense patterns include numerous arrests, although marketable job skills are present. Unstable childhoods, family pressure, and financial difficulties are typically present. The goals appropriate for this group include promoting stability in their professional and domestic endeavors, and achieving an improved utilization of the individual's potential along with an elimination of self-defeating behavior and emotional/psychological problems.

- **Limit Setting.** Offenders in this group are commonly considered to be successful and career criminals because of their long-term involvement in criminal activities. They generally enjoy "beating the system," they frequently act for material gain, and they show little remorse or guilt. Because of their value system, they easily adapt to prison environments and return to crime upon release. Goals for this group are problematic, but include changing the offender's basic attitudes and closely supervising his behavior within the community.

The information for the CMC is based on a structured interview with the offender. After a case has been classified, an individual treatment plan is developed. Results from the CMC have found that approximately 40 percent of probation caseloads are Selective Intervention, 15 percent are Environmental Structure, 30 percent are Casework Control, and 15 percent are Limit Setting.

Despite the advantages of the CMC, there are several shortcomings. One is the fact that risk and needs are separately assessed and not fully integrated. Another problem with this system is that the CMC component is time consuming to administer and the scoring is somewhat involved. In practice, many probation departments that use this instrument rely more heavily on the risk component, which is comprised of mainly static predictors.

Table 7.5
**Wisconsin Risk Assessment**

File _____ of _____

CLIENT NAME _____     CASE NUMBER _____
              Last                    First          MI

OFFICER _____     UNIT LOCATION _____
         Last                      Social Security Number

D A T E

**ARRESTED WITHIN (5) YEARS PRIOR TO ARREST FOR CURRENT OFFENSES (exclude traffic):**

0 No          4 Yes

**NUMBER OF PRIOR ADULT INCARCERATIONS IN A STATE OR FEDERAL INSTITUTION:**

0 No          3 1 - 2          6 3 and above

**NUMBER OF PRIOR ADULT PROBATION/PAROLE SUPERVISIONS**

0 None          4 One or more

**NUMBER OF PRIOR PROBATION/PAROLE REVOCATIONS RESULTING IN IMPRISONMENT (Adult or Juvenile):**

0 None          4 One or more

**AMOUNT OF TIME EMPLOYED IN LAST 12 MONTHS:**

0 More than 7 months     1 5 to 7 months     2 Less than 5 months     0 Not applicable

**NUMBER OF PRIOR FELONY CONVICTIONS (or Juvenile Adjudications):**

0 None          2 One          4 Two or more

0 None          3 One          6 Two or more          7 Three or more

**AGE AT ARREST LEADING TO FIRST FELONY CONVICTION (or Juvenile Adjudication):**

0 24 and over     2 20 - 23     4 19 and under

**AGE AT ADMISSION TO INSTITUTION OR PROBATION FOR CURRENT OFFENSE:**

0 30 and over     3 18 - 29     6 17 and under

0 30 and over     4 18 - 29     7 17 and under

### *RATE THE FOLLOWING BASED ON PERIOD SINCE LAST RE-ASSESSMENT*

**ALCOHOL USAGE PROBLEMS**

0 No interference with functioning     2 Occasional abuse; some disruption of functioning     4 Frequent abuse; serious disruption; needs treatment

0 No interference with functioning     2 Occasional abuse; some disruption of functioning     3 Frequent abuse; serious disruption; needs treatment

**OTHER DRUG USAGE PROBLEMS**

0 No interference with functioning     2 Occasional abuse; some disruption of functioning     4 Frequent abuse; serious disruption; needs treatment

0 No interference with functioning     1 Occasional abuse; some disruption of functioning     2 Frequent abuse; serious disruption; needs treatment

**ASSOCIATIONS**

0 Mainly with non-criminally oriented individuals     5 Mainly with negative individuals

**TYPE OF ARRESTS (indicate most serious, excluding traffic)**

0 None     2 Technical PV only     4 Misdemeanor arrest(s)     8 Felony arrest

**ATTITUDE**

0 No adverse difficulties/ motivated to change     2 Periodic difficulties/ uncooperative/dependent     5 Frequent hostile/negative criminal orientation

**Scale:** Max—17 and above
        Med—9-16
        Min—8 and below

**TOTAL**

Table 7.6
**Wisconsin Assessment of Client Needs**

File _____ of _____

CLIENT NAME _____ CASE NUMBER _____
Last                First           MI

OFFICER _____ UNIT LOCATION _____
Last                    Social Security Number

DATE

**EMOTIONAL AND MENTAL STABILITY**
**0** No symptoms of emotional and/or mental instability
**2** Symptoms limit but do not prohibit adequate functioning
**3** Symptoms prohibit adequate functioning and/or has Court or Board imposed condition
**8** Severe symptoms requiring continual attention and/or explosive, threatening and potentially dangerous to others and self

**DOMESTIC RELATIONSHIP**
**0** Stable/supportive relationship
**3** Some disorganization or stress but potential for improvement
**7** Major disorganization or stress

**ASSOCIATIONS**
**0** No adverse relationships
**2** Associations with occasional negative results
**4** Associations frequently negative
**6** Associations completely negative

**DRUG ABUSE**
**0** No disruption of functioning
**2** Occasional substance abuse; some disruption of functioning and/or has Court or Board conditions
**7** Frequent abuse; serious disruptions; needs treatment

**ALCOHOL USAGE**
**0** No disruption of functioning
**2** Occasional abuse; some disruption of functioning and/or has Court or Board conditions
**7** Frequent abuse; serious disruptions; needs treatment

**EMPLOYMENT**
**0** Satisfactory employment, no difficulties reported; or homemaker, student, retired, or disabled
**2** Underemployed
**4** Unsatisfactory employment; or unemployed but has adequate job skills/motivation
**5** Unemployed and virtually unemployable; needs motivation/training

**ACADEMIC/VOCATIONAL SKILLS/TRAINING**
**0** Adequate skills, able to handle everyday requirements
**2** Low skill level causing minor adjustment problems
**6** No identifiable skills and/or minimal skill level causing serious adjustment problems

**FINANCIAL MANAGEMENT**
**0** No current difficulties
**1** Situational or minor difficulties
**5** Chronic/severe difficulties

**ATTITUDES**
**0** No adverse difficulties/motivated for change
**2** Periodic difficulties/uncooperative/dependent
**4** Frequently hostile/negative/criminal orientation

**RESIDENCE**
**0** Suitable living arrangement
**2** Adequate living, i.e., temporary shelter
**4** Nomadic and/or unacceptable

**MENTAL ABILITY (INTELLIGENCE)**
**0** Able to function independently
**1** Some need for assistance; potential for adequate adjustment
**3** Deficiencies severely limit independent functioning

**HEALTH**
**0** Sound physical health; seldom ill
**1** Handicap or illness; interferes with functioning on a recurring basis
**2** Serious handicap or chronic illness; needs frequent medical care

**SEXUAL BEHAVIOR**
**0** No apparent dysfunction
**2** Real or perceived situations or minor problems
**6** Real or perceived chronic or severe problems

**OFFICER'S IMPRESSION OF NEEDS**
**0** Low
**3** Medium
**5** Maximum

**Scale:** Max—26 and above
Med—13-25
Min—12 and below

TOTAL

Box 7.2

### Actuarial versus Clinical Prediction

Actuarial or statistical prediction involves examining a group of offenders and identifying the factors associated with recidivism (or some other measure of outcome). With statistical prediction, offenders with a certain set of characteristics have a range of probabilities associated with success or failure. So for example, if we have 100 high-risk offenders, and our classification instrument indicated that the probability of failure for high-risk offenders is 75 percent, we are relatively confident that 75 out of 100 of those offenders will recidivate (assuming no intervention). Of course, we are predicting to the group and not the individual, so we do not know which 75 will fail. With clinical prediction, a trained professional gathers information and then uses his or her professional experience and judgment to render an opinion about the likelihood that an individual will fail or succeed. The evidence is very strong that actuarial or statistical prediction is more accurate than clinical prediction.

The third generation of classification instruments have successfully combined risk and needs, and are relatively easy to use. One example is the Level of Service Inventory-Revised (LSI-R) designed by Andrews and Bonta (1995). The LSI-R has been extensively tested and validated across North America. The LSI-R consists of 54 items in 10 areas. Information is collected primarily through a structured interview process. The LSI-R has been found to be one of the most valid instruments in predicting recidivism. There is also a juvenile version called the Youthful-Level of Service Inventory (Hoge & Andrews, 1996b).

More recently, the LSI-R was updated by re-organizing the original ten subcomonents into general and specific risk and need factors. This new instrument is called the Level of Service/Case Management Inventory (LS/CMI) (Andrews, Bonta & Wormith, 2004). It represents a significant improvement over the previous version (and other third generation classification instruments) as it emphasizes the link between assessment and case management. In addition to identifying risk and need factors, the LS/CMI acknowledges the role of personal strengths and specific responsivity factors in an offender's amenability to treatment. Figure 7.1 shows recidivism results from 561 probationers whose risk was assessed using the LS/CMI (see Andrews & Bonta, 2006). Recidivism rates increase directly with LS/CMI scores. A sample of some the LS/CMI categories is in Table 7.7.

Figure 7.1
**Level of Service/Case Management Inventory & Recidivism**

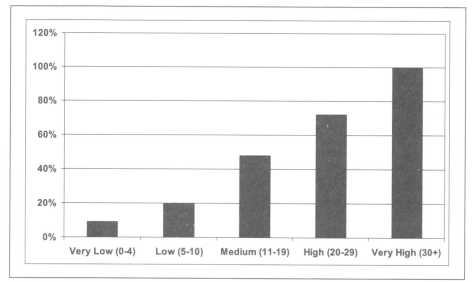

Source: Adapted from Andrews, D.A. and J. Bonta (2006). *The Psychology of Criminal Conduct,* p. 69. Newark, NJ: LexisNexis Matthew Bender.

Table 7.7
**Areas of the LS/CMI**

| **Section 1. General Risk/Need Factors** | **Section 5. Special Responsivity Considerations** |
|---|---|
| Criminal History | Motivation as a barrier |
| Education/Employment | Women, gender specific |
| Family/Marital | Low intelligence |
| Leisure/Recreation | Antisocial personality/psychopathy |
| Companions | |
| Alcohol/Drug Problem | |
| Procriminal Attitude/Orientation | **Section 9. Case Management Plan** |
| Antisocial Pattern | |
| | Program Targets and Intervention Plan |
| **Section 2. Specific Risk/Need Factors** | |
| Personal Problems with Criminogenic Potential | |
|    Diagnosis of "psychopathy" | |
|    Anger Management Deficits | |
|    Poor social skills | |
|    Underachievement | |
| History of Perpetration | |
|    Sexual assault, extrafamilial, child/adolescent –female victim | |
|    Physical assault (extrafamilial adult victim) | |
|    Gang participation | |

| Criminogenic Need | Goal | Intervention |
|---|---|---|
| 1. | | |
| 2. | | |

Source: Adapted from Andrews, D.A. and J. Bonta (2006). *The Psychology of Criminal Conduct,* pp. 293, 294. Newark, NJ: LexisNexis Matthew Bender.

There are also classification systems designed for certain types of offenders or need areas, such as the mentally disordered, sex offenders, and substance abusers. Some of these tools help to classify and recommend levels of intervention. Figure 7.2 shows the use of specialized assessment tools across the United States.

Figure 7.2
**Use of Specialized Assessment Tools by Probation, Parole, and Community Corrections Service Providers (in percent)**

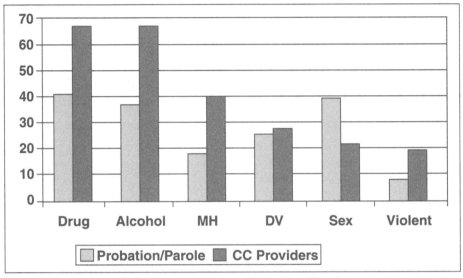

Source: Hubbard, D.J., L.F. Travis, and E.J. Latessa (2001). *Case Classification in Community Corrections: A National Survey of the State of the Art.* Washington, DC: National Institute of Justice; and Cincinnati, OH: Center for Criminal Justice Research, University of Cincinnati.

One of the major advantages of actuarial risk and need assessment tools is that they are standardized and objective, and help distinguish levels of risk or need (e.g., high, medium, low). Because they are based on statistical studies, they also reduce bias and false positive and false negative rates (Holsinger, Lurigio & Latessa, 2001).

In a recent national survey of probation and parole agencies concerning the use and practices surrounding class classification, Hubbard and her colleagues (2001) found that the vast majority of agencies reported using some actuarial instrument to assess and classify offenders. A summary of their findings is presented below:

- Almost 75 percent of the probation and parole agencies, and about 56 percent of the community corrections service providers reported that they classify using standardized and objective instruments.

- Large agencies were more likely to classify clients than were smaller agencies.

- Over 83 percent of the respondents reported that it was "absolutely" or "very necessary " to classify on risk, and 66 percent on needs.

- The most widely used instrument was the Wisconsin Risk and Need instrument, followed by the Level of Service Inventory.

- Nearly all respondents agreed that case classification makes their job easier, benefits the offender, creates a more professional environment, helps staff make better decisions, increases effectiveness of service delivery, and enhances fairness in decisionmaking.

- The most common uses of these tool were: officer workloads 75 percent, staff deployment 54 percent, development of specialized caseloads 47 percent, and sentencing decisions 20 percent.

- Nearly 80 percent of the agencies reported using the various instruments to reassess offenders.

Offender classification is not without its critics. Some argue that the instruments are nothing more than "educated guesses" (Smykla, 1986:127), while others are more concerned about their proper use and accuracy (Wilbanks, 1985; Greenwood & Zimring, 1985). Another major concern centers on the use of a risk instrument in one jurisdiction that has been developed and validated in another. Just because a risk instrument is accurate in one jurisdiction does not necessarily mean it will be effective in predicting outcome in another (Collins, 1990; Kratcoski, 1985; Wright, Clear & Dickson, 1984; Sigler & Williams, 1994). As Travis has stated, "Ideally, a risk classification device should be constructed based on the population on which it is to be used" (Travis, 1989).

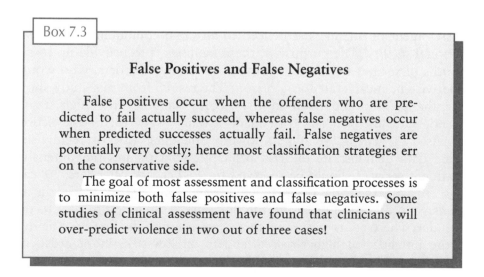

Box 7.3

**False Positives and False Negatives**

False positives occur when the offenders who are predicted to fail actually succeed, whereas false negatives occur when predicted successes actually fail. False negatives are potentially very costly; hence most classification strategies err on the conservative side.

The goal of most assessment and classification processes is to minimize both false positives and false negatives. Some studies of clinical assessment have found that clinicians will over-predict violence in two out of three cases!

Clear (1988:2) maintains that the implementation of these prediction instruments have two main advantages:

> First, they improve the reliability of decisions made about offenders—in a sense they make correctional officials more predictable. Second, they provide a basis on which corrections personnel can publicly justify both individual decisions and decision-making policies. In both cases, the advantage is grounded in the powerful appearance of 'scientific' decisionmaking.

There are a number of reasons that classification and assessment of offenders is important:

- Guides and helps structure decisionmaking;
- Reduces bias;
- Improves the placement of offenders for treatment and public safety;
- Helps manage offenders in a more effective manner;
- Aids in legal challenges; and
- Helps better utilize resources.

In addition the above advantages, the use of assessment tools based on dynamic factors is the ability to reassess the offender to determine whether or not there has been a reduction in risk score. This allows an agency to move beyond risk management to risk reduction, the ultimate goal of community corrections. Figure 7.3 illustrates the initial assessment and reassessment scores from a sample of youth supervised on probation. As can be seen from this figure, these data can help a probation department better focus its resources and strategies. Another example is demonstrated in Figure 7.4. This figure shows the results from the reassessment of offenders sentenced to an Ohio community-based correctional facility. The purpose of these facilities is to provide up to six months of secure, structured treatment to felony offenders, who would otherwise be incarcerated in a prison. The results from this study show that the greatest reduction in risk scores were for the highest-risk offenders, while low-risk offenders actually saw their risk scores increase. In general, treatment lowers offenders' risk of recidivism. These data demonstrate the risk principle, which states that intensive treatment services should be reserved for higher risk offenders. As can be seen from these data, when lower-risk offenders are placed in an intensive intervention program, the outcome is often detrimental to the offender. There are two reasons this effect occurs. The first may be due to the influence of higher-risk offenders on low-risk, more prosocial individuals. The second is probably due to the disruption of prosocial

Figure 7.3
**Youthful LSI: Assessment and Reassessment**

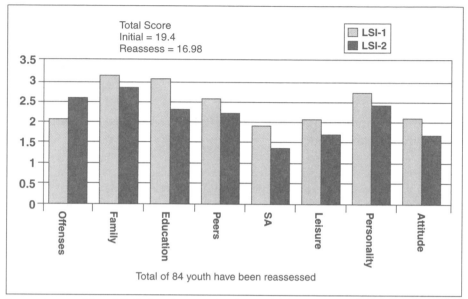

Source: Latessa, E.J. and C. Taylor (2001). *Using the Youthful Level of Service Inventory/Case Management in a Large Urban Court.* Cincinnati, OH: Center for Criminal Justice Research, University of Cincinnati.

Figure 7.4
**Results of Treatment as Measured by Changes in LSI-R Scores
(by Risk Category) (N = 559)**

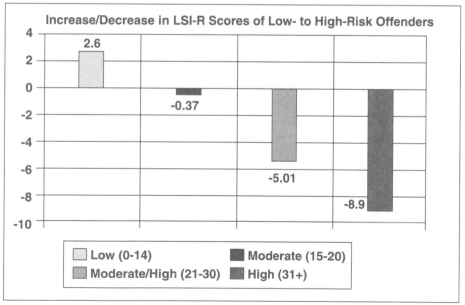

Source: Latessa, E.J. and C. Lowenkamp (2001). *Testing the LSI-R in Community-Based Correctional Facilities.* Cincinnati, OH: Center for Criminal Justice Research, University of Cincinnati.

networks and other social support mechanisms that low-risk offenders usually possess (or they would not be low risk!). For example, placement in a program such as the one described above usually results in loss of employment and disruption to the family.

## Principles of Offender Classification

Andrews, Bonta, and Hoge (1990:20) have identified four principles of effective classification:

- **Risk**—Higher risk offenders are characterized by greater criminogenic needs; Use a valid and reliable measure to assess offender risk; Target higher risk offenders for treatment;

- **Need**—Match offenders to programs that address their criminogenic needs; Target more criminogenic needs than non-criminogenic needs (3:1 ratio);

- **Responsivity**—Use potent behavior change strategies (i.e., social learning, cognitive-behavioral approaches); Deliver intervention in a style and mode that is consistent with the ability and learning style of the offender, and recognize that individuals may be more responsive to certain staff; and

- **Professional Discretion**—Having considered risk, need, and responsivity, decisions are made as appropriate under present conditions.

Through the work of a number of researchers, our understanding of classification and assessment, and the important role it plays in community corrections is becoming more apparent (Andrews, 1983 & 1989; Bonta & Motiuk, 1985; Gendreau, Goggin & Little, 1996; Jones, 1996; Kennedy & Serin, 1997).

Despite these concerns, the latest generation of classification instruments allows the probation or parole department an effective and fairly simple means of classifying and managing offenders. It is important to remember that instruments such as the CMC or LSI-R can be important and useful tools in assisting the community correctional agency and the supervising officer in case management. They will not solve all the problems faced by probation and parole agencies, nor will they fully replace the sound judgment and experience of well-trained probation and parole officers (Schumacher, 1985; Klein, 1989).

> **Box 7.4**
>
> ### Criminogenic Needs and Promising Targets
>
> Criminogenic needs refers to those crime-producing factors associated with criminal behavior. The new generation of risk assessment tools measures these needs. Some of the promising need factors which should be identified by researchers include the following:
>
> Changing antisocial attitudes
> Changing antisocial feelings
> Reducing antisocial peer associations
> Promoting familial affection and communication
> Promoting familial monitoring and supervision
> Increasing self-control and problem-solving skills
> Reducing chemical dependencies

## Standards of Classification

Travis and Latessa (1996) have identified 10 elements of effective classification and assessment. They include:

- **Purposeful.** Generally, the purpose of classification and assessment is to insure offenders are treated differentially within a system so as to insure safety, adequate treatment, and understanding.

- **Organizational Fit.** Organizations and agencies have different characteristics, capabilities, and needs.

- **Accuracy.** How well does the instrument correctly assess outcome? Is the offender correctly placed within the system? Basically, reliability and validity are the key elements to accuracy. Glick, Sturgeon, and Venator-Santiago (1998:73) explain reliability and validity thus: Reliability may be defined as hitting the same spot on a bull's eye all the time. If your system is reliable but not valid, you may be hitting the target consistently, but not the right spot.

- **Parsimony.** This refers to the ease of use, the economy of composition, and achieving accuracy with the least number of factors. In other words, short and simple.

- **Distribution.** How well does the system disperse cases across classification groups? If all offenders fall into the same group, there is little distribution.

- **Dynamism.** Is the instrument measuring dynamic risk factors that are amenable to change? Dynamic factors also allow you to measure progress and change in the offender. It also facilitates reclassification.

- **Utility.** To be effective, classification systems must be useful. This means that the staff achieve the purposes of classification and the goals of the agency.

- **Practicality.** Closely related to utility is the practical aspect of classification. The system must be practical and possible to implement. A process that is 100 percent accurate but impossible to apply in an agency does not help that agency. Similarly, a system that is easy to use, but does not lead to better decisions, is of no value.

- **Justice.** An effective classification and assessment process should produce just outcomes. Offender placement and service provision should be based upon offender differences that are real and measurable, and yield consistent outcomes, regardless of subjective impressions.

- **Sensitivity.** This is really a goal of the classification process. If all elements are met, the most effective classification and assessment process is sensitive to the differences of offenders. At the highest level, this would mean individualizing case planning.

---

| Box 7.5 |
| --- |

### Responsivity Factors

Recognizing differences in offenders that effect their engagement in treatment and their ability to learn is part of assessing responsivity. Developing a strategy to overcome these barriers is part of developing a good case plan. Some responsivity considerations include:

| General Population | Factors More Common with Offenders |
| --- | --- |
| Anxiety | Poor social skills |
| Self-Esteem | Inadequate problem-solving |
| Depression | Concrete-oriented thinking |
| Mental Illness | Poor verbal skills |
| Age | Social support for service |
| Intelligence | |
| Gender | |
| Race/Ethnicity | |
| Motivation | |

## Classification and Female Offenders

Several scholars have questioned the notion that the risk factors used to predict antisocial behavior for male offenders are similar to those and needed for females offenders (Chesney-Lind, 1989, 1997; Funk, 1999; Mazerolle, 1998). The neglect of female offenders has been a consistent criticism in many area of criminological and criminal justice research, from theory development to the development of correctional interventions (Belknap & Holsinger, 1998; Chesney-Lind & Sheldon, 1992; Funk, 1999). Furthermore, the lack of instruments that discriminate between males and females has been a common criticism of current risk/need assessment efforts (Funk, 1999). The basis for this criticism is twofold: (1) different factors may be involved in risk assessment for females, and (2) the risk factors may be similar, but exposure to these factors may present different challenges for female and male offenders (Funk, 1999; Gilligan & Wiggins, 1988; Chesney-Lind, 1989).

There is no question that there has been considerably less research conducted on female offenders than males; however, several studies that have examined risk factors and gender have found that instruments such as the LSI can be useful in assessing and classifying female offenders (Andrews, 1982; Bonta & Motiuk, 1985; Hoge & Andrews, 1996; Motiuk, 1993; Shields & Simourd, 1991; and Coulson, Ilacqua, Nutbrown, Giulekas, & Cudjoe, 1996). In a recent study examining risk prediction for male and female offenders, Lowenkamp, Holsinger, and Latessa (2001) added to this research by looking at 317 males and 125 female. They found that the LSI-R was a valid predictive instrument for female offenders. They also found that a history of prior abuse (sexual or physical), although more prevalent in female offenders, was not correlated with outcome. Although the debate will likely continue, it appears that the evidence is mounting that instruments such as the LSI can indeed be used to assess and classify offenders, both male and female.

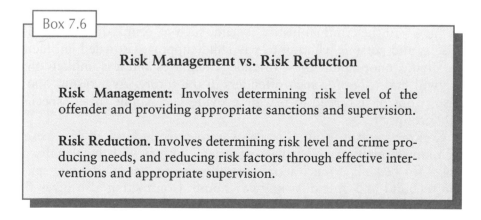

Box 7.6

**Risk Management vs. Risk Reduction**

**Risk Management:** Involves determining risk level of the offender and providing appropriate sanctions and supervision.

**Risk Reduction.** Involves determining risk level and crime producing needs, and reducing risk factors through effective interventions and appropriate supervision.

## Contracting for Services

As indicated in Chapter 6, recent events have called for a change in the role of the probation and parole officer. In addition to the increased demands of the surveillance aspect of supervision, other changes in this field have been geared toward enhancing the social service aspect of the probation or parole officer's role. The use of various types of contracts is one example of this development.

Contracts for a wide variety of client and administrative activities are particular to the unique responsibilities of community corrections (Jensen et al., 1987). These include:

- Residential programs (including halfway houses, house arrest, restitution centers, and facilities for juveniles, such as group or foster homes).

- Counseling and treatment programs for both general client groups and targeted offenders such as drug addicts and alcoholics.

- Administrative services for data processing, recordkeeping, evaluations, and so forth.

- Programs for victims of crime and crisis intervention. These would include traditional counseling services as well as programs designed to aid victims as they struggle with the criminal justice system and to help them file for victim compensation.

- Programs that conduct private pre-sentence investigation and develop sentencing alternatives for offenders.

- Dispute resolution, mediation programs, and pretrial services.

- Testing, ranging from employment/educational to urinalysis for drug or alcohol abuse.

Recently, stricter punishment policies have brought offenders that are "new" to the criminal justice system, such as drunk drivers, spouse abusers, and persons who fail to pay child support. Crowded jail facilities often cannot handle these offender categories and it is unlikely that they will find room for such offenders in the future. As a result, many jurisdictions have turned to private providers to handle these "specialized" groups.

Contracting can be an effective way to provide services. For example, many probation and parole agencies contract with local halfway houses for beds. It is much more cost-effective to "lease" the bed space than to build and operate a halfway house. Contracting also gives the agency the flexibility of being able to terminate the contract if the service fails to meet expectations or is no longer needed.

Many of these programs represent an attempt to treat some offenders in a nontraditional fashion and provide close ties between them and community programs. Such innovations can, when used with a particular type of client (such as mentally disordered offenders or drunk drivers), help offenders and relieve the burden of heavy caseloads upon a probation department. Their use could also permit a probation department to deploy its resources in a more efficient manner.

## Contracting with the Client

Another type of contract directly focuses upon the offender and the agency in an attempt to fully spell out the obligations of each party during the supervision period. As defined by Ankersmit (1976:28), setting the contract simply means reaching an agreement with the offender as to what goals he or she will work toward achieving. The basic idea is to use this device as a central point in the planning process, specifically including the probationer in this process. The contract, in this case, is between the supervising officer and the offender. The offender might agree to seek employment, pay child support, and study for a GED. The supervising officer agrees to help the offender meet his or her goals and to provide needed assistance and support. This type of "contract" is actually an extension of the conditions of probation or parole, and can be a useful tool in case planning. Although it is not known how many probation and parole agencies use "behavioral" contracts with offenders, Scott has identified two advantages of this approach:

1. The probationer is intimately involved in supervision planning from the very beginning of this process. As a result, the sentencing judge is provided with additional information on program plans and on the motivations of the offender.

2. Probationers have clear specifications of what is expected of them, including the possibility of early termination. In addition, the probation officer is provided with clearly specified objectives for supervision, and has a better idea of how to proceed with supervision plans. The hope is that contractual programming will result in a more efficient approach to probation management.

In short, it appears that contracting offers an opportunity to establish a system that strengthens and goes beyond the traditional standard special conditions of supervision. It can provide several benefits to both the offender and the department, and can lead to the efficient management of community services.

## Supervision Planning

Regardless of the approach used by an agency to deliver service, an essential ingredient to successful supervision is planning (Ellsworth, 1988). This includes the identification of the needs and problems of the offender, identifying the resources available and arranging for them, and evaluating the effectiveness of the supervision activities. The probation and parole populations under supervision today are different than those supervised 20 years ago. Not only are we seeing higher-risk offenders on probation due to prison and jail crowding, but the offender population is growing older (McCarthy & Langworthy, 1987; Burnett & Kitchen, 1989). With these changes comes a need to improve our planning of the actual supervision task. A solid supervision plan takes those risk, need, and responsivity factors that were identified in the assessment process and develops a plan or strategy to target or reduce those factors. Priorities are set, and the criteria to gauge offender progress are also developed.

One example of a case plan developed from the LSI can be seen in Table 7.8. This Table demonstrates how, following the assessment, the caseworker has identified the problem area, the objectives, and the strategies that will be used to target the risk factor. This example also allows the identification of responsibility, time frames, completion status, and strengths.

Table 7.8
**Supervision Problem: An Example**

| **Supervision Problems** |
| --- |
| Health: This offender has a documented history of heroin addiction dating back seven years and has two previous convictions for selling drugs to support a $100-a-day habit. |
| Family: Recently separated from his wife and two children but would like to be reunited with them. Several reports of wife abuse have been recorded. |
| Employment: Unemployed—occasional construction laborer. |
| For each supervision problem, a corresponding supervision objective is developed. |
| **Supervision Objectives** |
| Abstain from drug use, stabilize marital relationship, and assist offender to locate and maintain employment. |

After problems and objectives have been identified, the supervising officer formulates a plan for achieving those objectives. The methods selected are based on such considerations as the nature of the problem, the abilities and expertise of the officer, the availability of effective community resources, the attitude of the offender, and the exercise of authority necessary to insure the offender's participation.

A well thought-out initial supervision plan is the cornerstone of supervision activities. The plan need not be lengthy, but it should specify actions to be taken by the supervising officer, the responsibilities of the offender, and the role of any community resources.

In addition to developing the supervision or case plan, many agencies require periodic reviews. This review should include an evaluation of the dynamics of the offender's supervision problems as they have emerged over time. The review should also highlight the degree of progress achieved in meeting precisely established objectives and goals. Finally, the officer identifies new problems and revises the supervision plan to meet the current situation.

Undoubtedly, supervision planning varies from agency to agency, and often from officer to officer; however, regardless of the process or the format, there are common elements involved in supervision planning: recognizing problems, selecting objectives, developing a strategy, implementing that strategy and, finally, evaluating the effectiveness of the entire process.

## Use of Volunteers

Community correctional programs operate under a basic philosophy of reintegration: connecting offenders with legitimate opportunity and reward structures, and generally uniting the offender within the community. It has become quite apparent that the correctional system cannot achieve this without assistance, regardless of the extent of resources available. Reintegration requires the assistance and support of the community. One important resource for the community correctional agency is the use of volunteers. If used properly, these individuals can serve as an important asset for a community correctional agency.

This concept is certainly not a new one. The John Howard Association, the Osborne Association, and other citizen prisoners' aid societies have provided voluntary correctional-type services for many years. The volunteer movement developed in this country in the early 1820s, when a group of citizens known as the Philadelphia Society for Alleviating the Misery of Public Prisons began supervising the activities of inmates upon their release from penal institutions. This practice was later adopted by John Augustus, a Boston shoemaker, who worked with well over 2,000 misdemeanants in his lifetime (see Chapter 3).

Volunteerism is alive and well in corrections.[7] Judge Keith Leenhouts of the Royal Oak (Michigan) Municipal Court resurrected the concept some 20 years ago, and continues to serve as a driving force behind this now relatively accepted, and still growing, movement. In addition to the many local programs in existence, there are several national programs supporting volunteerism, such as VISTO (Volunteers in Service to Offenders), VIP (Volunteers in Probation), and the American Bar Association-sponsored National Volunteer Aide Program. Although exact numbers are not known, it is safe to say that there are thousands of volunteers serving more than 3,000 jurisdictions nationwide.

Proponents of the volunteer concept consider it to be one of the most promising innovations in the field, claiming that it can help alleviate the problem of excessive probation and parole caseloads, and contribute to rehabilitation and reintegration goals for the offender (Greenberg, 1988; Latessa, Travis & Allen, 1983). A good illustration of the effective use of volunteers can be seen in Lucas County (Toledo, Ohio). Here, probationers are screened according to risk. All "low-risk" probationers are assigned to one probation officer who, with the help of volunteers, supervises more than 1,000 clients.

Volunteers can range from student interns to older persons with time to devote. Some volunteers are persons that have a specific skill or talent to contribute, while others give their time and counsel.

## Scope of Services

Volunteerism generally refers to situations where individual citizens contribute their talents, wisdom, skills, time, and resources within the context of the justice system, without receiving financial remuneration. Volunteer projects operate on the premise that certain types of offenders can be helped by the services a volunteer can offer, and that such services can be provided at a minimal tax dollar cost and can result in significant cost savings.

By drawing upon the time, talents, and abilities of volunteers to assist in service delivery, community supervision officers can serve to broaden the nature of the services offered. Any community consists of persons who possess a diverse supply of skills and abilities that can be effectively tapped by volunteer programs. The National Center of Volunteers in Courts has reported that some 155 volunteer roles have actually been filled by volunteer persons in different jurisdictions. Scheier (1973) developed a list of more than 200 potential volunteer services including:

| | |
|---|---|
| addiction program volunteer | intake volunteer |
| case aide | newsletter editor |
| clerical courtroom assistance | presentence investigator |
| diagnostic home volunteer | recreation volunteer |
| educational aide | test administrator and scorer |
| foster parent | vocational service aide |
| fund-raiser | volunteer counselor |

In addition to the direct service offered, volunteers can supply a number of support services (Lucas, 1987). Volunteers often assist program operations in an administrative capacity. For example, a full-time volunteer for quite some time has supervised the well-known Royal Oak, Michigan program. The VISTO program in Los Angeles County (California) has likewise utilized volunteers to fill some of its clerical needs, such as handling supplies, photocopying, answering recruitment correspondence, and routine office contacts, as well as participating in research projects. In addition, many volunteers serve on advisory boards. Many nonprofit community agencies, such as halfway houses, rely on volunteers to serve on their boards of directors. There can be little doubt that volunteers can serve as a means of amplifying time, attention, and the type of services given to clients by the system. However, it is also important that an agency not become overreliant on volunteers, to the extent that they do not hire enough professional officers and staff.

## Summary

This chapter has discussed one of the most important aspects of probation and parole: supervision of the offender. We have noted that assignment of offenders to a probation or parole officer for supervision can follow several models. Some offenders are randomly assigned to caseloads, others are assigned based on geography or special problems, while yet others are classified through the use of prediction devices.

Once assignment is complete, the approach or philosophy of supervision usually centers on casework and brokerage. Casework follows a belief that the supervising officer should be the primary agent of change and thus "all things to all people." The brokerage approach assumes that the best place for treatment is in the community, and that the primary task of the probation or parole officer is to arrange for and manage community resources. While casework is the norm, in reality most probation and parole officers and agencies use techniques for both approaches.

Perhaps due to the prevalence of the casework approach, the tasks of supervision have traditionally been performed by a single officer. This has begun to change, as many agencies begin to recognize the team approach as a viable alternative to the single officer model.

This chapter has also addressed case management classification and supervision planning, and provided examples of the latest attempts to accomplish the many facets of community supervision. Perhaps one of the most important aspects of supervising the offender in the community is the determination of risk and need levels, and the provision of appropriate supervision and intervention.

Finally, the use of volunteers is not a new concept. Volunteers play an important role in community corrections, and if used properly can be a valuable asset to a community correctional agency.

## Review Questions

1. What are the assumptions of casework? Brokerage?

2. What are the limitations of casework in probation?

3. List three ways that caseloads are assigned.

4. How can risk/needs assessments be used in probation?

5. What are the 10 standards to good classification?

6. What are the four principles of classification?

7. Give three examples of responsivity characteristics and discuss ways they can impede an offender.

8. What is the difference between a static and a dynamic predictor?

9. Why do you think actuarial assessment tools have proven more reliable and valid than clinical assessment processes?

10. How can volunteers be used in probation?

## Key Terms

actuarial prediction

case management

classification system

contracting

conventional model

false negatives

false positives

numbers game

reassessment

responsivity

risk predictors

single-factor assignment

supervision planning

## Electronic Library

American Probation and Parole Association (www.appa-net.org).

International Community Corrections Association (www.icca.web.org).

Medical problems of inmates (www.ojp.usdoj.gov/bjs/pub/pdf/mpi97/pdf).

Prior abuse reported by inmates and probationers (www.ojp.usdoj.gov/bjs/pub/pdf/parip.pdf).

Profile of jail inmates (www.ojp.usdoj.gov/bjs/pub/pdy/pjim96.pdf).

Substance abuse and treatment, State and Federal prisoners (www.ojp.usdoj.gov/bjs/pub/pdf/satap95.pdf).

## Recommended Readings

Andrews, D.A. and J. Bonta (2006). *The Psychology of Criminal Conduct.* Newark, NJ: LexisNexis Matthew Bender.

Auerbach, B.J. and T.C. Castellano (1998). Successful Community Sanctions and Services for Special Offenders: Proceedings of the 1994 Conference of the International Community Corrections Association. Lantham, MD: American Correctional Association.

Dell'Apa, F., W.T. Adams, J.D. Jorgenson, and H.R. Sigurdson (1976). "Advocacy, Brokerage, Community: The ABC's of Probation and Parole." *Federal Probation*, 40(4):37-44.

Harlan, A.T. (1996). *Choosing Correctional Options that Work.* Thousand Oaks, CA: Sage.

Hoge, R.D. and D.A. Andrews (1996). *Assessing the Youthful Offender: Issues and Techniques*. New York, NY: Plenum Press.

Lowenkamp, C., A. Holsinger, and E. Latessa (2001). "Risk/Need Assessment, Offender Classification, and the Role of Childhood Abuse." *Criminal Justice and Behavior*, 28(5):543-563.1

Maruschak, L. and A. Beck (2001). *Medical Problems of Inmates, 1997*. Washington, DC; U.S. Bureau of Justice Statistics (http://www.ojp.usdoj.gov/bjs/pub/pdf/mpi97/pdf).

Van Voorhis, P. (1994). *Psychological Classification of the Adult Male Prison Inmate*. Albany, NY: State University of New York.

## Notes

[1]    Parole board refers to all agencies (commissions, board of charities, board of prison terms, and so on) whose duty it is to release inmates to the community, under supervision, prior to the expiration of the original sentence length. Resource: http://www.appa-net.org.

[2]    This point is eloquently argued by F.T. Cullen (1994). "Social Support as an Organizing Concept for Criminology." *Justice Quarterly*, 11:527-560. See also K. Scott and D. Wolfe (2000). "Change Among Batterers: Examining Men's Success Stories." *Journal of Interpersonal Violence*, 15(8):827-842.

[3]    For a good example of advocacy in probation and parole, see Frank Dell'Apa et al. (1976). "Advocacy, Brokerage, Community: The ABC's of Probation and Parole." *Federal Probation*, 40:37-44; and Claude T. Mangrum (1975). *The Professional Practitioner in Probation*, pp. 43-44. Springfield, IL: Charles C Thomas.

[4]    For recent discussions of advocacy, see D. Macallair (1994). "Disposition Case Advocacy in San Francisco's Juvenile Justice System: A New Approach to Deinstitutionalization." *Crime & Delinquency*, 40:84-95; D. Macallair (1993). "Reaffirming Rehabilitation in Juvenile Justice." *Youth and Society*, 25:104-125.

[5]    P. Hoffman (1994). "Twenty Years of Operational Use of a Risk Prediction Instrument: The United States Parole Commission's Salient Factor Score." *Journal of Criminal Justice*, 22:447-494. But see J. Proctor (1994). "Evaluating a Modified Version of the Federal Prison System's Classification Model: An Assessment of Objectivity and Predictive Validity." *Criminal Justice and Behavior*, 21:256-272.

[6]    Champion, D. (1994). *Measuring Offender Risk: A Criminal Justice Sourcebook*. Westport, CT: Greenwood Press; P. Van Voorhis (1994). *Psychological Classification of the Adult Male Prison Inmate*. Albany, NY: State University of New York Press.

[7]    American Correctional Association (1993). *Community Partnerships in Action*. Laurel, MD: ACA. See also American Correctional Association (1987). *Standards for Administration of Correctional Agencies*. Laurel, MD: ACA; and K. Celinska (2000). Volunteer Involvement in Ex-offenders' Readjustment." *Journal of Offender Rehabilitation*, 30(3/4):99-116.

# References

American Correctional Association (1993). *Community Partnerships in Action.* Laurel, MD: ACA.

American Correctional Association (1987). *Standards for Administration of Correctional Agencies.* Laurel, MD: ACA.

Andrews, D. (1989). "Recidivism Is Predictable and Can Be Influenced: Using Risk Assessments to Reduce Recidivism." *Forum on Correctional Research*, 1(2):11-17.

Andrews, D. (1982). *The Level of Services Inventory (LSI): The First Follow-up.* Toronto: Ontario Ministry of Correctional Services.

Andrews, D.A. (1983). "The Assessment of Outcome in Correctional Samples." In M. Lambert, E. Christensen, and S. DeJulio (eds.) *The Measurement of Psychotherapy Outcome in Research and Evaluation.* New York, NY: Wiley.

Andrews, D. and J. Bonta (1995). *LSI-R The Level of Service Inventory—Revised.* Toronto, ON: Multi-Health Systems, Inc.

Andrews, D.A. and J. Bonta (2006). *The Psychology of Criminal Conduct.* Newark, NJ: LexisNexis Matthew Bender.

Andrews, D., J. Bonta, and R. Hoge (1990). "Classification for Effective Rehabilitation Rediscovering Psychology." *Criminal Justice and Behavior*, 17:19-52.

Andrews, D.A., J. Bonta, and S.J. Wormith (2004). *The Level of Service/Case Management Inventory.* Toronto, ON: Multi-Health Systems, Inc.

Ankersmit, E. (1976). "Setting the Contract in Probation." *Federal Probation*, 41(2):28-33.

Auerbach, B. and T. Castellano (1998). Successful Community Sanctions and Services for Special Offenders: Proceedings of the 1994 Conference of the International Community Corrections Association, Lantham, MD: American Correctional Association.

Belknap, J. and K. Holsinger (1998). "An Overview of Delinquent Girls: How Theory and Practice have Failed and the Need for Innovative Changes." In R.T. Zaplin (ed.), *Female Crime and Delinquency: Critical Perspectives and Effective Interventions*, pp. 31-64. Gaithersburg, MD: Aspen.

Bonta, J. (1996). "Risk-Needs Assessment and Treatment." In A.T. Harlan, *Choosing Correctional Options That Work: Defining the Demand and Evaluating the Supply*, pp. 33-68. Thousand Oaks, CA: Sage Publications.

Bonta, J. and D. Andrews (1993). "The Level of Supervision Inventory: An Overview." *IARCA Journal*, 5(4):6-8.

Bonta, J. and L. Motiuk (1985). "Utilization of an Interview-Based Classification Instrument: A Study of Correctional Halfway Houses." *Criminal Justice and Behavior*, 12:333-352.

Bowers, S. (1950). "The Nature and Definition of Social Casework." In C. Kasius (eds.) *Principles and Techniques in Social Casework*, pp. 126-139. New York, NY: Family Services Association of America.

Bruce, A., A. Harno, E. Burgess, and J. Landesco (1928). *The Workings of the Interme-diate-Sentence Law and the Parole System in Illinois*. State of Illinois.

Bureau of Justice Statistics (2006). *Correctional Populations in the United States*. Washington, DC: U.S. Department of Justice.

Bureau of Justice Statistics (1997). *Correctional Populations in the United States*. Washington, DC: U.S. Department of Justice.

Burnett, C. and A. Kitchen (1989). "More Than a Case Number: Older Offenders on Probation." *Journal of Offender Counseling, Services and Rehabilitation*, 13:149-160.

Camp, C. and G. Camp (1997). *The Corrections Yearbook 1997*. South Salem, NY: The Criminal Justice Institute.

Carter, R. and L. Wilkins (1976). "Caseloads: Some Conceptual Models." In R.M. Carter and L.T. Wilkins (eds.) *Probation, Parole and Community Corrections*, pp. 391-401. New York, NY: John Wiley and Sons.

Celinska, K. (2000). "Volunteer Involvement in Ex-offenders' Readjustment." *Journal of Offender Rehabilitation*, 30(3/4):99-116.

Champion, D. (1994). *Measuring Offender Risk: A Criminal Justice Sourcebook*. Westport, CT: Greenwood Press.

Chesney-Lind, M. (1997). *The Female Offender*. Thousand Oaks, CA: Sage.

Chesney-Lind, M. (1989). "Girls' Crime and Women's Place: Toward a Feminist Model of Female Delinquency." *Crime &Delinquency*, 35:5-29.

Chesney-Lind, M. & Sheldon, R. (1992). *Girls, Delinquency, and Juvenile Justice*. Belmont, CA: Wadsworth.

Clear, T. (1988). "Statistical Prediction in Corrections." *Research in Corrections*, 1:1-39.

Clear, T. and K. Gallagher (1985). "Probation and Parole Supervision: A Review of Current Classification Practices." *Crime & Delinquency*, 31:423-444.

Collins, P. (1990). "Risk Classification and Assessment in Probation: A Study of Misdemeanants." Unpublished master's thesis, University of Cincinnati, Cincinnati, OH.

Coulson, G., G. Ilacqua, V. Nutbrown, D., Giulekas, and F. Cudjoe (1996). "Predictive Utility of the LSI for Incarcerated Female Offenders." *Criminal Justice and Behavior*, 23:427-439.

Cullen, F. (1994). "Social Support as an Organizing Concept for Criminology." *Justice Quarterly*, 11:527-560.

Dell'Apa, F., W. Adams, J. Jorgensen, and H. Sigurdson (1976). "Advocacy, Brokerage, Community: The ABC's of Probation and Parole." *Federal Probation*, 40(4):37-44.

Ellsworth, T. (1988). "Case Supervision Planning: The Forgotten Component of Intensive Probation Supervision." *Federal Probation*, 52(4):28-32.

Funk, S. (1999). "Risk Assessment for Juveniles on Probation." *Criminal Justice and Behavior*, 26:44-68.

Gendreau, P., C. Goggin, and T. Little (1996). *Predicting Adult Offender Recidivism: What Works?* Ottawa, CN: Solicitor General Canada.

Gilligan C. and G. Wiggins (1988). "The Origins of Morality in Early Childhood Relationships." In C. Gilligan, J. Ward, and J. Taylor (eds.) *Mapping the Moral Domain: A Contribution of Women's Thinking to Psychological Theory and Education*, pp. 111-138. Cambridge, MA: Harvard University Press.

Glick, B., W. Sturgeon, and C. Venator-Santiago (1998). *No Time to Play: Youthful Offenders in Adult Correctional System*. Lantham, MD: American Correctional Association.

Gordon, D. and J. Arbuthnot (1988). "The Use of Paraprofessionals to Deliver Home-Based Family Therapy to Juvenile Delinquents." *Criminal Justice and Behavior*, 15:364-378.

Greenberg, N. (1988). "The Discovery Program: A Way to Use Volunteers in the Treatment Process." *Federal Probation*, 52(4):39-45.

Greenwood, P. and F. Zimring (1985). *One More Chance: The Pursuit of Promising Intervention Strategies for Chronic Juvenile Offenders*. Santa Monica, CA: The Rand Corporation.

Hardman, D. (1959). "Authority in Casework: A Bread-and-Butter Theory." *National Probation and Parole Association Journal*, 5:249-255.

Hare, R., (1996). "Psychopathy: A Clinical Construct Whose Time Has Come." *Criminal Justice and Behavior*, 23:25-54.

Harlan, A. (1996). *Choosing Correctional Options That Work*. Thousand Oaks, CA: Sage.

Harlow, C. (1999). *Prior Abuse Reported by Inmates and Probationers*. Washington, DC: Bureau of Justice Statistics.

Harris, P. (1994). "Client Management Classification and Prediction of Probation Outcome." *Crime & Delinquency*, 40:154-174

Hoffman, P. (1994). "Twenty Years of Operational Use of a Risk Prediction Instrument: The United States Parole Commission's Salient Factor Score." *Journal of Criminal Justice*, 22:447-494.

Hoge, R. and D. Andrews (1996a). *Assessing the Youthful Offender: Issues and Techniques*. New York, NY: Plenum Press.

Hoge, R. and D. Andrews (1996b). *The Youthful Level of Service/Case Management Inventory*.

Holsinger, A., A. Lurigio, and E. Latessa (2001). "Practitioner's Guide to Understanding the Basis of Assessing Offender Risk." *Federal Probation*, 64(2):46-50.

Hubbard, D.J., L. Travis, and E. Latessa (2001). *Case Classification in Community Corrections: A National Survey of the State of the Art*. Washington, DC: National Institute of Justice, U.S. Department of Justice.

Jensen, C. (1987). *Contracting for Community Corrections Services.* Washington DC: U.S. Department of Justice, National Institute of Corrections.

Jones, P. (1996). "Risk Prediction in Criminal Justice." In A.T. Harlan, *Choosing Correctional Options that Work: Defining the Demand and Evaluating the Supply*, pp. 33-68. Thousand Oaks, CA: Sage Publications.

Kennedy, S. (1998). *Effective Interventions with Higher Risk Offenders.* Longmont, CO: National Institute of Corrections.

Kennedy, S. and R. Serin (1997). "Treatment Responsivity: Contributing to Effective Correctional Programming." *The ICCA Journal on Community Corrections*, 7(4):46-52.

Klein, A. (1989, Winter). "The Curse of Caseload Management." *Perspectives*, 13:27-28.

Kratcoski, P. (1985). "The Functions of Classification Models in Probation and Parole: Control or Treatment-Rehabilitation?" *Federal Probation*, 49(4):49-56.

Latessa, E.J. and C. Lowenkamp (2001). *Testing the LSI-R in Community-Based Correctional Facilities.* Cincinnati, OH: Center for Criminal Justice Research, University of Cincinnati.

Latessa, E.J. and C. Taylor (2001). *Using the Youthful Level of Service Inventory/Case Management in a Large Urban Court.* Cincinnati, OH: Center for Criminal Justice Research, University of Cincinnati.

Latessa, E., L. Travis, and H. Allen (1983). "Volunteers and Paraprofessionals in Parole: Current Practices." *Journal of Offender Counseling Services and Rehabilitation*, 8:91-105.

Lowenkamp, C., A. Holsinger, and E. Latessa (2001). "Risk/Need Assessment, Offender Classification, and The Role of Childhood Abuse." *Criminal Justice and Behavior*, 28(5):543-563.

Lucas, W. (1987). "Perceptions of the Volunteer Role." *Journal of Offender Counseling*, Services and Rehabilitation, 12:141-146.

Macallair, D. (1994). "Disposition Case Advocacy in San Francisco's Juvenile Justice System: A New Approach to Deinstitutionalization." *Crime & Delinquency*, 40:84-95.

Macallair, D. (1993). "Reaffirming Rehabilitation in Juvenile Justice." *Youth and Society*, 25:104-125.

Mangrum, C. (1975). *The Professional Practitioner in Probation.* Springfield, IL: Charles C Thomas.

Maruschak, L. and A. Beck (2001). *Medical Problems of Inmates.* Washington, DC: U.S. Bureau of Justice Statistics (www.ojp.usdoj.gov/bjs/pub/pdf/mpi97.pdf).

Mazerolle, P. (1998). "Gender, General Strain, and Delinquency: An Empirical Examination." *Justice Quarterly*, 15:65-91.

McCarthy, B. and R. Langworthy (1987). "Older Offenders on Probation and Parole." *Journal of Offender Counseling, Services and Rehabilitation*, 12:7-25.

Meeker, B. (1948). "Probation Is Casework." *Federal Probation*, 12(2):51-52.

Motiuk, L. (1993). "Where Are We in our Ability to Assess Risk?" *Forum on Correctional Research*, 5(1):14-18.

Mumola, C. (1999). *Substance Abuse and Treatment, States and Federal Prisoners, 1997.* Washington, DC: U.S. Bureau of Justice Statistics.

National Advisory Commission on Criminal Justice Standards and Goals (1973). *Corrections.* Washington, DC: U.S. Government Printing Office.

National Institute of Corrections. (1983). *Model Classification System.* Washington, DC.

Proctor, J. (1994). "Evaluating a Modified Version of the Federal Prison System's Classification Model: An Assessment of Objectivity and Predictive Validity." *Criminal Justice and Behavior*, 21:256-272.

Prochaska, J. and C. DiClemente (1986). "Toward a Comprehensive Model of Change." In W.R. Miller and S. Rollnick (eds.) *Motivational Interviewing: Preparing People to Change Addictive Behavior.* New York, NY: Guilford Press.

Scheier, I. (1970). "The Professional and the Volunteer: An Emerging Relationship." *Federal Probation*, 34(2):8-12.

Schumacher, M. (1985). "Implementation of a Client Classification and Case Management System: A Practitioner's View." *Crime & Delinquency*, 31:445-455.

Scott, K. and D. Wolfe (2000). "Change Among Batterers: Examining Men's Success Stories." *Journal of Interpersonal Violence*, 15(8):827-842.

Scott, R. (1978). "Contract Programming in Probation: Philosophical and Experimental Bases for Building a Model." *The Justice System Journal*, 4:49-70.

Shields, I. and D. Simourd (1991). "Predicting Predatory Behavior in a Population of Incarcerated Young Offenders." *Criminal Justice and Behavior*, 18:180-194.

Sigler, R. and J. Williams (1994). "A Study of the Outcomes of Probation Officers and Risk-Screening Instrument Classifications." *Journal of Criminal Justice*, 22:495-502.

Smykla, J. (1986). "Critique Concerning Prediction in Probation and Parole: Some Alternative Suggestions." *International Journal of Offender Therapy and Comparative Criminology*, 30-31, 125-139.

Studt, E. (1954). "Casework in the Correctional Field." *Federal Probation*, 17(3):17-24.

Travis, L. (1989). *Risk Classification in Probation and Parole.* Risk Classification Project, University of Cincinnati, Cincinnati, OH.

Travis, L. and E. Latessa (1996). "Classification and Needs Assessment Module." In *Managing Violent Youthful Offenders in Adult Institutions Curriculum.* Longmont, CO: National Institute of Corrections.

Trecker, H. (1955). "Social Work Principles in Probation." *Federal Probation*, 19(1):8-9.

Van Voorhis, P. (1994). *Psychological Classification of the Adult Male Prison Inmate*. Albany, NY: State University of New York Press.

Wilbanks, W. (1985). "Predicting Failure on Parole." In D. Farrington and R. Tarling (eds.) *Prediction in Criminology*, pp. 78-94. Albany, NY: SUNY Press.

Wong, S. (1997). Risk: Assessing the Risk of Violent Recidivism. Presentation at the American Probation and Parole Association, Boston, MA.

Wright, K., T. Clear, and P. Dickson (1984). "Universal Applicability of Probation Risk Assessment Instruments." *Criminology*, 22:113-134.

# Intermediate Sanctions

*If punishment makes not the will supple it hardens the offender.*

—John Locke

*The effects of our actions may be postponed but they are never lost. There is an inevitable reward for good deeds and an inescapable punishment for bad. Mediate this truth, and seek always to earn good wages from destiny.*

—Wu Ming Fu

## Intermediate Sanctions

No discussion of contemporary probation would be complete without examining the development and application of intermediate sanctions. Faced with overcrowded prison and jail systems, criminal justice professionals and policymakers are being forced to search for alternative ways to sanction and control criminal offenders.

A host of intermediate sanctions designed to treat the criminal offender in the community have been developed and implemented. The intermediate punishments described in this chapter include electronic monitoring, house arrest, community service, day reporting centers, day fines, intensive supervision, drug courts, and boot camps. The purposes of these intermediate interventions are to provide correctional alternatives to confinement.

The U.S. Department of Justice (1990:3) defines intermediate sanctioning as "a punishment option that is considered on a continuum to fall between traditional probation and traditional incarceration." Intermediate sanctions were largely developed out of the need to relieve the prison crowding[1] and satisfy the general publics' desire for new correctional alternatives. Thus, policymakers began to experiment with programs to punish, control, and reform offenders in the community. Figure 8.1 shows the percentage of probationers under several different types of sanctions. More than 10 percent are under some form of supervision other than regular. Two major issues confronting intermediate sanctions are: (1) offender diversion; and (2) public safety.

**Intermediate Sanctions**

Intermediate sanctions, ranging in severity from day fines to "boot camps," are interventions that are beginning to fill the sentencing gap between prison at one extreme and probation at the other. Lengthy prison terms may be inappropriate for some offenders; for others, probation may be too inconsequential and may not provide the degree of public supervision necessary to ensure public safety. By expanding sentencing options, intermediate sanctions enable the criminal justice system to tailor punishment more closely to the nature of the crime and the criminal. An appropriate range of punishments makes it possible for the system to hold offenders strictly accountable for their actions.

Source: V. Gowdy (1993). *Intermediate Sanctions*, p. 1. Washington, DC: U.S. Department of Justice.

Figure 8.1
**Probationers and Parolees Under Different Types of Supervision in 2002**

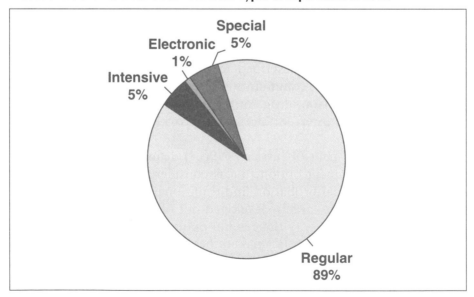

Source: Camp, C.G. and G.M. Camp (2003). *The 2002 Corrections Yearbook: Adult Corrections.* Middletown, CT: Criminal Justice Institute, p. 191.

# The Need for Intermediate Sanctions

With prison and jail populations at an all time high, most states have acknowledged that they will not be able to build their way out of the crisis. It should also be noted that the national annual incarceration expense for a single prisoner is over $21,000. Furthermore, with more than 76 percent of correctional agencies at or exceeding capacity, it is unlikely that there will be relief in the near future. Alternatives to long-term confinement are a necessity.

Despite the ever-increasing cost of incarceration, it is necessary for alternative sanctions to gain public, legislative, and judicial support (Finn, 1991). To earn sufficient support, an alternative to confinement must "be perceived as reasonably safe; address the public's desire for punishment through community control, nonpaid labor, and victim restitution; and offer an opportunity for positive change by providing treatment and employment skills" (American Correctional Association, 1990:2).

# Intensive Supervision

The most widely used community-based intermediate sanction that attempts to meet the above criteria is intensive supervision. Intensive supervision is most often viewed as an alternative to incarceration. Persons who are sentenced to intensive probation supervision are supposed to be those offenders who, in the absence of intensive supervision, would have been sentenced to imprisonment. However, intensive supervision is hardly a new idea. Previous programs of intensive supervision carried the common goal of maintaining public safety, but varied from the "new generation" of intensive supervision programs (ISPs) in very fundamental ways (Latessa, 1986).

Early versions of intensive supervision were based on the idea that increased client contact would enhance rehabilitation while allowing for greater client control. For example, California's Special Intensive Parole Unit experiments in the 1950s and the San Francisco Project in the 1960s were designed as intensive supervision, but they emphasized rehabilitation as the main goal. Later, with rehabilitation still as the main objective, experiments were "undertaken to determine the 'best' caseload size for the community supervision, despite the illogic of the proposition that a magical 'best' number could be found" (McCarthy, 1987:33). Nevertheless, the failure of these experiments to produce results fueled two decades' worth of cynicism about the general utility of community-based methods.

Burkhart (1986) and Pearson (1987) contend that today's ISPs emphasize punishment of the offender and control of the offender in the

---

Box 8.2

### Types of ISPs

ISPs are usually classified as prison diversion, enhanced probation, and enhanced parole. Each has a different goal.

**Diversion** is commonly referred to as a "front door" program because its goal is to limit the number of offenders entering prison. Prison diversion programs generally identify incoming, lower-risk inmates to participate in an ISP in the community as a substitute for a prison term.

**Enhancement** programs generally select already sentenced probationers and parolees and subject them to closer supervision in the community than regular probation or parole. People placed in ISP enhanced probation or enhanced parole programs show evidence of failure under routine supervision or have committed serious offenses deemed to be too serious for supervision on routine caseloads.

Treatment and service components in the ISPs included drug and alcohol counseling, employment, community service, and payment of restitution. On many of these measures, ISP offenders participated more than did control members; participation in such programs was found to be correlated with a reduction in recidivism. . . .

Source: J. Petersilia and S. Turner (1993). *Evaluating Intensive Supervision of Probation/Parole: Results of a Nationwide Experiment*, pp. 2, 7. Washington, DC: U.S. Department of Justice.

---

community at least as much as they do rehabilitation. Further, contemporary programs are designed to meet the primary goal of easing the burden of prison overcrowding.

Figure 8.2 illustrates the differences between the objectives of the original experiments with intensive supervision, and the so-called "new generation" programs. The early models were successful at accomplishing smaller caseloads and delivering more contacts and services; however, reductions in recidivism never materialized. Similarly, the more recent programs have reduced caseloads and significantly increased control and surveillance but have not had an appreciable impact directly on prison populations.[2]

Today, no two jurisdictions define intensive supervision in exactly the same way. However, one characteristic of all ISPs is that they provide for very strict terms of probation. As Jones (1991:1) points out: "Their common feature is that more control is to be exerted over the offender than that described as probation in that jurisdiction and that often these extra control mechanisms involve restrictions on liberty of movement, coercion into treatment programs, employment obligations, or all three." This increased level of control is usually achieved through reduced case-loads, increased number of contacts, and a range of required activities for participating offenders that can include victim restitution, community service, employment, random urine and alcohol testing, electronic monitoring, and payment of a probation supervision fee.

Figure 8.2
**Models of ISP Programs**

**Early ISP Program Model:**
Smaller ⟶ Increased ⟶ Improved Treatment ⟶ Reduced
Caseloads      Contacts      & Service Delivery      Recidivism

**New Generation ISP Program Model:**
Smaller ⟶ Increased ⟶ Improved Surveillance ⟶ Reduced
Caseloads      Contacts      & Control      Prison Population

Intensive supervision programs vary in terms of the number and type of contacts per month, caseload size, type of surveillance conducted, and services offered. In addition, programs vary depending upon whether they are staffed by specially trained officers or regular probation officers, and whether an officer "team" approach is used.

In 1986, Byrne conducted a survey on the use of intensive supervision in the United States. Byrne's interstate comparison found that "the numbers of direct personal contacts required ranged from two per month to seven per week. Some programs have specified no curfew checks while others specified three curfew checks per week" (Pearson, 1987:15). Ideally, supervising officers provide monitoring with a reduced caseload of about 15 offenders per officer. Yet, most officers carry caseloads of nearly 25 offenders. Offender entry into an intensive supervision program may be the decision of the sentencing judge, a parole board, a prison release board, or probation agency.

Table 8.1 shows some of the variation among selected ISPs. The types of clients served, the number of contacts made each month, and the recidivism rates vary greatly from program to program.

Many ISPs have revealed an increase in technical violations for ISP offenders as compared to offenders placed in other sentencing options, but no significant increase in the new offense rate (Erwin, 1987; Petersilia & Turner, 1993; Wagner & Baird, 1993). Most evaluations however, suggest that increased contact alone does not make a difference in terms of overall recidivism rates. In a recent study of ISPs in Ohio,

Table 8.1
**Intensive Supervision Probation/Parole**

| Author & Year | Site | Sample | Control Groups | Contacts | Recidivism |
|---|---|---|---|---|---|
| Jolin & Stipak (1991) | Oregon | N=70 Drug Users | 100 on EM 100 on Work Release Stratified random sample matched on risk | 5 counseling per wk & 3 self-help per wk., plus curfew & EM | 47% ISP 32% EM 33% WR |
| Erwin (1987) | Georgia | N=200 randomly selected from ISP | N=200 probationers N=97 prison releasees Matched samples | 5 per wk. ISP | 40% ISP 35.5% Probation 57.8% Prison |
| Pearson (1987) | New Jersey | N=554 parolees | N=510 | 20 per mo. | 24.7% ISP 34.6% CG |
| Byrne & Kelly (1989) | Massachusetts | N=227 High-Risk Probationers | N=834 ISP Eligible Offenders plus a 35% random sample of all offenders under supervision (N=2543) | 10 mo. ISP 2 mo. Probation | 56.6% ISP 60.9% Probation |
| Latessa (1993) | Ohio | All offenders in specialized ISP Units Alcohol=140 Drug=121 Sex=64 Mental=76 | N=424 regular probationers randomly selected | 6 mo. Alcohol & Drug 4.5 mo. Sex & Mental Health 1 mo. comparison | 42% Alcohol 59% Drug 22% Sex 27% MH 46% Probation |
| Latessa (1992) | Ohio | N=82 ISP randomly selected | N=101 randomly selected from regular probation | 7.5 mo. ISP 2.2 mo. Prob | 28% ISP 21% Probation |
| Latessa (1993) | Ohio | N=317 ISP N=502 High Risk ISP | N=424 randomly selected from regular probation | 4 mo. ISP 3 mo. High Risk 2 mo. Prob | 35% ISP 43% High 34% Probation |
| Fallen et al. (1981) | Washington | N=289 Low Risk parolees | N=102 matched parolees | 4 per mo. | 32.9% ISP 46.9% CG |
| Petersilia & Turner (1993) | Contra-Costra | N=170 | Randomly selected offenders placed in prison, probation, or parole | 12 per mo. | 29% ISP 27% CG |
| Petersilia & Turner (1993) | Los Angeles | N=152 | Randomly selected offenders placed in prison, probation, or parole | 24 per mo. | 32% ISP 30% CG |
| Petersilia & Turner (1993) | Seattle | N=173 | Randomly selected offenders placed in prison, probation, or parole | 12 per mo. | 46% ISP 36% CG |
| Petersilia & Turner (1993) | Ventura | N=166 | Randomly selected offenders placed in prison, probation, or parole | 24 per mo. | 32% ISP 53% CG |

Table 8.1—*continued*

| Author & Year | Site | Sample | Control Groups | Contacts | Recidivism |
|---|---|---|---|---|---|
| Petersilia & Turner (1993) | Atlanta | N=50 | Randomly selected offenders placed in prison, probation, or parole | 20 per mo. | 12% ISP 4% CG |
| Petersilia & Turner (1993) | Macon | N=50 | Randomly selected offenders placed in prison, probation, or parole | 20 per mo. | 42% ISP 38% CG |
| Petersilia & Turner (1993) | Santa Fe | N=58 | Randomly selected offenders placed in prison, probation, or parole | 20 per mo. | 48% ISP 28% CG |
| Petersilia & Turner (1993) | Dallas | N=221 parolees | Randomly selected offenders placed in prison, probation, or parole | 16 per mo. | 39% ISP 30% CG |
| Petersilia & Turner (1993) | Houston | N=458 parolees | Randomly selected offenders placed in prison, probation, or parole | 10 per mo. | 44% ISP 40% CG |
| Latessa, Travis, Fulton et al., (1998) | Iowa and Northeastern state | N=401 | Selected from urban probation department, and rural probation and parole caseload | Varied | 39% ISP 40% CG |
| Robertson, Grimes & Rogers (2001) | Mississippi | N=153 | Juvenile offenders placed on intensive probation, monitoring, on regular probation, or counselling with cognitive-behavioral (CB) therapy | 12 months | Benefit-cost ratio of subjects receiving CB therapy was almost twice that of intensive supervision and monitoring. |

Source: Compiled by authors.

Latessa, Travis, and Holsinger (1997) found that offenders in ISPs were less likely to be rearrested than offenders under other forms of correctional supervision; however, they were more likely to be subsequently incarcerated. They attributed this higher failure rate to revocations for probation violations. Latessa and his colleagues also concluded that ISPs in Ohio were saving the state over the cost of incarceration.

As currently designed, many ISPs fail to produce significant reductions in recidivism, or alleviate prison overcrowding. There does, however, appear to be a relationship between greater participation in treatment programs and lower failure rates (Petersilia & Turner, 1993; Johnson & Hunter, 1992, Jolin & Stipak, 1992; Paparozzi, n.d.; Pearson, 1987). This is one of the important issues facing intensive supervision. In a recent article summarizing the state of ISPs, Fulton, Latessa, Stichman, and Travis (1997:72) make the following conclusions:

- ISPs have failed to alleviate prison crowding;

- Most ISP studies have found no significant differences between recidivism rates of ISP offenders and offenders with comparison groups;

- There appears to be a relationship between greater participation in treatment and employment programs and lower recidivism rates;

- ISPs appear to be more effective than regular supervision or prison in meeting offenders' needs;

- ISPs that reflect certain principles of effective intervention are associated with lower rates of recidivism;

- ISPs provide intermediate punishment; and

- Although ISPs are less expensive than prison, they are more expensive than originally thought.

## Issues in Intensive Supervision

Intensive supervision, as a technique for increasing control over offenders in the community (and thereby reducing risk), has gained wide popularity.[3] A 1988 survey found that 45 states had or were developing intensive supervision programs. As of 1990, all states, plus the federal system, had some kind of intensive supervision program in place. This widespread acceptance has provided states with the needed continuum of sentencing options, so that offenders are being held accountable for their crimes while, at the same time, public safety is being maintained. This popularity of intensive supervision has generated much research, thereby raising several issues.

Current issues largely revolve around the effectiveness of intensive supervision. Yet, measures of success vary depending on the stated goals and objectives each program set out to address.[4] For instance, the goals of a treatment-oriented program differ from the goals of a program that places emphasis on offender punishment and control. However, it is possible to isolate two overriding themes of recent ISPs that raise several issues. First, "intensive probation supervision is expected to divert offenders from incarceration in order to alleviate prison overcrowding,[5] avoid the exorbitant costs of building and sustaining prisons, and prevent the stultifying and stigmatizing effects of imprisonment" (Byrne, Lurigio & Baird, 1989:10). Second, ISPs are expected to promote public safety through surveillance strategies, while promoting a sense of responsibility and accountability through probation fees, restitution, and community service activities (Byrne, Lurigio & Baird, 1989). These goals generate issues regarding the ability of ISP programs in reducing recidivism, diverting offenders from prison, and ensuring public safety.

The debate over control versus treatment has raged for many years. Recently, there has been a new movement, initiated by the American Probation and Parole Association, to develop a more balanced approach to ISP supervision (Fulton, Stone & Gendreau, 1994; Fulton, Gendreau & Paparozzi, 1996). This approach continues to support strict conditions and supervision practices, but within the context of more services, and higher quality treatment. Indeed, it appears that if ISP is going to live up to its promises, a new model must be developed.

## Day Reporting Centers

Unlike many other intermediate sanction alternatives, day reporting is of very recent vintage. While day reporting was used earlier in England, the first day reporting program in the United States was opened in Massachusetts in 1986 (McDevitt, 1988). This inaugural program was designed as an early release from prison and jail placement for inmates approaching their parole or discharge date. Participants in the program were required to report to the center each day (hence the name, "Day Reporting"), prepare an itinerary for their next day's activities, and report by telephone to the center throughout the day (Larivee, 1990). By 1992, there were six day reporting centers in operation in Massachusetts with average daily populations ranging from 30 to more than 100 offenders.

Parent (1990) reported that by the late 1980s, day reporting programs were operational in six states, and many more states were considering the option. The characteristics of these programs, and the clients they served varied considerably. As McDevitt and Miliano (1992:153) noted, "Although all centers have similar program elements, such as frequent client contact, formalized scheduling, and drug testing, the operations of different DRCs (day reporting centers) are quite varied. Therefore, it is difficult to define specifically what a day reporting center is; each center is unique."

Larivee (1990), in describing the development of day reporting centers in Massachusetts, noted that these centers were created for the purpose of diverting offenders from confinement in local jails. Offenders live at home, but must report once each day to the center, and are in telephone contact with the center four times each day. By 1990, there were seven centers serving eight counties and the state department of corrections. An evaluation of the Massachusetts day reporting centers reported that more than two-thirds of day reporting clients successfully completed programs and only two percent were returned to prison or jail for new crimes or escape (Curtin, 1990). An earlier evaluation of the Hampden County center (the first opened) reported more than 80 percent successful completion of the program and only one percent arrested for a new crime while in the program. Larivee concluded about the Massachusetts day reporting centers, "Every client in a day reporting center program would otherwise be incarcerated; additionally, no client is held in the center longer than he or she would be kept in jail . . . Only four percent of the clients were arrested for a new crime or escape, and none committed a violent offense."

---

Box 8.3

### Day Reporting Centers

Certain persons on pretrial release, probation, or parole are required to appear at day reporting centers on a frequent and regular basis in order to participate in services or activities provided by the center or other community agencies. Failure to report or participate is a violation that could cause revocation of conditional release or community supervision.

Reports indicate that offenders in these programs must not only physically report to their centers daily but also provide a schedule of planned activities, and participate in designated activities. In addition offenders must call the centers by phone throughout the day; they can also expect random phone checks by center staff both during the day and at home following curfew. In some programs, offenders must contact their respective centers an average of 60 times weekly and, in all but one, take random drug tests.

Source: V. Gowdy (1993). *Intermediate Sanctions*, p. 5. Washington, DC: U.S. Department of Justice.

---

Parent (1990) reported an assessment of 14 day reporting centers known to be in operation in 1989. Only three of the centers were operated by public agencies, with the other 11 being administered by private, nonprofit organizations. The programs ranged in capacity from 10 offenders to 150, with most being able to accommodate 50 or fewer. A survey of these centers revealed that successful completion of programs varied greatly by center, and by type of client. Probation and parole violators and those who had been denied discretionary parole release had successful completion rates of about one-third or less, while offenders received from institutional work release programs or diverted from jail had completion rates in excess of two-thirds (Parent, 1990:27). The survey also reported a range in center costs from less than $8 per day per offender to more than $50 per day. The mean cost was nearly $15 per day.

In 1993, Parent et al. (1995) replicated this survey, this time contacting 114 day reporting centers operating in 22 states. Fifty-four of these programs responded to the survey. Most of these responding programs indicated that they had opened after 1991. Most centers were still operated by private, nonprofit organizations, and there was still a wide variety in services, programming, and contact requirements. Newer centers, however, were more likely to be operated by public agencies than were the older ones.

When asked to identify the goals of their Day Reporting Center, respondents to the survey identified four purposes of the programs. The most important purpose, according to respondents, was to provide offenders with access to treatment services. Second most important was to reduce jail and prison crowding. Additional program goals included building political support for the program and the provision of surveillance/public safety.

The survey revealed wide variation in Day Reporting Center organizations, populations, costs, and effectiveness. Most centers were operated at the local level by agencies affiliated with the courts. Newer Day Reporting Centers were likely to serve a pre-imprisonment population, while the older centers primarily supervised offenders released from incarceration. Day Reporting Center populations included pretrial releasees, offenders diverted from imprisonment, probation and parole violators, and newly released prison and jail inmates. As Parent et al. observed (1995:22), "The average negative termination rate for all such programs is 50 percent, with a wide distribution that ranges from 14 to 86 percent." They found that characteristics of the day reporting programs were correlated with higher rates of negative termination. The survey did not provide any information specifically concerning the rearrest rates of program participants. Rather, "negative termination" refers to offenders removed from the program for rule violations, which would include the commission of a new crime.

Centers operated by private agencies were more likely to have high negative termination rates than were those operated by public agencies. Those centers that offered more services, and those using curfews had higher rates of negative terminations. Finally, policies towards violations of center rules were related to rates of negative termination. As would be expected, those centers with stricter policies and fewer alternatives within the program were more likely to experience high rates of negative terminations. It may also be that changes in day reporting populations to include a variety of offender types, and an increase in the number of expectations and conditions placed on these offenders (drug testing, mandatory treatment attendance, community service, curfews, etc.) combined to increase the likelihood of program failure. A final correlate of higher rates of negative terminations was line staff turnover. Programs that experienced higher rates of staff turnover also had higher rates of negative terminations. However, ". . . it is not clear which characteristic influences the other," as Parent et al. (1995:22) note.

---

Box 8.4

### Community Service

Community service requires that the offender complete some task that helps the community. It is considered a form of restitution, with labor rather than money being supplied. Common jobs include cleaning neighborhoods, working at nursing homes, painting schools, and doing assorted chores for the elderly. Community service can be a sentence in and of itself, or can be included with other sanctions, such as probation.

One high-profile case was Zsa Zsa Gabor, who was required to do community service after being convicted of slapping a Los Angeles police officer.

---

Day reporting programs offered a variety of services to program participants. Most centers offered job skills, drug abuse education, group and individual counseling, job placement, education, life-skills training, and drug treatment. While most services were provided in-house, it was common for drug treatment programs to be offered by providers not located at the Day Reporting Center. A recent trend in these centers noted in the survey as the tendency for the newer, public programs to co-locate social service programs with the day reporting program. The most common in-house programs (those offered at more than three-quarters of the Day Reporting Centers) were job-seeking skills, group counseling, and life-skills training.

The costs of these services are usually paid by the Day Reporting Center. For some programs, other agencies pay the costs of services such as drug treatment, transitional housing, and education and job placement assistance. Seldom are offenders required to pay for services. The costs of operation ranged from about $10 per offender day to more than $100 per offender day, with the average daily cost per offender

By permission of Johnny Hart and Creators Syndicate, Inc.

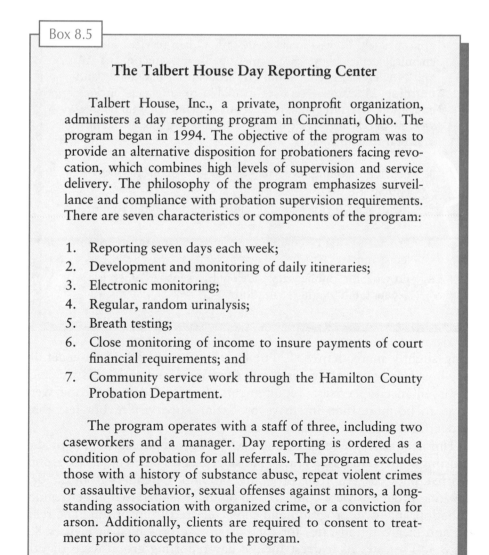

Box 8.5

### The Talbert House Day Reporting Center

Talbert House, Inc., a private, nonprofit organization, administers a day reporting program in Cincinnati, Ohio. The program began in 1994. The objective of the program was to provide an alternative disposition for probationers facing revocation, which combines high levels of supervision and service delivery. The philosophy of the program emphasizes surveillance and compliance with probation supervision requirements. There are seven characteristics or components of the program:

1. Reporting seven days each week;
2. Development and monitoring of daily itineraries;
3. Electronic monitoring;
4. Regular, random urinalysis;
5. Breath testing;
6. Close monitoring of income to insure payments of court financial requirements; and
7. Community service work through the Hamilton County Probation Department.

The program operates with a staff of three, including two caseworkers and a manager. Day reporting is ordered as a condition of probation for all referrals. The program excludes those with a history of substance abuse, repeat violent crimes or assaultive behavior, sexual offenses against minors, a long-standing association with organized crime, or a conviction for arson. Additionally, clients are required to consent to treatment prior to acceptance to the program.

---

Box 8.5—*continued*

Cases referred to the center are given a risk/needs assessment which includes Michigan Alcohol Scores Testing (MAST). Offenders must report to the center seven days each week, provide urine and breath tests as requested, and, if unemployed, must participate in employment-seeking activities. Offenders meet with center staff each afternoon to participate in program activities until 5:00 p.m., when they leave to return home or go to other arranged treatment activities. Offenders stay in the program between one to six months, based on judicial stipulation. The program currently serves about 10 offenders per day. The center provides in-house treatment including individual and group counseling by appropriately licensed/registered staff. Other services include chemical dependency, case management, introduction to AA and NA, life skills education, HIV education, budgeting, and nutrition. Additional services available to offenders include education, parenting, financial management, community service, mental health services, and leisure. The goals of the programs are identified as:

1.  Provide a community sanction option for probation violators;
2.  Identify problems facing offenders that may lead to criminality;
3.  Provide on-site or community referral to treat those problems; and
4.  Provide for public safety through intensive supervision, accountability, and retribution.

---

being slightly more than $35. Public centers were found to generally have lower daily operating costs, and costs increased with the stringency of surveillance/supervision requirements. Costs of day reporting were found to be more than intensive probation supervision, but less than residential treatment or incarceration.

Unfortunately, there have not been many empirical studies of day reporting centers. Latessa, Travis, Holsinger, and Hartman (1998) examined five pilot day reporting programs in Ohio. Offenders from the day reporting programs were compared to offenders supervised under regular probation, intensive program, and those released from prison. The rearrest and incarceration rates for each group are presented in Figures 8.3 and 8.4. The rates of rearrest for the day reporting group were slightly higher than those reported for the other groups. The incarceration rates indicate that the day reporting group performed slightly better than those offenders supervised under intensive supervision, worse than those on regular probation, and similar to those released from prison. Noteworthy, the authors also found that the quality of the treatment provided by the five day reporting centers in this study was judged to be poor.

Figure 8.3
**Ohio Day Reporting Study: Rearrest Rates**

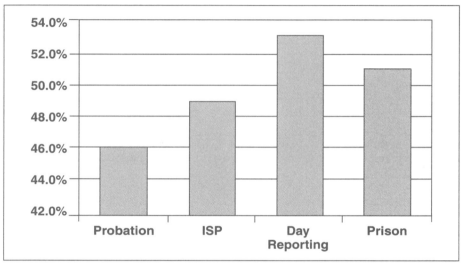

Source: E.J. Latessa, L.F. Travis, A. Holsinger, and J. Hartman (1998). *Evaluation of Ohio's Pilot Day Reporting Program: Final Report.* Cincinnati, OH: Division of Criminal Justice, University of Cincinnati.

## Day Fines

The fine is a common and widely accepted punishment imposed on misdemeanor and some less serious felony offenders (Zimmerman, et al. 1991). A fine is a penalty imposed by a court that requires the offender to pay a specific amount of money. The fine is a cash payment of a dollar amount assessed by the judge on an individual basis or determined by a published schedule of penalties. Fines may be paid in installments in many jurisdictions, or by use of the offender's credit card.

Monetary assessments are typically given to low-risk offenders, and the amount of this financial sanction tends to increase with the severity of the crime. Judges tend to employ rational discretion in these areas. Surprisingly, most fines are collected in large part if not in whole, and there is substantial evidence that the chance of further arrest and incarceration are significantly less for those assessed a fine than for those receiving a jail term, when the investigator controls for offender attributes and offense.[6]

Figure 8.4
**Ohio Day Reporting Study: Incarceration Rates**

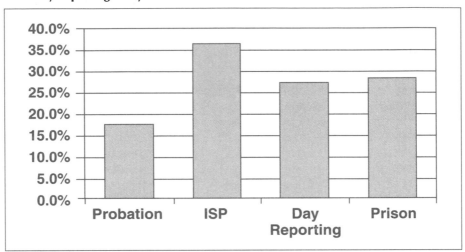

Source: E.J. Latessa, L.F. Travis, A. Holsinger, and J. Hartman (1998). *Evaluation of Ohio's Pilot Day Reporting Program: Final Report.* Cincinnati, OH: Division of Criminal Justice, University of Cincinnati.

Fines are an ancient and widely used penal measure, and noncustodial sanctions are not new in American sentencing. Sentencing judges on the federal level imposed fines in 21 percent of their felony cases in 1993. State judges imposed fines in 16 percent of their felony dispositions (Maguire & Pastore, 1994:533,541). What is new is a variation on financial sanctions known as the day fine, so called because the amount of the fine is tied to an offender's daily earnings, a practice common in European and some South American countries. In the United States, this is not a common practice, for fines have traditionally been based on the offense rather than the individual offender's ability to pay. With the movement toward intermediate punishments, day fines have been enthusiastically incorporated into sentencing systems and by judges, who are increasingly interested in a graduated progression of intermediate penalties: punishment based on an offender's ability to pay.

As sentencing judges become more familiar and comfortable with the day-fine approach, more will impose financial penalties that can be adjusted to individual circumstances and cases. Day fines have the additional potential of raising total collected fine revenues, and have been implemented not only in Staten Island, New York but also in numerous other jurisdictions across the country.[7]

> Box 8.6
>
> ### How Day Fines Work
>
> The general concept is simple: determining the amount of punishment to be administered to an offender is separated from a consideration of how much money that offender must pay. Judges determine how much punishment an offender deserves; this is then denominated into some unit other than money. These *punishment units* are then translated into monetary units based on how much money the offender makes per day.
>
> Practically speaking, the day-fine approach consists of a simple, two-step process. First, the court uses a "unit scale" or "benchmark" to sentence the offender to a certain number of day-fine units (for example, 15, 60, or 120 units) according to the gravity of the offense and without regard to income. To guide the court's choices, benchmarks or unit scales are typically developed by a planning unit of judges, prosecutors, and defense counselors familiar with the disposition patterns of a court.
>
> The value of each unit is then set at a percentage of the offender's daily income, and the total fine amount is determined by simple multiplication.
>
> Source: L. Winterfield and S. Hillsman (1993). *The Staten Island Day-Fine Project*, p. 1. Washington, DC: U.S. Department of Justice.

## Home Detention

House arrest, usually conjuring up images of political control and fascist repression, is court-ordered home detention in this nation, confining offenders to their households for the duration of sentence (Meecham, 1986). Introduced in 1984 in Florida, home detention rapidly spread throughout a nation searching for punitive, safe, and secure alternatives to incarceration (Maxfield & Baumer, 1990). The sentence is usually in conjunction with probation but may be imposed by the court as a separate punishment (as in Florida). Florida's Community Control program (FCCP) was designed to provide a safe diversion alternative, and help address the problem of prison population escalation and associated high costs (Flynn, 1986).

Participants may be required to make victim compensation, perform community work service, pay probation fees, undergo drug and alcohol testing and, in some instances, wear electronic monitoring equipment to verify their presence in the residence. (In some jurisdictions, house arrest is used on a pretrial basis,[8] as an isolated sentence, in conjunction with probation or parole, or with a prerelease status such as education or work furlough.) House arrest only allows the offender to leave her or his residence for specific purposes and hours approved by the court or supervising officer, and being absent without leave is a technical violation of conditions that may result in resentencing to jail or prison (Government Accounting Office, 1990).

Home detention is a punitive sentence and was designed in most cases to relieve institutional overcrowding. For many offenders it is their "last chance" to escape from being committed to prison. In addition to surveillance of the offender, home detention is viewed as a cost avoidance program, a "front-end" solution to prison overcrowding, and a flexible alternative for certain offenders (such as a pregnant offender until time of delivery). The use of telemonitoring devices, discussed below as "Electronic Monitoring Programs," can significantly increase the correctional surveillance of offenders.

The most significant critical argument[9] against home detention is that, by making a non-incarcerative control mechanism available to corrections, many petty offenders are brought under correctional control who would best be handled by diversion, fines, or mental health services. In general, such inclusive actions are viewed as "net widening," which occurs when offenders are sentenced to community control who might otherwise have received a lesser or even no sentence.

The National Council on Crime and Delinquency conducted an evaluation of the FCCP and concluded that the impact on prison crowding, offender behavior, and State correctional costs have been positive. With an estimated prison diversion rate of 54 percent, community control is cost-effective despite the combined effect of net widening and the punishments imposed on almost 10 percent of FCCP participants for technical violations. Furthermore, the new offense rate for community control offenders is lower than for similar offenders sentenced to prison and released without supervision. For every 100 cases diverted from prison, Florida saved more than $250,000 (Wagner & Baird, 1993).

Home detention is an option that has been widely used for many years with juvenile offenders, who are usually remanded to the care of their parents. It is also use for nonviolent adult offenders, and as mentioned previously, it is often used in conjunction with electronic monitoring.

## Electronic Monitoring

Home detention has a long history as a criminal penalty but its new popularity with correctional authorities is due to the advent of electronic monitoring, a technological link thought to make the sanction both practical and affordable. See Figure 8.5.

Figure 8.5
**Electronic Monitoring Devices in Use**

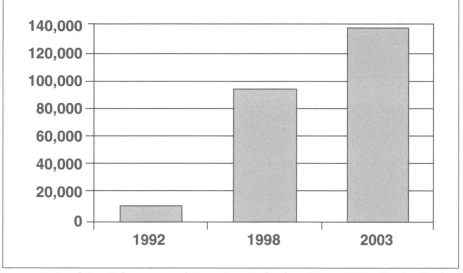

Source: National Law Enforcement and Corrections Technology Center (1999). *Keeping Track of Electronic Monitoring*. Washington, DC: NLECTC (http://www.nlectc.org/txtfiles/ElecMonasc.html). Data for 2003 estimated.

The concept of electronic monitoring is not new, having been proposed in 1964 by Schwitzgebel et al. as "electronic parole," and initially used to monitor the location of mental patients.[10] The first studies of home detention enforced by electronic monitoring began in 1986 and, by early 1992, there were at least 40,000 electronic monitors in use (Gowdy, 1993). It is used almost everywhere in the justice system after arrest. See Figure 8.6.

According to the Bureau of Justice Assistance (1989:3), the goals and objectives of electronic monitoring are to:

- Provide a cost-effective community supervision tool for offenders selected according to specific program criteria;

- Administer sanctions appropriate to the seriousness of the offense;

- Promote public safety by providing surveillance and risk control strategies indicated by the risk and needs of the offenders; and

- Increase the confidence of legislative, judicial, and releasing authorities in ISP designs as a viable sentencing option.

Figure 8.6
**Key Decision Points Where Electronic Monitoring (EM) Is Being Used**

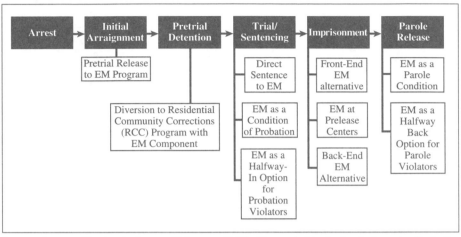

Source: Bureau of Justice Assistance (February, 1989). *Electronic Monitoring in Intensive Probation and Parole Programs.* Washington, DC: U.S. Department of Justice, p. 2.

Electronic monitoring can be active or passive. In active monitoring, a transmitter attached to the offender's wrist or ankle sends signals relayed by a home telephone to the supervising office during the hours the offender is required to be at home. Under passive monitoring, a computer program is used to call the offender randomly during the hours designated for home confinement. The offender inserts the wristlet or anklet into a verifier to confirm her or his presence in the residence. There does not appear to be any difference in recidivism between those on passive or active systems. Only about one in three offenders on home detention wear monitoring devices (Petersilia, 1987).

National surveys indicate that electronic monitoring was initially (1987) used for property offenders on probation but that a much broader range of offenders was being monitored (1989) than in the past. Monitoring has been expanded to include not only probationers but also to follow up persons after incarceration, to control those sentenced to community corrections, and to monitor persons before trial or sentencing.

A 1989 survey on telemonitoring found:

- Most jurisdictions using electronic monitoring tested some offenders for drug use, and many routinely tested all. Some sites charged for the testing; more than 66 percent charged offenders for at least part of the cost of leasing the monitoring equipment.

Box 8.7

## Electronic Supervision Tools: Lessons Learned

The providers of electronic monitoring technology and the practitioners that use them cannot ignore the down side to partial or misleading information presented in the media. Until the public information problem is adequately addressed, preferably through a joint effort, the public is at greater risk than it would otherwise be. The future development and implementation of cost-effective public safety strategies as well as the business climate for the electronic monitoring industry depends on successful resolution of the public relations dilemma.

Beginning in the mid-1980s, electronic monitoring emerged as one solution to burgeoning prison and jail populations and spiraling correctional costs. The design of the programs as well as technologies used varied widely. Anxious to show that something was being done to assure cost-effective expenditures of tax dollars, policymakers quickly embraced electronic monitoring of criminals—sometimes as a panacea for managing correctional populations and public safety concerns. Elevated by the excitement emanating from the field of criminal justice regarding the applications for electronic monitoring, entrepreneurs involved in the manufacture of technologies and operators of electronic monitoring case management centers moved quickly to provide new and improved equipment and services at reduced costs.

The convergence of criminal justice need for costeffective alternatives to incarceration and the business opportunities available within this environment resulted in grandiose promises and expectations. Industry manufacturers and practitioners shared purveyance of the message equally. It all sounded so right. Perhaps more importantly, it was what we wanted—even needed—to hear. With the technological hopes and promises of electronic monitoring, community corrections seemed to be moving into the next millennium retooled with the latest technological advances. However, as is the case with life in general, when something appears too good to be true it probably is. Often we in the business hear and vociferously contend that technology is only as good as the framework of policies and procedures within which it functions. Overconfidence in, and ignorance about, the limitations of technology result in an over-reliance and over-selling of technology to do that which it was never intended to do in the first place. In instances where under-funded and/or poorly designed programs rely on technologies to produce results that are impossible to achieve, the

Box 8.7—*continued*

fragile public image of community corrections is jeopardized. In the final analysis, electronic monitoring technology in and of itself makes more information readily available to practitioners without the need for an exorbitant commitment of human labor. In other words, taken out of a programmatic context, the technology makes us more efficient in that it assures that we do things better. Effectiveness, which assures that we do better things, however, is yet another matter. And here we must rely on well thought out and implemented program designs, programs that will process and react to efficiently delivered information in ways that are relevant to the public. Technological progress should not, as stated by Aldous Huxley in his book entitled *Ends and Means*, "merely provide us with more efficient means of going backwards."

Recognizing the negative impact of technologies that are mismatched to programs, and the relevance of program design to the ability to maximize public safety, the manufacturers of electronic monitoring technology and providers of monitoring services have advocated for standards as well as the maintenance of amicable relationships across the industry. The general standards that have been developed thus far fall far short of the mark in terms of their ability to link technologies and program practices to results that are valued by the public. At the same time, the sought after amicable relationships that would foster working together for the collective good of the industry, has been constrained by competitive product and service distinctiveness. Such competitiveness too often leads to an overselling of products and services in order to "win a bid." Under such circumstances, the public becomes confused, if not misled, about realistic purposes and expectations of electronic monitoring programs. In the end, both the industry and the profession lose credibility.

Source: Adapted from Paparozzi, M. and C. Wicklund (2002). "Electronic Supervision Tools: Lessons Learned" In A.H. Crowe, L. Sydney, P. Bancroft, and B. Lawrence (eds.) *Offender Supervision with Electronic Technology: A User's Guide*, pp. 16. American Probation and Parole Association: Lexington, KY.

- The average monitoring term in 1989 was 79 days. The longer the period of monitoring, the higher the odds of success. The chances of termination do not vary by type of offense, except that those committing major traffic violations committed fewer technical violations and new offenses.

- There were no significant differences in successful terminations among probationers, offenders on parole, or those in community corrections. All had successful terminations rates ranging between 74 and 86 percent. [West Palm Beach, Florida reported a 97 percent successful completion rate in 1992.]

- Rule violations resulted in reincarceration, brief confinement at a residential facility, intensified office reporting requirements, stricter curfews, or additional community service (Gowdy, 1993).

More recent evaluations in Oklahoma, Florida, Los Angeles, California, England and Wales,[11] Lake County, Illinois;[12] and Texas[13] indicated some success of electronic monitoring program, while others (Courtright, Berg, Mutchnick, 1997) have found little evidence that there is an impact on recidivism rates. Figure 8.7 shows the program termination from an electronic monitoring program operating in Cleveland, Ohio (Latessa, 1992). This program also gave program participants an exit survey. Table 8.2 shows offender responses to selected questions.

Figure 8.7
**Program Termination from Electronic Monitoring Program**

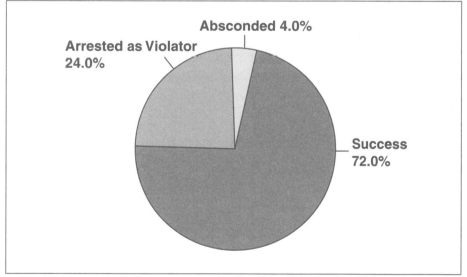

Source: E.J. Latessa (1991). *Report on Electronic Monitoring for the Cuyahoga County Adult Probation Department.* Cincinnati, OH: Department of Criminal Justice, University of Cincinnati.

Despite the widespread use of electronic monitoring and the support it has received by some, the empirical studies have not been as favorable. In a recent meta-analysis that included an examination of the research on electronic monitoring found that on average the effect size was .05, indicating that on average electronic monitoring *increased*

Table 8.2
**Results from Exit Interview with Electronic Monitoring Participants**

| | |
|---|---|
| Before this program have you ever served time in prison or jail? | |
| No | 44% |
| Yes | 56% |
| Do you think the program is better or worse than being in jail? | |
| Worse | 5% |
| Neither better nor worse | 13% |
| Better | 82% |
| To what extent did you find the transmitter comfortable or uncomfortable to wear? | |
| Uncomfortable | 25% |
| Neither comfortable nor uncomfortable | 44% |
| Comfortable | 31% |
| Since you have been on the monitoring program, how well do you get along with the people with whom you live? | |
| Better | 22% |
| About the same as before | 72% |
| Worse | 6% |
| While you were on the monitoring program, did you find that you had more or less money than you did before? | |
| Less money | 30% |
| About the same | 33% |
| More money | 37% |
| Since being on the monitoring program, do you find you have more or fewer friends? | |
| Fewer friends | 42% |
| About the same number of friends | 50% |
| More friends | 8% |
| Do you have the same friends now that you had when you began the monitoring program? | |
| Same friends | 65% |
| Different friends | 35% |
| Did you find the monitoring program better or worse than you expected it would be? | |
| Better | 44% |
| About as I expected it would be | 48% |
| Worse | 8% |
| Did anyone ask what the transmitter was? | |
| No | 30% |
| Yes | 70% |
| Were you able to violate any of the rules of the program without being caught by the monitoring equipment and/or the Probation Officer? | |
| No | 87% |
| Yes | 13% |

Source: E. Latessa (1991). *Report on Electronic Monitoring for Cuyahoga County Adult Probation Department.* Cincinnati, OH: Department of Criminal Justice, University of Cincinnati.

recidivism about five percent over comparison groups (Gendreau, Goggin, Cullen & Andrews, 2000). See Figure 8.8. Notice that the authors also examined the research on scared straight programs and found that on average they *increased* recidivism rates on average about 7 percent.

Figure 8.8
**Average Effect Size from Studies of Electronic Monitoring and Scared Straight Programs: Percent Increase in Recidivism**

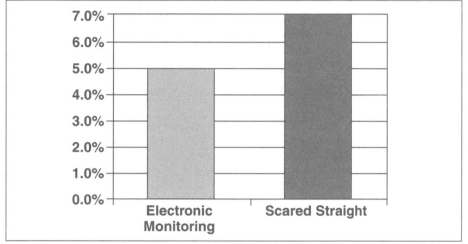

Source: Adapted from Gendreau, P., C. Goggin, F. Cullen, and D. Andrews (2000). "The Effects of Community Sanctions and Incarceration on Recidivism." *The Forum*, 12(2):10-13.

Perhaps the most interesting study involving electronic monitoring was recently conducted in Canada (Bonta, Wallace-Capretta & Rooney, 2000). In this study, offenders were first assessed with regard to risk and need factors using the LSI, and in addition to electronic monitoring, were required to attend an intensive treatment program. The results from this study are displayed in Figure 8.9. The combination of electronic monitoring and intensive treatment services resulted in a reduction of recidivism for high-risk offenders of about 20 percent, but more than *doubled* the recidivism rates for low-risk offenders. Undoubtedly, this is another example of the harm that can come from targeting low-risk offenders with intensive treatment and supervision programs.

## Community Residential Centers

Formerly known as "halfway houses," community residential centers (CRCs) are a valuable adjunct to community control and treatment services. Originally designed as residences for homeless men, they are now seen as a key nucleus of community-based correctional networks of residential centers, drug-free and alcohol-free living space, pre-release

Figure 8.9
**Recent Study of Intensive Rehabilitation Supervision in Canada**

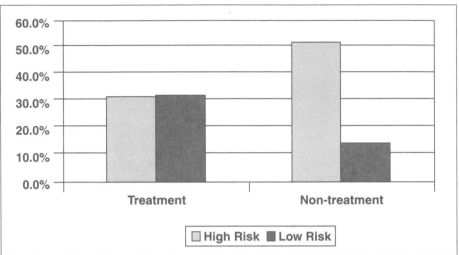

Source: Bonta, J., S. Wallace-Capretta, and J. Rooney (2000). "A Quasi-Experimental Evaluation of an Intensive Rehabilitation Supervision Program." *Criminal Justice and Behavior,* 27(3):312-329.

guidance centers, and private sector involvement with multiple-problemed offenders in need of intensive services. They also serve as noninstitutional residence facilities for a number of different classes of offenders, most of whom are high-need and pose medium-to-high risk to community corrections.

Community residential centers for criminal offenders have a long history in the United States (Hartmann et al., 1994). See Chapter 9. In the past, the typical use of community residential facilities was as "halfway houses." These programs were designed as transitional placements for offenders to ease the movement from incarceration to life in the free society. In time, some programs developed as alternatives to incarceration, so that the "halfway" aspect could mean either halfway into prison, or halfway out of prison.

CRCs are residential facilities for adjudicated adults or juveniles, or those subject to criminal or juvenile proceedings. They are intended as an alternative to confinement for persons not suited for probation or for those who need a period of readjustment to the community after imprisonment.

Between 1950 and 1980, the numbers and use of such halfway houses grew considerably. In the past 15 years, residential placements for criminal offenders have also undergone considerable role expansion. Increasingly, the population served by these programs has come to include large numbers of probationers and persons awaiting trial. In many jurisdictions, placement in a residential facility is available as a direct sentencing option to the judge. These changes in the role and population of residential programs supported the replacement of the traditional "halfway house" notion with the broader title of community residential center. There are many more CRCs providing transitional and extensive services for juveniles than for adults. Some CRCs specialize by client or treatment modality: women only, abused women, prerelease federal furloughers, drug-dependent, alcohol abusers, mentally ill, court diagnostic program, developmentally disabled, etc.

---

Box 8.8

### Community Residential Facility

Rush (1992) defines a residential facility as:
A correctional facility from which residents are regularly permitted to depart, unaccompanied by any official, for the purposes of using community resources, such as schools or treatment programs, and seeking or holding employment.

This definition is free of any reference to incarceration which was implicit in the term "halfway." Further, it does not necessitate the direct provision of any services to residents within the facility, and clearly identifies the program with a correctional mission. Thus, unlike the traditional "halfway house," the community residential facility serves a more diverse population and plays a broader correctional role. Traditional halfway houses are included within the category of residential facilities, but their ranks are swelled by newer adaptations, such as community corrections centers, prerelease centers, restitution centers, and the like.

---

DuPont (1985) explicitly identified a role for community residential facilities as an adjunct to traditional probation or parole supervision. Such facilities serve to increase both the punitive severity and public safety of traditional community-based corrections.

In an era when both correctional costs and populations grow yearly, planners, practitioners, and policymakers have supported a wide range of correctional alternatives. As Guynes (1988) observed, one effect of prison and jail crowding was a dramatic increase in the probation and parole populations. Further, Petersilia (1985), among others, suggests that these larger supervision populations are increasingly comprised of more serious and more dangerous offenders. Community residential facilities have come to be seen as an important option for the management and control of these growing and more dangerous offender populations (Walters, 1999).

Hicks (1987) observed that the use of residential placement as an alternative to incarceration or traditional community supervision has engendered some change in operations and philosophy. She terms it a movement "toward supervision rather than treatment." Thus in some cases, residential facilities provide little more than a place to live and access to community resources. The emphasis in these programs is upon custody and control rather than counseling and correction.

Unable or unwilling to underwrite the costs of prison for large numbers of convicted offenders, several jurisdictions have supported community residential facilities. As Hicks (1987:7) notes, ". . . budget weary legislators often view halfway houses as an inexpensive lunch." Residential programs, they hope, will provide public safety as well as incarceration, but at a fraction of the cost. As substitute prisons, however, the atmosphere of these programs has changed.

Traditional halfway houses still continue, where staff and programs are designed for the provision of direct services to residents. These programs continue to provide counseling, substance abuse treatment, educational and vocational training, and a variety of social services. In other, newer programs, especially those operated by corrections departments, the atmosphere is closer to that of a minimum security prison than a rehabilitative community.

As the foregoing discussion illustrates, it is not possible to describe the average residential facility. Diversity in population, program, size, and structure is the rule. It is, unfortunately, also not possible to know for certain how many such facilities are in operation today, or the number of offenders served by them. Hicks (1987:2) observed, "There are no national figures, only educated guesses . . ."

Given the lack of reliable data, it is possible to estimate that there are in excess of at least 1,000 residential facilities in operation today (Huskey, 1992:71). Further, it appears that the number of facilities has grown as much as 50 percent in the past decade.

It is not possible to estimate the number of offenders served by these facilities with any certainty. Length of residence is typically short, on the order of three to four months, meaning that a facility with 50 beds may serve 150 to 200 individuals annually. Based on the probability that a halfway house would serve three to four times as many residents as it had beds in each year, it is not unreasonable to assume that halfway houses serve well over 100,000 residents each year. Further, many of those in residential facilities are included in the totals of other correctional population counts such as the number of prison or furloughed inmates, or persons under parole supervision. Still, it is clear that the total number of residents in these facilities each year is substantial.[14]

Despite the long tradition of residential community correctional programs, the research literature is both sparse and inconclusive. There appear to be a number of reasons that residential programs have been largely ignored by correctional researchers.

First, residential facilities represent a relatively small part of the correctional system and, as mentioned above, it is often difficult to distinguish between residential facilities that serve only correctional clientele and those that serve a broader constituency. Second, many programs are operated by private entities, and are either unwilling or unable to facilitate research. Third, generalization is a problem since these programs are often markedly different from locale to locale, both in terms of the treatment offered, and the types of clients they accept. Finally, in evaluation research, it is often difficult to develop an adequate comparison group or to conduct a follow-up of residents. Despite these obstacles, there have been some notable attempts to evaluate the effectiveness of residential programs.

Latessa and Travis (1991) evaluated CRC treatment programs for adult offenders sentenced to probation and found that, in comparison with other similarly situated offenders, CRC clients exhibited more prior involvement in alcohol- and drug-treatment, and suffered from more psychiatric problems. Hence the study group was higher-need, higher-risk, and more likely to recidivate. The center's clients received more services and treatment in almost every area examined. Even though prior criminal histories would have predicted higher failure rates, the center's clients did as well as the comparison group in terms of re-offending. Employment services and enrolling in an educational program reduced recidivism. Clearly, for high-risk offenders, residential centers that provide specific client-needed services can be valuable assets in offender control and outcome, particularly for community control clients whose technical violations are a result of high needs otherwise unaddressed within the community. While further research is required to better understand the relationships, the data from the Latessa and Travis study and others tend to support the following observations:

- Residential community correctional groups display greater service needs than do regular probation or parole groups.

- Many of these needs, such as psychiatric and drug/alcohol abuse history, are related both to positive adjustment and to new criminal convictions. Offenders in residential facilities are more likely to receive a variety of treatment and counseling services.

- Based on group characteristics at intake, an a priori assumption that CRC groups would demonstrate a higher rate of recidivism and lower social adjustment seems reasonable.

- Generally, no such difference in outcome has been observed, and residential groups have received considerably more treatment interventions. This may indicate that program participation is beneficial for this group.

It appears that residential community correctional facilities will continue to grow and develop new programs. In large part this will be a response to the crowding of local and state correctional institutions.

## Shock Incarceration Programs

Technically, shock incarceration programs, or boot camps as they are commonly known, are institutional correctional programs, not community-based ones. However, they are considered intermediate sanctions, and are a distant cousin to shock probation programs (see Chapter 7).[15] The most recent shock incarceration programs, or boot camps as they are more commonly called, appeared first in Georgia (1983) and Oklahoma (1984). The concept spread quickly and, in 2000, 54 boot camp programs had opened in 41 state correctional jurisdictions, and handled more than 21,000 inmates in 2000 (Camp & Camp, 2000:120, 122, 197), in addition to many programs developed and being considered in cities and counties, and for juveniles (Gover, MacKenzie & Styve, 2000).

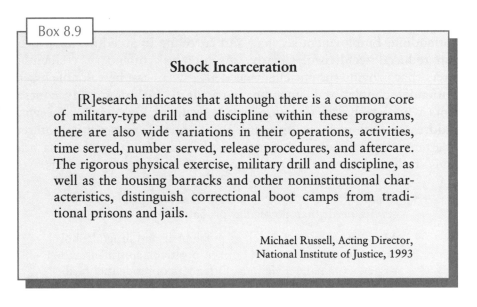

Box 8.9

**Shock Incarceration**

[R]esearch indicates that although there is a common core of military-type drill and discipline within these programs, there are also wide variations in their operations, activities, time served, number served, release procedures, and aftercare. The rigorous physical exercise, military drill and discipline, as well as the housing barracks and other noninstitutional characteristics, distinguish correctional boot camps from traditional prisons and jails.

Michael Russell, Acting Director,
National Institute of Justice, 1993

While labeled a recent innovation, the basic elements of boot camp were present in the Elmira Reformatory in 1876, designed by Zebulon Reed Brockway. In its current developments, boot camp combines elements of military basic training and traditional correctional philosophy, particularly rehabilitation. Although there is no generic boot camp because individual programs vary in form and objectives, the typical boot camp is targeted at young, nonviolent offenders.[16] Once in the camp, the participant is subjected to a regimen of: (1) military drills and discipline; (2) physical exercise; (3) hard physical labor; (4) specialized education and training; and (5) counseling and treatment for substance abuse and addiction.

Most boot camp programs require the inmates to volunteer, offering as an incentive an incarceration period of a few months, compared to the much longer periods they would have spent in prison or on probation. Generally, a state boot camp graduate is released to parole, intensive supervision, home confinement, or some type of community corrections.

The philosophy behind the prison boot camps is simple. Offenders who can be turned around before they commit a major crime can improve their own opportunities for living a successful life free of incarceration. Traditional prisons generally have not been viewed as successful in rehabilitating offenders.

According to boot camp advocates, the population at greatest risk of entering prison is the young adult who is poorly educated, comes from a low-income background, has not had proper role models or discipline, has little or no work skills, and is subjected to an environment in which drug use and drug trafficking are common. Because many misdirected young persons have become productive citizens after exposure to military training, the boot camp endeavors to provide this same discipline and direction to persons who still have a chance of being diverted from a life of crime and incarceration.

The boot camp concept appeals to diverse elements of the justice system. For the offender, it offers a second chance. He or she generally will be returned to the community in a much shorter period without the stigma of having been in prison. For the judge, it is a sentencing option that provides sanctions more restrictive than probation but less restrictive than a conventional prison. For the correctional system, it allows the placement of individuals outside the traditional prison environment and reduces costs and crowding by moving the persons through the system in less time.

The boot camp concept also appeals to groups with diverse views on the objectives of corrections. For those who believe that corrections should focus more on rehabilitation, the shorter sentence, structured environment, supervision after release, and emphasis on training and treatment can be found in the boot camp. For those who believe that prisons should serve as punishment and a deterrent, the highly disciplined environment, military-style drills, physical exercise, and work within a correctional setting exist in the boot camp. Although boot camps are most often associated with prisons, probation and parole agencies also operate boot camps. According to Camp and Camp (2000:197), 19 probation and parole agencies operated 32 boot camps, and served almost 3,000 offenders in 1999.

Results from studies of the effectiveness of boot camp programs in reducing recidivism have not been positive. Some programs have abandoned the military-style training and incorporated educational, wilderness, job corps, and industrial components (Gowdy, 1993). A recent outcome study conducted in Texas (1999) compared the rearrest rates of four different types of community facilities for adult offenders: boot camps, treatment centers, intermediate sanction facilities (used for probation violators), and substance abuse treatment facilities. The results are presented in Figure 8.10.

Figure 8.10
**Rearrest Rates for Residents Discharged from Community Correctional Facilities in Texas: Two Year Follow-up (in percent)**

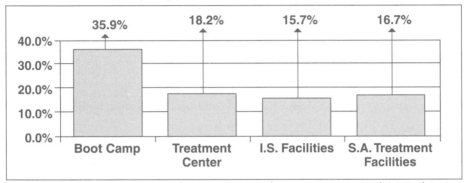

Source: *Community Corrections Facilities Outcome Study*, Texas Department of Criminal Justice, January 1999.

The boot camp reported rearrest rates nearly double the other programs. It should also be noted that when risk and need scores from a standardized assessment tool were compared for offenders in all four programs, the only difference was in the need scores, with the boot camp residents reporting *fewer* higher need offenders than the other options. Finally, a meta-analysis conducted by researchers in Washington State (Aos, Phipps, Barnoski & Lieb, 1999) found that, on average, juvenile boot camps increased recidivism rates about 11 percent. Some other findings from boot camp evaluations make the following conclusions:

- Low- or moderate-risk juvenile and adult offenders who are subjected to high level of supervision (boot camps) actually do worse than those left on traditional probation (Altschuler & Armstrong, 1994).

- High percentages of minority youth are served by boot camps: conclusion is that boot camp model fails to connect with this population.

- Some evidence that the rate of recidivism declined in boot camp programs for adults where offenders spent three hours or more per day in therapeutic activity and had some type of aftercare (MacKenzie & Souryal, 1994).

- In general, studies have found similar recidivism rates for those who completed boot camps and comparable offenders who spent long periods of time in prison.

More recent evaluations of boot camps have also produced unfavorable results regarding their effectiveness in reducing recidivism (Bottcher & Ezell, 2005; Weis, Whitemarsh & Wilson, 2005).

Despite their continued popularity, there are several reasons that boot camps are not producing the desired reductions in recidivism. Boot camps tend to:

- Bond delinquent and criminal groups together;

- Target noncrime producing needs such as physical conditioning, drill and ceremony, and self-esteem;

- Mix low-, medium-, and high-risk offenders together;

- Model aggressive behavior.


## Drug Courts

Although some might not consider drug courts an intermediate sanction, it appears that they fall into this category when you consider that they usually combine close probation supervision with substance abuse treatment in an attempt to keep the offender from being incarcerated. Indeed, the phenomenal growth and expansion of drug court can be largely attributed to the dissatisfaction of traditional methods of dealing with drug offenders, and the belief that drug courts will reduce substance abuse and criminal behavior through close judicial monitoring and community-based treatment services. As of 1998 there were a total of 275 drug courts in operation, serving an estimated 90,000 offenders (Drug Court Programs Office, 1998), with another 155 drug courts in the planning stages.

According to Belenko (1998), drug courts differ from traditional courts in several important ways. First, drug courts attempt to manage cases quickly, and make provisions for the treatment to start as soon as possible after arrest. Second, drug courts have adopted a collaborative rather than an adversarial approach found in most traditional courts.

Third, the judges in drug courts are actively involved in the cases, holding regular status hearings, meeting regularly with treatment providers and probation officers, and providing feedback to the offender. Finally, drug courts focus on providing treatment services rather than simply increasing sanctions.

Despite the rapid expansion of drug courts, there is limited research on their effectiveness, although evaluations are starting to emerge. For example, research by Goldkamp (1994) on the first drug court (Dade County, Florida) found lower incarceration rates, longer time to rearrest, and less frequent arrests among drug court participants. However, he also found higher failure-to-appear rates among drug court clients, but attributed them to the requirement of frequent appearances. Other studies have found similar results (Hepburn, Johnston & Rogers, 1994; Peters & Murrin, 2000; Peters, Haas & Murrin, 1999; Listwan, Shaffer & Latessa, 2001). Other studies, however, have failed to show evidence of a reduction in criminal behavior as measured by rearrest (Belenko, Fagan & Dumanovsky, 1994; Deschenes & Greenwood, 1994; Granfield, Eby & Brewster, 1998; Harrell, 1998; Johnson & Latessa, 1998; Johnson, Sundt, Holsinger & Latessa, 1998).

Johnson, Hubbard, and Latessa (2000) have identified some ways that drug courts can increase their effectiveness:

- Improve the assessment of offenders by using standardized and objective instruments that provide levels of risk and need, and which cover all major risk and need factors, not just substance abuse;

- Use behavioral and cognitive treatment strategies;

- Provide at least 100 hours of direct treatment services, and make sure the level of treatment is matched to the need and risk of the offender;

- Provide structured aftercare;

- Monitor the delivery of treatment services.

Drug courts will continue to play an important role in community corrections. In many ways they represent the future, and the hope that we will see the collaboration of close supervision practices and high quality and effective treatment and services for offenders. Based in part on the popularity of drug courts, several jurisdictions have started other specialization courts, including those for the mentally ill and for domestic violence offenders. Only time will tell if these initiatives prove to be effective.

# Effectiveness of Intermediate Sanctions

There are many justifications for the use of intermediate sanctions as an alternative to incarceration. However, given the investment that many jurisdictions and states have made in these options, the question of how effective they are in reducing recidivism is an important one. In a 1998 National Institute of Justice study of what works, Sherman and his associates listed a number of intermediate sanctions that have not demonstrated effectiveness. Included were correctional boot camps, shock probation, home detention with electronic monitoring, intensive supervision programs, and wildness programs for youthful offenders. In a recent meta-analysis of intermediate sanctions, Gendreau, Goggin, and Fulton (1996) addressed this question. They examined research results from 44 ISP programs, 16 restitution programs, 13 boot camps, 13 scared straight programs, nine drug-testing programs, and six electronic monitoring programs. They found virtually no effect on recidivism, and where they did find some effect it appeared that some sanctions slightly increased recidivism! They conclude that "the 'get tough' revolution has been an abject failure when it comes to reducing recidivism."

# Summary

Intermediate sanctions have become a vital component of contemporary corrections. Two developments have led to a search for innovative and cost-effective programs: prison and jail crowding, and the development of new technologies, such as electronic monitoring and readily available drug testing. Not only are institutions crowded; probation, parole, and community corrections are also impacted by the waves of offenders caught in the arms of the law.

Our review of intermediate sanctions provides both insight into the reasons for the volume of clients, but also programs and strategies for managing the risks posed by different types of offenders who need differing treatments and supervision. Intermediate sanctions will likely continue, despite the mixed findings concerning their effectiveness. The critical question is whether or not we can take what we have leaned from programs that are demonstrating reductions in recidivism and apply it to approaches that are not working. Day reporting centers, drug courts, and other treatment-based options appear to offer the best hope that we can currently foresee for delivering effective interventions and services to offenders in the community. Change will continue. This is an exciting time for corrections as a field and for students wishing to impact on the futures of clients and the safety of communities.

## Review Questions

1.  Explain the difference between fines and day fines.

2.  Why are boot camps so popular among the general public?

3.  What roles do CRCs play in corrections?

4.  What are the two basic types of electronic monitoring programs?

5.  What are some of the limitations of electronic monitoring programs?

6.  What do we know about the effectiveness of intensive supervision programs?

7.  Why are day reporting programs gaining popularity?

8.  Explain how drug courts differ from traditional courts.

9.  What are some of the reasons that boot camps have failed to reduce recidivism?

## Key Terms

boot camp programs
community service programs
day fines
day reporting centers
drug courts
electronic monitoring
fines

home detention
intensive supervised probation
intermediate sanctions
meta-analysis
net widening
shock incarceration

## Electronic Library

American Correctional Association (www.corrections.com/aca)

American Probation and Parole Association (www.appa-net.org)

Drug Courts Programs Office, Office of Justice Programs (www.ojp.usdoj.gov/dcpo/)

Netherlands Ministry of Justice (in English) (www.minjust.nl:8080/a_beleid/thema/them- ind.htm).

Talbert House (www.talberthouse.org)

# Recommended Readings

Byrne, J., A. Lurigio, and J. Petersilia (1993). *Smart Sentencing*. Beverly Hills, CA: Sage.

Fulton, B., S. Stone, and P. Gendreau (1994). *Restructuring Intensive Supervision Programs: Applying "What Works."* Lexington, KY: American Probation and Parole Association.

Marciniak, L. (2000). "The Addition of Day Reporting to Intensive Supervised Probation." *Federal Probation*, 64(2):34-39.

Morris, N. and M. Tonry (1990). Between Prison and Probation: Intermediate Punishments in a Rational Sentencing System. Oxford: Oxford University Press.

Petersilia, J. (1998). *Community Corrections: Probation, Parole, and Intermediate Sanctions*. New York, NY: Oxford Press.

Sherman, L., D. Gottfredson, D. MacKenzie, J. Eck, P. Reuter, and S. Bushway (1998). *Preventing Crime: What Works, What Doesn't, What's Promising*. National Institute of Justice, Research in Brief, Washington, DC: U.S. Department of Justice.

# Notes

[1]    Blumstein argues that the nation has not to date been able to meet the demand for additional prisons to build their way out of the crowding crisis. A. Blumstein (1995). "Prisons." In J. Wilson and J. Petersilia (eds.) (1995). *Crime*, pp. 387-419. San Francisco, CA: Institute for Contemporary Studies. See also D. Garland (Ed.) (2001). "Special Issue on Mass Imprisonment in the USA." *Punishment and Society*, 3(1):5-199.

[2]    Not all new generation ISP programs have abandoned the treatment approach. See T. Clear and E.J. Latessa (1993). "Probation Office's Roles in Intensive Supervision versus Treatment." *Justice Quarterly*, 10:441-462. The American Probation and Parole Association is working with several states to modify their ISP programs from a control/surveillance orientation to one more treatment focused (www.appa-net.org).

[3]    J. Byrne and F. Taxman (1994). "Crime Control Policy and Community Corrections Practice." *Evaluation and Program Planning*, 17:227-233. See also F. Cullen, P. Van Voorhis, and J. Sundt (1996). "Prisons in Crisis: The American Experience." In R. Matthews and P. Francis (eds.) *Prisons 2000: An International Perspective on the Current State and Future of Imprisonment*. New York, NY: Macmillan.

[4]    Fulton, B., S. Stone, and P. Gendreau (1994). *Restructuring Intensive Supervision Programs: Applying 'What Works'."* Lexington, KY: American Probation and Parole Association. See also Cullen, F. and P. Gendreau (2000). "From Nothing Works to What Works." *The Prison Journal*, 81(3):313-338.

[5]    For example, J.T. Whitehead, et al. found that intensive probation in Tennessee resulted in both diversion and net widening. They argued that if diversion is the only objective of intensive probation then the efforts might be misguided. See J. Whitehead, L. Miller, and L. Myers (1995). "The Diversionary Effectiveness of Intensive Supervision and Community Corrections Programs." In J. Smykla and W. Selke (eds.) *Intermediate Sanctions: Sentencing in the 1990s*, pp. 135-151. Cincinnati, OH: Anderson Publishing Co. See also Bonta, J., S. Wallace-Capretta and J. Rooney (2000). "Can Electronic Monitoring Make a Difference?" *Crime & Delinquency*, 46(1):61-75.

[6]    Gordon, M. and D. Glaser (1991). "The Use and Effects of Financial Penalties in Municipal Courts." *Criminology*, 29(4):651-676.

[7]    Day-fine sentences are being implemented in Maricopa County, Arizona, and in Oregon, Iowa, and Connecticut.

[8]    A discussion of the issues can be found in J. Goldkamp (1993). "Judicial Responsibility for Pretrial Release Decisionmaking and the Information Role of Pretrial Services." *Federal Probation*, 57(1):28-34. See also J. Rosen (1993). "Pretrial Services—A Magistrate Judge's Perspective." *Federal Probation*, 57(1):15-17, and E. McCann and D. Weber (1993). "Pretrial Services: A Prosecutor's View." *Federal Probation*, 57(1):18-22.

[9]    See in particular S. Rackmill (1994). "An Analysis of Home Confinement as a Sanction." *Federal Probation*, 58(1):45-52. An empirical analysis can be found in Stanz, R. and R. Tewksbury (2000). "Predictors of Success and Recidivism in a Home Incarceration Programs." *Prison Journal*, 80(3):326-344.

[10]    R. Schwitzgebel, R. Schwitzgebel, W. Pahnke, and W. Hurd (1964). "A Program of Research in Behavioral Electronics." *Behavioral Scientist*, 9(3):233-238. See also R.K. Gable (1986). "Application of Personal Telemonitoring to Current Problems in Corrections." *Journal of Criminal Justice*, 14(2):173-182; and J. Lilly, R. Ball, and W. Lotz (1986). "Electronic Jail Revisited." *Justice Quarterly*, 3(3):353-361.

[11]    Mair, G. Evaluating Electronic Monitoring in England and Wales. Paper presented at the annual meeting of the American Society of Criminology, San Francisco, November 18, 1989. See also J. Lilly (1990). "Tagging Revisited." *The Howard Journal*, 29(4):229-245; and National Association for the Care of Offenders and the Prevention of Crime (1989). *The Electronic Monitoring of Offenders*. London, NACRO.

[12]    K. Cooprider (1992). "Pretrial Bond Supervision: An Empirical Analysis with Policy Implications." *Federal Probation*, 56(3):41-49.

[13]    Enor, R., C. Block, and J. Quinn, et al. (1992). *Alternative Sentencing: Electronically-Monitored Correctional Supervision*. Briston, IN: Wyndham Hall.

[14]    Estimating the size of the community corrections residential facility population is hazardous at best. In her 1987 article, however, Hicks reported interviews with representatives of California, Texas, and the Federal Bureau of Prisons. These officials estimated that by 1988, the combined total of offenders served in residential facilities for these three jurisdictions would exceed 7,000. Given that these numbers do not include probationers or misdemeanants in all three jurisdictions, a conservative extrapolation yields an estimated 70,000 offenders in residential facilities during 1988. This represents about 10 percent of the prison population for that year.

[15]    Shock probation originated in Ohio in 1965, and was designed to give first-time young adult offenders a "taste of the bars." Offenders were to be sentenced to prison, and then within 30-120 days be released on probation. It was assumed that the physical and psychological hardships of prison life would "shock" the offender straight.

[16]    The bulk of the following section is drawn from Government Accounting Office, Prison Boot Camps. Washington, DC: U.S. Department of Justice, 1993.

## *References*

Altschuler, D. and T. Armstrong (1994). *Intensive Aftercare for High-Risk Juveniles: A Community Care Model.* Program Summary. Washington, DC: Office of Juvenile Justice and Delinquency Prevention, Office of Justice Programs, U.S. Dept. of Justice.

American Correctional Association (1990). *Intermediate Punishment: Community-Based Sanctions.* Baltimore, MD: United Book Press.

Aos, S., P. Phipps, R. Barnoski, and R. Lieb (1999). *The Comparative Costs and Benefits of Programs to Reduce Crime: A Review of the National Research Findings with Implications for Washington State.* Washington State Institute for Public Policy, Olympia, WA.

Belenko, S. (1998). "Research on Drug Courts: A Critical Review." *National Drug Court Institute Review*, 1(1):1-43.

Belenko, S., J. A. Fagan, and T. Dumanovsky (1994). "The Effects of Legal Sanctions on Recidivism in Special Drug Courts." *Justice System Journal*, 17:53-81.

Blumstein, A. (1995). "Prisons." In J. Wilson and J. Petersilia (eds.) *Crime*, pp. 387-419. San Francisco, CA: Institute for Contemporary Studies.

Bonta, J., S. Wallace-Capretta, and J. Rooney (2000). "A Quasi-Experimental Evaluation of An Intensive Rehabilitation Supervision Program." *Criminal Justice and Behavior*, 27:312-329.

Bottcher, J. and M.E. Ezell (2005). "Examining the Effectiveness of Boot Camps: A Randomized Experiment with a Long-term Follow-up." *Journal of Research in Crime and Delinquency*, 42:309-332.

Bureau of Justice Assistance (1989). *Electronic Monitoring in Intensive Probation and Parole Programs.* Washington, DC: U.S. Department of Justice.

Burkhart, W. (1986). "Intensive Probation Supervision: an Agenda for Research and Evaluation." *Federal Probation*, 50(2):75-77.

Byrne, J. and L. Kelly (1989). "Restructuring Probation as an Intermediate Sanction: An Evaluation of the Massachusetts Intensive Probation Supervision Program." Final Report to the National Institute of Justice. Washington, DC: U.S. Department of Justice.

Byrne, J., A. Lurigio, and C. Baird (1989). "The Effectiveness of the New Intensive Supervision Programs." *Research in Corrections*, 2.

Byrne, J., A. Lurigio, and J. Petersilia (1993). *Smart Sentencing.* Beverly Hills, CA: Sage.

Byrne, J. and F. Taxman (1994). "Crime Control Policy and Community Corrections Practice." *Evaluation and Program Planning*, 17:227-233.

Camp, C. and G. Camp (1997). *The Corrections Yearbook 1997*. South Salem, NY: Criminal Justice Institute.

Camp, C. and G. Camp (2000). *The 2000 Corrections Yearbook: Adult Corrections*. Middletown, CT: Criminal Justice Institute.

Clear, T. and E. Latessa (1993). "Probation Office's Roles in Intensive Supervision versus Treatment." *Justice Quarterly*, 10:441-462

Cooprider, K. (1992). "Pretrial Bond Supervision: An Empirical Analysis with Policy Implications." *Federal Probation*, 56(3):41-49.

Courtright, K., B. Berg, and R. Mutchnick (1997). "Effects of House Arrest with Electronic Monitoring on DUI Offenders." *Journal of Offender Rehabilitation*, 24 (3/4):35-51.

Cullen, F. and P. Gendreau (2000). "From Nothing Works to What Works." *The Prison Journal*, 81(3):313-338.

Cullen, F., P. Van Voorhis, and J. Sundt (1996). "Prisons in Crisis: The American Experience." In R. Matthews and P. Francis (eds.) *Prisons 2000: An International Perspective on the Current State and Future of Imprisonment*. New York, NY: Macmillan.

Curtin, E. (1990). "Day Reporting Centers." In A. Travisino (ed.) *Intermediate Punishment: Community-Based Sanctions*, pp. 72-73. Laurel, MD: American Correctional Association.

Deschenes, E. and P. Greenwood (1994). "Maricopa County's Drug Court: An Innovative Program for First Time Drug Offenders on Probation." *Justice System Journal*, 17:99-115.

Drug Court Programs Office, Office of Justice Programs (1998). *Drug Court Activity*. Washington, DC: U.S. Department of Justice.

DuPont, P. (1985). *Expanding Sentencing Options: A Governor's Perspective*. Washington, DC: National Institute of Justice.

Enor, R., C. Block, and J. Quinn (1992). *Alternative Sentencing: Electronically-Monitored Correctional Supervision*. Bristol, IN: Wyndham Hall.

Erwin, B. (1987). *Final Report: Evaluation of Intensive Probation Supervision in Georgia*. Atlanta, GA: Georgia Department of Corrections.

Fallen, D., C. Apperson, J. Holt-Milligan, and J. Roe (1981). *Intensive Parole Supervision*. Olympia, WA: Department of Social and Health Services, Analysis and Information Service Division, Office of Research.

Finn, P. (1991). "State-by-State Guide to Enforcement of Civil Protection Orders." *Response to the Victimization of Women & Children*, 14(78):3-12.

Flynn, L. (1986). "House Arrest." *Corrections Today*, 48(5):64-68.

Fulton, B., P. Gendreau, and M. Paparozzi (1996). "APPA's Prototypical Intensive Supervision Program: ISP As It Was Meant To Be." *Perspectives*, 19(2):25-41.

Fulton, B., E. Latessa, A. Stichman, and L.F. Travis (1997). "The State of ISP: Research and Policy Implications." *Federal Probation*, 61(4):65-75.

Fulton, B, S. Stone, and P. Gendreau (1994). *Restructuring Intensive Supervision Programs: Applying "What Works."* Lexington, KY: American Probation and Parole Association.

Gable, R. (1986). "Application of Personal Telemonitoring to Current Problems in Corrections." *Journal of Criminal Justice*, 14:173-182.

Garland, D. (ed.) (2001). "Special Issue on Mass Imprisonment in the USA." *Punishment and Society*, 3(1):5-199.

Gendreau, P., C. Goggin, and B. Fulton (1996). "Intensive Supervision in Probation and Parole." In C. Hollin (ed.) *Handbook of Offender Assessment and Treatment.* Chichester, UK: John Wiley & Son.

Gendreau, P., C. Goggin, F. Cullen, and D. Andrews (2000). "The Effects of Community Sanctions and Incarceration on Recidivism." *Forum*, 12 (2):10-13.

Goldkamp, J. (1994). "Miami's Treatment Drug Court for Felony Defendants: Some Implications of Assessment Findings." *Prison Journal*, (74(2):110-157.

Goldkamp, J. (1993). "Judicial Responsibility for Pretrial Release Decisionmaking and the Information Role of Pretrial Services." *Federal Probation*, 57(1):28-34.

Gordon, M. and D. Glaser (1991). "The Use and Effects of Financial Penalties in Municipal Courts." *Criminology*, 29:651-676.

Gover, A., D. MacKenzie, and G. Styve (2000). "Boot Camps and Traditional Facilities for Juveniles." *Journal of Criminal Justice*, 28(1):53-68.

Government Accounting Office (1993). *Prison Boot Camps.* Washington, DC: U.S. Department of Justice.

Government Accounting Office (1990). *Intermediate Sanctions.* Washington, DC: USGAO.

Gowdy, V. (1993). *Intermediate Sanctions.* Washington, DC: U.S. Department of Justice.

Granfield, R., C. Eby, and T. Brewster (1998). "An Examination of the Denver Drug Court: The Impact of a Treatment-Oriented Drug Offender System." *Law and Policy*, 20(2):183-202.

Guynes, R. (1988). *Difficult Clients, Large Caseloads Plague Probation, Parole Agencies.* Washington, DC: U.S. Department of Justice.

Harrell, A. (1998). *Drug Courts and the Role of Graduated Sanctions.* National Institute of Justice Research Brief, Washington, DC: U.S. Department of Justice.

Hartmann, D., P. Friday, and K. Minor (1994). "Residential Probation: A Seven-Year Follow-Up Study of Halfway House Discharges." *Journal of Criminal Justice*, 22:503-515.

Hepburn J., C. Johnston, and S. Rogers (1994). *Do Drugs Do Time: An Evaluation of the Maricopa County Demand Reduction Program.* National Institute of Justice Research Brief. Washington, DC: U.S. Department of Justice.

Hicks, N. (1987). "A New Relationship: Halfway Houses and Corrections." *Corrections Compendium*, 12(4):1,5-7.

Huskey, B. (1992). "The Expanding Use of Community Reintegration Centers." *Corrections Today*, 54(8):70-74.

Johnson, G. and R. Hunter (1992). *Evaluation of the Specialized Drug Offender Program for the Colorado Judicial Department*. Boulder, CO: University of Colorado, Center for Action Research.

Johnson S., D. Hubbard, and E. Latessa (2000). "Drug Courts and Treatment: Lessons to Be Learned from the 'What Works' Literature." *Corrections Quarterly Management*, 4(4):70-77.

Johnson, S. and E. Latessa (1998) *Evaluation of the Hamilton County Drug Court*. Report for the Supreme Court of Ohio, Columbus.

Johnson, S., J. Sundt, A. Holsinger, and E. Latessa (1998). "The Effects of Drug Court Programming on Recidivism: The Cincinnati Experience." Paper presented at the American Society of Criminology annual meeting, Washington, DC.

Jolin, A. and B. Stipak (1992). "Drug Treatment and Electronically Monitored Home Confinement: An Evaluation of a Community-Based Sentencing Option." *Crime & Delinquency*, 38:158-170.

Jolin, A. and B. Stipak (1991). *Clackamas County Community Corrections Intensive Drug Program: Program Evaluation Report*. Oregon City, OR: Clackamas County Community Corrections Division.

Jones, M. (1991). "Intensive Probation Supervision in Georgia, Massachusetts, and New Jersey." *Criminal Justice Research Bulletin*, 6(1):1-9.

Larivee, J. (1990). "Day Reporting Centers: Making Their Way from the U.K. to the U.S.." *Corrections Today*, (October):86-89.

Latessa, E. (2000). "Incorporating Electronic Monitoring into the Principles of Effective Interventions." *Journal of Offender Monitoring*, 13(4):5-6.

Latessa, E. (1993a). *An Evaluation of the Lucas County Adult Probation Department's IDU and High Risk Groups*. Cincinnati, OH: Department of Criminal Justice, University of Cincinnati.

Latessa, E. (1993b). *Profile of the Special Units of the Lucas County Adult Probation Department*. Cincinnati, OH: Department of Criminal Justice, University of Cincinnati.

Latessa, E. (1992). *A Preliminary Evaluation of the Montgomery County Adult Probation Department's Intensive Supervision Program*. Cincinnati, OH: Department of Criminal Justice, University of Cincinnati.

Latessa, E. (1991). *Report on Electronic Monitoring for the Cuyahoga County Adult Probation Department*. Cincinnati, OH: Department of Criminal Justice, University of Cincinnati.

Latessa, E. (1986). "Cost Effectiveness of Intensive Supervision." *Federal Probation*, 50(2):70-74.

Latessa, E. and L. Travis (1991). "Halfway Houses or Probation: A Comparison of Alternative Dispositions." *Journal of Crime and Justice*, 14:53-75.

Latessa, E., L. Travis, B. Fulton, and A. Stichman (1998). *Evaluating the Prototypical ISP: Results from Iowa and Connecticut*. Cincinnati: Division of Criminal Justice, University of Cincinnati.

Latessa, E., L. Travis, and A. Holsinger (1997). *Evaluation of Ohio's Community Corrections Act Programs and Community Based Correctional Facilities Final Report.* Cincinnati, OH: Division of Criminal Justice, University of Cincinnati.

Latessa, E., L. Travis, A. Holsinger, and J. Hartman (1998). *Evaluation of Ohio's Pilot Day Reporting Program Final Report.* Cincinnati, OH: Division of Criminal Justice, University of Cincinnati.

Lilly, J. (1990). "Tagging Revisited." *The Howard Journal*, 29:229-245.

Lilly, J., R. Ball, and R. Lotz (1986). "Electronic Jail Revisited." *Justice Quarterly*, 3:353-361.

Listwan, S., D. Shaffer, and E. Latessa (2001). *The Erie County Drug Court: Outcome Evaluation Findings.* Center for Criminal Justice Research, University of Cincinnati, Cincinnati.

McCann, E. and D. Weber (1993). "Pretrial Services: A Prosecutor's View." *Federal Probation*, 57(1):18-22.

McCarthy, B. (ed.) (1987). *Intermediate Punishments: Intensive Supervision, Home Confinement, and Electronic Surveillance.* Monsey, NY: Willow Tree Press.

McDevitt, J. (1988) *Evaluation of the Hampton County Day Reporting Center.* Boston, MA: Crime and Justice Foundation.

McDevitt, J. and R. Miliano (1992). "Day Reporting Centers: An Innovative Concept in Intermediate Sanctions." In J. Byrne, et al. (eds.) *Smart Sentencing*, pp. 153-165. Newbury Park, CA: Sage.

MacKenzie, D. and C. Souryal (1994). *Multisite Evaluation of Shock Incarceration.* Washington, DC: National Institute of Justice, Office of Justice Programs, U.S. Deptartment of Justice.

Maguire, K. and A. Pastore (eds.) (1994). *Sourcebook of Criminal Justice Statistics 1994.* Washington, DC: U.S. Department of Justice.

Mair, G. (1989). "Evaluating Electronic Monitoring in England and Wales." Paper presented at the annual meeting of the American Society of Criminology, San Francisco, California.

Marciniak, L. (2000). "The Addition of Day Reporting to Intensive Supervised Probation." *Federal Probation*, 64(2):34-39.

Maxfield, M. and T. Baumer (1990). "Home Detention with Electronic Monitoring: Comparing Pretrial and Postconviction Programs." *Crime & Delinquency*, 36:521-536.

Meecham, L. (1986). "House Arrest: The Oklahoma Experience." *Corrections Today*, 48:102-110.

Morris, N. and M. Tonry (1990). *Between Prison and Probation: Intermediate Punishments in a Rational Sentencing System.* Oxford: Oxford University Press.

National Association for the Care of Offenders and the Prevention of Crime (1989). *The Electronic Monitoring of Offenders.* London, NACRO.

National Law Enforcement and Corrections Technology Center (1999). *Keeping Track of Electronic Monitoring.* Washington, DC: NLECTC (http://www.nlectc.org/txtfiles/ElecMonasc.html).

Netherlands Ministry of Justice (1993). *Dutch Penal Law and Policy: Alternative Sanctions for Juveniles in the Netherlands*. The Hague: NMJ (www.minjust.nl:8080/a_belied/thema/them_ind.htm).

Paparozzi, M. (n.d.). *An Evaluation of the New Jersey Board of Parole's Intensive Supervision Program*. Unpublished Report.

Paparozzi, M. and C. Wicklund (2002). "Electronic Supervision Tools: Lessons Learned" In A.H. Crowe, L. Sydney, P. Bancroft, and B. Lawrence (eds.) *Offender Supervision with Electronic Technology: A User's Guide*, pp. 16. American Probation and Parole Association: Lexington, KY.

Parent, D. (1990). *Day Reporting Centers for Criminal Offenders—A Descriptive Analysis of Existing Programs*. Washington, DC: National Institute of Justice.

Parent, D., J. Byrne, V. Tsarfaty, L. Valade, and J. Esselman (1995). *Day Reporting Centers: Volume 1*. Washington, DC: National Institute of Justice.

Pearson, F. (1987). *Research on New Jersey's Intensive Supervision Program*. New Brunswick, NJ: Administrative Office of the Courts.

Peters, R., A. Haas, and M. Murrin (1999). "Prediction of Retention and Arrest in Drug Courts." *National Drug Court Insittute Review*, 2(1):33-60

Peters, R. and R. Murrin (2000). "Effectiveness of Treatment Based Drug Courts in Reducing Criminal Recidivism." *Criminal Justice and Behavior*, 27(1)72-96.

Petersilia, J. (1998). *Community Corrections: Probation, Parole, and Intermediate Sanctions*. New York, NY: Oxford Press.

Petersilia, J. (1987). *Expanding Options for Criminal Sentencing*. Santa Monica, CA: Rand Publications.

Petersilia, J. (1985). *Probation and Felon Offenders*. Washington, DC: U.S. Department of Justice.

Petersilia, J. and S. Turner (1993). *Evaluating Intensive Supervised Probation/Parole Results of a Nationwide Experiment*. Washington, DC: U.S. Department of Justice.

Rackmill, S. (1994). "Prisoner Handbook, Camp Reams Shock Incarceration Program: An Analysis of Home Confinement as a Sanction." *Federal Probation*, 58(1):45-52.

Robertson, A.A., P.W. Grimes, and K.E. Rogers (2001). "A Short-run Cost-Benefit Analysis of Community-Based Interventions for Juvenile Offenders." *Crime & Delinquency*, 47(2):265-284.

Rosen, J. (1993). "Pretrial Services—A Magistrate Judge's Perspective." *Federal Probation*, 57(1):15-17.

Rush, G. (1992). *The Dictionary of Criminal Justice*. Guilford, CT: Duskin.

Schwitzgebel, R., R. Schwitzgebel, W. Pahnke, and W. Hurd (1964). "A Program of Research in Behavioral Electronics." *Behavioral Scientist*, 9:233-238.

Sherman, L., D. Gottfredson, D. MacKenzie, J. Eck, P. Reuter, and S. Bushway (1998). *Preventing Crime: What Works, What Doesn't, What's Promising*. National Institute of Justice, Research in Brief, Washington, DC: U.S. Department of Justice.

Stanz, R. and R. Tewksbury (2000). "Predictors of Success and Recidivism in a Home Incarceration Programs." *Prison Journal*, 80(3):326-344.

U.S. Department of Justice (1990). *Survey of Intermediate Sanctions*. Washington, DC: U.S. Government Printing Office.

Wagner, D. and C. Baird (1993). *Evaluation of the Florida Community Control Program*. Washington, DC: U.S. Department of Justice.

Walters, G. (1999). "Short-term Outcomes of Inmates Participating in the Lifestyle Change Program." *Criminal Justice and Behavior*, 26(3):322-327.

Weis, R., S.M. Whitemarsh & N.L. Wilson (2005). "Military-style Residential Treatment for Disruptive Adolescents: Effective for Some Girls, All Girls, When, and Why?" *Psychological Services*, 2:102-122.

Whitehead, J., L. Miller, and L. Myers (1995). "The Diversionary Effectiveness of Intensive Supervision and Community Corrections Programs." In J. Smykla and W. Selke (eds.) *Intermediate Sanctions: Sentencing in the 1990s*, pp. 135-151. Cincinnati, OH: Anderson Publishing Co.

Winterfield, L. and S. Hillsman (1993). *The Staten Island Day-Fine Project*. Washington, DC: U.S. Department of Justice.

Zimmerman, S., B. Rivera, and M. Seis (1991). "An Indirect Assessment of Public Tolerance for Day Fines." Paper presented at the annual meeting of the Academy of Criminal Justice Sciences, Nashville, TN.

# Community Residential Correctional Programs

## 9

[Community Residential Centers] play a vital role in the criminal justice system. They provide additional sentencing options for the court, protect public safety, provide individualized and intensive service aimed at reducing recidivism, and are cost-effective.

—Bobbie L. Huskey

Community residential programs for criminal offenders have a long history in the United States (Latessa & Travis, 1992; Hartmann et al., 1994). Until very recently, the typical residential community correctional facility was known as a "halfway house," a transitional residence for criminal offenders (Wilson, 1985).

---

Box 9.1

### Halfway House

Community-based residential facility for offenders who are either about to be released from an institution or who, immediately after release, are in the initial stages of return to society. In the last three decades, some halfway houses have been designed as alternatives to jail or prison incarceration, primarily for probationers. Halfway now could mean halfway into or out of prison.

---

This chapter places such programs in the larger context of corrections in the community, explaining the historical factors that contributed to the emergence of the halfway house movements; models of halfway houses; and their current operations and practices, effectiveness, costs, and futures. We begin with an explanation of the development of the halfway house over time.

# Historical Development of the Halfway House in America

The halfway house concept began first in England and Ireland during the early 1800s, advocating transitional residences for criminal offenders. It spread quickly across the ocean; in 1817, the Massachusetts Prison Commission recommended establishing a temporary residence to house destitute offenders after release from prison (Cohn, 1973:2):

> The convicts who are discharged are often entirely destitute. The natural prejudice against them is so strong that they find great difficulty in obtaining employment. They are forced to seek shelter in the lowest receptacles; and if they wish to lead a new course of life, are easily persuaded out of it; and perhaps driven by necessity to the commission of fresh crimes. It is intended to afford a temporary shelter in this building, if they choose to accept it, to such discharged convicts as may have conducted themselves well in prison, subject to such regulations as the directors may see fit to provide. They will here have a lodging, rations from the prison at a cheap rate, and . . . a chance to occupy themselves in their trade, until some opportunity offers of placing themselves there they can gain an honest livelihood in society. A refuge of this kind, to this destitute class, would be found, perhaps, humane and political.

The Commission making this recommendation believed that ex-inmates needed an accepting transitional house immediately after release and a supportive environment to assist in the process of establishing a law-abiding and independent existence. It was also motivated by the intention to reduce the unacceptably high rate of recidivism among newly released inmates (Seiter & Carlson, 1977). Unfortunately, the Massachusetts Legislature feared that ex-prisoners might "contaminate" each other if housed together, neutralizing their newly instilled crime resistance learned in prison.

The concept, however, found fertile ground in other locations and under private sponsorship. In 1845, the Isaac T. Hooper Home in New York City opened under the auspices of the Quakers, and today operates as the Women's Prison Association and Hooper Home, serving female clients. Perhaps the most significant halfway house program in this earlier era was Hope House, established by Maud and Ballington Booth in 1896, in New York City. Supported both financially and morally by the Volunteers of America, other Hope Halls opened across the nation (Chicago, San Francisco, New Orleans, etc.). This earlier movement and Hope Halls in particular did not last. Parole was introduced and implemented widely in the early 1900s, as a means for controlling and helping ex-inmates after release from prison. The belief in likely and malevolent contamination from association with other parolees continued. The Great Depression weakened financial support for these privately operated homes, already under-funded. Phase I of the development of the halfway house ended shortly thereafter, not to revive until the 1950s.

The rebirth of the halfway house movement resulted, in part, from a growing awareness of the ineffectiveness of institutional corrections. High recidivism rates were interpreted as indications of ineffectiveness of prison as a venue for rehabilitation. The growing dissatisfaction with prisons was buttressed by new evidence that parolees face problems in the transition from imprisonment to a free society, evidence of the need for supportive services in the transition to community life. In 1954, numerous

Photo 9.1

A modern halfway house. Courtesy of Connecticut Halfway Houses, Inc.

halfway houses opened in America (such as Crenshaw House in Los Angeles, and Dismas House in St. Louis, under the direction of Father Charles Dismas), England, and Canada. Private and religious groups pioneered in both the historical and revival phases of development of the halfway house.

Earlier in the revival phase, most houses used individualized treatment, counseling, employment referrals, and substance abuse counseling, reflecting the general correctional philosophy found within the prison: the medical model. Persons not yet committed to predatory criminal lifestyles, younger, and more malleable offenders were believed ideal clients for the medical model. Then Attorney General Robert Kennedy suggested in 1961 that federal funds be used to establish publicly operated halfway houses for juvenile and youthful offenders, leading to the establishment of the Prisoner Rehabilitation Act of 1965. This legislation authorized the Bureau of Prisons to establish community-based residences for adult and youthful pre-release offenders, as well as to transfer federal prisoners to privately sponsored halfway houses. In

1968, the Law Enforcement Assistance Administration began to provide substantial funds for establishing non-federal houses, a thrust that continued until 1980.

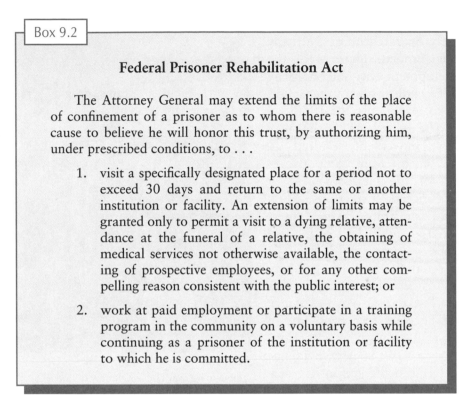

Box 9.2

**Federal Prisoner Rehabilitation Act**

The Attorney General may extend the limits of the place of confinement of a prisoner as to whom there is reasonable cause to believe he will honor this trust, by authorizing him, under prescribed conditions, to . . .

1. visit a specifically designated place for a period not to exceed 30 days and return to the same or another institution or facility. An extension of limits may be granted only to permit a visit to a dying relative, attendance at the funeral of a relative, the obtaining of medical services not otherwise available, the contacting of prospective employees, or for any other compelling reason consistent with the public interest; or

2. work at paid employment or participate in a training program in the community on a voluntary basis while continuing as a prisoner of the institution or facility to which he is committed.

Perhaps the most significant event in Phase II was the development of the International Halfway House Association (IHHA) in 1964.[1] This group, motivated by the absence of state and local support for halfway houses, established a voluntary professional organization of halfway house administrators and personnel (Wilson, 1985). IHHA (now known as the International Community Corrections Association) conducted numerous training workshops, sponsored training programs and conferences, and affiliated with the American Correctional Association.[2] The organization grew from 40 programs in 1966 to more than 1,800 in 1982,[3] and now holds annual conferences that deal with "what works" in correctional intervention. As a result of these and related efforts, few cities and counties run their own residential treatment centers, and state programs that operate halfway houses usually contract with private-sector, nonprofit halfway houses to provide services.

---

Box 9.3

### Day Reporting Centers

Community centers to which adults and sometimes juveniles report in lieu of incarceration or as a condition of probation. A variety of community or in-house programs may be offered, including individual and group counseling, job readiness training, Alcoholics Anonymous 12-Step Programs, drug abuse education, and so on. Participants usually return to their individual homes at night.

### Restitution Centers

Community residential centers for offenders ordered by the court to make financial payments to victims. Offenders may also be remanded as a condition of probation. The offender must seek and obtain employment, make restitution to victims, reimburse the center for room and board, and set aside any residual earnings for use after release. Center programs usually require curfews, strict alcohol and drug abstinence, and participation in community or in-house programs.

### Work Furlough Centers

Residential facility for sentenced offenders released from a correctional institution for work during the day. Residents typically spend nights and weekends in the facility and must participate in available community or in-house programs. Participants are generally charged a per diem fee for services, room, and board.

---

## Uses of Halfway Houses

Over the past 50 years, as suggested above, the numbers, roles, and uses of halfway houses increased considerably. There has been considerable role expansion in residential placements of adult (and juvenile) offenders. For the most part, the increase has been in the services provided to new groups: probationers, the accused awaiting trial, and offenders directly sentenced for treatment, ordered by a judiciary eager to secure services and supervision for offenders. Judges are usually unwilling to incarcerate clients likely to give up criminal behavior if a supportive and facilitating community environment could be provided in which the offenders remediate their needs and improve their functioning. These changes in roles, sentencing alternatives, clients, and use of halfway houses have rendered "halfway house" an obsolete term, one that has been replaced by the more accurate "community corrections residential facility." Rush (1992) defines such facilities as:

> A correctional facility from which residents are regularly permitted to depart, unaccompanied by any official, for the purposes of using community resources, such as school or treatment programs, and seeking or holding employment. This definition not only deletes the term "halfway" but also defines a correctional mission for the facility. The definition does not require centers to provide direct services to clients. Halfway houses are thus subsumed under the larger umbrella term, further reflecting the more diverse populations served, as well as broader correctional mission and such newer programs as day, restitution, and work-release centers.

Another major factor influencing the development and use of community residential centers in the United States has been a shift in the ideology of corrections, from rehabilitation to "reintegration," a term introduced by the President's Commission on Law Enforcement and Administration of Justice in 1967.

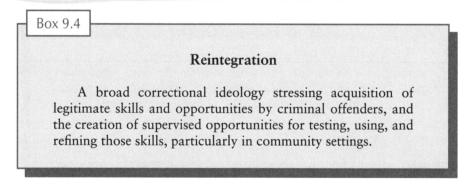

Box 9.4

**Reintegration**

A broad correctional ideology stressing acquisition of legitimate skills and opportunities by criminal offenders, and the creation of supervised opportunities for testing, using, and refining those skills, particularly in community settings.

This correctional philosophy places priority on keeping offenders in the community whenever possible, rather than commitment to prison. It also stresses the role of the community in corrections. Thus the new ideology, new developments stressing community placement in local correctional programs, and existing halfway houses contributed to an accelerating expansion of community correctional residential programs. This thrust was further expanded by three factors:[4] (1) widespread correctional acceptance of the reintegration mission, (2) success of the reintegration movement in the mental health field, and (3) the lower costs of halfway houses as compared to prisons.[5] Prison overcrowding in the 1980s and early 1990s, resulting from the War on Drugs, further accelerated the shift (Allen & Simonsen, 1992, Allen & Simonsen, 2001).

---

Box 9.5

### Community Residential Centers

Community residential centers (CRCs) are nonconfining residential facilities to adjudicated adults or juveniles, or those subject to criminal or juvenile proceedings. They are intended as an alternative for persons not suited to probation or who need a period of readjustment to the community after imprisonment.

There are more CRCs providing transitional and extensive services for juveniles than adults. Some CRCs specialize by client or treatment modality: for example, women only, abused women, prerelease federal furloughers, drug-dependent or alcohol abusers, the mentally ill, those identified by the court diagnostic program, or the developmentally disabled.

---

From 1980 through the present, prison inmates have increased dramatically, with now more than 2,100,000 prisoners held in Federal or State prisons and local jails (Bureau of Justice Statistics, 2005), creating a lack of prison capacity and extensive prison overcrowding. The primary reason for the burgeoning prison population is believed to be the "War on Drugs," reflecting both the conservative emphases on retributive justice and the nation's unwillingness to address the causes of crime (Allen, 1995). Three major results of this development have been (1) an increase in the number of offenders placed on probation and parole, (2) an increase in the seriousness and dangerousness of offenses of those placed into traditional community-based supervision,[6] and (3) a heightened demand for community residential treatment facilities to provide transitional placement for offenders and to respond to such special needs populations as narcotics and drug abusers, offenders driving under the influence of alcohol or drugs, mental health clients. Community residential facilities and programs expanded and changed to address these new demands and women offenders.[7] Community residential facilities and programs expanded and changed to address these new demands, required programs, and heightened supervision levels (Huskey, 1992). Before addressing programs for these clients, it is necessary to understand the models on which the programs operate. Figure 9.1 shows the number of halfway houses in operation in about 30 states and the Federal Government between 1997 and 2000 (Camp & Camp, 2000). The number of inmates served in these facilities are presented in Figure 9.2. These data indicate that in 2000, nearly 30,000 inmates were served in just over 50 percent of the states (Camp & Camp, 2000).

Figure 9.1
**Halfway Houses in Operation, 1994-1999**

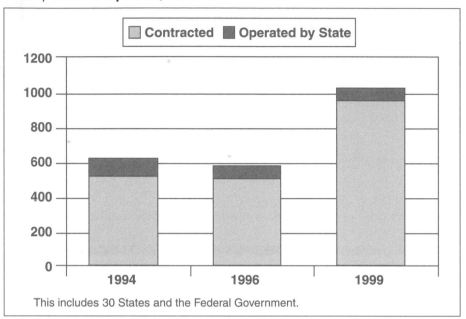

Source: Camp, C. and G. Camp (1997). *The Corrections Yearbook 1997*. South Salem, NY: The Criminal Justice Institute, Inc.; and Camp, C. and G. Camp (2000). *The 2000 Correction Yearbook: Adult Corrections*. Middletown, CT: Criminal Justice Institute, Inc., p. 124.

Figure 9.2
**Inmates Located at Halfway Houses 1994-1999**

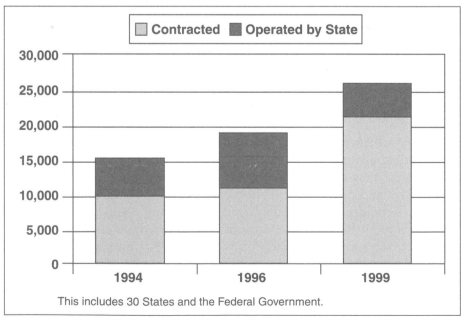

Source: Camp, C. and G. Camp (1997). *The Corrections Yearbook 1997*. South Salem, NY: The Criminal Justice Institute, Inc.; and Camp, C. and G. Camp (2000). *The 2000 Correction Yearbook: Adult Corrections*. Middletown, CT: Criminal Justice Institute, Inc., p. 124.

## Models of Community Residential Programs

It should be remembered that Phase II of the development of community residential programs has been underway for more than 30 years. Thus, the models under which halfway houses and related community programs operate have also undergone significant change. We start by examining an earlier model in a less complex environment.

In 1976, Allen et al. studied halfway houses and probation. These researchers developed three alternative models of halfway houses, based on referral service. This trichotomy is useful in depicting how halfway houses interface with the criminal justice system, as well as the advantages and services these programs offer to their clients. The trichotomy can be found in Figure 9.3 (Latessa & Allen, 1982).

Figure 9.3
**Alternative Models of Halfway Houses**

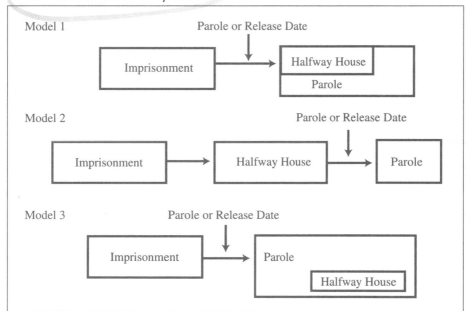

Source: E. Latessa and H. Allen (1982). "Halfway Houses and Parole: A National Assessment." *Journal of Criminal Justice,* 10:153-163.

Model 1 is the standard and most frequent pattern of referral to halfway house programs. In this model, an inmate granted a conditional release (such as parole, shock probation, or shock parole) enters a halfway house during the initial parole period. This model provides services to parolees who need support during their period of release. The length of residency in the halfway house may be specified before referral but usually is a shared decision to be made collaboratively by the supervision officer, house staff, and client. Typically, this decision is based on such factors as resident's readiness to leave the house, employment, savings, and alternative residential plan. After leaving the house, the offender generally continues on parole supervision. This model has been found to successfully reduce recidivism (Bouffard, MacKenzie & Hickman, 2000).

---

**Box 9.6**

### Model

A picture or representation showing the parts of a system. Models suggest the ways that segments of the criminal justice system (courts, probation, prisons, etc.) fit together and interrelate. One implication of a model is that change in one part of the system will have an impact on the other parts of the system. A simplified demonstration of this is seen when law enforcement agencies increase arrests; judicial personnel, probation officers, and jail facilities face increased workloads.

---

Model 2 is similar to the first in that inmates' release plans call for placement in a halfway house as the initial phase of their release process. Unlike the first, however, halfway house residency occurs prior to formal granting of parole and subsequent supervision as a parolee. Typically, these inmates have been scheduled for a definite release date before moving from the prison to the halfway house. These clients remain inmates, serving the remainder of their sentences in residency at a halfway house. Halfway house residency provides needed and significant services in the prison-community transition. Additional benefits include continuation of jurisdiction by the referring correctional agency, ability to return the inmate to incarceration without formal violation of parole, development of a more positive attitude toward the halfway house by the resident, and less expensive after-care service that can be more legitimately compared to imprisonment, rather than the costs of parole.[8] The U.S. Bureau of Prisons was a leader in initiating this model for using halfway houses,[9] and continues to use this model on a pre-release basis.[10]

The third model of halfway house use, also based on the reintegration model of corrections, differs by time of placement into the program. With Model 3, offenders on probation and inmates granted parole are assigned to the community without initially residing in a halfway house. If such clients may be reverting to criminal behavior or encounter unanticipated problems that might be resolved by program services of or a period of residency in a halfway house, the supervising agency may remand the offender to the residential setting for a short period. If and when conditions warrant, the client could then be returned to a lower level of supervision. It should be noted here that some residential correctional programs are large and can provide services and programs at many points in the supervision process, as will be explored below. Model 3 appears to best suggest the organization and practices of multi-service agencies in larger urban settings.

---

Box 9.7

### Bureau of Prisons and Halfway Houses

The goal of BOP's halfway house program is to provide federal prison inmates a transition back to the communities where they will live upon release from federal custody. Besides subsistence and housing, BOP guidelines state that halfway house operators are required to offer inmates job counseling, academic and vocational training, family reconciliation services, access to substance abuse programs, post-release housing referrals, and community adjustment services. . . . In 1999, BOP reported it had contracts with 285 operators; this includes both profit and nonprofit operators. According to BOP's figures, halfway house contracts ranged from 1 to 150 beds for a total of 6,987 beds as of October 1990. Halfway house operators are reimbursed based on a daily rate for each inmate. The daily rates averaged $42. In comparison, BOP averaged nearly $58 for each inmate in a federal prison during 1999.

Source: U.S. Government Accounting Office, 2000.

---

In addition to the models described above, halfway houses take on a wide range of functions and services depending on their size, mission, and resources. Figure 9.4 illustrates a continuum of types of programs based on the services they provide. Some halfway houses provide shelter, food, and minimal counseling and referral services. These programs are considered supportive halfway houses. Examples of these types of programs might include shelters and drop-in centers. Halfway houses that offer a full range of services can be considered interventive programs. These are programs that offer a full range of treatment services. Most programs fall somewhere in the middle.

Figure 9.4
**Types of Halfway Houses Based on Services**

SUPPORTIVE◄————————————►INTERVENTIVE

Minimal services program          Total treatment
Minimal staff                     Specialized staff
Short-term                        Long-term stay
Referral service

It should be obvious that roles of halfway houses as residential probation and after-care centers within the correctional process are varied in both operation and focus. Although all three models acknowledge the need for a residential setting at some point in the transition back to the community, there are various approaches and strategies for meeting these needs. To understand the range of alternatives, we will examine a rural community residential treatment center, as well as a larger urban counterpart.

## Rural Community Programs

Rural correctional programs serve a wide range of offenders and are themselves diverse. Whereas the "Mom and Pop" stereotype possibly typical of the earliest developments of rural community corrections has surely died,[11] what has emerged is an increasingly diversified pattern of local programs that solidly reflect the concept of "residential community corrections programs."[12] See, for example, Hilltop House (Durango, Colorado), Portage House (Stevens Point, Wisconsin), or Re-Entry House (western upper peninsula in Michigan).

Community residential correctional programs in rural settings face differing challenges. They are smaller, and fewer employment opportunities and treatment programs in rural areas for the offenders. Residents are drawn from a small pool of eligible offenders. These programs face and must overcome community suspicion that the center's existence may attract recalcitrant offenders who will move their base of criminal activities to the local area, the "importation" reaction. Decreased societal tolerance for certain offender types (such as rapists, child molesters, and drug pushers), coupled with concerns over public safety and demands for increased supervision have great potential to restrict treatment, job and educational placement, access to existing treatment programs, and funding from community sources. Many facilities must work hard to interface with referral sources (probation and parole agencies, for example), and develop liaisons with other services offered by mental health, drug, alcohol, family counseling, and court agencies.

Box 9.8

### Rural Community Corrections

Community corrections in its rural expression is the remnant of the grassroots folkart of the original concept. Rural programs are generally not larger than 40 beds (a LARGE rural program) and are concerned about the importation of offenders regularly into their community, the meeting of the next payroll, the expense of travel to training as opposed to the cost of training itself. The rural program generally is not faced with the challenge of adequately accessing and implementing brokerages to existing treatment in their community; we are worried about how to create, fund, and perpetuate treatment. Our "community" may be a town of 12,000 serving a catchment area of several hundred miles. Our worries are not typically of gang behavior between "Crips and Bloods." They may, however, include the American Indian in any of its numerous tribal groups, the rural hispanic or black, all in the delicately interwoven and overwoven social fabric of the lineages of a rural community. Every individual job truly means the future of our programs. The failure of one client can affect the future political support of our program; a single incident cannot only destroy a program but also the potential efforts of any program to replace it (Berry, 1990:6-7).

These opportunities and challenges face Hilltop House,[13] a 28-bed private, nonprofit agency providing residential services to male offenders, and outpatient services to delinquents and victims referred from local, state, and federal sources. In its earliest days, this small program would close in the winter and re-open in the spring, housing not more than 12 clients referred from one judicial district. It now serves a much wider catchment area, working with six district court judges.

Photo 9.2
Substance abuse group. Courtesy of Talbert House, Inc.

Hilltop House began to grow in this environment, even though encountering the conservative political swing that demanded longer sentences, less diversion, and specialized programs to assist the higher-need clients the justice system was processing. This demand was met by:

- Developing liaisons with other court referral units and probation officers.

- Working with non-incarcerated populations (such as misdemeanant offenders, persons driving under the influence, self-referred persons with drug and alcohol abuse problems, youth referred by their parents, and so on).

- Developing new service programs in the areas of incest treatment and domestic violence, and urinalysis collection and testing for a county youth home, private schools, social services, employers, individuals, and parents.

- Developing a sexual abuse treatment team, using workers from a number of agencies and providing service to offenders, their non-offending spouses, victims, and other adults who had been molested as children (AMACs). This multi-agency approach was expanded to include juvenile restitution, a program using many volunteers as mediators and providing subsidized employment and monitored restitution payments, as well as group therapy to reconcile victims and their offenders, and develop empathy among juvenile offenders.

Hilltop House appears to serve the specific needs of the community, develop resources to plan and initiate specialized services, and maximize the therapeutic gains for clients, victims, and citizens. Individuals who resolve conflicts, personal problems, challenges, development problems, and the impacts of being victimized, are more likely to become constructive citizens and lower the crime rate in their community.

---

Box 9.9

### America's Community Residential Centers

A national survey of CRCs in 1991 found more than 1,000 agencies. The most common type of residential programs were a combination of drug treatment and work release centers. The three most frequent types of services provided to clients were job development, drug testing, and counseling. In descending order, their clients were prison pre-releasees, inmates, and probationers. In 1991 alone, more than 16,000 offenders were diverted from incarceration. The rate of program completion is high (more than 70%), and the failure rate (rearrest while in program) was only three percent! (Huskey, 1992:70).

## Metropolitan Residential Programs

Residential community correctional programs for offenders that are located in urban areas are more numerous and diverse than those in rural areas. In addition, many of the largest programs make extensive use of existing community services, especially if these are needed adjuncts to a treatment plan for an individual client. Treatment generally falls into two categories: individual and group, and most halfway houses conduct detailed intake assessments to determine the needs of their clients. Figure 9.5 shows an example of a Halfway House Intake Form.

Although halfway houses usually offer a range of programs and services, the most common include employment, substance abuse, and cognitive restructuring. Employment programming usually includes job readiness training, resume writing and interviewing skills, job placement, and transportation assistance.

Programs for drug abusers might include methadone maintenance, weekly and unscheduled urinalysis, 12-Step programming, groups, Alcoholic Anonymous and Narcotics Anonymous, and detoxification. It should be noted that in 1999, more than 60 percent of all male arrestees tested positive for at least one drug, including alcohol (Drug Use Forecasting, 2000), and about one in four tested for a major drug (PCP, heroin, crack, or cocaine). The rate for female jail inmates was even higher than for males; 28 percent tested positive for opiates compared to 17 percent for males. Alcohol and drug abuse is a risk factor for many offenders, and such clients have high needs for treatment that community residential correctional facilities can meet.[14]

Box 9.10

### Alcoholics and Treatment

Many community corrections center programs focus on Alcoholics Anonymous as part of the overall abstinence program. This may mean requiring residents to work the 12 steps of AA, demonstrate understanding of the program, design a post-release plan, chair an AA meeting, and participate in the affairs of the program. The latter might include house chores (vacuuming, cleaning restrooms, shoveling snow, cleaning ashtrays, etc.), attending house meetings, remaining sober and clean, working outside the program, and seeking specialized treatment. If the resident's family unit is not broken, reconciliation counseling might be required. If appropriate, the resident might be required to participate in meetings of Adult Children of Alcoholics (ACAs), or child sexual abuse and domestic violence programs. When alcohol is the underlying cause of criminal behavior, an individually designed, monitored, and supportive program may sharply reduce criminal activity.

Figure 9.5
**Halfway House Intake Form (Form A-2)**

---

## GENERAL INFORMATION

**1.** ☐☐☐☐☐☐☐☐☐☐☐☐☐  ☐  ☐☐☐☐☐☐☐☐☐☐☐☐☐
   (First)              (Middle)         (Last)              Client Name

**2.** ☐☐☐☐☐☐ Client T.H. ID #

**3.** ☐☐-☐☐-☐☐☐☐ Client SS #

**4.** ☐ Admission Status:
   (1) New Admission
   (2) Re-Admission (within fiscal year)
   (3) Re-Admittance after Escape/Absconding
       (within fiscal year)
   (4) Legal Status Altered

**5.** ☐☐ / ☐☐ / ☐☐ Date of Birth (mo/day/yr)

**6.** ☐ Sex (1) Male   (2) Female

**7.** ☐ Race
   (AI) American Indian    (OR) Oriental
   (BL) Black              (WH) White
   (HI) Hispanic           (Specify) Other _____

**7a.** ☐ Appalachian   (1) Yes   (2) No

**8.** ☐ Current Marital Status
   (1) Single      (4) Married
   (2) Divorced    (5) Separated
   (3) Widowed     (6) Common Law

**9.** ☐☐ Number of Dependents (financial responsibility other than self)

**10.** ☐☐ Number of Children

**11.** ☐ Legal Responsibility for Children?    (1) Yes (2) No

**12.** ☐☐☐☐☐ Zip Code of Last Community Address

**13.** ☐ Homeless Before Arrest?    (1) Yes (2) No

**14.** ☐ Place to Live When Discharged?    (1) Yes (2) No

**15.** ☐ Primary Source of Income (at present)
   (1) Public Assistance    (5) Family
   (2) Investments          (6) No Income
   (3) Full-Time Employment (7) Other _____
   (4) Part-Time Employment

**15a.** ☐☐☐☐☐ Total Income Last Year (Nearest Dollar)

**16.** ☐☐☐☐☐ Court Costs Owed (Nearest Dollar)

**17.** ☐☐☐☐☐ Restitution Owed (Nearest Dollar)

---

## CRIMINAL HISTORY

Note: When answering questions 19-30, if the information is not available from the referral source, use client-reported answers.

18.  ☐☐☐☐ . ☐☐☐  Ohio Revised Code for which convicted.

19.  ☐☐  Number of prior felony convictions (adult/juvenile).

20.  ☐☐  Number of prior adult felony commitments in a state or federal institution (when sentenced).

21.  ☐☐  Age at admission to institution (or probation) for current offense.

22.  ☐☐  Number of offenses (including current offense) committed while under parole/probation supervision.

23.  ☐☐  Number of offenses (including current offense) involving drugs/alcohol.

24.  ☐☐  Number of prior arrests during the past five years, prior to incarceration.

25.  ☐☐  Number of offenses (including current offense) for auto theft.

26.  ☐☐  Number of offenses (including current offense) involving serious injury to the victim.

27.  ☐☐  Number of offenses (including current offense) involving the use of a weapon.

28.  ☐☐  Has this individual been previously convicted for the same offense? (1) Yes   (2) No

29.  ☐☐  Was the current conviction for multiple crimes? (1) Yes   (2) No

30.  ☐☐  Was the offender employed at the time of arrest? (1) Yes   (2) No

Figure 9.5—*continued*

## EDUCATION AND EMPLOYMENT HISTORY

31. ☐☐ Years of education attained (last grade completed).

32. ☐☐ Highest diploma/degree received and name major subject area where applicable.
(1) None
(2) G.E.D.
(3) High School
(4) College     Associate/Major   _____
                    Bachelor/Major   _____
                    Master's/Major   _____
                    Doctoral/Major   _____

33. ☐☐ Years of vocational training.

34. ☐☐ Certification of vocational training awarded
(1) Yes _____ Trade
(2) No

### Enter 1 for YES   2 for NO for Questions 35-37

35. ☐☐ Physical/Health impairments (e.g., amputee, paraplegic, deaf, blind, serious illness, debilitating effect of age)

36. ☐☐ Mental capacity impairment (e.g., diagnosed mental retardation, diagnosed borderline MR)

37. ☐☐ Behavioral impairment (e.g., mental and/or emotional condition or disorders that require the treatment of a qualified mental health professional).

38. ☐☐ Number of jobs held in the last two years in the community prior to incarceration.

39. ☐☐ Longest stay on the job in the last two years in the community (number of months).

## CLIENT/STAFF ASSISTANCE ASSESSMENT

### Enter 1 for YES   2 for NO for Questions 40-55

40. ☐ Does client feel he/she needs assistance while in residency?

41. ☐ Does this individual need employment assistance?

42. ☐ Does this individual need assistance in academic or vocational training?

43. ☐ Does this individual need assistance in financial management?

44. ☐ Does individual need assistance in the area of domestic relations (e.g., marriage, family, etc.)?

45. ☐ Does this individual need assistance in the area of emotional or mental health?

46. ☐ Is this individual currently required to take medication for any psychological condition?

47. ☐ Does this individual need assistance for a substance abuse (alcohol/drug) problem?

48. ☐ Does this individual need assistance with securing suitable living arrangements?

49. ☐ Does this individual need assistance for a learning disability?

50. ☐ Has medication ever been prescribed for a psychological condition (e.g., nerves)?

51. ☐ Has client had prior psychiatric hospitalization?

52. ☐ Has client ever attempted suicide?

53. ☐ Was client ever a victim of child abuse?

54. ☐ Was client ever a victim of domestic violence?

55. ☐ Was client ever a victim of sexual abuse or incest?

## DRUG/ALCOHOL HISTORY

56. ☐☐ # times client had prior drug/alcohol treatment.

57. ☐☐ # months prior outpatient treatment.

58. ☐☐ Successful? (1) Yes (2) No (3) NA

59. ☐☐ # months prior inpatient treatment.

60. ☐☐ Successful? (1) Yes (2) No (3) NA

61. ☐☐ # months prior Halfway House treatment.

62. ☐☐ Successful? (1) Yes (2) No (3) NA

63. ☐ Has client participated in a halfway house **program** before this occasion?
(1) Yes       (2) No

64. ☐☐ Longest period of drug/alcohol abstinence in community (months) **or** (99) No problem

Staff member completing form

_____

Date _____

Rev. 061992

Recently, there has been increased attention to the effectiveness of cognitive behavioral programs. These interventions involved targeting the antisocial attitudes, values, and beliefs that many offenders have. Cognitive programming attempts to restructure the thinking of offenders, and develop new skills that can be used to improve their problem-solving abilities. Many halfway houses today offer criminal thinking groups, and other cognitive interventions aimed at anger and violence reduction, sexual behavior, negative peer associations, and improved problem-solving techniques.

Another group of problem offenders are those with both mental illness and substance abuse problems. County community health boards and criminal courts can both use services for these offenders. These offenders are called "dual diagnosed," and they pose a special problem for community corrections. Although there is research that indicates that the major predictors of recidivism are the same for mentally disordered offenders as non-mentally disordered offenders (Bonta, Law & Hanson, 1998; Solicitor General of Canada, 1998), the availability of treatment services in the community is a often lacking for this special need group. Peters and Hills (1999:95):

> Offenders placed under community supervision who have co-occurring mental health and substance abuse disorders are quite diverse in symptom presentation, severity and chronicity of disorders. These individuals often have severe mental health disorders, and simultaneously use different types of drugs, presenting considerable challenges to treatment programs for this population. Many offenders with co-occurring disorders would benefit from specialized treatment services in the community.

Unfortunately, there are relatively few programs that are specifically designed to deal with the dual diagnosed offender. Most of these programs are located in large urban areas. One such program is the Substance Abuse-Mental Illness (SAMI) program operated by Talbert House in Cincinnati, Ohio. This program has been in operation for more than six years, and has served nearly 500 offenders over that period of time. (www.talberthouse.org/aboyt/services/same.html)

Many urban communities across the nation face the problem of finding treatment opportunities that permit reintegration of high-need offenders, such as described above. Increasingly, these counties are turning to private sector, profit and nonprofit residential programs for assistance. Figure 9.6 suggests how such residential and community programs can interface with traditional justice agencies in provision of services.

Figure 9.6
**A Reintegration Model**

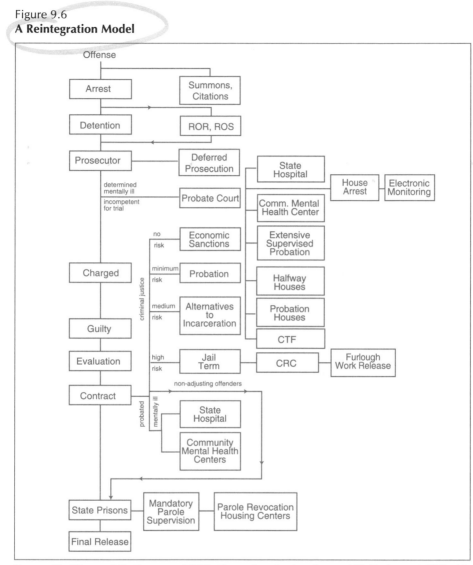

Source: H. Allen and C. Simonsen (1995). *Corrections in America*, p. 665. Englewood Cliffs, NJ: Prentice-Hall.

Community residential correctional programs of these types exist across the nation and will increase in number and importance in the coming years. The private sector providing these programs, facilities and centers will grow as cities and counties, facing fiscal and policy crises, accept and introduce these programs in their local areas.

## Effectiveness of Community Residential Programs

The question of the effectiveness of halfway houses, along with other community corrections programs, is addressed in Chapter 11. A brief summary statement is included here to place both phases of the halfway house movement in perspective.

Evaluation of the effectiveness of halfway houses and, more recently, residential community correctional programs, requires that they be considered across three dimensions: humaneness, recidivism, and cost studies (Latessa & Allen, 1982). There is little doubt that halfway houses, during both phases, were and are more humanitarian that imprisonment. Halfway house programs were established in part to address the devastating economic and psychological effects of prisons and prisonization on most inmates. Prison crowding, gross idleness of inmates, absence of meaningful work and vocational training, unhealthy and unsafe physical plants, prison rape, and gang conflicts within prisons make prisons less than the pinnacle of humanitarianism (Donnelly & Forschner, 1987). Halfway houses are more humane, although the conservative punishment emphasis in the last two decades raises policy questions about whether American correctional policy ought to be so (Latessa & Allen, 1982).

Photo 9.3
Mental health program. Courtesy of Talbert House, Inc.

The weight of evidence to date demonstrates that halfway houses are cost effective in terms of expenditure of public funds when compared to institutional placement. Further, their programs achieve some

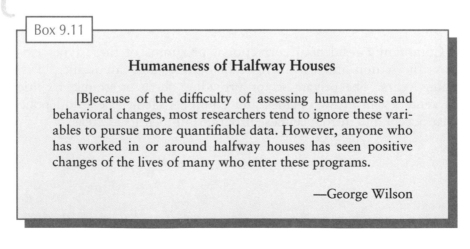

Box 9.11

### Humaneness of Halfway Houses

[B]ecause of the difficulty of assessing humaneness and behavioral changes, most researchers tend to ignore these variables to pursue more quantifiable data. However, anyone who has worked in or around halfway houses has seen positive changes of the lives of many who enter these programs.

—George Wilson

if not all stated objectives, including the maintenance of offenders' community ties and making community resources available to offender clients (Dowell et al., 1985). On average, halfway houses cost about $50 per day, and one recent study concluded that halfway houses tend to be more cost effective under private rather than public management (Pratt &Winston, 1999).

The issue of recidivism is much more complex, particularly with regard to halfway houses. The diversity of halfway houses, as well as the range of types of offenders they serve (parolees, probationers, pretrial detainees, work releasees, and furloughees, not to mention state, county, and federal offenders) make it difficult to develop adequate comparison groups for follow-up studies.[15] The recidivism studies of CRC residents that exist indicate success with about 71 percent of the clients, and in-program rearrest rates of two to 17 percent (Huskey, 1992). Follow-up recidivism studies of alcohol-abusing clients show success rates ranging from 70 to 80 percent; driving-under-the-influence (DUI) rates can be significantly reduced with residential treatment, significantly raising the DUI survival rates (Langworthy & Latessa, 1993; Langworthy & Latessa, 1996; Pratt, Holsinger & Latessa, 2000). For clients who graduate from CRC programs, success rates can be as high as 92 percent (Friday & Wertkin, 1995). On the whole, follow-up recidivism studies indicate that halfway house residents perform no worse than offenders who receive other correctional sanctions. There is also some evidence that offenders placed in halfway houses have more needs than other offenders (Latessa & Travis, 1991). Latessa (1998) has examined a number of halfway houses across the country. He has several criticisms that are noteworthy:

- Many halfway houses fail to adequately assess offenders, and there are few distinctions made between offenders based on risk;

- In general, qualifications of staff are low, and there is a great deal of staff turnover;

- Most halfway houses offer a wide range of "eclectic" treatment, with little if any theoretically based treatment models in place; and

- Despite some notable exceptions, most halfway houses can be classified as one step above "three hots and a cot."

In several recent studies of a halfway houses, Leon et al. (1999), and Munden et al. (1999) voiced similar concerns about poor offender assessment practices, frequent staff turnover, change in leadership, inadequate resources, and insufficient emphasis on treatment. Lowenkamp and Latessa (2004) recently demonstrated the importance of assessing the risk level of offenders before assigning them to community-based correctional facilities (CBCFs). Figures 9.7 and 9.8 illustrate the recidivism rates for individual CBCF programs. Consistent with the risk principle (see Chapter 11), the CBCF programs generally increased the recidivism rates of low risk offenders by 4 percent, but decreased the recidivism rates of higher risk offenders by 8 percent.

Box 9.12

**Community-Based Correctional Facilities**

In one of the more unique attempts to provide residential treatment programs, Ohio has developed a correctional alternative called Community-Based Correctional Facilities or CBCFs. Currently there are 19 operating CBCFs in Ohio. The size of the facilities ranges from 54 to 200 offenders, and several serve both males and females. Funding for the CBCFs is provided by the state, however, the operation and management of the CBCF is left to a local judicial corrections board. In some instances, the local courts operate the facilities, and in other cases, private providers are retained. The CBCFs are secure facilities, however, treatment is the primary focus. Ohio has also developed similar juvenile programs called Community Correctional Facilities. Some states such as Texas, have similar programs.

## The Future of Residential Community Corrections

Predicting future correctional trends is difficult due to possible national policy changes, economic fluctuations, crime trends, and public sentiment. One thing is evident: public sentiment for increasing punishment of offenders in the hope of lessening crime[16] remains strong. Thus it is reasonable to expect increased numbers of offenders in jails and prisons, and on probation, parole, and other community correctional programs.

Despite the increased use of punishment, the future of residential community correctional programs appears promising. Probation populations are at an all-time high, and approximately 95 percent of prison inmates will return to the community. Halfway houses and other community-based programs will be needed to assist in their reintegration. Early release programs, such as work and educational furlough and pre-parole release, will also increase, furthering the demand for services of halfway houses and related programs.

Figure 9.7
**Treatment Effects for Low-Risk Offenders**

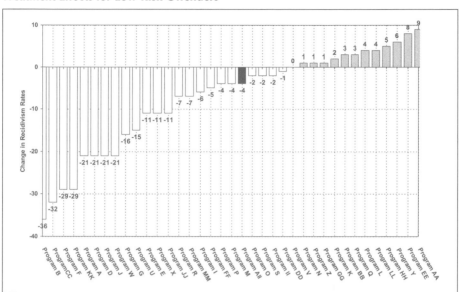

Source: Lowenkamp, C.T., and E.J. Latessa (2004). "Residential Community Corrections and the Risk Principle: Lessons Learned in Ohio." In *Ohio Corrections Research Compendium, Volume II.* Columbus, OH: Ohio Department of Research and Corrections.

Figure 9.8
**Treatment Effects for High-Risk Offenders**

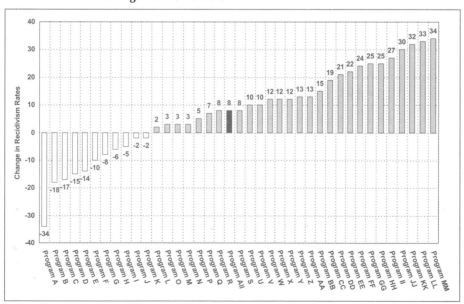

Source: Lowenkamp, C.T., and E.J. Latessa (2004). "Residential Community Corrections and the Risk Principle: Lessons Learned in Ohio." In *Ohio Corrections Research Compendium, Volume II.* Columbus, OH: Ohio Department of Research and Corrections.

It is also likely that local units of government will increasingly turn to private-sector providers for correctional (and perhaps law enforcement) programs, contracting with larger numbers of halfway houses to provide lower-cost and diverse services that government cannot otherwise fund. To do less would decrease reintegration services and increase the possibility of offenders returning to prisons for committing new crimes in local communities. Indeed, one of the issues facing community corrections is the increased privatization of services and programs. While nonprofit providers have always been the mainstay of traditional halfway houses, the influx of for-profit providers will likely change the face of this industry. Figure 9.9 shows the average daily cost per inmate of halfway houses. These data clearly show that programs operated by contractors are lower cost than those operated by the states.

Figure 9.9
**Halfway House Daily Costs per Inmate 1991-1999**

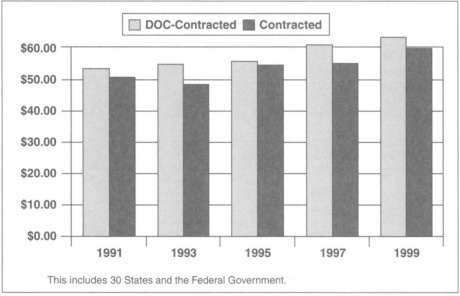

This includes 30 States and the Federal Government.

Source: Camp, C. and G. Camp (2000). *The 2000 Corrections Yearbook: Adult Corrections*, p. 125. Middletown, CT: Criminal Justice Institute, Inc.

Halfway houses and related programs will also need to increase the quality and effectiveness,[17] of programs to serve the demands of clients, communities, and corrections. To do this, they will need to maintain relationships with justice agencies, strengthen community ties and acceptance, adopt treatment models that have demonstrated effectiveness, and assist in insuring the safety of the community in reintegrating offenders. Future research will also be needed to address the roles and effectiveness of community residential correctional programs. Fortunately, there is a movement underway to improve the effectiveness of community correctional programs. This movement is being supported by the National Institute of Corrections[18] and the International Community Corrections Association, and is based on the work of scholars such as Paul Gendreau, Don Andrews, Francis Cullen, and others. Through their research we continue to learn about "what works" with offenders (Cullen & Gendreau, 2001).

## Summary

Halfway houses have been part of the correctional scene since the early 1800s. Originally designed to assist offenders who had been released from prison, today, many halfway houses serve as both halfway "in" and halfway "out" facilities. Often called community residential correctional programs, these facilities include both privately and publicly operated programs, and range from "three hots and cot," to programs designed to meet all of an offender's treatment needs. Although halfway houses are often overlooked, they represent an important part of community corrections.

Community corrections centers serving high-risk clients have produced evidence of both lower recidivism and cost effectiveness. Such centers are more humane, less expensive, and more effective in ensuring public safety. Community corrections centers will remain a major segment of community corrections, and will be increasingly specialized to serve a wider variety of high-risk clients.

## Review Questions

1. Why did Phase I of the halfway house movement die in the 1930s?

2. Explain the revival of the halfway house movement in the 1950s.

3. Define residential community correctional center.

4. What are some of the services offered by halfway houses?

5. What are the advantages of halfway houses?

6. What is "substance abuse?" Debate: is it a disease or a learned behavior?

7. Define "reintegration" and discuss ways that halfway houses can lower crime.

8. What are some of the criticisms of halfway houses?

## Key Terms

"CRCs"

cost effective

day reporting centers

dual diagnosed offenders

halfway house

humaneness

reintegration

residential community correctional program

restitution centers

work furlough centers

## Electronic Library

Colorado's experience with offenders on halfway houses (http://www.cdpsweb.state.co.us/ors/pdf/docs/comcor01.pdf).

Halfway house use by the Federal Bureau of Prisons, The Bureau in Brief (www.bop.gov/ipapg/ipabib.html).

International Community Corrections Association (www.iccaweb.org).

Inmate views on halfway houses (www.lvrj.com/lvrj_home/2001/Apr-15-Sun-2001/news/15812376.html).

Mentally disordered offenders and community corrections (http://www.sgc.gc.ca/epub/Corr/e199805a/e199805a.htm).

Moral panic over a high notoriety crime situations (www.cjcj.org/jpi/washpost082299.html).

Prison population changes (www.ojp.usdoj.gov/bjs/pub/press/p00pr.htm).

Talbert House service programs (www.talberthouse.org/about/services.html).

Women's Prison Association and Home (New York) (ajacobs@wpaonline.org).

Community residential programming for women offenders and their children (www.nicic.org/pubs/2000/period180.pdf).

## Recommended Readings

Allen, H., E. Carlson, E. Parks, and R. Seiter (1978). *Program Models: Halfway Houses*. Washington, DC: U.S. Department of Justice.

Latessa, E. and L. Travis (1992). "Residential Community Correctional Programs." In Byrne J. and A. Lurigio (eds.) *Smart Sentencing? An Examination of the Emergence of Intermediate Sentencing*, pp. 166-181. Beverly Hills, CA: Sage.

Wilson, G. (1985). "Halfway House Programs for Offenders." In L. Travis (ed.) *Probation, Parole and Community Corrections*, pp. 151-164. Prospect Heights, IL: Waveland.

## Notes

[1]    This organization is now known as the International Community Corrections Association, publishes the ICCA Journal, and sponsors local, state, regional, national, and international conferences and training programs concerned with halfway houses and community alternatives. Contract ICCA Central Office, P.O. Box 1987, LaCrosse, WI 54602 (www.iccaweb.org).

[2]    The American Correctional Association, 4380 Forbes Boulevard, Lanham, MD 20706-4322 (www.corrections.com/aca/).

[3]    The National Institute of Corrections lists more than 1,200 programs in its 1989 Directory of Residential Community Corrections Facilities in the United States. The Directory does not list all small programs, particularly in rural areas. National Institute of Corrections, 1860 Industrial Circle, Suite A, Longmont, CA 80501 (www.nicic.org).

[4]    Harry E. Allen, Eric Carlson, Evalyn Parks, and Richard Seiter (1978). *Program Models: Halfway Houses* (Washington, DC: U.S. Department of Justice).

[5]    Halfway houses for juveniles tend to be more cost-effective than detention. Pratt, T. and M. Winston (1999). "The Search for the Frugal Grail." *Criminal Justice Policy Review*, 10(3):447-471.

[6]    Petersilia, J., S. Turner, J. Kahan, and J. Peterson (1985). *Granting Felons Probation: Risks and Alternatives*, p. 15. Santa Monica, CA: Rand.

[7]    Chapple, K. (2000). "Community Residential Programming for Female Offenders and Their Children." *Responding to Women Offenders in the Community*. Washington, DC: National Institute of Corrections, pp. 31-35 (www.nicic.org/pubs/2000/period180.pdf).

[8]    This question is explored in more detail in Nancy Hicks (October, 1987). "Halfway Houses and Corrections." Corrections Compendium, 12:1-7. See also G. Wilson (1985). "Halfway House Programs for Offenders." In L. Travis (ed.) *Probation, Parole and Community Corrections*, pp. 158-159. Prospect Heights, IL: Waveland; Latessa, E., and L. Travis (1992). "Residential Community Correctional Programs." In Byrne, J., and A. Lurigio (eds.) *Smart Sentencing? An Examination of the Emergence of Intermediate Sentencing*, pp. 166-181. Beverly Hills, CA: Sage; and Latessa, E., and H. Allen (1982). "Halfway Houses and Parole: A National Assessment." *Journal of Criminal Justice*, 10:153-163.

[9]    Federal Bureau of Prisons (2001). The Bureau in Brief (www.bop.gov/ipapg/ipabib.html). See also Thevenot, C. (April 15, 2001). "Halfway House: Training for Freedom." Las Vegas Review-Journal (www.lvrj.com/lvrj_home/2001/Apr-15-Sun-2001/news/15812376.html).

[10]   Harold Valentine (1991). *Prison Alternatives: Crowded Federal Prisons Can Transfer More Inmates to Halfway Houses*. Washington, DC: U.S. Government Accounting Office. The Bureau of Prisons under utilizes their contracted bedspace, further exacerbating their prison overcrowding problem.

11    This nostalgic view of warm-hearted older rural Americans trying to help the less successful, down-trodden and sodden of the Depression years by feeding any who ask, putting transients to work chopping wood or hauling water, and allowing the more needy to sleep in the barn has many adherents. No doubt this pattern of early philanthropic assistance was found in many sites, and continues in isolated locales. These "Mom and Pop" programs, often unofficial, were undoubtedly major sources of humanitarian assistance to the needy in some if not most of the nation during the early Twentieth Century, providing "three hots and a cot." If they exist today, they are an endangered species.

12    See IARCA Journal for a description of some more successful programs in rural America and urban England (Leeds Alternative to Care and Custody Scheme, and Roundabout Group). *IARCA Journal*, 3 (July, 1990).

13    See Thomas Berry (July, 1990). "Rural Community Corrections and the Challenge: Providing Comprehensive Services." IARCA Journal, 3:6-7.

14    Barbara Owen found that alcohol frequently accompanied drug use among parolees in California, leading to most parole violations. Barbara Owen (1991). "Normative Aspects of Alcohol and Parole Performance." *Drug Problems*, 18:453-476. See also, Langworthy, R., and E. Latessa (1993). "Treatment of Chronic Drunk Drivers: The Turning Point Project." *Journal of Criminal Justice*, 21:265-276; and Division of Criminal Justice Office of Research and Statistics (2000). *Executive Summary: 2000 Community Corrections Study Results* (www.cdpsweb.state.co.us/ors/pdf/docs/comcor01.pdf).

15    It is important to note that studies that do not employ a control group make it very difficult to gauge the effectiveness of programs, at least in terms of recidivism.

16    Judging from official crime statistics and victimization studies, the crime rate in the nation has been dropping for the past 10 years. Yet politicians and agencies with vested interests in maintaining concern over crime, have come to believe that public safety will be enhanced by "locking up criminals and throwing away the prison keys." This assumption is at least debatable and could be patently wrong.

17    There is some evidence that staff attributes within programs influence program effectiveness and recidivism. Staff selection and training, as well as program developments, could be improved by matching personality and attitudinal attributes. See Johnson J., and J. Bonta (1985). "Characteristics of Staff and Programs in Correctional Halfway Houses." *Journal of Offender Counseling, Services and Rehabilitation*, 9:39-51.

18    For more information about this movement, write: NIC at 320 1st St. NW, Washington, DC 20534 (www.nicic.org).

# References

Allen, H. (1995). "The American Dream and Crime in the Twenty-First Century." *Justice Quarterly*, 12:427-445.

Allen, H., E. Bowman, E. Carlson, E. Parks, and R. Seiter (1976). "Halfway Houses in the United States: An Analysis of the State of the Art." Paper presented at the International Halfway House Association, Guilford, England.

Allen, H., E. Carlson, E. Parks, and R. Seiter (1978). *Program Models: Halfway Houses*. Washington, DC: U.S. Department of Justice.

Allen, H. and C. Simonsen (2001). *Corrections in America*. Englewood Cliffs, NJ: Prentice-Hall.

Allen, H. and C. Simonsen (1995). *Corrections in America*. Englewood Cliffs, NJ: Prentice-Hall.

Allen, H. and C. Simonsen (1992). "Prison Overcrowding and the Conservative Ideology Revisited." Paper presented at the annual meeting of the Academy of Criminal Justice Sciences, Pittsburgh.

Berry, T. (1990). "Rural Community Corrections and the Challenge: Providing Comprehensive Services." *IARCA Journal*, 3(July):6-7.

Bonta, J., M. Law, and K. Hanson (1998). "The Prediction of Criminal and Violent Recidivism Among Mentally Disordered Offenders: A Meta-Analysis." *Psychological Bulletin*, 123(2):123-142.

Bouffard, J., D. MacKenzie, and L. Hickman (2000). "Effectiveness of Vocational Education and Employment Programs for Adults Offenders." *Journal of Offender Rehabilitation*, 31(1/2):1-42.

Bureau of Justice Statistics (2001). Nation's State Prison Population Falls in Second of 2000—First such Decline Since 1972. (www.ojp.usdoj.gov/bjs/pub/press/p00pr.htm).

Bureau of Justice Statistics (1995). *Correctional Populations in the United States*. Washington, DC: U.S. Department of Justice.

Camp, C. and G. Camp (2000). *The 2000 Corrections Yearbook: Adult Corrections*. Middletown, CT: Criminal Justice Institute.

Camp, C. and G. Camp (1997). *The Corrections Yearbook*. South Salem, NY: The Criminal Justice Institute, Inc.

Chapple, K. (2000). "Community Residential Programming for Female Offenders and Their Children." *Responding to Women Offenders in the Community*. Washington, DC: National Institute of Corrections, pp. 31-35

Cohn, J. (1973). *A Study of Community-Based Correctional Needs in Massachusetts*. Boston, MA: Massachusetts Department of Corrections.

Cullen, F. and P. Gendreau (2001). "From Nothing Works to What Works." *The Prison Journal*, 81(3):313-338.

Division of Criminal Justice Office of Research and Statistics (2001). Executive Summary: 2000 Community Corrections Results (www.cdpsweb.state.co.us/ors/pdf/docs/com cor01.pdf).

Donnelly, P. and B.E. Forschner (1987). "Predictors of Success in a Co-Correctional Halfway House: A Discriminant Analysis." *Journal of Crime and Justice*, 10:1-22.

Dowell, D., C. Klein, and C. Krichmar (1985). "Evaluation of a Halfway House for Women." *Journal of Criminal Justice*, 13:217-226.

Drug Use Forecasting (2000). *Annual Report on Adult and Juvenile Arrestees*. Washington, DC: National Institute of Justice.

Federal Bureau of Prisons (December 14, 2001). *The Bureau in Brief* (www.bop.gov/ipapg/ipabib.html).

Friday, P. and R. Wertkin (1995). "Effects of Programming and Race on Recidivism: Residential Probation." In Smykla J. and W. Selke (eds.) *Intermediate Sanctions: Sentencing in the 1990s*, pp. 209-217. Cincinnati, OH: Anderson Publishing Co.

Greenfield, L. and S. Minor-Harper (1991). *Women in Prison*. Washington, DC: U.S. Department of Justice.

Hamm, M. and J. Kite (1991). "The Role of Offender Rehabilitation in Family Violence Policy: The Batterers Anonymous Experiment." *Criminal Justice Review*, 16:227-248.

Hartmann, D., P. Friday, and K. Minor (1994). "Residential Probation: A Seven-Year Follow-Up Study of Halfway House Discharges." *Journal of Criminal Justice*, 22(6):503-515.

Hicks, N. (1987). "Halfway Houses and Corrections." *Corrections Compendium*, 12(October):1-7.

Huskey, B. (1992). "The Expanding Use of CRCs." *Corrections Today*, 54(8):70-74.

Johnson, J. and J. Bonta (1985). "Characteristics of Staff and Programs in Correctional Halfway Houses." *Journal of Offender Counseling, Services and Rehabilitation*, 9:39-51.

Langworthy, R. and E. Latessa (1996). "Treatment of Chronic Drunk Drivers: A Four-Year Follow-Up of the Turning Point Project." *Journal of Criminal Justice*, 24:273-281.

Langworthy, R. and E. Latessa (1993). "Treatment of Chronic Drunk Drivers: The Turning Point Project." *Journal of Criminal Justice*, 21:265-276.

Latessa, E. (1998). *Public Protection Through Offender Risk Reduction: Putting Research Into Practice*. Washington, DC: National Institute of Corrections.

Latessa, E., and H. Allen (1982). "Halfway Houses and Parole: A National Assessment." *Journal of Criminal Justice*, 10:153-163.

Latessa, E., R. Langworthy, and A.Thomas (1995). *Community Residential Treatment Program Evaluation for Talbert House Inc.* Cincinnati, OH: Division of Criminal Justice, University of Cincinnati.

Latessa, E. and L. Travis (1992). "Residential Community Correctional Programs." In Byrne, J.,and A. Lurigio (eds.) *Smart Sentencing? An Examination of the Emergence of Intermediate Sentencing*, pp. 166-181. Beverly Hills, CA: Sage.

Latessa, E. and L. Travis (1991). "Halfway House or Probation: A Comparison of Alternative Dispositions." *Journal of Crime and Justice*, 14(1):53-76.

Leon, A., S. Dziegielewski, and C. Tubiak (1999). "A Program Evaluation of a Juvenile Halfway House: Considerations for Strengthening Program Components." *Evaluation and Program Planning*, 22:141-153.

Lowenkamp, C.T., and E.J. Latessa (2004). "Residential Community Corrections and the Risk Principle: Lessons Learned in Ohio." In *Ohio Corrections Research Compendium, Volume II*. Columbus, OH: Ohio Department of Research and Corrections.

Michaels, D., D. Zoloth, and P. Alcabes (1992). "Homelessness and Indicators of Mental Illness Among Inmates in New York City's Correctional System." *Hospital and Community Psychiatry*, 32:150-154.

Munden, D., Tewksbury, R., and E. Grossi (1999). "Intermediate Sanctions and the Halfway Back Program in Kentucky." *Criminal Justice Policy Review*, 9:431-449.

National Institute of Corrections (1989). 1989 Directory of Residential Community Corrections Facilities in the United States. Longmont, CO: National Institute of Corrections.

Owen, B. (1991). "Normative Aspects of Alcohol and Parole Performance." *Drug Problems*, 18:453-476.

Pratt, T. and M. Winston (1999). "The Search for the Frugal Grail." *Criminal Justice Policy Review*, 10(3):447-471.

Pratt, T., A. Holsinger, and E. Latessa (2000). "Treating the Chronic DUI Offender: 'Turning Point' Ten Years Later." *Journal of Criminal Justice*, 28:271-281.

Peters, R. and H. Hills (1999). "Community Treatment and Supervision Strategies for Offenders with Co-Occurring Disorders: What Works?" In Latessa, E., (ed.) *What Works Strategic Solutions: The International Community Corrections Association Examines Substance Abuse*, pp. 81-136. Laurel, MD: ACA Press.

Petersilia, J., S. Turner, J. Kahan, and J. Peterson (1985). *Granting Felons Probation: Risks and Alternatives*. Santa Monica, CA: Rand.

President's Commission on Law Enforcement and Administration of Justice (1967). *Corrections*. Washington, DC: U.S. Government Printing Office.

Rush, G. (1992). *The Dictionary of Criminal Justice*. Guilford, CT: Duskin.

Seiter R. and E. Carlson (1977). "Residential Inmate Aftercare: The State of the Art." *Offender Rehabilitation*, 4:78-94.

Solicitor General of Canada (1998) *Mentally Disordered Offenders* (http://www.sgc.gc.ca/epub/Corr/e199805a/e199805a.htm).

Thevenot, C., (2001). "Halfway House: Training for Freedom." *Las Vegas Review-Journal* (www.lvrj.com/lvrj_home/2001/Apr-15-Sun-2001/news/15812376.html).

Twill, S., L. Nackerbud, E. Risler et al. (1998). "Changes in Measured Loneliness, Control and Social Support Among Parolees in a Halfway House." *Journal of Offender Rehabilitation*, 27(3/4):77-92.

Valentine, H. (1991). *Prison Alternatives: Crowded Federal Prisons Can Transfer More Inmates to Halfway Houses*. Washington, DC: U.S. Government Accounting Office.

Wilson, G. (1985). "Halfway House Programs for Offenders." In Travis, L. (ed.) *Probation, Parole and Community Corrections*, pp. 151-164. Prospect Heights, IL: Waveland.

## 10

# Special Populations in Community Corrections

[America's War on Drugs] has, in fact, been
responsible for a massive increase in prison
populations that has been borne dispropor-
tionately by minority offenders.
                —Robert Johnson and Hans Toch

Successful sex offender management requires
more governmental funding. Unfortunately,
public aversion to spending money on sex offenders undercuts their management.
                —R.J. Konopasky

## Introduction

We now come to a chapter that deals with special populations of offenders We have chosen to focus on four specific types of clients: sex offenders, substance abusers, mentally disordered offenders, and female
offenders. These categories do not exhaust the list of possible types of
special category offenders.[1]

## The Sex Offender

Each state has differing laws that regulate sexual conduct, and correctional systems typically deal with three special needs groups of sexual
offenders: rapists, child molesters (pedophiles), and prostitutes. Each of
these categories has differing motivations, modes of operation, challenges, and dangers. Almost all are handled, either initially or later, by
community corrections. We begin with a brief discussion of public opinion and fear, two factors that color both legal and treatment issues with
sex offenders.

Box 10.1

**Sex Offenders**

Persons who have committed a sexual act prohibited by law, such as rape, incest, child molestation, or prostitution for sexual, economic, psychological, or situational reasons.

On a given day, there are approximately 234,000 offenders convicted of rape or sexual assault under the care, custody or control of corrections agencies. Nearly 60 percent of these sex offenders are under conditional supervision in the community.

The median age of the victims of imprisoned sexual assaulters was less than 13 years old; the median age of rape victims was about 22 years.

An estimated 24 percent of those serving time for rape and 19 percent of those serving time for sexual assault had been on probation or parole at the time of the offense for which they were in State prison three years earlier.

Source: Bureau of Justice Statistics (2002). Criminal Offenders Statistics (www.ojp.usdoj.gov/bjs/crimoff.htm).

## Public Opinion and Fear

With the possible exception of the violent offender, no type of correctional client evokes more concern from the public than the sex offender. Sex offenders, especially child molesters, are treated with both disdain and violence. Few offenders are as stigmatized or reviled as child molesters.

Many Americans fear sex assaulters, gang rapists, serial rapists, stranger rapists, child abductors, and child abusers. Rape is one of the most feared events as well as a frightening and misunderstood crime. Others feel that treatment of sexual assaulters is undeserved and ineffective. Politicians tend to follow public opinion,[2] despite the evidence that there is widespread support for treatment and rehabilitation of offenders ranging from the very young to geriatric prisoners. Opinion polls overestimate the amount of support for punitive approaches to special need clients, particularly for juveniles (Cullen & Moon, 2002). There is no doubt that public sentiment works against the establishment and funding of treatment programs and options. Yet there is substantial evidence that treatment works (Sherman, Gottfredson & MacKenzie, 1997; Lipton, Pearson & Wexler, 1999; Yates, 2002). Specifically, three

Box 10.2

## Dangerous Sex Offenders

Washington State's 1990 Community Protection Act was the first law authorizing public notification when dangerous sex offenders are released into the community. It was thought that sex offender registration laws are necessary because:

- Sex offenders pose a high risk of re-offending after release from custody.

- Protecting the public from sex offenders is a primary governmental interest, and the rights of sex offenders take backseat to public interest.

- Releasing certain information about sex offenders to public agencies and the general public will contribute to public safety.

It took the brutal 1994 murder-rape of Megan Kanka (1994) to prompt public demand for broad-based community notification. President Clinton signed Megan's Law in 1996, and it allows the States discretion to establish criteria for disclosure, but compels them to make personal and private information about registered sex offenders available to the public. It was believed that such notification:

- Assists law enforcement agencies during investigations.

- Establishes legal grounds to hold offenders.

- Deters sex offenders from committing new offenses.

- Offers citizens information useful in protecting their children from victimization.

Some States mandate registration and penalize non-registration with imprisonment. One link to State procedures can be found at www.klasskids.org/pg-legmeg.htm.

Sex offender registration has been criticized as a flawed strategy for controlling sex crime, reflecting a skewed view of sex offenders, and encouraging vigilantism. Probation and parole agents' responsibilities were negatively impacted.

Sources: Presser, L. and E. Gunnison (1999). "Strange Bedfellows." *Crime & Delinquency*, 45(3):299-315; and Zavitz, R. and M. Farkas (200). "The Impact of Sex-Offender Notification on Probation/Parole in Wisconsin." *International Journal of Offender Therapy and Comparative Criminology*, 44(1):8-21.

Table 10.1
**Meta-analyses Demonstrating Treatment Reduces Sexual Recidivism**

|  | Number of Studies | Percent Reduction |
|---|---|---|
| Gallagher, Wilson, Hirschfield, Coggeshall, and MacKenzie (1999) | 25 | 21% |
| Hanson et al. (2002) | 43 | 12% |
| Lösel and Schmucker (2005) | 69 | 37% |

meta-analyses on the topic have been conducted, and the results from each review indicate that treatment has an appreciable impact on recidivism. First, Gallagher, Wilson, Hirschfield, Coggeshall, and MacKenzie (1999) located a total of 25 studies and found a 21 percent reduction in sexual recidivism overall. Second, Hanson et al. (2002) reviewed 43 studies involving more than 9,000 sex offenders and found a 12 percent reduction in sexual recidivism. More recently, Lösel and Schmucker (2005) quantitatively synthesized 69 studies and found a 37 percent reduction in sexual recidivism compared to controls. See Table 10.1, above.

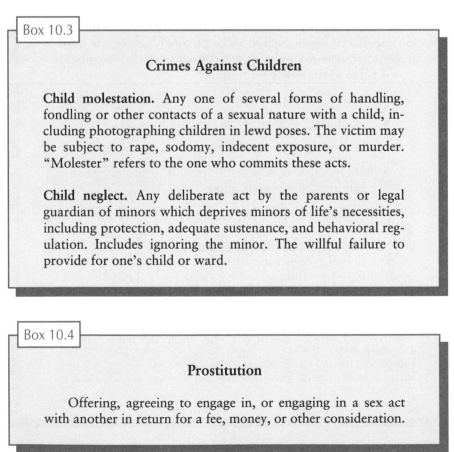

Box 10.3

**Crimes Against Children**

**Child molestation.** Any one of several forms of handling, fondling or other contacts of a sexual nature with a child, including photographing children in lewd poses. The victim may be subject to rape, sodomy, indecent exposure, or murder. "Molester" refers to the one who commits these acts.

**Child neglect.** Any deliberate act by the parents or legal guardian of minors which deprives minors of life's necessities, including protection, adequate sustenance, and behavioral regulation. Includes ignoring the minor. The willful failure to provide for one's child or ward.

Box 10.4

**Prostitution**

Offering, agreeing to engage in, or engaging in a sex act with another in return for a fee, money, or other consideration.

## The Rapist

There are many different types of rapists, including date rapists, stranger rapists, family rapists, acquaintance rapists, gang rapists, homosexual rapists, and serial rapists. All have three things in common: a victim or victims, sexual intercourse or attempted sexual intercourse with persons against their will, and force or threat of use of force. Most of the victims are female and view rape as a brutal personal assault. Many rape victims feel that the act was not as much sexually motivated as much as it was a physical assault fed by a desire for violent coercion and power. In this light, rape should be seen as an act of violence, not an act fueled primarily by sexual arousal. Almost never is the female responsible for the act, although defense attorneys may use this line of argument in their efforts to blame the victim.

---

**Box 10.5**

### Rape

Sexual intercourse or attempted sexual intercourse with persons against their will, by force or threat of force. Date rape is forcible rape in which the victim has consented to the company of the offender but has not agreed to have sexual intercourse.

Statutory rape is sexual intercourse with a person who has consented in fact but is deemed, because of age, to be legally incapable of consent.

---

### Forcible Rape

The definition of rape and forcible rape varies across jurisdictions and the Federal Bureau of Investigation (FBI) defines rape as the carnal knowledge of a female forcibly and against her will, including assaults and attempts to commit rape by force or threat of force. Not included are statutory rape (without force) and other sex offenses. This definition does not define rape of a male as forcible rape.

The extent of forcible rape in the nation is only estimated. The FBI reported 90,100 rapes of females in 2000, but the National Crime Victimization Survey (Rennison, 2001) estimates three times that number for females age 12 and older. This suggests that only one in three of the incidents were reported to the police. Many victims fail to report because they are embarrassed, blame themselves, feel the police will not act, anticipate that they, as the victim, will be blamed for the crime, or know their rapist and fear retaliation (their assaulters were fathers, brothers, uncles, friends, or neighbors).

A darker side of rape can be seen when examining sexual assault of young children. The Bureau of Justice Statistics (2000) reported that, in each sexual assault category except forcible rape, children below the age of 12 were about half the victims. They represent one in eight forcible rapes, and females under age 12 represent one in six of the reported rapes. Almost one-half of the offenders of victims under age 6 were family members, as were four in 10 offenders who sexually assaulted juveniles age 12 through 17. Knowing that a child under age 6 was assaulted in the residence suggests the most likely offender was a juvenile acquaintance age 12 through 17 or a family member age 24 through 34. Schmalleger (1999:69) reports:

> . . . 20 percent of female victims under age 12 had been raped by their fathers, 26 percent were attacked by other relatives, and 50 percent were assaulted by friends and acquaintances. Only four percent of rape victims under 12 were attacked by strangers.

Both the official and victimization statistics significantly under-report rape. Other victim studies suggest that at least 20 percent of adult women and 12 percent of adolescent girls have experienced sexual abuse or assault sometimes in their lives.[3]

---

**Box 10.6**

### Child Abuse

Any act of commission or omission that endangers or impairs a child's physical or emotional health and development: sexual abuse, exploitation, negligent treatment, and maltreatment by a person who is responsible for the child's welfare.

The major forms are (a) physical, including neglect or lack of adequate supervision; (b) emotional, including deprivation; and (c) sexual. The abuser is someone usually close to the victim, such as mother, father, stepparent, grandparent, or other caretaker who engages in a repeated pattern of behavior. Rarely is the abuser a total stranger.

---

**Box 10.7**

### Incest

Sexual relations between close relatives other than husband and wife.

## Stranger-to-Stranger Rape

When victims are attacked by strangers, the attack is likely to be more violent, and the attacker likely to be armed and to threaten the victims. The offender is likely to be a substance abuser (Hsu & Starzynskki, 1990). The victim is likely to be harmed physically; the viciously harmed female is more likely to report the attack. Most victims were not provocateurs (Warren, Reboussin, Hazelwood, et al., 1999).

Serial rapists (offenders raping several victims in three or more separate events) are particularly problematic among the stranger-to-stranger category, for many of the victims are killed or simply "disappear." Recent studies of serial rapists suggest they are more likely to be white rather than minority status, select victims based on sexual attractiveness and vulnerability (Stevens, 1999), rape their victims for longer periods of time and use more profanity, be sadistic, and to escalate levels of violence over time (Knight, Warren, Reboussin, et al., 1998). A study of United Kingdom serial rapists indicates itinerancy and mobility. A majority of attacks were initiated within five miles of the victim's residence. Offenders tended to target locations where numbers of suitable victims were available, and rapists spent considerable time "prowling" or "hunting" over those larger areas in search of victims, occasionally stumbling over victims during relatively sophisticated property offenses. Perpetrators are more likely to have anti-social ("psychopathic") personalities (Davies & Dale, 1996). Victims of serial rapists generally require extensive therapy over long periods of time, sometimes in therapeutic communities (Winick & Levine, 1992).

## Acquaintance Rape

At least one-half of the rapes reported to police involve someone known to the victim, including family members, friends, and suitors. The victimization incidents involving female victims under age 12 suggest this type of rape is vastly under-reported. We focus briefly on date rape and marital rape in order to comprehend the dynamics of and treatment facing offenders and the correctional system,

Date rape, often defined as unlawful forced sexual intercourse with a woman against her will, occurs within the context of a dating or courting relationship. Date rape is a frequent event and not limited to this nation. A survey of Canadian college women found that one in four had sexual relations when they did not want to during the past year.[4] An estimated 15-25 percent of all college women in the nation are victims of rape or attempted rape. The actual incidence is probably higher, as many victims blame themselves for not being more forceful in their own defense, or for using drugs or alcohol prior to the rape. [Date rape differs

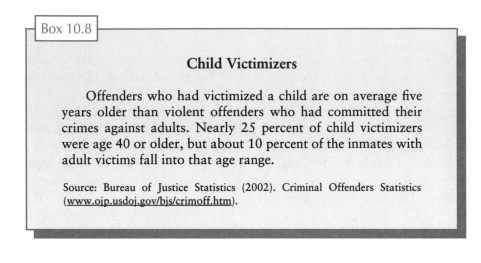

Box 10.8

### Child Victimizers

Offenders who had victimized a child are on average five years older than violent offenders who had committed their crimes against adults. Nearly 25 percent of child victimizers were age 40 or older, but about 10 percent of the inmates with adult victims fall into that age range.

Source: Bureau of Justice Statistics (2002). Criminal Offenders Statistics (www.ojp.usdoj.gov/bjs/crimoff.htm).

from campus gang rape in that usually only one perpetrator is involved in date rape, the victim and victimizer know each other intimately, the event is not generally viewed by others, and the sexual assault is better viewed as a coercive sexual encounter than as a violent rape.]

The perpetrator may feel that he has invested so much time and money in his date that he is owed sexual relations, that sexual intimacy is a validating element in the progression of the relationship, that other couples in similarly lengthy dating processes had begun sexual activities, or that "she said 'no' but really meant 'yes'." Perhaps one in 10 date rapes are reported to the police, because victims are embarrassed or frightened, some do not perceive date rape as "real rape" which they believe requires an attack by a stranger, or fear they will be stigmatized or victimized by the police. Some men (particularly adolescents) have difficulty relating to women and treat them more as sexual objects who should be responsive to their sexual appetites, rather than as worthy and independent partners who should be treated as such (Kerschner, 1996). Stereotyped relations and perceptions abound in the area of rape.

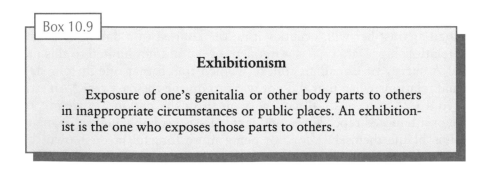

Box 10.9

### Exhibitionism

Exposure of one's genitalia or other body parts to others in inappropriate circumstances or public places. An exhibitionist is the one who exposes those parts to others.

## Marital Rape

Marital or spousal rape is rape by a male domiciled with his wife, although the rapist/victim role can be reversed. Generally, it is spousal rape if the husband forces her to have nonconsensual intercourse. Until recently, a legally married man could not be prosecuted for raping his wife under the "marital exemption:" a woman entering marriage was believed to implicitly give her consent to sexual intercourse at the behest of her husband. Over the last two decades, research into spousal abuse has identified marital rape as one part of a continuing pattern of spousal abuse, sometimes accompanied by sadistic and violent beatings. Every person is worthy of protection under the law, and almost every state has now enacted legislation defining marital rape as a crime.

The extent of marital rape is unknown, but is a persistent problem in a large number of marriages (Straus, 1988). It is under-reported in part because society tends to blame and judge rape victims harshly. Women assaulted by their husbands have reported that the assault was one of a series of similar attacks (Riggs, Kilpatrick & Resnick, 1992) occurring in three cycles: tension building, acute battering, and subsequent contrite behavior by the husband, with recurrent cycles. Considerable evidence suggests that homes in which spousal rape occurs are characterized by high levels of tension and distrust among spouses and their children (Mahoney & Williams, 1998). A study in Great Britain found 13 percent of wives had sexual intercourse with their husbands against their will and, in total, one in five had been raped either inside or outside of marriage (Painter & Farrington, 1998). Finally, multiple sexual victimization (such as incest and marital rape) is a co-occurring problem among victims and, to some extent, among perpetrators. New psychotherapy models and treatments are needed (Walker, 2000).

This review of sexual offenders suggests the heterogeneity of these crimes and acts of violence. As a result, treatment programs are as varied as crime type; some treatment programs fail to focus on those factors contributing to the commission of the crime and thus erroneously address objectives that would not lessen re-offending. A study of sex offender treatment in Vermont outlined the goals of an institutional treatment program:

- Get the offender to accept responsibility for his actions and the harm done to the victim and others.

- Deal with distorted thinking used to justify his actions.

- Teach the offender to understand the impact of his behavior on victims and to show more empathic behavior with other people around them (recognize others' emotional distress, identify another's perspective, communicate empathy toward others, etc.).

- Address such competency issues as anger management, substance abuse treatment issues, communicating with opposite gender adults, improving dating skills, and seeking therapy.

- Deal with sexual arousal to reduce inappropriate object arousal and enhance arousal with an appropriate adult partner.

- Plan relapse prevention that teaches the offender how and when to intervene in his own patterns of behavior that lead up to a sexual offense (drinking and remaining aloof, alone and physically inactive can build up to fantasizing about a victim, and this requires such personal intervention as initiating counseling, attending Alcoholics Anonymous group meetings, and calling a designated crime prevention hotline). Relapse prevention includes teaching offenders how to recognize the chain of events leading up to their current offense and to practice strategies for breaking this chain.

- Plan for release into the community and set up a support team of people who know the offender's issues and can provide support and monitoring, including sex offender-specific outpatient treatment.

Six years after release, five percent of the men who completed the Vermont treatment program had committed another sexual offense and were caught, in contrast to 30 percent of the men who got only partial treatment (left the program or were expelled from the program for rules violations). Thirty percent of the incarcerated men who refused to enter the program were arrested again for some form of sexual abuse (Cumming, 2001).

A recent study of adolescent sexual assaulters from a Wisconsin secure juvenile correctional institution included perpetrators of sexual assault against children, rapists of same age or older victims, and non-sex offense adjudicated adolescents. The rapists and child offender groups completed a mandatory, serious sex offender treatment program that included group psychotherapy, general education, sex education, behavior management programming, and individual and family therapy. Eight years later, adolescent sex offenders were found to less frequently offend sexually than did the non- sex-offending adolescent delinquents, although all three groups were significantly more likely to be involved with sexual assaults than was the general male population in the nation.

Perhaps the most sophisticated review of effectiveness of treatment on various types of sexual offenders was undertaken by Yates (2002). She concluded that treatment can significantly reduce sexual reoffending for a variety of offenders, both juvenile and adult, if behavioral-specific treatments are based on diagnosis of needs, development of a treatment plan, delivery of treatment in a coherent fashion by competent therapists under direction of a supervisor, and review and revamping of treatment if it is not working. She concluded that dynamic risk factors are amenable to change and will lower criminal reoffending. These factors include attitudes, values and beliefs; criminogenic peers; and instability of employment. For juveniles, treatment targets include:

- Increasing responsibility and accountability for behavior;

- Addressing cognitive, affective and behavioral factors which support sexual offending;

- Reducing deviant sexual arousal;

- Improving relationships among family members;

- Enhancing victim empathy;

- Improving social skills;

- Developing healthy attitudes towards relationships and sex;

- Reducing the effects of personal trauma; and

- Targeting cognitive distortions

Yates reported on treatment effectiveness of adolescents six years after a comprehensive, cognitive-behavioral, relapse prevention sexual offender program. Effectiveness was measured by recidivism, comparing a treatment group with a similar non-treatment group. The results are found in Table 10.2. Treated sex offenders recidivated significantly less frequently and less violently. Sex offender criminal behavior is amenable to intervention and the preponderance of evidence is that treatment works for most perpetrators (although there remain considerable challenges to develop effective treatment for the relatively rare psychopathic sex offender).

Table 10.2
**Comparison of Recidivism of Treated and Untreated Adolescent Sex Offenders**

| Group: | Recidivated sexually | Recidivated violently but not sexually | Recidivated nonviolently |
|---|---|---|---|
| Treated | 5.2% | 18.9% | 20.7% |
| Untreated | 17.8 | 32.2 | 50.0 |

Source: Yates, P. (2002). "What Works: Effective Intervention with Sex Offenders." In Allen, H. (ed.) *What Works: Risk Reduction: Interventions for Special Needs Offenders*, p. 148. Lanham, MD: American Correctional Association.

Box 10.10

### Psychopathy

Hare defines the clinical construct of psychopathy by a combination of interpersonal, affective and lifestyle characteristics. Interpersonally, psychopaths are arrogant, callous, dominant, grandiose, manipulative, and superficial. Affectively, they lack guilt or anxiety, and are short-tempered and unable to form strong emotional bonds with others. Interpersonal and affective characteristics are frequently found with a socially deviant lifestyle that includes impulsive and irresponsible behavior, and a tendency to ignore or flagrantly violate social conventions and mores. While not all psychopaths come to the attention of the criminal justice system, they are at high risk of violence and aggression. In maximum security prisons, they may constitute 20-25 percent of the general population.

Sources: Hare, R. (2002). "Psychopathy as a Risk Factor for Violence." In Allen, H. (ed.) *What Works: Risk Reduction: Interventions for Special Needs Offenders*, pp. 165-184. Lanham, MD: American Correctional Association.

Box 10.11

### Female Sex Offenders

The extent of female sex offending, like that of males, is vastly underreported. Compared with men, very few women are convicted of sex offenses (except those associated with prostitution) and a substantial proportion of those convicted are convicted as accomplices of men. Only two to five percent of sex offenders are female.

Female sex offenders have commonly been physically and sexually abused as children, and are more likely to be young, poorly educated, from lower socioeconomic status, have few social supports, and be "willing to do anything to fit in." They are less likely than men to use physical force (or will use it less) than do men, and are less likely to be predatory. Unlike male sexual offenders, females are less likely to deny what they have done and more likely to accept responsibility earlier. They typically offend against female children; male victims, female infant, and adult victims are rare.

## Substance Abusers

Substance abuse is the unauthorized possession of any controlled substance, whether it is nonmedical use of psychotherapeutic drugs, illicit substances, or inhalation of common household products. Alcohol, probably the most commonly abused substance, is illegal for minors to possess but is widely used by Americans. There are significant social, economic, and personal costs in substance abuse. Substance abuse has also been cast in a legal perspective, rather than the set of medical problems it represents, and has given rise to "dope fiend" stereotypes and frequent incarceration.

Each year, drug and alcohol abuse contributes to the death of more than 120,000 Americans. Drugs and alcohol cost taxpayers more than $294 billion annually in preventable health care costs, extra law enforcement, auto crashes, crime, and lost productivity. Families of victims of drunk drivers suffer enormous hurt, not to mention the crimes of higher insurance premiums and costs, lost productivity, jail and prison overcrowding, and repeat criminal behaviors from unaddressed alcohol problems. While the overall use of drugs in the nation has fallen 50 percent in the past 20 years, adolescent drug use has increased during the past decade. However, since 1996, drug use by youth has leveled off, with the past several years showing a moderating trend in drug use among adolescents, although the use of inhalants has increased slightly.[5]

---

**Box 10.12**

### Drug Abuse

**Drug.** Any chemical substance used for psychological or physical purposes.

**Drug Abuse.** Any offense involving the use, possession, manufacture, or distribution of illegal or controlled substance (e.g., cocaine, crack, marijuana, heroin, methamphetamine). Includes "designer" drugs.

**Drug addict.** A person with dependency upon a given substance, including narcotics and controlled substances, alcohol, or prescription medicines.

---

In calendar 2000, an estimated 14 million Americans were current illicit drug users, meaning they had used an illicit drug during the month prior to an interview. This is more than six percent of the population age 12 or older. According to data from a 2004 survey, approximately 110 million Americans age 12 or older (46 percent of the population) report using illicit drugs at least once in their lifetime (SAMHSA, 2005). Furthermore, a total of 15 percent of the general population reported using an illicit drug in the past year, and 8 percent reported use within the past month. Drug use varies by employment. An estimated 15 percent of unemployed adults were current illicit drug users in 2000, compared with eight percent of part-time employed adults and six percent of full-time employed adults.

Just under four million Americans are dependent on illicit drugs, representing almost two percent of the total population aged 12 and older.[6] Another eight million Americans are dependent on alcohol (about four percent of the population). Overall, almost five percent of the American people are dependent on either alcohol or drugs.

Marijuana is the most commonly used illicit drug, used by about 75 percent of current illicit drug users. Men continue to have higher rate of current illicit drug use than women. Finally, some two million youths age 12 through 17 had used inhalants (glue, shoe polish, gasoline, lighter fluid, etc.) at sometimes in their lives as of 2000; this constitutes about nine percent of youth. A total of 45.7 percent of high school seniors reported having ever used marijuana/hashish in 2004. A total of 8.1 percent reported ever having used cocaine, and 1.5 percent reported ever used heroin (Bureau of Justice Statistics, 2005). See Table 10.3 for a review of the reported drug and alcohol use by high school seniors in 2004. The majority of high school seniors report they could fairly easily or very easily obtain drugs (Table 10.4).

Table 10.3
**Percent of High School Seniors Who Used Cocaine, 1989-2004**

| Year | Within 12 Months | Past 30 Days |
|------|------------------|--------------|
| 1989 | 6.5 | 2.8 |
| 1990 | 5.3 | 1.9 |
| 1991 | 3.5 | 1.4 |
| 1992 | 3.1 | 1.3 |
| 1993 | 3.3 | 1.3 |
| 1994 | 3.6 | 1.5 |
| 1995 | 4 | 1.8 |
| 1996 | 4.9 | 2 |
| 1997 | 5.5 | 2.3 |
| 1998 | 5.7 | 2.4 |
| 1999 | 6.2 | 2.6 |
| 2000 | 5 | 2.1 |
| 2001 | 4.8 | 2.1 |
| 2002 | 5 | 2.3 |
| 2003 | 4.8 | 2.1 |
| 2004 | 5.3 | 2.3 |

Source: University of Michigan, Monitoring the Future, Press Release, *Overall teen drug use continues gradual decline, but use of inhalants rises*, December 21, 2004.

Table 10.4
**Percent of High School Seniors Reporting They Could Obtain Drugs Fairly Easily or Very Easily (2000)**

| Drug | Percent |
|------|---------|
| Marijuana | 88.5% |
| Amphetamines | 57.1 |
| Cocaine | 47.8 |
| LSD | 46.9 |
| Crack | 42.6 |
| Barbiturate | 37.4 |
| Tranquilizers | 33.8 |
| Heroin | 33.5 |

Source: Bureau of Justice Statistics (2001). Drug Use (www.ojp.udoj.gov/bjs/dcf/du.htm).

Data from 2004 indicate that marijuana and cocaine use is the most prevalent among persons age 18 to 25 (see Table 10.5). Overall, an estimated seven million persons (about three percent of the population) drove under the influence of an illicit drug during the last 12 months, but this rate tripled (to almost 11 percent) among young adults aged 18 to 25.

Table 10.5
**Drug Use by Age of Respondent, 2004**

| Drug use | Age of Respondent | | |
|----------|-------|-------|-------------|
| | 12-17 | 18-25 | 26 or older |
| **Marijuana** | | | |
| Last month | 7.6% | 16.1% | 4.1% |
| Last year | 14.5% | 27.8% | 7.0% |
| **Cocaine** | | | |
| Last month | 0.5% | 2.1% | 0.7% |
| Last year | 1.6% | 6.6% | 1.7% |

Source: SAMSHA, Office of Applied Studies, 2004 National Survey on Drug Use and Health: National Findings, September 2005. (www.oas.samhsa.gov/NSDUH/.2k4results/2k4results.htm#high)

## Alcohol Abuse

Almost one-half of Americans ages 12 or older report being current drinkers of alcohol, translating to an estimated 104 million people. Overall, heavy drinking was reported by almost six percent of the population ages 12 and older (13 million people). Some 10 million people age 12 to 20 reported drinking alcohol in the month prior to a national survey (27 percent of the age group). Almost seven million were binge drinkers and two million were heavy drinkers. [Binge drinking is defined as the consumption of the equivalent of one-half gallon of liquor in a single day.] Young adults aged 18 to 22 enrolled full-time in college were more likely than their peers not enrolled to report any use, binge drinking and heavy use of alcohol (62, 41 and 16%, respectively). Unfortunately, one in ten Americans age 12 and older (2000) had driven under the influence of alcohol at least once in the 12 months prior to the national survey, a figure even more concentrated in the age group 18-25 (20%).

---

**Box 10.13**

### Use of Alcohol by Convicted Offenders

Among the nine million convicted offenders under the jurisdiction of corrections agencies in 2003, nearly 2.6 million, or about 36 percent, were estimated to have been drinking at the time of the offense. The vast majority (about two million) of these alcohol-involved offenders were sentenced to supervision in the community: 1.7 million on probation and more than 260,000 on parole.

Alcohol use at the time of the offense was commonly found among those convicted of public-order crimes, a type of offense most highly represented among those on probation and in jail. Among violent offenders, 41 percent of probationers and 41 percent of those in local jails, 38 percent of those in state prisons, and one in five of those in federal prisons were estimated to have been drinking when they committed the crime.

Source: Bureau of Justice Statistics (2002). *Criminal Offenders Statistics* (www.ojp.usdoj.gov/bjs/crimoff.htm). Data extrapolated from 1996 statistics.

---

An estimated 2.8 million people (more than one percent of the population) had received some kind of drug or alcohol treatment in the 12 months prior to the national survey in 1999. Of this group, 1.6 million received treatment of illicit drugs and 2.3 million for alcohol.

Programs that treat drunk driving fall into one of three major categories: (1) long-term treatment designed to cure pathological drinking; (2) programs that prevent the drunk driver from driving; and (3) educational programs intended to correct poor judgment. Outcome studies suggest that individualized treatment over an extended time period generally create promising results from chronic drunk drivers.

# Criminal Justice System Involvement

Despite generally declining rates of drug use (and stable rates of alcohol use) over the past two decades, drug arrests have risen significantly over the same time period. According to the FBI's Uniform Crime Report (2000:226), roughly 1,024,000 drug violation arrests were made in 2000, up sharply from 580,900 in 1980 (an increase of 76%). These arrests have resulted in a dramatic increase in prison and jail populations. According to the Bureau of Justice Statistics (2000), an estimated 250,000 State and Federal inmates were imprisoned for drug-related offenses, compared to 148,600 in 1990. About 112,000 people were held in jails for drug-related offenses, compared to 20,400 in 1983.

# Substance Abuse and Treatment

Offenders coming to the attention of the correctional system are, in general, extensively involved in the abuse of drugs and alcohol. The further the offender penetrates into the correctional system, the greater the risk posed and higher the personal needs, and more difficult management issues become. The difficulty is in part due to the filtering system by which offenders are processed, and in part to the impacts of incarceration and imprisonment on offenders, their families, economic situation and prospects. In addition, many offenders are made more hostile, recalcitrant, and hardened by the experience of imprisonment, particularly in institutions providing few services and primarily warehousing offenders. We examine the relationship between substance abuse and crime by legal status: probationers, jail inmates, prisoners, and parolees.

## *Probationers*

The first national survey of adults on probation in 1995 found that nearly 70 percent reported past drug use (Bureau of Justice Statistics, 2000). One in three said they were using illegal drugs in the month before the offense, and slightly more than one in seven were on drugs when they committed their offense. More than 20% (one in five) were on probation for driving under the influence of drugs or alcohol, and one in four said they had been drinking at the time of their offense. One-third reported prior binge drinking; a fifth were on probation for a DWI offense. In sum, about two-thirds of probationers may be characterized as alcohol- or drug-involved offenders. The survey also found that one in six probationers reported having participated in a drug treatment program while serving their sentence, and one in three said they had received treatment for alcohol abuse. Overall, almost four in 10 had received some treatment for substance abuse since beginning their probation. Details on probationer abuse of alcohol and drugs can be found in Table 10.6.

Table 10.6
**Percent of Probationers Under the Influence at Time of Offense**

| Offense | Alcohol | Drugs* |
|---|---|---|
| All probationers | 40% | 14% |
|    Non-DWI offenders | 25 | 16 |
| Severity of Offense | | |
|    Felony | 28 | 18 |
|    Misdemeanor | 58 | 8 |
| Type of Offense | | |
|    Violent | 41 | 11 |
|    Property | 19 | 10 |
|    Drug | 16 | 32 |
|    Public-order | 75 | 6 |

*Includes marijuana/hashish, cocaine/crack, heroin/opiates, barbiturates, stimulants, hallucinogens, and other illegal drugs.

Source: Mumola, C. and T. Bonczar (1998). *Substance Abuse and Treatment of Adults on Probation*. Washington, DC: Bureau of Justice Statistics, p. 1 (www.ojp.usdoj.gov/bjs/pub/pdf/satap95.pdf).

## *Jail Inmates*

In 2002, the date of the most recent national survey, 68 percent of jail inmates were found to be dependent on drugs or alcohol at the time of their offense (Bureau of Justice Statistics, 2005) This represents an increase from 1996. About 30 percent of convicted jail inmates were under the influence of drugs at the time of the offense. Specifically, 13.6 percent of convicted jail inmates had used marijuana, and 10.6 percent had used cocaine or crack cocaine.

Offenders in local jails reported extensive prior drug use. Over one-half said they used drugs in the month before the offense. Jail inmates were even more likely than probationers to report using drugs in the month before the offense. A total of 16.4 percent reported committing their offense to get money to buy drugs. See Table 10.7. Among inmates who had used alcohol or drugs in the month before their offense, 47 percent participated in treatment or programs while under correctional supervision (Bureau of Justice Statistics, 2005). A total of 18% of jail inmates who met the criteria for drug dependence or abuse and 17%

who met the criteria for alcohol dependence or abuse had received treatment since their admission to jail. Some jail inmates manage to continue to use drugs in jail, and about one in 10 were positive when tested for drugs. The major sources of drugs smuggled into jails are staff; almost half of the jails dismissed employees when they test positive for drug use.

Table 10.7
**Drug Use Among Jail Inmates, 2002**

| | |
|---|---|
| **Convicted Inmates** | |
| under the influence at the time of offense | 28.8% |
| use in the month before | 54.6% |
| active drug involvement | 68.7% |
| | |
| **Drug Used at the Time of Offense** | |
| Marijuana/Hashish | 13.6% |
| Cocaine/Crack | 10.6% |
| Heroin/Opiates | 4.1% |

Source: Karberg, J.D. and D.J. James (2005). *Substance Dependence, Abuse and Treatment of Jail Inmates, 2002*. Washington, DC: Bureau of Justice Statistics, p. 5 (www.ojp.usdoj.gov/bjs/abstract/sdatji02.htm).

## State and Federal Prisoners

The latest survey on substance abuse by and treatment of State and Federal inmates found that 32% of State prisoners and 26% of Federal prisoners reported the use of alcohol or drugs while committing their offense (Durose & Langan, 2005). While only a fifth of State prisoners were drug offenders, 83 percent reported past drug use and 57 percent were using drugs in the month before their offense. [These are somewhat higher figures than an earlier (1991) survey.] Some 37 percent of state prisoners were drinking at the time of their offense.

About 32 percent of State and 26 percent of Federal prisoners reported committing their offense while under the influence of drugs.

About 40 percent of state and 30 percent of federal prisoners reported prior binge drinking experiences; more than 40 percent of both had driven drunk in the past. Overall, three in four state and four in five federal prisoners may be characterized as alcohol- or drug-involved offenders. In 2004, an estimated 269,200 prisoners who had used drugs in the month before the offense reported taking part in drug treatment or other drug programs since admission to prison (Durose & Langan, 2005). This figure represented a one third increase since 1997.

Table 10.8
**Substance Abuse and Treatment Among State and Federal Prisoners, 2002**

|  | Percentage of Prisoners | |
|---|---|---|
| **Self-reported Drug Use** | **2004** | **1997** |
| **In month before offense** | | |
| State | 56 | 57 |
| Federal | 50 | 45 |
| **At the time of the offense** | | |
| State | 32 | 33 |
| Federal | 26 | 22 |
| **Uses Regularly** | | |
| State | 69 | 70 |
| Federal | 64 | 57 |
| **Ever Used** | | |
| State | 83 | 83 |
| Federal | 79 | 73 |

Source: Durose, M.R. and P. Langan (2005). *State Court Sentencing of Convicted Felons, 2002.* Washington, DC: Bureau of Justice Statistics, p. 23 (www.ojp.usdoj.gov/bjs/abstract/scsc02st.htm).

## Parolees

Many drug-involved offenders are sentenced to imprisonment for the instant offense, which may or not be a drug law violation. While in prison, most will receive little treatment, treatment of inadequate duration, or ineffective treatment and will be released into the community, typically with little effort to link treatment needs with community resources. Re-entry services may well not have coordinated with existing social services, and parolees fail to receive the support and supervision needed. In some states, such as California, more prison inmates return as parole revocations than as new commitments from court. The 2000 national survey of illicit drug use found that more than one in five on parole or other supervised release from prison had used an illicit drug in the past month, a rate four times that of adults not on parole.

In general, the number of correctional facilities that operated primarily as alcohol or drug treatment programs increased 8% from 233 in 1995 to 249 in 2000. Furthermore, facilities with drug or alcohol treatment as a main focus increased from 192 to 200, whereas community-based facilities with this specialty rose from 41 to 49. More than 80% of these facilities were State operated, whereas about 10% were private contract facilities, and 8% were Federal institutions. Community-based facilities, on the other hand, were nearly evenly split between privately operated institutions (55%) and State facilities (45%) (Bureau of Justice Statistics, 2003).

Overall, a total of 96% of correctional facilities offered counselling in 2000. Both drug and alcohol counselling were available in about 90% of the facilities. This pattern was similar among Federal, State and privately operated facilities (Bureau of Justice Statistics, 2003).

## Driving While Intoxicated

No discussion of the relationship between substance abuse and crime would be complete without exploring driving while under the influence of alcohol or drugs (DWI). In 1997, an estimated 513,200 offenders were on probation, or in jail or prison for DWI: 454,500 on probation, 41,100 in jail, and 17,600 in State prison. DWI offenders accounted for nearly one in seven probationers, one in 14 jail inmates, and two percent of State prisoners.

Compared to other offenders, DWI offenders are older, better-educated, and more commonly white and male. Of DWI offenders, about one-half of those in jail reported drinking for at least four hours prior to their arrest, while about one-half on probation reported drinking at least three hours. About one-half the DWI offenders in jail reported consuming about six ounces of ethanol (equivalent to about 12 beers or six glasses of wine); about one-half those on probation reported consuming four ounces of ethanol. The estimated average blood alcohol concentration (BAC) of DWI offenders in jail was .24 grams of alcohol per decilitre of blood (g/dl); for those on probation, the g/dl was .19. Most States have legal definitions of drunk driving that presume drunk driving at the .08 or .10 g/dl level.

One-third of DWI offenders on probation (compared to about two-thirds of those in jail) reported prior DWI sentences. Of DWI offenders, one in three in jail and one in 12 on probation reported three or more prior DWI offenses; more than one in three on probation and almost half in jail exhibited indicators of past alcohol dependence. More than two-thirds of the DWI offenders in jail and almost one-half on probation reported a domestic dispute while under the influence of alcohol.

Of DWI offenders on probation, over one-half reported receiving alcohol treatment or participating in a self-help program sometimes in their lives. More probationers than jail inmates reported that, since their sentence began, they had received alcohol treatment (46 versus 4%) or had participated in such self-help groups as Alcoholics Anonymous or Narcotics Anonymous (62 versus 17%). Because these data were obtained primarily from self-reports, they should be interpreted as minimal estimates. The true figures of use and abuse are probably much higher.

Substance abusers pose many problems for corrections. Alcohol use, commonly viewed as a recreational behavior, has pharmacological characteristics that include loss of coordination, reduction of inhibitions, impairment of judgment, confused understanding, and psychological excitation. Thus a drunk driver's trip home can become vehicular homicide; drunk drivers killed almost 50,000 persons in 2000. A domestic dispute can become domestic violence and aggravated assault, and a night of drinking can become an auto theft.

Even when drug offenders are referred to treatment instead of prison, treatment is not always forthcoming. In California, an initiative was passed in 2000, requiring treatment instead of jail or prison for first- and second-time nonviolent drug offenders. More than one in three such offenders were not in treatment in 2002, a rate better than results in Arizona, which started a similar program in 1997.[7] Other states may have treatment programs that provide better compliance between constitutional requirements and treatment.

Langworthy and Latessa (1993, 1996) evaluated the effectiveness of the Turning Point Multiple DWI Treatment Program in Cincinnati, Ohio, which is an alternative correctional program for dealing with the convicted and sentenced habitual drunk driver in a community-based residential setting. This chemical dependency program for multiple DWI offenders requires clients to serve a minimum of 30 days in county jail, and then enter a mandatory 28-day residential program. The program is a comprehensive treatment regimen and includes individualized alcohol treatment, family counseling and educational service. Clients are required to develop and implement an individual treatment plan that promotes personal change and requires active participation in Alcoholics Anonymous (or Narcotics Anonymous). Pratt, Holsinger, and Latessa (2000) followed the Turning Point cohort for 10 years. In contrast to a comparison group, treatment group member with three or more DWIs and 30 days in jail avoided new offenses. The treatment's effect was found to be stable, contributing from 10 to 30 percent in the reduced reoffending of the group.

Substance abusers present problems for probation and parole officers, as well as community treatment providers. Because some abusers (such as cocaine users and alcoholics) can become assaultive when under the influence, dealing with them can be dangerous. Much remains to be done to create, fund, and continue public and private service providers, as well as to get individuals to recognize the pattern of their own substance abuse and to decide to change that pattern. This is a major thrust behind drug courts, drug therapy, counseling, and employment programs.

Probation and parole officers consider drug and alcohol monitoring for use and abuse of substances (as well as treatment) to be major parts of their job requirements. Because few probation and parole officers (POs) are equipped for or skilled in substance abuse assessment, urinalysis and treatment, existing social services must be identified, accessed, and utilized. POs help clients identify their alcohol or drug problems through assessment, obtain the needed services, refer clients to agencies and monitor compliance. After addressing substance abuse problems,

POs can then address the offender's lack of employment, marital difficulties, and emotional issues that are usually secondary to the problems of alcoholism or drug addiction.

## Mental Health Disorders

In 2005, the Bureau of Justice Statistics estimated that over 1.2 million offenders with mental illnesses were incarcerated in the nation's jails and prisons (James & Glaze, 2006). About 56 percent of State prisoners, 45 percent of Federal prisoners, and 64 percent of local jail inmates reported having a mental health problem. Most have co-occurring substance abuse problems, either alcohol or drugs (or both).

For constitutional and policy reasons, most mental health facilities existing at mid-twentieth century have closed, and those remaining primarily service court-ordered forensic patients remanded by courts, including those not guilty by reason of insanity or guilty but mentally ill, those who are a danger to self and others, and those transferred by probate court order due to mental illnesses associated with or as a result of imprisonment. A few are dangerous sex offenders who have completed their sentences but were ordered into mental health facilities due to the perceived probability of their repeating heinous crimes.

The Sentencing Project (2002:2) argues that mental disorders among prisoners occur at least five times the rate found in the general population, and represent the criminalization of the mentally ill: "the increased likelihood of people with mental illness being processed through the criminal justice system instead of through the mental health system." Criminalization of the mentally ill has occurred because:

- the deinstitutionalization movement that began in the 1960s was predicated on local communities providing sufficient mental health services, but funding was not forthcoming to underwrite treatment in the community.

- of reductions in treatment spending and availability, including fragmentation of treatment services.

- barriers arose to involuntary commitment, including a court-ordered finding that the detained are either a clear and present danger to self or others, or so markedly disabled by their conditions as not to be able to care for themselves. Involuntary hospitalization also requires legal representation and a full judicial hearing.

In addition, U.S. Supreme Court decisions require that persons involuntarily detained under the color of treatment must receive treatment. Many states cannot or will not fund treatment services.

Box 10.14

## Mental Illness and Prisons

Most people familiar with justice system will understand that the courts are concerned with the three major types of pleas that could be entered in the pre-adjudication phases: "incompetent to stand trial," "not guilty by reason of insanity," and "guilty but mentally ill." In addition, there are two categories of post adjudication offenders whose special psychological needs pose problems for institutional corrections: inmates whose mental health deteriorates to episodic crises and those sentenced to death who become mentally disturbed.

For some inmates, the impacts of prison life overwhelm their usual coping patterns. Some factors that lead to "prison psychosis" include the routine of the prison, fear of other inmates, forced homosexual behavior, assault and fear of assault, deterioration in affairs and circumstances of family on the outside of prison, depression, etc. When the psychological crisis comes, correctional administrators frequently transfer affected inmates to prison infirmaries or psychological treatment wards, or initiate inmate transfer to a mental health system. Long-term and intensive psychotherapy for "mentally ill" inmates, however, is believed to be rare. Treatment for episodic mental crisis tends to remain at the first-aid level in many states.

Death rows do not usually contain a large proportion of a prison's population but consume a disproportionate share of the per-inmate cost due to the demands of observing, caring, and maintaining death row. That includes a lower staff-inmate ratio, mail processing, death-watch officer workload, closer custody during recreational periods, and so on. Some inmates on death row become mentally ill and, as such, cannot be executed. (*Ford v. Wainwright*, 106 S. Ct. 2595, 1986). The state has an additional burden of determining if the death-row inmate is sane, establishing some procedure to restore the inmate to sanity, and then certifying the sanity of the patient-inmate. Because this would be tantamount to a "death sentence" and thus not a favor for the inmate, it is unlikely mental health physicians would undertake that process alone or with any great enthusiasm. It remains for the states to develop procedures for identifying, diagnosing, treating, and certifying the sanity of death-row inmates who claim to be insane.

Is the mentally disordered person more prone to criminal behavior? Or does the criminal justice system respond to such misfits in a legal manner only because the mental health sys-

Box 10.14—*continued*

tem has been rendered helpless to deal with most of them? Steadman and Manahan have studied that relationship and have made some rather interesting discoveries:

- The correlation of crime among the mentally disordered appears to be the same as the correlates of crime among any other group: age, gender, race, social class, and prior criminality.

- Likewise, the correlates of mental disorder among criminal offenders appear to be the same as those in other population: age, socioeconomic status, and previous disorder. Populations characterized by the correlates of both crime and mental disorders (e.g., low social class) can be expected to show high rates of both, and they do.

Source: Steadman, H. and J. Monahan (1984). *Crime and Mental Disorder: An Epidemiological Approach*, p. 5. Washington DC: Bureau of Justice Statistics.

## Female Offenders

Male offenders constitute the majority (84%) of adults under correctional control. The much smaller female offender population is primarily handled within the community corrections system, although the number of imprisoned females is increasing faster than that of male prisoners. In this section, we look at the crimes that place females under correctional control, the process by which they are assigned to and exit from community corrections, and the special problems female offenders face.

## Female Corrections Populations

In 2000, there were more than 952,000 women under care, custody or control of adult criminal justice authorities, and almost 9,000 juvenile females were under secure and nonsecure state-managed and contract institutions. This translates into a rate of nearly one percent of American adult females having some correctional status on any given day. About 85 percent were supervised in the community, and 15 percent were confined in jails and prisons. Most violent female offenders are not confined; about 65,000 women convicted of violence are under

Box 10.15

### Developmentally Disabled Prisoners

Few jails or prisons have sufficient facilities and programs to handle the special needs of developmentally disabled offenders, and hospitals and other health facilities are seldom capable of administering correctional programs with sufficient security to protect society's rights. Without alternatives, judges are left with no other choice than to sentence those individuals to prison.

- Some mentally retarded offenders require incarceration because of the seriousness of their crimes or their records as repeat offenders, but most other mentally retarded offenders could be diverted from prison to community treatment programs while still ensuring the safety of the community.

- There is tremendous variation in estimates of the number of mentally retarded persons incarcerated in prison: earlier research indicates that the percentage of those offenders is higher than the percentage within the general population, while the most recent studies place the percentage at about the same level as that within the general population.

- Mentally retarded offenders are often used by their peers, reflecting their great need for approval and acceptance. They have no long-term perspective and little ability to think in a causal way to understand the consequences of their actions.

- Retarded persons are often victimized or abused by other inmates.

- Identifying offenders who have special needs is essential for planning individualized programs. Due process, functional diagnosis and evaluation performed by specially trained staff utilizing sophisticated assessment tools and procedures are essential.

- Because the developmentally challenged are usually undetected, the violations of the legal rights of such persons are frequent.

- Criminal justice and corrections personnel are not presently trained to handle the special problems and needs of such offenders.

Box 10.15—*continued*

- Matters of competency relating to diminished mental capacity should be considered at the first point of contact with criminal justice system and at each decision point in the continuum.

- Developmentally disabled offenders should be assigned to programs that meet their individual needs; some may be mixed in with the regular prison population; some need a segregated environment; some would benefit most from a community setting; and others might be placed in a regular mental retardation group home or guardianship arrangement.

- The survey of local jurisdictions revealed the need for training about the developmentally challenged for criminal justice personnel who normally do not distinguish between the developmentally challenged and mental illness; the need for early identification of such persons once they come into contact with the criminal justice system; and the need for more community resources; particularly residential programs, to serve this category of offenders.

supervision by probation authorities compared to some 3,300 in local jails, 21,000 in state prisons, and almost 1,000 in federal prisons. Among convicted female drug traffickers, almost 58,000 are on probation, 5,300 in local jails, 13,500 in state prisons, and almost 5,300 in federal prison. See Table 10.9.

## Women Serving a Sentence

Nearly two-thirds of women under probation supervision are white, but nearly two-thirds of those confined in local jails and state and federal prisons are minority: Black, Hispanic, and other races. Those on probation or in local jails are younger than those in prisons; nearly one-quarter of federal prison inmates are at least 45 years old. Adult women under correctional control are substantially less likely than the general population to never have been married.

Yet nearly seven out of 10 women under correctional sanction have minor children under the age of 18. These females report an average of 2.1 minor children, and these estimates translate into more than 1.3

million minor children as the offspring of women under correctional sanction. About two-thirds of state prison inmates had lived with their children prior to entering prison.

Table 10.9
**Types of Sentences Imposed by State Court, Female Felons, 2002**

| Most Serious Conviction Offense | Percent of Felons Sentenced to: | | | |
| --- | --- | --- | --- | --- |
| | Incarceration | | Nonincarceration | |
| | Prison | Jail | Probation | Other |
| *All Offenses* | 25% | 31% | 40% | 3% |
| *Violent Offenses* | 32% | 31% | 34% | 3% |
| Murder | 81 | 7 | 11 | 1 |
| Sexual assault* | 44 | 27 | 25 | 4 |
| Robbery | 50 | 24 | 24 | 1 |
| Aggravated assault | 23 | 35 | 39 | 3 |
| Other violent | 37 | 31 | 29 | 3 |
| *Property Offenses* | 22 | 31 | 44 | 3 |
| Burglary | 39 | 43 | 25 | 3 |
| Larceny | 19 | 33 | 45 | 3 |
| Fraud | 22 | 27 | 48 | 3 |
| *Drug Offenses* | 26 | 28 | 41 | 5 |
| Possession | 21 | 30 | 43 | 6 |
| Trafficking | 29 | 27 | 40 | 4 |
| *Weapons* | 27 | 33 | 35 | 5 |
| *Other Offenses* | 27 | 39 | 33 | 3 |
| *Includes rape | | | | |

Source: Durose, M.R. and P. Langan (2005). *State Court Sentencing of Convicted Felons, 2002.* Washington, DC: Bureau of Justice Statistics, p. 23 (http://www.ojp.usdoj.gov/bjs/abstract/scsc02 st.htm).

Female prisoners generally have more difficult economic circumstances than male prisoners prior to entering prison. About four in 10 women in state prison reported that they had been employed full-time prior to their arrest, but more than one-third of the employed females had earned incomes of less than $600 per month prior to arrest. Nearly 30 percent of female inmates reported receiving welfare assistance.

Health issues were more problematic for female than male offenders. About 3.5 percent of the female inmate population was HIV-positive. About one-half of the confined female offenders reported they had been using alcohol, drugs, or both at the time of the offense for which they had been incarcerated. Drug use was reported more often than alcohol use. On every measure of drug abuse (ever used, using regularly, using in the month before the offense, and using at the time of the offense), female offenders had higher rates of use than male offenders. Male offenders, on the other hand, had higher alcohol use on every measure of alcohol ingestion. An estimated 25 percent of women on probation, 30 percent of women in local jails and in state prisons, and 15 percent of women in federal prison had been consuming alcohol at the time of their offense. Nearly one in three women serving time in state prisons said that they had committed the offense that brought them to prison in order to obtain money to support their need for drugs.

Photo 10.1

Maricopa County inmates wearing prison stripes work on Sheriff Joe Arpaio's female chain gang cleaning up trash in Phoenix, Arizona. Photograph by Eric Drotter, courtesy of AP/Wide World Photos.

Nearly 56 percent of women substance abusers in state prisons reported having received treatment for their alcohol and drug abuse, and one in five said treatment had occurred since entry to prison. Another one-third said they had joined a voluntary program (such as Alcoholics Anonymous and Narcotics Anonymous) since entering prison.

Forty-four percent of women under correctional authority reported that they were physically or sexually assaulted at some time during their lives. Forty-eight percent of women reporting an assault said that it had occurred before age 18.

## Women in Jail

Women in jail are more disadvantaged than are males. First, the number of women in local jails increased to more than 68,000 in 2000, up 330 percent from 1983[1] Almost one-half of this increase resulted from drug violations (Snell, 1992:1). More than one in three females were in jail in 2000 for drug offenses, an increase from one in eight in 1983. Among convicted female inmates, nearly two-fifths reported that they had committed their first offense under the influence of drugs, and one-quarter reported the drug to be cocaine or crack. Approximately four in ten used drugs daily. About one in four convicted female jail inmates reported that they committed their current offense to get money

Photo 10.2
Female on street-cleaning work detail, San Francisco jail. San Francisco Sheriff's Department/Sheriff's Work Alternative Program. Photograph by Harry Allen.

to buy drugs. Some two-thirds of the jailed women had children under the age of 18, and most of these were with either a grandparent or father.

A recent study of mental illness among female jail inmates (Teplin, Abrams & McClelland, 1997) in Chicago found that 80 percent of their representative sample met the criteria for at least one lifetime psychiatric disorder, most commonly drug and alcohol abuse or dependence, and post-traumatic stress disorder. Rates for all psychiatric disorders (particularly depression) were significantly higher than those of the general population. Investigators concluded that few female jail inmates received in-facility treatment, primarily because inmate's needs far exceeded current resources.

Women who use drugs often have low self-esteem and little self-confidence and may feel powerless. In addition, minority women may face additional cultural and language barriers that can hinder or affect treatment and recovery. Many drug-using women do not seek treatment because they are afraid. They fear not being able to take care of or keep their children, reprisals from their spouses or boyfriends, and punishment from the authorities in the community. Many women report that their drug-using-male partners initiated them into drug abuse. Finally, research[9] indicates that drug-dependent women have great difficulty abstaining from drugs, when the lifestyles of their male partner is one that supports drug use.

Approximately 40 percent of the female jail inmates grew up in a single-parent household, and an additional 17 percent lived in a household without either parent. Close to one-third of all women in jail had a parent or guardian who abused drugs or alcohol, and four in 10 reported that another family member (usually brother or sister) had been incarcerated.

This brief examination of jail inmates suggests a group of offenders with high needs who were frequently victimized as they were growing up. Broken homes, sexual and physical abuse, minority status, and parental/guardian abuse of alcohol or drugs characterizes a large portion of the female population. This segment of offenders is not generally likely to receive effective treatment for the major, underlying problems. After an average stay of less than six months, most will be returned to the community to continue to break their drug dependences and, for the most part, their efforts will fail without intensive assistance. It is possible for drug-dependent women, of any age, to overcome the illness of drug addiction. Those who have been most successful have had the help and support of significant others, family members, treatment providers, friends and the community. We discuss specific issues later in this chapter.

## Parole

Despite the recent emphasis on studying female offenders, relatively little is known about females on parole. In 2000, females were an estimated 12 percent of all parolees, up from eight percent in 1990. That translates into more than 87,000 female parolees. The growth in the number of female paroles reflects higher offending rates, arrests per offense, increased commitments to prison per arrest, and parole recommitments (parolees who failed on parole were returned to prison, from which they will be later be re-paroled). The lifetime likelihood of a female going to state or federal prison is now more than one percent, although Hispanic women have a 50 percent higher likelihood than do white women. Black non-Hispanic women, have a likelihood seven times that of white women.[10]

Most women sent to prison have several factors that will work against successful reintegration following parole. Drug and alcohol use, unemployment and few occupational skills, a history of sexual abuse, and incomplete education are difficult to overcome when treatment is a low priority to resource-strapped systems.[11] There is a gap between institutional treatment and transition to the community.[19] Absent meaningful treatment, one should not be surprised at recidivism indicators.

Overall, about 45 percent of women for whom supervision was ended in calendar 1996 were returned to prison or had absconded. Prior arrest history was an important predictor of post-prison recidivism. Among women with only one arrest for which they had been imprisoned, 21 percent were rearrested within three years (Greenfield & Snell, 1999:11). Nearly

Photo 10.3
Sixteen-year-old youthful offender on electronic monitoring in lieu of detention.

eight out of 10 women with 11 or more priors were rearrested over the next three years. Females who had secured employment and stable living arrangements by the time of discharge tended to do significantly better than those who did not (Hohman, McGaffigan & Segars, 2000).

## Substance Abuse Treatment

There is widespread need for effective treatment programs for substance abuse by female offenders. Research has shown that women receive the most benefit from drug treatment programs that provide comprehensive services for meeting their basic needs, including access to the following:

- food, clothing, and shelter
- transportation
- job counseling and training
- legal assistance
- literacy training and educational opportunities
- parenting training
- family therapy
- couples counseling
- medical care
- child care
- social services
- social support
- psychological assessment and mental health care, and
- assertiveness training

A comprehensive spectrum of services is needed for female offenders at every level of the criminal justice system. After all, almost all return to unconditional release into the community. Traditional drug treatment programs may not be appropriate for female offenders because those programs may not provide the services needed. In addition, research also suggests that, for female offenders, a continuing relationship with a treatment provider is an important factor throughout treatment. Any individual may experience lapses and relapses during the treatment process. Learning how to identify and avoid circumstances that may lead to relapse is important. This is a treatment thrust for many community programs, particularly therapeutic communities (Lockwood & Inciardi, 1998).

Jail-based projects include therapeutic communities (Sisters in Sober Treatment and Empowered Recovery or SISTERS, San Francisco, California; and Stepping Out, San Diego) have a wide range of treatment programs (modalities). Aftercare (post-jail release) components provide intensive outpatient services and sober living, job development and placement assistance, referrals to supportive services, and a mutual-help group created for and by ex-offenders (Kassebaum, 1999). Prison-based therapeutic communities are becoming more numerous and their clients have significantly lower relapse and recidivism rates than do those who do not enroll (Nielsen, Scarpitti & Inciardi, 1996).

The state of Georgia faced a correctional population with 10 percent of the males and 27 percent of the females classified as mental health cases. The Georgia Board of Pardons and Parole reported on the Georgia Treatment and Aftercare for Probationers and Parolees (TAPP) program to boost post-prison support for Georgia's mentally ill and retarded offenders. A TAPP mental health professional in each service area acts as case manager to nonviolent mental health offenders returned to the area, monitoring offenders' behavior and arranging ongoing community support and treatment. Such transitional programs are examples of the needed coordination between incarceration and gradual reintegration into the community for female offenders (Georgia Board of Pardons and Parole, 2000). Such coordination is needed throughout the community corrections system.

## Summary

Our discussion of the special needs offender suggests that they are not a unitary group of similarly situated offenders, but a complex combination of individuals facing problems of living complicated by self-defeating behaviors that require change. Each group has certain distinct characteristics and problems that are related to offense situations and basic needs, almost all of which are not effectively addressed. While they are alike in that they have been convicted of criminal activities, underlying those events are unaddressed social, personal, and medical needs best handled through treatment. Future corrections will need to apply a range of classification systems to determine the most effective way to manage any group of offenders and maximize public safety.[10]

## Review Questions

1. Explain "special needs" offenders.

2. What effects have public fears had on treatment of sex offenders?

3. Differentiate between date rape and campus gang rape.

4. Defend the proposition: The first responsibility of probation officers is to force the client to address his or her alcohol/drug dependency.

5. Does treatment for sex offenders work?

6. How has substance abuse increased both jail and prison populations?

7. Why are offenders with mental health disorders concentrated in correctional systems?

8. Explain why criminalization of the mentally ill has occurred.

9. How can corrections better respond to developmentally disabled offenders?

10. Why are diversion programs the most effective means to integrate substance abusers?

## Key Terms

special category offenders
sex offender
dangerous sex offenders
Megan's Law
rape
forcible rape
child molestation
prostitution
child abuse
serial rapists
incest
drug abuse

drug addict
date rape
exhibitionism
marital rape
relapse prevention
substance abuse
psychopath
binge drinking
DWI
criminalization of the mentally ill
mentally handicapped offenders
developmentally disabled offenders

## Electronic Library

Child Rape and Megan's Law (www.klaaskids.org/pg-legmeg.htm).

Drug Abuse by Probationers (www.ojp.usdoj.gov/bjs/pub/pdf/satap95.pdf).

Drug Use in Jails (www.ojp.usdoj.org/bjs/pub/pdf/duttj.pdf).

DWI Offenders (www.ojp.usdoj.gov/bjs/pub/pdf/dwiocs.pdf).

Female Sex Offenders (www.csc-scc.gc.ca/text/pblct/forum/e082/e082m.shtml).

Incestuous fathers (www.csc-scc.gc.ca/text/pblct/forum/e082/e082i.shtml).

Illicit Drug Use (www.samhsa.gov/oas/NHSDA/2kNHSDA/highlights.htm).

Managing sex offenders (www.csc-scc.gc.ca/text/pblct/forum/e082/e082n.shtml).

Mentally Ill Offenders in the Criminal Justice System (www.sentencingproject.org/news/pub9089.pdf).

Offenders with Mental Impairment (www.tdcj.state.tx.us/publications/tcomi/).

Prisoners and Substance Abuse (www.ojp.usdoj.gov/bjs/pub/pdf/satsfp97.pdf).

Sexual Offender Treatment in Vermont (www.mountainpridemedia.org/oitm/issues/2001/sep2001/fea03_treatment.htm).

Substance Abuse-National Challenge (www.samhsa.gov/oas/NHSDA/2kHHSfacts.htm).

## Recommended Readings

Hammett, R., C. Roberts, and S. Kennedy (2001). "Health-Related Issues in Prison Reentry." *Crime & Delinquency*, 47(3):390-409.

Lowenkamp, C., A. Holsinger, and E. Latessa (2001). "Risk/Need Assessment, Offender Classification, and the Role of Childhood Abuse." *Criminal Justice and Behavior*, 28(5):543-563.

The Sentencing Project (2002). *Mentally Ill Offenders in the Criminal Justice System: An Analysis and Prescription.* Washington, DC: TSP (www.sentencingproject.org/news/pub9089.pdf).

Travis, J. (2000). *But They All Come Back: Rethinking Prisoner Reentry.* Washington, DC: Office of Justice Programs.

## Notes

[1]    Other special needs offenders include geriatric offenders and HIV-infected clients. Gang members (security threat groups) are usually subsumed under institutional corrections.

[2]    Kerschener, R. (1996). "Adolescent Attitudes Toward Rape." *Adolescence*, 31(121):29-33.

[3]    Browne, A. (1992). "Violence Against Women." *Journal of the American Medical Association*, 267:3184-3189.

[4]    DeKeserdy, W., M. Schwartz, and K. Tait (1993). "Sexual Assault and Stranger Aggression on a Canadian Campus." *Sex Roles*, 28(2):263-277.

[5]    U.S. Department of Health and Human Services (2001). Substance Abuse—A National Challenge (w); University of Michigan News and Information Services (2004). Overall Teen Drug Use Continues Gradual Decline; but use of inhalants rises (w)

[6]    For a study of drugged druggists, see Dabney, D. and R. Hollinger (2002). "Drugged Druggists." *Justice Quarterly*, 19(1):181-213.

[7]    Thompson, D. (2002). "Study: One-third of Drug Offenders Not in Treatment." *Desert Sun*, (April 10, 2002), p. A5.

[8]    Bureau of Justice Statistics (2002). *Jail Populations by Age and Gender, 1990-2000*. Washington, DC: BJS (www.ojp.usdoj.gov/bjs/glance/tables/jailagtab.htm).

[9]    National Institute of Drug Abuse (2002). *Treatment Methods for Women* (www.drugabuse.gov/infofax/treatwomen.html).

[10]    Bureau of Justice Statistics (1997). *Lifetime Likelihood of Going to State or Federal Prison*, p. 6 (www.ojp.usdoj.gov/bjs/pub/pdf/llgsfp.pdf).

[11]    Curry, L. (2001). "Tougher Sentencing, Economic Hardships, and Rising Violence." *Corrections Today*, 63(1):74-76.

## References

Allen, H. (ed.) (2002). *What Works? Risk Reduction: Interventions for Special Needs Offenders*. Lanham, MD: American Correctional Association.

Allen, H. and C. Simonsen (2001). *Corrections in America*. Upper Saddle River, NJ: Prentice Hall.

Almanac of Policy Issues (2000). *Drug Policy* (www.policyalmanac.org/crime/drugs.shtml).

Atkinson, J. (1999). *Female Sex Offenders* (www.cscscc.gc.ca/text/pblct/forum/e082/e082m.shtml).

Beck, A. and P. Harrison (2001). *Prisoners in 2000*. Washington, DC: Bureau of Justice Statistics.

Bernier, L., M. Mailloux, G. David, and H. Cote (1999). *An Innovative Treatment Approach for Incestuous Fathers* (www.csc-scc.gc.ca/text/pblct/forum/e082/e082i.shtml).

Browne, A. (1992). "Violence Against Women." *Journal of the American Medical Association*, 267:3184-3189.

Bureau of Justice Statistics (2006). *Drug Use and Dependence, State and Federal Prisoners, 2004* (www.ojp.usdoj.gov/bjs/dcf/dt.htm).

Bureau of Justice Statistics (2005). *Substance Dependence, Abuse, and Treatment of Jail Inmates, 2002* (w).

Bureau of Justice Statistics (2003). *Census of State and Correctional Facilities, 2000* (www.ojp.usdoj.gov/bjs/dcf/dt.htm).

Bureau of Justice Statistics (2002). *Criminal Offenders Statistics* (www.ojp.usdoj.gov/bjs/crimoff.htm).

Bureau of Justice Statistics (2002). *Jail Populations by Age and Gender, 1990-2000.* Washington, DC: BJS (www.ojp.usdoj.gov/bjs/glance/tables/jailagtab.htm).

Bureau of Justice Statistics (2001). *Drugs and Crime Facts*, p. 3 (www.ojp.usdoj.gov/bjs/dcd/du/htm).

Bureau of Justice Statistics (2001). *Drug Use* (www.ojp.usdoj.gov/bjs/dcf/du.htm).

Bureau of Justice Statistics (1997). *Lifetime Likelihood of Going to State or Federal Prison*, p. 6 (www.ojp.usdoj.gov/bjs/pub/pdf/llgsfp.pdf).

Cullen, F. and M. Moon (2002). "Reaffirming Rehabilitation: Public Support for Correctional Treatment." In Allen, H. (ed.) *What Works? Risk Reduction: Interventions for Special Needs Offenders*, pp. 7-26. Lanham, MD: American Correctional Association.

Cumming, G. (2001). *Sex Offender Treatment in Vermont* (www.mountainpridemedia.org/oitm/issues/2001/sep2001/fea03_treatment.htm).

Curry, L. (2001). "Tougher Sentencing, Economic Hardships, and Rising Violence." *Corrections Today*, 63(1):74-76.

Dabney, D. and R. Hollinger (2002). "Drugged Druggists." *Justice Quarterly*, 19(1):181-213.

Davies, A. and A. Dale (1996). "Locating the Stranger Rapist." *Medicine, Science and the Law*, 36(2):146-156.

DeKeserdy, W., M. Schwartz, and K. Tait (1993). "Sexual Assault and Stranger Aggression on a Canadian Campus." *Sex Roles*, 28(2):263-277.

Durose, M.R. and P. Langan (2005). *State Court Sentencing of Convicted Felons, 2002.* Washington, DC: Bureau of Justice Statistics, p. 23 (http://www.ojp.usdoj.gov/bjs/abstract/scsc02st.htm).

Editors (2002). "Budget Cuts Affect Drug Treatment." *Correctional News*, 8(3):1.

Federal Bureau of Investigation (2001). *Crime in the United States 2000.* Washington, DC: Federal Bureau of Investigation.

Gallagher, C.A., D.B. Wilson, P. Hirschfield, M. Coggeshall, and D.L. MacKenzie (1999). "A Quantitative Review of the Effects of Sex Offender Treatment on Sexual Reoffending." *Corrections Management Quarterly*, 3, 19-29.

Georgia Board of Pardons and Parole (2000). *FY 2000 Annual Report* (www.pap.state. ga.us/2000AR/ass_m_i_off.htm).

Greenfield, L. and T. Snell (1999). *Women Offenders*. Washington, DC: Bureau of Justice Statistics (www.ojp.usdoj.gov/bjs/pub/pdf/wo.pdf).

Hall, G. (2001). "Sex Offender Recidivism Revisited." In Latessa, E., A. Holsinger, J. Marquart and J. Sorensen (eds.) *Correctional Contexts*. Los Angeles, CA: Roxbury.

Hanson, R.K., A. Gordon, A.J.R. Harris, J.K. Marques, W. Murphy, V.L. Quinsey, and M.C. Seto (2002). "First Report of the Collaborative Outcome Data Project on the Effectiveness of Psychological Treatment for Sex Offenders." *Sexual Abuse: A Journal of Research and Treatment*, 14, 167-192.

Hohman, M., R. McGaffigan, and L. Segars (2000). "Predictors of Successful Completion of a Post-Incarceration Drug Treatment Program." *Journal of Addictions and Offender Counseling*, 21(1):12-22.

Hsu, L. and Starzynski, J. (1990). "Adolescent Rapists and Adolescent Child Sexual Assaulters." *International Journal of Offender Therapy and Comparative Criminology*, 34(1):23-30.

Hubbard, D., L. Travis, and E. Latessa (2001). *Case Classification in Community Corrections: A National Survey of the State of the Art*. Cincinnati, OH: Center for Criminal Justice Research, University of Cincinnati.

James, D.J., and L.E. Glaze (2006). "Mental Health Problems of Prison and Jail Inmates." *Bureau of Justice Statistics Report*, NDJ 213600 (w).

Kassebaum, P. (1999). *Substance Abuse Treatment for Women Offenders*. Rockville, MD: Center for Substance Abuse Treatment (www.treatment.org/taps/tap23.pdf).

Kerschener, R. (1996). "Adolescent Attitudes about Rape." *Adolescence*, 31(121):29-33.

Klaaskids Foundation (2002). *Megan's Law* (www.klaaskids.org/pg-legmeg.htm).

Knight, R., J. Warren, R. Reboussin, et al. (1998). "Predicting Rapist Type from Crime-scene Variables." *Criminal Justice and Behavior*, 25(1):46-80.

Konopasky, D. (1999). *Managing Sex Offenders* (www.csc-scc.gc.ca/text/pblct/forum/e082/e082n.shtml).

Langworthy, R. and E. Latessa (1996). "Treatment of Chronic Drunk Drivers." *Journal of Criminal Justice*, 24(3):273-281.

Langworthy, R. and E. Latessa (1993). "Treatment of Chronic Drunk Drivers: The Turning Point Project." *Journal of Criminal Justice*, 21(3):265-276.

Latessa, E. and R. Langworthy (1990). *Evaluation of the Turning Point Project for Talbert House, Inc.* Cincinnati, OH: Department of Criminal Justice, University of Cincinnati.

Lipton, D., F. Pearson, and H. Wexler (1999). *National Evaluation of the Residential Substance Abuse Treatment for State Prisoners Program*. New York, NY: Development and Research Institutes.

Lockwood, D. and J. Inciardi (1998). "Developing Comprehensive Prison-Based Thera-peutic Community Treatment for Women." *Drugs and Society*, 13 (1/2):193-212.

Lösel, F., and M. Schmucker (2005). "The Effectiveness of Treatment for Sexual Of-fenders: A Comprehensive Meta-analysis." *Journal of Experimental Criminology*, 1, 117-146.

Lowenkamp, C., A. Holsinger, and E. Latessa (2001). "Risk/Need Assessment, Of-fender Classification, and the Role of Childhood Abuse." *Criminal Justice and Be-havior*, 28(5):543-563.

Mahoney, P. and L. Williams (1998). "Sexual Assault in Marriage." In J. Jasinski and L. Williams (eds.) *Partner Violence*. Thousand Oaks, CA: Sage Publications.

Maruschak, L. (1999). *DWI Offenders under Correctional Supervision* (www.ojp. usdoj.gov/bjs/pub/pdf/dwiocs.pdf).

Mumola, C. (1999). *Substance Abuse and Treatment, State and Federal Prisoners, 1997* (www.ojp.usdoj.gov/bjs/pub/pdf/satsfp97.pdf).

Mumola, C. and T. Bonczar (1998). *Substance Abuse and Treatment of Adults on Pro-bation, 1995* (www.ojp.usdoj.gov/bjs/pub/pdf/satap95.pdf).

National Institute of Drug Abuse (2002). *Treatment Methods for Women* (www. drugabuse.gov/infofax/treatwomen.html).

Nielsen, A., F. Scarpitti, and J. Inciardi (1996). "Integrating the Therapeutic Commu-nity and Work Release for Drug-Involved Offenders." *Journal of Substance Abuse Treatment*, 13(4):349-358.

Osher, F. and Y. Han (2002). "Jails as Housing for Persons with Serious Mental Ill-ness." *American Jails*, 16(1):36-40.

Out In The Mountains (2001). *Sex Offender Treatment in Vermont* (www.mountain pridemedia.org/oitm/issues/2001/sep2001/fea03_treatment.htm).

Painter, K. and D. Farrington (1998). "Sexual and Nonsexual Marital Aggression." *Ag-gression and Violent Behavior*, 3(4):369-389.

Pratt, T., A. Holsinger, and E. Latessa (2000). "Treating the Chronic DWI Offender." *Journal of Criminal Justice*, 28(4):271-281.

Presser, L. and E. Gunnison (1999). "Strange Bedfellows." *Crime & Delinquency*, 45(3):299-315.

Rennison, C. (2001). *Criminal Victimization 2000*. Washington, DC: Bureau of Justice Statistics.

Riggs, D., D. Kilpatrick, and H. Resnick (1992). "Long-Term Psychological Distress As-sociated with Marital Rape and Aggravated Assault." *Journal of Family Violence*, 7(4):283-296.

Rush, G. (1991). *The Dictionary of Criminal Justice*. Guilford, CT: Duskin.

Schmalleger, F. (1991). *Criminal Justice Today*. Upper Saddle River, NJ: Prentice Hall.

The Sentencing Project (2002). *Mentally Ill Offenders in the Criminal Justice System: An Analysis and Prescription*. Washington,DC:TSP (www.sentencingproject.org/ news/pub9089.pdf).

Sherman, L., D. Gottfredson, D. MacKenzie, et al. (1997). *Preventing Crime: What Works? What Doesn't? What's Promising?* Washington, DC: Office of Justice Programs.

Snyder, H. (2000). *Sexual Assault of Young Children as Reported to Law Enforcement.* Washington, DC: Bureau of Justice Statistics.

Stephan, J. (2001). *Census of Jails, 1999* (www.ojp.usdoj.gov/bjs/pub/pdf/cj99.pdf).

Stevens, D. (1999). *Inside the Mind of a Serial Rapist.* San Francisco, CA: Austin and Winfield.

Straus, M. (ed.) (1988). *Abuse and Victimization Across the Life Span.* Baltimore, MD: Johns Hopkins Press.

Substance Abuse and Mental Health Services Administration (2002). *Highlights: 2000 National Household Survey on Drug Abuse* (www.samhsa.gov/oas/NHSDA/2k NHSDA/highlights.htm).

Teplin, L., K. Abrams, and G. McClelland (1997). "Prevalence of Psychiatric Disorders Among Incarcerated Women." *Archives of General Psychiatry*, 53(2):505-512.

Texas Council on Offenders with Mental Impairments (2001). *Biennial Report* (www.tdcj.state.tx.us/publications/tcomi).

Thompson, D. (2002). "Study: One-third of Drug Offenders Not in Treatment." *Desert Sun*, (April 10, 2002), p. A5.

Travis, L. (2000). *But They All Come Back: Rethinking Prisoner Reentry.* Washington, DC: Office of Justice Programs (www.ncjrs.org/pdffiles1/nij/181413.pdf).

U.S. Department of Health and Human Services (2001). *Substance Abuse: A National Challenge* (www.samhsa.gov/oas/NHSDA/2kHHSfacts.htm).

Walker, L. (2000). *The Battered Woman Syndrome.* New York, NY: Springer.

Warren, J., R. Reboussin, R. Hazelwood, N. Gibbs, S. Trumbetta, and A. Cummings (1999). "Crime Scene Analysis and the Escalation of Violence in Serial Rape." *Forensic Science International*, 100(1/2):37-56.

West, M., C. Hromas, and P. Wenger (2000). *State Sex Offender Treatment Programs: 50-State Survey* (www.doc.state.co.us/admin_reg/PDFs/So-report-send2.pdf).

Wilson, D. (2000). *Drug Use, Testing, and Treatment in Jails.* (www.ojp.usdoj.gov/bjs/pub/pdf/duttj.pdf).

Winick, C. and A. Levine (1992). "Marathon Therapy: Treating Female Rape Survivors in a Therapeutic Community." *Journal of Psychoactive Drugs*, 24(1):49-56.

Yates, P. (2002). "What Works? Effective Intervention with Sex Offenders." In H. Allen (ed.) *What Works? Risk Reduction: Interventions for Special Needs Offenders*, pp. 115-164. Lanham, MD: American Correctional Association.

Zavitz, R. and M. Farkas (2000). "The Impact of Sex-Offender Notification on Probation/Parole in Wisconsin." *International Journal of Offender Therapy and Comparative Criminology*, 44(1):8-21.

# The Effectiveness
# of Corrections
# in the Community

## 11

With few and isolated exceptions, the rehabilitative efforts that have been reported so far have not had an appreciable effect on recidivism.

—Robert Martinson

The data have continued to accumulate, testifying to the potency of offender rehabilitation programs.

—Paul Gendreau

After examining more than two decades of correctional research, Martinson's (1974) now famous conclusion had a tremendous impact on the field of corrections. Whatever the limitations of the Martinson study, and there were many, the conclusion drawn by many was that treatment or rehabilitation is not effective.[1] Thus, what became known as the "nothing works" doctrine, led to renewed efforts to demonstrate the effectiveness of correctional programs.[2] Fortunately, there has been a great deal of research since Martinson that has added significantly to the body of knowledge about correctional effectiveness.

The effectiveness of community-based correctional programs has been debated and studied for many years. As more and more offenders have been diverted or released to the community, the question of effectiveness has become increasingly important. Many critics of both probation and parole point to discretionary abuses, the arbitrary nature of the indeterminate sentence, the disparity in sentencing practices by judges, the failure of rehabilitation and supervision, and the inadequate delivery of services. In an attempt to offset some of these criticisms, mandatory and determinate sentencing systems have been imposed, sentencing tribunals have been formed, parole boards have adopted and implemented decision-making guidelines, probation and parole departments have tested new and innovative service delivery strategies, and intermediate sanctions have been developed. But these, too, are open to attack and are frequently criticized.

Much has been written about the effectiveness of probation and parole. We know that the use of discretionary parole release has declined dramatically over the past few years. In 1977, 72 percent of those released from prison were released on discretionary parole, in 1989 only 39 percent were so paroled, and by 1999 less than 20 percent. However, more than 80 percent of those released from prison received supervision in the community (Jankowski, 1990). At the end of 2005, over 4.9 million adult men and women were under Federal, State, or local probation or parole jurisdiction (Bureau of Justice Statistics, 2006). This represented an increase of 0.6% in the probation and parole population. This ever-increasing number of offenders placed on probation and parole has resulted in large caseloads and workloads for probation and parole departments.

There is also an acute shortage of residential programs and halfway houses. We continually experiment with service systems components— such as brokerage, casework, house arrest, day-reporting, electronic monitoring, intensive and specialized caseloads, and volunteer-paraprofessionals—but, again, we know little about the actual effectiveness of these strategies in community corrections. In short, there have been nearly as many innovative programs and reported results as there are probation and parole agencies. The question of effectiveness remains and, because it is so essential, it should be closely examined.

Perhaps the most limiting aspect of effectiveness studies has been the neglect given to other performance measures. By simply comparing recidivism rates, researchers have ignored some of the main effects that community correctional programs are designed to achieve. The quality of contacts and services provided to probationers and parolees need to be adequately defined and gauged, as does the effect of officer style

Photo 11.1
Drug abuse is a contributing factor to outcome supervision.
Photograph by Beth Sanders.

and attitude on outcome. There are also relatively few cost-benefit or cost-effectiveness studies. The importance of this type of information should not be overlooked. These types of studies can help community correctional agencies make more efficient selections in terms of the resources they will employ and the strategies to be used to deliver those resources. For example, Petersilia (1991) distinguishes between "passive" research designs and "active" ones. She argues that passive designs only look at the program in operation and ignore the selection of participants and levels of treatment. Without this kind of information it is difficult to determine which attributes of a correctional program are effective.

Finally, a list of effectiveness indicators should include the degree of humaneness that community supervision affords offenders and their families, and the impact of these alternatives on reducing prison populations and overcrowded conditions in jails and prisons. We have come to realize that we cannot incarcerate everyone that breaks the law.[3] Yet, probation and parole are often an afterthought, particularly when it comes to resource allocation.

There is little doubt that recidivism, no matter how it may be defined, should remain a main criterion; however, the need to measure additional outcome indicators appears obvious. Indeed, there has been a great deal of criticism directed at the research conducted in the area of correctional programming. This chapter will examine some of those criticisms as well as address what is generally known about the effectiveness of community corrections, particularly probation and parole.

## Limitations of Effectiveness Studies

Evaluating the effectiveness of community corrections is not easy even under the best of circumstances. First, political, ethical, and programmatic reasons may not permit random assignment of offenders to membership in the treatment or control group. Nonrandom assignment forces the evaluator to statistically make the groups comparable, an honored tradition in empirical research but one that delivers results that are hard to communicate to policymakers and program directors (and sometimes to other researchers).

Even in the best of circumstances in achieving random assignment, for the same reasons mentioned above, treatment or program effects "bleed over" to the control group or the intended treatment is inappropriately or unevenly applied. This makes it difficult to determine whether the treatment group members received needed treatment, and whether the control group remained "treatment free." After all, no program and no client exist in a vacuum; historical accidents can affect both groups, or one group more than another, or accidentally reinforce negative treatment effects in one group or another.

Another major problem in evaluating treatment effectiveness in community corrections is that it is rare to have only one treatment in operation at a time. For example, an offender ("Bob") may be sentenced initially to probation and restitution. The victim-offender interaction and mediation may have very positive effects on Bob's attitudes and behavior. His drinking problem, however, may lead the probation officer to recommend that the court tighten the conditions of probation to include mandatory daily participation in Alcoholics Anonymous (AA), from which Bob derives much immediate and long-term benefit. Former antisocial friends may become reacquainted with Bob, and misdemeanor crime may occur. Alerted by Bob's subsequent arrest, the PO may have Bob (a failure?) assigned to individual counseling that includes relapse prevention techniques that assist him in identifying high-risk situations and coping with them. After three years of probation, when the victim's losses have been compensated, and with Bob securely employed in a job with a future and now voluntarily participating in AA, it is impossible to determine which of the treatment program elements will have been most effective in turning Bob around, and his reintegration. Was it probation supervision? Quality of PO supervision? Mediation and remorse associated with restitution? AA support and direction? Relapse prevention techniques? Employment? or some combination of treatment elements? Because "probation" is a generic term that can refer to a combination of treatment, supervision, and intermediate sanctions ("punishing smarter"), what element should be recognized as the "best intervention?"

Finally, we need to deal with the question of whether Bob should be labeled a "success" or "failure" in corrections. Defining "failure" may mean using outcome indicators: arrest, reconviction or probation revocation, or incarceration (jail or prison). If the research design defines "success" as the absence of arrest, Bob failed: he was arrested. Yet the overall picture indicates that the arrest was just one critical incident in the long-range process of reintegration, one that Bob and his probation officer managed to overcome. Yet that single arrest incident in the three-year period would, from the perspective of reintegration, misclassify the probationer into the "failure" category. The bulk of evidence, however, clearly indicates that Bob was a success!

Thus the analyses that follow should be seen in light of these three major problems: research design and implementation, difficulty in separating effects of various treatment programs, and definition of outcome. With these limitations in mind, let us now turn to the question of effectiveness of treatment. As we do this, keep firmly in mind the argument by Gendreau (1996:118): ". . . programs that [included principles of effective intervention] reduced recidivism in the range of 25-70% with an average of about 50%. . . ."

## Correctional Effectiveness

While the debate over correctional effectiveness will surely continue for some time, those attempting to evaluate and measure the worth of various strategies and programs found in corrections face a most difficult dilemma—defining "effectiveness."

### Measuring Outcome and Recidivism

A large part of the problem lies in the desire on the part of researchers and practitioners alike to define failure or success in clear-cut, "either/or" terms. See Figure 11.1. Unfortunately, very few programs can be categorized in definitive terms. There is a strong need to view success or failure on a continuum, rather than as a win or lose dichotomy. For example, an offender may complete a sentence of probation yet have erratic employment and numerous technical violations. This individual is certainly not as successful as one who finishes probation, gains upward mobility in a job, makes restitution, supports a family, and incurs no new charges of any type; still, both these cases may be classified as successes. There is also a great deal of difference between the offender who is caught on a minor charge or a technical violation, and one who commits a serious new felony. For example, in California and other states there is evidence that the number of parolees being revoked for technical violations is increasing dramatically (Austin, 1987). Some consider a new arrest a failure, while others count only those who are incarcerated.[4]

Figure 11.1
**Placement and Successful Termination During 2005 for Probationers and Parolees**

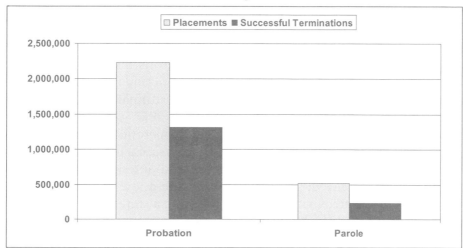

Source: Bureau of Justice Statistics (2006). *Probation and Parole in the United States, 2005.* Washington, DC: Bureau of Justice Statistics, p. 4, 6-7, 9 (http:www.ojp.usdoj.gov/bjs/abstract/ppus05.htm).

---

Box 11.1

### Parole Violation

A parolee can be returned to prison for committing a new criminal act or failing to conform to the conditions of parole. The latter is frequently known as a technical parole violation: a rule violation that is not a criminal act but is prohibited by the conditions of the parole agreement. The latter might include persistent consumption of alcohol, failure to observe curfew, refusal to make victim restitution, failure to file required reports, and so on. In a recent study of parole revocations, Austin (2000) found that 54 percent of parolees in California were returned for technical violations, 36 percent in Georgia, 57 percent in Missouri, 55 percent in Ohio, and 53 percent in Texas. Drug use accounts for many of the violations, and often there are few intermediate punishments for parole officers to use. Prison treatment programs for drug abuse are generally insufficient, and community resistance to implementing treatment centers is considerable. Clearly, prisoner reentry is a major issue facing corrections and policymakers.

---

In addition to this problem, there is no consensus on the indicators of effectiveness. While most agree that recidivism should be a primary performance measure, there is no agreement on its definition or on the indicators to be used for its measurement. Indeed, one study of parole supervision found that the nature of the outcome criteria had a significant effect upon the interpretation of results (Gottfredson, Mitchell-Herzfeld & Flanagan, 1982). Researchers tend to define recidivism in terms that fit the available data, yet we know official sources are inadequate at best. Community follow-up and appropriate comparison groups are the exception rather than the rule when examining the recidivism of probationers and parolees. There is also some evidence that the amount of time given to the follow-up period may have a significant effect on the reported recidivism rates (Hoffman & Stone-Meierhoefer, 1980; Nicholaichuk, Gordon & Gu, 2000).[5]

Correctional outcome, which is usually operationalized as recidivism, has inherent limitations. The indicators used to measure recidivism, length of follow-up, and external and internal factors affect recidivism rates. Indeed, the best way to insure a low recidivism rate is to define it very narrowly (e.g., incarceration in a state penal institution) and to utilize a very short follow-up period.

Too often, arrest (and only arrest) is used as a primary indicator when measuring recidivism, and consequently, program success or failure. Certainly arrest may serve as an indicator of post-program (or post-release) performance, but in and of itself arrest has many limitations. Some of the other factors that are overlooked when considering the impact of a correctional program or criminal sanction, even when arrest is being used, are time until arrest; offense for which an offender was arrested (type of offense as well as severity level); whether or not the offender were convicted; and, if convicted, what the resulting disposition was.

An example of this can be seen from the results of a study of community corrections in Ohio. Figure 11.2 show the results from a three-year follow-up of offenders supervised in the community between 1991 and 1993. Four groups were used for this study: offenders supervised under regular probation and intensive supervised probation (ISP), those who were released from a community-based correctional facility (CBCF) and those released from prison. In this graph, the rearrest rates of the group groups are presented. These data indicate that the ISP and CBCF groups performed better than the regular probation and the prison groups (i.e., lower recidivism rates), at least when measured by rearrest. However, when we examine Figure 11.3 we see a somewhat different picture of recidivism. In this example, the incarceration rates for the same four groups are presented. Here we see that the ISP and CBCF groups had the highest failure rates (when defined as subsequent incarceration). Of course what this figure does not show is that the majority of those ISP and CBCF offenders who were incarcerated were as a result of a technical violation. Regular probationers who received a

Figure 11.2

**Offenders Supervised Under Community Corrections in Ohio: Percent Rearrested During a Three-Year Follow-Up**

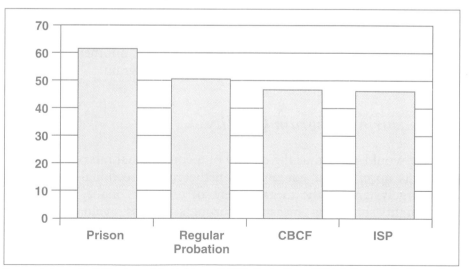

Source: Latessa, E., F. Travis, and A. Holsinger (1997). *Evaluation of Ohio's Community Corrections Acts Programs and Community Based Correctional Facilities.* Cincinnati, OH: Division of Criminal Justice, University of Cincinnati.

Figure 11.3

**Offenders Supervised Under Community Corrections in Ohio: Percent Incarcerated in a Penal Institution During a Three-Year Follow-Up**

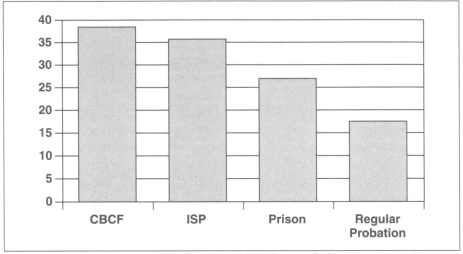

Source: Latessa, E., F. Travis, and A. Holsinger (1997). *Evaluation of Ohio's Community Corrections Acts Programs and Community Based Correctional Facilities.* Cincinnati, OH: Division of Criminal Justice, University of Cincinnati.

technical violation were often placed in ISP or a CBCF and, since the majority of the offenders in the prison group were released without parole supervision, they were not subject to revocation.

Despite these limitations, recidivism remains the most important measure of public protection. When legislators and other public officials ask if a program works, recidivism is what they are generally referring to. Outcome studies provide much of our knowledge about the effectiveness of correctional programs in reducing recidivism. Unfortunately, outcome studies usually are focused on the results of intervention and provide little, if any, useful information about why a program is or is not effective. Besides the measurement of outcome, another factor that can influence recidivism rates is the quality of a program.

## *Measuring Program Quality*

Few would argue that the quality of a correctional intervention program has no effect on outcome. Nonetheless, correctional researchers have largely ignored the measurement of program quality. Traditionally, quality has been measured through process evaluations. This approach can provide useful information about a program's operations; however, these types of evaluations often lack the "quantifiability" of outcome studies. Previously, researchers' primary issue has been the development of criteria or indicators by which a correctional program

Box 11.2

## Three Methods of Research Review

With all the studies that are conducted and published each year, it is often difficult to sort through all the research. There are three major techniques that researchers use to summarize and understand research findings:

### Literature Review

The first and most common method for reviewing research is called the literature review. Using this approach, the researcher reads the studies that are available on a topic and then summarizes what they think the major conclusions are from that body of research. The advantages to this approach are that most of us are familiar with the technique, it is easy to do, and it allows the reader to consider a wide range of issues. The disadvantages include the potential for bias of the reviewer, and the selection of studies to review.

### Ballot Counting

The second approach is called ballot counting. With this technique, the researcher gathers the research studies on a particular topic and then "counts" the number of studies that show or do not show some effect. This is the approach that Robert Martinson used to arrive at his now famous conclusion that "nothing works." He gathered 231 studies on correctional intervention, divided them into topics (e.g., education programs, work programs, etc.) and then determined that there were more studies that showed no effect than were those that did. Thus his conclusion was based on a tallying of the number of studies that showed no effect (by the way, 48% of the studies he reviewed showed a positive effect). This approach is also relatively easy to do; however, because the majority wins, it tells us little about the programs that do report positive effects.

### Meta-Analysis

The third approach that has become increasingly popular with researchers is called meta-analysis. This approach uses a quantitative synthesis of research findings in a body of literature. Meta-analysis computes the "effect size" between the treatment and outcome variable—in our case, recidivism. The effect size can be negative (treatment increases recidivism), zero, or positive (treatment reduces recidivism). Meta-analysis

Box 11.2—*continued*

also has some limitations. First, meta-analysis is effected by "what goes into it": what studies are included in the analysis. Second, how factors are coded can also be an important issue (e.g., into what treatment categories). There are major advantages, however, to meta-analysis. First, it is possible to control for factors that might influence the size of a treatment effect (e.g., size of sample, quality of research design, length of treatment). Second, it provides a quantifiable result that can be replicated and tested by other researchers. Third, meta-analysis helps build knowledge about a subject such as correctional treatment in a precise and parsimonious way.

All three approaches allow us to review a large body of knowledge; however, given the advantages of meta-analysis, it is becoming more popular with researchers. As we will see, the approach is not as important as what we can learn from the research.

can be measured. While traditional audits and accreditation processes are one step in this direction, thus far they have proven to be inadequate. For example, audits can be an important means to ensure if a program is meeting contractual obligations or a set of prescribed standards; however, these conditions may not have any relationship to effective intervention. It is also important to note that outcome studies and assessment of program quality are not necessarily mutually exclusive. Combining outcome indicators with assessments of program quality can provide a more complete picture of an intervention's effectiveness. Fortunately, there has been considerable progress in identifying the hallmarks of effective programs (Andrews, Zinger, Hoge, Bonta, Gendreau & Cullen, 1990; Cullen & Applegate, 1998; Gendreau & Paparozzi, 1995; Gendreau & Ross, 1979, 1987; Palmer, 1995). This issue will be examined later in this chapter.

## Parole Effectiveness

What is actually known about the effectiveness of probation and parole, and other community correctional alternatives, and what should be future research priorities? The next section summarizes what is generally concluded about selected topic areas of interest in parole effectiveness. This discussion of topic areas is basically organized along the general flow of criminal justice decision points as they relate to parole; however, most of the findings also pertain to probation, particularly those on supervision and innovative programs.

## Institutional Factors

Several aspects of the institutional experience are thought to be related to parole and its effectiveness, such as length of time incarcerated, prison behavior, institutional programs, and parole conditions imposed as conditions of release.

### Time Served

Early research that examined the effects of the amount of time served in prison on parole has generally concluded that the shorter the amount of time served, the greater the likelihood of successful parole (Gottfredson, Gottfredson & Garofalo, 1977; Eichman, 1965).

Similarly, Smith, Goggin and Gendreau (2002) conducted a meta-analysis of the prison literature. The results included a total of 27 studies comparing community-based offenders (e.g., probationers) to inmates, as well as 23 studies comparing prisoners who served longer sentences to prisoners who served shorter sentences. Results indicated that offenders who were imprisoned had recidivism rates approximately 7 percent higher than community-based offenders, and inmates who served longer sentences had a recidivism rate that was 3 percent higher than inmates with shorter sentences (Smith, Goggin & Gendreau, 2002). See Figure 11.4.

Figure 11.4
**Percent Increase in Recidivism by Type of Sanction**

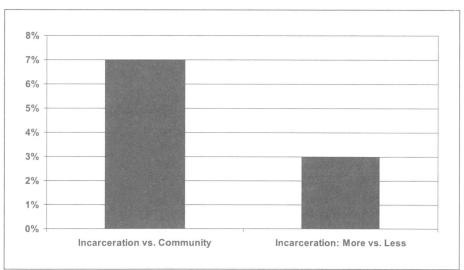

Source: Smith, P., Goggin, C., & Gendreau, P. (2002). *The Effects of Prison Sentences and Intermediate Sanctions on Recidivism: Age, Gender, and Race* (Research Report). Ottawa, Ontario: Solicitor General of Canada, Corrections Research Branch.

Most researchers, however, have concluded that longer prison terms have an adverse effect upon parolee chances of success, implying that the negative aspects of prisonization seem to intensify with time. For example, in his study of shock probationers, Vito (1978) concluded that even a short period of incarceration has a negative impact. The question that remains unanswered by this research is: Are there any characteristics of inmates who have served more time that are also associated with an unfavorable parole outcome?

## Prison Programs

Does participation in prison programs have an effect on recidivism? Existing research on the effectiveness of institutional programs and prison behavior has been limited in its scope. Most such programs are analyzed in relation to institutional adjustment, disciplinary problems, and impact of program participation on the parole-granting process. The few evaluations that included a parole period usually show little if any positive effects with regard to recidivism. A recent study by Smith (2006), however, examined the relationship between program participation and recidivism in a Canadian sample of 5,469 federal offenders. Results indicated that programs targeting criminogenic needs reduced post-release recidivism by 9 percent for moderate risk offenders, and 11 percent for high risk offenders. German correctional researchers recently evaluated the effectiveness of social therapy programs across eight prisons, and the results were remarkably similar (Egg, Pearson, Cleland & Lipton, 2000). The overall average reduction in recidivism for what is generally described as moderate to high risk adult incarcerates was 12 percent.

Most research that has examined prison behavior has not found a relationship between prison behavior and success on parole (von Hirsch & Hanrahan, 1979; Morris, 1978). However, a study by Gottfredson, Gottfredson, and Adams (1982), found that there is some relation between institutional infractions and infractions while on parole, after controlling for prior record (Finchamp, 1988). French and Gendreau (2004) also examined the relationship between participation in prison-based programs and misconducts/post-release recidivism using meta-analytic techniques. Prison-based programs targeting criminogenic needs reduced misconducts by 26 percent, and reduced post-release recidivism by 14 percent (French & Gendreau, 2004). Overall, however, there has not been a great deal of attention given to the relationship between institutional programs, prison behavior, and subsequent success or failure on parole.

## Work and Education Programs

Two areas that have received some attention are work and education programs for offenders. Although the literature on education programs is inconclusive, the evidence does seem to suggest that educational programs[6] can positively affect inmate behavior and recidivism (Linden & Perry, 1982; Ayers, Duguid, Montague & Wolowidnyk, 1980; Roberts & Cheek, 1994; Eskridge & Newbold, 1994). A recent study by MacKenzie and Hickman (1998:17,23) examined 12 correctional education programs for adult offenders. Of the 12 studies, eight produced results suggesting that correctional education may have a positive impact on the rate of recidivism. They also concluded that while there were some inconsistencies in the findings, the preponderance of evidence suggested that vocational education programs were effective in reducing recidivism.

---

Box 11.3

### Vocational and Academic Indicators of Parole Success

Schumaker et al. (1990) reported on the effects of in-prison vocational and academic coursework for 760 inmates who were followed on parole for 12 months. Their employment information and criminal activity rates (technical violations and new arrests) were gathered. The vocational/academic groups generally had the lowest criminal activity rates and the highest employment rates. Those who had earned a General Education Diploma had the lowest criminal activity rate, and the control group who did not participate in vocation/academic programming had the highest criminal activity rate.

Stevens and Ward (1997) tracked North Carolina inmates who had earned their associate and/or baccalaureate degrees while imprisoned, and found that prison inmates who earned their degrees tended to become law-abiding citizens significantly more often that did inmates who did not advance their education.

Sources: R. Schumaker, D. Anderson, and S. Anderson (1990). "Vocational and Academic Indicators of Parole Success." *Journal of Correctional Education*, 41:8-13; and D. Stevens and C. Ward (1997). "College Education and Recidivism." *Journal of Correctional Education*, 48(3):106-111.

Likewise the literature on work programs[7] does not convincingly demonstrate reduced recidivism (Zeisel, 1982; Vito, 1985b). Gendreau and Ross (1987:380; MacKenzie & Hickman, 1998), however, provide some principles that should be followed with regard to work programs: (1) they must enhance practical skills, (2) develop interpersonal skills and minimize prisonization, and (3) ensure that work is not intended as punishment alone.

In a study that reviewed the available research on corrections-based education, vocational, and work programs, Wilson and his associates (1999) looked at 33 studies. The majority of the studies they reviewed reported that the education or work programs had reduced recidivism, with the average reduction between four and 14 percent. Despite these promising findings, the researchers did not believe the research provided sufficient evidence of the effectiveness of these programs. This was attributed to a lack of high quality studies.

## Therapeutic Communities

In recent years, prison-based therapeutic communities (TCs) have made a resurgence (See Box 11.4). This is due in part to increased federal funding. Although there is a great deal of variation in how therapeutic communities operate, the essential ingredient is the principle that all staff and offenders provide therapeutic experiences. TCs are more common in prisons, however, many operate in community based facilities, such as halfway houses.

A number of studies have shown that TCs can have an appreciable effect on recidivism rates, especially, when community follow-up aftercare is provided (see Martin, Butzin, Saum & Inciardi, 1999; Wexler, Melnick, Lowe & Peters, 1999; Knight, Simpson & Hiller, 1999). Figure 11.5 shows the results from one such program operating in Delaware.

## Faith-Based Programs

One of President Bush's initiatives has been the expansion of faith-based programs in human service. While faith-based programs have a long history in corrections, there has been surprisingly little empirical research conducted on its effectiveness, and the results are mixed. Religious programs in prisons may help inmates cope; however, research indicates that offenders who had poor coping skills prior to prison have poor coping skills in prison (Porporino & Zamble, 1984). Since 1985, 23 studies have explored relationship between religion and deviance in the general population. Eighteen of those studies show evidence that

Box 11.4

## Therapeutic Communities

Therapeutic communities or TCs as they are commonly known, are eclectic in nature and offer an intense self-help model that focuses on the whole person. Staff and offenders are intimately involved in the treatment process. Confrontation and accountability are key ingredients of a TC. Offenders who engage in appropriate behavior are given "pull-ups" (positive reinforcement) by other offenders and staff, while those who engage in behavior detrimental to them or others are given "haircuts" (confronted about their behavior). One of the criticisms leveled at TCs is their use of shaming and other degrading sanctions. For example, some TCs have been known to have offenders wear diapers like a baby, sit in chairs for long periods of time, wear dunce hats, and other punishments designed to change the behavior of the participant.

Figure 11.5
**Therapeutic Community Treatment: Arrest Rates After a Three Year Follow-Up (percent arrested)**

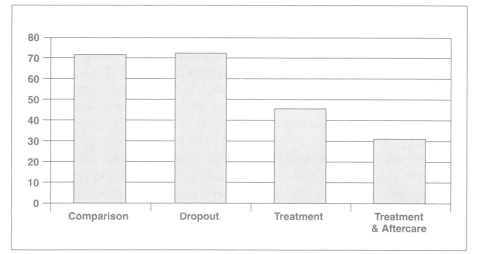

Source: Martin, S., C. Butzin, C. Saum, and J. Inciardi (1999). "Three-Year Outcomes of Therapeutic Community Treatment for Drug-Involved Offenders in Delaware." *The Prison Journal*, 79(2):294-320.

religiosity reduces deviance (that is, people of strong faith are generally less criminal than non-believers); however, this does not appear to translate well into correctional programming.

Only two studies have examined effects of religious participation on institutional adjustment and infractions. In 1984, Johnson studied 782 inmates in Florida. The results indicated no differences in disciplinary problems or institutional adjustment for religious and nonreligious inmates. In 1992, Clear et al. studied non-random sample of 769 inmates in 20 prisons in 12 states. They concluded that a prisoner's religious participation had a significant and positive relationship to prison adjustment. They also found other factors played a role such as age and race of offender.

Similarly, only three studies have examined religion and post-release behavior. In 1987, Johnson et al. studied inmates released from four adult male prisons in New York. One group participated in Prison Fellowship Program (PFP); one did not. The results from this research indicated that the level of participation influenced prison adjustment, however, the direction was not always as anticipated:

- High level of involvement PFP participants less likely to commit infractions than low or moderate participants

- However, high PFP participants received more serious infractions

- High PFP participants were significantly less likely to be rearrested during the follow-up, but this relationship was strongest for whites and nonsignificant for African-Americans.

Young et al. (1995) followed a group of 180 federal inmates trained as volunteer prison ministers who attended special seminars, and a matched control group. Overall, the seminar group had a significantly lower rate of recidivism and maintained a higher survival rate than did the control group. Seminars were most effective with lower-risk subjects, whites and women.

A more recent study by Sumter (1999) followed inmates from the Clear, Stout, and Dammer (1992) study. There were no differences in the recidivism rates between "religious" and "nonreligious" inmates; furthermore, regardless of how many times they attended chapel, inmates who had a greater religious orientation in terms of values were less likely to recidivate. Sumter also found that offenders who attended religious programs upon release were less likely to recidivate; however no relationship existed between attending inside and outside prison. Participation in religious programs was certainly no panacea: 66 percent of "religious" prisoners experienced one or more arrests in the follow-up period. Sumter concluded that religion as a correctional program is complicated and multifaceted—as personal as it is social—and becomes more complicated in a prison setting. Inmates embrace religion for a number of reasons, some heartening (spirituality and coping mechanism), and some cynical (get snacks, time out of cell, more freedom, looks good for parole). What we do know is that prisons distort everything. What may seem like a quest for spiritual awakening on the surface can simply be a way to get around the strictures of confinement. Related to this is the fact that we have little understanding of precisely how religion works, or what the best definition of "religious" might be (conversion, weekly service attendance, number of books read in Bible study, punitive versus redemptive orientation, or frequency of participation in such religious rites as attending church, participation in services, tithing, frequency of prayer, or proselytizing.) Regardless of the findings on faith based correctional programs, most of us would agree that pursuit of religious understanding is a basic human right—prisoners who wish to engage in spiritual expression should be encouraged to do so, but this is true regardless of what the research finds. It does not mean that faith-based programs will have a significant effect on recidivism rates.

Given all the contradictions from the research, it is often difficult to determine what, if any, effects prison-based treatment has on offender behavior. In a large study that was conducted by researchers in Washington State (Aos et al., 1999), the research examined all the available studies and conducted a meta-analysis to determine effect sizes on recidivism. As can been in Figure 11.6, they found that Life Skills programs produced no reductions in recidivism, but subsidizing jobs for offenders age 27 and over produced reductions of 24 percent.

## Parole Conditions

Offenders who are granted parole are required to follow rules and conditions. Failure to do so can lead to reincarceration. With regard to the imposition of parole conditions, a nationwide survey of 52 parolee field supervision agencies, Allen and Latessa (1980) found 49 had residency requirements as a condition of parole, and 47 had an employment requirement. The Travis and Latessa (1984) survey found similar results. In spite of the widespread requirement of parole conditions, the literature produced only three studies that were directly related to the imposition of these conditions and parole effectiveness. Although two studies (Beasley, 1978; Morgan, 1993) showed a relationship between stability of residency and parole success, the lack of research in this area makes generalization difficult.

Figure 11.6
**Washington State Study of the Average Effect Sizes of Prison Programs**
**(average percent reduction in recidivism)**

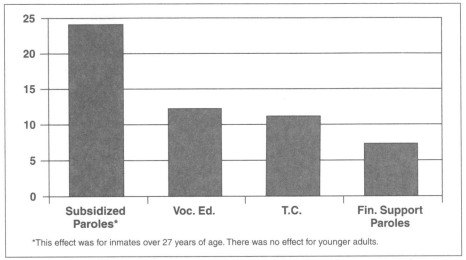

*This effect was for inmates over 27 years of age. There was no effect for younger adults.

Source: Aos, S. et al. (1999). *The Comparative Costs and Benefits of Programs to Reduce Crime.* Olympia, WA: Washington State Institute for Public Safety.

One of the most important conditions of parole is the requirement to report regularly to a parole officer, and not to leave a prescribed area such as the county without permission. Offenders who fail to report or whose whereabouts are unknown are called absconders. A study by Williams, McShane, and Dolny (2000) found that 27 percent of parolees in California were listed as absconders, and another study conducted by Schwaner (1997) in Ohio found 11 percent. Absconders have problems with alcohol abuse, have been convicted of a property crime, and have a history of prior parole violation and absence of suitable housing (Buckholtz & Foos, 1996). Despite these high numbers of absconders, there has been little research on this subject.

## Parole Release

Primarily in response to the supporters of determinate sentencing,[8] researchers have increasingly turned their attention to evaluating the success of parole supervision.

Critics of parole supervision rely on two basic arguments to support their views. The first is that parole supervision simply is not effective in reducing recidivism (Citizens' Inquiry on Parole and Criminal Justice, 1975; Wilson, 1977). The second, more philosophical argument is that supervision is not "just" (von Hirsch & Hanrahan, 1979). A more plausible conclusion is that the evidence is mixed; that parole supervision is effective in reducing recidivism rates among parolees (Flanagan, 1985).

Several studies have compared parolees to mandatory releases, but they have failed to control for possible differences in the selection of the groups (Martinson & Wilks, 1977). Other studies that have been controlled for differences have reported favorable results (Lerner, 1977; Gottfredson, 1975), and yet other studies have reported less positive results (Waller, 1974; Nuttal et al., 1977; Jackson, 1983). In one study, Gottfredson, Mitchell-Herzfeld, and Flanagan (1982:292) concluded "much of our data does indicate an effect for parole supervision, an effect that varies by offender attributes, and an effect that appears not to be very large." The existing evidence seems to be in favor of parole supervision, although there is no clear consensus as to its effectiveness.

Even the most outspoken critics of parole agree that the agencies responsible for the task of supervision are often understaffed, their officers undertrained, underpaid, and overworked. They are inundated with excessively large caseloads, workloads, and paperwork. Community services are either unavailable or unwilling to handle parolees, and as a consequence parole officers are expected to be all things to all people. As indicated in Chapter 6, they are also expected to perform the dual roles of surveillance-policeman and rehabilitator-treatment agent.

There is some evidence that, by shortening the amount of time on parole, we could save a considerable amount of money and time, and not seriously increase the risk of failure. Most data seem to indicate that the majority of failures on parole occur during the first two years (Hoffman & Stone-Meierhoefer, 1980; Flanagan, 1982) and drop significantly thereafter. There is also some evidence that early release into the community and from parole incurs no higher risk to the community and, in fact, is justifiable on cost considerations (Holt, 1975), a conclusion echoed by MacKenzie and Piquero (1994:244-245). It is also important to note that easing the offender back into the community through community residential centers and furlough programs can facilitate the early release process. The definition and purpose of community residential centers and furloughs are found in Box 11.5 and Box 11.6, respectively.

A Washington State (1976) 10-year follow-up of parolees found that the first year of parole was critical, with more than one-half of those paroled returning to prison during this time period. In this study, there were more failures in the second, than in first, six months after release. It was also found that those convicted of murder and manslaughter were less likely to recidivate, and that property offenders—especially those convicted of burglary, auto theft, and forgery—had the highest failure rate. As expected, younger parolees did significantly worse than those 40 years of age or older. Blacks did slightly worse than whites after the first six months, and Native Americans did significantly worse than all other groups.

Box 11.5

### America's Community Residential Centers

Community residential centers (also known as halfway houses) are residential facilities where probationers, furloughees, and parolees may be placed when they are in need of a more structured setting. The primary purpose of a halfway house is to limit an offender's freedom while encouraging reintegration into society through employment, education, treatment, habilitation, restitution, training, compliance with financial sanctions, and other activities designed to rehabilitate the offender and deter future crime (Ohio Community Corrections Organization, 1993).

Box 11.6

### Furloughs

Furlough is a phased re-entry program designed to ease the offender's transition from prison to the community. Furloughs include escorted or unescorted leaves from confinement, granted for designated purposes and time periods (funerals, dying relatives, etc.), before the formal sentence expires. Primarily used for employment, vocational training, or education, furlough in effect extends the limits of confinement to include temporary residence in the community during the last months of confinement. Furloughees are frequently required to reside in community residential centers. Furloughs allow parole boards to observe the offender's behavior in the community and may lead to faster release from parole supervision for those adjusting favorably. Because furloughees are closely screened and supervised in the community, failure rates appear to be low. For example, Ohio reports a nine percent return to prison rate for calendar 1992 (Ohio Community Corrections Organization)

It is important to note that many of the failures on parole supervision are a result of technical violations (TVs), that is, failure to abide by the conditions imposed by the parole board. TVs can range from a positive drug test, to failure to report as directed. Some states have reported that the reincarceration rates for parolees have dropped; Texas reported their high of 50 percent in 1992 declined to 31 percent in 1997, and Pennsylvania reported a decline from 50 percent in 1994 to 39 percent in 1996. The reasons offered for these declines are not know, but possible explanations include an older parole population, and lower-risk offenders being sent to prison. Figures 11.7 and 11.8 illustrate the reason for failure for probationers and parolees.

Figure 11.7
**Probationers Returned to Custody During 2005**

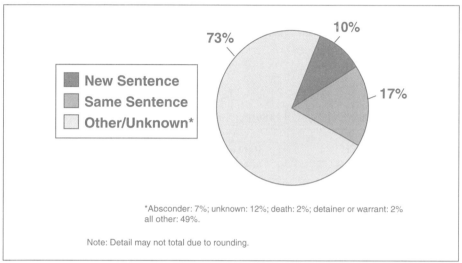

Source: Bureau of Justice Statistics (2006). *Probation and Parole in the United States, 2005*. Washington, DC: Bureau of Justice Statistics, p. 5-6 (www.ojp.usdoj.gov/bjs/abstract/ppus05htm).

Figure 11.8
**Parolees Returned to Prison During Year 2005**

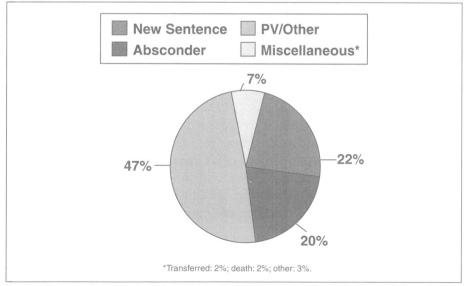

Source: Bureau of Justice Statistics (2006). *Probation and Parole in the United States, 2005*. Washington, DC: Bureau of Justice Statistics, p. 7,9 (www.ojp.usdoj.gov/bjs/abstract/ppus05htm).

Studies of parole success by type of offense repeatedly indicate that those who commit murder are among the best parole risks (Neithercutt, 1972). The reasons for this conclusion vary; the explanation most frequently offered is that most murderers tend to be first offenders who have committed crimes of passion. Another reason cited is age; because most convicted murderers spend a great amount of time incarcerated, they tend to be older (and more mature) when released, usually after the high-crime-risk years of 16 to 29. See Table 11.1.

Table 11.1
**Age of Parolees and Likelihood of Failure**

| Age at time of prison release | Rate of return to prison by years after release from prison | | | | | | |
|---|---|---|---|---|---|---|---|
| | YEARS | | | | | | |
| | 1 | 2 | 3 | 4 | 5 | 6 | 7 |
| 18-24 years old | 21% | 34% | 41% | 45% | 48% | 49% | 50% |
| 25-34 | 12 | 21 | 28 | 33 | 37 | 41 | 43 |
| 35-44 | 7 | 14 | 18 | 22 | 26 | 30 | 34 |
| 45+ | 2 | 4 | 6 | 8 | 10 | 11 | 12 |
| All Ages | 14 | 23 | 29 | 34 | 37 | 40 | 42 |

Source: Adopted from A.J. Beck (1987). "Recidivism of Young Parolees." Bureau of Justice Statistics.

In a study of murderers that had been given a death sentence, and then had that sentence commuted when *Furman v. Georgia* was overturned, Vito, Wilson, and Latessa (1991) found that 43.5 percent of the death row inmates in Ohio were paroled and that 25 percent were returned to prison (recidivated). These results were very similar to those found in Texas, where 19 percent of the paroled *Furman* cases recidivated (Marquart & Sorensen, 1988), and in Kentucky, which had a 29 percent failure rate (Vito & Wilson, 1988). Overall, studies examining murderers were found to generate consistent findings and conclusions over time.

Table 11.2
**Failure Rates of Parolees**

| Percent of Young Parolees Who within 6 Years of Release from Prison Were— | | | |
|---|---|---|---|
| | Rearrested | Reconvicted | Reincarcerated |
| All Parolees: | 69% | 53% | 49% |
| Sex: | | | |
| Male | 70% | 54% | 50% |
| Female | 52 | 40 | 36 |
| Race: | | | |
| White | 64% | 49% | 45% |
| Black | 76 | 60 | 56 |
| Hispanic | 71 | 50 | 44 |
| Other | 75 | 65 | 63 |
| Education: | | | |
| Less than 12 yrs. | 71% | 55% | 51% |
| High School Graduate | 61 | 46 | 43 |
| Some College | 48 | 44 | 31 |
| Paroling Offense: | | | |
| Violent Offense | 64% | 43% | 39% |
| Murder | 70 | 25 | 22 |
| Robbery | 64 | 45 | 40 |
| Assault | 72 | 51 | 47 |
| Property Offense | 73 | 60 | 56 |
| Burglary | 73 | 60 | 56 |
| Forgery/Fraud | 74 | 59 | 56 |
| Larceny | 71 | 61 | 55 |
| Drug Offense | 49% | 30% | 25% |

Source: Adopted from A.J. Beck (1987). *Recidivism of Young Parolees.* Bureau of Justice Statistics.

A recent study by Austin (2001:331) has examined the important issue of prisoner re-entry. He concluded "it is not clear that parolees, in the aggregate, pose as large a public safety problem as some believe."

In order to summarize, we have selected data from a national study of parole recidivism (Beck, 1987). These data confirm two important points with regard to parole effectiveness; (1) recidivism rates vary depending upon the definition of recidivism, and (2) the type of offense and age are important factors in determining parole success. Other findings included the following:

- Approximately 10 percent of the persons paroled accounted for 40 percent of the subsequent arrest offenses.

- About one-fifth of the subsequent arrests occurred in states other than the original paroling state.

- An estimated 37 percent of the parolees were rearrested while still on parole.

- Recidivism rates were highest in the first two years after an offender's release from prison. Within one year, 32 percent of those paroled had been arrested; within two years, 47 percent had been rearrested.

- Recidivism was higher among men, blacks, and persons who had not completed high school than among women, whites, and high school graduates.

- Almost three-quarters of those paroled for property offenses were rearrested for a serious crime compared to about two-thirds of those paroled for violent offenses.

- Approximately one-third of both property offenders and violent offenders were rearrested for a violent crime upon release from prison.

- The longer the parolee's prior arrest record, the higher the rate of recidivism—more than 90 percent of the parolees with six or more previous adult arrests were rearrested compared to 59 percent of the first-time offender.

- The earlier the parolee's first adult arrest, the more likely the chances for rearrest—79 percent of those arrested and charged as an adult before the age of 17 were rearrested, compared to 51 percent of those first arrested at the age of 20 or older.

- Time served in prison had no consistent impact on recidivism rates—those who had served six months or less in prison were about as likely to be arrested as those who had served more than two years.

## Probation Effectiveness

As with parole, the quality of probation research is dubious. Unlike parole, which is found on state and federal levels, probation still remains primarily a local governmental function. The fact is that probation can be found at local, state, and federal levels; that there are municipal and county probation departments; and that probation serves both misdemeanants and felons. These combined with the problems discussed previously, make research in probation very difficult to conduct. Indeed, much of the research has been limited to only the several probation departments to which researchers have been welcome. This event gives us a limited sense of the true picture of probation.

---

Box 11.7

## Estimated Time to Serve

As we go to press, Congress is considering a proposal to require prison inmates to serve a larger percentage of their sentences. If the current average sentence remained the same for violent offenders and the required policy were to be to serve 85 percent of the current sentence, the predicted times served would be increased by:

- for new admissions, 26 months;

- for prisoners now present, 84 months;

- for releases, an average of 33 months longer in prison.

Based on current sentences, the estimated time predicted to be served would be:

| Percent of sentence served | Prison admissions | Prisoners present | Prison releases |
|---|---|---|---|
| Current | 62 months | 100 months | 43 months |
| 75% | 78 months | 162 months | 67 months |
| 85% | 88 months | 188 months | 76 months |
| 100% | 104 months | 216 months | 89 months |

Source: L. Greenfield (1995). *Prison Sentences and Time Served for Violence.* Washington, DC: U.S. Department of Justice.

---

As with parole, the research on probation effectiveness will be divided into sections. However, unlike our presentation of parole, the research on probation will be divided into five groups: studies that compare the performance of offenders receiving alternative dispositions; studies that simply measure probation outcome without comparison with any other form of sanction; studies that measure probation outcome and then attempt to isolate the characteristics which tend to differentiate between successful and nonsuccessful outcomes; studies that examine the cost effectiveness of probation; and studies that examine probation combined with therapeutic drug courts.

## Probation versus Alternative Dispositions

To examine the effectiveness of probation compared to other dispositions we looked at six studies. Three of the studies compared recidivism rates of individuals placed on probation with individuals sentenced to incarceration. Babst and Mannering's study (1965) compared similar types of offenders who were imprisoned or placed on probation. The sample consisted of 7,614 Wisconsin offenders who were statistically comparable in original disposition, county of commitment, type of offense committed, number of prior felonies, and marital status. Parolees were followed for two years, and probationers were followed for two years or until discharge from probation, whichever came first. Violations were defined as the commission of a new offense or the violation of probation/parole rules. The findings of this study showed that, for offenders with no prior felony convictions, the violation rate was 25 percent for probationers and 32.9 percent for parolees. For offenders with one prior felony conviction, violation rates were 41.8 percent for probationers and 43.9 percent for parolees; for offenders with two or more felonies, the rates were 51.8 percent for probationers and 48.7 percent for parolees. With respect to the difference in violation rates for first offenders (which was statistically significant at the .05 level), Babst and Mannering note that this finding could be a result of the fact that parolees are a more difficult group to supervise or could actually show that, at least for first offenders, incarceration does more harm than good.

Another study done in Wisconsin (Wisconsin Division of Corrections, 1965) compared the performance of burglars, who had no previous felony convictions, sentenced to prison or placed on probation. While this study also attempted to investigate the characteristics associated with successful and nonsuccessful probationers and parolees, we will simply report at this point that the violation rate (based on a two-year follow-up, using the same definition of violation rate as Babst and Mannering, above) for burglars placed on probation was 23 percent, and for burglars who were incarcerated and then placed on parole was 34 percent. Thus, it appears that, as with the Wisconsin study, probation was more successful than parole.

The Pennsylvania Program for Women and Girl Offenders, Inc. (1976) compared recidivism rates between all women placed on state probation or released on state parole during a two-year period. Recidivism was defined as any technical violation of probation or parole or any new criminal charge. The findings showed that, overall, women placed on probation had a 35.6 percent recidivism rate. When only women with no prior convictions were considered, the probationers had a 24 percent recidivism rate, and the parolees had a 23.1 percent rate. The differences between these rates were not statistically significant.

Vito (1978) compared regular probationers with shock probationers (who served at least 30 days in prison). He found that shock probationers had a 40 percent higher probability of failure than those released to regular supervision. Vito and Allen (1981:16) concluded:

> . . . the fact of incarceration is having some unknown and unmeasurable effect upon (the more unfavorable) performance of shock probationers. . . . It could be that the negative effects of incarceration are affecting the performance of shock probationers.

Whereas these four studies compared probation with some form of incarceration, a California study (California Department of Justice, 1969) compared violation rates among offenders placed on probation, offenders sentenced to probation following a jail term, and offenders given straight jail sentences. The study examined the performance of a cohort of offenders, all of whom had an equal exposure of one full year in the community. For the probation group, cohort status was gained on the date of the beginning of the probation period; for the group receiving jail sentences, cohort status began on the date of release from jail. To evaluate the relative effectiveness of these dispositions, three violation levels were used: "none" or no known arrest for a technical violation or a new offense, "minor" or at least an arrest and perhaps a conviction resulting in a jail sentence of less than 90 days or probation of one year or less, and "major," signifying at least a conviction resulting in a jail sentence of not less than 90 days or a term of probation exceeding one year. Because each case was followed for only one year, the final outcome of a violation occasionally did not occur until after the year was over. If it could be inferred that the disposition or sentence was the result of an arrest that did occur within the follow-up year, the action was included in the violation rate.

The findings of this study are illustrated in Table 11.3. Those offenders receiving jail sentences without the benefit of probation services have the worst record of recidivism.

Table 11.3
**Violation Levels of Sentenced Offenders in California**

| Sentence | Violations | | |
|---|---|---|---|
| | None | Minor | Major |
| Probation only | 64.7% | 23.7% | 11.6% |
| Jail, then probation | 50.3% | 31.7% | 18.0% |
| Jail only | 46.6% | 29.5% | 23.9% |

Source: California Department of Justice (1969).

These studies illustrate that, as a disposition, probation appears to be more effective than incarceration, even for a short period of time. This may be due, in part, to the fact that probationers immediately return to the community, their jobs, and their families.

Finally, an Alaska Study (Alaska Department of Health and Social Services, 1976) utilized an experimental design to compare the performance of misdemeanant offenders receiving probation supervision with offenders officially on probation but not required to report to the probation unit. The groups were created by random assignment to the experimental group (under supervision) or the control group (no supervision) and were followed for periods ranging from two months to slightly more than two years. Performance was assessed by means of recidivism, defined as the conviction for a new offense. The findings of the study showed that 22 percent of the experimental group members and 24 of the control group members had been convicted of new offenses during the follow-up period.

Given the paucity of research and the caution with which recidivism data must be approached, it is nearly impossible, not to mention inappropriate, to attempt to draw any definitive conclusions from these studies about the effectiveness of probation compared to other alternative dispositions. Nonetheless, it appears from the limited research that has been conducted that the following tentative conclusions can be reached. Of the studies that compared probation to incarceration, it tentatively appears that probation may have a significant impact on first offenders. It may also be suggested that the severity of violations appears to increase in proportion to the severity of the disposition. It does not appear that the provision of probation supervision for misdemeanants is more effective than an unsupervised probation period.

## Probation Outcome

There were a number of studies that reported recidivism rates only for probationers. Thirteen of these were reviewed, but one should remember that definitions of failure, follow-up periods, and the types of offenders differ significantly from one study to another. Table 11.4 includes the author, types of instant offenses committed by the probationers in the study, and the definition of failure used in the study, the length of follow-up, and the failure rates.

These summary descriptions illustrate many of the problems associated with attempting to assess probation effectiveness. The type of offenders constituting the samples (as represented by instant offenses) varies, as do the definitions used in each study to characterize failure. Four studies computed failure rates while offenders were on probation, and the length of follow-up periods ranged from several months to many years.

Table 11.4
**Studies Reporting Recidivism Rates for Probationers**

| Study | Instant Offense | Failure | Follow-Up | Failure Rate (%) |
|---|---|---|---|---|
| Caldwell (1951) | Internal revenue laws (72%) | Convictions | Post-probation 5½-11½ yrs. | 16.4 |
| England (1955) | Bootlegging (48%) & forgery | Convictions | Post-probation 6-12 yrs. | 17.7 |
| Davis (1955) | Burglary, forgery & checks | Two or more violations (technical & new offense) | To termination 4-7 yrs. | 30.2 |
| Frease (1964) | Unknown | Inactive letter, Bench warrant & revocation | On probation 18-30 mos. | 20.2 |
| Landis et al. (1969) | Auto theft, forgery & checks | Revocation (technical & new offense) | To termination | 52.5 |
| Irish (1972) | Larceny & burglary | Arrests or convictions | Post-probation Minimum 4 yrs. | 41.5 |
| Missouri Div. Probation & Parole (1976) | Burglary, larceny & vehicle theft | Arrests & convictions | Post-probation 6 mos.- 7 yrs. | 30.0 |
| Kusuda (1976) | Property | Revocation | To termination 1-2 yrs. | 18.3 |
| Comptroller General (1976) | Unknown | Revocation & post-release conviction | Post-probation 20 mo. average | 55.0 |
| Irish (1977) | Property | Arrests | Post-probation 3-4 yrs. | 29.6 |
| Petersilia (1985) | Felony probationers | Arrests | Tracked over 40 mos. | 65.0 |
| McGaha, Fichter & Hirschburg (1987) | Felony probationers | Arrests | Tracked over 40 mos. | 22.3 |
| Vito (1986) | Felony probationers (excluding drug offenses) | Arrests | Tracked over 40 mos. | 22.0 |
| Maxwell, Bynum, Gray, & Combs (2000) | Felony probationers | Revoked | Tracked over 30 mos. | 47.0 |

Source: Adapted and updated from H.E. Allen, E.W. Carlson, and E.C. Parks (September, 1979).
*Critical Issues in Adult Probation: Summary,* p. 35. National Institute of Law Enforcement and Criminal Justice. New studies have been added over time.

Most of the studies reviewed here stated that their purpose was to assess "probation effectiveness;" however, unlike the five studies examined earlier, none of these studies defined a base (such as a failure rate for comparable parolees or offenders on summary probation) against which to compare findings in order to support a claim that probation is an effective alternative for rehabilitating offenders.

In a recent study of 1,700 probationers in Michigan (Maxwell et al., 2000) found that only 24 percent of probationers had no technical violations during a 30-month follow-up period. The results are summarized in Figure 11.9. Treatment related violations, such as dirty urine or failing to attend treatment programs accounted for the largest proportion of violations, followed by failure to appear. Only 13 percent of the violations were for a new crime.

Figure 11.9
**Michigan Study of Probationer Recidivism (percentage)**

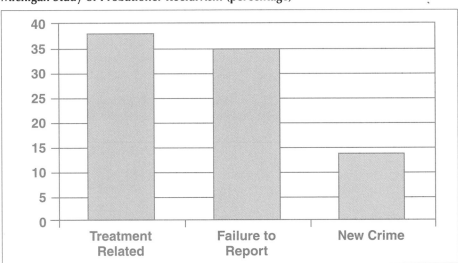

Source: Maxwell, S., T. Bynum, M. Gray, and T. Combs (2000). "Examining Probationer Recidivism in Michigan." *Corrections Compendium*, 25(12):1-4, 18-19.

Recently, MacKenzie and her colleagues (1999:445) studied the impact of probation on the criminal activities of offenders. They concluded that probation alone had an effect on property and dealing crimes. Probation was not significantly associated with reductions in personal crimes of forgery and fraud offenses. The conclusion reached by the authors was that "probation may be more effective than previously thought."

In one of the more critical studies of probation effectiveness, Petersilia (1985) examined 1,672 felony probationers from two counties in California over a 40-month period. She found that more than 67 percent were re-arrested and 51 percent were convicted for a new offense.

Petersilia concluded that felony probationers posed a significant risk to the community. Critics of the Petersilia study quickly pointed out that two urban counties in California are not representative of the rest of the states or the country. Two replication studies, one in Kentucky (Vito, 1986) and one in Missouri (McGaha, Fichter & Hirschburg, 1987) found quite different results. In both Kentucky and Missouri, felony probationers were re-arrested at about one-third of the rate as those in California.

---

**Box 11.8**

### Probationers Rearrested for a Felony Within Three Years

State courts in 32 counties across 17 states sentenced 79,000 felons to probation in 1986. Within three years of sentencing, while still on probation, 43 percent were rearrested for a felony. An estimated 18 percent of the arrests were for a violent crime (murder, rape, robbery, or aggravated assault); 33 percent were for a drug offense (drug trafficking or drug possession).

Of each 100 felony probationers tracked for three years:

- 26 went to prison,
- 10 went to jail, and
- 10 absconded.

These findings are based on a follow-up survey of felons on probation, using a sample that represented a fourth of the total 306,000 felons sentenced to probation in 1986. The survey used state criminal history files and probation files to obtain information. It was not based on a nationally representative sample; 39 percent of the follow-up cases were from a single state (California). Nevertheless, based on 12,370 sample cases representing 79,043 felons placed on probation in the counties and states studied, the follow-up represents the largest survey of its kind ever done.

Source: Bureau of Justice Statistics National Update (1994). Washington, DC: U.S. Department of Justice, p. 10.

---

One suggested reason for these differences is the effects of budget cuts on probation staffs in California. Caseloads of over 300 are commonplace, and there is virtually no enforcement of probation conditions (Snider, 1986). In spite of the reasons, it is important to note that the effectiveness of felony probation is still very much in debate.

Morgan (1993) studied 266 adult felony probationers in Tennessee to determine factors associated with favorable probation outcome and those that would predict success. She found that only 27 percent of the probationers failed and that females, married probationers, and those with higher levels of education were most likely to succeed. Factors significantly related to probation failure were prior felonies, prior probation, prior institutional commitment, and probation sentence length (the longer the sentence, the more likely the failure).

The review of these studies demonstrates that little progress has apparently been made over the past few years toward an adequate assessment of probation. The conclusions drawn by the authors of these studies, however, appear to suggest that there exists an unwritten agreement or rule of thumb that probation can be considered to be effective, and that a failure rate above 30 percent indicates it is not effective. This tendency is suggested by the comments in Table 11.5.

## Probation Outcome and Statistics

In addition to measuring the effectiveness of probation, a number of studies have also attempted to isolate characteristics that could be related to offender rehabilitation. Table 11.6 presents a summary of the major factors that were found in each study to be statistically correlated with failure. Keeping in mind the methodological differences among the studies in terms of definition of failure and specification of follow-up period, it appears that the one characteristic most commonly found to be associated with failure is the probationer's previous criminal histories. Other factors frequently cited are: the youthfulness of the probationer, marital status other than married, unemployment, and educational level below the eleventh grade.

Factors such as employment and education are dynamic factors that are correlated with outcome. Since these are areas that can be addressed during supervision, one can reasonably view these factors positively; we have a clear indication of offender needs, and they can be improved. On the other hand, a question remains as to whether probation and parole officers are addressing these needs adequately. When probation and parole agencies fail to meet offender needs that are correlated with outcome, the result is often higher failure rates.

Table 11.5
**Evaluations of Effectiveness of Probation**

| Year | Author | Failure Rate | Comments |
|------|--------|--------------|----------|
| 1951 | Caldwell | 16% | [P]robation is an effective method of dealing with federal offenders . . . |
| 1955 | England | 18% | A reconviction rate of less than one-fifth or one-quarter . . . is an acceptable performance for a probation service. |
| 1976 | Missouri | 30% | Probation is an effective and efficient way of handling the majority of offenders in the State of Missouri. |
| 1976 | Comptroller | 55% | [P]robation systems we reviewed were achieving limited success in protecting society and rehabilitating offenders. |
| 1977 | Irish | 30% | [S]upervision program is effectively accomplishing its objective. |
| 1985 | Petersilia | 65% | Felony probation does present a serious threat to public safety. |
| 1986 | Vito | 22% | Felony probation supervision appears to be relatively effective in controlling recidivism . . . |
| 1987 | McGaha et al. | 22% | In Missouri, it does not appear that the current use of felony probation poses a high risk to the security of the community. |
| 1991 | Whitehead | 40% | [C]alls for drastically reduced use of probation for felony offenders are only partially in order. |
| 1994 | Morgan | 27% | [I]nadequate employment and unemployment are major impediments to achieving successful probation adjustment and . . . outcome. |
| 1997 | Mortimer and May | 18% | Electronic monitoring and probation orders yield comparable success rates. |

Source: Adapted and updated from H.E. Allen, E.W. Carlson, and E.C. Parks (September 1979). *Critical Issues in Adult Probation: Summary*, p. 36. National Institute of Law Enforcement and Criminal Justice; J. Petersilia (1985). "Probation and Felony Offenders." *Federal Probation*, 49(2):4-9; G. Vito (1986). "Felony Probation and Recidivism: Replication and Response." *Federal Probation*, 50(4):17-25; J. McGaha, M. Fichter, and P. Hirschburg (1987). "Felony Probation: A Re-Examination of Public Risk." *American Journal of Criminal Justice*, 12:1-9; J.T. Whitehead (1991). "The Effectiveness of Felony Probation: Results from an Eastern State." *Justice Quarterly*, 8:525-543; K. Morgan (1993). "Factors Influencing Probation Outcome: A Review of the Literature." *Federal Probation*, 57(2):23-29. E. Mortimer and C. May (1997). *Electronic Monitoring in Practice*. London, UK: U.K. Home Office.

Table 11.6
**Studies Reporting Factors Related to Probationer Recidivism**

| Study | Previous Criminal History | Youth | Status Other Than Married | Not Employed | Low Income (Below $400) | Education Below 11th Grade | Abuse of Alcohol or Drugs | Property Offender | On-Probation Maladjustment | Imposition of Conditions |
|---|---|---|---|---|---|---|---|---|---|---|
| Caldwell (1951) | Significant correlation | Significant correlation | Significant correlation | Significant correlation | Significant correlation | Significant correlation | | * | | |
| England (1955) | Significant correlation | Significant correlation | Significant correlation | Significant correlation | Significant correlation | Significant correlation | | * | | Significant correlation |
| Davis (1955) | Significant correlation | Significant correlation | | | | | | Significant correlation | Significant correlation | |
| Frease (1964) | Significant correlation | | Significant correlation | | ! | Significant correlation | Significant correlation | | | Significant correlation |
| Landis (1969) | Significant correlation | Significant correlation | Significant correlation | Significant correlation | Significant correlation | Significant correlation | Significant correlation | | Significant correlation | |
| Irish (1972) | Significant correlation | Significant correlation | Significant correlation | Significant correlation | Significant correlation | Significant correlation | Significant correlation | Significant correlation | * | |
| MO Div. of Prob. & Parole (1976) | Significant correlation | Significant correlation | Significant correlation | Significant correlation | + | Significant correlation | Significant correlation | Significant correlation | | |
| Kusuda (1976) | | Significant correlation | Significant correlation | Significant correlation | ! | * | Significant correlation | * | | |
| Comptroller General (1976) | | | | | | | | * | | |
| Irish (1977) | Significant correlation | | | | | | | * | Significant correlation | |
| Petersilia (1985) | Significant correlation | Significant correlation | Significant correlation | Significant correlation | | | | Significant correlation | | |
| Benedict (1998) | Significant correlation | Significant correlation | Significant correlation | | | Significant correlation | Significant correlation | | Significant correlation | Significant correlation |

* In these studies, instant & post-probation offenses committed by probationers were predominantly "property;" however, a correlation between property offenses & recidivism was not investigated.

! Correlation only with income between $100 and $400; those who make less than $100 & those who made above $400 both had an equal probability of success.

+ Correlation only with income between $100 and $700; those who made less than $100 or above $700 both had an equal probability of success.

Source: Adapted from H.E. Allen, E.W. Carlson and E.C. Parks (September 1979). *Critical Issues in Adult Probation: Summary*, p. 37. National Institute of Law Enforcement and Criminal Justice.

---

Box 11.9

### Shock Probation

Shock probation (also known as "reconsideration of sentence" or "shock therapy") is a program allowing sentencing judges to reconsider the offender's original sentence to imprisonment and then recall the inmate for a sentence to probation within the community under conditions deemed appropriate. It is presumed that a short term of incarceration would "shock" the offender into abandoning criminal activity and into pursuit of law-abiding behavior. It can be seen as an alternative disposition for sentencing judges who wish to control probationer behavior through deterrence and tourniquet sentencing. It is a last-ditch program used by some judges in the difficult decision of how best to protect the public while maximizing offender reintegration. In more recent years, it has become a "front end" solution to prison overcrowding.

Vito (1985a) found reincarceration rates to range from 10 to 26 percent across many studies; Boudouris and Turnbull (1985) found a rearrest/revocation rate of 39 percent in Iowa over a longer follow-up period. The latter also found that sex and substance abuse offenders were most responsive to shock incarceration, and that the cost-savings of sentencing offenders to shock probation would be substantial.

---

## Cost Effectiveness

While the public has demanded tougher sentences, it has become increasingly apparent that the cost associated with more incarceration and prison construction is astronomical. Estimates place the cost of constructing a maximum-security prison at approximately $80,000 per bed, and the annual cost of maintenance and housing inmates at more than $21,000 (Camp & Camp, 2000:88). The acute shortage of prison space, despite the opening of 371 new prisons since 1991, and constructing an additional 558,000 beds since 1992 (Camp & Camp, 2000:76), has made incarceration a scarce resource. Many states are faced with severe budget deficits, and legislators and the public are reluctant to vote for new prison construction. Yet there is also ample evidence that once prisons are built they are filled. In addition, 19 states are under court order to increase services or reduce or limit their prison populations or the population in a specific prison (American Correctional Association, 2000:16). Because of the increasingly high cost associated with incarceration, researchers have begun to focus on the cost effectiveness of alternatives.

---

Box 11.10

### Probation as a Correctional Alternative

Morgan reviewed the probation outcome literature through 1991 and concluded that probation is effective as a correctional alternative. Failure rates ranged from 14 to 60 percent for a group that had already committed crime; success rates vary from 40 to 86 percent.

Factors more frequently associated with failure on probation included age, sex, marital status, low income, prior criminal record, and employment status. Those most likely to fail were unemployed or underemployed young males with a low income and prior criminal record. The reconviction offenses of those who failed were more likely to be minor misdemeanors rather than felonies. Probationers who were adequately employed, married with children, and had lived in their area for at least two years were most often successful when placed on probation.

Source: K. Morgan (1993). "Factors Influencing Probation Outcome: A Review of the Literature." *Federal Probation*, 57:23-29.

---

In light of these factors, and in addition to the research aimed at measuring effectiveness in terms of recidivism, there have been attempts to demonstrate cost effectiveness of probation. Typically, with criminal justice agencies, costs are usually divided into three types: processing, program, and client-centered. Processing costs include monies spent in identifying and selecting individuals for a given program. Program costs are expenditures associated with incarceration and include direct costs, such as loss of earning, and indirect costs, such as psychological effects upon of alienation/prisonization, social stigma, and other detrimental effects upon the prisoner's marriage and family (Nelson, 1975).

Similarly, the benefits generated by probation could include savings to society through the use of diversion, wages, and taxes generated by the participants, and reduced crime or recidivism rates (Vito & Latessa, 1979:3). In addition there are the costs associated with failure, such as the monetary loss and grief experienced by the victims.

The studies that provided the most thorough financial comparisons were those that treated the cost-benefit analysis as their primary focus, and considered direct and indirect costs and benefits.

In one of the most comprehensive studies of probation costs, Frazier (1972) attempted to develop realistic cost information on probation and incarceration for the purpose of comparison. A number of estimates were used to compare the indirect costs associated with incarceration.

These factors included the average wage and average months employed per year, the average taxes paid on gross wages, and the cost of welfare support for children whose wage-earning parent had been incarcerated. These figures were based upon data collection from a representative sample of 115 inmates, and were then extended to the entire inmate population in Texas for 1970. The authors concluded that if 3,000 inmates were diverted, a one-year savings of $5,715,000 could be generated, and this, in 1970 dollars.

There have been several other cost-benefit analyses, however, that tend to include cost comparisons as part of a large research effort, and thus are plagued by errors of omission, and incomplete costs or benefit identifications (Erwin, 1984; Pearson, 1985; Wetter, 1985; Latessa, 1985; Latessa, 1986; System Sciences, 1982). Despite their limitations, these studies also support the contention that probation is a cost-effective alternative to incarceration. In one recent study that included cost effectiveness as part of a larger research effort, Latessa, Travis & Holsinger (1997) compared the cost of four correctional options (regular probation, ISP, Community Based Correctional Facilities, and Prison). Figure 11.10 shows the average cost per offender by from supervision through discharge. This shows that probation and ISP are clearly cheaper alternatives to residential and institutional options. They went on to conclude:

- Compared to incarceration, placement in ISP or CBCFs program produces savings and revenues between $4,500 and $5,000 per offender when compared to imprisonment.

- ISP and CBCF programs were more expensive than regular probation, but substantially less expensive than imprisonment.

- If only half of the offenders served in the community had been incarcerated, the state realized a savings of $49 million.

- Offenders in the ISP and CBCFs paid more than $3.4 million in court costs, fines, and restitution, and $1.7 million in the value of community service and labor over a three year period.

In a recent review of seven cost-benefit analysis studies that have been conducted on correctional alternatives, Welsh and Farrington (2000) found that for each dollar spent on programs, the public received a return of $1.13 to $7.14 in various savings. Likewise, Cohen (1998) determined the monetary value of saving a high-risk youth at between $1.7 and $2.3 million. Likewise, Aos and his associates (1999) calculated the cost savings from selected correctional programs based on expected reductions in recidivism rates (see Table 11. 7).

Figure 11.10
**Average Cost of Supervision Through Discharge in Ohio**

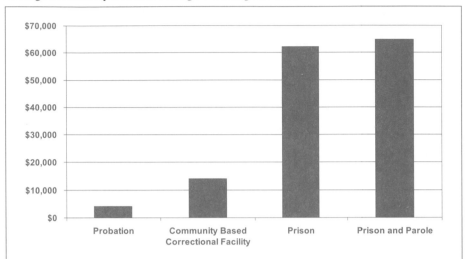

Source: Latessa, E. (2006). Cincinnati, OH: Cincinnati Division of Criminal Justice, University of Cincinnati.

Table 11.7
**Cost Savings from Selected Correctional Programs**

| | |
|---|---|
| Juvenile Boot Camps | Taxpayers receive $0.42 for every dollar spent |
| In-Prison Vocational Education | Taxpayers receive $2.30 for every dollar spent |
| Adult Basic Education | Taxpayers receive $1.71 for every dollar spent |
| In-Prison Therapeutic Communities | Taxpayers receive $0.76 for every dollar spent |
| Sex Offender Treatment Programs | Taxpayers receive $0.25 for every dollar spent |
| Life Skills Programs | Taxpayers receive $0.00 for every dollar spent |
| Job Counseling and Job Search for Inmates Leaving Prison | Taxpayers receive $2.84 for every dollar spent |
| Drug Courts | Taxpayers receive $1.69 for every dollar spent |
| Subsidized Jobs for Inmates Leaving Prison | Taxpayers receive $0.67 for every dollar spent |
| Adult Intensive Supervision Programs | Taxpayers receive $0.39 for every dollar spent |
| Case Management Substance Abuse Programs | Taxpayers lost $0.15 for every dollar spent |

Adopted from Aos, S., P. Phipps, R. Barnoski, and R. Lieb (1999). *The Comparative Costs and Benefits of Programs to Reduce Crime*. Olympia, WA: Washington State Institute for Public Policy.

## Probation and Drug Courts

As a response to the high number of offenders who have a substance abuse problem, drug courts have become a commonplace and important part of community based corrections. Because these offender remains in the community, probation plays a critical role in drug courts. The increase in the number of drug courts across the country is staggering. At the present time, there are over 1,100 drug courts operating throughout the United States, serving an estimated 230,000 offenders (Koetzle-Shaffer, 2006). One major reason for this growth stems from the popular view that drug courts will reduce substance abuse and criminal recidivism through frequent judicial monitoring and community-based treatment services. By adding a community-based treatment component, these specialized courts represent a major shift in how drug involved offenders are processed and given access to treatment services. It should be noted that some jurisdictions are now introducing courts that deal specifically with the mentally ill and other "special" groups; however, these "therapeutic" courts are too new to have any research available on effectiveness.

## Effectiveness of Drug Courts

Despite the rapid expansion of drug courts, their growing prevalence, and popularity, there is limited research to support their widespread effectiveness. It is difficult to determine if drug courts are effective because they differ substantially between jurisdictions. Similarly, it is difficult to identify which components or combination of features are contributing to success or failure. There is some evidence, however, to suggest that drug courts have been successful at reducing drug use and recidivism among program participants.

Evaluations of drug courts are finally beginning to emerge in the literature base. For example, research by on the impact of the first drug court to emerge in 1989 in Dade County, Florida, has provided insight into the drug court model. Outcome findings include lower incarceration rates, longer time to rearrest, and less frequent rearrest among participants (Goldkamp, 1994). However, Goldkamp (1994) did find higher failure to appear rates among drug court participants, but attributes these rates to the frequency of appearances required by the court. Further, an analysis of the Maricopa County Drug Court demonstrated reductions in recidivism and an overall delay in rearrest rates among drug court participants (Hepburn, Johnston & Rogers, 1994). Data from the Escambia County Drug Court indicate that graduates are sig-

Box 11.11

### Substance Abuse Programs

General estimates indicate that as many as 80 percent of all offenders have some form of substance abuse problem (particularly alcohol and drugs). Mauser et al. (1994) estimate total annual societal losses at $144 billion, not including pain and suffering of victims and family members, costs of crimes to victims, diminished health of substance abusers, or use of medical resources. As a result, the justice system has responded with specialized probation caseloads and counseling, community substance abuse programs, chemical dependency counseling, etc. Halfway houses offer residential settings for delivery of substance abuse and family counseling, life skills and crisis management training, and so on. Jail programs usually include Alcoholics Anonymous and Narcotics Anonymous, Sober Living Programs, and transfer to specialized care treatment centers.

Despite the stereotypical belief that nothing works, many studies show that substance abuse treatment can be effective in reducing recidivism rates. The research on substance abuse treatment can be summarized as follows:

- There is no "magic bullet"—no one treatment approach works with everyone.

- In general, treatment is superior to no treatment.

- Drug addiction is a chronic relapsing condition. Applying short term, education-based treatment services will not effectively reduce it. Treatment should be at least 100 hours of direct service over a three- to four-month period; however, intensive treatment programs lasting over one year might begin to see diminishing results.

- Traditional models used by substance abuse programs, such as drug/alcohol education and 12-step programs, have not been found as effective as cognitive-behavioral models.

- Aftercare services increase treatment effectiveness.

- Criminality is a significant factor that independently affects a treatment outcome.

nificantly less likely to be rearrested in comparison to non-graduates of the program (Peters, Haas & Murrin, 1999; Peters & Murrin, 2000). Finally, a recent meta-analysis conducted by Koetzle-Shaffer (2006) determined that drug courts reduced recidivism by 9 percent. Results also indicated that adult drug court programs tended to be more effective than juvenile drug court programs. Her quantitative review included a total of 83 effect sizes, representing 76 distinct drug courts and 6 aggregated drug court programs (Koetzle-Shaffer, 2006).

In an effort to predict treatment success, researchers explored the relationship between individual characteristics and treatment success. Specifically, Schiff and Terry (1997:305) explored the impact of a treatment oriented drug court in Broward County, Florida, and found that "higher education levels and decreased levels of prior crack cocaine use increase the chances of program graduation." In addition, a study of the Denver Drug Court found that offenders with more extensive involvement with drugs are more likely to be revoked from treatment (Granfield, Eby & Brewster, 1998). Similarly, one study of the Dade County Drug Court reported that defendants who reported high levels of drug use at program entry showed the poorest performance in the program (Goldkamp & Weiland, 1993). Finally, reports from the Escambia County Drug Court explored the differences between graduates and non-graduates and found several differences. Specifically, graduates had fewer prior arrests, were more likely to have completed high school or obtained a GED certificate, report full time employment, report living with their parents, and were less likely to report cocaine as their drug of choice (Peters et al., 1999). In the meta-analysis conducted by Koetzle-Shaffer (2006), important moderators included the amount of leverage that the drug court holds over participants, the involvement of qualified, competent staff members, and adequate treatment intensity.

Although a great deal of the research on drug courts is promising, other studies are providing reason for pause. For example, a number of courts across the county have failed to show evidence of a reduction in criminal behavior as measured by rearrest (Belenko, et al. 1994; Deschenes & Greenwood 1994; Granfield, et al. 1998; Harrell, 1998; Johnson & Latessa, 1998; Johnson, Sundt, Holsinger & Latessa, 1998). Although it is difficult to determine why some programs are failing to show evidence of effectiveness, the correctional treatment literature provides a strong case that the quality and content of the treatment programs may have an impact (Johnson et al., 2000).

Box 11.12

### The Drug Court Model

Drug courts differ from traditional court models in several key ways. One major departure pertains to how cases are managed. Specifically, drug courts manage cases quickly and make provisions for the intervention to occur as soon as possible after arrest (Belenko, 1998). Potential clients are often taken immediately to the treatment agency for assessment and orientation. Prompt identification of drug involved offenders and immediate intervention capitalizes on the crisis of arrest, making it difficult to deny their addictions. Furthermore, minimizing the time from arrest to disposition is believed to maximize an offender's motivation for change (Defining Drug Courts, 1997).

By acknowledging that the system must be involved in drug abuse treatment, drug courts have adopted a collaborative rather than the adversarial approach found in traditional courts (Drug Court Programs Office, 1998). Prosecutors and defense counselors work together with judges, treatment professionals, and probation officers to provide the best opportunity for the offender's success. In fact, Belenko (1998) concludes that drug courts are able to retain clients in treatment longer. Specifically, "it is estimated that about 60 percent of those who enter drug courts are still in treatment (primarily outpatient drug-free) after one year" (Belenko, 1998:21).

In traditional courts, judicial monitoring is hindered by burdened court dockets. Drug court judges, however, are key players in the treatment and supervision of drug-involved offenders (Goldkamp, 1994; Tauber, 1994; Drug Court Programs Office, 1997). In the drug court model, judges hold regular status review hearings with the offender, the counsel, and often a representative from the service provider. These hearings provide an opportunity for the judge to monitor participants' progress in treatment, provide feedback (both positive and negative) to participants, and maintain offender accountability. Moreover, the treatment agencies have a systematic opportunity to give feedback to judges thus allowing for the opportunity to reward and/or hold the offender more accountable.

Finally, in addition to the role of the judge, community based treatment is a crucial component of many drug courts. Experience and research demonstrates that drug addiction is a chronic, relapsing condition not effectively addressed by increasing sanctioning (Fagan, 1994). In contrast, research reveals that drug addiction is responsive to appropriate treatment. There is a growing body of evidence indicating that

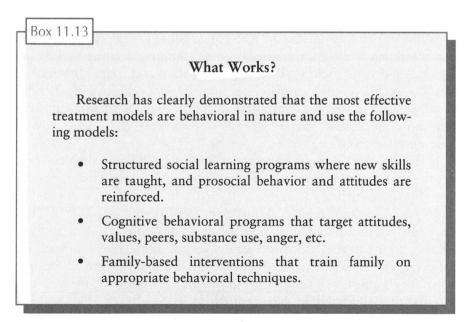

Box 11.12—*continued*

drug treatment–especially intensive, long-term treatment–can successfully reduce drug use and criminality, even when treatment is involuntary (Anglin & Hser 1990; Anglin, Brecht & Maddahian 1989; Prendergast, Anglin & Wellisch 1995). In short, the drug court movement has been shaped by both the failure of past efforts to meaningfully reduce drug related crime and the improved knowledge about the nature of drug addiction and its treatment.

## What Works in Correctional Intervention?

As discussed earlier in this chapter, the importance of evaluating correctional programs, especially those operating in the community, has never been more pronounced. Vast sums are being spent on correctional programming, and the public is demanding programs that work. The critical questions the remainder of this chapter will address are: "What works"?, What do we know about program effectiveness?, and What harm is done when we fail to develop effective programs?

Box 11.13

### What Works?

Research has clearly demonstrated that the most effective treatment models are behavioral in nature and use the following models:

- Structured social learning programs where new skills are taught, and prosocial behavior and attitudes are reinforced.

- Cognitive behavioral programs that target attitudes, values, peers, substance use, anger, etc.

- Family-based interventions that train family on appropriate behavioral techniques.

One of the most important areas of contemporary concern for correctional officials is the design and operation of effective correctional intervention programs. This is particularly relevant because there is consistent evidence that the public supports rehabilitation programs for offenders (Applegate, Cullen & Fisher, 1997). Furthermore, survey research also reveals strong support for public protection as an important goal of corrections (Applegate et al., 1997). Consequently, disagreements arise, focusing on what the best methods may be to achieve these and other correctional goals. On one side are advocates for more punitive policies such as an increased use of incarceration, punishing smarter (e.g., boot camps), or simply increasing control and monitoring if the offender is supervised in the community. Those advocating these strategies of crime control do so on the basis of the often-interrelated goals of punishment—deterrence, retribution, and incapacitation. The limits of these approaches have been outlined and debated by others (Currie 1985, Bennett, DiIulio & Walters, 1996). The ultimate effect of most of these policies has been described as "penal harm" (Clear, 1994).

As Cullen and Applegate (1998) imply, the most disheartening aspect of these "get-tough" policies is their dismissal of the importance of programming that is designed to rehabilitate offenders. Cullen and Applegate further question whether the penal harm movement's rejection of rehabilitation is sound public policy. As many states have found, simply locking up offenders and "throwing away the key" has proven to be a very expensive approach to crime control. This approach is also very limited, since the vast majority of offenders will one day return to society. Many will return at best unchanged, and at worst with many more problems and intensified needs for service (Petersilia, 1992). For those advocating incapacitation, one must also ask what should be done with offenders while incarcerated? Some scholars, such as Cullen and Applegate, do not believe that incapacitation and rehabilitation are mutually exclusive. Furthermore, because the vast majority of offenders are supervised in the community at differing degrees of intensity, it is even more important that we develop programs that work toward reducing recidivism.

Many of the "intermediate sanctions" that have been developed over the past few years are but a few examples of "programs" that often fail to live up to their expectations, particularly in terms of reductions in recidivism (Latessa, Travis & Holsinger, 1997; Petersilia, 1997). These results are often attributed to policies that emphasize control and surveillance over treatment and service delivery (Fulton, Latessa, Stichman & Travis, 1997). While programs such as boot camps, Scared Straight, and other "punishing smarter" programs remain popular, there is little evidence that they will lead to reductions in recidivism. Figure 11.11 shows some of the results from various studies. Unfortunately, the evidence seems to indicate that in some cases, punishing smarter programs actually increase recidivism rates.

Figure 11.11
**Effects of Punishing Smarter Programs on Recidivism\***

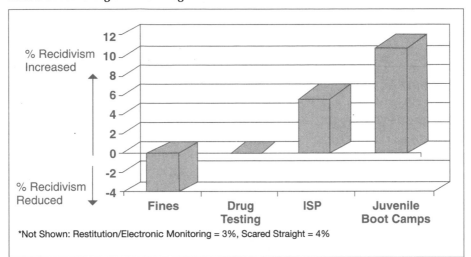

*Not Shown: Restitution/Electronic Monitoring = 3%, Scared Straight = 4%

Sources: Gendreau, P. et al. (2000). "The Effects of Community Sanctions and Incarceration on Recidivism." *FORUM,* 12(2):10-13; Aos, S. et al. (1999). *The Comparative Costs and Benefits of Programs to Reduce Crime.* Washington State Institute for Public Safety.

In a recent study funded by the National Institute of Justice, Sherman and his colleagues (1998) summarized what does not work in reducing recidivism.

- Correctional boot camps using traditional military basic training

- Drug prevention classes focused on fear and other emotional appeals, including self-esteem, such as DARE

- School-based leisure-time enrichment programs

- "Scared Straight" programs where juvenile offenders visit adult prisons

- Shock probation, shock parole, and split sentences adding time to probation or parole

- Home detention with electronic monitoring

- Intensive supervision

- Rehabilitation programs using vague, unstructured counseling

- Residential programs for juvenile offenders using challenging experiences in rural settings

Despite the punitive movement, there is increasing evidence that correctional treatment can be effective in reducing recidivism among offenders (Andrews, Zinger, Hoge, Bonta, Gendreau & Cullen, 1990; Gendreau & Andrews, 1990; Cullen & Gendreau, 1989; Redondo, Sanchez-Meca & Garrido, 1999; Van Voorhis, 1987). Nonetheless, some scholars remain unconvinced (Antonowicz & Ross, 1994; Lab & Whitehead, 1988; Logan & Gaes, 1993). The debate surrounding treatment effectiveness has been on going since Martinson's proclamation that "nothing works," with many still clinging to this mantra, despite evidence to the contrary. Principle among the reasons for disbelief in the potential effectiveness of correctional programming is the failure to measure outcome properly, and the lack of quality programs.

---

Box 11.14

### House Arrest and Electronic Monitoring

House arrest requires offenders to remain within the confines of their residences and obey a curfew, and is generally used with probation but can be used as a "stand alone" program for pretrial defendants, for convicted offenders as an alternative to incarceration, and for intensive probation and parole supervision. Supervising officers verify the presence of participants by telephone or face-to-face checks. Evaluations indicate that the impact on prison crowding, offender behavior, and state correctional costs have been favorable. Only 10 percent of Florida participants received additional punishment for technical violations, and the reoffense rate for community control offenders is lower than for similar offenders sentenced to prison (Wagner & Baird, 1993).

Electronic monitoring provides technological verification of the offender's whereabouts, and is used to monitor house arrestees and curfew observation. It is also used to follow up parolees, control those sentenced to community corrections, and monitor pretrial defendants. Recent technological developments allow for on-site testing for alcohol consumption. Home detention with electronic monitoring was successful for 73 percent of participants in a pretrial release program. Defendants most likely to complete home detention lived with a spouse or opposite-gender roommate. Of the 27 percent failures, about one-half were technical violators and the other one-half absconded. Electronic monitoring programs with probationers, offenders on parole, and those in community corrections report successful termination rates ranging from 74 to 86 percent, although rates as high as 97 percent have been achieved (Gowdy, 1993).

Gendreau (1996) has examined hundreds of correctional and rehabilitation programs that attempt to intervene with offenders. Others
have conducted similar studies (Lipsey & Wilson, 1997) and have come
to the same conclusion: rehabilitation can be effective in reducing recidivism. For example, citing the work of Lipsey (1992), Gendreau (1996)
found that 64 percent of the offender rehabilitation studies (that had
control groups) reported reductions in favor of the treatment group; the
average reduction in recidivism was 10 percent. When the studies were
categorized by the general type of program (employment, relapse prevention, etc.), reductions in recidivism averaged 18 percent. Figure
11.12 is based on a meta-analysis conducted by Lipsey. This figure
shows the expected recidivism rates when various programming characteristics are factored into probation.

Figure 11.12
**Expected Recidivism with Various Intervention Characteristics for
Non-Institutionalized Juvenile Offenders**

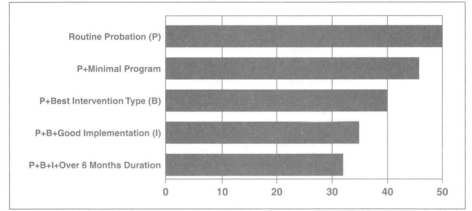

Source: Lipsey, M. (1999). "Can Intervention Rehabilitate Serious Offenders?" *Annals of the
American Academy of Political and Social Science*, 564:142-166.

Gendreau and Paparozzi (1995) also found that, when rehabilitation programs incorporated at least some of eight principles of effective
intervention, those programs reduced recidivism in the range of 25-70
percent, with the average about 50 percent. Principles of effective intervention are as follows:

1. Programs have intensive services that are behavioral in
   nature, that occupy 40-70 percent of the offender's time in
   a program and are from three to nine months in duration.
   [Behavioral means using positive reinforcers to strengthen
   behavior, such as rewarding "doing good" with attendance
   at sports events, praise, and approval.] Further, behavioral
   strategies are essential to effective service delivery.

2. Behavioral programs target the criminogenic needs of high-risk offenders, such as antisocial attitudes, peer associations, and chemical dependencies.

3. Programs incorporate responsivity between offender, therapist, and program. Simply said, treatment program should be delivered in a manner that facilitates the offender's learning new prosocial skills.

4. Program contingencies and behavioral strategies are enforced in a firm but fair manner; positive reinforcers are greater than punishers by at least 4:1.

5. Therapists relate to offenders in interpersonally sensitive and constructive ways and are trained and supervised accordingly. Treatment is systematically delivered by competent therapists and treaters.

6. Program structure and activities disrupt the delinquency network by placing offenders in situations (with people and in places) where prosocial activities predominate.

7. Provide relapse prevention in the community by such tactics as planning and rehearsing alternative prosocial responses, anticipating problem situations, training significant others (family and friends) to provide reinforcement for prosocial behavior, and establishing a system for booster sessions.

8. A high level of advocacy and brokerage as long as the community agency offers appropriate services.

Similarly, Gendreau (1996) lists those interventions that have not been found to be effective in reducing recidivism:

- Counseling for everyone
- Talking cures
- Nondirective, relationship-oriented therapy
- Radical nonintervention
- Traditional medical model approaches
- Intensive services directed to low-risk offenders
- Intensive services oriented to non-crime-producing needs

One example of a program that was not effective in reducing recidivism is found in Table 11.8. In a recent review of substance abuse treatment, Lightfoot (1997) identified effective and ineffective types of treatment. Interestingly, the types of effective and ineffective treatment models for substance abusers mirrors the findings from studies of other

---

Box 11.15

### Acupuncture Treatment for Drug-Dependent Offenders

Acupuncture is defined as "the Chinese medical art of inserting fine needles into the skin to relieve pain or disability" (Wensel, 1990:5). A number of advocates claim that acupuncture can be an effective remedy for drug addiction (Smith, et al., 1982 & 1984; Smith et al., 1984).

In 1992 Latessa and Moon published the results from a study they conducted on a outpatient drug treatment program for felony probationers. The program participants were randomly divided into three groups; an experimental group, which received acupuncture on a regular basis, a control group, which did not receive acupuncture, and a placebo group, which received an acupuncture-like simulation. They concluded that, "With regard to outcome there is no evidence that acupuncture had any appreciable effect on program completion, arrests, convictions, or probation outcome" (1992:330).

Source: E.J. Latessa and M.M. Moon (1992). "The Effectiveness of Acupuncture in an Outpatient Drug Treatment Program." *Journal of Contemporary Criminal Justice*, 8:317-331.

---

offender types. Similarly, Taxman (2000) made similar conclusions when she reviewed the research on substance abuse treatment. Her findings are summarized in Table 11.9.

Gendreau concludes that many programs in the past and present lack most of the effective components listed above. When these are present, reductions in recidivism are high. His arguments suggest that the "nothing works in corrections" position is not only premature, it is inaccurate. A program focused on behavioral change, organized with the principles of effective treatment in mind in the various components and subsystems of community-based corrections, could significantly improve how we handle and rehabilitate offenders. Rehabilitation does appear to work, but it also seems that the programs that meet the above principles are more effective than those that do not. One important question, however, is how do we determine the degree to which a program meets the principles of effective intervention? Gendreau and Andrews (1994) accomplished this through the development of an instrument known as the Correctional Program Assessment Inventory (CPAI). The most current version of the instrument is the CPAI-2000 (Gendreau & Andrews, 2001).

Table 11.8
**Review of Drug Treatment Effectiveness by Lightfoot (1997)**

---

What treatment types were effective in quasi-experimental and/or controlled studies:

---

- Social-Learning Based Treatments
- Aversion Therapy: Electrical/Chemical Counter-conditioning
- Covert Sensitization
- Contingency Management/Contingency Contracting
- Broad Spectrum Therapies
- Individualized Behavior Therapy
- Community Reinforcement
- Behavior Self-Control Thinking
- Relapse Prevention

---

What treatment types showed no clear evidence of effectiveness from controlled studies:

---

- Acupuncture
- Education
- Lectures
- Bibliotherapy
- Self-help
- Alcoholics Anonymous
- Narcotics Anonymous
- Al-Anon
- Adult Children of Alcoholics
- Psycho-therapy
- Supportive
- Confrontational
- Pharmacotherapies

Source: Lightfoot, L. (1997). "What Works in Drug Treatment." Presented at the International Community Corrections Association annual meeting.

The CPAI is a tool that has been used for assessing correctional intervention programs. The CPAI assesses a program on six primary areas: (1) program implementation and leadership; (2) offender assessment and classification; (3) characteristics of the program; (4) characteristics and practices of the staff; (5) evaluation and quality control; and (6) miscellaneous items such as ethical guidelines and levels of support. One advantage of the CPAI is that is allows researchers to quantify the degree to which a program meets the principles of effective intervention. Each section of the CPAI is scored as "very satisfactory" (70% to 100%), "satisfactory" (60% to 69%), "satisfactory but needs improvement" (50% to 59%) or "unsatisfactory" (less than 50%).

Table 11.9
**Review of Drug Treatment Effectiveness by Taxman (2000)**

---

What treatment types were successful at reducing recidivism?

---

- Directive Counseling
- Behavior Modification
- Therapeutic Community
- Moral Reasoning
- Social Competency Cognitive Behavior Models
- Emotional Skill Development
- Cognitive Skills
- Behavioral Skills

---

What treatment types showed no clear evidence of effectiveness of reduced recidivism?

---

- Nondirective counseling
- Reality Therapy
- Psychosocial education
- 12-step or other self-help groups
- Psychoanalytical

Source: Taxman, F.S. (2000). "Unraveling 'What Works' for Offenders in Substance Abuse Treatment Services." *National Drug Court Institute Review*, Vol. II, 2.

To date, researchers from the University of Cincinnati have assessed over 400 correctional programs across the country. The types of programs assessed include residential facilities, halfway houses, ISPs, work release centers, therapeutic communities, day reporting programs, school based programs, boot camps, substance abuse treatment programs, and a variety of special programs for offenders. Figure 11.13 shows the percentages of programs that scored in each category. Only eight percent of the programs assessed scored in the "very satisfactory" range, while more than 70 percent scored either "satisfactory but needs improvement," or "unsatisfactory" category. A similar study conducted by Matthews, Hubbard, and Latessa (2001) found that, of the correctional programs they studied, the majority did not adequately assess offender risk or need factors, did not utilize effective treatment models, do no adequately train their staff, and do not evaluate their programs or the performance of the offenders they served. These results indicate that many programs are not meeting the principles of effective intervention.

Figure 11.13
**Percentage of Programs in Each CPAI Category (based on 4000 CPAI assessments across a wide variety of programs)**

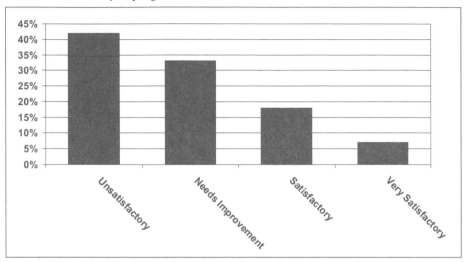

Source: Division of Criminal Justice. University of Cincinnati, Cincinnati, OH.

Although there was a great deal of variation between (and within) programs, Latessa and Holsinger (1998) have summarized some of the major strengths and weakness in each of the CPAI areas across the programs they assessed:

- **Program Implementation and Leadership.** Strengths: Effective programs have strong leadership and involvement of the program director. For the most part we have found qualified and experienced program directors, who were involved in designing the program. They tend to be involved in the hiring and training of staff, and in many instances they provide some direct services to offenders. It is also important for the support of a program that the values and goals of the program be consistent with existing values in the community or institution in which it resides, and that there be a documented need for the program. Support for the program also depends on perceptions of cost-effectiveness. We usually find that most correctional programs meet these conditions. Weaknesses: There are two flaws that are common in this area. Effective programs are based on strong theoretical models that are derived from the treatment literature. Regardless, many of the correctional intervention programs we examined were basically designed with little regard for the empirical research on what works with the type of offenders they were serving. In addition, effective programs are usually begun on a pilot basis to work out the logistics. Thus far we have found few programs that piloted their treatment components before full implementation.

- **Offender Assessment and Classification.** Strengths: The vast majority of programs we studied have stated criteria for admissions, receive appropriate clients, and have a rational legal/clinical basis for the exclusion of certain types of offenders. We also found that in general, most programs attempt to assess some offender characteristics related to risk and need. Weaknesses: While many programs did indeed attempt to assess offenders regarding risk and need, doing so did not involve the incorporation of a standardized, objective, actuarial instrument. The absence of actuarial risk/needs assessment instruments was particularly evident in programs that deal with juvenile offenders. Even when a standardized assessment is being performed at some point in the offender's entry/progress, it is seldom found that the information gathered is being used to distinguish offenders by risk. In other words, even when proper (and potentially beneficial) assessments are being performed, the information is not influencing the decision-making process, let alone service delivery. In addition, it is generally found that staff assessments of offenders are based on a quasi-clinical approach that does not result in a summary score. Likewise, it has been very rare to find that programs are routinely measuring with standardized instruments responsivity characteristics, such as levels of motivation, intelligence, or psychological development.

- **Characteristics of the Program.** Strengths: Effective intervention programs focus the vast majority of their efforts on targeting criminogenic needs and behaviors. In general we have found that many correctional intervention programs target these behaviors (although we still find programs that provide intensive services and treatment in noncrime producing areas, such as self-esteem). Another common strength was that many programs have criteria for program completion, and upon discharge many offenders are routinely referred to programs and services that help meet their needs. Weaknesses: Offenders typically have not been spending a significant percentage of their time in structured programs. In addition, the amount of services and treatment provided has not been varying by risk and need levels. Yet another characteristic of an effective program is the use of a treatment model that has been found to be effective. Because programs are rarely designed around a theoretical model, was not surprising to find a lack of a consistently applied treatment model in place. In general, the major shortcomings found when considering the "Characteristics of Program" portion of the CPAI include: lack of programmatic structure; incomplete or nonexistent treatment manuals; few rewards to encourage program participation and compliance; the ineffective use of punishment; staff being allowed to design their own interventions regardless of the treatment literature base; a host very obvious and definable, yet ineffective treatment models. This area of the CPAI also examines the extent to which matching occurs between offenders and staff, offenders and programs, and staff and programs. Even when matching is found to occur, it is uncommon to observe it being based on specific responsivity criteria. In addition, it is very rare to find a program that includes family and/or friends of the offender in the treatment process. Finally, many programs failed to provide aftercare services or booster sessions.

- **Characteristics and Practices of the Staff.** Strengths: Although there is a great deal of variation from program to program with regarding staff quality, for the most part we found educated and experienced staff working with offenders. Often staff were selected on personal characteristics such as life experience, fairness, firmness, and problem-solving skills. We also found that staff usually had input in the structure of the programs, and that ongoing training was provided. Weaknesses: Staff turnover was often a problem with some types of correctional programs (e.g., halfway houses), and we rarely found staff who had received sufficient training on the interventions and treatments utilized by the program. Clinical supervision was not routinely provided, and staff were rarely assessed on service-delivery skills.

- **Evaluation and Quality Control.** Programs that study themselves tend to be more effective than programs that do not. Data provide insight into program and offender performance, help identify who is successful and who is not, and allow adjustments to be made. Strengths: File review and case audits were usually conducted. Weaknesses: Periodic, objective, and standardized assessment of offenders to see if criminogenic factors were being reduced was uncommon. In short, most programs do not develop meaningful performance measures (to measure either program or offender performance over time). We also found that the majority of programs were not tracking offenders after they have left the program, and formal evaluations involving comparison groups were the exception.

- **Other Items.** Strengths: Most of the programs we examined score well in this area. In general, offender records are complete and are kept in a confidential file. Changes that jeopardize programs, funding, or community support are rare. Weaknesses: Some programs do not have ethical guidelines for intervention, and public agencies tend not to have advisory boards, while those operated by nonprofits do.

Two investigators have recently assessed the predictive validity of the CPAI. Nesovic (2003) reviewed 173 studies (including a total of 266 effect sizes) from the offender treatment literature and reported a mean correlation of $r = .46$ between program scores (i.e., overall CPAI score) and recidivism. Lowenkamp, Latessa and Smith (2006) used the CPAI to conduct 38 in situ reviews of offender treatment programs with matched controls, and reported a mean correlation of $r = .42$ between program scores and recidivism. See Figure 11.14 for a graph demonstrating the difference in recidivism rates between treatment and comparison groups based on the CPAI total scores.

While these results indicate that the majority of correctional programs assessed are not fully meeting the principles of effective intervention, they also provide some useful information on how to improve the quality of correctional interventions.

Figure 11.14
**Difference in Recidivism Rates between Treatment and Comparison Groups Based on the CPAI Measure Total Score**

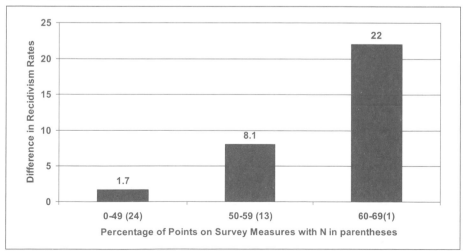

Adapted from: Lowenkamp, C. T., Latessa, E. J., & Smith, P. (2006). "Does Correctional Program Quality Really Matter? The Impact of Adhering to the Principles of Effective Intervention." *Criminology and Public Policy, 5* (3):575-594.

Box 11.16

### Sex Offender Treatment: Does It Work?

The typical justice response to sex offenders involves punishment and incapacitation by eliminating offender access to victims. Because almost all sex offenders return to the community, incapacitation without treatment does not reduce reoffending. In Vermont, the cost of a relapse (justice and victim services) is estimated to be more than $138,000.

McGrath (1994) provides a synopsis of 68 outcome studies and clearly shows that treatment in the community is effective, particularly more recent programs that use relapse prevention treatment models delivered in group therapy sessions. Typical treatment goals include accepting responsibility for the offense, developing empathy with the victim, improving social competence, controlling deviant sexual arousal, and developing relapse prevention skills. More recent treatment programs (since 1980) appear to be more effective.

Re-offending rates for treated offenders are 80 percent less than for untreated offenders; persons who complete treatment programs (versus dropping out) are 77 percent less likely to recidivate. Sex offenders treated in relapse prevention (versus behavioral change) groups are 73 percent less likely to re-offend. Finally, the re-offending rate for sex offenders treated since 1980 is six percent. Furby et al. (1989) argue it is no more than 10 percent but argue for longer follow-up periods after treatment.

McGrath concludes that results from the 68 sex offender outcome studies reviewed show that treatment works, is cost effective, and can be provided in communities under probation control.

Source: R. McGrath (1995). "Sex Offender Treatment: Does It Work?" *Perspectives*, 19:24-26.

## The Harm of Ineffective Programs

This chapter has outlined what many of the pertinent issues have been when evaluating program effectiveness. It has become apparent that the way recidivism is measured may need to be reconsidered in order to more fully understand the essence of a program's crime-reducing potential. Further, and perhaps more importantly, measuring other indicators or program performance, such as program quality if often neglected. The result of allowing ineffective correctional strategies to continue is quite likely to be harmful, which manifests itself in several

---

Box 11.17

### Probation Supervision of the Mentally Disordered Offender

Despite claims by mental health advocates that "people with mental illness pose no more of a crime threat than do other members of the general public," (National Mental Health Association, 1987), strong evidence suggests that this is not the case. However, for the correctional system, the issue of whether the mentally ill are more "dangerous" than members of the general public is not a particularly relevant question. For mentally ill individuals who have been convicted of an offense, a more appropriate question is whether they pose more of a risk than other offender groups being supervised in the community?

In a recent study, Latessa (1996) compared arrest, conviction, and probation outcome data for several groups under probation supervision. The probation groups included: sex offenders, drug offenders, high-risk offenders, regularly supervised offenders, and mentally disordered offenders. He found that mentally disordered offenders performed as well, and in some cases better, than other probation groups. He concluded that mentally ill offenders can and are being supervised in the community without increasing risk to public safety.

Source: E.J. Latessa (1996). "Offenders with Mental Illness on Probation," *Community Corrections in America: New Directions and Sounder Investments for Persons with Mental Illness and Co-Disorders*. Washington, DC: National Institute of Corrections and the National Coalition for Mental and Substance Abuse Health Care in the Justice System.

---

ways. First, the undermining of confidence and support. When faced with the existence of ineffective correctional treatment strategies, judges, legislators, and the public lose confidence in correctional efforts, which in turn undermines support for effective programs. In the realm of public opinion regarding correctional sanctions, some bad apples may indeed spoil the entire bushel—programs that are effectively reducing recidivism based on what we know works can be harmed by programs that are not. In short, if ineffective strategies continue to flourish, the risk of returning to a "nothing works" doctrine will undoubtedly increase. Second, there is a tendency to seek "quick fix" solutions that have no empirical support. The result has often been programs that promise a quick fix to the problem of criminal behavior, or what Cullen (Personal Communication, n.d.) refers to as correctional "quackery." There is no panacea approach to changing offender behavior. Those searching for a "magic pill" for reducing crime and changing human behavior will not only be disappointed, but will at best perpetuate the myth that there is some simple solution, and at worst erode faith in the potential for effective intervention. Finally, offenders get all the blame. Perhaps the greatest harm that is perpetuated is that which is done to the offender. When we use programs that are not effective, the offender receives the blame, not the program. Too often we hear judges say that they have already sent the offender to some program, and that they have failed. This "failure" is then used to justify even harsher punishments. Sending an offender to a program that does not adequately meet the principles of effective intervention should not be expected to change criminal behavior. Blaming the offender absolves us from designing and operating high quality and effective intervention programs.

---

**Box 11.18**

### Restorative Justice

The concept of restorative justice remains problematic to define. The term has been used interchangeably with community justice, transformative justice, peacemaking criminology, and relational justice (Bazemore & Walgrave, 1999). Perhaps the best definition is offered by Marshall (1999:5): "Restorative justice is a process whereby all the parties with a stake in a particular offence come together to resolve collectively how to deal with the aftermath of the offence and its implications for the future."

Despite the difficulties in defining restorative justice, the concept has become increasingly popular in correctional settings. While some have argued that restorative justice should not be evaluated using traditional criminal justice outcome measures like recidivism (Zehr, 1989), the essential question remains "is restorative justice effective?"

In a recent meta-analysis of restorative justice Latimer, Dowden, and Muise (2001) found that studies of restorative justice programs demonstrated that it was an effective method of improving victim/offender satisfaction, increasing offender compliance with restitution, and decreasing the recidivism of offenders when compared to more traditional approaches such as incarceration, probation, court-ordered restitution. However, the authors also concluded that restorative justice programs, while yielding average effect sizes for reducing recidivism of about seven percent, were nowhere near what studies of promising correctional treatment programs had found (effect sizes of about 30%).

## Summary

During the past few years there have been a number of meta-analysis studies that have focused on the positive results of correctional treatment programs (Gendreau & Ross, 1987; Van Voorhis, 1987; Garrett, 1985; Palmer, 1991). Meta-analysis refers to a type of research method that examines other studies on a specific subject or topic. These studies have been very critical of the "nothing works" doctrine put forth by Martinson and others (Whitehead & Lab, 1989). However, as Palmer (1991:331) states:

> . . . . the research designs of many individual studies that comprised the meta-analyses and literature reviews were much less than excellent and were in that respect open to valid questions.

Even though there appear to be programs and interventions that are effective, the research conducted to date has been hampered by many constraints and limitations and, as a result, is less than adequate.

Part of this dilemma rests with the concept of effectiveness. While, as noted above, most would agree that recidivism should be a primary performance measure, there is no consensus on its definition or the indicators to be used for its measurement. Researchers often ignore other performance measures of effectiveness, especially those examining the management or supervisory aspects of parole and probation, and the quality of correctional programs.

## *Review Questions*

1. What are some of the indicators of effectiveness used in correctional research?

2. List the three major ways that research studies are summarized.

3. Why is it so difficult to predict recidivism?

4. List some of the factors that are related to outcome for parolees.

5. How does probation compare to other correctional alternatives with regard to outcome?

6. List the principles of effective intervention.

7. What are the six areas of the Correctional Program Assessment Inventory?

8. According to Latessa and Holsinger, what percentage of correctional program can be classified as "very satisfactory"?

9. Why do you believe drug courts have become some popular?

10. What does not work with offenders?

11. What are the most effective treatment models?

## Key Terms

ballot counting

cost effectiveness

drug courts

length of follow-up

literature review

meta analysis

outcome measures

parole conditions

parole violation

principles of effective intervention

program quality

recidivism

restorative justice

shock probation

therapeutic community

## Electronic Library

Evaluation of Intensive Parole of Juveniles (www.wa.gov/wsipp/crime/pdf/jraparole.pdf).

Pretrial Release of the Homeless (www.cjcj.org/hrp/hrp.pdf).

Mental Health and Treatment of Probationers and Inmates (www.ojp.usdoj.gov/bjs/pub/pdf/mhtip.pdf).

Trends in State Parole (www.ojp.usdoj.gov/bjs/pub/pdf/tsp00.pdf).

Outcomes of Drug Treatment, Federal Offenders (www.bop.gov/orepg/oretriadpref.pdf).

Problems of Reentry into the Community (www.ncjrs.org/pdffiles1/nij/184253.pdf).

## Recommended Readings

Andrews, D., I. Zinger, R. Hoge, J. Bonta, P. Gendreau, and F. Cullen (1990). "Does Correctional Treatment Work? A Clinically Relevant and Psychologically Informed Meta-Analysis." *Criminology*, 28:369-404.

Aos, S., P. Phipps, R. Barnoski, and R. Lieb (1999). *The Comparative Costs and Benefits of Programs to Reduce Crime: A Review of National Research Findings with Implications for Washington State*. Olympia, WA: Washington State Institute for Public Policy.

Cullen, F. and B. Applegate (1998). *Offender Rehabilitation*. Brookfield, MA: Ashgate Darthmouth.

Gendreau, P. (1996). "The Principles of Effective Intervention with Offenders." In A. Harland (ed.) *Choosing Correctional Options That Work: Defining the Demand and Evaluating the Supply*. Thousand Oaks, CA: Sage.

Lipsey, M. (1999). "Can Intervention Rehabilitate the Serious Delinquent?" *Annals of the American Academy of Political and Social Science*, 564:142-166.

Martinson, R. (1974). "What Works?—Questions and Answers About Prison Reform." *The Public Interest*, 35:22-54.

## Notes

[1]   For a discussion of the limitations and criticism of the Martinson study see Palmer, T. (1975). "Martinson Revisited." *Journal of Research in Crime and Delinquency*, 12:133-152; and Cullen, F. and P. Gendreau (2001). "From Nothing Works to What Works." *Prison Journal*, 81(3):313-338.

[2]   Francis T. Cullen eloquently argues that rehabilitation reduces recidivism across programs by about 50 percent when interventions are based on principles of effective treatment. Cullen, F. (1994). "Social Support as an Organizing Concept for Criminology." *Justice Quarterly*, 11:52-59.

[3]   For a discussion of the various alternative definitions of recidivism see Champion, D. (1988). *Felony Probation, Problems and Prospects*. New York, NY: Praeger, pp. 95-97; Palmer, T. (1995). "Programmatic and Nonprogrammatic Aspects of Successful Intervention: New Directions for Research." *Crime & Delinquency*, 41:101-131; and National Policy Committee of American Society of Criminology (2001). *The Use of Incarceration in the U.S.* (www.asc41.com/policypapers.html).

[4]   Gendreau, P. and M. Paparozzi (1995). "Examining What Works in Community Corrections." *Corrections Today*, 56(8):28-30, and Petersilia, J. (2001). "Prisoner Reentry." *Prison Journal*, 81(3):360-375.

[5]   There is evidence that for some offender groups, such as sex offenders and habitual drunk drivers, a follow-up period of at least 10 years is necessary in order to adequately gauge recidivism. This is due to the low probability of being apprehended for these types of crimes.

[6]   See the excellent collection of articles by Vito, G. (ed.) (1994). "Education in Correctional Settings." *The Prison Journal*, 74:395-473, and Gallagher, C.A., D.B. Wilson, and P. Hischfield (1999). "A Quantitative Review and Description of Corrections-Based Education, Vocation and Work Programs." *Corrections Management Quarterly*, 3(4):8-18.

<sup>7</sup>    For a synopsis of inmate participation in institutional work programs, see Camp, C. and G. Camp (2000). *The 2000 Corrections Yearbook: Adult Corrections*. Middletown, CT: The Criminal Justice Institute.

<sup>8</sup>    California adopted a determinate sentencing system in 1977 that, despite literally hundreds of revisions, is deemed seriously flawed. See N. Holt (1995). "California's Determinate Sentencing: What Went Wrong?" *American Probation and Parole Association Perspectives*, 19(3):19-23; and Editors (2002). "States Overhauling Sentencing Structures." *Corrections News*, 8(1):1.

## *References*

Alaska Department of Health and Social Services (1976). *Misdemeanants Probation Project*. Juneau, AK: Division of Corrections.

Allen, H., E. Carlson, and E. Parks (1979). *Critical Issues in Adult Probation*. Washington, DC: National Institute of Law Enforcement and Criminal Justice.

Allen, H. and E. Latessa (1980). *Parole Effectiveness in the United States: An Assessment*. San Jose, CA: San Jose State University Research Foundation.

American Correctional Association (2000). *Directory*. Laurel, MD: ACA.

Andrews, D, I. Zinger, R. Hoge, J. Bonta, P. Gendreau, and F. Cullen (1990). "Does Correctional Treatment Work? A Clinically Relevant and Psychologically Informed Meta-Analysis." *Criminology*, 28:369-404.

Anglin, M. and Y. Hser (1990). "Treatment of Drug Abuse." In M. Tonry and J.Q. Wilson (eds.) *Drugs and Crime*. Chicago, IL: University of Chicago Press: 393-460.

Anglin, M., M. Brecht, and E. Maddahian (1989). "Pretreatment Characteristics and Treatment Performance of Legally Coerced Versus Voluntary Methadone Maintenance Admissions." *Criminology*, 27(3), 537-555.

Antonowicz D. and R. Ross (1994). "Essential Components of Successful Rehabilitation Programs for Offenders." *International Journal of Offender Therapy and Comparative Criminology*, 38:97-104.

Aos, S., P. Phipps, R. Barnoski, and R. Lieb (1999). *The Comparative Costs and Benefits of Programs to Reduce Crime: A Review of National Research Findings with Implications for Washington State*. Olympia, WA: Washington State Institute for Public Policy.

Applegate, B., F. Cullen, and B. Fisher (1997). "Public Support for Correctional Treatment: The Continuing Appeal of the Rehabilitative Ideal." *The Prison Journal*, 77:237-258.

Austin, J. (2001). "Prisoner Reentry: Current Trends, Practices, and Issues." *Crime & Delinquency*, 47:314-334.

Austin, J. (1987). *Success and Failure on Parole in California: A Preliminary Evaluation*. Washington, DC: U.S. Department of Justice.

Ayers, D., S. Duguid, C. Montague, and S. Wolowidnyk (1980). *Effects of the University of Victoria Program: A Post-Release Study*. Ottawa, CN: Ministry of the Solicitor General of Canada.

Babst, D. and J. Mannering (1965). "Probation versus Imprisonment for Similar Types of Offenders." *Journal of Research in Crime and Delinquency*, 2:60-71.

Bazemore, G., and L. Walgrave. (1999) *Restorative Juvenile Justice: Repairing the Harm of Youth Crime*. Monsey, NY: Criminal Justice Press.

Beasley, W. (1978). "Unraveling the Process of Parole: An Analysis of the Effects of Parole Residency on Parole Outcome." Paper presented at the meeting of the American Society of Criminology, Atlanta, GA.

Beck, A. (1987). *Recidivism of Young Parolees*. Washington, DC: Bureau of Justice Statistics Special Report.

Belenko, S. (1998). "Research on Drug Courts: A Critical Review." *National Drug Court Institute Review*, 1(1):1-43.

Belenko, S., J. Fagan, and T. Dumanovsky (1994). "The Effects of Legal Sanctions on Recidivism in Special Drug Courts." *Justice System Journal*, 17, 53-81.

Benedict, W., L. Huff-Corzine, and J. Corzine (1998). "'Clean Up and Go Straight': Effects of Drug Treatment on Recidivism Among Felony Probationers."*American Journal of Criminal Justice*, 22(2):169-187.

Bennett, W., J. DiIulio, Jr., and J. Walters (1996). *Body Count: Moral Poverty . . . and How to Win America's War Against Crime and Drugs*. New York, NY: Simon and Schuster.

Boudouris, J. and B. Turnbull (1985). "Shock Probation in Iowa." *Journal of Offender Counseling, Services and Rehabilitation*, 9(4):53-67.

Bucholtz, G. and R. Foos (1996). *Profiling Parole Violators at Large*. Columbus, OH: Department of Rehabilitation and Correction.

Bureau of Justice Statistics (2006). *Probation and Parole in the United States, 2005*. Washington, DC: U.S. Department of Justice.

Bureau of Justice Statistics (2001). *Correctional Populations in the United States*. Washington, DC: Department of Justice.

Bureau of Justice Statistics (1999). *Correctional Populations in the United States*. Washington, DC: U.S. Department of Justice.

Bureau of Justice Statistics National Update (1994). Washington, DC: U.S. Department of Justice

Caldwell, M. (1951). "Review of a New Type of Probation Study Made in Alabama." *Federal Probation*, 15(2):3-11.

California Department of Justice (1969). *Superior Court Probation and/or Jail Sample: One Year Follow-Up for Selected Counties*. Sacramento, CA: Division of Law Enforcement, Bureau of Criminal Statistics.

Camp, C. and G. Camp (2000). *The 2000 Corrections Yearbook: Adult Corrections*. Middletown, CT: Criminal Justice Institute.

Champion, D. (1988). *Felony Probation, Problems and Prospects*. New York, NY: Praeger.

Citizens' Inquiry on Parole and Criminal Justice (1975). *Prison Without Walls: Report on New York Parole*. New York, NY: Praeger.

Clear, T.R. (1994). *Harm in American Penology: Offenders, Victims, and Their Communities.* Albany State University of New York Press.

Clear, T.R., B.D. Stout, and H.R. Dammer (1992). "Does Involvement in Religion Help Prisoners Adjust to Prison?" *NCCD Focus*, November:1-7.

Clear, T.R., B. Stout, L. Kelly, P. Hardyman, and C. Shapiro (1992). *Prisoners, Prisons and Religion: Final Report.* New Jersey: School of Criminal Justice, Rutgers University.

Cohen, M. (1998). "The Monetary Value of Saving a High-Risk Youth." *Quantitative Criminology*, 14:5-32.

Comptroller General of the United States (1976). *State and County Probation: Systems in Crisis, Report to the Congress of the United States.* Washington, DC: U.S. Government Printing Office.

Cullen, F.T. (n.d.). Personal Communication.

Cullen, F. (1994). "Social Support as an Organizing Concept for Criminology." *Justice Quarterly*, 11:52-59.

Cullen, F. and B. Applegate (1998). *Offender Rehabilitation.* Brookfield, MA: Ashgate Darthmouth.

Cullen, F. and P. Gendreau (2001). "From Nothing Works to What Works." *Prison Journal*, 81(3):313-338.

Cullen, F. and P. Gendreau (1989). "The Effectiveness of Correctional Rehabilitation: Reconsidering the 'Nothing Works' Debate." In L. Goodstein and D. MacKenzie (eds.) *American Prisons: Issues in Research and Policy*, pp. 23-44. New York, NY: Plenum.

Currie, E. (1985). *Confronting Crime: An American Dilemma.* New York, NY: Pantheon.

Deschenes, E. and P. Greenwood (1994). "Maricopa County's Drug Court: An Innovation Program for First Time Drug Offenders on Probation." *Justice System Journal*, 17 (1):99-115.

Editors (2002). "States Overhauling Sentencing Structures." *Corrections News*, 8(1):1.

Egg, R., F.S. Pearson, C.M. Cleland and D.S. Lipton (2000). "Evaluations of Correctional Treatment Programs in Germany: A Review and Meta-analysis." *Substance Use and Misuse*, 35:1967-2009.

Eichman, C. (1965). "The Impact of the Gideon Decision Upon Crime and Sentencing in Florida: A Study of Recidivism and Socio-Cultural Change." Unpublished master's thesis, Florida State University, Tallahassee, FL.

England, R. (1955). "A Study of Postprobation Recidivism Among Five Hundred Federal Offenders." *Federal Probation*, 19(3):10-16.

Erwin, B. (1984). *Georgia's Intensive Supervision Program: First Year Evaluation.* Atlanta, GA: Department of Offender Rehabilitation.

Eskridge, C. and G. Newbold (1994). "Corrections in New Zealand." *Federal Probation*, 57(3):59-66.

Fagan, J. (1994). " Do Criminal Sanctions Deter Drug Crimes?" In MacKenzie, D. and C. Uchida (eds.) *Drugs and Crime: Evaluating Public Policy Initiatives*. Thousand Oaks, CA: Sage.

Finchamp, D. (1988). "An Examination of the Validity of the California Department of Corrections' Custodial Classification System." Unpublished doctoral dissertation, Claremont Graduate School.

Flanagan, T. (1985). "Questioning the 'Other' Parole: The Effectiveness of Community Supervision of Offenders." In L. Travis (ed.) *Probation, Parole and Community Corrections*, pp. 167-184. Prospect Heights, IL: Waveland.

Flanagan, T. (1982). "Risk and the Timing of Recidivism in Three Cohorts of Prison Releasees." *Criminal Justice Review*, 7:34-45.

Frazier, R. (1972). "Incarceration and Adult Felon Probation in Texas: A Cost Comparison." Unpublished master's thesis, Institute of Contemporary Corrections and the Behavioral Sciences, Sam Houston State University, Huntsville, TX.

Frease, D. (1964). *Factors Related to Probation Outcome*. Olympia, WA: Washington Department of Institutions, Board of Prison Terms and Paroles.

French, S. and P. Gendreau (2006). "Reducing Prison Misconducts: What Works!" *Criminal Justice and Behavior*, 33(2):185-218

Fulton, B., E. Latessa, A. Stichman, and L. Travis (1997). "The State of ISP: Research and Policy Implications," *Federal Probation*, 61(4):65-75.

Furby, L., M. Weinrott, and L. Blackshaw (1989). "Sex Offender Recidivism: A Review." *Psychological Bulletin*, 105:3-30.

Gallagher, C.A., D.B. Wilson, and P. Hischfield (1999). "A Quantitative Review and Description of Corrections-Based Education, Vocation and Work Programs." *Corrections Management Quarterly*, 3(4):8-18.

Garrett, C. (1985). "Effects of Residential Treatment on Adjudicated Delinquents: A Meta-Analysis." *Journal of Research in Crime and Delinquency*, 22:287-308.

Gendreau, P. (1996). "The Principles of Effective Intervention with Offenders." In A. Harland (ed.) *Choosing Correctional Options that Work: Defining the Demand the Evaluating the Supply*. Thousand Oaks, CA: Sage.

Gendreau, P. and D. Andrews (2001). *The Correctional Program Assessment Inventory-2000*. Saint John, NB, Canada: University of New Brunswick.

Gendreau, P. and D. Andrews (1994). *The Correctional Program Assessment Inventory*, Fifth Edition. Saint John, NB, Canada: University of New Brunswick.

Gendreau, P. and D. Andrews (1990). "Tertiary Prevention: What the Meta-Analysis of the Offender Treatment Literature Tells Us About 'What Works.'" *Canadian Journal of Criminology*, 32:173-184.

Gendreau, P., C. Goggin, F. Cullen, and D. Andrews (2000). "The Effects of Community Sanctions and Incarceration on Recidivism." *FORUM*, 12(2):10-13.

Gendreau, P. and M. Paparozzi (1995). "Examining What Works in Community Corrections." *Corrections Today*, (February):28-30.

Gendreau, P. and R. Ross (1987). "Revivification of Rehabilitation: Evidence from the 1980s." *Justice Quarterly*, 4:349-407.

Gendreau, P. and R. Ross (1979). "Effective Correctional Treatment: Bibliography for Cynics." *Crime & Delinquency*, 25:463-489.

Goldkamp, J. (1994). "Miami's Treatment Drug Court for Felony Defendants: Some Implications of Assessment Findings." *Prison Journal*, 74(2):110-157.

Goldkamp, J. and D. Weiland (1993). "Assessing the Impact of Dade County's Felony Drug Court." *National Institute of Justice Research Brief*, Washington DC: U.S. Department of Justice.

Gottfredson, D. (1975). "Some Positive Changes in the Parole Process." Paper presented at the meeting of the American Society of Criminology.

Gottfredson, D., M. Gottfredson, and M. Adams (1982). "Prison Behavior and Release Performance." *Law and Policy Quarterly*, 4:373-391.

Gottfredson, D., M. Gottfredson, and J. Garofalo (1977). "Time Served in Prison and Parolee Outcomes Among Parolee Risk Categories." *Journal of Criminal Justice*, 5:1-12.

Gottfredson, M., S. Mitchell-Herzfeld, and T. Flanagan (1982). "Another Look at the Effectiveness of Parole Supervision." *Journal of Research in Crime and Delinquency*, 18:277-298.

Gowdy, V. (1993). *Intermediate Sanctions*. Washington, DC: U.S. Department of Justice.

Granfield, R., C. Eby, and T. Brewster (1998). "An Examination of the Denver Drug Court: The Impact of a Treatment-Oriented Drug-Offender System." *Law and Policy*, 20(2):183-202.

Greenfield, L. (1995). *Prison Sentences and Time Served for Violence*. Washington, DC: U.S. Department of Justice.

Harrell, A. (1998). *Drug Courts and the Role of Graduated Sanctions*. National Institute of Justice. Washington DC: U.S. Department of Justice.

Hepburn, J., C. Johnston, and S. Rogers (1994). *Do Drugs, Do Time: An Evaluation of the Maricopa County Demand Reduction Program*. Washington, DC: National Institute of Justice.

Hoffman, P. and B. Stone-Meierhoefer (1980). "Reporting Recidivism Rates: The Criterion and Follow-Up Issues." *Journal of Criminal Justice*, 8:53-60.

Holt, N. (1995). "California's Determinate Sentencing: What Went Wrong?" *American Probation and Parole Association Perspectives*, 19(3):19-23Holt, N. (1975). *Rational Risk Taking: Some Alternatives to Traditional Correctional Programs*. Proceedings: Second National Workshop on Corrections and Parole Administration, Louisville, Kentucky.

Irish, J. (1972). *Probation and Its Effects on Recidivism: An Evaluative Research Study of Probation in Nassau County, New York*. New York, NY: Nassau County Probation Department.

Jackson, P. (1983). *The Paradox of Control: Parole Supervision of Youthful Offenders*. New York, NY: Praeger.

Jankowski, L. (1990). *Probation and Parole 1989*. Washington, DC: Bureau of Justice Statistics Bulletin.

Johnson, B.R. (1984). "Hellfire and Corrections: A Quantitative Study of Florida Prison Inmates." Doctoral dissertation, Florida State University.

Johnson, S., D. Hubbard, and E. Latessa (2000). "Drug Courts and Treatment: Lessons to be Learned from the 'What Works' Literature." *Corrections Management Quarterly*, 4(4):70-77.

Johnson, S. and E. Latessa (1998). "Evaluation of the Hamilton County Drug Court." Report for the Supreme Court of Ohio.

Johnson, S., J. Sundt, A. Holsinger, and E. Latessa (1998). "The Effects of Drug Court Programming on Recidivism: The Cincinnati Experience." Presented at American Society of Criminology Annual Meetings.

Knight, K., D. Simpson, and M. Hiller (1999). "Three-Year Reincarceration Outcomes for In-Prison Therapeutic Community Treatment in Texas." *The Prison Journal*, 79:337-351.

Koetzle-Shaffer, D. (2006). "Reconsidering Drug Court Effectiveness: A Meta-analytic Review." Unpublished doctoral dissertation. University of Cincinnati.

Kusuda, P. (1976). "Probation and Parole Terminations." Madison, WI: Wisconsin Division of Corrections.

Lab, S. and J. Whitehead (1988). "An Analysis of Juvenile Correctional Treatment," *Crime & Delinquency*, 28:60-85.

Landis, J., J. Mercer, and C. Wolff (1969). "Success and Failure of Adult Probationers in California." *Journal of Research in Crime and Delinquency*, 6:34-40.

Latessa, E. (1996). "Offenders with Mental Illness on Probation." *Community Corrections in America: New Directions and Sounder Investments for Persons with Mental Illness and CoDisorders*. Washington, DC, National Institute of Corrections and the National Coalition for Mental and Substance Abuse Health Care in the Justice System.

Latessa, E. (1986). "The Cost Effectiveness of Intensive Supervision." *Federal Probation*, 50(2):70-74.

Latessa, E. (1985). *The Incarceration Diversion Unit of the Lucas County Adult Probation Department Report Number Six*. Cincinnati, OH: University of Cincinnati.

Latessa, E. and A. Holsinger (1998). "The Importance of Evaluating Correctional Programs: Assessing Outcome and Quality." *Corrections Management Quarterly*.

Latessa, E. and M. Moon (1992). "The Effectiveness of Acupuncture in an Outpatient Drug Treatment Program." *Journal of Contemporary Criminal Justice*, 8:317-331.

Latessa, E., L. Travis, and A. Holsinger (1997). Evaluation of Ohio's Community Corrections Act Programs and Community Based Correctional Facilities, Cincinnati, OH: Division of Criminal Justice, University of Cincinnati.

Latimer, J., C. Dowden, and D. Muise (April 2001). The Effectiveness of Restorative Justice Practices: A Meta Analysis. Research and Statistics Division, Department of Justice, Canada.

Lerner, M. (1977). "The Effectiveness of a Definite Sentence Parole Program." *Criminology*, 15:32-40.

Lightfoot, L. (1997). "Treating Substance Abuse and Dependence in Offenders: A Review of Methods and Outcome." Paper presented at the International Community Corrections Association meeting, Cleveland, OH.

Linden, R. and L. Perry (1982). "The Effectiveness of Prison Education Programs." *Journal of Offender Counseling, Services and Rehabilitation*, 6:43-57.

Lipsey, M. (1999). "Can Intervention Rehabilitate Serious Delinquent?" *Annals of the American Academy of Political and Social Science*, 564:142-166.

Lipsey, M. (1992). "Juvenile Delinquency Treatment: A Meta-Analytic Inquiry into the Variability of Effects." In T. Cook, H. Cooper, D. Cordray, H. Hartmann, L. Hedges, R. Light, T. Louis, and F. Mosteller (eds.) Meta-Analysis for Explanation, pp. 83-127. New York, NY: Russell Sage Foundation.

Lipsey, M. and D. Wilson (1997). "Effective Interventions for Serious Juvenile Offenders," in R. Loeber and D. Farrington (eds.) *Serious and Violent Juvenile Offenders: Risk Factors and Successful Interventions,* pp. 313-345. Thousand Oaks, CA: Sage.

Logan, C. and G. Gaes (1993) "Meta-Analysis and the Rehabilitation of Punishment." *Justice Quarterly*, 10:245-263.

Lowenkamp, C.T., E.J. Latessa and P. Smith (2006). "Does Correctional Program Quality Really Matter? The Impact of Adhering to the Principles of Effective Intervention." *Criminology and Public Policy*, 5 (3):201-220.

McGaha, J., M. Fichter, and P. Hirschburg (1987). "Felony Probation: A Re-Examination of Public Risk." *American Journal of Criminal Justice*, 12:1-9.

MacKenzie, D., L., Browning, S. Skroban, and D. Smith (1999). "The Impact of Probation on the Criminal Activities of Offenders." *Journal of Research in Crime and Delinquency*, 36(4):423-453.

MacKenzie, D. and L. Hickman (1998). *What Works in Corrections? An Examination of the Effectiveness of the Type of Rehabilitation Programs Offered by Washington State Department of Corrections*. Report to the State of Washington Legislature Joint Audit and Review Committee, College Park, MD: Dept. of Criminology and Criminal Justice, University of Maryland.

MacKenzie, D. and A. Piquero (1994). "The Impact of Shock Incarceration Programs on Prison Crowding." *Crime & Delinquency*, 40:222-249.

Marquart, J. and J. Sorensen (1988). "Institutional and Post-Release Behavior of Furman-Commuted Inmates in Texas." *Criminology*, 26:667-693.

Marshall, Tony F (1999). *Restorative Justice: An Overview* Home Office. Research Development and Statistics Directorate. London, UK

Martin, S., C. Butzin, C. Saum, and J. Inciardi (1999). "Three-Year Outcomes of Therapeutic Community Treatment for Drug-Involved Offenders in Delaware." *The Prison Journal*, 79:294-320.

Martinson, R. (1974). "What Works?—Questions and Answers About Prison Reform." The Public Interest, 35:22- 54.

Martinson, R. and J. Wilks (1977). "Save Parole Supervision." *Federal Probation*, 42(3):23-27.

Matthews, B., D. Jones Hubbard, and E. Latessa (2001). " Making the Next Step: Using Evaluability Assessment to Improve Correctional Programming." *Prison Journal*, 81(4):454-472.

Mauser, E., K. van Stelle, and D. Moberg (1994). "The Economic Impact of Diverting Substance-Abusing Offenders into Treatment." *Crime & Delinquency*, 40(4):568-588.

Maxwell, S., T. Bynum, M. Gray, and T. Combs (2000). "Examining Probationer Recidivism in Michigan." *Corrections Compendium*, 25(12):1-4,18-19.

Missouri Division of Probation and Parole (1976). *Probation in Missouri, July 1, 1968 to June 30, 1970: Characteristics, Performance, and Criminal Reinvolvement*. Jefferson City, Missouri.

Morgan, K. (1993). "Factors Influencing Probation Outcome: A Review of the Literature." *Federal Probation*, 57(2):23-29.

Morris, N. (1978). "Conceptual Overview and Commentary on the Movement Toward Determinacy." In *Determinate Sentencing: Proceedings of the Special Conference on Determinate Sentencing*. Washington, DC: National Institute of Law Enforcement and Criminal Justice.

Mortimer, E. and C. May (1997). *Electronic Monitoring in Practice*. London, UK: U.K. Home Office.

National Mental Health Association (1987). *Stigma: A Lack of Awareness and Understanding*. Alexandria, VA: National Mental Health Association.

National Policy Committee of American Society of Criminology (2001). *The Use of Incarceration in the U.S.* (www.asc41.com/policypapers.html).

Neithercutt, M. (1972). "Parole Violation Patterns and Commitment Offense." *Journal of Research in Crime and Delinquency*, 9:87-98.

Nelson, C.W. (1975). "Cost-Benefit Analysis and Alternatives to Incarceration." *Federal Probation*, 39(4):45-50.

Nesovick, A. (2003). *Psychometric Evaluation of the Correctional Program Assessment Inventory*. Dissertation Abstracts International, 64 (09), 4674B. (UMI No. AAT NQ83525).

Nicholaichuk, T., A. Gordon, D. Gu (2000). "Outcome of an Institutional Sexual Offender Treatment Program." *Sexual Abuse*, 12(2):139-153.

Nuttal, C.P. and Associates (1977). *Parole in England and Wales*. Home Office Research Studies No. 38. London: Her Majesty's Stationery Office.

Ohio Community Corrections Organization (1993). *Ohio's Community Corrections Bench Book*. Columbus, OH: OCCO.

Palmer, T. (1995). "Programmatic and Nonprogrammatic Aspects of Successful Intervention: New Directions for Research." *Crime & Delinquency*, 41(1):101-131.

Palmer, T. (1991). "The Effectiveness of Intervention: Recent Trends and Current Issues." *Crime & Delinquency*, 37(3):330-346.

Palmer, T. (1975). "Martinson Revisited." *Journal of Research in Crime and Delinquency*, 12(2):133-152.

Pearson, F. (1985). "New Jersey's Intensive Supervision Program: A Progress Report." *Crime & Delinquency*, 31:393-410.

Pennsylvania Program for Women and Girl Offenders, Inc. (1976). Report on Recidivism of Women Sentenced to State Probation and Released from SCI Muncy 1971-73. Philadelphia, PA.

Peters, R.H. and M.R. Murrin (2000). "Effectiveness of Treatment-Based Drug Courts in Reducing Criminal Recidivism." *Criminal Justice and Behavior*, 27(1):72-96.

Peters, R., A. Haas, and M. Murrin (1999). "Predictors of Retention and Arrest in Drug Courts." *National Drug Court Institute Review*, 2(1):33-60.

Petersilia, J. (2001). "Prisoner Reentry." *Prison Journal*, 81(3):360-375.

Petersilia, J. (1997). "Probation in the United States." In M. Tonry (ed.) *Crime and Justice: A Review of Research*, Vol. 22 (149-200), Chicago, IL: University of Chicago Press.

Petersilia, J. (1992) "California's Prison Policy: Causes, Costs, and Consequences," *The Prison Journal*, 72:8-36.

Petersilia, J. (1991). "The Value of Corrections Research: Learning What Works." *Federal Probation*, 55(2):24-26.

Petersilia, J. (1985). "Probation and Felony Offenders." *Federal Probation*, 49(2):4-9.

Porporino F. and E. Zamble (1984). "Coping with Imprisonment." *Canadian Journal of Criminology*, 264(4):403-421.

Prendergast, M., D. Anglin, and J. Wellisch (1995). "Up to Speed: Treatment for Drug-Abusing Offenders Under Community Supervision." *Federal Probation*, 59(4):66-75.

Redondo, S., J. Sanchez-Meca, and V. Garrido (1999). "The Influence of Treatment Programmes on the Recidivism of Juvenile and Adult Offenders: An European Meta-Analytic Review." *Psychology, Crime and Law*, 5:251-278.

Roberts, R. and E. Cheek (1994). "Group Intervention and Reading Performance in a Medium Security Prison Facility." *Journal of Offender Rehabilitation*, 20:97-116.

Schiff, M. and C.W. Terry III (1997). "Predicting Graduation from Broward County's Dedicated Drug Treatment Court." *The Justice System Journal*, 19(3):291-310.

Schumaker, R., D. Anderson, and S. Anderson (1990). "Vocational and Academic Indicators of Parole Success." *Journal of Correctional Education*, 41:8-13.

Schwaner, S. (1997). "They Can Run, But Can They Hide? A Profile of Parole Violators at Large." *Journal of Crime and Justice*, 20(2):19-32.

Sherman, L., D. Gottfredson, D. MacKenzie, J. Eck, P. Reuter, and S. Bushway (1998). *Preventing Crime: What Works, What Doesn't, What's Promising*. National Institute of Justice Research in Brief.

Smith, M.O., J. Aponte, R. Bonilla-Rodriquez, N. Rabinowitz, F. Cintron, and L. Hernandez (1984). "Acupuncture Detoxification in a Drug and Alcohol Treatment Setting." *American Journal of Acupuncture*, 12(July-September):251-255.

Smith, M.O., R. Squires, J. Aponte, N. Rabinowitz, and R. Bonilla-Rodriquez (1982). "Acupuncture Treatment of Drug Addiction and Alcohol Abuse." *American Journal of Acupuncture*, 10(April-June):161-163.

Smith, P. (2006). "The Effects of Incarceration on Recidivism: A Longitudinal Examination of Program Participation and Institutional Adjustment in Federally Sentenced Adult Male Offenders." Unpublished doctoral dissertation. University of New Brunswick.

Smith, P., C. Goggin and P. Gendreau (2002). "The Effects of Prison Sentences and Intermediate Sanctions on Recidivism: General Effects and Individual Differences." Ottawa, Ontario: Public Works and Government Services Canada (Cat. No. JS42-103/2002).

Snider, R.M. (1986). "The High Risks of Felony Probation." *California Lawyer*, (March):33-37.

Stevens, D. and C. Ward (1997). "College Education and Recidivism." *Journal of Correctional Education*, 48(3):106-111.

Sumter, M.T. (1999). *Religiousness and Post-Release Community Adjustment*. Doctoral Dissertation. Florida State University.

System Sciences (1982). Executive Summary National Evaluation Program—Phase II Intensive Evaluation of Probation. Bethesda, MD.

Taxman, F. (2000). "Unraveling 'What Works' for Offenders in Substance Abuse Treatment Services." *National Drug Court Institute Review*, Vol. II, 2.

Tauber, J. (1994). "Drug Courts: Treating Drug-Using Offenders Through Sanctions, Incentives." *Corrections Today*, 56(1):28-35.

Travis, L. and E. Latessa (1984). "A Summary of Parole Rules—Thirteen Years Later: Revisited Thirteen Years Later." *Journal of Criminal Justice*, 12:591-600.

Van Voorhis, P. (1987). "Correctional Effectiveness: The High Cost of Ignoring Success." *Federal Probation*, 51(1):56-62.

Vito, G. (ed.) (1994). "Education in Correctional Settings." *The Prison Journal*, 74:395-473.

Vito, G. (1986). "Felony Probation and Recidivism: Replication and Response." *Federal Probation*, 50(4):17-25.

Vito, G. (1985a). "Developments in Shock Probation: A Review of Research Findings and Policy Implications." *Federal Probation*, 48(2):22-27.

Vito, G. (1985b). "Putting Prisoners to Work: Policies and Problems." *Journal of Offender Counseling Services and Rehabilitation*, 9:21-34.

Vito, G. (1978). "Shock Probation in Ohio: A Comparison of Attributes and Outcomes." Unpublished doctoral dissertation, Ohio State University, Columbus.

Vito, G. and H. Allen (1981). "Shock Probation in Ohio: A Comparison of Outcomes." International *Journal of Offender Therapy and Comparative Criminology*, 25:70-75.

Vito, G. and E. Latessa (1979). "Cost Analysis in Probation Research: An Evaluation Synthesis." *Journal of Contemporary Criminal Justice*, 1:3-4.

Vito, G. and D. Wilson (1988). "Back from the Dead: Tracking the Progress of Kentucky's Furman-Commuted Death Row Population." *Justice Quarterly*, 5:101-111.

Vito, G., D. Wilson, and E. Latessa (1991). "Comparison of the Dead: Attributes and Outcomes of Furman-Commuted Death Row Inmates in Kentucky and Ohio." In R.M. Bohm (ed.) *The Death Penalty in America: Current Research*, pp. 101-111. Cincinnati, OH: Anderson Publishing Co.

von Hirsch, A. and K. Hanrahan (1979). *The Question of Parole: Retention, Reform, or Abolition*. Cambridge, MA: Ballinger.

Waller, I. (1974). *Men Released from Prison*. Toronto, CN: University of Toronto Press.

Wagner, D. and C. Baird (1993). *Evaluation of the Florida Community Control Program*. Washington, DC: U.S. Department of Justice.

Washington Department of Social and Health Sciences (1976). *Who Returns? A Study of Recidivism for Adult Offenders in the State of Washington*. Olympia, WA.

Welsh, B. and D. Farrington (2000). "Correctional Intervention Programs and Cost-Benefit Analysis." *Criminal Justice and Behavior*, 27:115-133.

Wensel, L. (1990). *Acupuncture in Medical Practice*. Reston, VA: Reston Publishing.

Wexler, H., G. Melnick, L. Lowe, and J. Peters (1999). "Three-Year Reincarceration Outcomes for Amity In-Prison Therapeutic Community and Aftercare in California." *The Prison Journal*, 79:321-337.

Wetter, R. (1985). *Descriptive Analysis of the Intensive Supervision Program*. Frankfort, KY: Office of Administrative Services Planning and Evaluation Branch, Kentucky Corrections Cabinet.

Whitehead, J. (1991). "The Effectiveness of Felony Probation: Results from an Eastern State." *Justice Quarterly*, 8:525-543.

Whitehead, J. and S. Lab (1989). "A Meta-Analysis of Juvenile Correctional Treatment." *Journal of Research in Crime and Delinquency*, 26:276-295.

Williams, F., M. McShane, and H.M. Dolny (2000). "Predicting Parole Absconders." *The Prison Journal*, 80:24-39.

Wilson, D., C. Gallagher, M. Coggeshall, and D. MacKenzie (1999). "Corrections-Based Education, Vocation, and Work Programs." *Corrections Management Quarterly*, 3(4):8-18.

Wilson D., C. Gallagher, and D. MacKenzie (2000). "A Meta-Analysis of Correctional-Based Education, Vocation and Work Programs for Adult Offenders." *Journal of Research in Crime and Delinquency*, 37(4):347-368.

Wilson, R. (1977). "Supervision (the other parole) Also Attacked." *Corrections Magazine*, 3(3):56-59.

Wisconsin Division of Corrections (1965). *A Comparison of the Effects of Using Probation Versus Incarceration for Burglars with No Previous Felony Convictions*. Madison.

Young, M., J. Gartner, and T. O'Connor (1995). "Long-Term Recidivism Among Federal Inmates Trained as Volunteer Prison Ministers." *Journal of Offender Rehabilitation*, 22(1/2):97-118.

Zeisel, H. (1982). "Disagreement Over the Evaluation of the Controlled Experiment." *American Journal of Sociology*, 88:378-389.

Zehr, H. (1989). "Justice: Stumbling Toward a Restorative Ideal," pp. 1-15. In *Justice: The Restorative Vision*. Occasional papers of the MCC Canada Victim Offender Ministries Program and the MCC U.S. Office of Criminal Justice, Number 7. Elkhard, IN: Mennonite Central Committee and Kitchener, Ontario Canada Victim Offender Ministries Programs.

# The Future of Corrections in the Community

## 12

Show people that there are programs nationwide where violent or habitual felons are assured prison beds only because many of the nuisance shoplifters, technical probation violators, or petty thieves are being punished in other meaningful ways. Make the public understand that dangerous offenders will still be put in prison; that intermediate sanctions are necessary to reintegrate offenders so they have a better chance of becoming successful citizens and not continuing lives of crime.

—M. Castle
Governor of Delaware

## Introduction

As the nation enters the twenty-first century, it is legitimate to ask what corrections will look like by the year 2010, and what changes one might find. Both are legitimate questions and offer opportunities to effect closure in the area of corrections in the community. In 2005, there were over seven million people under correctional supervision. About 59 percent of those were on probation and another 11 percent were on parole, or 70 percent under community supervision (see Table 12.1). The other 30 percent were incarcerated in jails and prisons. Taken together, we incarcerate more adult residents in this nation (738 per 100,000 residents) than any other major western country, even Russia (594) (Bureau of Justice Statistics, 2005). See Figure 12.1. This high rate is due in large part to policies that encourage the use of incarceration and, some would say, over-use of incarceration for property and drug offenders (Fish, 2000).

Table 12.1
**Persons Under Adult Correctional Supervision, 1995-2005**

| Correctional Program | 1995 | 2000 | 2003 | 2005 |
|---|---|---|---|---|
| Probation | 3,077,861 | 3,826,209 | 4,120,012 | 4,162,536 |
| Prison | 1,078,542 | 1,316,333 | 1,390,270 | 1,446,269 |
| Parole | 679,421 | 723,898 | 769,925 | 784,408 |
| Jail | 507,044 | 621,149 | 691,301 | 747,529 |
| | 5,342,868 | 6,487,589 | 6,971,517 | 7,140,742 |

Source: Bureau of Justice Statistics (2006). *Probation and Parole in the United States, 2005.* Washington, DC: Bureau of Justice Statistics, p. 1 (http://www.ojp.usdoj.gov/bjs/abstract/ppus05.htm)

Figure 12.1
**International Incarceration Rates per 100,000 of the National Population**

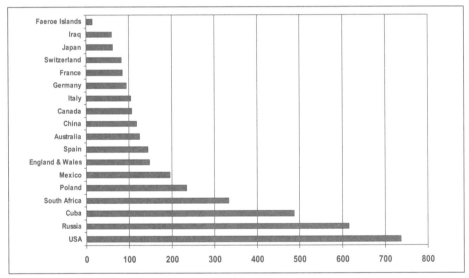

Source: International Centre for Prison Studies: University of London (http://www.prisonstudies.org/).

The use of imprisonment, of course, varies greatly by group. Although African-Americans make up about 14 percent of the total population, they represent one-half of the jail and prison group. This turns out to be about one in 12 adult African-American men aged 14 to 54; there are more African-Americans under incarceration than the total number of African-American men of any age enrolled in college throughout the nation. Disproportionate minority confinement is widespread (although the Juvenile Justice Institute in 2000 demonstrated that it can be sharply reduced). See Figure 12.2.

Figure 12.2
**Age-Specific Imprisonment Rates for Males: 2005 ( in percent)**

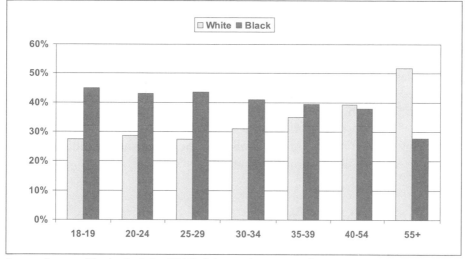

Source: Bureau of Justice Statistics (2006). *Prisoners in 2005.* Washington, DC: U.S. Department of Justice, p. 8 (http://www.ojp.usdoj.gov/bjs/abstract/p00.htm).

No doubt this higher rate reflects the differential rate of involvement of African-Americans in violent crimes; it also reflects effects of the War on Drugs, a "crass attempt to purchase the votes of affluent white Americans" (Cullen et al., 1996).[1] The War on Drugs cannot reasonably have any major effect on the sale, distribution, or use of illicit controlled substances (GAO, 1997). The War on Drugs will continue well into the twenty-first century (Zimring & Block, 1997).

At the present time, then, the correctional population in the United States totals more than seven million offenders, or about one in 30 adult residents in America. The bulk of offenders are on probation or under parole supervision. The incarcerated group has more than two million, with most of those inmates incarcerated in prison. We estimate that the increase in incarcerated offenders will continue unabated well into the twenty-first century.

As dire as these projections are, there are major developments and trends under way that can significantly improve both the protection of

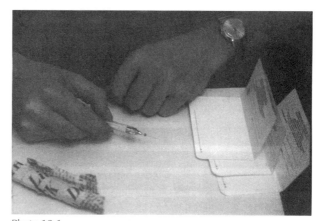

Photo 12.1
The "War on Drugs." Courtesy of Talbert House, Inc.

the public and reintegration of the offender. Far better would be the implementation of more fundamental structural transformations in underclass communities and among those locked out from participation in the American dream, and addressing racism and injustice before America resegregates along racial and class lines (Allen, 1995).

The dominant conservative political ideology[2] makes such transformation less likely, and major change in this area will certainly not be addressed well into the twenty-first century. The future of change in corrections lies in implementing and expanding intermediate sanctions through "transformative rationality" (Musheno et al., 1989:137), the sustaining over time of broad policy principles while simultaneously adapting those polices to local situations.

## Intermediate Sanctions

The reader should be familiar with intermediate sanctions from Chapters 2 and 8, and will recall that these are correctional interventions that fill the sentencing gap between probation and prison (Allen & Simonsen, 2001:211). Their dominant characteristic is that they allow increased surveillance and control over the offender: they have been advanced as a means of avoiding prison crowding and reintegrating offenders. These are depicted in Figure 12.3, and range across 13 distinct programs, each increasingly punitive and controlling. Some of these programs, of course, are themselves composed of different technologies and usefulness, and many permit effective treatment.

## Public Acceptance

The public tends to perceive corrections as being a choice between "mere" probation and imprisonment,[3] a false dichotomy that implies that public safety is met only when major offenders and miscreants are locked away, out of sight and for long periods of time. It should be apparent at this point that public protection does not mean only prison or that anything short of incarceration will endanger public safety. Castle (1989:1) argued:

1.  Nationwide, about one in [38] persons is under the control of correctional authorities.

2.  [In the 1980s], national per capita expenditures grew 21 percent, but correctional expenditures grew 65 percent.

3.  The nations's prison population doubled during the 1980s [and will double again by 2003] . . . If you include the jail population, that's [two] million people behind bars.

Figure 12.3
**A Range of Sentencing Options: Rank by Level of Punishment**

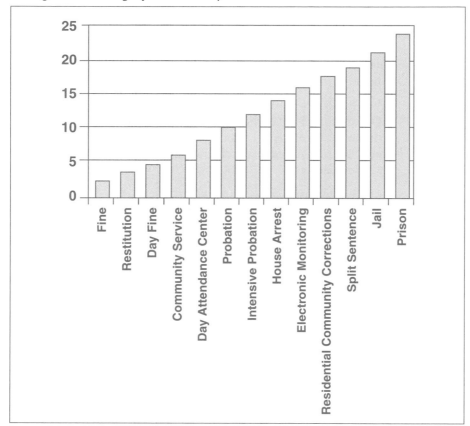

Source: Adapted from J. Byrne (1990). "The Future of Intensive Probation Service." *Crime & Delinquency*, 36(1):29.

4. The growth of America's prison population is more than 10 times that of the general population.

5. It would take the total state tax collected from 15 Delaware residents to pay for just one [prison] resident for only one year.

Policymakers in the State of Delaware, convinced that it was not possible to build their way out of the prison crowding problem and that the public held strong preferences for reintegration of offenders,[4] decided to develop and expand community corrections. Their policy priorities were: (1) to remove violent offenders from the community, (2) to restore the victims to the preoffense status by restitution and compensation, and (3) to rehabilitate offenders. The result was a continuum of programs comprising five levels of increasingly restrictive and punitive sanctions that included cost control mechanisms. The system was de-

signed to allow offenders to earn their way out of prison by good behavior, work, and conformity to rules, or to worm their way into the
prison system by repeated criminal activity and nonconformity to supervision rules. The system is spread over five "levels."

- Level 5 is full incarceration with complete institutional
  control.

- Level 4 is quasi-incarceration in which an offender is supervised from 9 to 23 hours a day in such programs as
  community treatment centers, electronically monitored
  house arrest, attendance centers, and residential drug
  treatment centers.

- Level 3 is intensive, direct supervision over 1-8 hours per
  day, during which offenders are subject to curfew checks,
  employment checks, and frequent monitoring for attendance in treatment programming.

- Level 2 is "normal" field supervision, generally probation,
  with from 0 to 1 hour of supervision per day.

- Level 1 is the lowest level of supervision.

The system allows the sentencing judge wide latitude in sentencing both
the offender and the offense.

## Creating Change

Prisons, of course, will continue to play a vital role in corrections in
future years, yet may be called upon to play decreasingly important
functions as they cease to be the central element of corrections. This will
require an agenda for change, and the most effective way would be to
encourage local communities to address better ways to manage crime
and criminals in their own communities. This in turn would require
leadership at the state governmental level to sentence "smarter," not
just tougher. Is there a politician existing in today's political environment who believes taking a "soft" approach to crime will help in win-
ning an election? The problem to be addressed is not "softer or
harsher," but a recognition that what is needed is a philosophy for organizing corrections.

Before describing the prescriptive approach to organizing a system
that will incarcerate the truly dangerous, make victims whole, and rehabilitate the changeable, it is necessary to identify the coming crisis in
corrections that will contribute to the major changes. The crisis is only
in part the overcrowding of prisons, and the fiscal hurdle of finding
funds to support institutional corrections, even if this might mean de-

creasing allocations to other functions of government. After all, education, welfare,[5] and the economic infrastructure can be and have been choked off in the interest of retribution and disabling offenders (Allen, 1995). Rather, the crisis is in the philosophical basis of corrections.

When the "nothing works in corrections" argument arose, many scholars and practitioners who should have known better abandoned the rehabilitation model. Corrections lost its organizing theme or premise. Now that the abandonment of rehabilitation has been recognized as both premature and erroneous,[6] the stage is set for a considerable and acrimonious battle over the "conscience" or purpose of handling offenders. Unfortunately, that will not occur until we are well into the twenty-first century, and will probably by triggered at that time by students and powerful constituents (senior citizens, parents, school administrators, etc.) tired of increased taxes and decreased services, the outcomes of increasing neglect by policymakers and politicians (Greene & Schiraldi, 2002). The "Great Debate" is imminent.

We choose to focus on boot camp programs to identify and discuss the dimensions of the crisis to come. Since their inception in 1983, boot camp programs have been implemented in at least 66 jail, prison and probation/parole agencies. Advocates of this politically popular program point to alleged benefits of boot camp ("will make a man[7] out of that kid," "teach the offender discipline," "build up physical and moral fiber," "nothing works like punishment," and so on). Some programs have extensive program components, such as learning to read and write, obtaining a general education diploma (GED), learning survival skills, and breaking drug dependency. At least 14,700 offenders graduated from boot camps in 2000 (Camp & Camp, 2000:120). Few scholars or practitioners, however, openly admit that the primary purpose of the program has a quite different objective: managing prison population growth by facilitating early release of basically drug-problemed but low-risk offenders who, if community corrections were more developed and coordinated, should never have been imprisoned. Boot camps have become and probably will remain a permanent part of the correctional scene, despite the negative results emerging from most program evaluations.[8]

More than 100 evaluations of boot camp programs have been conducted and, by the end of 2001, 87 books, articles and national surveys on adult and juvenile, as well as misdemeanant and felony programs, had been published in the United States, alone. With rare exceptions, most evaluations did not find reduced recidivism; some show that gains made during program participation quickly evaporate ("wash out") after the offender is released back into the community. Although well-intentioned and mostly staffed by an enthusiastic and optimistic cadre, boot camps have two fatal flaws: they fail to treat effectively, and they model aggressive behavior.

Box 12.1

## New Correctional Policies

The Justice Policy Institute recently proposed new correctional policies primarily aimed at reducing prison overcrowding, as well as over-reliance on incarceration for non-violent and non-sale drug law violators. The over-all thrust was to strengthen corrections in the community. Among their recommendations were the following:

- Reform "mandatory minimum" sentencing laws by returning sentencing discretion to judges.

- Retain minimum-risk nonviolent offenders in community corrections settings and programs. This would reduce prison populations by 40 percent.

- Except for the violent and persistent, women offenders should be handled in community corrections, especially if they are primary care givers to dependent children.

- Create a sentencing presumption for community treatment and supervision for nonviolent offenders who face primary responsibility for care of their offspring.

- Release and divert nonviolent elderly offenders to community supervision.

- Divert petty drug offenders, particularly those convicted only of possession, to community-based treatment in lieu of incarceration in jail or prison.

- Increase control supervision for probationers and parolees who violate a drug-related condition of community, rather than incarceration.

- Reduce the length of community supervision for offenders convicted of low-level offending.

- Establish and fund day-attendance centers.

Box 12.1—*continued*

- Shorten sentence length by earlier parole of low-risk offenders and requiring a set period of halfway house residence or community release under a "diminished liberty" plan.

- Use "summary" or unsupervised release for low-risk parolees.

- Use intermediate sanctions to address technical probation or parole violations.

- Reduce criminogenic conditions and promote public health and economic well-being for families in high-risk urban environments.

Allen (2002) also identified promising programs and thrusts that would reduce criminogenic conditions: family strengthening interventions, visiting nurse programs for prenatal and infant care, aggressive and mandatory interventions in domestic violence cases, and treatment for mental health and substance abuse problems for juveniles.

Sources: Allen, H. (2002). "Preliminary Remarks." In H. Allen (ed.) *Risk Reduction: Interventions for Special Needs Offenders*. Landham, MD: American Correctional Association; and Greene, J. and V. Schiraldi (2002). Cutting Correctly: New Prison Policies for Times of Fiscal Crisis (www.cjcj.org/cutting/cutting_es.html).

Treatment can be defined as the diagnosis of an offender's needs, the design of a specific program to address these concrete and criminogenic needs, the application of that program by competent staff supervised by experienced professionals, routine review of the adequacy of delivery of the service and redesign of the individual's program until it is effective, and graduated release into the community with supervision and assistance. Treatment also requires follow-up of the graduates over time and documentation of outcome, the latter to help "fine-tune" treatments for incoming offenders. Said differently, "treatment" requires diagnosis, classification, delivery of the intervention, and case monitoring and long-term follow-up. We know of no boot camp program in the nation that meets these basics of treatment.

Contemporary community corrections is called upon (see below) to do more with less, to be more effective, and to protect through service and surveillance. Meeting this challenge will require more resources, trained professionals, competent administrators, and demonstrated effectiveness. It is no longer enough to be "well meaning." A new breed of correctional practitioner, theorist, manager and specialist is needed; the principles of effective treatment must be implemented. And vital to achieving the new community corrections is the recognition that "more of the same" is no longer acceptable.

Lest the reader misunderstand, we are not berating boot camp programs per se, but identifying the basic philosophical problem that underlies community as well as institutional corrections. The need is for vision, mission, and training. Competence, focus, diagnosis, classification, and individualized treatment must be incorporated as part of the mission. Students entering corrections who can dedicate themselves to accepting the challenge of crime in a free society would be warmly welcomed.

## Establishing a Community Correctional System

The first step is deciding on the goals of the correctional system (incapacitation, restitution, rehabilitation, and so on), and their priority. Second, a commission should be established, possibly by legislative act, to devise a workable scheme to gain control of prison population and resource problems. The commission should serve as the open forum for debate and research on intermediate sanctions, as well as implementing an accountability system. The commission might best be charged with defining the scope and continuum of acceptable sanctions, as well as accepting testimony from concerned groups and activists. The Commission might be best served by calling for a moratorium on prison construction.[9] Third, public opinion leaders, such as legislators, jurists, and media leaders, should be informed of proposed changes and made part of the developmental process. The judiciary should be charged and empowered to develop sentencing standards and guidelines for possible adoption across jurisdictions. Monitoring of the program, sentencing compliance, concerns, and effectiveness should be coordinated through the commission as part of accountability for the system. This was the basic process used for the highly successful Delaware system.

## Conclusion

The nation cannot build itself out of current prison and management crises, but states and local jurisdictions can manage and control not only the prison populations but also the costs and integrity of the justice system that deals with post-offense corrections. By developing a logical set of sentencing policies with clear goals and a wide range of sentencing options and sanctions, the nation would begin to address public safety on a more sound foundation. In addition, an aggressive public education and information initiative is necessary for public acceptance. In the long run, corrections must hold offenders accountable to the public and the legal system for their criminal behaviors, and politicians must be held accountable to the public for their actions.

Many issues face community corrections: risk management and handling of special needs populations, officer safety and work conditions, and the appropriate use of technology, such as drug testing and electronic monitoring. We have confidence that the field will rise to the challenge. We base this faith on our knowledge of the professionals who work in and will come to the field. Because of these dedicated individuals, the future of corrections in the community is bright, and the achievement of a logical, coherent and safe system for handling criminal offenders is attainable. In doing this, we must remember that corrections is above all else a human issue, that change is not easy, and that partners in change are necessary. Corrections has a bright future.

## Electronic Library

New Correctional Policies (www.cjcj.org/cutting/cutting es.html).

Rates of Incarceration In Various Countries (www.sentencingproject.org/brief/usvsrus. pdf).

Reducing Disproportionate Minority Confinement (www.cjcj.org/portland/portland web.html).

Recommended Readings

Ambrosio, T. and V. Schiraldi (1997). *From Classrooms to Cell Blocks. A National Perspective*. Washington, DC: Justice Policy Institute.

Green, J. and V. Schiraldi (2002). *Cutting Correctly: New Prison Policies for Times of Fiscal Crisis* (www.cjcj.org/cutting/cutting es.html).

Klofas, J. and S. Stojkovic (1995). *Crime and Justice in the Year 2010*. Belmont, CA: Wadsworth.

Muraskin, R. and A. Roberts (2002). *Visions for Change: Crime and Justice in the Twenty-First Century*. Upper Saddle River, NJ: Prentice-Hall.

## Notes

[1]    This statement is not meant to imply that nonwhites are not concerned about drugs and crime. Surveys indicate that both white and nonwhite Americans are concerned about drug abuse and the effects of drugs on communities.

[2]    Jacobs and Helms found that shifts in the incarceration rate are related to the strength of the Republican Party and whether it were an election year. D. Jacobs and R. Helms (1996). "Toward a Political Model of Incarceration." *American Journal of Sociology*, 102(2):323-351.

[3]    Those interested in the death penalty and public opinion should see H. Bedeau (1997). *The Death Penalty in America: Current Controversies*. New York, NY: Oxford University Press.

[4]    Cullen, F. and M. Moon (2002). "Reaffirming Rehabilitation: Public Support for Correctional Treatment." In Allen, H. (ed.) *Risk Reduction: Interventions for Special Needs Offenders*. Lanham, MD: American Correctional Association, pp. 7-26.

[5]    There is a clear and negative impact of welfare on crime, particularly cash and public housing programs. For bibliotherapy, see J. Zhang (1997). "The Effect of Welfare Programs on Criminal Behavior." Economic Inquiry, 35(1):120-137; and Hirsch, A. (2001). "The World Was Never a Safe Place for Them." *Violence Against Women*, 7(2):159-175.

[6]    Allen, H. (2002). "Introductory Remarks." In Allen, H. (ed.), supra note 4:1-6.

[7]    Most boot camp participants are male (13,700 of 14,700 graduates in 2000) but there are at least 21 boot camps for females.

[8]    Stinchcomb, J. and W. Terry (2002). "Predicting the Likelihood of Rearrest Among Shock Incarceration Graduates." *Crime & Delinquency*, 47(2):221-242.

[9]    Ambrosio, T. and V. Schiraldi (1997). *From Classrooms to Cell Blocks: A National Perspective*. Washington, DC: Justice Policy Institute.

## References

Allen, H. (ed.) (2002). *Risk Reduction: Interventions for Special Needs Offenders*. Lanham, MD: American Correctional Association.

Allen, H. (1995). "The American Dream and Crime in the 21st Century." *Justice Quarterly*, 12:427-444.

Allen, H. and C. Simonsen (2001). *Corrections in America*. Upper Saddle River, NJ: Prentice-Hall.

Ambrosio, T. and V. Schiraldi (1997). *From Classrooms to Cell Blocks: A National Perspective*. Washington, DC: Justice Policy Institute.

Bedeau, H. (1997). *The Death Penalty in America: Current Controversies*. New York, NY: Oxford University Press.

Bureau of Justice Statistics (2005). *Probation and Parole in the United States, 2005* (www.ojp.usdoj.gov/bjs/abstract/pp05.htm).

Byrne, J. (1990). "The Future of Intensive Probation Service." *Crime & Delinquency*, 36(1):3-32.

Camp, C. and G. Camp (2000). *The 2000 Corrections Yearbook: Adult Corrections*. Middletown, CT: The Criminal Justice Institute.

Castle, M. (1989). *Alternative Sentencing: Selling It to the Public*. Washington, DC: U.S. Department of Justice.

Cullen, F. and M. Moon (2002). "Reaffirming Rehabilitation: Public Support for Correctional Treatment." In Allen, H. (ed.) *Risk Reduction: Interventions for Special Needs Offenders*. Lanham, MD: American Correctional Association.

Cullen, F., P. Van Voorhis, and J. Sundt (1996). "Prisons in Crisis: The American Experience." In R. Matthews and F. Francis (eds.) *Prisons 2000: An International Perspective on the Current State and Future of Imprisonment*, pp. 21-52. New York, NY: Macmillan.

Fish, J. (ed.) (2000). "The Drug Policy Debate." *Fordham University Law*, 28(6):3-361.

General Accounting Office (1997). *Drug Control: Observations on Elements of the Federal Drug Control Strategy*. Washington, DC: USGAO.

Greene, J. and V. Schiraldi (2002). *Cutting Correctly: New Prison Policies for Times of Fiscal Crisis* (www.cjcj.org/cutting/cutting_es.htm).

Hirsch, A. (2001). "The World Has Never Been a Safe Place for Them." *Violence Against Women*, 7(2):159-175.

Jacobs, D. and R. Helms (1996). "Toward a Political Model of Incarceration." *American Journal of Sociology*, 102(2):323-357.

Juvenile Justice Institute (2002). *Reducing Disproportionate Minority Confinement*. (www.cjcj.org/portland/portland_web.html).

Klofas, J. and S. Stojkovic (1995). *Crime and Justice in the Year 2010*. Belmont, CA: Wadsworth.

Muraskin, R. and A. Roberts (2002). *Visions for Change: Crime and Justice in the Twenty-First Century*. Upper Saddle River, NJ: Prentice-Hall.

Musheno, M., D. Palumbo, S. Maynard-Moody, and J. Levine (1989). "Community Corrections as an Organizational Innovation: What Works and Why." *Journal of Research in Crime and Delinquency*, 26:136-167.

Stinchcomb, J. and W. Terry (2002). "Predicting the Likelihood of Rearrest Among Shock Incarceration Graduates." *Crime & Delinquency*, 47(2):221-242.

Zhang, J. (1997). "The Effect of Welfare Programs on Criminal Behavior: A Theoretical and Empirical Analysis." *Economic Inquiry*, 35(1):120-137.

Zimring, F. and M. Block (1997). *Two Views on Imprisonment Policies*. Washington, DC: U.S. Institute of Justice.

# Glossary

The authors are grateful to the Law Enforcement Assistance Administration for the publication of the *Dictionary of Criminal Justice Data Terminology*, from which many of the following terms and definitions have been extracted. It is in the spirit of that effort to standardize criminal justice terminology that we have decided to include this section. We hope that students, especially those new to the field, will take the time to read and absorb the meanings of these tools of the trade. To obtain more detailed information about the terms in this glossary, write to U.S. Department of Justice, National Criminal Reference Service, Washington, DC 20531.

Abscond (corrections). To depart from a geographical area or jurisdiction prescribed by the conditions of one's probation or parole, without authorization.

Abscond (court). To intentionally absent or conceal oneself unlawfully in order to avoid a legal process.

Acquittal. A judgment of a court, based either on the verdict of a jury or a judicial officer, that the defendant is not guilty of the offense(s) for which he or she has been tried.

Adjudicated. Having been the subject of completed criminal or juvenile proceedings, and convicted, or adjudicated a delinquent, status offender, or dependent.

Adjudication hearing. In juvenile proceedings, the fact-finding process wherein the juvenile court determines whether or not there is sufficient evidence to sustain the allegations in a petition.

Adult. A person who is within the original jurisdiction of a criminal, rather than a juvenile, court because his or her age at the time of an alleged criminal act was above a statutorily specified limit.

Alias. Any name used for an official purpose that is different from a person's legal name.

Alternative facility. An alternative place of limited confinement that may be an option for certain kinds of offenders. Such facilities may include treatment settings for drug-dependent offenders, minimum security facilities in the community that provide treatment and services as needed, work/study-release centers, and halfway houses or shelter-type facilities. All of these are less secure than the traditional jail but offer a more stimulating environment for the individual.

Appeal. A request by either the defense or the prosecution that a case be removed from a lower court to a higher court in order for a completed trial to be reviewed by the higher court.

Appearance. The act of coming into a court and submitting to the authority of that court.

Appearance, first (initial appearance). The first appearance of a juvenile or adult in the court that has jurisdiction over his or her case.

Appellant. A person who initiates an appeal.

Arraignment. The appearance of a person before a court in order that the court may inform the individual of the accusation(s) against him or her and enter his or her plea.

Arrest. Taking a person into custody by authority of law for the purpose of charging him or her with a criminal offense or initiating juvenile proceedings, terminating with the recording of a specific offense.

Arson. The intentional destruction or attempted destruction, by fire or explosive, of the property of another or of one's own property with the intent to defraud.

Assault. Unlawful intentional inflicting, or attempted or threatened inflicting, of injury upon another.

Assault, aggravated. Unlawful intentional causing of serious bodily injury with or without a deadly or unlawful intentional attempting or threatening of serious bodily injury or death with a deadly weapon.

Assault, simple. Unlawful intentional threatening, attempted inflicting, or inflicting of less than serious bodily injury, in the absence of a deadly weapon.

Assault with a deadly weapon. Unlawful intentional inflicting, or attempted or threatened inflicting, or injury or death with the use of a deadly weapon.

Assault on a law enforcement officer. A simple or aggravated assault, in which the victim is a law enforcement officer engaged in the performance of his or her duties.

Assigned council. An attorney, not regularly employed by a government agency, assigned by the court to represent a particular person(s) in a particular criminal proceeding.

Attorney/lawyer/counsel. A person trained in the law, admitted to practice before the bar of a given jurisdiction, and authorized to advise, represent, and act for other persons in legal proceedings.

Backlog. The number of pending cases that exceeds the court's capacity, in that they cannot be acted upon because the court is occupied in acting upon other cases.

Bondsman-secured bail. Security service purchased by the defendant from a bail bondsman. The fee for this service ranges upward from 10 percent and is not refundable. The bail bondsman system, which permits a private entrepreneur to share with the court the decision on pretrial release, has been criticized for many years and is becoming obsolete in more progressive jurisdictions.

Booking. A police administrative action officially recording an arrest and identifying the person, the place, the time, the arresting authority, and the reason for the arrest.

Boot camp programs. A form of shock incarceration program usitlizing a program of military regimen, physical execise, specialized education and training. Boot camp programs generally permit earlier release of clients under contional release.

Burglary. Unlawful entry of a structure, with or without force, with intent to commit a felony or larceny.

Camp/ranch/farm. Any of several types of similar confinement facilities, usually in a rural location, which contain adults or juveniles committed after adjudication.

Case. At the level of police or prosecutorial investigation, a set of circumstances under investigation involving one or more persons; at subsequent steps in criminal proceedings, a charging document alleging the commission of one or more crimes; a single defendant; in juvenile or correctional proceedings, a person who is the object of agency action.

Case (court). A single charging document under the jurisdiction of a court; a single defendant.

Caseload (corrections). The total number of clients registered with a correctional agency or agent during a specified time period, often divided into active and inactive or supervised and unsupervised, thus distinguishing between clients with whom the agency or agent maintains contact and those with whom it does not.

Caseload (court). The total number of cases filed in a given court or before a given judicial officer during a given period of time.

Caseload, pending. The number of cases at any given time that have been filed in a given court, or are before a given judicial officer, but have not reached disposition.

Cash bail. A cash payment for a situation in which the charge is not serious and the scheduled bail is low. The defendant obtains release by paying in cash the full amount, which is recoverable after the required court appearances are made.

CCH. An abbreviation for computerized criminal history.

Charge. A formal allegation that a specific person(s) has committed a specific offense(s).

Charging document. A formal written accusation, filed in a court, alleging that a specified person(s) has committed a specific offense(s).

Check fraud. The issuance or passing of a check, draft, or money order that is legal as a formal document, signed by the legal account holder but with the foreknowledge that the bank or depository will refuse to honor it because of insufficient funds or a closed account.

Child abuse. Willful action or actions by a person causing physical harm to a child.

Child neglect. Willful failure by the person(s) responsible for a child's well-being to provide for adequate food, clothing, shelter, education, and supervision.

Citation (to appear). A written order issued by a law enforcement officer directing an alleged offender to appear in a specific court at a specified time in order to answer a criminal charge.

Citizen dispute settlement. The settlement of interpersonal disputes by a third party or the courts. Charges arising from interpersonal disputes are mediated by a third party in an attempt to avoid prosecution. If an agreement between the parties cannot be reached and the complainant wishes to proceed with criminal processing, the case may be referred to court for settlement.

Commitment. The action of a judicial officer ordering that an adjudicated and sentenced adult, or adjudicated delinquent or status offender who has been the subject of a juvenile court disposition hearing, be admitted into a correctional facility.

Community corrections. A general term used to refer to various types of non-institutional correctional programs for criminal offenders and juvenile delinquents. These programs (diversion, pre-trial release, probation, restitution and community service, day attendance centers, halfway houses, and parole) form a continuum of options for dealing with offenders in the community.

Community facility (nonconfinement facility, adult or juvenile). A correctional facility from which residents are regularly permitted to depart, unaccompanied by any official, to use daily community resources such as schools or treatment programs, or to seek or hold employment.

Community residential treatment centers. Formerly known as halfway houses, these centers provide residential settings from which clients leave for work, education, training and treatment. Curfews and supervision are required.

Community service (community work order). A period of service to the community as a substitute for, or in partial satisfaction of, a fine. This disposition is generally a condition of a suspended or partially suspended sentence or of probation. The offender volunteers his or her services to a community agency for a certain number of hours per week over a specified period of time. The total number of hours, often assessed at the legal minimum wage, is determined by the amount of the fine that would have been imposed or that portion of the fine is suspended.

Complaint. A formal written accusation made by any person, often a prosecutor, and filed in a court, alleging that a specified person(s) has committed a specific offense(s).

Complaint denied. The decision by a prosecutor to decline a request that he or she seek an indictment or file an information or complaint against a specified person(s) for a specific offense(s).

Complaint granted. The decision by a prosecutor to grant a request that he or she seek an indictment or file an information or complaint against a specified person(s) for a specific offense(s).

Complaint requested (police). A request by a law enforcement agency that the prosecutor seek an indictment or file an information or complaint against a specified person(s) for a specific offense(s).

Conditional diversion. At the pretrial stage, suspension of prosecution while specific conditions are met. If conditions are not satisfied during a specified time period, the case is referred for continued prosecution.

Conditional release. The release of a defendant who agrees to meet specific conditions in addition to appearing in court. Such conditions may include remaining in a defined geographical area, maintaining steady employment, avoiding contact with the victim or with associates in the alleged crime, avoiding certain activities or places, participating in treatment, or accepting services. Conditional release is often used in conjunction with third-party or supervised release.

Confinement facility. A correctional facility from which the inmates are not regularly permitted to depart each day unaccompanied.

Convict. An adult who has been found guilty of a felony and who is confined in a federal or state confinement facility.

Conviction. A judgment of a court, based either on the verdict of a jury or a judicial officer or on the guilty plea of the defendant, that the defendant is guilty of the offense(s) for which he or she has been tried.

Correctional agency. A federal, state, or local criminal justice agency, under a single administrative authority, of which the principal functions are the investigation, intake screening, supervision, custody, confinement, or treatment of alleged or adjudicated adult offenders, delinquents, or status offenders.

Correctional day programs. A publicly financed and operated nonresidential educational or treatment program for persons required, by a judicial officer, to participate.

Correctional facility. A building or part thereof, set of buildings, or area enclosing a set of buildings or structures operated by a government agency for the custody and/or treatment of adjudicated and committed persons, or persons subject to criminal or juvenile justice proceedings.

Correctional institution. A generic name proposed in this terminology for those long-term adult confinement facilities often called "prisons," "federal or state correctional facilities," or "penitentiaries," and juvenile confinement facilities called "training schools," "reformatories," "boys ranches," and the like.

Correctional institution, adult. A confinement facility having custodial authority over adults sentenced to confinement for more than a year.

Correctional institution, juvenile. A confinement facility having custodial authority over delinquents and status offenders committed to confinement after a juvenile dispassion hearing.

Corrections. A generic term that includes all government agencies, facilities, programs, procedures, personnel, and techniques concerned with the investigation, intake, custody, confinement, supervision, or treatment of alleged or adjudicated adult offenders, delinquents, or status offenders.

Count. Each separate offense, attributed to one or more persons, as listed in a complaint, information, or indictment.

Court. An agency of the judicial branch of government, authorized or established by statute or constitution, and consisting of one or more judicial officers, which has the authority to decide on controversies in law and dispute matters of fact brought before it.

Court of appellate jurisdiction. A court that does not try criminal cases but does hear appeals.

Court of general jurisdiction. Of criminal courts, a court that has jurisdiction to try all criminal offenses, including all felonies and that may or may not hear appeals.

Court of limited jurisdiction. Of criminal courts, a court of which the trial jurisdiction either includes no felonies or is limited to less than all felonies and which may or may not hear appeals.

Crime (criminal offense). An act committed or omitted in violation of a law forbidding or commanding it for which an adult can be punished, upon conviction, by incarceration and other penalties or a corporation penalized, or for which a juvenile can be brought under the jurisdiction of a juvenile court and adjudicated a delinquent or transferred to adult court.

Crime Index offenses (index crimes). A UCR classification that includes all Part I offenses with the exception of involuntary (negligent) manslaughter.

Crimes against businesses (business crimes, commercial crimes). A summary term used by the National Crime Panel reports, including burglary and robbery (against businesses).

Crimes against households (household crimes). A summary term used by the National Crime Panel reports, including burglary (against households), household larceny, and motor vehicle theft.

Crimes against persons. A summary term used by UCR and the National Crime Panel reports, but with different meanings:

UCR
Murder
Nonnegligent (voluntary) manslaughter
Negligent (involuntary) manslaughter
Forcible rape
Aggravated assault

National Crime Panel
Forcible rape
Robbery (against person)
Aggravated assault
Simple assault
Personal larceny

Crimes against property (property crime). A summary term used by UCR, both as a subclass of the Part I offenses and as a subclass of Crime Index offenses, but with different meanings: As a subset of UCR Part I offenses:

> Robbery
> Burglary
> Larceny-theft
> Motor vehicle theft
> As a subset of UCR Crime Index offenses

> Burglary
> Larceny-theft
> Motor vehicle theft

Crimes of violence (violent crime). A summary term used by UCR and the National Crime Panel, but with different meanings: As a subset of UCR Index Crimes:

> Murder
> Nonnegligent (voluntary) manslaughter
> Forcible rape
> Robbery
> Aggravated assault
> As a subset of National Crime Panel crimes against persons
> Forcible rape
> Robbery (against persons)
> Aggravated assault
> Simple assault

Criminal history record information. Information collected by criminal justice agencies on individuals, consisting of identifiable descriptions and notations of arrests, detentions, indictments, informations, or other formal criminal charges, and any disposition(s) arising therefrom, including sentencing, correctional supervision, and release.

Criminal justice agency. Any court with criminal jurisdiction and any other government agency or subunit that defends indigents, or of which the principal functions or activities consist of the prevention, detection, and investigation of crime; the apprehension, detention, and prosecution of alleged offenders; the confinement or official correctional supervision of accused or convicted persons; or the administrative or technical support of the above functions.

Criminal proceedings. Proceedings in a court of law undertaken to determine the guilt or innocence of an adult accused of a crime.

Culpability. The state of mind of one who has committed an act that makes him or her liable to prosecution for that act.

Day attendance center. A highly structured non-residential program utilizing sanctions, services and supervision and coordinated from a center's office. Used for preparole releasees, work and study releases and furloughees.

Day fines. A financial penalty system based on an offender's daily income, rather than fixed schedule of dollar amounts to be imposed by the court.

Defendant. A person against whom a criminal proceeding is pending.

Defense attorney. An attorney who represents the defendant in a legal proceeding.

Delinquency. Juvenile actions or conduct in violation of criminal law and, in some contexts, status offenses.

Delinquent. A juvenile who has been adjudicated by a judicial officer of a juvenile court as having committed a delinquent act, which is an act for which an adult could not be prosecuted in a criminal court.

Delinquent act. An act committed by a juvenile for which an adult could not be prosecuted in a criminal court, but for which a juvenile can be adjudicated in a juvenile court.

Dependency. The legal status of a juvenile over whom a juvenile court has assumed jurisdiction because the court has found his or her care by parent, guardian, or custodian to fall short of a legal standard or proper care.

Dependent. A juvenile over whom a juvenile court has assumed jurisdiction because the court has found his or her care by parent, guardian, or custodian to fall short of a legal standard of proper care.

Detention. The legally authorized holding in confinement of a person subject to criminal or juvenile court proceedings until the point of commitment to a correctional facility or release.

Detention center. A government facility that provides temporary care in a physically restricting environment for juveniles in custody pending court disposition.

Detention facility. A generic name proposed in this terminology as a cover term for those facilities that hold adults or juveniles in confinement pending adjudication, adults sentenced for one year or less of confinement, and in some instances post-adjudicated juveniles, including facilities called "jails," "county farms," "honor farms," "work camps," "road camps," "detention centers," "shelters," "juvenile halls," and the like.

Detention facility, adult. A confinement facility of which the custodial authority is 48 hours or more and in which adults can be confined before adjudication or for sentences of one year or less.

Detention facility, juvenile. A confinement facility having custodial authority over juveniles confined pending and after adjudication.

Detention hearing. In juvenile proceedings, a hearing by a judicial officer of a juvenile court to determine whether a juvenile is to be detained, to continue to be detained, or to be released, while juvenile proceedings are pending in his or her case.

Diagnosis or classification center. A functional unit within a correctional institution, or a separate facility, that holds persons held in custody in order to determine to which correctional facility or program they should be committed.

Dismissal. A decision by a judicial officer to terminate a case without a determination of guilt or innocence.

Disposition. The action by a criminal or juvenile justice agency that signifies that a portion of the justice process is complete and jurisdiction is relinquished or transferred to another agency or that signifies that a decision has been reached on one aspect of a case and a different aspect comes under consideration, requiring a different kind of decision.

Disposition, court. The final judicial decision, which terminates a criminal proceeding by a judgment of acquittal or dismissal or which states the specific sentence in the case of a conviction.

Disposition hearing. A hearing in juvenile court, conducted after an adjudicatory hearing and subsequent receipt of the report of any predisposition investigation, to determine the most appropriate disposition of a juvenile who has been adjudicated a delinquent, a status offender, or a dependent.

Disposition, juvenile court. The decision of a juvenile court, concluding a disposition hearing, that a juvenile be committed to a correctional facility, placed in a care or treatment program, required to meet certain standards of conduct, or released.

Diversion. The official halting or suspension, at any legally prescribed processing point after a recorded justice system entry, of formal criminal or juvenile justice proceedings against an alleged offender, and referral of that person to a treatment or care program administered by a nonjustice agency or a private agency, or no referral.

Driving under the influence of alcohol (drunk driving). The operation of any vehicle after having consumed a quantity of alcohol sufficient to potentially interfere with the ability to maintain safe operation.

Driving under the influence of drugs. The operation of any vehicle while attention or ability is impaired through the intake of a narcotic or an incapacitating quantity of another drug.

Drug law violation. The unlawful sale, transport, manufacture, cultivation, possession, or use of a controlled or prohibited drug.

Early release. Release from confinement before the sentence has been completed. Early release to supervision means less jail time and, with more rapid turnover, low jail populations and capacity requirements. Early release may come about through parole, time off for good behavior or work performed, or modification of the sentence by the court. The last procedure is usually associated with sentences to jail with a period of probation to follow. Although there are some objections to its use, "probation with jail" is a common disposition in some jurisdictions. More often than not, these sentences are in lieu of a state prison term.

Electronic monitoring. A computer-based system for validating the presence of a client under house arrest or confinement while awaiting trial.

Embezzlement. The misappropriation, misapplication, or illegal disposal of legally entrusted property with intent to defraud the legal owner or intended beneficiary.

Escape. The unlawful departure of a lawfully confined person from a confinement facility or from custody while being transported.

Expunge. The sealing or purging of arrest, criminal, or juvenile record information.

Extortion. Unlawful obtaining or attempting to obtain the property of another by the threat of eventual injury or harm to that person, the person's property, or another person.

Felony. A criminal offense punishable by death or by incarceration in a state or federal confinement facility for a period of which the lower limit is prescribed by statute in a given jurisdiction, typically one year or more.

Filing. The commencement of criminal proceedings by entering a charging document into a court's official record.

Finding. The official determination of a judicial officer or administrative body regarding a disputed matter of fact or law.

Fine. The penalty imposed on a convicted person by a court requiring that he or she pay a specified sum of money. The fine is a cash payment of a dollar amount assessed by the judge in an individual case or determined by a published schedule of penalties. Fines may be paid in installments in many jurisdictions.

Forgery. The creation or alteration of a written or printed document that, if validly executed, would constitute a record of a legally binding transaction, with the intent to defraud by affirming it to be the act of an unknowing second person. Defining features: Making or altering a written or printed document or record. Act being falsely attributed to an unknowing second person. Intent being to deprive illegally a person of property or legal rights.

Fraud. An element of certain offenses consisting of deceit or intentional misrepresentation with the aim of illegally depriving a person of property or legal rights.

Fugitive. A person who has concealed himself or herself or fled a given jurisdiction in order to avoid prosecution or confinement.

Furlough. A prison releae program peermittingn the inate to pursue education, vocational trainig, or employment in the community. Furlough clients typically remain inmates and can easily be returned to incarceration settings with minimal difficulty.

Group home. A nonconfining residential facility for adjudicated adults or juveniles or those subject to criminal or juvenile proceedings, intended to reproduce as closely as possible the circumstances of family life and at the minimum, providing access to community activities and resources.

Halfway house. A nonconfining residential facility for adjudicated adults or juveniles or those subject to criminal or juvenile proceedings, intended as an alternative to confinement for persons not suited for probation or needing a period of readjustment to the community after confinement.

Hearing. A proceeding in which arguments, evidence, or witnesses are heard by a judicial officer or administrative body.

Hearing, probable cause. A proceeding before a judicial officer in which arguments, evidence, or witnesses are presented and in which it is determined whether there is sufficient cause to hold the accused for trial or whether the case should be dismissed.

Homicide. Any killing of one person by another.

Homicide, criminal. The causing of the death of another person without justification or excuse.

Homicide, excusable. The intentional but justifiable causing of the death of another or the unintentional causing of the death of another by accident or misadventure, without gross negligence. Not a crime.

Homicide, justifiable. The intentional causing of the death of another in the legal performance of an official duty or in the circumstances defined by law as constituting legal justification. Not a crime.

Homicide, willful. The intentional causing of the death of another person, with or without legal justification.

Indictment. A formal written accusation made by a grand jury and filed in a court alleging that a specified person(s) has committed a specific offense(s).

Information. A written formal accusation, filed in a court by a prosecutor, that alleges a specific person has committed a specific offense.

Infraction. An offense punishable by fine or other penalty, but not by incarceration.

Inmate. A person in custody in a confinement facility.

Institutional capacity. The officially stated number of inmates or residents that a correctional facility is designed to house, exclusive of extraordinary arrangements to accommodate overcrowded conditions.

Intake. The process during which a juvenile referral is received and a decision is made by an intake unit to file a petition in juvenile court, to release the juvenile, to place the juvenile under supervision, or to refer the juvenile elsewhere.

Intake unit. A government agency or agency sub-unit that receives juvenile referrals from police, other government agencies, private agencies, or persons and screens them, resulting in closing of the case, referral to care or supervision, or filing of a petition in juvenile court.

Intensive supervised probation. A propgram of increased surveillance of offenders who are deemed too risky for regular probation requirements. Can be used for diversion of offenders, enhancement programs, and those failing under lower supervision in the community.

Jail. Confinement facility, usually administered by a local law enforcement agency, intended for adults but sometimes also containing juveniles, that holds persons detained pending adjudication and/or persons committed after adjudication for sentences of one year or less.

Jail (sentence). The penalty of commitment to the jurisdiction of a confinement facility system for adults, of which the custodial authority is limited to persons sentenced to one year or less of confinement.

Judge. A judicial officer who has been elected or appointed to preside over a court of law, whose position has been created by statute or by constitution and whose decisions in criminal and juvenile cases may only be reviewed by a judge or a higher court and may not be reviewed de novo.

Judgment. The statement of the decision of a court that the defendant is convicted or acquitted of the offense(s) charged.

Judicial officer. Any person exercising judicial powers in a court of law.

Jurisdiction. The territory, subject matter, or person over which lawful authority may be exercised.

Jurisdiction, original. The lawful authority of a court or an administrative agency to hear or act upon a case from its beginning and to pass judgment on it.

Jury, grand. A body of persons who have been selected and sworn to investigate criminal activity and the conduct of public officials and to hear the evidence against an accused person(s) to determine whether there is sufficient evidence to bring that person(s) to trial.

Jury, trial (petit jury; jury). A statutorily defined number of persons selected according to law and sworn to determine certain matters of fact in a criminal action and to render a verdict of guilty or not guilty.

Juvenile. A person subject to juvenile court proceedings because a statutorily defined event was alleged to have occurred while his or her age was below the statutorily specified limit of original jurisdiction of a juvenile court.

Juvenile court. A cover term for courts that have original jurisdiction over persons statutorily defined as juveniles and alleged to be delinquents, status offenders, or dependents.

Juvenile justice agency. A government agency, or sub-unit thereof, of which the functions are the investigation, supervision, adjudication, care, or confinement of juveniles whose conduct or condition has brought or could bring them within the jurisdiction of juvenile court.

Juvenile record. An official record containing, at a minimum, summary information pertaining to an identified juvenile concerning juvenile court proceedings, and, if applicable, detention and correctional processes.

Kidnapping. Unlawful transportation of a person without his or her consent or without the consent of his or her guardian, of a minor.

Larceny (larceny-theft). Unlawful taking or attempted taking of property, other than a motor vehicle, from the possession of another.

Law enforcement agency. A federal, state, or local criminal justice agency of which the principal functions are the prevention, detection, and investigation of crime and the apprehension of alleged offenders.

Law enforcement officer (peace officer, police officer). An employee of a law enforcement agency who is an officer sworn to carry out law enforcement duties or is a sworn employee of a federal prosecutorial agency who primarily performs investigative duties.

Level of government. The federal, state, regional, or local county or city location of administrative and major funding responsibility of a given agency.

Manslaughter, involuntary (negligent manslaughter). Causing the death of another by recklessness or gross negligence.

Manslaughter, vehicular. Causing the death of another by grossly negligent operation of a motor vehicle.

Manslaughter, voluntary (nonnegligent manslaughter). Intentionally causing the death of another with reasonable provocation.

Misdemeanor. An offense usually punishable by incarceration in a local confinement facility for a period of which the upper limit is prescribed by statute in a given jurisdiction, typically limited to one year or less.

Model Penal Code. A generalized modern codification of that which is considered basic to criminal law, published by the American Law Institute in 1962.

Monitored release. Recognizance release with the addition of minimal supervision or service; that is, the defendant may be required to keep a pretrial services agency informed of his or her whereabouts, and the agency reminds the defendant of court dates and verifies the defendant's appearance.

Motion. An oral or written request made by a party to an action, before, during, or after a trial, that a court issue a rule or order.

Motor vehicle theft. Unlawful taking, or attempted taking, of a motor vehicle owned by another with the intent to deprive the owner of it permanently or temporarily.

Murder. Intentionally causing the death of another without reasonable provocation or legal justification, or causing the death of another while committing or attempting to commit another crime.

Nolo contendere. A defendant's formal answer in court to the charges in a complaint, information, or indictment in which the defendant states that he or she does not contest the charges and which, though not an admission of guilt, subjects the defendant to the same legal consequences as does a plea of guilty.

Offender (criminal). An adult who has been convicted of a criminal offense.

Offender, alleged. A person who has been charged with a specific criminal offense(s) by a law enforcement agency or court but has not been convicted.

Offense. An act committed or omitted in violation of a law forbidding or commanding it.

Offenses, Part I. A class of offenses selected for use in UCR, consisting of those crimes that are most likely to be reported, that occur with sufficient frequency to provide an adequate basis for comparison, and that are serious crimes by nature and/or volume.

ANNOTATION. The Part I offenses are:
1. Criminal homicide
   a. Murder and nonnegligent (voluntary) manslaughter
   b. Manslaughter by negligence (involuntary manslaughter)
2. Forcible rape
   a. Rape by force
   b. Attempted forcible rape
3. Robbery
   a. Firearm
   b. Knife or cutting instrument
   c. Other dangerous weapon
   d. Strongarm
4. Aggravated Assault
   a. Firearm
   b. Knife or cutting instrument
   c. Other dangerous weapon
   d. Hands, fist, feet, etc.,—aggravated injury
5. Burglary
   a. Forcible entry
   b. Unlawful entry—no force
   c. Attempted forcible entry
6. Larceny-theft (larceny)
7. Motor vehicle theft
   a. Autos
   b. Trucks and buses
   c. Other vehicles

Offenses, Part II. A class of offenses selected for use in UCR, consisting of specific offenses and types of offenses that do not meet the criteria of frequency and/or seriousness necessary for Part I offenses.

ANNOTATION. The Part II offenses are:
Other assaults (simple,* nonaggravated)
Arson*
Forgery* and counterfeiting*
Fraud*
Embezzlement*
Stolen property: buying, receiving, possessing
Vandalism
Weapons: carrying, possessing, etc.
Prostitution and commercialized vice
Sex offenses (except forcible rape, prostitution, and commercialized vice)
Narcotic drug law violations

Gambling
Offenses against the family and children
Driving under the influence*
Liquor law violations
Drunkenness
Disorderly conduct
Vagrancy
All other offenses (except traffic law violations)
Suspicion*
Curfew and loitering law violations (juvenile violations)
Runaway* (juveniles)

Terms marked with an asterisk (*) are defined in this glossary, though not necessarily in accord with UCR usage. UCR does not collect reports of Part II offenses. Arrest data concerning such offenses, however, are collected and published.

Pardon. An act of executive clemency that absolves the party in part or in full from the legal consequences of the crime and conviction.

> ANNOTATION. Pardons can be full or conditional. The former generally applies to both the punishment and the guilt of the offender and blots out the existence of guilt in the eyes of the law. It also removes his or her disabilities and restores civil rights. The conditional pardon generally falls short of the remedies of the full pardon, is an expression of guilt, and does not obliterate the conviction. (U.S. Supreme Court decisions to pardons and their effects are directly contradictory, and thus state laws usually govern pardons.)

Parole. The status of an offender conditionally released from a confinement facility, prior to the expiration of his or her sentence, and placed under the supervision of a parole agency.

Parole agency. A correctional agency, which may or may not include a parole authority and of which the principal function is the supervision of adults or juveniles placed on parole.

Parole authority. A person or a correctional agency that has the authority to release on parole those adults or juveniles committed to confinement facilities, to revoke parole, and to discharge from parole.

Parolee. A person who has been conditionally released from a correctional institution before the expiration of his or her sentence and who has been placed under the supervision of a parole agency.

Parole violation. A parolee's act or a failure to act that does not conform to the conditions of his or her parole.

**Partial confinement.** An alternative to the traditional jail sentence, consisting of "weekend" sentences, that permit offenders to spend the work week in the community, with their families, and at the jobs; furloughs, which enable offenders to leave the jail for a period of a few hours to a few days for specific purposes—to seek employment, take care of personal matters or family obligations, or engage in community service; or work/study release, under which offenders work or attend school during the day and return to the detention facility at night and on weekends.

**Penalty.** The punishment annexed by law or judicial decision to the commission of a particular offense, which may be death, imprisonment, fine, or loss of civil privileges.

**Percentage bail.** A publicly managed bail service arrangement that requires the defendant to deposit a percentage (typically 10 percent) of the amount of bail with the court clerk. The deposit is returned to the defendant after scheduled court appearances are made, although a charge (usually 1 percent) may be deducted to help defray program costs.

**Person.** A human being, or a group of human beings considered a legal unit, which has the lawful capacity to defend rights, incur obligation, prosecute claims, or be prosecuted or adjudicated.

**Personally secured bail.** Security that is put up by the defendant or the defendant's family. This arrangement is generally out of reach of the less affluent defendant.

**Petition (juvenile).** A document filed in juvenile court alleging that a juvenile is a delinquent, a status offender, or a dependent and asking that the juvenile be transferred to a criminal court for prosecution as an adult.

**Petition not sustained.** The finding by a juvenile court in an adjudicatory hearing that there is not sufficient evidence to sustain an allegation that a juvenile is a delinquent, status offender, or dependent.

**Plea.** A defendant's formal answer in court to the charges brought against him or her in a complaint, information, or indictment.

**Plea bargaining.** The exchange of prosecutorial and/or judicial concessions, commonly a lesser charge, the dismissal of other pending charges, a recommendation by the prosecutor for a reduced sentence or a combination thereof, in return for a plea of guilty.

**Plea, final.** The last plea to a given charge, entered in a court record by or for a defendant.

**Plea, guilty.** A defendant's formal answer in court to the charges in a complaint, information, or indictment, in which the defendant states that the charges are true and that he or she has committed the offense as charged.

Plea, initial. The first plea to a given charge, entered in a court record by or for a defendant.

Plea, not guilty. A defendant's formal answer in court to the charges in a complaint, information, or indictment, in which the defendant states that he or she is not guilty.

Police department. A local law enforcement agency directed by a chief of police or a commissioner.

Police officer. A local law enforcement officer employed by a police department.

Population movement. Entries and exits of adjudicated persons, or persons subject to judicial proceedings, into or from correctional facilities or programs.

Predisposition report. The document resulting from an investigation by a probation agency or other designated authority, which has been requested by a juvenile court, into the past behavior, family background, and personality of a juvenile who has been adjudicated a delinquent, a status offender, or a dependent, in order to assist the court in determining the most appropriate disposition.

Presentence report. The document resulting from an investigation undertaken by a probation agency or other designated authority, at the request of a criminal court, into the past behavior, family circumstances, and personality of an adult who has been convicted of a crime, in order to assist the court in determining the most appropriate sentence.

Prior record. Criminal history record information concerning any law enforcement, court, or correctional proceedings that have occurred before the current investigation of, or proceedings against, a person; or statistical description of the criminal histories of a set of persons.

Prison. A confinement facility having custodial authority over adults sentenced to confinement for more than one year.

Prisoner. A person in custody in a confinement facility or in the personal custody of a criminal justice official while being transported to or between confinement facilities.

Prison (sentence). The penalty of commitment to the jurisdiction of a confinement facility system for adults, whose custodial authority extends to persons sentenced to more than one year of confinement.

Privately secured bail. An arrangement similar to the bail bondsman system except that bail is provided without cost to the defendant. A private organization provides bail for indigent arrestees who meet its eligibility requirements.

Probable cause. A set of facts and circumstances that would induce a reasonably intelligent and prudent person to believe that an accused person had committed a specific crime.

Probation. The conditional freedom granted by a judicial officer to an alleged offender, or adjudicated adult or juvenile, as long as the person meets certain conditions of behavior. One requirement is to report to a designated person or agency over some specific period of time. Probation may contain special conditions, as discussed in the conditions of suspended sentence. Probation often includes a suspended sentence but may be used in association with the suspension of a final judgment or a deferral of sentencing.

Probation agency (probation department). A correctional agency of which the principal functions are juvenile intake, the supervision of adults and juveniles placed on probation status, and the investigation of adults or juveniles for the purpose of preparing presentence or predisposition reports to assist the court in determining the proper sentence or juvenile court disposition.

Probationer. A person required by a court or probation agency to meet certain conditions of behavior who may or may not be placed under the supervision of a probation agency.

Probation officer. An employee of a probation agency whose primary duties include one or more of the probation agency functions.

Probation (sentence). A court requirement that a person fulfill certain conditions of behavior and accept the supervision of a probation agency, usually in lieu of a sentence to confinement but sometimes including a jail sentence.

Probation violation. An act or a failure to act by a probationer that does not conform to the conditions of his or her probation.

Prosecutor. An attorney employed by a government agency or subunit whose official duty is to initiate and maintain criminal proceedings on behalf of the government against persons accused of committing criminal offenses.

Prosecutorial agency. A federal, state, or local criminal justice agency whose principal function is the prosecution of alleged offenders.

Pro se (in propria persona). Acting as one's own defense attorney in criminal proceedings: representing oneself.

Public defender. An attorney employed by a government agency or subdivision, whose official duty is to represent defendants unable to hire private counsel.

Public defender's office. A federal, state, or local criminal justice agency or subunit of which the principal function is to represent defendants unable to hire private counsel.

Purge (record). The complete removal of arrest, criminal, or juvenile record information from a given records system.

Rape. Unlawful sexual intercourse with a person, by force or without legal or factual consent.

Rape, forcible. Sexual intercourse or attempted sexual intercourse with a person against his or her will, by force or threat of force.

Rape, statutory. Sexual intercourse with a person who has consented in fact but deemed, because of age, to be legally incapable of consent.

Rape without force or consent. Sexual intercourse with a person legally of the age of consent but who is unconscious or whose ability to judge or control his or her conduct is inherently impaired by mental defect or intoxicating substances.

Recidivism. The repetition of criminal behavior; habitual criminality.

Referral to intake. In juvenile proceedings, a request by the police, parents, or other agency or person that a juvenile intake unit take appropriate action concerning a juvenile alleged to have committed a delinquent act or status offense or to be dependent.

Release from detention. The authorized exit from detention of a person subject to criminal or juvenile justice proceedings.

Release from prison. A cover term for all lawful exits from federal or state confinement facilities primarily intended for adults serving sentences of more than one year, including all conditional and unconditional releases, deaths, and transfers to other jurisdictions, excluding escapes:

> Transfer of jurisdiction
> Release on parole
> Conditional release
> Release while still under jurisdiction of correctional agency, before expiration of sentence
>
> Discretionary
> Release date determined by parole authority
>
> Mandatory
> Release date determined by statute
> Discharge from prison
> Release ending all agency jurisdiction
> Unconditional release
>
> Discretionary
> Pardon, commutation of sentence

>Mandatory
>Expiration of sentence
>Temporary release
>Authorized, unaccompanied temporary departure for educational, employment, or other authorized purposes
>Transfer of jurisdiction
>Transfer of jurisdiction of another correctional agency or a court
>Death
>Death from homicide, suicide, or natural causes
>Execution
>Execution of sentence of death

In some systems release on "parole" represents only discretionary conditions release. It is recommended that mandatory conditional release be included, as both types describe conditional releases with subsequent parole status.

**Release on bail.** The release by a judicial officer of an accused person who has been taken into custody, upon the accused's promise to pay a certain sum of money or property if he or she fails to appear in court as required, a promise that may or may not be secured by the deposit of an actual sum of money or property.

**Release on own recognizance.** The release, by a judicial officer, of an accused person who has been taken into custody, upon the accused's promise to appear in court as required for criminal proceedings.

**Release, pretrial.** A procedure whereby an accused person who has been taken into custody is allowed to be free before and during his or her trial.

**Release to third party.** The release, by a judicial officer, of an accused person who has been taken into custody, to a third party who promises to return the accused to court for criminal proceedings.

**Residential treatment center.** A government facility that serves juveniles whose behavior does not necessitate the strict confinement of a training school, often allowing them greater contact with the community.

**Restitution.** Usually a cash payment by the offender to the victim of an amount considered to offset the loss incurred by the victim or the community. The amount of the payment may be scaled down to the offender's earning capacity, and/or payments may be made in installments. Sometimes services directly or indirectly benefiting the victim may be substituted for cash payment.

**Restorative justice.** Any victim-centered approach that views crime as a violation against individuals, their families and communities, and seeks to repair the harm done by the crime through mediation, reparation and empowerment of both victim and offender. Violators are held accountable for the offense and required to repair all or part of the damage, while being restored to the community.

Retained counsel. An attorney, not employed or compensated by a government agency or sub-unit or assigned by the court, who is privately hired to represent a person(s) in a criminal proceeding.

Revocation. An administrative act performed by a parole authority removing a person from parole, or a judicial order by a court removing a person from parole or probation, in response to a violation by the parolee or probationer.

Revocation hearing. An administrative and/or judicial hearing on the question of whether or not a person's probation or parole status should be revoked.

Rights of defendant. Those powers and privileges that are constitutionally guaranteed to every defendant.

Robbery. The unlawful taking or attempted taking of property that is in the immediate possession of another, by force or the threat of force.

Robbery, armed. The unlawful taking or attempted taking of property that is in the immediate possession of another, by the use or threatened use of a deadly or dangerous weapon.

Robbery, strongarm. The unlawful taking or attempted taking of property that is in the immediate possession of another by the use or threatened use of force, without the use of a weapon.

Runaway. A juvenile who has been adjudicated by a judicial officer of a juvenile court as having committed the status offense of leaving the custody and home of his or her parents, guardians, or custodians without permission and failing to return within a reasonable length of time.

Seal (record). The removal, for the benefit of the subject, of arrest, criminal, or juvenile record information from routinely available status to a status requiring special procedures for access.

Security. The degree of restriction of inmate movement within a correctional facility, usually divided into maximum, medium, and minimum levels.

Security and privacy standards. A set of principles and procedures developed to ensure the security and confidentiality of criminal or juvenile record information in order to protect the privacy of the persons identified in such records.

Sentence. The penalty imposed by a court on a convicted person, or the court decision to suspend imposition or execution of the penalty.

Sentence, indeterminate. A statutory provision for a type of sentence to imprisonment in which, after the court has determined that the convicted person shall be imprisoned, the exact length of imprisonment and parole supervision is afterward fixed within statutory limits by a parole authority.

Sentence, mandatory. A statutory requirement that a certain penalty shall be imposed and executed upon certain convicted offenders.

Sentence, suspended. The court decision postponing the pronouncement of sentence upon a convicted person or postponing the execution of a sentence that has been pronounced by the court.

Sentence, suspended execution. The court decision setting a penalty but postponing its execution.

Sentence, suspended imposition. The court decision postponing the setting of a penalty.

Shelter. A confinement or community facility for the care of juveniles, usually those held pending adjudication.

Sheriff. The elected or appointed chief officer of a county law enforcement agency, usually responsible for law enforcement in unincorporated areas and for operation of the county jail.

Sheriff, deputy. A law enforcement officer employed by a county sheriff's department.

Sheriff's department. A law enforcement agency organized at a county level, directed by a sheriff, that exercises its law enforcement functions at the county level, usually within unincorporated areas, and operates the county jail in most jurisdictions.

Shock Probation (shock parole). A judicial program permitting judges to incarcerate offenders in prison and then recall for resentencing, based on the belief that a short period of confinements will "shock" the offender into abandoning criminal activity. Shock parole is typically a parole-board early release option to expedite community supervision of low risk inmates.

Speedy trial. The right of the defendant to have a prompt trial.

Stationhouse citation. An alternative to pretrial detention, whereby the arrestee is escorted to the precinct police station or headquarters rather than the pretrial detention facility. Release, which may occur before or after booking, is contingent upon the defendant's written promise to appear in court as specified on the release form.

Status offender. A juvenile who has been adjudicated by a judicial officer of juvenile court as having committed a status offense, which is an act or conduct that is an offense only when committed or engaged in by a juvenile.

Status offense. An act or conduct that is declared by statute to be an offense, but only when committed or engaged in by a juvenile, and that can be adjudicated only by a juvenile court.

Subjudicial officer. A judicial officer who is invested with certain judicial powers and functions but whose decisions in criminal and juveniles cases are subject to de novo review by a judge.

Subpoena. A written order issued by a judicial officer requiring a specified person to appear in a designated court at a specified time in order to serve as a witness in a case under the jurisdiction of that court or to bring material to that court.

Summons. A written order issued by a judicial officer requiring a person accused of a criminal offense to appear in a designated court at a specified time to answer the charge(s). The summons is a request or instruction to appear in court to face an accusation. As an alternative to the arrest warrant, it is used in cases on which complaints are registered with the magistrate or prosecutor's office.

Supervised release. A type of release requiring more frequent contact than monitored release does. Typically, various conditions are imposed and supervision is aimed at enforcing these conditions and providing services as needed. Some form of monetary bail also may be attached as a condition of supervised release, especially in higher-risk cases.

Suspect. A person, adult or juvenile, considered by a criminal justice agency to be one who may have committed a specific criminal offense but who has not been arrested or charged.

Suspended sentence. Essentially a threat to take more drastic action if the offender again commits a crime during some specified time period. When no special conditions are attached, it is assumed that the ends of justice have been satisfied by conviction and no further action is required, as long as the offender refrains from involvement in new offenses. Suspended sentences may be conditioned on various limitations as to mobility, associates, or activities or on requirements to make reparations or participate in some rehabilitation program.

Suspicion. Belief that a person has committed a criminal offense, based on facts and circumstances that are not sufficient to constitute probable cause.

Theft. Larceny, or in some legal classifications, the group of offenses including larceny, and robbery, burglary, extortion, fraudulent offenses, hijacking, and other offenses sharing the element of larceny.

Third-party release. A release extending to another person the responsibility for ensuring the defendant's appearance in court. This may be a person known to the defendant or a designated volunteer. Third-party release may be a condition of unsecured bail, with the third party as a cosigner.

Time served. The total time spent in confinement by a convicted adult before and after sentencing, or only the time spent in confinement after a sentence of commitment to a confinement facility.

Training school. A correctional institution for juveniles adjudicated to be delinquent or status offenders and committed to confinement by a judicial officer.

Transfer hearing. A preadjudicatory hearing in juvenile court in order to determine whether juvenile court jurisdiction should be retained or waived for a juvenile alleged to have committed a delinquent act(s) and whether he or she should be transferred to criminal court for prosecution as an adult.

Transfer to adult court. The decision by a juvenile court, resulting from a transfer hearing, that jurisdiction over an alleged delinquent will be waived and that he or she should be prosecuted as an adult in a criminal court.

Trial. The examination of issues of fact and law in a case or controversy, beginning when the jury has been selected in a jury trial, the first witness is sworn, or the first evidence is introduced in a court trial and concluding when a verdict is reached or the case is dismissed.

Trial, court (trial, judge). A trial in which there is no jury and a judicial officer determines the issues of fact and law in a case.

Trial, jury. A trial in which a jury determines the issues of fact in a case.

Unconditional discharge. As a posttrial disposition, essentially the same as unconditional diversion. No savings are obtained in criminal justice processing costs, but jail populations may be reduced; conditions of release are imposed for an offense in which the defendant's involvement has been established.

Unconditional diversion. The cessation of criminal processing at any point short of adjudication with no continuing threat of prosecution. This type of diversion may be voluntary referral to a social service agency or program dealing with a problem underlying the offense.

Unsecured bail. A form of release differing from release on recognizance only in that the defendant is subject to paying the amount of bail if he or she defaults. Unsecured bail permits release without a deposit or purchase of a bondsman's services.

Venue. The geographical area from which the jury is drawn and in which trial is held in a criminal action.

Verdict. In criminal proceedings, the decision made by a jury in a jury trial, or by a judicial officer in a court trial, that a defendant is either guilty or not guilty of the offense(s) for which he or she has been tried.

Verdict, guilty. In criminal proceedings, the decision made by a jury in jury trial, or by a judicial officer in a court trial, that the defendant is guilty of the offense(s) for which he or she has been tried.

Verdict, not guilty. In criminal proceedings, the decision made by a jury in a jury trial, or by a judicial officer in a court trial, or by a judicial officer in court trial, that the defendant is not guilty of the offense(s) for which he or she has been tried.

Victim. A person who has suffered death, physical or mental suffering, or loss of property as the result of an actual or attempted criminal offense committed by another person.

Warrant, arrest. A document issued by a judicial officer that directs a law enforcement officer to arrest a person who has been accused of an offense.

Warrant, bench. A document issued by a judicial officer directing that a person who has failed to obey an order or notice to appear be brought before court.

Warrant, search. A document issued by a judicial officer that directs a law enforcement officer to conduct a search for specified property or persons at a specific location, to seize the property or person, if found, and to account for the results of the search to issuing judicial officer.

Witness. A person who directly perceives an event or thing or who has expert knowledge relevant to a case.

Youthful offender. A person, adjudicated in criminal court, who may be above the statutory age limit for juveniles but is below a specified upper age limit, for whom special correctional commitments and special record sealing procedures are made available by statute.

# Name Index

# Subject Index

# About the Authors

Edward J. Latessa is a Professor and Head of the Division of Criminal Justice at the University of Cincinnati. Dr. Latessa has published more than 110 works in the area of criminal justice, corrections, and juvenile justice. He is co-author of seven books including *Corrections in the Community*, and *Corrections in America*. Professor Latessa has directed more than 100 funded research projects, including: studies of day reporting centers, juvenile justice programs, drug courts, intensive supervision programs, halfway houses, and drug programs. He and his staff have also assessed more than 450 correctional programs throughout the United States. Dr. Latessa is a consultant with the National Institute of Corrections, and he has provided assistance and workshops in more than 40 states. Dr. Latessa served as President of the Academy of Criminal Justice Sciences (1989-90). He has also received several awards, including: the August Vollmer Award from the American Society of Criminology (2004), the Simon Dinitz Criminal Justice Research Award from the Ohio Department of Rehabilitation and Correction (2002), the Margaret Mead Award for dedicated service to the causes of social justice and humanitarian advancement by the International Community Corrections Association (2001), the Peter P. Lejins Award for Research from the American Correctional Association (1999), ACJS Fellow Award (1998), ACJS Founders Award (1992), and the Simon Dinitz Award by the Ohio Community Corrections Organization.

Paula Smith is an Assistant Professor, Division of Criminal Justice and Associate Director, Corrections Institute at the University of Cincinnati. She received her Ph.D. in Psychology from the University of New Brunswick. Her research interests include offender classification and assessment, correctional rehabilitation, the psychological effects of incarceration, program implementation and evaluation, the transfer of knowledge to practitioners and policymakers, and meta-analysis. She has authored several articles, book chapters, and conference presentations on the above topics. In addition to her research experience, Smith has frontline experience working with a variety of offender populations, including juvenile offenders, sex offenders, and perpetrators of domestic violence. Currently, she provides technical assistance to criminal justice agencies throughout the United States and Canada.